CORPVS CHRISTIANORVM

Continuatio Mediaeualis

235A

CORPVS CHRISTIANORVM

Continuatio Mediaeualis

235A

GERARDI MAGNI

OPERA OMNIA

cura et studio
Instituti Titus Brandsma
in Vniuersitate Radbodi Nouiomagensi
ad fidem codicum manu scriptorum
edita

Pars II, 2

TURNHOUT
BREPOLS ✠ PUBLISHERS
2016

GERARDI MAGNI

SCRIPTA CONTRA SIMONIAM ET PROPRIETARIOS

cura et studio

Rijcklof HOFMAN
et
Marinus VAN DEN BERG

TURNHOUT
BREPOLS PUBLISHERS
2016

CORPVS CHRISTIANORVM

Continuatio Mediaeualis

in ABBATIA SANCTI PETRI STEENBRVGENSI
a reuerendissimo Domino Eligio DEKKERS
fundata
nunc sub auspiciis Vniuersitatum
UNIVERSITEIT ANTWERPEN
VRIJE UNIVERSITEIT BRUSSEL UNIVERSITEIT GENT
KATHOLIEKE UNIVERSITEIT LEUVEN
UNIVERSITÉ CATHOLIQUE DE LOUVAIN
edita

editionibus curandis praesunt
Rita BEYERS   Alexander ANDREE   Emanuela COLOMBI
Georges DECLERCQ   Jeroen DEPLOIGE
Paul-Augustin DEPROOST   Anthony DUPONT   Jacques ELFASSI
Guy GULDENTOPS   Hugh HOUGHTON   Mathijs LAMBERIGTS
Johan LEEMANS   Paul MATTEI   Gert PARTOENS
Marco PETOLETTI   Dominique POIREL   Paul TOMBEUR
Marc VAN UYTFANGHE   Wim VERBAAL

parandis operam dant
Luc JOCQUÉ   Bart JANSSENS
Paolo SARTORI   Christine VANDE VEIRE

D/2016/0095/196
ISBN 978-2-503-56640-5
Printed in the EU on acid-free paper

© 2016, Brepols Publishers n.v., Turnhout, Belgium

All rights reserved. No part of this publication may be reproduced,
stored in a retrieval system, or transmitted, in any form or by any means,
electronic, mechanical, photocopying, recording, or otherwise,
without the prior permission of the publisher.

PREFACE

For more than twenty years now I have prepared my editions at the Titus Brandsma Instituut in Nijmegen, a congenial community where professed monks work together in harmony with lay co-workers. In a way, this form of collaboration is comparable to Grote's cohabitation during three years in the Carthusian monastery Monnikhuizen, not in the least because of the impulses stimulating my spiritual growth. The stimulus which Grote received from Carthusians is definitely equalled by the support which I get from Carmelite Friars. Last year, my closest professed colleague Rudolf van Dijk O.Carm. passed away at an advanced age, while at the same time my closest lay fellow worker Charles Caspers changed course in research focus, a situation comparable to the transfer of Grote's close friend and mentor Heinrich Egher from Kalkar from the charterhouse near Arnhem to the recently founded house of the Order in Roermond. These developments left me as the sole representative of *Deuotio Moderna* research at core level in the institute, although I am now and then reassured that research into this movement remains a 'spearhead' of the research programme.

Fortunately, help arrived from a quarter which is in the end not that unexpected after all. When asked, Marinus van den Berg at once willingly agreed to collaborate with me, and to take over the edition of the Middle Dutch texts in this volume. His situation resembles that of Geert Grote even more than mine, for his status as an associate researcher of the Titus Brandsma Instituut shows considerable overlap with that of Grote as a paying guest in Monnikhuizen. Also, he has a long-standing relationship with the institute, as Rudolf van Dijk's close collaborator with the annotated Modern Dutch translation of the works of Alijt Bake, and as the editor of the spiritual treatises transmitted in the *Gaesdoncksetraktatenhandschrift*, a codex destroyed during the Second World War, of which photographs survive in the Brandsma Collectie in the Titus Brandsma Instituut.

At the end of our work on this edition, it is our pleasure to thank the many colleagues and friends who have contributed to this final result. Keepers of manuscript collections have kindly put at our disposal manuscript material in their care. I recollect with much gratitude especially the lively e-mail correspondence with Dr. Annelen Ottermann (Stellvertretende Amtsleiterin, Wissenschaftliche Stadtbibliothek, Mainz). We received much support and help from colleagues at the Titus Brandsma Instituut, most notably from Charles Caspers, Henk Rutten, Lieneke Lok and Ria Heerema. As always, Luc Jocqué of Brepols Publishers has been immensely helpful. In the course of the preparation of this particular volume, he has in addition with exemplary patience and friendliness processed several consecutive versions of the texts here edited. We are equally grateful to the Regular Canonesses of Saint Augustine who lived until 1997 at Soeterbeeck, the last representatives of the *Deuotio Moderna* movement in the Netherlands directly descending from the Congregatie of Windesheim, who generously destined their legacy to be used for scholarly research into the *Deuotio Moderna* movement.

But our main and most important support comes from our wives – they gave us free rein to indulge in work which for us is fun at the same time. We therefore dedicate this book to Bernadette Smelik and Mari-Anne van den Berg.

Rijcklof Hofman / Marinus van den Berg
Nijmegen / Hilversum, 27 May 2016

BIBLIOGRAPHY

Primary sources

Ambr., *Off.* = Ambrosivs Mediolanensis, *De officiis* – ed. M. Testard (*CC SL*, 15), Turnhout, 2000.

Apvl., *Mag.* = *Apulei Platonici Madaurensis Opera quae supersunt*, Vol. 2, Fasc. 1, *Pro se de magia liber (Apologia)* – ed. R. W. O. Helm (*Bibl. Teubneriana*), ed. 4., Lipsiae, 1963, uel Apvleivs of Madavros, *Pro se de magia (Apologia)* – ed. V. J. C. Hunink, Amsterdam, 1997.

Arch., *Comm. Decr.* = *Guidonis à Baiiso Archidiaconi Bononiensis iuris utriusque peritissimi Rosarium, seu in Decretorum volumen Commentaria, Nicolai Superantii, patricii Veneti, iuris cons. & Equitis Hierosolymitani, ac etiam Petri Albignani Tretii iuris cons. Adnotationibus illustrata, cum summariis & indice rerum ac uerborum, notatu dignorum, locupletissimo*, Venetiis: Apud Iuntas, 1601, repr. on CD-rom, Roma: Bibliotheca Apostolica Vaticana, ed. Gaetano Colli, 2001.

Arch., *Comm. vium* = *Guidonis à Baiiso Archidiaconi Bononiensis iuris utriusque peritissimi in Sextum Decretalium Commentaria, nonnullorum doctissimorum hominum adnotationibus illustrata, cum summariis & indice rerum ac uerborum, notatu dignorum, locupletissimo*, Venetiis: Apud Iuntas, 1606, repr. on CD-rom, Roma: Bibliotheca Apostolica Vaticana, ed. Gaetano Colli, 2001.

Arist., *Ethic. Lat.* = Aristoteles, *Ethica Nicomachea. Translatio Roberti Grosseteste Lincolniensis siue 'Liber ethicorum'* (A: *Recensio pura*, B: *Recensio recognita* [a Guill. Morbeka reuisa]) – ed. R. A. Gauthier (*Aristoteles Latinus*, uol. 26.1-3, fasc. 3-4), Leiden, Bruxelles, 1972-1974.

Arist., *Metaph. Lat.* = Aristoteles, *Metaphysica*, l. 1-14, *rec. et transl. Guillelmi de Moerbeka* – ed. G. Vuillemin-Diem (*Aristoteles Latinus*, uol. 25.3), Leiden, 1995.

Arist., *Pol. Lat.* = *Aristotelis Politicorum libri octo cum uetusta translatione Guilelmi de Moerbeka* – ed. F. Susemihl, Leipzig, 1872 [editio noua in *Aristoteles Latinus*, 29.2 praeparatur].

Arist., *Post. Lat.* = Aristoteles, *Analytica posteriora. Translationes Iacobi, Anonymi siue "Ioannis", Gerardi et Recensio Guillelmi de Moerbeka* – ed. L. Minio-Paluello et B. G. Dod (*Aristoteles Latinus*, 4.1-4), Bruges etc., 1968.

Ps. Arist., *Probl.* = Ps. Aristoteles, sec. uersionem latinam a Bartholomaeo de Messana s. xiii factam, *Problemata*, edition of the text of

Aristotle in the form of lemmata in this incunable: PETRVS DE ABANO, *Expositio problematum Aristotelis cum textu*, Venetiis: ap. Ioh. Herbort de Seligenstat, 1482, available online at: http://visualiseur.bnf.fr/Visualiseur?destination=Gallica&O=NUMM-58529.

ARN. GHEYL., *Gnot.* = ARNOLDVS GHEYLOVEN (ARNOLDVS THEODERICI DE HOLLANDIA DE ROTTERDAM), *Gnotosolitos paruus* (*e codice Seminarii Leodiensis 6 F 18 editus*) – ed. A. G. Weiler (*CC CM*, 212), Turnhout, 2008.

AVG., *Ciu. Dei* = AVGVSTINVS HIPPONENSIS, *De ciuitate Dei* – ed. B. Dombart – A. Kalb (*CC SL*, 47-48), Turnhout, 1955.

AVG., *Contra Faustum* = AVGVSTINVS HIPPONENSIS, *Contra Faustum* – ed. J. Zycha (*CSEL*, 25), Wien etc., 1891, p. 251-797.

AVG., *Ep.* = AVGVSTINVS HIPPONENSIS, *Epistulae*, Pars 3, *Epp.* 124-184 – ed. A. Goldbacher (*CSEL*, 34, 1; 34, 2; 44), Wien etc., 1895-1923.

AVG., *Exp. Gal.* = AVGVSTINVS HIPPONENSIS, *Expositio epistulae ad Galatas* – ed. J. Divjak (*CSEL*, 84), Wien, 1971, p. 55-141.

AVG., *In Ioh. tract.* = AVGVSTINVS HIPPONENSIS, *In Iohannis euangelium tractatus* – ed. R. Willems (*CC SL*, 36), Turnhout, 1954.

AVG., *Lib. arb.* = AVGVSTINVS HIPPONENSIS, *De libero arbitrio* – ed. W. M. Green (*CC SL*, 29), Turnhout, 1970, p. 211-321.

AVG., *Reg.* = AVGVSTINVS HIPPONENSIS, *Regula tertia uel Preceptum* – ed. L. Verheijen, *La Règle de Saint Augustin*, I. *Tradition manuscrite*, Paris, 1967, p. 417-437.

AVG., *Serm.* = AVGVSTINVS HIPPONENSIS, *Sermones de uetere testamento* – ed. C. Lambot (*CC SL*, 41), Turnhout, 1961.

AVG., *Trin.* = AVGVSTINVS HIPPONENSIS, *De trinitate libri XV* – ed. W. J. Mountain aux. Fr. Glorie (*CC SL*, 50-50A), Turnhout, 1968.

AVG., *Vera rel.* = AVGVSTINVS HIPPONENSIS, *De uera religione* – ed. K.-D. Daur (*CC SL*, 32), Turnhout, 1962, p. 187-260.

PS. AVG., *Serm.* 393 = PS. AVGVSTINVS HIPPONENSIS, *Sermo* 393 – ed. Maurinorum (*PL*, 39, c. 1713-1715).

BAS., *Reg.* = *Basilii Regula a Rufino latine uersa* – ed. K. Zelzer (*CSEL*, 86), Wien etc., 1986, p. 5-221.

BEDA, *In Luc.*; *In Marc.* = *Bedae Venerabilis Opera*. Pars 2. *Opera exegetica*, Vol. 3. *In Lucae Euangelium expositio*; *In Marci Euangelium expositio* – ed. D. Hurst (*CC SL*, 120), Turnhout, 1960.

BENED., *Reg.* = BENEDICTVS DE NVRSIA, *Regula* – ed. A. de Vogüé (*SC*, 181, p. 412-490; *SC*, 182, p. 508-674), Paris, 1972.

BERN., *Dil. Deo* = BERNARDVS CLARAEVALLENSIS, *Liber de diligendo Deo*, in *S. Bernardi Opera*, vol. 3, *Tractatus et opuscula* – ed. J. Leclercq et H. M. Rochais, Roma, 1963, p. 119-154.

BERN., *Ep.* 7 = BERNARDVS CLARAEVALLENSIS, *Epistola 7 ad Adam monachum*, in *S. Bernardi Opera*, vol. 7, *Epistolae*. I. *Corpus epistolarum*, 1-180 – ed. J. Leclercq et H. M. Rochais, Roma, 1974, p. 31-46.

BERN., *Praec.* = BERNARDVS CLARAEVALLENSIS, *De praecepto et dispensatione*, in *S. Bernardi Opera*, vol. 3, *Tractatus et opuscula* – ed. J. Leclercq et H. M. Rochais, Roma, 1963, p. 255-294.

BERN., *Serm. Cant.* = BERNARDVS CLARAEVALLENSIS, *Sermones super Cantica Canticorum*, in *S. Bernardi Opera*, vol. 1-2 – ed. J. Leclercq, C. H. Talbot et H. M. Rochais, Roma, 1957-1958.

BERN. PARM., *Glos. ord. in Decret.* = *Decretales D. Gregorii Papæ .IX. suae integritati unà cum glossis* [sc. Bernardi Parmensis] *restitutae, cum priuilegio Gregorii XIII. pont. max. et aliorum principum*, Romae, 1582 (available online at http://digital.library.ucla.edu/canonlaw); editio ultima, Parisiis, 1612, etiam adhibita est, sed minus frequenter.

BONIFACIVS PAPA VIII, cfr infra, s.v. *Decret.*, VI.

BRIX., *Glos. ord. in* GRAT., *Decr.* = *Decretum Gratiani emendatum et notationibus* [sc. Bartholomaei Brixiensis] *illustratum, Gregorii XIII. pont. max. iussu editum*, Romae, 1582 (available online at http://digital.library.ucla.edu/canonlaw); editio ultima, Parisiis, 1612, etiam adhibita est, sed minus frequenter.

CASS., *Coll.* = IOHANNES CASSIANVS, *Collationes* 24 – ed. M. Petschenig (*CSEL*, 13), Wien etc., 1886.

CIC., *Cato maior* = MARCVS TVLLIVS CICERO, *Cato maior de senectute* (*M. Tulli Ciceronis scripta quae manserunt omnia*, fasc. 47) – ed. K. Simbeck (*Bibl. Teubneriana*), Leipzig, 1917, p. 3-43.

CIC., *Off.* = MARCVS TVLLIVS CICERO, *De officiis* (*M. Tulli Ciceronis Scripta quae manserunt omnia*, fasc. 48) – iterum recogn. C. Atzert (*Bibl. Teubneriana*), Lipsiae, 1932.

Clem. = *Clementis papae V constitutiones*, in *Corpus iuris canonici*, pars secunda: *Decretalium collectiones* – ed. E. Friedberg, Leipzig, 1881, c. 1129-1200.

Conc. oecum. decr., COD = *Conciliorum oecumenicorum decreta* – ed. Centro di documentazione, Istituto per le scienze religiose, Bologna, curantibus G. Alberigo, P.-P. Joannou, Cl. Leonardi, P. Prodi, consultante H. Jedin, Basileae etc., 1962.

DDS = *Dictionnaire de droit canonique, contenant tous les termes du droit canonique, avec un sommaire de l'histoire et des institutions et de l'état actuel de la discipline*, publ. sous la dir. de R. NAZ, T. 1-7, Paris, 1935-1965.

Decret. = *Decretales Gregorii papae IX*, in *Corpus iuris canonici*, pars secunda: *Decretalium collectiones* – ed. E. Friedberg, Leipzig, 1881, c. 1-928.

Decret., VI = *Liber sextus decretalium d. Bonifacii papae VIII. suae integritati restitutus*, in *Corpus iuris canonici*, pars secunda: *Decretalium collectiones* – ed. E. Friedberg, Leipzig, 1881, c. 933-1124.

DION., *Cael. hier.*; *Eccl. Hier.* = DIONYSIVS AREOPAGITA sec. Iohannem Scotum Eriugenam, *De ecclesiastica hierarchia* – ed. Pierre Chevallier avec son équipe de Solesmes, *Dionysiaca. Recueil donnant l'ensemble des traductions latines des ouvrages attribués au Denys de l'Aréopage et synopse marquant la valeur de citations presque innombrables allant seules depuis trop longtemps remises enfin dans leur contexte au moyen d'une nomenclature rendue d'un usage très facile*, T. 1-2, [Bruges], 1937, T. 2, p. 727-1039, l. 3 (*Cael. hier.*); T. 2, p. 1071-1476 (*Eccl. Hier.*).

DION., *Diu. nom.* = DIONYSIVS AREOPAGITA sec. Iohannem Saracenum, *De diuinis nominibus* – ed. Pierre Chevallier avec son équipe de Solesmes (cfr previous entry), T. 1, p. 5-561, l. 4.

DION., *Ep.* 8 = DIONYSIVS AREOPAGITA sec. Iohannem Saracenum, *Epistula 8, ad Demophilum monachum* – ed. Pierre Chevallier avec son équipe de Solesmes (cfr previous entry), T. 2, p. 1501-1571, l. 4.

DON., *Mai.* = AELIVS DONATVS, *Ars maior*, in L. HOLTZ, *Donat et la tradition de l'enseignement grammatical. Étude sur l'Ars Donati et sa diffusion (IVe-IXe siècle) et édition critique*, Paris, 1981, p. 603-674.

Extrau(ag). comm. = *Extrauagantes decretales, quae a diuersis Romanis pontificibus post .VI. emanauerunt*, in *Corpus iuris canonici*, pars secunda: *Decretalium collectiones* – ed. E. Friedberg, Leipzig, 1881, c. 1237-1312.

FLAV. IOS., *Ant.* = [FLAVIVS IOSEPHVS], *The Latin Josephus. The Antiquities, books I-V* – ed. F. Blatt (*Acta Jutlandica*, 30, 1; *Acta jutlandica*, Humanistisk serie, 44), København, 1958; copy used for Bks. 6-20: *Flavii Iosephi, patria Hierosolymitani, religione Iudaei, inter Græcos historiographos, cum primis facundi, opera quædam Ruffino presbytero interprete, in quibus post ultimam aliorum æditionem, loca nec pauca, nec omnino leuis momenti ex uetustissimorum codicum collatione restituta comuenies, lector*, Basileae, apvd Io. Frobenivm, 1524 (mense septembri); Permalink: http://www.mdz-nbn-resolving.de/urn/resolver.pl?urn=urn:nbn:de:bvb:12-bsb10139723-4; textus graecus: FLAVIVS JOSEPHVS, *Jewish antiquities*, Bks. 14-15 – ed. A. Wikgren; Bks. 18-19 – ed. L. H. Feldman (Cambridge, Mass.: Loeb, Vol. 489, 1963; Vol. 433, 1965); FLAVIVS IOSEPHVS, *Judean antiquities 1-4* – tr. and comm. L. H. Feldman; *Judean antiquities 15* – tr. and comm. J. W. van Henten (FLAVIUS JOSEPHUS, *Translation and commentary*, Vol. 3; Vol. 7B), Leiden etc., 2000; 2014.

GAVFR. (PS. BERN. CLAR.), *Coll. Sim.* = GAVFRIDVS (PS. BERNARDVS CLARAEVALLENSIS), *Declamationes de colloquio Simonis cum Iesu* (*PL*, 184, c. 437-476).

Ger. Mag., *Artic.* = Gerardvs Magnvs, *Articuli uiginti quattuor de focaristis* – ed. R. Hofman, in Ger. Mag., *Focar.*, p. 519-538.

Ger. Mag., *Cura past.* = Gerardvs Magnvs, *Consilium de cura pastorali* – ed. R. Hofman, hoc uolumine.

Ger. Mag., *Ep.* 17; 19; 41; 42; 44; 45; 46 = Gerardvs Magnvs, *Epistola* 17; 19; 41; 42; 44; 45; 46 – ed. R. Hofman, hoc uolumine.

Ger. Mag., *Epp.* 1-75 = *Gerardi Magni Epistolae* – ed. W. Mulder (*Tekstuitgaven van Ons geestelijk erf*, 3), Antwerpen, 1933.

Ger. Mag., *Focar.* = Gerardvs Magnvs, *Sermo ad clerum Traiectensem de focaristis*, in Gerardi Magni *Opera Omnia*, Pars II.1. *Sermo ad clerum Traiectensem de focaristis – Opera minora contra focaristas* – ed. Rijcklof Hofman (*CC CM*, 235), Turnhout, 2011, p. 299-464.

Ger. Mag., *Leeringhe* = Gerardvs Magnvs, *Tractatus de simoniaca receptione sororum in conuentibus Tertii Ordinis* – ed. M. van den Berg, hoc uolumine.

Ger. Mag., *Locat.* = Gerardvs Magnvs, *Consilium de locatione cure pastoralis* – ed. R. Hofman, hoc uolumine.

Ger. Mag., *Merckelijc onderwijs* = Gerardvs Magnvs, *Een merckelijc onderwijs op die punten van der Derder Regulen des salighen vaders sinte Francisci* – ed. H. van Engen, 'Twee onuitgegeven brieven van Geert Grote over de derde orde van Sint-Franciscus', *Ons geestelijk erf*, 79 (2005), p. 105-145, at p. 131-136.

Ger. Mag., *Obseru.* = Gerardvs Magnvs, *Obseruationes quattuor de presbyteris fornicariis notoriis* – ed. R. Hofman, in Ger. Mag., *Focar.*, p. 571-576.

Ger. Mag., *Sim(onia) beg.* = Gerardvs Magnvs, *De simonia ad beguttas* – ed. M. van den Berg, hoc uolumine.

Ger. Mag., *Stat.* = Gerardvs Magnvs, *Statuta domus a magistro Gerardo feminis deuotis destinatae* – ed. M. van den Berg, hoc uolumine.

Ger. Mag., *Tract. paup.* = Gerardvs Magnvs, *Sermo in festo palmarum de paupertate* – ed. R. Hofman, hoc uolumine.

Ger. Mag., *Turrim* = Gerardi Magni *Contra turrim Traiectensem* – ed. R. Hofman (*CC CM*, 192), Turnhout, 2003, p. 745-814.

Gloss. ord. in Bibl. = *Biblia Latina cum glossa ordinaria. Facsimile reprint of the Editio princeps (Strassburg 1480-1481)* – with an introd. by M. T. Gibson and K. Froehlich, Turnhout, 1992.

Grat., *Decr.* = *Corpus iuris canonici*, pars prior: *Decretum magistri Gratiani* – ed. E. Friedberg, Leipzig, 1879.

Greg. Magn., *Dial.* = Grégoire le Grand, *Dialogues*, T. 1-3 – ed. A. de Vogüé, trad. P. Antin (*Sources chrétiennes*, 251; 260; 265), Paris, 1978-1980.

Greg. Magn., *Ep.* = Gregorivs Magnvs, *Registrum epistolarum* – ed. D. Norberg (*CC SL*, 140-140A), Turnhout, 1982.

GREG. MAGN., *Hom.* = GREGORIVS MAGNVS, *Homiliae in euangelia* – ed. R. Étaix (*CC SL*, 141), Turnhout, 1999.

GREG. MAGN., *Hom. Ez.* = GREGORIVS MAGNVS, *Homiliae in Hiezechihelem prophetam* – ed. M. Adriaen (*CC SL*, 142), Turnhout, 1971.

GREG. MAGN., *Moral.* = GREGORIVS MAGNVS, *Moralia in Iob* – ed. M. Adriaen (*CC SL*, 143-143B), Turnhout, 1979-1985.

GREG. MAGN., *Reg. Past.* = GREGORIVS MAGNVS, *Regula pastoralis* – ed. F. Rommel (*SC*, 381-382), Paris, 1992.

GREG. VII, *Reg.* = *Das Register Gregors VII. Gregorii VII registrum* – ed. E. Caspar (*MGH, Epp. Sel.*, t. 2.1-2), Berlin, 1920-1923.

GREGORIVS PAPA IX, cfr supra, s.v. *Decretales*.

GVIL. ALT., *Summa* = MAGISTER GVILLELMVS ALTISSIODORENSIS, *Summa aurea* (Vol. 1-5) – cura et studio Jean Ribaillier, Paris, Grottaferrata (Roma), 1980-1987.

GVIL. RHED., *App. ad Sum. Raym.* = GVILLELMVS RHEDONENSIS, *Apparatus ad Summam Raymundi*, in *Summa sancti Raymundi de Peniafort Barcinonensis O.P. de poenitentia et matrimonio cum glossis Ioannis de Friburgo... nunc primum in lucem edita*, Romae, 1603; the copy kept at the Bayerische Staatsbibliothek München is available on-line at http://reader.digitale-sammlungen.de/resolve/display/bsb10635019.html, or by searching for 'Raimundus' and 'Summa' in the search screen 'Suche nach Digitalisaten im OPAC der BSB' at http://www.digitale-sammlungen.de/.

HELIN., *Serm.* = HELINANDVS FRIGIDI MONTIS, *Sermones* (*PL*, 212, 481C-720C)

HENR. BOIC, *Dist.* = *Henrici Boich Lugdunensis iuris utriusque doctoris clarissimi In quinque decretalium libros commentaria, postrema hac editione, majori quam ante studio recognita & ab erroribus ex vetustate contractis repurgata*, continentia *Distinctiones in quinque libros Decretalium*, Venetiis, 1576; the copy kept at the Bayerische Staatsbibliothek München is available on-line by searching for 'Bohic' in the field 'digitale sammlungen' (top left) at http://www.digitale-sammlungen.de/.

HENR. GAND., *Quodl.* 2 = HENRICVS DE GANDAVO, *Quodlibet* II – ed. R. Wielockx (*Henrici de Gandavo Opera omnia*, 6), Leuven, 1983.

HIER., *Adu. Iou.* = S. HIERONYMVS PRESBYTER, *Aduersus Iouinianum* (*PL*, 23, c. 221-352).

HIER., *Comm. in Ezech.* = *S. Hieronymi presbyteri Opera*. Pars 1. *Opera exegetica* 4. *Commentariorum in Hiezechielem libri* 14 – ed. F. Glorie (*CC SL*, 75), Turnhout, 1964.

HIER., *Comm. in Proph. Min.* = *S. Hieronymi presbyteri Opera*. Pars 1. *Opera exegetica* 6. *Commentarii in prophetas minores* – ed. M. Adriaen (*CC SL*, 76-76A), Turnhout, 1969.

HIER., *In Math.* = *S. Hieronymi presbyteri Opera.* Pars I. *Opera exegetica* 7. *Commentariorum in Matheum libri* 4 – ed. D. Hurst, M. Adriaen (*CC SL*, 77), Turnhout, 1969.

Homil. Vadst. = *Homiletica Vadstenensia ad religiosos et sacerdotes* – ed. M. Berggren (*CC CM*, 229), Turnhout, 2009.

HOST., *Summa* = *Summa D. Henrici cardinalis Hostiensis... una cum summariis & adnotationibus R. patris domini N. Superantii*, Lyon, 1537, repr. Aalen, 1962, uel *Henrici de Segusio cardinalis Hostiensis Summa aurea ad uetustissimos codices summa fide diligentiáque nunc primùm collata, atque ab innumeris erroribus, quibus scatebat hactenus, repurgata, cum antiquis Nic. Superantii, atque eruditis recèns ex summa F. Martini Abbatis... adiectis adnotationibus*, Venetiis, 1574, available online at http://web.colby.edu/canonlaw/2009/09/24/liber-extra-decretalists.

HRAB. MAVR., *Exp. in Matth.* = HRABANVS MAVRVS, *Expositio in Matthaeum* – ed. B. Löfstedt (*CC CM*, 174-174A), Turnhout, 2000.

INNOC., *Comm. Decret.* = *Divina Innocentii IIII. pontificis maximi... in V. libros Decretalium commentaria, A D. L. Paulo Rosello adnotationibvs... ornata*, Venetiis, 1570, repr. Frankfurt, 1968, uel *Innocentii IIII. pontificis maximi super libros quinque Decretalium commentaria... nouisque insuper summariis additis et Margarita Baldi de Ubaldis Perusini*, Francofurti ad Moenum, 1570, available online at http://web.colby.edu/canonlaw/2009/09/24/liber-extra-decretalists.

IOH. ANDR., *Glos. ord. in Sext., Clem.* = *Liber sextus decretalium D. Bonifacii Papae .VIII. suae integritati una cum Clementinis, & Extrauagantibus, earumque glossis* [sc. Iohannis Andreae] *restitutus, cum priuilegio Gregorii XIII. pont. max. et aliorum principum*, Romae, 1582 (available online at http://digital.library.ucla.edu/canonlaw); editio ultima, Parisiis, 1612, etiam adhibita est, sed minus frequenter.

PS. IOH. CHRYS., *Opus imperf.* = PS. IOHANNES CHRYSOSTOMVS, *Opus imperfectum* (*PG*, 56, c. 611-946).

IOH. FRIB., *Summa Conf.* = IOHANNES FRIBVRGENSIS, *Summa Confessorum*, editio princeps, Augsburg, Günther Zainer, 1476 (Hain, 7365, cfr E. Hertrich *et al.*, *Bayerische Staatsbibliothek, Inkunabelkatalog*, Bd. 3, Wiesbaden, 1988, p. 414-415); the copy kept at the Bayerische Staatsbibliothek München is available on-line by searching for "Johannes de Friburgo" in the search screen 'Suche nach Digitalisaten im OPAC der BSB' at http://www.digitale-sammlungen.de/.

ISID., *Et.* = ISIDORVS HISPALENSIS, *Etymologiarum siue Originum Libri XX* – ed. W. M. Lindsay (*Oxford Classical Texts*), Oxford, 1911.

IVO CARN., *Serm.* = IVO CARNOTENSIS, *De ecclesiasticis sacramentis et officiis ac praecipuis per annum festis sermones* (*PL*, 162, c. 505A-610B).

IVST., *Dig.* = IVSTINIANI *Institutiones* – rec. P. Krueger; *Digesta* – rec. Th. Mommsen, retr. P. Krueger (*Corpus iuris ciuilis*, vol. 1), Berolini, 1928 (ed. stereotypa quinta decima).

LACT., *Diu. inst.* = *L. Caeli Firmiani Lactanti Opera omnia.* Ps. 1. *Diuinae institutiones et epitome diuinarum institutionum* – rec. S. Brandt (*CSEL*, 19), Vindobonae etc., 1890.

LIV., *A.u.c.* = TITVS LIVIVS, *Ab urbe condita* – ed. W. Weissenborn et M. Müller (*Bibl. Teubneriana*), Leipzig, 1932.

PETRVS LOMB., *Sent.* = *Magistri Petri Lombardi, Parisiensis Episcopi, Sententiae in IV libris distinctae* – ed. Collegium S. Bonaventurae ad Claras Aquas [i.e. V. Doucet], ed. tert., T. I, Pars 1, *Prolegomena*; Pars 2, *L. I-II*, Grottaferrata (Romae), 1971; T. II, *L. III-IV*, ibid., 1981.

PLIN., *Nat. hist.* = PLINIVS MAIOR (CAIVS PLINIVS SECVNDVS), *Naturalis historia* – ed. L. Ian – C. Mayhoff (*Bibl. Teubneriana*), Leipzig, 1892-1909.

RAYM., *Summa* = *Sancti Raymundi de Pennaforte ordinis praedicatorum Summa, ad manuscriptorum fidem recognita & emendata sacrorumque canonum, qui in codicibus & anterioribus editionibus tantummodo allegantur, testimoniis aucta, juxta editionem anni* MDCCXX, *quam P. Honoratus Vincentius Laget procurauit*, Verona, 1744, editio critica:

RAYM., *Summa de paen.* = RAIMVNDVS DE PENNAFORTE, *Summa de paenitentia* – cur. X. Ochoa et A. Diez (*Universa bibliotheca iuris*, vol. 1, t. B), Roma, 1976, or cfr *Summa sancti Raymundi de Peniafort Barcinonensis O.P. de poenitentia et matrimonio cum glossis Ioannis de Friburgo... nunc primum in lucem edita*, Romae, 1603; the copy kept at the Bayerische Staatsbibliothek München is available on-line at http://reader.digitale-sammlungen.de/resolve/display/bsb10635019.html, or by searching for 'Raimundus' and 'Summa' in the search screen 'Suche nach Digitalisaten im OPAC der BSB' at http://www.digitale-sammlungen.de/.

Reg. ord. tert. edita in *Bullarum, Diplomatum et Privilegiorum Sanctorum Romanorum Pontificum Taurinensis Editio* – ed. F. Gaude, Augustae Taurinorum, 1859, T. 4, p. 90-95.

RVF., *Summa* = *Die Summa Decretorum des Magister Rufinus* – ed. H. Singer, Paderborn, 1902.

RVP. TVIT., *Apoc.* = RVPERTVS TVITIENSIS, *Commentarium in Apocalypsim Iohannis apostoli* (*PL*, 169, c. 827A-1214C).

SEN., *Dial.* = L. ANNAEVS SENECA, *Dialogorum liber 2. De constantia sapientis*, in *Dialogorum libri 12* – ed. E. Hermes, in *L. Annaei Senecae Opera quae supersunt* (*Bibl. Teubneriana*), Vol. 1.1, Leipzig, 1905, p. 21-45.

SEN., *Ep.* = L. ANNAEVS SENECA, *Ad Lucilium epistularum moralium quae supersunt* – ed. O. Hense, in *L. Annaei Senecae Opera quae supersunt*, Vol. 3 (*Bibl. Teubneriana*), Lipsiae, 1898, p. 1-599.

PS. SEN., *Mor.* = PS. SENECA, *De moribus* – ed. F. [G. H. C.] Haase, in *L. Annaei Senecae Opera quae supersunt, Supplementum* (*Bibl. Teubneriana*), Lipsiae, ed. altera stereotypa, 1902, p. 463-467 (= PS. MARTINVS BRACCARENSIS, *Libellus de moribus* (*PL*, 72, c. 29A-32C)); super auctorem cfr MEERSSEMAN, *Seneca*, p. 49-58.

SINGER, *Thesaurus prouerbiorum* = S. SINGER (begr.), *Thesaurus prouerbiorum medii aeui. Lexikon der Sprichwörter des romanisch-germanischen Mittelalters*, Bd. 1-13, Berlin etc., 1995-2002.

Stat. synod. Leod. = *Les statuts synodaux de Jean de Flandre, évêque de Liège (1288)* – éd. critique précédée d'une étude de leur sources et de leur contenu, publiée par J. Avril (*Bulletin de la Société d'Art et d'Histoire du Diocèse de Liège*, t. 61), Liège, 1996.

SVET., *Caes.* = C. SVETONIVS TRANQVILLVS, *De uita Caesarum libri 8* – ed. M. Ihm (*Bibl. Teubneriana*), Lipsiae, 1908.

SVSO, *Hor.* = *Heinrich Seuses Horologium sapientiae* – ed. P. Künzle (*Spicilegium Friburgense*, 23), Freiburg/Schweiz, 1977, textum circiter a. 1350-1400 in uulgari Brabantina lingua conuersum ed. Zr. H. van de Wijnpersse, *Oerloy der ewigher wijsheit* (*Horologium sapientiae door Henricus Suso O.P.*), Groningen, 1938.

THOM., *Perf.* = THOMAS AQVINAS, *De perfectione spiritualis vitae* – cura et studio fratrum praedicatorum, in *Sancti Thomae de Aquino Opera omnia iussu Leonis XIII p. m. edita*, T. 41B, Romae, 1970.

THOM., *Sent.* (L. 1 – L. 4, d. 1-22) = *S. Thomae Aquinatis Ordinis Praedicatorum... Scriptum super Sententiis Magistri Petri Lombardi episcopi Parisiensis*, 1-4. *Scriptum super primo – quarto libro Sententiarum* – ed. noua curâ; *uel* recognouit atque iterum edidit R. P. [P. F.] Mandonnet O.P., M. F. Moos O.P., Paris, 1929-1947.

THOM., *Sent.* (Lib. 4, d. 23-50) = *Sancti Thomae Aquinatis Opera omnia*, T. 7/2, *Commentum in quartum librum Sententiarum magistri Petri Lombardi*, Parmae, 1858, p. 872-1259.

THOM., *Sent. pol.* = THOMAS AQVINAS, *Sententia libri politicorum* – cura et studio fratrum praedicatorum, in *Sancti Thomae Aquinatis doctoris angelici Opera omnia*, T. 48, Roma, 1971.

THOM., I = THOMAS AQVINAS, *Pars prima summae theologiae a q. 1 ad q. 49*, et *Pars prima summae theologiae a q. 50 ad q. 119* – cura et studio fratrum eiusdem [praedicatorum] ordinis, in *S. Thomae Aquinatis doct. ang. Opera omnia iussu impensaque Leonis XIII p. m. edita*, T. 4-5, Roma, 1888-1889.

THOM., I-II = THOMAS AQVINAS, *Prima secundae summae theologiae a q. 1 ad q. 70*, et *Prima secundae summae theologiae a q. 71 ad q. 114* – cura et studio fratrum eiusdem [praedicatorum] ordinis, in *S. Thomae Aquinatis doct. ang. Opera omnia iussu impensaque Leonis XIII p. m. edita*, T. 6-7, Roma, 1891-1892.

THOM., II-II = THOMAS AQVINAS, *Secunda secundae summae theologiae* – cura et studio fratrum eiusdem [praedicatorum] ordinis, in *S. Thomae Aquinatis doct. ang. Opera omnia iussu impensaque Leonis XIII p. m. edita*, T. 8-10, Roma, 1895-1899.

THOM., III = THOMAS AQVINAS, *Summae theologiae tertia pars* – cura et studio fratrum eiusdem [praedicatorum] ordinis, in *S. Thomae Aquinatis doct. ang. Opera omnia iussu impensaque Leonis XIII p. m. edita*, T. 11-12, Roma, 1903-1905.

THOM. KEMP., *Chron.* = THOMAS A KEMPIS, *Chronica Montis S. Agnetis*, in *Thomae Hemerken a Kempis canonici regularis ordinis S. Augustini Opera Omnia*, Bd. 7 – ed. M. J. Pohl, Freiburg im Breisgau, 1922, p. 333-478.

THOM. KEMP., *Dial.* = THOMAS A KEMPIS, *Dialogus nouiciorum*, in *Thomae Hemerken a Kempis canonici regularis ordinis S. Augustini Opera Omnia*, Bd. 7 – ed. M. J. Pohl, Freiburg im Breisgau, 1922, p. 3-329.

VAL. MAX., *Mem.* = VALERIVS MAXIMVS, *Facta et dicta memorabilia* – ed. C. Kempf (*Bibl. Teubneriana*), Leipzig, 1888.

VIRG., *Geo.* = P. VIRGILIVS MARO, *Georgicon liber* – ed. R. A. B. Mynors (*Oxford Classical Texts*), Oxford, 1969.

SECONDARY LITERATURE

ACQUOY, *Epistolae* = J. G. R. ACQUOY, *Gerardi Magni Epistolae XIV*, Amsterdam, 1857.

BBKL = *Biographisch-bibliographisches Kirchenlexikon*, Bd. 1-14, *Ergänzungen* 1-18, Bd. 15-21, Begr. und hrsg. von F. W. BAUTZ, fortgef. von T. BAUTZ, Hamm (Westf.), later Herzberg, Nordhausen, 1970-1998 (-2010), on-line version at http://www.bautz.de/bbkl/.

DE BEER, *Spiritualiteit* = K. C. L. M. DE BEER, *Studie over de spiritualiteit van Geert Groote*, Brussel – Nijmegen, 1938.

CHARLAND, *Artes praedicandi* = Th. M. CHARLAND, *Artes praedicandi. Contribution à l'histoire de la rhétorique au Moyen Âge*, Paris – Ottawa, 1936.

CMD-NL = G. I. LIEFTINCK – J. P. GUMBERT, *Manuscrits datés conservés dans les Pays-Bas. Catalogue paléographique des manuscrits en écriture latine portant des indications de date*, T. 1, 1-2, Amsterdam, 1964; T. 2, 1-2, Leiden etc., 1988.

CLARISSE, 'Groete' = J. CLARISSE, 'Over den geest en de denkwijze van Geert Groete (Groot, de Groot), kenbaar uit zijne schriften', *Archief voor kerkelijke geschiedenis, inzonderheid van Nederland*, 2 (1830), p. 245-395; 3 (1831), p. 1-90; 8 (1837), p. 3-383.

CONSTABLE, *Letters* = G. CONSTABLE, *Letters and Letter-collections (Typologie des sources du moyen âge occidental*, A-2, 17), Turnhout, 1976.

COURTENAY, *Rotuli* = W. J. COURTENAY, E. D. GODDARD (ed.), *Rotuli Parisienses. Supplications to the Pope from the University of Paris*, Vol. 1. *1316-1349*; Vol. 2. *1352-1378*, Leiden etc., 2002-2004.

COWDREY, *Gregory VII* = H. E. J. COWDREY, *Pope Gregory VII, 1073-1085*, Oxford, 1998.

DEPAIRE, *Croisiers* = J.-P. DEPAIRE, *La bibliothèque des Croisiers de Huy, de Liège et de Namur*, 2 vols, Liège, 1969-1970.

DUMBAR, *Deventer* = G. DUMBAR, *Het kerkelyk en wereltlyk Deventer, behelzende eene uitvoerige beschryving van stats oirsprong, verscheide benaemingen, gelegenheit... als ook een omstandigh verhael der beurtenissen van oude tyden af...: uit echte bezegelde brieven, kloosterschriften, en oude aentekeningen, meest alle nooit voorhene gedrukt, en verscheide voornaeme schryveren*, Deventer, 1732.

VAN DIJK, 'Briefschaften' = R. VAN DIJK, 'Die Überlieferung der Briefschaften von Geert Grote', *Quaerendo*, 41 (2011), p. 172-182.

VAN DIJK, 'Kartuizers' = R. Th. M. VAN DIJK, 'Tussen kartuizers en cisterciënzers. De brieven van Geert Grote aan de abdij van Kamp', in *A Fish Out of Water? From Contemplative Solitude to Carthusian Involvement in Pastoral Care and Reform Activity. Proceedings of the Symposium Ordo pre ceteris commendatus. Held in Zelem, Belgium, September 2008* – ed. S. J. Molvarec – T. Gaens, Leuven, 2013, p. 127-163.

VAN DIJK, *Prolegomena* = R. Th. M. VAN DIJK, *Prolegomena ad Gerardi Magni Opera Omnia. Pars I, 1. Die Forschungslage des gesamten Schrifttums (mit Ausnahme des Stundenbuches)* = *Gerardi Magni Opera Omnia*, Vol. I (*CC CM*, 192), Turnhout, 2003, p. 17-744.

VAN DIJK, 'Raadgevingen' = R. Th. M. VAN DIJK, 'Raadgevingen voor een kartuizernovice. Geert Grote en zijn *Brief over een nieuwe monnik*', in R. VAN DIJK, *Twaalf kapittels over ontstaan, bloei en doorwerking van de Moderne Devotie* – ed. Ch. Caspers en R. Hofman, Hilversum, 2012, p. 19-43.

VAN DIJK, *Salome* = R. Th. M. VAN DIJK O.Carm., *Salome Sticken (1369-1449) en de oorsprong van de Moderne Devotie*, met medewerking van R. Hofman, en met een eerste kritische editie van de *Statuten van het Meester-Geertshuis*, bezorgd door M. van den Berg, Hilversum, 2015.

ELM, 'Reformbemühungen' = K. ELM, 'Spätmittelalterliche Reformbemühungen unter den Zisterziensern im Rheinland und in den Niederlanden', in *Die niederrheinischen Zisterzienser im späten Mittelalter* – ed. R. Kottje, Köln, 1992, p. 3-20.

ELM, 'Westfälisches Zisterziensertum' = K. ELM, 'Westfälisches Zisterziensertum und spätmittelalterliche Reformbewegung', in *Mittelalterliches Ordensleben in Westfalen und am Niederrhein* – ed. K. Elm, Paderborn, 1989.

ELM – FEIGE, 'Verfall' = K. ELM – P. FEIGE, 'Der Verfall des zisterziensischen Ordenslebens im späten Mittelalter'; 'Reformen und Kongregazionsbildungen der Zisterzienser im Spätmittelalter und früher Neuzeit', in *Die Zisterzienser. Ordensleben zwischen Ideal und Wirklichkeit. Eine Ausstellung des Landschaftsverbandes Rheinland, Rheinisches Museumsamt, Brauweiler; Aachen, Krönungssaal des Rathauses, 3. Juli-28. September 1980* [– ed. K. Elm, P. Joerißen, H. J. Roth], Köln, Bonn, 1980, p. 237-254.

VAN ENGEN, 'Brieven' = H. VAN ENGEN, 'Twee onuitgegeven brieven van Geert Grote over de derde orde van Sint-Franciscus', *Ons geestelijk erf*, 79 (2005), p. 105-145.

VAN ENGEN, *Derde Orde* = H. VAN ENGEN, *De derde orde van Sint-Franciscus in het middeleeuwse bisdom Utrecht. Een bijdrage tot de institutionele geschiedenis van de Moderne Devotie*, Hilversum, 2006.

VAN ENGEN, 'Managing the Common Life' = J. VAN ENGEN, 'Managing the Common Life: The Brothers at Deventer and the Codex of the Household (The Hague, MS KB 70 H 75)', in *Schriftlichkeit und Lebenspraxis im Mittelalter* – ed. H. Keller, C. Meier and T. Scharff, München, 1999, p. 111-169.

VAN ENGEN, *Sisters and Brothers* = J. VAN ENGEN, *Sisters and Brothers of the Common Life*, Philadelphia, 2008.

VAN ENGEN, 'Writings' = J. VAN ENGEN, 'The Writings of Master Geert Grote of Deventer, Deacon (1340-84)', *Ons geestelijk erf*, 78 (2004), p. 345-368.

ÉPINEY-BURGARD, *Gérard Grote* = G. ÉPINEY-BURGARD, *Gérard Grote (1340-1384) et les débuts de la Dévotion Moderne*, Wiesbaden, 1970.

ÉPINEY-BURGARD, *Lettres* = G. ÉPINEY-BURGARD, *Gérard Grote, fondateur de la Dévotion Moderne, Lettres et traités. Présentation, traduction et notes*, Turnhout, 1998.

FIERENS, *Suppliques d'Urbain V* = A. FIERENS, *Suppliques d'Urbain V (1362-1370). Textes et analyses (Analecta Vaticano-Belgica. Documents relatifs aux anciens diocèses de Cambrai, Liège, Thérouanne et Tournai*, vol. 7), Rome etc., 1914.

GAENS, 'Carthusian influences' = T. GAENS, 'Fons hortorum irriguus, ceteras irrigans religiones. Carthusian influences on monastic reform in Germany and the Low Countries in the 15th century', in *A Fish Out of Water? From Contemplative Solitude to Carthusian Involvement in Pastoral Care and Reform Activity. Proceedings of the Symposium Ordo pre ceteris commendatus. Held in Zelem, Belgium, September 2008* – ed. S. J. Molvarec – T. Gaens, Leuven, 2013, p. 51-103.

GOERING, 'Internal forum' = J. GOERING, 'The Internal Forum and the Literature of Penance and Confession', in HARTMANN et al., History, Ch. 12, p. 379-482.

GOUDRIAAN, 'Grote on simony' = K. GOUDRIAAN, 'Geert Grote, On simony to the Beguines, and Church Reform', in *Die räumliche und geistige Ausstrahlung der Devotio Moderna – zur Dynamik ihres Gedankengutes (Die Devotio Moderna. Sozialer und kultureller Transfer (1350-1580)*, Bd. 2) – ed. I. Kwiatkowski and J. Engelbrecht, Münster, 2013, p. 115-140.

HARTMANN et al., History = W. HARTMANN, K. PENNINGTON (ed.), *The history of medieval canon law in the Classical Period, 1140-1234. From Gratian to the Decretals of pope Gregory IX*, Washington, D.C., 2008.

HOFMAN, 'Brulocht' = Ioannis Rusbrochii *Ornatus spiritualis desponsationis* Gerardo Magno interprete, cura et studio R. Hofman (*CC CM*, 172), Turnhout, 2000.

HOFMAN, 'Crutched Friars' = 'The early reception of the *Deuotio moderna* among the Crutched Friars', *Church History and Religious Culture*, 93.4 (2013), p. 505-534.

HOFMAN, *Focar.* = Gerardi Magni *Opera Omnia*, Pars II.1. *Sermo ad clerum Traiectensem de focaristis – Opera minora contra focaristas*, cura et studio Rijcklof HOFMAN (*CC CM*, 235), Turnhout, 2011.

HOFMAN, 'Functionaliteit' = R. HOFMAN, 'De functionaliteit van handschriften uit de Moderne Devotie', in *Geen povere schoonheid: bijdragen over laat-middeleeuwse kunst in verband met de Moderne Devotie* – ed. K. Veelenturf, Nijmegen, 2000, p. 169-194.

HOFMAN, 'Recipients' = R. HOFMAN, 'The recipient(s) of Geert Grote's *Letters* 15, 27 and 85', in *Ons geestelijk erf*, 87 (2016) (forthcoming).

HULLU, 'Statuten' = J. DE HULLU (ed.), 'De Statuten van het Meester Geertshuis te Deventer', in *Archief voor Nederlandsche Kerkgeschiedenis*, 6 (1897), p. 63-76 (edition on p. 65-74).

KIENZLE, *Sermon* = B. M. KIENZLE (dir.), *The sermon* (*Typologie des sources du Moyen Âge occidental*, fasc. 81-83), Turnhout, 2000.

KLAUSMANN, 'Satzungen' = Th. KLAUSMANN, 'Die ältesten Satzungen der Devotio moderna', in *Kirchenreform von unten. Gerhard Zerbolt von Zutphen und die Brüder vom gemeinsamen Leben* – ed. N. Staubach, Frankfurt am Main, 2004, p. 24-43.

KRÄMER, *Handschriftenerbe*, 1989-1990 = S. KRÄMER, *Handschriftenerbe des deutschen Mittelalters* (*Mittelalterliche Bibliothekskataloge Deutschlands und der Schweiz*, Ergänzungsband 1, Teil 1-2), München, 1989-1990.

KRAUß, *Devotio moderna* = S. KRAUß, *Die "Devotio moderna" in Deventer. Anatomie eines Zentrums der Reformbewegung*, Berlin, 2007.

KUYS, *Kerkelijke* = J. KUYS, *Kerkelijke organisatie in het middeleeuwse bisdom Utrecht*, Nijmegen, 2004.

LAENEN, *Introduction* = J. LAENEN, *Introduction à l'histoire paroissiale du diocèse de Malines. Les institutions*, Bruxelles, 1924.

Lexicon Nederl. = *Lexicon Latinitatis Nederlandicae Medii Aeui. Woordenboek van het middeleeuws Latijn van de Noordelijke Nederlanden*, composuit J. W. FUCHS adiuuante O. WEIJERS, Leiden, 1970-2005.

LYNCH, *Simoniacal entry* = J. H. LYNCH, *Simoniacal entry into religious life from 1000 to 1260. A social, economic and legal study*, Columbus, 1976.

MEERSSEMAN, *Seneca* = G. G. MEERSSEMAN, 'Seneca maestro di spiritualità nei suoi opuscoli apocrifi dal XII al XV secolo', *Italia medioevale e umanistica*, 16 (1973), p. 43-135.

MERTENS, 'Lezen met de pen' = Th. MERTENS, 'Lezen met de pen. Ontwikkelingen in het laatmiddeleeuws geestelijk proza', in *De studie van de Middelnederlandse letterkunde, stand en toekomst. Symposium Antwerpen 22-24 september 1988* – ed. F. P. van Oostrom, F. Willaert, Hilversum, 1989, p. 187-200.

MIXSON, J. D., *Poverty's proprietors. Ownership and mortal sin at the origins of the Observant Movement*, Leiden etc., 2009.

MOLL, 'Sermoen' = W. MOLL, 'Geert Groote's Sermoen voor Palmzondag over de vrijwillige armoede volgens handschriften der vijftiende eeuw', *Studiën en Bijdragen op 't gebied der Historische Theologie*, 2 (1872), p. 425-469 (Text p. 432-469).

MULDER, *Epp.*: cfr supra, GER. MAG., *Epp.* 1-75.

MULDERS, *Archidiakonat* = H. J. B. MULDERS, *Der Archidiakonat im Bistum Utrecht bis zum Ausgang des 14. Jahrhunderts. Eine rechtshistorische Studie zum kirchlichen Verfassungsrecht*, Utrecht [etc.], 1943.

PANSTERS, *Deugden* = K. PANSTERS, *De kardinale deugden in de Lage Landen, 1200-1500*, Hilversum, 2007.

PENNINGTON – MÜLLER, 'Decretists' = K. PENNINGTON – W. P. MÜLLER, 'The Decretists. The Italian school', in HARTMANN *et al.*, *History*, p. 121-173.

POST, 'Oorkonden' = R. POST, 'Geert Groote in Pauselijke oorkonden', *Mededeelingen van het Nederlandsch historisch Instituut te Rome*, 2ᵉ Rks., 5 (1935), p. 31-49.

POST, *Kerkgeschiedenis* = R. R. POST, *Kerkgeschiedenis van Nederland in de Middeleeuwen*, Utrecht, 1957.

POST, *Modern Devotion* = R. R. POST, *The Modern Devotion. Confrontation with Reformation and Humanism*, Leiden, 1968.

POST, 'Statuten' = R. POST, 'De statuten van het Mr. Geertshuis te Deventer', *Archief voor de Geschiedenis van het Aartsbisdom Utrecht*, 71 (1952), p. 1-46 (parallel edition ibid., p. 3-21).

POST, Supplieken = R. R. POST, *Supplieken gericht aan de pausen Clemens VI, Innocentius VI en Urbanus V, 1342-1366*, 's-Gravenhage, 1937.

Repertorium Germanicum = *Repertorium Germanicum. Verzeichnis der in den päpstlichen Registern und Kameralakten vorkommenden Personen, Kirchen und Orte des Deutschen Reiches, seiner Diözesen und Territorien vom Beginn des Schismas bis zur Reformation*, hrsg. vom Königlich Preußischen Historischen Institut in Rom, Teil 1. *Verzeichnis der in den Registern und Kameralakten Clemens' VII. von Avignon vorkommenden Personen, Kirchen und Orte des Deutschen Reiches, seiner Diözesen und Territorien, 1378-1394*, bearb. von E. GÖLLER, Berlin, 1916.

RÜTHING, 'Briefe' = H. RÜTHING, 'Vier neue Briefe Geert Grootes', *Ons geestelijk erf*, 40 (1966), p. 392-406.

RÜTHING, *Egher* = H. RÜTHING, *Der Kartäuser Heinrich Egher von Kalkar 1328-1408*, Göttingen, 1967.

SCHÖLER, *"Ama nesciri"* = M. SCHÖLER, *"Ama nesciri". Spuren des Wirkens des Bibliothekars Conradus de Grunenberg († 1465/66) in der Bibliothek der Kölner Kreuzbrüder (Libelli Rhenani*, Bd. 11), Köln: Erzbischöfliche Diözesan- und Dombibliothek, 2005.

SCHOENGEN, *Narratio* = M. SCHOENGEN (ed.), *Jacobus Traiecti alias de Voecht, Narratio de inchoatione domus clericorum in Zwollis, met akten en bescheiden betreffende dit Fraterhuis*, Amsterdam, 1908.

SINGER, *Thesaurus prouerbiorum* = S. SINGER, *Thesaurus prouerbiorum medii aeui. Lexikon der Sprichwörter des romanisch-germanischen Mittelalters*, Bd. 1-13, Berlin etc., 1995-2002.

TIECKE, *Werken* = J. G. J. TIECKE, *De werken van Geert Groote*, Nijmegen, 1941.

VENNEBUSCH, *Handschriften* = J. VENNEBUSCH, *Die theologischen Handschriften des Stadtarchivs Köln*, Teil 2. *Die Quart-Handschriften der Gymnasialbibliothek*; Teil 3. *Die Oktav-Handschriften der Gymnasialbibliothek*, Köln; Wien, 1980; 1983.

VERDAM, *Handwoordenboek* = J. VERDAM, *Middelnederlandsch handwoordenboek. Onveranderde herdruk en van het woord 'sterne' af opnieuw bewerkt door C. H. Ebbinge Wubben*, 's-Gravenhage, 1932.

De VREESE, *Simonia*, 1940 = W. DE VREESE (ed.), *Geert Groote, De simonia ad beguttas. De Middelnederlandsche tekst opnieuw uitgegeven met inleiding en aantekeningen*, 's-Gravenhage, 1940.

WACKERS, 'Latinitas' = P. WACKERS, 'Latinitas en Middelnederlandse letterkunde: ter inleiding', in *Verraders en bruggenbouwers. Verkenningen naar de relatie tussen Latinitas en de Middelnederlandse letterkunde* – ed. P. Wackers et al., Amsterdam, 1996.

WALTHER, *Prouerbia* = H. WALTHER (ed.), *Prouerbia sententiaeque latinitatis medii aeui. Lateinische Sprichwörter und Sentenzen des Mittel-*

alters in alphabetischer Anordnung, Bd. 1-6, Göttingen, 1963-1969; *Nova series. Prouerbia sententiaeque latinitatis medii ac recentioris aeui. Lateinische Sprichwörter und Sentenzen des Mittelalters und der frühen Neuzeit in alphabetischer Anordnung, aus dem Nachlaß von Hans Walther* hrsg. *von* Paul Gerhard SCHMIDT, Bd. 7-9, ibid., 1982-1986.

WANSEM, *Broederschap* = C. [J. M.] VAN DER WANSEM, *Het ontstaan en de geschiedenis der Broederschap van het Gemene Leven tot 1400*, Leuven, 1958.

WEILER, 'Grote en begijnen' = A. G. WEILER, 'Geert Grote en begijnen in de begintijd van de Moderne Devotie', *Ons geestelijk erf*, 69 (1995), p. 114-132.

WEILER, *Norm* = A. G. WEILER, *Volgens de norm van de vroege kerk*, Nijmegen, 1997.

WEITZEL, *Simonie* = J. WEITZEL, *Begriff und Erscheinungsformen der Simonie bei Gratian und den Dekretisten*, München, 1967.

WERNER, *Sprichwörter* = J. WERNER, *Lateinische Sprichwörter und Sinnsprüche des Mittelalters aus Handschriften gesammelt*, 2. überarb. Aufl. von Peter Flury, Darmstadt, 1966.

VAN ZIJL, *Gerard Groote* = Th. P. VAN ZIJL, *Gerard Groote, ascetic and reformer (1340-1384)*, Washington, D.C., 1963.

INTRODUCTION

CHAPTER I

GEERT GROTE AND THE PROBLEMS OF SIMONY AND PROPRIETARISM

I.1 INTRODUCTION

Shortly after his death already, Grote's biographers singled out his attempts to improve the moral standards of contemporary clergymen among his most noteworthy pursuits. His efforts in this field basically came down to opposition against two forms of abuse in the world of the clergy, incontinence and corruption.[1] What seemed to him the most proper attitude towards priests who shared their life and house with a member of the weaker vessel is set out in detail in the treatises edited in the previous volume of *Gerardi Magni Opera omnia*.[2] In the present volume his essays against three closely related topics are edited: firstly, corrupt practices in connection with the acquisition of and functioning in ecclesiastical offices, and secondly, the widespread custom to require an admission fee from prospective residents in religious institutions. Together with corrupt ordination, these evils were in Grote's days generally together referred to as different forms of simony,[3] a widespread abuse, aptly defined by Brigide Schwarz as 'jede Vergabe von Ämtern, bei der – nach Ansicht der Kritiker – bestimmte Vorteile für den Verleihenden eine Rolle gespielt hatten'.[4]

---

[1] His struggle against simony has earlier been analyzed in detail, on the basis of older editions, by VAN ZIJL, *Gerard Groote*, p. 243-273, and by ÉPINEY-BURGARD, *Gérard Grote*, p. 230-235.
[2] Cfr GER. MAG., *Focar*. (*Corpus Christianorum, Continuatio Mediaeualis*, 235), passim.
[3] Cfr for a historical sketch of the development of such misuses WEITZEL, *Simonie*, p. 48-56 and passim; cfr also below, section I.2.
[4] Cfr B. SCHWARZ, 'Die Entstehung der Ämterkäuflichkeit an der Römischen Kurie', in *Ämterhandel im Spätmittelalter und im 16. Jahrhundert* – ed. I. Mieck, Berlin, 1984, p. 61-65, at p. 61.

Closely related to simoniacal practices in relation with monastic entry is a tolerant attitude towards personal possessions belonging to individual residents in religiously living communities, a custom known as proprietarism.

Corrupt acquisition of (*Locat.*; *Ep.* 17) and misconduct in (*Cura past.*; *Ep.* 19) pastoral positions are the subject matter in the first four essays edited below; improper requirements for admission, required from prospective residents, presented suggestively as bribery by Grote, are discussed in the next essays, in part written in the vernacular (*Simonia beg.*; *Leeringhe sym.*; *Ep.* 44). Grote's views on such entrance fees are foreshadowed in the *Statutes* which he composed after he had decided to put his parental home at the disposal of devout unmarried women in 1374. In view of the remarkable overlap between these texts, which belong to such different genres, I decided that an edition of the *Statutes* had to be incorporated in this collection. I was really fortunate that Marinus van den Berg quite willingly agreed to prepare editions of all three texts originally composed in Middle Dutch.

Poverty, interpreted by Grote as a recommendable indifference, even a negative attitude towards personal belongings and property, is the subject matter of a sermon delivered by him to a religious community on Palm Sunday (*Tract. paup.*), whereas its opposite, the vice of proprietarism, is discussed in the remaining essays, all of them letters to Cistercian communities (*Ep.* 41; *Ep.* 42; *Ep.* 45; *Ep.* 46). It seems not unlikely that Grote developed his views on proprietarism under the influence of Henricus de Coesfeldia (†1410), who functioned as prior in the Carthusian community Monnikhuizen near Arnhem precisely in the period when Grote lived there as a paying guest for three years between 1374 and 1379 – Henricus is among other things known for his virulent views on proprietarism.[5]

Each of the texts edited in this volume is summarized in detail below, as first item in the chapters on the individual texts. Some general outlines are sketched in this general introduction, which may serve to place the individual texts in the context of Grote's

---

[5] This was recently suggested for the first time by GAENS, 'Carthusian influences', p. 58-59, who draws attention to the parallels between Henricus' *De tribus uotis* and Grote's *Ep.* 41. Gaens characterizes this treatise by Henricus *ibid.*, p. 52-56, and investigates the influence, reception and Nachleben of this work *ibid.*, p. 68-77.

age. First, however, the more notable discoveries which I made in the course of the preparation of this edition must be highlighted briefly.

I.1.1 A summary of the more conspicuous new insights presented in this volume

Some paragraphs of greater general importance are somewhat hidden in the separate introductions to the individual texts. It seems wise therefore to draw attention to a number of new insights here.

First, I observe in section I.3 below, fn. 59, that Grote betrays a sound knowledge of canon law in all of his treatises, but that his allusions to Roman law are quoted secondhand. This confirms that he never studied in Orléans, where students interested in Roman law had to turn to, as Roman law was not taught in Paris.

Next, section III.2 includes the description of manuscript *H2* (Den Haag, Koninklijke Bibliotheek, 78 J 55), containing one of the two still extant 'letter collections', the witness which Mulder used in 1933 as main basic manuscript for his edition of Grote's letters. I there argue among various other points that this collection has its provenance, but not origin in the Benedictine abbey Saint-Jacques in Liège, and that the small collection of letters *H1*, at present bound in the same manuscript, has been transcribed from *H2* in that abbey in 1439; this date therefore is a *terminus ante quem* for *H2*, but I further argue that *H2* should be redated to s. XVa, and that the place where *H2* has been written, and therefore its origin, possibly is the Heer-Florenshuis in Deventer. The interrelationship between the 'letter collections' and witnesses transmitting individual letters, and the comparatively good quality of the text in the 'letter collections', is addressed directly below, in section I.2.1.

Another important witness is the manuscript containing several new letters, not known to Mulder in 1933, and for the first time published by Rüthing in 1966; I propose tentatively in Ch. IX.3 that this witness was transcribed around 1500 from an exemplar having its origin in the Koblenz charterhouse St. Beatusberg, which also may mean that the 'new' letters 82-85 were written by Grote not to the Carthusian community in Monnikhuizen, as Rüthing proposed, but to the community in Koblenz.

In addition, I propose in section IX.2 a new recipient for *Ep.* 27, a newly professed anonymous Cistercian rather than Matthew from Tiel,[6] and in section V.2 a new main subject for *Ep.* 19, namely that the priest John in this letter might perhaps be identical with the John who gave away his house in Deventer to the first community of brethren around Florens rather than just an anonymous repentent priest.

The new collation of the two versions of the *Statutes* of the Meester-Geertshuis in Deventer, text 5 in the edition, exemplifies the poor quality of the transcripts published by Post in 1952, inferior also to the diplomatic edition of the long version *D* as published by De Hullu in 1896. Also, the new insights in the genesis of the long final version *D* and its relation to the short earlier version *L*, as proposed by Rudolf van Dijk in 2015 on the basis of earlier work by Th. Klausmann mainly, are now for the first time available in the modern scholar's *lingua franca*, English, in Ch. VI.

As regards *Simonia beg.*, Goudriaan's recent suggestion that the three chapters in this conglomerate are in fact three separate 'essays' on the same subject matter, originally destined for different addressees,[7] although attractive in itself, is called into question again in the introduction to this text in Ch. VII.1 below, on the basis of the many cross-references in the text among others. Also, it is argued in Ch. VIII that the transcript of *Leeringhe*, as made in 1531 by the lay Franciscan Friar Peter Jansz, cannot possibly be taken as an accurate and conscientious copy of Grote's original text.

And finally, it is (cautiously!) suggested in section XIV.1.1 that one of Grote's most polished and literary products,[8] his *Sermon on the occasion of Palm Sunday about ‹voluntary› poverty*, was written for the community of the Cistercian abbey of Kamp-Lintfort in the Niederrhein region, and perhaps delivered there by Grote in person, either on 15 March 1383 or on 3 April 1384.

I.1.2 Some further observations on the *Letters* and the 'letter collections'

The texts edited in this volume include several essays and letters transmitted both independently and also in the so-called

---

[6] Cfr on this apart from Ch. IX.2 below also HOFMAN, 'Recipients'.

[7] Cfr GOUDRIAAN, 'Grote on simony', p. 120-123.

[8] Cfr on this judgment ÉPINEY-BURGARD, *Lettres*, p. 137, and ÉPINEY-BURGARD, *Gérard Grote*, p. 223.

corpora epistolarum (or in the case of *Epp.* 17; 19 exclusively so), the three collections of letters compiled in the close proximity of Grote during his lifetime or shortly after his death.[9] Although a reasonable case can certainly be made for a decision to omit texts evidently composed as letters from an edition of essays, I have nevertheless decided to include all 'letters' or 'letter-like amalgams of genres' discussing simony and proprietarism in this edition. A valid argument in favour of this choice obviously is the overlap in subject matter. However, I was enticed to this choice by another argument also: after I had finished the collation of *Cura past.*, I was struck by the good quality and relatively deviant position in the stemma of the version of that text as transmitted through both letter collections, *L* and *H2*. I therefore hoped to be able to get new insight in the genesis and origin of the letter collections by comparing the quality of the witnesses of other texts transmitted independently as well as through these collections.

When the version in *LH2* could in these cases also compete with the best independent witnesses, this would confirm that the collections originated in Grote's personal surroundings. In this connection, it seems apt to highlight a few considerations in this introduction already.

At some places, a comparison between readings in the letter collections *LH2* on the one hand and parallel readings in other witnesses for specific letters on the other hand may shed light on the text in the common exemplar of *LH2* (cfr section IV.4.1 below). An interesting example occurs in *Ep.* 44, 54. The independent manuscripts *KOB* here transmit a superior reading, "columpna et firmamentum", an obvious *lectio difficilior*, whereas the scribes of *LH2* were clearly hesitant about what to do with the text which they found in their exemplar. In *L* we find "columpna et firma fundamentum", in *H2* "fundamentum" in the main hand *H2¹*, which was corrected between the lines with super-

---

[9] Cfr on the three 'letter collections' of Grote now primarily VAN DIJK, 'Briefschaften', p. 172-182, for a succinct evaluation of their possible genesis and character VAN ENGEN, 'Writings', p. 349-353, for a detailed description of the collection which originated in Namur HOFMAN, 'Crutched Friars', p. 521-529, where I have corrected my in part mistaken views in HOFMAN, *Focar.*, p. 135-138. The collections are evaluated in VAN DIJK, *Prolegomena*, p. 478-563, manuscripts described ibid., p. 190-203 (*H2*); 270-284 (*L*); 287-300 (*M*). The origin and connections of *H2* are discussed in connection with the detailed description of the manuscript, below, in section III.2.

scribed "firma" in the hand of the corrector $H2^2$. All of this points to an originally correct "columpna et firmamentum" in the common exemplar, which was then 'emended' into "columpna et fundamentum". In itself, this emendation is perfectly understandable: 'column' quite naturally suggests "fundamentum" (fundament) rather than "firmamentum", as this latter word was much more common in the fifteenth century in the derived sense 'firmament' than in the original, literal sense 'strengthening'. The embarrassment of the scribes of *LH2* at this place therefore reveals that their common exemplar went through a correction process before the actual copy was released for further use.

Another error in the common exemplar of *LH2* is revealed in *Ep.* 46, where the reading of the two other (fragmentary) witnesses should be preferred: in l. **21**, *WKk* transmit "nullo modo" against "a nullo" in *L* and "nullo" in *H2*, pointing to a misread abbreviation "nllo°" representing "nullo modo" in their common exemplar, with attempt at emendation in *L*, but not in *H2*.

A disputable decision taken by Mulder about *Ep.* 42

In his edition of Grote's collected letters, Mulder convincingly argues that Grote's letters to the abbot (*Epp.* 41; 43; 44) and community (*Ep.* 42) of the Cistercian abbey near Kamp-Lintfort should be linked to the election of William of Cologne, who took up his office on 7 November 1382.[10] He further associates *Ep.* 42 (written to the community of monks in the abbey) with the first letter to the abbot himself (*Ep.* 41), in which Grote congratulates him with his election and gives him advice about proper behaviour when confronted with proprietarism (cfr further section X.1). This association, however, is not motivated, and it is also inconsistent with the sequence of the letters in all three collections, in which *Ep.* 42 precedes *Ep.* 44. As observed in sections XI.2-3, the recently discovered witness from Koblenz only transmits *Epp.* 45; 42; 44. If *Ep.* 42 should indeed really be associated with *Ep.* 41, it cannot be explained why that letter is missing in the Koblenz codex. In addition, there are strong parallels between the contents of *Epp.* 42 and 44. It seems inevitable to escape the conclusion, therefore, that Grote wrote to the community in Kamp to ask them to sup-

---

[10] Cfr MULDER, *Epp.*, p. xli-xlii.

port their abbot in his attempts to tackle simony in relation with entry into religious life in the Cistercian nunnery Ter Hunnepe near Deventer.

The *consilia* on corrupt practices

Next, it should be stressed at the outset already that Grote personally took the initiative to struggle against clerical incontinence and monastic proprietarism, but that most of his essays against simony were prompted by others, excepting his *Ep.* 17, which sprung from sincere personal indignation about a case of straightforward and hardly disguised deceit in relation to the acceptance of a pastoral position, committed moreover by a younger brother of one of Grote's close allies in Deventer – was this just indignation, or perhaps worry about the implications for Grote's own reputation also?

The remaining essays on simony generally had the form of *consilia*, formal pieces of advice given by a (juridical) expert at the request of individuals who were not well versed in juridical intricacies. This consideration shows well in which two fields Grote established his priorities. In a way, there is no need to be shocked or surprised about this. During an earlier stage of his career in his pre-conversion period, Grote had very probably himself been guilty of the same corrupt practices which he condemned so fiercely after his conversion. Early on in his academic career already, Reinier Post has assembled all documents still preserved in the papal archives in which Grote's name is mentioned in connection with requests for the assignment of prebends.[11] A fresh analysis of all relevant documents, in section I.3 below, confirms that Grote applied for at least four prebends in collegiate churches and for one position as parish priest, submitted to Popes Urban V and Gregory XI between 1362 and 1371. These Popes issued for him several provisions, or letters containing papal consent to propose a candidate as suitable for a given ecclesiastical position which had not become vacant yet, in the end resulting in canonries in the collegiate church of St Mary in Aachen and the Dom in Utrecht, accorded between 1365 and 1371 (cfr on this issue further section I.3 below). In the light of these earlier solicitations,

---

[11] POST, 'Oorkonden', assessed in detail in section I.3 below.

it cannot really come as a surprise that Grote seriously opposed trading in offices involving *cura animarum* or pastoral care, but that he had much fewer qualms in *Locat.*[12] about applications submitted by secular canons in collegiate churches.

This seems the proper place also to point to a clue which sheds light on the anteriority of *Locat.* on *Cura past.* This clue was mentioned by Mulder already in 1933, and taken up by Tiecke in 1941.[13] As it is, Grote alludes in *Cura past.*, **123-128**, to an argument which he had also discussed in *Locat.*, with these specific references: "prout scripsi eciam in quadam questione" and "Hec probaui in eadem questione", preceding and following his repeated argument.

I.2 VIEWS ON SIMONY IN THE SECOND HALF OF THE MIDDLE AGES

Each of the texts edited in this volume is summarized in detail below, in general as first item in the chapters on the individual texts. Some general outlines are now sketched in this introduction, which may serve to place the individual texts in the context of Grote's age.

"Inter crimina ecclesiastica simoniaca haeresis obtinet primum locum", writes Johannes of Freiburg (*c.* 1250-1314) at probably the most prominent place of his manual for confessors, at the very beginning of the first *Title* of his *Summa confessorum*.[14] He goes

---

[12] *Locat.* **1-6**: "Queritur an quis possit locare sub annuo censu curam animarum aut regimen una cum prouentibus et redditibus ipsi cure debitis. Respondeo que sequuntur. Primum quod obuentiones, oblationes et redditus alicuius cure possunt locari sub annuo censu, si sine regimine locentur, id est, si regimen non locetur."

[13] Cfr MULDER, *Epp.*, p. 314, fn. 4, where he refers to a less adequate parallel passage in *Cura past.*, and TIECKE, *Werken*, p. 163-166 (and briefly already p. 103-104). Tiecke discusses the two passages which to his mind are most close to one another, printing them in parallel columns (cfr on this ÉPINEY-BURGARD, *Gérard Grote*, p. 232). However, the compared passages show a general overlap only, while another passage in *Locat.* than the one chosen by him comes really close to the argument briefly repeated in *Cura past.*, cfr the *app. font.* to the editions below at *Locat.*, **383-388** and esp. **481-494**, and at *Cura past.*, **123-130**.

[14] IOH. FRIB., *Summa Conf.*, L. 1, t. 1, a.q.1 (f. 4ra); Johannes quotes here as well as in most of what follows *uerbatim* from his main source, the *Summa de paenitentia* compiled by his fellow Dominican friar Raymundus de Peñaforte. Cfr on Johannes succinctly *BBKL* 3 (1992), c. 361-362, in greater detail L. BOYLE, 'The "Summa confessorum" of John of Freiburg and the popular-

on directly after that in the first *Quaestio* to provide a definition of simony: "Simonia est studiosa uoluntas emendi uel uendendi aliquid spirituale uel annexum spirituali". Neither the qualification of simony as the greatest of all crimes and as a heresy nor this definition is original. Pope Gregory I already, quoted by Gratian, qualified simony as heretical, because it disregards Christ's precept *"gratis accepistis, gratis date"* (*Matth.* 10, 8) and because the offender subordinates the gifts of the Holy Ghost to personal (ab)use.[15] The definition given by Johannes does not occur in the *Decretum*,[16] but it was formulated in these words shortly afterwards by Rufinus in his *Summa decretorum* (1157-1159),[17] and taken over virtually unmodified by most later canonists.

Simony is accorded an equally prominent place and censured just as severely by many other influential opinion makers in the fields of morality and Church law during the high and later Middle Ages. Gratian, for instance, discusses simony in the first *Causa* of the second part of the *Decretum*, and it is the subject matter of the first *Title* in Bk. 5 ('On crime') of Gregory IX's *Decretales*,[18] and accordingly has the same prominence in all commentaries and *Summae* following the order of these great collections. However, it seems nevertheless apt to quote both remarks from Johannes' manual, as Grote himself recommends this *Summa* as standard

---

ization of the moral teaching of St Thomas and of some of his contemporaries', in *St. Thomas Aquinas, 1274-1974, Commemorative studies* – ed. A. A. Maurer *et al.*, Toronto, 1974, 2, p. 245-268, on Johannes and Grote HOFMAN, *Focar.*, p. 63-67. On penitential literature cfr now the useful introduction by J. GOERING, 'Internal forum', in HARTMANN *et al.*, *History*, Ch. 12, p. 379-482, on Johannes briefly *ibid.*, p. 423, on his sources Raymundus and William p. 419-422.

[15] GRAT., *Decr.*, C.1 q.1 c.117 (c. I, 403-404), quoting from GREG. MAG., *Ep.* 5, 63 (p. 368, 35-57), for the greater part also available in *Ep.* 5, 58 (p. 355, 29 – 356, 47) and in *Ep.* 6, 7 (p. 376, 30-47). WEITZEL, *Simonie*, p. 34-35, discusses the original *locus*, and presents a summary with full references to the detailed analysis of later quotations up to Huguccio *ibid.*, p. 149-150.

[16] Quite remarkably, Gratian does not provide a clear-cut definition of simony. But from the arrangement and choice of authorities in the *Decretum* it can be deduced unequivocally that he indeed considered simony as a crime in its own right, as is set out clearly by WEITZEL, *Simonie*, p. 26-39.

[17] RUF., *Summa, In C.1* (p. 197-198), cfr for further discussion WEITZEL, *Simonie*, p. 65-66, and for a summary with full references to the detailed analysis of later quotations up to Huguccio *ibid.*, p. 149. On Rufinus cfr most recently PENNINGTON – MÜLLER, 'Decretists', in HARTMANN *et al.*, *History*, p. 135-136, with further references.

[18] C.1 q.1 c.1-130 (c. I, 357-438); X 5.3.1-46 (c. II, 749-767 ed. Friedberg).

vade mecum on moral issues, penance and confession for the repentant parish priest John in his *Ep.* 19 (l. **136-140**), edited in this volume.

Pope Gregory the Great's straightforward condemnation in the late sixth century does not mean that simony was much of an issue in the early Middle Ages. His views were generally neglected by most ecclesiastical authorities for the next five centuries. Charges of simony effectively obtained a firm footing during the period of the Gregorian Reform for the first time, in the second half of the eleventh century, as has been argued convincingly by J. H. Lynch.[19] In his superb monograph on the great Pope Gregory VII (1073-1085), H. E. J. Cowdrey devotes a separate chapter to Gregory's ideas on Christian morality and spirituality, as distinct from his political actions.[20] In this section he writes *inter alia*: it was "in the central years of his pontificate that he [Gregory VII] sought what might be called the over-all moral rearmament of Latin Christendom". He legislated about this especially during synods convened in Rome between November 1078 and Lent 1080. In his quest for moral reform, Gregory VII focused on four abuses, which were in his view closely related to each other: (1) lay interference with ecclesiastical appointments, often leading to (2) lay investiture, and (3) corrupt practices or simony connected with such appointments, whether lay people were involved or not, and (4) clerical incontinence.[21] This led among others to jurisprudence against the first two forms of simony briefly mentioned above (in section I.1, viz. simoniacal ordination and simoniacal assignment of ecclesiastical offices with accompanying benefices),[22] in chapters 9 and 11 and in decrees 4, 5 and 7 of the proceedings which were issued after the synod held in November 1078, which were disseminated widely in the Western Christian world after the synod.[23] However, the new laws and

---

[19] Cfr LYNCH, *Simoniacal entry*, most notably Ch. 3, p. 61-81.
[20] Cfr COWDREY, *Gregory VII*, Ch. 8. 'Gregorian ideas' (p. 495-583), quoted words *ibid.*, p. 508.
[21] Discussed by COWDREY, *Gregory VII*, § 8.5-8.8, p. 536-550.
[22] Termed 'simonistische Spendung der Sakramente' and 'simonistische Ausübung der Jurisdiktion', the latter subdivided in 'simonistische Amtsverleihung'; 'Veräußerung kirchlicher Einkommensquellen' and 'simonistische Wahl' by WEITZEL, *Simonie*, in his discussion of the phenomena on p. 48-56.
[23] The proceedings of the 1078 synod are available in Gregory's *Register*, GREG. VII, *Reg.*, 6.5b (p. 2, 400-406); cfr for a discussion and a summary in

decretals had not led to drastic changes in Grote's days. As Van Zijl rightly observes,[24] "[a]lthough the system of proprietary churches had been abolished long before, the right of patronage which was acquired by the building or endowment of a church was in practice not much different from the earlier proprietary right". As a consequence, many prospective parish priests were more interested in the benefice than in the pastoral tasks. Especially when the benefice was a lucrative one yielding much annual profit, they were prepared to bribe their way into such a position. Formally, they did not acquire the spiritual thing itself simoniacally, but the *annexum spirituali* only, which, however, was an equally serious crime, as is set out by Gratian already.[25]

Conversely, the legislation on simoniacal entry, which had to be implemented in any case formally by conscientious prelates, could also unjustly be diverted to personal (ab)uses, in efforts to break someone's career, by ingeniously discrediting a person's behaviour.[26]

The acquirement of a clerical position, in practice most often a position as parish priest, was bound to run the risk of the involvement of bribes and other corrupt practices precisely because of the system developed to fund such positions, which had arisen in the course of the first half of the Middle Ages. This system consisted in the close interconnection between spiritual office and accompanying benefice, or material livelihood sustaining a par-

---

English of the main regulations COWDREY, *Gregory VII*, p. 508-511. On the threefold subdivision of simony ("munus ab obsequio, a manu, a lingua") cfr below.

[24] VAN ZIJL, *Gerard Groote*, p. 261-270 (discussing *Locat.*), at p. 262. Cfr. on the Church in general in Grote's days E. DELARUELLE, E.-R. LABANDE et P. OURLIAC, *L'église au temps du Grand Schisme et de la crise conciliaire (1378-1449)*, Vol. 1-2 (*Histoire de l'église depuis les origines jusqu'à nos jours*, T. 14), Paris, 1962-1964, on the Papal court in Avignon J. FAVIER, *Les Papes d'Avignon*, Paris, 2006.

[25] Cfr WEITZEL, *Simonie*, p. 43, with fn. 103 referring to the relevant *loci* in the *Decretum* (a.C.1 q.3 c.1; C.1. q.3 c.7; c.12).

[26] A case in which canon law regulations were in this manner unjustly applied in Reims during the generation preceding the one of Grote's arrival in Paris for further study is analyzed and described in great detail in W. J. COURTENAY, K. B. SHOEMAKER, 'The Tears of Nicholas. Simony and Perjury by a Parisian Master of Theology in the Fourteenth Century', *Speculum*, 83:3 (2008), p. 603-628.

ish priest (or other ecclesiastical dignitary).[27] Such a benefice was most often provided for, in whole or in part, by wealthy local lay people, who thereby became patrons. These patrons had by Grote's days inevitably the right of presentation (*ius praesentandi*), which means that in case of a vacancy in the benefice the patron may propose to the bishop or his deputy, the archdeacon, who were empowered with the right of collation, the name of a suitable person for the vacant office. In view of the considerable financial advantages of many benefices, not the most suitable, but the most wealthy applicant for a vacant position was often able to bribe his way to a lucrative position. And when a candidate did not obtain the benefice he desired, he could still try to obtain it by turning to the Papal court.[28]

With respect to the form of simony involving gifts in exchange for entry into a religious community, Lynch observes that this became an issue at an even later date for the first time, starting only after Gratian had devoted a *Quaestio* to the topic (C.1 q.2 c.1-10)

---

[27] The system and the manner in which it functioned in the Low Countries have most recently been described succinctly, but clearly by KUYS, *Kerkelijke*, p. 50-53; 57-59, with – for the earlier period – reference to the analysis in R. R. POST, *Eigenkerken en bisschoppelijk gezag in het diocees Utrecht tot de XIIIe eeuw*, Utrecht, 1928, p. 105-107; 140-142; 174-179. Cfr further on benefices in Grote's days G. MOLLAT, *La collation des bénéfices ecclésiastiques sous les papes d'Avignon (1305-1378)*, Paris, 1921, some details on the Low Countries in H. NÉLIS, 'La collation des bénéfices ecclésiastiques en Belgique sous Clément VII', *Revue d'histoire ecclésiastique*, 28 (1932), p. 34-39, and on the part of the revenues that slipped away to the papacy J. FAVIER, *Les finances pontificales à l'époque du Grand Schisme d'Occident, 1378-1409*, Paris, 1966. Not relevant for the discussion of corrupt practices at local level are B. SCHIMMELPFENNIG, 'Der Ämterhandel an der römischen Kurie von Pius II. bis zum Sacco di Roma (1458-1527), and B. SCHWARZ, 'Die Entstehung der Ämterkäuflichkeit an der Römischen Kurie', both in *Ämterhandel im Spätmittelalter und im 16. Jahrhundert* – ed. I. Mieck, Berlin, 1984, p. 3-41; 61-65, as these essays are mostly restricted to trading of official positions at lower levels at the papal court at a later date. Moreover, such trading was generally no longer seen as simoniacal, corrupt or undesirable from a juridical or theological viewpoint, as the positions discussed did not encompass directly spiritual aspects.

[28] Cfr on the gradually growing influence of the Popes on the collation of lucrative benefices e.g. H. JEDIN, 'Kann der Papst Simonie begehen?', in *Kirche des Glaubens, Kirche der Geschichte. Ausgewählte Aufsätze und Vorträge*, Bd. 2. *Konzil und Kirchenreform*, Freiburg, 1966, p. 164-284, and for a good and concise summary W. M. PLÖCHL, *Geschichte des Kirchenrechts*, Bd. II. *Das Kirchenrecht der abendländischen Christenheit, 1055 bis 1517*, 2. erw. Aufl., Wien, 1962, p. 72ss.

in the *Decretum* around the middle of the twelfth century. However, in this *Quaestio* the single most relevant canon, attributed to Pope Boniface I (418-422), turns out to be a forgery,[29] and measures against simoniacal entry remained lax and halfway until the innovations put in motion by Pope Innocent III (1198-1216).[30]

Effectively, he implemented measures to improve discipline regarding a number of ecclesiastical issues, initially set in motion during the Third Lateran Council in 1179 by Pope Alexander III (1159-1181).[31] As regards simony, Lynch observes: "The texts of Alexander III [i.e. a canon issued during a Council in Tours in 1163 and canon 10 "Monachi non pretio", issued during Lateran III in 1179] were significant in at least three ways for the development of the issue of simoniacal entry into religious life. First, they took an issue that was, so to speak, invented by Gratian and his commentators and gave it full legal standing as a crime with punishments tailored to it. Second, Alexander's decisions to condemn simoniacal entry at Tours and at the Lateran gave the issue a major dose of publicity in two of the largest ecclesiastical gatherings of the second half of the twelfth century. Finally, and most significantly, these three texts of Alexander became, in their turn, a stimulus to further canonical discussion and elaboration." Especially important with respect to its further divulgement, and in the context of its reception by Grote also, is the incorporation of the Lateran canon in Gregory IX's *Decretales*, as X 3.35.2,[32] as it pro-

---

[29] Cfr LYNCH, *Simoniacal entry*, p. 95-96 and fn. 46. P. LANDAU, 'Fälschungen zum Begriff des Benefiziums und der Simonie im *Decretum Gratiani*. Ein Beitrag zur Entstehungsgeschichte des kirchlichen Benefiziums im kanonischen Recht und zu Papst Alexander II', in *Päpste, Pilger, Pönitentiarie. Festschrift für Ludwig Schmugge zum 65. Geburtstag* – ed. A. Meyer, C. Rendtel, M. Wittmer-Butsch, Tübingen, 2004, p. 3-13, argues that Grat., *Decr.*, C.1 q.2 c.2 (as well as C.3 q.3 c.1-2) are later forgeries, which have been inspired by two decretals issued by Pope Alexander II (1061-1073).

[30] Cfr LYNCH, *Simoniacal entry*, p. 179-202.

[31] Although Lynch writes that Alexander was the first canonist on the papal throne, following the identification of the Pope with the canonist Rolandus, it has since been proved that the two persons are not identical, cfr esp. J. T. NOONAN, 'Who was Rolandus?', in *Law, church, and society. Essays in honor of Stephan Kuttner* – ed. K. Pennington, R. Somerville, Philadelphia, 1977, p. 21-48; R. WEIGAND, 'Magister Rolandus und Papst Alexander III', *Archiv für katholisches Kirchenrecht*, 149 (1980), p. 3-44, on Rolandus most recently PENNINGTON – MÜLLER, 'Decretists', p. 131-135.

[32] *Decret.*, X 3.35.2 (c. II, 596-597), reiterating Conc. Lat. III, c. 10 (a. 1179, *COD*, p. 193).

hibited not only simoniacal entry, but also proprietarism. Also, this canon for the first time unambiguously prescribes that an entrant disqualifies for holy orders when guilty of simony, and that a simoniacal monastic superior must be deposed.

These and similar initiatives set the trend towards change in the morality of both secular and regular clergy, a topic for which Innocent III, the first truly effective pope since Alexander III, was motivated by conviction and training. After much preliminary work and thinking, he convened the majority of the ecclesiastical and lay decision makers to an ecumenical council in 1215, the Fourth Lateran Council. After the council, seventy canons on a variety of topics were promulgated. Among them were four canons addressing various forms of simony (*Const.* 63-66):[33] "Canon 63 forbade payments for installing or consecrating prelates. Canon 65 forbade bishops to extort money for filling positions. Canon 66 ordered that the sacraments be provided for free, provided that the 'laudable customs' of giving gifts by the laity were observed. Canon 64 was devoted to simony in the entrance to religious houses", summarizes Lynch.[34] These four canons all found their way into Gregory IX's *Decretales* eventually (X 5.3.39-42), and thus they were disseminated incredibly widely.

However, such formal jurisprudence did not always result in wide application of the new rules. Concerning simoniacal entrance, for instance, financial problems confronted a much greater number of religious houses now that a major source of income had been legislated away, especially in the case of female religious communities. This made proper enforcement of the law not a really feasible option for bishops and archdeacons at local level, who had many other duties on their minds.[35] Also, required entry fees, "tainted by force or agreement", could easily be circumvented by suggesting to prospective candidates voluntary or semi-voluntary gifts or offerings, expected after an applicant had safely settled in his or more often her new communal life. In view of Grote's letters to the Cistercian abbot of Kamp, Lynch's

---

[33] Edited in *COD*, p. 240-241. For further discussion of these canons cfr LYNCH, *Simoniacal entry*, p. 193-195, for their inclusion in *Decret.*, X 5.3.39-42 (c. II, 765-766 ed. Friedberg), *ibid.*, p. 203-204.
[34] LYNCH, *Simoniacal entry*, p. 193.
[35] Discussed in greater detail by LYNCH, *Simoniacal entry*, p. 207-210.

observation[36] that Cistercian nunneries were especially unresponsive in conforming to the new legislation is for us highly relevant.[37] Finally, the number of arrangements made simply out of sheer incapability to cope at local level with the intricacies of university-made law, sneered at as 'ignorance' or "simplicitas" by Grote and his fellow educated intellectuals, should not be underestimated.[38]

Corrupt practices were in the eyes of the canonists not restricted to deals involving the transfer of money. They all endorsed a definition originally formulated by – again – Pope Gregory the Great, who was the first to distinguish between three different subcategories of simony, which I quote once more from Grote's favourite authority Johannes Friburgensis: "aliud est munus ab obsequio, aliud munus a manu, aliud munus a lingua. Munus quippe ab obsequio est subiectio (seruitus *Ioh. Frib.*) indebite impensa, munus a manu pecunia, munus a lingua fauor".[39] This threefold differentiation was for the first time effectively divulged on a wide scale thanks to Gratian,[40] in a literary quotation from Gregory,[41] but also in a paraphrase quoted from Pope Urban II,[42] itself again quoted by

---

[36] LYNCH, *Simoniacal entry*, p. 161-163; 211-212. For the context of the Cistercian nunneries in the Niederrhein region, which were dependent on the main North-Western house of the Order in Kamp-Lintfort, cfr in this context most notably ELM, 'Reformbemühungen'; ELM, 'Westfälisches Zisterziensertum', and ELM – FEIGE, 'Verfall'.

[37] Cfr LYNCH, *Simoniacal entry*, p. 215.

[38] Cfr LYNCH, *Simoniacal entry*, p. 219-222.

[39] Cfr IOH. FRIB., *Summa Conf.*, L. 1, t. 1, q. 7 (f. 5va), in a sloppy quotation from GREG. MAGN., *Hom. in Eu.*, L. 1, Hom. 4 (p. 31, 117-122), and with reference to RAYM., *Summa de paen.*, L. 1 t. 1 § 4. Since Grote's rendering in *Cura past.* (14-17) follows Johannes more closely than St Gregory, we can be sure that he quotes indirectly through Johannes.

[40] The full reception of Pope Gregory's *dictum* by Gratian is analyzed by WEITZEL, *Simonie*, p. 46-47, with references to all relevant *loci* in the *Decretum*.

[41] On the decisive role of Gregory VII in disseminating Gregory the Great's ideas cfr COWDREY, *Gregory VII*, p. 509-510, where he writes: "Gregory followed Gregory the Great by for the first time in his pontificate specifying not only those in which money passed but also those which were conferred in return for favours or services (*decr.* 5 [of the proceedings of the November 1078 synod])".

[42] Cfr GRAT., *Decr.*, C.1 q.1 c.114 (c. II, 402, 37 – 403, 7) and *Decr.*, C.1 q.3 c.8 (c. II, 414, 16-21) respectively.

St Thomas.[43] The elements in the definition are paraphrased by Joseph Weitzel as 'ungeschuldete Dienstleistungen', 'Geld und geldwerte Sachen', and 'Fürbitten für einen unwürdigen Kandidaten oder die Bitte eines unwürdigen Bewerbers' respectively.[44] In the context of Grote's essays against simony, it is certainly a meaningful classification also, as he attacks all three forms of simony: "munus ab obsequio" is offered to the lay patron by the female relatives of the prospective parish priest in *Cura past.* (14-21), and in a way substitution in office and taking the place of someone else (*Ep.* 17) can be taken similarly. "Munus a manu" can best be proved by the "pactio" or formal agreement between (lay) patron and leaseholder, one of the focal points in *Locat.*, as well as by the exchange of money for a place in a religious house, as in the essays against simoniacal entry. "Munus a lingua", finally, or improper support for an unworthy candidate is disapproved of by Grote in *Ep.* 17, *Cura past.* and once again in all essays on simoniacal entry in a (semi-)religious community.

A further distinction in relation to these three forms of simony is first formulated by Rufinus.[45] He differentiates between an intention to acquire a spiritual good, when the wish to trade in it has no practical effect, which is a sin punishable by God only, and its actual acquisition, which often involved the sealing of the transaction with a "pactio" or agreement. This latter form can be prosecuted in Church law, as the deal can be proved on the basis of the "pactio". This distinction is important for Grote also, especially in *Locat.*

I.3 Has Grote committed simony himself according to his own standards before his conversion?

It remains to be investigated whether Grote had been guilty of simoniacal practices himself before his conversion. From the re-

---

[43] Cfr Thom., *Sent.*, l. 4 d.25 q.3 a.3 arg. (p. 914, c. 1), explained *ibid.*, co. (p. 914, c. 2); II-II, q. 100 a. 5 s.c. (T. 9, p. 362, a. 5, c. 1).

[44] Weitzel, *Simonie*, p. 151, where Weitzel summarizes his analysis of the consistent reception of this threefold subdivision of simony in the decretists up to Huguccio, with full references.

[45] Relevant *loci* collected by Weitzel, *Simonie*, p. 66-67, with further discussion. The same differentiation is a matter for discussion for Huguccio also, on C.1 q.1 c.21, cfr Weitzel, *Simonie*, p. 136 and fn. 8-9.

CHAPTER I   39

cords preserved in the Archivum Secretum Vaticanum[46] and from various other sources, R. Post has early on in his academic career already assembled all supplications and documents relating to requests for ecclesiastical offices (mainly canonries and/or prebends) submitted to the Pope by or in the name of a cleric called Gerardus Grote from the Diocese of Utrecht.[47] All in all, he was able to trace nine different documents in which the names Gerardus Groet(e) or Gerardus Magni/Magnus are mentioned.

Although Post managed to assemble all documents mentioning a Geert Grote, this does not necessarily mean that all documents submitted by this person (or these persons) to the papal administration have indeed been recovered, as the papal archives have come down to us in an incomplete form.[48]

The two earliest documents date from 1351 (29 May and 9 July), and they consist in papal provisions, or letters containing papal consent to propose a candidate as suitable for a given ecclesiastical position which had not become vacant yet,[49] issued by Pope

---

[46] It should be noted at the outset that the *Registra supplicationum* were renumbered after a reorganization in 1925-1927, cfr e.g. R. Ch. LOGOZ, *Clément VII (Robert de Genève). Sa chancellerie et le clergé romand au début du Grand Schisme (1378-1394)*, Lausanne, 1974, p. xvi. This means that references in source publications predating this date differ from the actual modern shelf marks (for an overview of the actual shelf marks cfr http://www.archiviosegretovaticano.va/en > activity > publications > Registra Supplicationum). In what follows, both references are given when appropriate. A convenient introduction to the intricacies of the fourteenth-century materials preserved in the Vatican Archives is F. BOCK, *Einführung in das Registerwesen des Avignonesischen Papsttums* (= *Quellen und Forschungen aus italienischen Archiven und Bibliotheken*, 31), Rome, 1941. Still authoritative on the papal chancery in the fourteenth century is H. BRESSLAU, *Handbuch der Urkundenlehre für Deutschland und Italien*, Leipzig, 1889, 3. Aufl., Berlin, 1958, Bd. 1, p. 287-322.

[47] Cfr POST, 'Oorkonden'.

[48] The inadequate transmission of documents which must have existed in the past, as well as the poor practices of the staff responsible for the filing of documents have been suggested or suspected often already, cfr COURTENAY, *Rotuli*, Vol. 1, p. 2-5. This unfortunate situation is now confirmed beyond doubt by the careful reconstruction of lost *rotuli* through letters of provision in the three volumes of COURTENAY's *Rotuli*. The kind of research necessary to effectuate a correct reconstruction of lost *rotuli* is descibed *ibid.*, Vol. 1, p. 5-16.

[49] All supplications and bulls to and from the papal chancery are drawn up in a formulaic manner, and consist of the same elements formulated in the same manner; cfr the introductory sections in e.g. FIERENS, *Suppliques d'Urbain V*, p. vi-xvii, or *Repertorium Germanicum*, Teil 1, p. 59*-98*.

Clement VI (1342-1352) for a cleric from the Diocese of Utrecht called Gerardus Magni (note the genetive ending in the cognomen, not observed by Post), at that date an illuminator, rubricator and penwork artist working in the Benedictine abbey la Chaise Dieu (Dép. Haute-Loire in Auvergne), where the Pope had been a monk himself and where he was buried after his death later on in 1352. In his letters of provision he granted twice an *expectans* or formal, papally recognized authorization to compete for a benefice in two churches in Utrecht, the Cathedral and the collegiate church of St John.[50] On the basis of the date of the documents alone, which were issued when our Geert Grote was eleven years old and still lived with his uncle in Deventer, Post argues that the person mentioned in these documents must have been a namesake of the preacher from Deventer. Post associates two other documents with this namesake also, both emanating from or handed in at the court of Anti-Pope Clement VII in Avignon, in 1380 (2 May) and 1382.[51] In the earlier document, a letter of provision,[52] Pope Clement assigns his papal chaplain and auditor William de Ortolano the charge to take care that Gerardus Groete gets hold of a vacant benefice in yet another collegiate church in Utrecht, St Peter's. The later document[53] is a supplication, submitted by a local baron, Gijsbert of Vianen and Goy, asking papal favours for a number of protégés, among them one Gemerdus

---

[50] Discussed by Post, *ibid.*, p. 31-37. Relevant bulls mentioned in G. BROM, *Bullarium Trajectense. Romanorum Pontificum diplomata quotquot olim usque ad Urbanum Papam VI (an. 1378) in veterem Episcopatum Trajectensem destinata reperiuntur*, collegit et auspiciis Societatis Historicae Rheno-Trajectinae edidit G. Brom, Vol. 1-2, Hagae-Comitis, 1891-1896, Vol. 2, p. 39, no. 1401; p. 41, no. 1408, quoted from Archivum Secretum Vaticanum, Reg. Aven., T. 62, f. 168r; f. 352r respectively; preceding supplications edited in POST, *Supplieken*, p. 212, no. 324; p. 216, no. 333, from Archivum Secretum Vaticanum, Reg. Suppl., Vol. 23, f. 17v; 63r respectively. None of the supplications handed in by this namesake is listed in COURTENAY, *Rotuli*, as they have not been incorporated in the *rotuli* presented at the papal court on behalf of the University of Paris.

[51] Discussed by Post, *ibid.*, p. 43-49, mentioned in *Repertorium Germanicum*, Teil 1 – ed. Göller, p. 32, c. 2; p. 34, c. 2; available on-line also at http://www.romana-repertoria.net/, in the database 'RG Online'.

[52] Preserved in Archivum Secretum Vaticanum, Reg. Aven., T. 224, f. 326rv, register described in *Repertorium Germanicum*, p. 18*.

[53] Preserved in Archivum Secretum Vaticanum, Reg. Suppl., Vol. 64, f. 136r, mentioned in *Repertorium Germanicum*, p. 32, c. 2, register described under the old file number Reg. Suppl., Vol. 61, *ibid.*, p. 8*.

CHAPTER I 41

Groet, surely a notary's slip of the pen for Gerardus Groet.[54] For him the baron requested the assignment of a vacant canonry with full prebend in the cathedral church. Baron Gijsbert also was the brother of the Avignonese candidate when the episcopal see of Utrecht had become vacant in 1379, who had tasted defeat against the successful Roman candidate Floris van Wevelinckhoven (1379-1393),[55] the well-known supporter of the *Deuotio moderna* movement. This circumstance alone makes him an unlikely associate of our Geert Grote, who supported the Roman Pope Urban VI (1378-1389), although not wholeheartedly. In addition, several remarks in the supplication refer to other benefices claimed by this namesake, among them canonries in the collegiate churches of St John and St Peter in Utrecht, as well as an altar in the Utrecht cathedral and a canonry in the Lebuinus church in Deventer, some of them precisely the canonries mentioned in the earlier documents dating from 1351, when our Geert was only eleven years old.[56] Post convincingly argues that these documents therefore cannot be associated with our Geert Grote.

---

[54] Some remarks testifying to the notorious inaccuracy of papal notaries are assembled by Fierens in his introduction to *Suppliques d'Urbain V (1362-1370)*, p. xvii.

[55] Cfr on this episode POST, *Kerkgeschiedenis*, 1, p. 286-288.

[56] The text of the supplication has been paraphrased in Dutch by Post, *ibid.*, p. 45-46, the literal text of the relevant part of the supplication reads as follows: "Supplicat S. V. deuota creatura uestra G. dominus de Vianen et de Goy baro Traiectensis diocesis quatenus sibi in personas infrascriptas dignemini facere gratias speciales [...] Item quatenus dilecto suo clerico Gemerdo [*sic*] Guet [*sic*; Groet *in margine corr.* 'B', = Pontius Beraldi, corrector litterarum apostolicarum, cfr H. BRESSLAU, *Handbuch der Urkundenlehre für Deutschland und Italien*, Leipzig, 1889, 3. Aufl., Berlin, 1958, Bd. 1, p. 261 fn. 3] dicte diocesis specialem gratiam facientes de canonicatu et prebenda cum supplemento ecclesie Traiectensis uacantibus per priuationem per dictum dominum cardinalem de persona Michaelis Moliaert factis, de quibus sic uacantibus dictus cardinalis Henrico de Reno clerico dicte diocesis gratiose prouidit, qui litteris super huiusmodi prouisionem nondum confectis matrimonium cum quadam muliere per uerba legum de presenti contraxit, sic aut per huiusmodi matrimonium uel alias quouismodo uacantibus eciam si sit dispositum dicte sedis generaliter uel specialiter reseruatis, eidem Gerardo dignemini misericorditer prouidere, non obstante quod de canonicatibus et prebendis sancti Petri et sancti Iohannis Traiectensis ac sancti Lebuini Dauentriensis dicte diocesis ecclesiarum et quodam altari sito in dicta ecclesia Traiectensi certo modo uacantibus apostolica auctoritate extitit prouisis, quorum possessio nondum et cetera, et cum aliis non obstantibus ut supra."

42   INTRODUCTION

The five remaining documents indeed deal with prebends for which our Geert Grote had actually applied.[57] All of his requests directed at the papal administration in Avignon date from the time when he had completed his studies in the arts in Paris (1357), was accorded a *licentia ubique docendi* (11 May 1358),[58] and studied canon law and other subjects there,[59] without, however, actively participating in teaching and intellectual research.[60] The first of them occurs in a *rotulus*, or collective scroll of supplications for ecclesiastical dignities presented at the papal court, handed in by the Board of the University of Paris to the administration in 1362, shortly after the coronation of Pope Urban V (1362-1370).[61] It is subdivided in supplications on behalf of members of the higher faculties, with the Faculty of Arts as tail end. The requests made by members of this largest of all faculties are further subdivided in the respective nations, with Grote's supplication logically occurring in the section submitted by the English(-German) nation, to which he was attached.[62] His name occurs somewhat further

---

[57] All five applications are succinctly discussed by ÉPINEY-BURGARD, *Gérard Grote*, p. 27-28, a conveniently short text which in fact summarizes POST, 'Oorkonden', p. 37-43. An even shorter summary of this period in Grote's life is printed in A. G. WEILER, *Geert Grote und seine Stiftungen* (*Nachbarn*, Teil 30), Bonn, 1984, p. 7-10; I owe this reference to Marinus van den Berg.

[58] Relevant entries from the cartulary of Paris University and its supplement (*Auctarium*) listed in ÉPINEY-BURGARD, *Gérard Grote*, p. 20-23, where the date quoted in fn. 13 from the *Auctarium*, T. 1, c. 207, 47, should of course be MCCCLVII rather than MDCCCLVII.

[59] In quotations from law texts in all of his treatises Grote betrays a sound knowledge of canon law, but all of his allusions to Roman law are quoted secondhand. This confirms that he never studied in Orléans, where Roman law was taught.

[60] This seems an inevitable conclusion, as his name is not included in O. WEIJERS, *Le travail intellectuel à la Faculté des arts de Paris. Textes et maîtres (ca. 1200-1500)*, T. 3. *Répertoire des noms commençant par G* (*Studia Artistarum*, 6), Turnhout, 1998.

[61] On the circumstances with respect to the preparation and settlement of such *rotuli* cfr briefly COURTENAY, *Rotuli*, Vol. 1, p. 5-9, on this particular *rotulus* Vol. 2, p. 6. A convenient recent introduction to the manner in which the University of Paris was organized and functioned in the Middle Ages is O. WEIJERS, *A scholar's paradise. Teaching and debating in medieval Paris*, Turnhout, 2015.

[62] The *rotulus* has been preserved in Archivum Secretum Vaticanum, Reg. Suppl., T. 36, f. 75v-160r (formerly 77v-163r), requests by the English nation on f. 151r-160r (formerly 154r-163r), request by Grote on f. 158v (161v), no. 6, edited in COURTENAY, *Rotuli*, Vol. 2, p. 79-237, the supplication by and letter of provision for Grote *ibid.*, p. 231, the supplication only also in FIERENS, *Suppliques d'Urbain V (1362-1370)*, p. 101, no. 363, with a pre-1925-1927 file reference to

down in the list, and this means that he had not yet reached prominence in the University community.[63] The *rotulus* submits for 'magister' (no further specifications) Gerardus Grote a request for a provision on a canonry in the collegiate church of St Mary in Aachen with the prospect of a prebend at a later date after the decease of one of the canons endowed with a prebend, a request which was confirmed on 27 November 1362. Less than two months later, on 16 January 1363, a second canonry "sub expectatione maioris prebende", this time in Soest in Westphalia in the Diocese of Cologne, was requested for "Gherhardo Grote... magistro in artibus Parisius, scolari in legibus" in another *rotulus*. "This *rotulus*", writes Courtenay,[64] "was prepared at Avignon by German masters from various universities and *studia*, most of whom had probably travelled there at the beginning of Urban's pontificate.

Reg. Suppl., T. 34, both in abbreviated form; the introductory section for all nine applicants from the English nation printed before no. 360 on p. 221 ed. Courtenay = p. 160-161 ed. Fierens. The full text on Grote reads as follows: "Magistro Gerardo Grote de Dauantria, Trajectensis diocesis, de canonicatu et prebenda ecclesie B. Marie Aquensis, Leodiensis diocesis, dignemini prouidere"; the resulting letter of provision, confirmed on the same date, and passed down in Archivum Secretum Vaticanum, Reg. Avin., 150, f. 612, is mentioned in H. V. SAUERLAND, *Urkunden und Regesten zur Geschichte der Rheinlande aus dem vatikanischen Archiv (Publikationen der Gesellschaft für rheinische Geschichtskunde*, 23), Gesammelt und bearb. von H. S., Bd. 5, *1362-1378*, Bonn, 1910, p. 15, no. 41, and in BROM, *Bullarium*, 2, p. 123, no 1721, with reference to volume number: T. 1 (referring to the first year of the pontificate of Urban V, rather than to Reg. Aven. 150); cfr also POST, *Supplieken*, p. 370.

[63] COURTENAY, *Rotuli*, Vol. 1, p. 23 notes: "This [the fact that later dates were sometimes assigned by the papal administration to letters of provision further down in a *rotulus*, resulting in posteriority when vacant positions were granted], in turn, provided incentive to university masters to seek as high a position on the *rotulus* as possible, or to seek a position less in demand". The same is true, incidentally, for his friend Henricus Egher de Kalkar, whose supplication for a position in the collegiate church in Werden occurs two places further down in the *rotulus* than Grote's supplication. The supplication by and letter of provision for Heinrich Egher, who according to information in the supplication had acquired a canonry with prebend in the collegiate church St. Georg in Cologne already, most recently printed in COURTENAY, *Rotuli*, Vol. 2, p. 231, the provision also mentioned in SAUERLAND, *Urkunden*, Bd. 5, p. 14, no. 37. Cfr for the context and Heinrich's career at the University of Paris RÜTHING, *Egher*, p. 53-56; it is not clear to me why Rüthing identifies "ecclesia Werdensis" in the papal documents with "Stift St. Suitbert in Kaiserswerth".

[64] Quoted from COURTENAY, *Rotuli*, Vol. 2, p. 245, fn. 6, in a note accompanying the introductory section of the *rotulus*.

The list was assembled in December 1362."[65] In view of the detailed specifications in the request about major and minor prebends, it cannot be doubted that a canonry was meant in the St. Patrokli-Dom, a collegiate community only surpassed in importance in the diocese by the see in Cologne.[66] From the comment added at the end by the notary we learn that this supplication was refused, but that Grote did in fact receive a canonry in the collegiate Noordmonster- or St Peter's church in Middelburg, with the prospect of a prebend at a later date. The required prestigious canonry in Soest went to someone else, for somewhat further down in the *Registrum supplicationum* we read, in the entry for Conrad Hoklein (more probably Hoklem) de Gogh, that it was given to him.[67]

More than two years passed before we find Grote's name in the papal archives again, in the second *rotulus* submitted by the Board of the University of Paris. Obviously, Grote's prestige had increased in the intervening years, for his supplication had been placed at the second position this time, in the list submitted by

---

[65] Archivum Secretum Vaticanum, Reg. Suppl., T. 37 (old 35), f. 175r-178v, most recent edition in COURTENAY, *Rotuli*, Vol. 2, p. 245-259, entry on Grote *ibid.*, p. 248, entries on Dutch requests (among them Grote) also printed in POST, *Supplieken*, p. 386-387, no. 665 (with incorrect date '17 Jan.'), both in abbreviated form, which in expanded form reads "Item quatenus Gherhardo Grote, clerico Trajectensis diocesis, magistro in artibus Parisius, scolari in legibus, de canonicatu sub expectatione maioris prebende ecclesie Sozatiensis Coloniensis diocesis, ubi maiores et minores prebende existunt, dignemini prouidere – non obstantibus statutis etc. quibus caueri dicitur quod nullus maiorem prebendam in dicta ecclesia assequi ualeat nisi prius gradatim et per optionem de minoribus ad maiores ascendat, ut in forma – Habeat canonicatum sub expectatione prebende in ecclesia Middelburgensi [Maddeburgen. *Ms.*] diocesis Trajectensis"; introductory section printed by FIERENS, *Suppliques d'Urbain V*, p. 163-164; although some other supplications from German dioceses are printed in SAUERLAND, *Urkunden*, Bd. 5, p. 23-24, from Reg. Suppl., T. 37 (35), many other ones, including that by Grote, are missing here.

[66] Cfr most recently E. [Edeltraud] KLUETING, 'Die Klosterlandschaft des Herzogtums Westfalen im Hochmittelalter', in *Das Herzogtum Westfalen*, Bd. 1. *Das kölnische Herzogtum Westfalen von den Anfängen der kölner Herrschaft im südlichen Westfalen bis zur Säkularisation 1803* – ed. H. [Harm] Klueting, Münster, 2009, p. 70f.

[67] His supplication, and the accompanying provision, are printed in COURTENAY, *Rotuli*, Vol. 2, p. 249, an entry again missing in SAUERLAND, *Urkunden*, p. 23-24; he also applied for and ultimately received a canonry in Mainz, cfr COURTENAY, *Rotuli*, Vol. 2, p. 232 and 338.

CHAPTER I

the English nation on 16 June 1365.[68] Grote now asked for a canonry with the prospect of a full prebend (that is including a supplement) in the cathedral church of the Diocese of Utrecht. According to the elucidation in the *rotulus*, he had so far not acquired any benefice at all. Obviously, he still waited until one of the prospected benefices finally became vacant through the death or (less likely) withdrawal of the actual occupant in the collegiate churches of either Aachen or Middelburg.

Less than a year later Grote temporarily decided to change course, for in a personal request dated 7 February 1366 he asked the Pope to assign him an advance appointment in the parish church in 'Oeldekerken' (probably to be identified with modern Ouderkerk aan de Amstel[69]), which implies pastoral care for a flock,[70] but also required presence in the parish church, in accor-

---

[68] This time, the higher faculties and the Faculty of Arts did not together submit their supplication lists on the same date. The *rotulus* submitted by the Faculty of Arts was most likely handed in on 16 June 1365, as this is the date of the letters of provision, where extant. The abbreviated data in the *rotulus* have been edited in COURTENAY, *Rotuli*, Vol. 2, p. 288-317, on the basis of MS Archivum Secretum Vaticanum, Reg. Suppl., T. 43, f. 101r-108r; Grote's supplication printed *ibid.*, p. 315 (abbreviated, as it is in POST, *Supplieken*, p. 457, no. 799; it is not clear to me why Post mentions 17 May 1365 as date for the *rotulus*; again not in SAUERLAND, *Urkunden*). The full text, on f. 107v in the manuscript, reads: "Item Gherardo Grote, clerico Traiectensis diocesis, nullum beneficium ecclesiasticum assecuto, de canonicatu sub expectatione prebende ac supplementi ecclesie Traiectensis simul uel successiue uacantibus uel uacaturis", with the papal approval "Fiat ad collationem" directly following. That Grote still dwelled in Paris around this date is confirmed by an entry dated 16 June 1365 in the cartulary, cfr H. S. DENIFLE, E. L. M. CHATELAIN, *Chartularium Universitatis Parisiensis, sub auspiciis consilii generalis facultatum Parisiensium ex diversis bibliothecis tabulariisque collegit et cum authenticis chartis contulit H. D.* T. III. *Ab anno 1350 usque ad annum 1394*, Parisiis, 1894, p. 132, an entry missed by ÉPINEY-BURGARD.

[69] Cfr W. MULDER, 'Guillaume de Salvarvilla', *Ons geestelijk erf*, 5 (1931), p. 166-211, at p. 195 fn. 42.

[70] Archivum Secretum Vaticanum, Reg. Suppl., T. 45 (old 42), f. 77r, no. 1, supplication printed in FIERENS, *Suppliques d'Urbain V*, p. 615, no. 1610, as: "Supplicat S. V. Gerardus Grote, clericus Traiectensis diocesis, magister in artibus Parisius et studens in legibus, qui plus quam per 7 annos post suum magisterium in naturalibus, moralibus et aliis diuersis speculatiuis scientiis multum laborauit, quatenus sibi prouideatur (*om.* Fierens) de parrochiali ecclesia in Oeldekerken dicte Traiectensis diocesis (20 march. argenti secundum communem estimationem), si ex eo quod Petrus Jacobi de Compostella canonicatum et prebendam [ecclesie] S. Iohannis Traiectensis fuerit assecutus, uacet, dignemini eidem Gerardo prouidere, non obstante quod canonicatum sub expectatione prebende ecclesie B. Marie Aquensis, Leodiensis diocesis, obtineat", also printed, with slight variations, by SAUERLAND,

dance with general legislation, and in particular with a local Utrecht stipulation still valid when he applied for this position, and transmitted in the synodal statutes issued by Bishop Guy of Hainaut (1301-1317) after the diocesan synod of 1310, and renewed successively in 1318 by his successor Frederik van Sierck (1317-1322) and in 1343 by Jan van Arkel (1342-1364).[71] In the request he mentions that he is still based in Paris, now not only involved in legal studies, but also in sciences, morality and speculative arts. The position in this parish church had become vacant, says the request, because the former substitute parish priest ("uicarius") Petrus Jacobi de Compostella had apparently acquired a canonry with prebend in the collegiate church of St John in Utrecht, vacant because of the decease of the former occupant Petrus de Sancto Michaele, on condition that he gave up his vicariate.[72] However, Grote was probably never in fact appointed as pastor, for Petrus Jacobi is still referred to as "perpetuus uicarius parochialis ecclesie in Oudekerke" in a later papal document, dated 24 April 1371,[73] which assigns him yet another canonry with prebend in another Utrecht collegiate church (St Peter's).

Urkunden, p. 177, no. 474. This supplication is not mentioned in COURTENAY, *Rotuli*, Vol. 2, as it does not form part of a collective *rotulus* submitted by the Board of the University or of the Faculty of Arts.

[71] Edited in J. G. C. JOOSTING (ed.), *Bronnen voor de geschiedenis der kerkelijke rechtspraak in het Bisdom Utrecht in de Middeleeuwen*, Vijfde deel, Vierde Afdeeling, *Provinciale en synodale statuten*, Vijfde Afdeeling, *Seendrechten* (*Werken der Vereeniging tot uitgave der Bronnen van het Oude Vaderlandsche Recht*, 2ᵉ reeks, 16), 's-Gravenhage, 1914, p. 89-90, as decision 28 in the statutes issued in 1310, *ibid.*, p. 69-99, confirmation edited *ibid.*, p. 100-101, as decision 1 of the statutes of 1318 (*ibid.*, p. 100-105) and p. 106-107, as decision 3 of the statutes of 1343 (*ibid.*, p. 105-108).

[72] Relevant document transmitted in Archivum Secretum Vaticanum, Reg. Suppl., T. 45, f. 65v, cfr BROM, *Bullarium*, 2, p. 150, no. 1817.

[73] Cfr BROM, *Bullarium*, 2, p. 197, no. 1997. Petrus Jacobi probably did acquire this canonry, for a document from 19 March 1372 mentions a new occupant of the position in the parish at that date, Johannes de Dryel, who failed to be ordained priest at the requested date; relevant document printed in C. TIHON, *Lettres de Grégoire XI (1371-1378)*, T. 1-3. *Textes et analyses*; T. 4. *Déscription des sources et tables* (*Analecta vaticano-belgica. Documents relatifs aux anciens diocèses de Cambrai, Liège, Thérouanne et Tournai*, Vol. 11; 20; 25; 28), Bruxelles [etc.], 1958-1975, at T. 2 (1962), p. 49, no. 1490. This failure led to much juridical fuss with a new applicant, Gerardus de Zile (Ziil), cfr apart from this document the references in BROM, *Bullarium*, 2, p. 213, no. 2047 dated 19 April 1372; p. 257, no. 2186 dated 28 April 1374; p. 266, no. 2204 dated 8 Jan. 1375 (*sic leg.*); p. 278, no. 2232 dated 11 July 1375.

CHAPTER I 47

After this temporary deviation Grote steered back to his original course. This is clear from the next document preserved in the Vatican archives in which he is mentioned. After the death of Urban V on 19 December 1370 and the coronation of Gregory XI as his successor on 30 December 1370, many universities, among them that of Paris, hastily finished *rotuli*. Again the Paris *rotulus* has not survived, but a cluster of letters of provision intended for Paris masters and all of them signed and dated on 27 January 1371 by Pope Gregory XI testifies to the likelihood of its submission shortly before this date.[74] Among them is a letter for Grote, according him a right on a canonry, albeit without prebend, in the Dom in Utrecht.[75] The *rotulus* was prepared and sent to Avignon in the surprisingly short period of two weeks. The fact that Grote had his name included in it is undeniable evidence that he was present in Paris at the time of its confection, or less likely, present in Avignon at the time of its presentation to the Pope. More importantly, the *non obstante* section mentions that he finally had acquired a benefice in Aachen, in the period therefore between 17 May 1365 and 27 January 1371. Furthermore, it is clear from a letter sent much later on (21 October 1383) to Pope Urban VI by Grote's old friend Guillaume de Salvarvilla that Grote had also acquired the prebend in the Dom in Utrecht at an unspecified moment between January 1371 and October 1375.[76] If it is true that

---

[74] Cfr the longer account in COURTENAY, *Rotuli*, Vol. 2, p. 7-8 and p. 353 fn. 1.

[75] All letters of provision probably resulting from this *rotulus* are edited in COURTENAY, *Rotuli*, Vol. 2, p. 353-453; the one intended for Grote is printed in abbreviated form *ibid.*, p. 434, on the basis of Archivum Secretum Vaticanum, Reg. Av. 177, f. 80 (not f. 180, sic BROM, *Bullarium*, 2, p. 181-182, no. 1910), as: "Gerardo Groete, qui in artibus duodecim anni sunt elapsi magister fuit et in legibus et aliis speculatiuis scientiis diu studuit, confertur canonicatus ecclesie Traiectensis et prebenda reseruata (sub expectatione prebende *Brom*), non obstante quod canonicatum et prebendam ecclesie B. Marie de Aquisgrani, Leodiensis diocesis, obtineat", with following papal confirmation; also printed in excerpt by Brom and in greater detail by SAUERLAND, *Urkunden*, p. 280, no. 713; TIHON, *Lettres de Grégoire XI*, T. 1, p. 131, no. 256 and by A.-M. HAYEZ, J. MATHIEU, M.-F. YVAN, A. MARCHANDISSE (ed.), *Grégoire XI (1370-1378). Lettres communes analysées d'après les registres dits d'Avignon et du Vatican*, T. 1. *1371-1372*, Rome, 1992, no. 7883.

[76] The letter was written in connection with the ban on preaching with which Grote was struck after he had delivered his sermon against focarists, cfr for the context Hofman, *Focar.*, Introduction, Ch. I.5.1, p. 113-115. Salvarvilla characterizes his friend as follows: "Vir quidam uenerabilis, nomine Gherardus Magni [thus *only* in Mulder's basic manuscript *H2*, all other wit-

Grote had personal motifs in writing his little tract against raising the height of the Dom tower, and that this treatise was prepared in anticipation of a diocesan synod held in Utrecht in October 1371,[77] it seems possible to suggest that he acquired this second benefice in 1371 already, fairly early on during Gregory XI's pontificate.

In his letter, Salvarvilla also states that Grote gave up his prebends and his personal riches after his conversion ("propter Deum"), a decision proudly mentioned by at least some of his biographers also.[78] He renounced these benefices in any case before 11 October 1375, for at that date his Aachen canonry and benefice came in the possession of someone else, Godfried Lutzelenburch from Aachen, vacant "per liberam resignationem a Gerardo Groyt de Dauantria in manibus Remboldi de Flodorp, uice decani, et capituli dicte ecclesie, extra Romanam curiam sponte factam et dum idem Gerardus dictos canonicatum et prebendam adhuc obtineret (8 kal. iunii proxime preteriti)".[79] It seems especially significant how carefully the registration of this resignation is formulated, in such a manner that it is juridically ruled out that Grote can come back on his extraordinary decision.

From the description of Grote's activities while applying for benefices from 1362 until 1371, we can deduce at least one important conclusion: he spent more than twelve years in Paris after he had obtained his degree of master in the arts in 1358, studying law, speculative theology and moralities. He nowhere mentions his studies in medicine in his supplications, probably because he did not deem them relevant for his prospective canonries.

---

nesses read "Magnus"], dyaconus Traiectensis diocesis, in scientiis liberalibus, naturalibus et moralibus ac etiam in theologia et iure canonico eruditus, qui dudum propter Deum omnia sua beneficia, scilicet prebendas Traiectenses et Aquenses, ac etiam patrimonium suum satis largum reliquit, modica dicti patrimonii parte retenta pro tenui uictu suo, cui mundus crucifixus est et ipse mundo, factus est magnus hereticorum persecutor, iustitie et unitatis ecclesie zelator et feruidus predicator in dicta dyocesi contra uitia laycorum et clericorum. Nichil ab illis quibus predicat recipiens seu requirens, nullum temporale seu ecclesiasticum petit beneficium, sed desiderat, ut liberius et sine impedimento predicare possit, habere super hec commissionem auctoritate apostolica." (GER. MAG., *Epp.* – ed. Mulder, p. 223).

[77] Cfr on this suggestion HOFMAN, *Turrim*, Introduction, p. 759-764.
[78] Cfr the discussion in ÉPINEY-BURGARD, *Gérard Grote*, p. 38.
[79] The relevant papal document is printed in SAUERLAND, *Urkunden*, p. 462, no. 1160; TIHON, *Lettres de Grégoire XI*, T. 3 (1964), p. 178-179, no. 3373.

When we now turn to the texts written by Grote against simony after his conversion and try to determine which practices he opposed most vehemently, we face some rather interesting observations. Quite important in this context is a passage in the treatise *De simonia ad beguttas* (**491-516**). Grote here addresses the procedure when a new canon is chosen, and he states straightforwardly that any cleric can apply for such a position, whether rich or poor. When a newly appointed canon remunerates the members of the selection committee afterwards, says Grote, this cannot be interpreted as bribing or simony, for such remuneration is customary, it occurs after rather than before a choice has been made, and the new canon in general shows his appreciation with gifts funded with capital from his new prebend. Objections against such practices are therefore inappropriate. He also addresses this issue immediately at the beginning of *Locat*. Here he states that ecclesiastical offices can always be rented on an annual basis, provided that they do not involve pastoral care (4-7).

When his activities before his conversion and his behaviour and decisions after it are evaluated in combination, these together lead to the inevitable conclusion that Grote's views were strict, even rigorist, as far as positions involving pastoral care were concerned, but that he never felt the need to show remorse for his own applications for canonries lacking pastoral duties, not even after his conversion.

I.4 SOME NOTES ON GROTE'S USE OF SOURCES

As a follow-up to my observations in the introduction to *Focar*.,[80] I have collected a few examples here also of the manner in which Grote uses his sources, and more specifically of the manner in which he disguises his direct source, thereby suggesting that he is much more well-read than is actually the case. As in *Focar*., Grote finds inspiration for the development of his argumentation in his sources in texts edited in this volume also. An interesting example of this method of developing the line of reasoning suggested in his direct source is found in *Simonia beg*., in

---

[80] Cfr for an analysis of this mode of operation other examples adduced in HOFMAN, *Focar*., p. 56-58; 65-67, and especially 69-83; these findings are summarized on p. 83-84.

the section (l. **419-477**) dealing with inappropriate appraisal of other persons or *acceptio personarum*, a topic discussed in the New Testament already. The very combination of sources strongly suggests that the entire section ultimately depends on Question 63 in II-II of St Thomas' *Summa theologiae*, as Grote quotes or alludes to all authorities adduced there. Significantly, he omits to mention the name of his main source altogether. A similar behaviour can be observed in his use of biblical material in *Tract. paup.* Some striking examples in this sermon are: a quotation from *I Tim.* 6, 18 in l. **439-440** seems direct, but Grote in fact quotes through THOM., II-II, q. 66 a. 2 co. (T. 9, p. 85, c. 2, especially art. 2, l. 12-18): in the preceding lines **426-438** he enlarges upon text from this article in the *Summa theologiae*, in which the same clause from *I Tim.* is quoted. Significantly, both Grote and Thomas insert "et" between "tribuere" and "communicare", which is missing in the original biblical text; in l. **976-978** Grote suggests that he quotes from AVG., *Ciu. Dei* 19, 13 (p. 679, 10-11), but the quotation is indirect, through THOM., II-II, q. 29 a. 1 co., ad 1 (T. 8, p. 236, a. 1, c. 2, 7-26). In other texts this conduct can be observed also. Thus, Grote suggests to quote directly from 'sancti patres' in *Ep.* 41 (**35-39**), but his paraphrase from Gregory the Great's *Dialogues* is remarkably similar to the paraphrase in the quotation from a decretal issued by Pope Innocent III, quoted in *Decret.*, X 3.35.6. It seems certain therefore that Grote quotes Gregory the Great through the decretal; cfr *app. font. ad loc.*

Here perhaps also belongs a deliberate conflation of two biblical passages in this sermon, in l. **576-577**. Grote mixes up *Matth.* 5, 3 ("Blessed are the poor in spirit: for theirs is the Kingdom of Heaven") and *Luc.* 6, 20 ("Blessed be ye poor: for yours is the Kingdom of God"), quoting Matthew literally yet omitting the phrase "in spirit", but adding a reference to *Luke*, in order to be able to apply this famous beatitude to actual rather than intellectual poverty. In *G* this subtlety is inadvertently spoilt by adding "in spirit". Elsewhere, in l. **660-666**, Grote quotes from *Ps.* 30 (31), 12-14, but so loosely that Moll suggested in a note that he surely did so by heart, without consulting the biblical text. However, most people in the Middle Ages, and especially the well educated ones among them, knew their Psalter by heart. There must therefore be a different reason for his paraphrasing version. Elsewhere, in *Cura past.*, he seems to quote by heart indeed. In l. **266-270**, he refers to "quodam *Sermone super Cantica*" (viz. BERN., *Serm.*

Cant., 18, 1, 2-3), thus revealing that he remembers the passage, but that he does not have his source at hand. This is especially clear from the inadvertent use of "amphora", while St Bernard uses "concha".

Conversely, as has been observed in the analysis of the sources used in *Focar.* also, he sometimes follows a lead to a given source through intermediate authorities. After that, he quotes the ultimate source in greater length than his direct source. A fine example is the quotation in *Cura past.* from Ps. Dionysius, *Letter to Demophilus*, in l. **223-234**. This source is quoted by St Thomas directly in the neighbourhood of a *locus* exploited by Grote, but Grote quotes more from Ps. Dionysius than St Thomas, and he must therefore have consulted the ultimate source himself. In this particular instance, direct use of Ps. Dionysius is confirmed by another quotation from the same source somewhat earlier on in *Cura past.* (l. **138-141**), which Grote concludes by observing: "Multa hic de capitulo eodem Dyonisii possent dici, sed sufficiunt hec intelligenti", a remark which clearly suggests that he had direct access to Ps. Dionysius. This happens also for instance in *Simonia beg.* In the passage on *acceptio personarum* demonstrably quoted from St Thomas, to which I referred above already also, St Thomas quotes a single verse only from the *Epistola Iacobi* (*Iac.* 2, 1). Grote expands the quotation, citing no less than six verses from the same letter (*Iac.* 2, 1-6, in l. **434-447**). Another very interesting example also comes from *Simonia beg.* In l. **604-612**, the paragraph introducing the second main section of the treatise, Grote has literally translated a passage originally written in Latin by himself, which he originally composed for *Turrim*, **57-60**, and which in turn depends on St Thomas, I-II, q. 93 a. 3 sed c, co. (T. 7, p. 164, c. 1-2). St Thomas quotes a phrase from the biblical book *Prou.*, Grote has extended the quotation by adding three other biblical verses.[81] If it is accepted that *Turrim* predates

---

[81] Elsewhere, he also turns to the original source through the secondary source, for instance in *Simonia beg.*, **855-859**, where Grote gives more details from a biblical passage (*IV Reg.* 5, 20-27) than his direct source, in this case St Thomas Aquinas (THOM., II-II, q. 100 a. 1 ad 4 (T. 9, p. 353, c. 2, 13-17)), cfr GRAT., *Decr.*, C.1 q.1 c.11 (c. I, 361, 1-3); similarly, he suggests direct use of St Augustine's *De trinitate* in *Simonia beg.*, **1002-1007**. However, the quoted fragment occurs in Bk. 2, whereas Grote refers his readers to Bk. 3: this error strongly suggests the use of an indirect source, which unfortunately could

his conversion, he apparently had started to compile a sort of card-index box before his conversion, which he still used long after that, as the same quotation is also employed in the introductory section of *Focar*. It remains to be investigated, however, how much of all of this ultimately comes from Johannes Friburgensis.

Some of the sources used come as a surprise, as they diverge from what is to be expected. This is most notably so for the extensive use of Seneca's *Letters to Lucilius* in *Tract. paup.*, a subject dealt with in greater detail in section XIV.1.3 below. In *Ep.* 17 (57-62) Justinian's *Digestae* seem cited directly, although it might be possible that he quotes through the decretalist Archidiaconus, as is argued in the *app. font. ad loc.*

Another unusual source certainly is Rupert of Deutz (*c.* 1075-1129), a Benedictine monk from the Diocese of Liège mainly known for his theoretical treatise on the Eucharist (*De diuinis officiis*) and his commentaries on most books of the Bible.[82] It cannot be ruled out that Grote had access to at least some works written by him. Since Rupert's *floruit* preceded the emergence of scholastic theology by a few decades only, interest in his written output rapidly diminished shortly after his death. Nevertheless, the wording of a colon in *Locat.* (**86**) strikingly coincides word for word with a phrase in Rupert's *Commentary on the Apocalypse*, nowhere else formulated in precisely the same manner. An argument in favour of use of Rupert is that the phrase occurs in a section where he addresses the two main evils in the Church, fornication and simony (the main topic of *Locat.*),[83] in a comment on *Apoc.* 2, 14-15. St John here compares the behaviour of some of the Christians in Pergamos to that of Balaam, the prophet who in exchange for earthly compensation suggested to the Old Testament King Balac to seduce the Israelites into fornication and eating things sacrificed to idols (described in *Num.* 22-25). Two other arguments, however, plead against use of Rupert,

---

not be traced, and which therefore perhaps consisted in a *catena* or collection of excerpted quotations.

[82] Cfr on Rupert e.g. J. H. VAN ENGEN, *Rupert of Deutz*, Berkeley, 1983, on the *Apocalypse commentary ibid.*, p. 275-282.

[83] Van Engen, *Rupert*, comments on this section: "The message to Pergamus Rupert turned into his single most vivid and angry condemnation of the 'simony and immorality which now threaten the whole Church'" (*ibid.*, p. 277).

viz. firstly, that Grote quotes precisely these verses from *Apoc.* elsewhere, in connection with his struggle against focarists,[84] without any reference to the commentary by Rupert, and secondly, that Rupert's *Commentary on the Apocalypse* never knew a wide dissemination anyway, not even in the twelfth century before the rise of scholasticism, and was especially little known in the Low Countries.[85]

I.5 EDITORIAL PRINCIPLES

The editions in this volume form part of the *Gerardi Magni Opera Omnia*; in all volumes belonging to these *Opera Omnia* the editorial principles will essentially be the same, although of course individual works require additional principles due to their specific nature.[86] In this volume, this is the case for the three texts originally composed in Middle Dutch. The additional principles are set out in section I.5.2 below.

Elements relevant for texts in both Latin and Middle Dutch

When a text edited in this volume is transmitted in more than one witness, the edition is based on a basic manuscript, ideally a witness of which it can be proved or for which it is relatively likely that it is close to Grote's lost autograph of a given text. The version of the text in this basic manuscript is in general followed, but I depart from it when a given reading is transmitted in the basic manuscript only, or in the basic manuscript and very few other manuscripts. Such deviating readings have during a later stage in the constitution of the text been changed in such a way that read-

---

[84] The precise *loci* are: GER. MAG., *Focar.* 2 (568-577), p. 326 – ed. Hofman; *Arg.* 28-31, p. 566 – ed. Hofman; *Ep.* 20 – ed. W. Mulder, p. 77; *Ep.* 35 – ed. W. Mulder, p. 148 (cfr on these latter to *loci* also Hofman, *Focar.*, Intr., p. 117-118 and fn. 223.

[85] R. HAACKE, 'Die Überlieferung der Schriften Ruperts von Deutz', *Deutsches Archiv*, 16 (1960), p. 397-436, lists twelve extant and ten lost witnesses, mostly from Bavaria and Austria, the most Northern ones having as their provenance Rupert's 'home' abbeys Deutz near Cologne (s. XII, lost) and Saint-Laurent in Liège (s. XII, extant). Cfr also the summary lists in H. SILVESTRE, 'Les manuscrits des œuvres de Rupert', *Revue bénédictine*, 88 (1978), p. 286-289 (listing fourteen extant copies).

[86] This section has been written by Marinus van den Berg and Rijcklof Hofman together.

ings transmitted in the majority of the witnesses, but also in all branches of the stemma, were preferred for the final version of the text. The considerations which have lead to the choice for a particular manuscript have been set out in detail in the section on the relations between the various manuscripts transmitting a given text.

For interpunction most scribes use slash (/) and dot in heightened position (·) only. We have often disregarded the scribes' interpunction, as it impedes the clarity of the sentence structure. In view of an easier accessibility of Grote's texts, punctuation is based on the Germanic system, without, however, overloading the text with punctuation marks. At the end of manuscript lines, scribes sometimes use, but elsewhere omit a hyphen, executed as a slash (/).

As regards the use of capital letters, we do not follow scribal practices, as the scribes use capitals in other positions than modern readers are used to. Rather, we have chosen to stick to modern conventions, using capitals at the beginning of new sentences, for proper names and place names, and in words referring to God.

Rubrics and underlining in the manuscripts are disregarded, just like mediaeval section marks (usually ¶, representing modern §). The subdivision in paragraphs in the edition is based on the contents of the texts, sometimes but not always in accordance with the subdivision and usage of the scribes.

Evident mistakes and errors have been corrected. ⟨ ⟩ indicates a necessary emendation or addition, as for instance in *Locat.*, **140**, the proper name "Archidiaconus", for which the manuscripts present such diverse variants as "Ancisidorensis *N*, Archisidorensis *ZX*, Archisideren- *E*, Antesidorensis", or in *Simonia beg.*, **96**, where manuscript "staet" should evidently be read as "slaet" in "de syne hant an de ploech ⟨slaet⟩". [ ] indicates a necessary omission, as in *Locat.*, **297**, "certum est quod", or *Simonia beg.*, **43**, "Want de [de] Derde Orde". All such instances are explained or discussed in the *app. crit.* Evident mistakes have only been corrected when the manuscript reading(s) are clearly impossible in content, or grammatically incorrect. Restraint is clearly in order here, as it is not always clear which liberties the scribes felt free to permit themselves without change in meaning, especially in the case of Middle Dutch texts.

CHAPTER I

Quotations and use of quotation marks

In most of his original works, Grote quotes sometimes excessively long passages *uerbatim* from predecessors or in his day generally acknowledged authorities. In order to avoid fully italicized pages in the edition, it has been decided to print biblical quotations in italics, but to adopt a different policy for quotations from other texts. These are printed in roman type, between "double quotation marks", and introduced by a colon (:). Words or phrases within a quotation which differ from the text as edited in standard editions are nevertheless incorporated in the quotation, as it is indicated in the *apparatus fontium* whether or not a quotation is *uerbatim*. When quotations are attributed, the author's name is in roman type, spelt in accordance with the best manuscripts, the title of the quoted work is in italics, written in accordance with the best manuscripts (i.e. not regularized); a capital letter is used for the first letter of the first word of the title only. References in the text to Books, Chapters, etc. are in roman type, but *incipits* of sections (e.g. of the *Decretum*) mentioned by Grote in his references are in italics. When Grote quotes from commentaries arranged by lemmata and mentions such specific lemmata in his own text, these are between 'single quotation marks'.

Single quotation marks after a colon are also used for words not integrated in the sentence in accordance with Latin syntax. This happens for instance in a passage in *Locat.* (l. **99**), where Grote explains the biblical phrase "*Fel amaritudinis*": "'*Fel amaritudinis*' est intrinseca fellica malitia". "Double quotation marks" are used for direct speech only, when introduced by *uerba dicendi*.

Also, we have decided to respect Grote's notorious sloppiness in quotations. As a result, references to the same *locus* may differ from one another at different places in the edition.

Apparatuses

Apparatus fontium – Traced sources are listed in two separate apparatuses, one for biblical quotations, and one for all other quotations. Within these apparatuses there are three divisions: (1) unlabeled (uerbatim), which means that a given passage is reproduced word for word, although orthographic differences and minor inflectional changes are allowed; (2) *paene ad litt.*, indicating that only a few differences exist between the source and Grote's text; (3) *cfr*, indicating that the source has a similar passage, but that many differences exist.

These three categories take precedence in ordering the list of sources. If a given passage has more than one type of source, the types are separated by a semi-colon. If a passage has more than one source reference within one of these types, the authors are arranged chronologically and also separated by a semi-colon.

Apparatus criticus – The critical apparatus is basically negative: the lemma from the text is quoted only when confusion might arise, or when it is not at once clear for which word in the text a variant is transmitted in a given manuscript. When a variant extends over more than two words, the intermediate words are replaced by a dash. Words quoted from the text or from manuscripts are in roman type, all other elements are in italics. In variants quoted from individual manuscripts the exact spelling in the manuscript is retained, without any form of normalization. Unimportant orthographical variants are not recorded (thus, "ebulicione" for "ebullitione" is not recorded, but "bullitione" is).

The order in which the witnesses are listed in the *apparatus* for texts transmitted in more than one witness is as follows: first, those readings from the basic manuscript (which is mentioned in the *conspectus siglorum* preceding each of the edited texts) that have not been adopted in the text are listed. When this reading is transmitted in other witnesses also, these are then listed, preceded by "etiam". After that follow readings from other witnesses, in the order in which the 'families' are listed in the *conspectus siglorum* of the respective texts.

I.5.1 Orthography and related matters in Latin texts

The orthography of none of the scribes of individual manuscripts is consistent. Because of this observation, the orthography needs to be standardized. As a rule, classical orthography is followed, unless manuscripts unanimously and consistently transmit medieval spelling. Not surprisingly, this is the case for the spelling of the original diphthongs /ae, oe/, which without exception are spelt "-e-" ("celum", "fedus"), and for intervocalic /h/, which is fairly consistently spelt "-ch-" ("michi, nichil"). Due to the *hybrida* or *cursiva* scripts in which most Grote manuscripts are written, it is very difficult to decide whether scribes wrote "-c-" or "-t-"

for the alveolar fricative /s/ (spelled "-c-") before /e, i/. It has therefore been decided to standardize and to print the etymologically correct forms ("gratia, fiducia"). Likewise, the etymologically correct forms are printed for the orthographical variants "-i-/-y-" ("immo" versus "presbyter"), for the sequence "-xs-" ("exsequi" versus "extensus"), and for the phoneme /k^w/ ("loquuntur, quotidie"). Also, "-m-" is consistently written in words like "quicumque". Except for "omnis" and declined forms and compounds such as "omnipotens" and the very frequently used adverb "omnino", the phonetical combination /mn/ is with very few exceptions universally spelled "-mpn-" in the manuscripts, as in "columpna, dampnum, (con)dempnare, solempnis" and declined forms and derivatives. These manuscript spellings have been retained in the edition. The decision to regularize a fourteenth-century text in accordance with more or less classical standards seems justified, since a regularized spelling facilitates the consultation of databases and search machines.

Apart from these more general principles, it has been decided to adhere to the spelling transmitted in all manuscripts or in the vast majority of them in a few instances, most often involving personal names. Thus, "Matheus" and declined forms are virtually universally transmitted with single "-t-".

In words which are not names the following universally and consistently transmitted spellings are adopted in this edition: "diffini-" for "defini-", "dyocesis" and declined forms. In the use of "hii, hiis" for "hi, his" most scribes are consistent. Deviant spellings occurring in *Focar.* for various words pop up again in this volume. Thus, we find here also "caracter" and declined forms, universally spelled without "-h-" for more classic "character-", and therefore adopted in the edition (in *Locat.*, **54**; **124**; **135** and *Cura past.*, **161-162**). Also, "glosa" occurs again for "glossa" (in such diverse texts as *Locat.*, **651**; *Cura past.*, **35**; *Ep.* **45**, **108**; *Tract. paup.*, **354**, but also *Simonia beg.*, **21** = *Leeringhe*, **80**), as well as "omelia" (only in *Simonia beg.*, **650**; **718**; **837**), and "sathane" (gen. sg.) for "satane" (in *Ep.* **41**, **56** and *Ep.* **44**, **7**). 'Hierarchy' and derivatives are spelled "ierarchie" etc. in *Locat.*, **42**; **153** ("gherarchia" in *DZ*) and *Cura past.*, **139**; **204**; **240** (Iherarchia *Di*) (and three other instances in the direct neighbourhood). Similarly "Ierusalem" is only once thus spelled in *El* (*Tract. paup.*, **2**), elsewhere consistently spelled "Iherusalem" (*Ep.* **45**, **47** (Iherozolimis *LM*) and *Tract. paup.*, **2**; **149**; **156**; **210**; **1177**); "fantastici" is spelled with initial 'f' for /f/ (*Tract. paup.*, **961**). I refrain this time from observations on pronounciation. After some hesitation, I have decided to spell "immo" as "ymmo", the spelling most often transmitted. As in *Focar.*, the word "idololatria" is consistently spelled "ydolatria" in *Locat.*, **359** and *Ep.* **41, 64**, in all witnesses.

Also in *Locat.*, in l. **415**; **518**; **523**, most manuscripts transmit "emolimentum (-ta)" for "emolumentum (-ta)". For the word "presbyter" and its derivatives the scribe in *E* consistently writes "prespiter" etc. Note that the corrector correctly writes "presbyter" etc.

As regards grammar, I note two noticeable details. About half of the manuscripts transmitting *Cura past.* read in the phrase "aliquid canonicum" in l. **7** "aliquid" as a substantive, modified by an adjective "canonicum". Four other manuscripts, however, clearly read "aliquod canonicum", taking "canonicum" as a substantive noun preceded by a modifying indefinite pronoun.[87] After some hesitation, I have decided to follow the majority of the manuscripts. No other instances of substantive "aliquid" occur in *Cura past.* In *Focar.*, substantively used "aliquid" when modified is most often accompanied by a dependent clause in the genitive (e.g. **2545**; **2793** "aliquid sui ordinis"), but two cases similar to the one here in *Cura past.* also occur, **1005** "aliquid contrarium legi uniuersali positiue" and **3526-3527** "...spero me aliquid modicum alias dicturum et scripturum".

Usually, Grote is well aware of the rules for declination of cardinal numbers. In *Cura past.*, **281-283**, however, a case is found where the declinable cardinal numbers "duo milia" are not declined, most probably because they are preceded by indeclinable "mille": "ad mille uel ad duo milia, et non dico ouium, ymmo leonum et ursarum pro parte et insensibilium quorundam animalium curam regendam", for correct "ad mille uel ad duorum milium...", perhaps "ad mille uel ad duarum milium".

I.5.2 Editorial policy with regard to texts in Middle Dutch

In the editions of the Middle Dutch texts *Statuten van het Meester-Geertshuis*, *De simonia ad beguttas* and *Een zuverlike leeringhe* I adhere in general to the same principles as Rijcklof

---

[87] *Kh* is defective here, two manuscripts are erroneous, aliud *Tc*, quid *W*.

CHAPTER I

Hofman with respect to the Latin texts. This means that the orthography of the manuscript witnesses is rendered as accurately as possible. Although all Middle Dutch texts in this volume have come down to us in *codices unici*, I have chosen not to edit them diplomatically. Firstly, both *Simonia beg.* and *Leeringhe* are available in editions on the basis of diplomatic transcripts already, and the two versions of the *Statutes* in transcripts which almost conform to this principle (cfr sections VII.2, VIII.1, and VI.3 below). And secondly, everything that the editor comes across in the manuscript, is faithfully represented in such a diplomatic edition: ideally, he reproduces the manuscript layout in modern typeface, maintaining rubrics, miniatures, original foliation, initials and capitals, abbreviations (which are expanded in italics), spelling and interpunction, and even the numbers of characters in a line. Corrections in the main hand are given side by side with those entered by later users of the manuscript. This is done in such a way that the modern reader is exactly aware of the manner in which the scribe has handled all of this.

Rather than doing this, I have in my transcripts modified the manuscript texts in order to facilitate the reading process, as the text must be sensible and understandable for a modern audience.

(1) All abbreviations have been expanded in accordance with forms written out in full elsewhere in the same text when applicable, and following prevailing conventions in other cases. Italics have therefore been avoided, as common abbreviations only occur in the texts edited in this volume:

> (a) tildes (˜) over letters represent common abbreviations, such as -m-: "e*m*mermeer"; -n-: "werke*n*, ordina*n*cie", -de-: "en*de*, un*de*";
> (b) apostrophe (') represents -er-: "he*r*en, he*r*, woe*r*den, donck*er*, barmhe*r*ticheit";
> (c) letter/stroke combinations are limited to the two conventional strokes through the lower shaft of -p-, representing -per- and -pro-: "pe*r*sonen, pe*r*soen", and "*pro*phane";
> (d) further conventual abbreaviations used are 7ca > "et cetera", xpi > "Cristi, Christi"; xpo > "Christo", xpc > "Christus", vo(e)rs / > "vorse*ghet*, vors*creven*", Jt / > "It*em*, erfg / ₂ "erf*genamen*";
> (e) Ə, 9 stands for -con- in "*con*firmiert, *con*sciencie";
> (f) superscript -u- between -qᵘa- in q*u*ame"".

(2) Medieval use of -u-, -v-, -w- and -i-, -j- differs from modern conventions. In my editions, use of these letters is normalized. As regards the close central rounded vowel [ü] (German 'ü', IPA num-

ber 318) and the voiced bilabial fricative [β] (as in English 'v[ast]'), these are in the manuscript consistently both written 'v' in initial position, but 'u' when occurring elsewhere in a word. These mutually interchangeable written versions of the same writing symbol are transcribed in all positions of all words as 'v' when they represent the sound [β] (examples: "erve, avete" (= ooft 'fruit')), and as 'u' when representing the close central rounded vowel [ü] (examples: short vowel [ü]: "onghebunden", long vowel [ü:]: "luden, uetghesadt, uytgesat, ute", sometimes in the manuscripts written as -w- (examples: "wtkiest > uutkiest, wtghenamen > uutghenamen")). Similarly, 'uu' and 'w' in the manuscript are transcribed 'w' when representing the voiced labiodental fricative [v] (as in 'W[illiam], IPA number 129) (examples: "pawes (= paus, 'pope'), scouwenden"). In a similar manner, the scribal usage of the written symbols -i-, -j- is transcribed as 'j' when representing the voiced palatal approximant [j] (IPA number 153), and as 'i' when representing the close front unrounded vowel [i] (IPA number 301) (examples: "Jenighen > ienighen, Jtem > Item").

(3) The scribes differentiate between 'y' and 'ij'. I follow their usage, also in instances where there is no Modern Dutch equivalent. 'I, j, ij' are always written with a dot in the edition, sometimes against scribal usage.

(4) Divergent written representations of 'r, s' have been adapted to modern usage.

(5) The most conspicuous point in which I departed from scribal usage is the orthography of word clusters. For the readers' convenience, words which are written separately in the manuscripts, but which yet belong together, are printed in combination in the edition. This is the case for instance with conjunctions (("ten waer > tenwaer", "in den dat > inden dat"), pronominal adverbs ("daer in > daerin"), compound verbal forms ("uet gheet > uetgheet", "weder zegghen > wederzegghen"), compound substantives ("mynre broderen > mynrebroderen") and adjectives.

Where words are written together which according to modern standards should be taken as separate entities, I have separated the constituent elements, as for instance in the case of combinations consisting of preposition and article ("nader > na der", "inder > in der", "vanden > van den"), conjunction and pronoun ("datmen > dat men"), finite verbal form and pronoun ("salmen > sal men") and negative particles preceding finite verbal forms ("enghevet > en ghevet").

In this category also belong clitics, which are sometimes written separately, but in other instances together, in proclisis with the following word or in enclisis with the preceding word. Enclitically written personal pronouns such as "se" (she) occur independently elsewhere; I have therefore consistently printed them separately. Enclises such as "ment (= men 't)", "mitten" have been printed in the form in which they occur in the manuscript, so as to leave no doubt. I have done the same with the proclisis in "teten (= te eten)".

Here also belong different spellings for the same word. I have not emended such instances, as the morphology in the manuscripts is quite capricious.

CHAPTER II

A *CONSILIVM* ON THE LEGITIMACY OF LETTING
AN ECCLESIASTICAL POSITION INVOLVING PASTORAL CARE

II.1 SUMMARY OF CONTENTS

In this *consilium*, Grote answers an enquiry about the legitimacy of leasing out or letting a position as clergyman in exchange for a fixed (annual) rent, formally subdivided into seven distinct arguments. He first states that there are no objections when no pastoral care is involved (4-7).[1] When this is the case, however, leasing out (l. 8-13, the second argument) as well as letting (l. 14-17, the third and longest argument, beginning here but continuing until l. 332) should be considered as simony, both when it is for a short or long fixed period and when the duration of the period is not specified (320-332). As it is, in his view, a competence involving pastoral care, together with ecclesiastical dignities involving juridical powers and competence obtained through ordination,[2] should be considered as pre-eminently spiritual – they should for this reason under no circumstances be associated with temporal gain or profit (17-37). Only a sincere and spiritually oriented disposition regarding life, knowledge and consecration qualifies a person for these three types of spiritual offices (38-53). By using the term "potestas" or 'competence', Grote probably deliberately takes up the terminology used in the account of Simon the magician's efforts to acquire spiritual competences in exchange for money ("*Da michi hanc potestatem, ut cuicumque manus imposuero, accipiat Spiritum sanctum*", 'Give me also this power, that on whomsoever I lay hands, he may receive the Holy Ghost' (*Act.* 8, 19)), with the further intention to enrich himself

---

[1] On a possible personal aspect in relation with this view, cfr the discussion above, section I.3. The contents of this treatise are also discussed in detail in VAN ZIJL, *Groote*, p. 264-270 and analyzed briefly in ÉPINEY-BURGARD, *Gérard Grote*, p. 232-234.
[2] Grote relies on *Decret.*, X 5.3.15. Cfr on this standard subdivision above, section I.2, and in greater detail WEITZEL, *Simonie*, p. 48-56.

through them, as described in *Act.* 8, (4-)14-25, an episode discussed in detail by Grote in the next section (62-78).

Grote concludes that this double form of simony is to be feared in everyone who similarly tries to acquire spiritual powers in return for money, with personal enrichment as his motive (79-91). Still in accordance with the story in *Act.*, he goes on to conclude that such a person is not motivated by spiritual considerations and inevitably exercises his function in an unfair manner (79-106). Also, because of the chance of repeated unfair execution of tasks pertaining to a spiritual office, the simoniacal acquirement of spiritual powers is in canon law considered and punished as a more severe offense than their simoniacal provision (107-123).

For each of the three competences mentioned already (those involving pastoral care, juridical powers and proper functioning in holy orders) ordination as priest is required. When a deacon carries out pastoral tasks, therefore, he is expected to obtain ordination within a year (124-136).

Grote then inserts a short excursus on juridical powers. In the case of archdeacons, who need not necessarily be ordained as priests, these are more limited than those of their spiritual superiors, the bishops, and they can primarily be put to use to correct and guide the parish priests supervised by them.[3] Bishops, on the other hand, fully possess all three competences, and they are entitled to accord them to others and to supervise their proper execution (137-154; 164-172). Acquiring this high rank through simony, after having been ordained as priest only in order to acquire the episcopate, is the worst form of simony (155-163). This in the context not fully relevant excursus may be taken as a guarded allusion to an actual event, and may as such help to suggest a possible date of composition for this otherwise undated *consilium*. It may perhaps refer to the ordination, first as priest and then as bishop, of Raynaldus de Vianen on the see of Utrecht in 1378 by the Avignonese Pope Clement VII. This Avignonese rival of the Roman candidate Floris van Wevelinckhoven (supported by Pope Urban VI) was the brother of a local baron, who also requested the assignment of a vacant canonry with full prebend in the cathedral church in Utrecht for a namesake of Grote

---

[3] Cfr on the function and prerogatives of the archdeacon, esp. in the Diocese of Utrecht, primarily MULDERS, *Archidiakonat, passim.*

in 1382, in a *rotulus* submitted to the administration of Clement VII in Avignon.[4] Raynaldus contested the see for two years, between 1378 and 1380, when he gave up his claims. His appointment was widely seen as simoniacal.[5] Alternatively, the stress on the position and rights of archdeacons, equally out of place in the context, may perhaps suggest that this *consilium* was written at the request of Grote's old friend Salvarvilla shortly after his appointment by Urban VI as archdeacon of Brabant in the diocese of Liège in 1382.[6]

After this excursus, Grote returns to a discussion of the tasks and obligations of priests. In principle, ordination as priest only results in an allowance to consecrate bread and wine during the Eucharist (Grote labels this as being a "simplex presbyter"). After he has acquired a pastoral office (labelled as "ordo" combined with "potestas"), a priest is entitled, but also obliged to perform other tasks, most notably absolving and preaching (**173-189**). The consequence of acquisition of executive powers through money inevitably is that pastoral tasks are carried out in a simoniacal manner, and the ultimate aim of a simoniacal priest is not just functioning in office, but the acquirement of money through his office (**185-206**). Also, the acceptance of a position as an active parish priest (**207-216**) carries with it considerable spiritual responsibilities, among them the possibility to absolve (i.e. to grant or deny parishioners the prospect of salvation, **207-228**) and to act as celebrant (**229-235**).[7] To acquire such a position in a corrupt manner through money harms the reputation of the Church, and it should be seen as deceit of parishioners (**236-243**). Precisely because a parish priest can offer parishioners access to eternal life in Heaven, simoniacal acquirement of a parish should be considered a greater crime than simoniacally acquiring a position involving juridical decisions here on earth about external, worldly matters (**244-263**), despite the fact that such external transgressions

---

[4] Cfr on this supplication also above, section I.3.

[5] Cfr on this rival bishop POST, 'Oorkonden', esp. p. 43-49, and for a summary version POST, *Kerkgeschiedenis*, I, p. 274; 287-288.

[6] Cfr on Salvarvilla's stay in Liège esp. W. MULDER, 'Guillaume de Salvarvilla', *Ons geestelijk erf*, 5 (1931), p. 186-211, esp. 209-211.

[7] On Grote's veneration for the priesthood, on which he writes a *laudatio* in the introductory part of *Focar.*, cfr the discussion in both VAN ZIJL, *Groote*, p. 243-261 and ÉPINEY-BURGARD, *Gérard Grote*, p. 226-230. The subject is also touched upon briefly in HOFMAN, *Focar.*, p. 103-106.

are in general more heavily punished in courts of human justice, as they are more easily proven (264-284).

Grote then addresses ambition, another vice acting as incentive to acquire a local parish (285-294). Actively soliciting a position is therefore generally considered as an equally despicable subcategory of simony (termed "munus a lingua", discussed above in section I.1) (295-304), unless an applicant's underlying motive is not personal gain or ambition, but a sincere desire to serve his parishioners (305-319).

The briefly formulated fourth and fifth arguments belong together closely, and can be summarized together. When a candidate rents a position annually for a fixed price in the expectance of financial gain, he should refund to the Church any revenues from the accompanying benefice exceeding what is necessary for life sustenance (333-348), a point ventilated also in *Cura past.* and in *Ep.* 19 (cfr the *app. font.*). When the inner motivation of a candidate applying for a position consists in "the guarantee of a lifelong income, he places the temporal above the spiritual" (349-361),[8] an opinion also found in *Cura past.*

In the sixth argument Grote approaches the same topic from a different angle, by focusing on the applicant's intention.[9] For this he distinguishes between two different applicants for a position as parish priest. On the one hand, an insincere one whose main intention is personal gain, but who effectively circumvents a charge of simony by avoiding to sign a formal contract (described in 362-365; 368-376; 385-388), and on the other hand a sincere one, who wishes to serve his parishioners and makes up a contract in good faith (described in 365-367; 377-385, plausibility of the existence of such a person denied below, 565-573). In actual practice, the sincere one is punishable by law for simony because of his contract, whereas the insincere one is more guilty of simony in the eyes of God, but not punishable in a human court of justice, in which only apparent and external offenses are judged (363-392, cfr 420-424).

In order to counter such awkward practices, Grote insisted on judging applicants' intentions in the confessional. In Van Zijl's

---

[8] Quoted from VAN ZIJL, *Groote*, p. 266.
[9] Cfr on this section also VAN ZIJL, *Groote*, p. 267-268, whose summary is paraphrased here in part.

words,[10] "In case of a benefice without *cura animarum*, Groote required only a change of intention [and when this failed to occur, refusal of absolution, 393-405]. In case of a benefice involving the *cura animarum* he required [on penalty of refusal of absolution]: (1) change of intention to the effect that the spiritual well-being of the souls should become the principal motive; (2) worthiness for the pastoral office, i.e., sufficient knowledge and exemplary life; (3) readiness to carry out pastoral duties without any compensation, provided the priest had a living from other sources [406-424]". These same requirements also figure prominently in *Cura past.* among the standards which a prospective priest should meet.[11]

In the seventh argument Grote goes one step further by suggesting that a sincere applicant who has agreed to pay a fixed price or annual rent for a position, in accordance with unfortunately normal practice, should set an example by restituting to the Church any goods or wealth that remain after the necessities of life have been catered for (a view also expressed in *Ep.* 19, edited further down in this volume), and by resignedly suffering the punishment required by canon law (425-448).

After that Grote opposes in his eighth and second longest argument (449-589) a practice which was fairly widespread in his day, and which came down to an argumentation that in the case of temporary appointments "transactions were said to concern only the revenues, not the spiritual office for which they were given" (449-454; 518-525).[12] Relying on a decretal supposedly issued by Pope Paschal I (transmitted as GRAT., *Decr.*, C.1 q.3 c.7 (c. I, 413, 11-20)), he argued that revenues and office were intimately connected with each other (449-466), and that an office should be accorded to worthy applicants only (481-494). In the same context he wonders why a difference was made between temporary and permanent appointments, and why a similar intertwining was not equally self-evident in the case of prebends (467-480). Because of this inextricable interconnection, any agreement on occupying a pastoral office with accompanying benefice in

---

[10] *Ibid.*, p. 267-268 fn. 77.
[11] The same requirements are summarily enumerated in *Cura past.*, 78-83, and discussed in greater detail *ibid.*, 86-98 (first requirement); 203-251 (second requirement); 178-188 (third requirement).
[12] Quoted from VAN ZIJL, *Groote*, p. 267.

exchange for a fixed (annual) rent must necessarily be taken as simony (**495-525**), no matter what form of smoke screen might be put up (**495-506**; **518-525**) to disguise a practice which was and remained objectionable and which therefore caused scandal among parishioners (**526-530**), although it was unfortunately nevertheless widespread (**512-517**; **558-564**). When secular positions would be leased out in a similar manner to the highest bidder, such transactions would even among pagan philosophers before the introduction of the Christian faith have given rise to considerable indignation (**531-543**). In a religious context, such practices ruin the Church and its reputation, and they inevitably lead to the appointment of greedy, unworthy, uneducated and/or unfitting pastors (**544-564**). No applicant with sincere intentions should agree to collaborate in this horse trading, as his bad example scandalizes sincere parishioners, induces bad or weak characters to sink even lower, and estranges ignorant elements among his flock from God (**565-589**).

Grote then turns to a discussion of the questionable trick by which applicants suggested that they only rented the benefice with its lucrative revenues, but that they voluntarily took on the collateral obligations associated with their office. This procedure was tolerated by the Church and labelled as mental simony, for which a culprit was accountable to God only in the confessional. Thus the Church avoided that "while you gather up the tares you also uproot the wheat with them" (*Matth.* 13, 29) (**590-607**). In Grote's view this misguided tolerance towards manifestly corrupt practices originates in indifference among prelates and, more importantly, in an attempt to avoid even greater damage for the Church, but he doubts whether the Fathers of the early Church would have been just as indulgent when confronted with such straightforward simony (**608-624**; **644-660**, cfr **679-705**). He is prepared to show appreciation only in cases where either the intention was sincere and no contract was made up (Grote refers to X 5.3.46), or where a strict distinction was maintained between on the one hand the contract regulating the profits of a benefice and on the other hand the intention to serve as parish priest (Grote refers to Pope Innocent IV's commentary on X 5.4.3) (**625-643**). As an explanation why this unfortunate situation was never altered, he refers to the system of patronage itself, in which corrupt patrons of local parish churches were able to influence decisions in local courts successfully, at the expense of unwilling but nevertheless ineffectual ecclesiastical authorities or sincere, but poor clerics (**661-676**).

Much of this remains unchanged because it is considered to belong in the domain of intentions, which are not judged in court, but in the confessional. Conscientious repentant parish priests can nevertheless force a way out of this awkward situation by setting an example and by publicly denouncing themselves and their past behaviour, in word and deed. By way of penance, they should refund their gains to the Church or use them to do works of charity (**677-696**), a theme elaborated in much greater detail in *Ep.* 19.

And despite the tolerant attitude displayed by most prelates (**697-705**, with reference to the comparable preceding section in **654-660**), he incites in a moving final appeal all priests to implement such restitution of gains or alternatively to compensate badly treated parties as a proper form of satisfaction, when they hear a penitent confess to any form of simony in the confessional (**706-725**). Grote ends his *consilium* with a polite humility topos which nevertheless in no way conceals where he stands himself (**726-743**).

II.2 EDITORIAL HISTORY, SUPPLEMENT

Locat. has been printed once only, by J. Clarisse in his 1837 *editio princeps*,[13] on the basis of the manuscript Utrecht, UB, 206 (4 B 10), which he gave the siglum *C*, a siglum also used in the present edition to denote this witness. In footnotes, Clarisse printed variant readings from a second Utrecht witness (UB, 174 (1 L 14)), labelled *A* by him and therefore by me also. Unfortunately, he hardly adopted any readings form this superior witness in the main text. The discussion and summaries of this treatise by Van Zijl and Épiney depend on this edition.[14] In the margin of my edition, I have inserted references to the pagination of Clarisse's edition and to the foliation of the basic manuscript *D*.

---

[13] Cfr CLARISSE, 'Groete', 8 (1837), 'Bijlage N° 3', p. 13-27, and cfr on the Utrecht witnesses *A C* below, section II.3.1-2, with further references to HOFMAN, *Focar.*, p. 172-174 (*A*); 192 (*C*).

[14] Cfr VAN ZIJL, *Groote*, p. 264-273 and ÉPINEY-BURGARD, *Gérard Grote*, p. 227-235.

CHAPTER II 69

II.3 THE MANUSCRIPTS

The manuscripts transmitting *Locat.* have been subdivided in two separate groups. Those that have been selected for the edition on the basis of arguments developed and motivated in section II.4 on the relations between the manuscripts are discussed first, the other ones after that.

II.3.1 Manuscripts used for the edition

Most manuscripts used for the edition of *Locat.* (*NAKhXZ*) are described in greater detail elsewhere; cfr, in the sequence of the *conspectus siglorum* below, HOFMAN, *Focar.*, p. 167-168, for *N*;[15] HOFMAN, *Focar.*, p. 172-174 for *A*;[16] HOFMAN, *Focar.*, p. 237-238 for *Kh*;[17] HOFMAN, *Focar.*, p. 253, for *X*;[18] HOFMAN, *Focar.*, p. 188 for *Z*.[19]

D Köln, Historisches Archiv der Stadt Köln, GB 4° 249, a. 1418, Or.: Deventer, most probably Heer-Florenshuis, Prov.: Köln, Crutched Friars, cfr VAN DIJK, *Prolegomena*, p. 229-231.

The larger part of this important quarto (215×145) paper manuscript, i.e. eight sexterniones together constituting f. 22-117 (quires 4-11^{12}, of f. 1-175) was begun in Deventer in 1418 by Conrad Scheych

---

[15] Den Haag, Koninklijke Bibliotheek, 79 K 22 (olim Neuss, Archiv Schram, 5), s. XIVd-XVa, Or.: probably but not demonstrably Deventer, Heer-Florenshuis (Brethren of the Common Life), Prov.: Neuss, Regular Canonesses of St Augustine, cfr VAN DIJK, *Prolegomena*, p. 327-328; the text of *Locat.* occurs on f. 132r-142v, as first of the three works by Grote, written by hand 4 on a separate quire (12$^{14\text{-}2}$).
[16] Utrecht, Bibliotheek der Rijksuniversiteit, 174 (1 L 14), s. XVc, Or. (?), Prov.: Utrecht, Nieuwlicht (Carthusians), cfr VAN DIJK, *Prolegomena*, p. 357-358; the text of *Locat.* occurs on f. 168r-176r, directly following *Focar.* and *Ep.* 57, and after an intervening text followed by *Cura past.*
[17] Köln, Diözesan- und Dombibliothek, 1092, s. XVb, Prov.: Hohenbusch, monastery of the Crutched Friars, cfr VAN DIJK, *Prolegomena*, p. 220-222, description and digital images available through http://www.ceec.uni-koeln.de; the text of *Locat.* occurs on p. 232-245, as first of the four complete Grote texts.
[18] Wolfenbüttel, Herzog August Bibliothek, 18. 32 Aug. 4°, Grote part s. XVc, before 1466, Prov.: unknown, cfr VAN DIJK, *Prolegomena*, p. 388-389; the text of *Locat.* occurs on f. 271v-283v, preceded by *Cura past.*
[19] Paderborn, Erzbischöfliche Akademische Bibliothek, Ba 12, s. XVa (1407), Or.: Zwolle, Bethlehem or St. Agnietenberg (Windesheim Regular canons), Prov.: Böddeken, St. Meinulph (Windesheim Regular canons), cfr VAN DIJK, *Prolegomena*, p. 331-332; the text of *Locat.* occurs on f. 156-161, directly preceding *Focar.*

from Grünberg,[20] at that time a student in Deventer, who was professed as friar in the house of the Crutched Friars in Cologne in 1420, after he had finished his studies in Deventer. He remained as librarian in that house for the rest of his life. We know that he copied this part of the manuscript in Deventer from two entries in his hand, an *explicit* on f. 37v: "...scripta per me Conradum Scheych de Grunenberg fratrem et seruum inutilem, finita Dauentrie anno Domini 1418°",[21] and a remark giving insight in small accidents, entered on f. 68r: one night a tomcat had urinated on the folium which Conrad had left opened, spoiling the paper. The next morning he wrote: "Confundatur cattus! Confundatur pessimus cattus qui minxit super librum istum in nocte Dauentrie, ... etc.".[22] The text of Grote's *Locat.*, on f. 22r-31r, followed by *Cura past.*, on f. 31v-35r, written in *cursiua libraria* script, occurs between these two annotations, which therefore prove that these two texts were copied in Deventer. In view of the place where he worked, but also in view of the extremely good quality of this transcript, it is very likely that Conrad transcribed these texts from Grote's autograph. After that he filled the remainder of this set of sexterniones with copies of other texts preserved in the Heer-Florenshuis, among which Heinricus de Frimaria's *De decem preceptis* (f. 38-73) and Bk. 4 of the *Vitaspatrum* (f. 90v-109v). From Grote's *Ep.* 12, written to Balduinus from Amsterdam,[23] then prior of the charterhouse Monnikhuizen (which Grote had left himself a short while before), we know that

---

[20] Cfr on Conrad and on this manuscript HOFMAN, 'Functionaliteit', p. 173-180, and especially SCHÖLER, "*Ama nesciri*". His death is recorded in the minutes of the general chapter for 1466: "Hoc anno obierunt (...) fr Conradus Koloniensis (...)" (A. VAN DE PASCH, *Definities der generale kapittels van de orde van het Heilig Kruis 1410-1786*, Brussel, 1968, p. 128).

[21] An illustration of this *explicit* can be found in SCHÖLER, "*Ama nesciri*", p. 43, Abb. 3.

[22] An illustration of this folium, with an expanded version of the note as well as a picture of a cat drawn by Conrad, and full comment, can be found in SCHÖLER, "*Ama nesciri*", p. 92-94, and Abb. 17.

[23] Cfr on this identification of the recipient of *Ep.* 12 Chr. DE BACKER†, 'De kartuize Monichusen bij Arnhem. Prosopografie samen met de regesten van de zopas ontdekte oorkondenschat', in *Amo te, sacer ordo Carthusiensis. Jan de Grauwe, passionné de l'Ordre des Chartreux* – ed. F. Hendrickx – T. Gaens, Leuven, 2012, p. 133-204, at p. 134-135, version revised by the editors of id., *id.*, in *Historia et spiritualitas Cartusiensis. Colloquii quarti internationalis Acta, Gandavi – Antverpiae – Brugis, 16-19 Sept. 1982* – ed. J. de Grauwe, Destelbergen, 1983, p. 69-155, identification here at p. 70-71.

Grote possessed an incomplete copy of this Bk. 4, and that he tried to acquire a complete text through Monnikhuizen.[24] This text was apparently still not yet complete in Deventer by 1418, for the copying work was interrupted in mid-quire in mid-sentence on f. 109v in 1418, and only later completed, on f. 90v-174r, in s. xvb in Cologne by Jacobus de Vace,[25] who lived in the house in Cologne in that period, and who continued the writing of the text first on the quire which had in part remained empty, and after that on additional quires which can be dated to s. xvb through their watermarks. A second hand *D2*, responsible for corrections in the text, is mentioned at some places in the *app. crit.* The corrections added in this hand have probably been entered by Conrad himself, in the 1450's, for there is a remarkable similarity between the correction "formate" in the margin on f. 23ra and Conrad's later handwriting.[26]

E   Erlangen, Universitätsbibliothek, 543, a. 1456, cfr VAN DIJK, *Prolegomena*, p. 179-180.

This small folio (285×205) paper manuscript consists nowadays of 28 f. only, but it must have been more bulky originally, as the foliation starts with f. 67. It has been written in two-column layout in *hybrida currens* script. In the *explicit* of *Locat.* the scribe, who identifies himself as a priest 'Nicolaus', writes: "finitum necnon scriptum per me Nicolaum presbiterum in superiori Eschpach, anno Domini .MCCCCL. sexto in crastino decollacionis beati Iohannis baptiste, quod tunc erat feria secunda, quia predictum festum fuerat die dominico". The feast of the "decollatio" of John the Baptist is on 29 August, which means that Nicolaus finished his work on 30 August, which fell in 1456 on a Monday, as he writes himself.

II.3.2   Other manuscript witnesses

Some of the manuscripts not used for the edition of *Locat.* are described in greater detail elsewhere also (*Eb VCT*); following the

---

[24] Cfr GROTE, *Ep.* 12, p. 40-41 ed. Mulder, at p. 41, l. 4-6: "Ceterum peto michi mitti reliquam partem *Moralium* papiream cum Heynrico et *Vitas Patrum*, in qua deficit michi una pars de quatuor, et Liram, *Super Regum*".
[25] Cfr VENNEBUSCH, *Handschriften*, Teil 2 (1980), p. 255-259, at p. 256.
[26] Cfr for an illustration of Conrad's handwriting at an advanced age SCHÖLER, "*Ama nesciri*", p. 59-60, Abb. 14-15.

alphabetical order of the libraries in which these witnesses are presently kept, cfr HOFMAN, *Focar.*, p. 179-180 for *Eb*;[27] HOFMAN, *Turrim*, p. 767-768 for *V*;[28] HOFMAN, *Focar.*, p. 192 for *C*;[29] HOFMAN, *Focar.*, p. 254 for *T*.[30]

L Lübeck, Stadtbibliothek, theol. lat. 64 (olim Ff 5; 11; 80), s. XVc, Prov.: probably Lübeck or its surroundings, cfr VAN DIJK, *Prolegomena*, p. 285-286.

This folio (325×220) paper manuscript contains on f. 159r-165v the text of *Locat.*, written in single column layout in *cursiua* script datable to s. XVc, in style comparable to the *hybrida* script used in the *Artic.* and *Focar.* witness *M2/Ma*. The scribe may have been familiar with canonical literature, as is suggested by additions in titles not transmitted elsewhere (cfr e.g. **6** uices] suas *add. L*).

M Mainz, Stadtbibliothek, I 507, *c.* 1450, Prov.: Mainz, St. Jakob (Benedictines), later Mainz, St. Michael (Carthusians), cfr VAN DIJK, *Prolegomena*, p. 315.

This witness contains on f. 101r-105v *Cura past.*, followed directly by *Locat.* on f. 105v-117r. Both texts have been written in *cursiua libraria* script datable around 1450.

---

[27] Berlin, Staatsbibliothek zu Berlin – Preußischer Kulturbesitz, theol. lat. qu. 240, s. XVbc (*c.* 1450-1460), Prov.: Erfurt, Benedictines, cfr VAN DIJK, *Prolegomena*, p. 137-138; this witness transmits *Locat.* on f. 4r-19r between *Ep.* 70 and *Focar.*; the contents of this witness almost exclusively consist in works by Grote and Gerard Zerbolt.

[28] Köln, Historisches Archiv der Stadt Köln, GB 4° 37, s. XVa (before 1419), Or.: Deventer, Heer-Florenshuis (Brethren), Prov.: Vollenhove, Sint-Janskamp (Brethren), later prov.: Cologne, Crutched Friars. This important witness originating in the close proximity of Grote himself transmits on f. 75v-84r *Locat.* and a fragment from *Ep.* 73, elsewhere in the same manuscript *Turrim*; *Ep.* 21 (fragment); *Notab.*, supplemented with *Ep.* 65 and *Gener. medit.*, originally present in the same codex, but later transferred to ms. Köln, HA, GB 4° 249 by Conrad Scheych. Cfr for the fragments of *Cura past.* transmitted on f. 84r below, Ch. IV.3.2.

[29] Utrecht, Bibliotheek der Rijksuniversiteit, 206 (4 B 10), s. XVa (*c.* 1420), Prov.: Utrecht, St Mary and the twelve Apostles (Windesheim Regular Canons), cfr VAN DIJK, *Prolegomena*, p. 359-360; this witness transmits *Locat.* on f. 31v-38v directly after *Focar.*

[30] Wolfenbüttel, Herzog August Bibliothek, 35. 1 Aug. fol., s. XVc (1466), 317 f., Prov.: Riddagshausen, St. Maria (Cistercians), cfr VAN DIJK, *Prolegomena*, p. 389-391; this witness (transcribed from *X*) transmits *Locat.* on f. 241ra-247rb directly after *Cura past.*

II.4 Procedure in establishing a stemma

II.4.1 Choosing a basic manuscript

The text of *Locat.* is transmitted in 13 manuscripts.[31] The first step in editing the text had to consist in the choice of a basic manuscript. For his *editio princeps*, J. Clarisse used the inferior Utrecht manuscript *C* (UB, 206 (4 B 10), c. 1420) as basic manuscript, supplemented with variants from the second Utrecht witness *A* (Utrecht, UB, 174 (1 L 14), s. XVc), printed in the footnotes, but not used for the establishment of a critical text. On the basis of my experiences with Clarisse's transcripts of *Focar.* and *Artic.*, it seemed foolish to have too much faith in the accuracy of his collation work. Moreover, *C* also transmits *Focar.*, and the version of that text in *C* is not surprisingly close to Grote's autograph.[32] I therefore decided to disregard Clarisse's work altogether, and to prepare a preliminary version of part of the text on the basis of three witnesses which perhaps offered some guarantee of having a good text. All three have known or probable connections with the Heer-Florenshuis in Deventer, where Grote's autographs ended up after his death:[33] *D* (Köln, HA, GB 4° 249), a manuscript according to its explicit copied in Deventer in 1418 by Conrad Scheych; *V* (Köln, HA, GB 4° 37), a manuscript having as its provenance the house of the Brethren of the Common Life established in 1398 in Vollenhove near Zwolle, which was led by one of Grote's earliest and closest allies, the blind Johannes van Ommen; *N* (Den Haag, KB, 79 K 22), the manuscript used as basic manuscript for both *Turrim* and *Focar.*

On the basis of the version of the text as transmitted in *DVN*, I established a preliminary and possibly comparatively reliable first version of l. 1-198 of the text edited below, which could serve as a starting point for the choice of a basic manuscript. It soon

---

[31] All witnesses are conveniently listed in VAN DIJK, *Prolegomena*, p. 459. They are described in detail in sections II.3.

[32] On the version of *Focar.* in *C* cfr HOFMAN, *Focar.*, p. 192; 216-217. After I started comparing the collated version of *DVN* with the text printed by Clarisse, it turned out immediately that *DVN* agree much more often with *A* than with *C*.

[33] As regards *D*, arguments in favour of this supposition are discussed above, in section II.3.1, and as regards *V* and *N*, I refer to the discussion in HOFMAN, *Turrim*, p. 767-768 and HOFMAN, *Focar.*, p. 172-174 respectively.

turned out that the scribe in *N* had incorporated quite a few variant readings in the body of the text when compared to the version in *DV*, and occasionally *AC* also. Most of these were later corrected by a second hand into readings in accordance with the text in the other witnesses. This second hand obviously supervised the work of the original scribe. However this may be, the version transmitted in *N* is less unequivocally close to Grote's autograph than in the case of *Focar.*, and to a slightly lesser extent *Turrim*. The preliminary version was then compared to the text transmitted in all thirteen witnesses. For this, selected text was first collated in all extant copies, as has been done in the case of *Focar.* and *Artic.* For *Locat.*, I collated l. 1-99 below in all witnesses first. One of the manuscripts only, viz. *D*, transmits in this first selected passage a text which is most often in accordance with that in the majority of other witnesses, in all instances where one or more of the other ones have a deviant reading; *D* was therefore chosen as basic manuscript. The text of the preliminary version was then adapted to the version of the text as transmitted in the basic manuscript *D*. In accordance with the regulations set out in section I.5, containing the editorial principles, readings transmitted in *D* only or in *D* and very few other manuscripts were during a later stage changed in such a way that diverging readings transmitted in the majority of the witnesses, but also in all branches of the stemma, were preferred for the final version of the text.

Next, it seemed wise to reduce the relatively large number of witnesses at an early stage. On the basis of the first collation exercise already, it turned out that several manuscripts could be allocated to two distinct groups: *XTEb* on the one hand and *VKb* on the other hand belong together closely, as will be argued in detail in sections II.4.2.1-2 below. For the edition, collation work was reduced to the witnesses *XKb*, and *TEbV* were not collated any further.

In order to eliminate more manuscripts, a second collation exercise was necessary. For this purpose, I selected two randomly chosen passages, first the concluding paragraphs of the text, l. **697-743** in the edition below, and after that l. **99-198**. For these portions of the text all witnesses except *TEb* were collated. On the basis of this second collation exercise, I was able to prove that *C* belonged in the neighbourhood of *KbV*. The main distinguishing variants occur in l. **139-140**, where *KbVC* together omit "aut – Anchisidorensis [thus spelled in *D*]", and in l. **156-157**, where all

CHAPTER II 75

three manuscripts read "si tunc presbyter, ut oportet, propter episcopatum efficitur" for "si presbyter, ut oportet, propter episcopatum habendum efficitur".[34]

Variants in l. 711-715 clearly show that the stemma as a whole can be split up in two distinct branches. Most manuscripts (*D N C Z X* (representing *T Eb*) *E M*) here transmit the version:

> Si dixeris: "c. finale, Extra, *De symonia*, dicit 'sufficere per solam penitentiam satisfacere Creatori', m a x i m e   i n   i l l i s   q u e ecclesia uoluntarie pretextu (*om. N¹, corr. N²*) propter (*om. D¹, suppl. D², per C*) occultationem (-is *D¹*) interiorum (*om. NC*) s u s t i n e t", respondeo quod uerum est, sed in ueris penitentibus.

whereas some other ones (*Kh VAL*) transmit:

> Si dixeris: "c. finale, Extra, *De symonia*, dicit 'sufficere per solam penitentiam satisfacere Creatori', s a l t e m   i n   h i i s   q u o s ecclesia uoluntarie pretextu occultationis interioris s u s t i n e t", respondeo quod uerum est, sed in ueris penitentibus.

The relevant discrepancy, here printed in expanded typeface, should be taken as 'especially in those aspects which the Church... tolerates' against 'in any case in those persons whom the Church... supports'. The latter alternative seems the more corrupt one, created under the influence of following "sed in ueris penitentibus", which necessitated a further change from "pretextu propter occultationem interiorum" into "pretextu occultationis interioris". A few other, mostly minor variants corroborate this grouping, but they show at the same time that *N* occasionally agrees with *KhA* against the other witnesses.[35]

While a more detailed argumentation justifying this grouping will follow below, in sections II.4.2.1-2, these variants, as well as the certain Deventer origin of *D*, and the probable origin of *N* in the same city, already enabled me to present a full stemma at this stage, and to allocate two German manuscripts, *LM*, both of them transmitting a particular bad version of *Locat.*, in the neighbourhood of groups which had been established previously: *L* near

---

[34] More variants grouping these three manuscripts together are discussed below, in section II.4.2.2 Group υ (MSS *Kh V – C*).
[35] Cfr e.g., 368 coinquinat] coinquinet *NKhA* also in *Z*; 410-411 habere talem curam *tr. NKhA*; 736 concordat] concordet *NKhA*; cfr for 739 immundus sum et; a talibus next note also.

group υ (*Kb VC*)[36] and *M* near groups ζξ (*ZX* (*TEb*) *E*); *M* is here closer to *Z* than to *XE*, as is proved by two readings where *M* agrees with *Z* and the majority of other manuscripts against

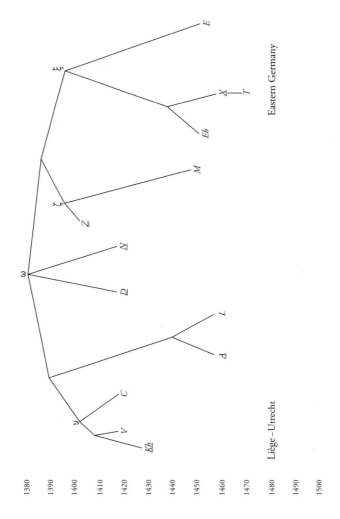

---

[36] Other variants proving that *L* belongs in the neighbourhood of *Kb* (*VC*) *A* are for instance: **16** patet – et²] *om. Kb VL*, **49** spiritualioribus] spiritualibus *Kb VCL*, **67** scilicet] *om. Kb VCL*, and in the second collated passage **739** immundus sum et] *om. Kb VALX*; a talibus] ab aliis *Kb VAL*.

CHAPTER II 77

shared errors in XE: 170 regere] *Mcett.*, gerere XE; 175-176 absoluendum] *Mcett.*, soluendum XE.[37] In view of the great number of idiosyncratic readings not recurring anywhere else, it was most welcome that this more or less precise allocation removed the necessity to collate these two manuscripts any further. In the stemma, manuscripts which have been used for the edition appear underlined.

II.4.2.1 Conglomerate ζξ

That the manuscripts in groups ζ and ξ belong in each other's neighbourhood, has been set out above in section II.4.1, in the paragraphs introducing the stemma. Apart from the variants in l. 170 and 175-176 discussed there, they share some other variants, among them 332 quas] quos ZXE; 471 iurium] numerum ZEb (for X, here missng) E.[38]

Here, it is necessary to prove also that none of these manuscripts has been transcribed from the early and good witness Z. This can be done by listing a few idiosyncratic variants transmitted in Z only, but not in any of the other manuscripts. Some significant examples are: 91 dilectionem] delectationem Z; 130 cure] turbe *sic* Z; 247 solum] *om.* Z; 271 et forum] in foris Z; 319 precibus] *om.* Z; 479 habet] que Z.

Group ξ (MSS $XTEb - E$)

As in the case of *Artic.*, the text of *Locat.* (and of *Ep.* 73) in T has been transcribed from the one in X.[39] Another witness is closely related to XT also, viz. Eb. This is immediately clear from the combined facts that most deviations present in X also occur in T and Eb, but that T and Eb have additional variants not occurring in X.[40] The most significant shared deviation is a garbled se-

---

[37] Variants proving that M belongs in the neighbourhood of ZX (representing EbT) E are for instance: 10 annos] ad *praem.* ZEM; 40 in¹] *om.* $XEML$; 162 in³] *om.* XEM.

[38] Cfr also the minor variants 417 sunt] *om.* ZXE, also transmitted in the basic manuscript D; 432 ecclesia] eciam ZXE; 510 coram] cum ZXE.

[39] The arguments proving that a consecutive series of eight texts in T was transcribed from X are discussed in detail in HOFMAN, *Focar.*, Ch. III.3.2, p. 253-254. Cfr for common variants in *Locat.* e.g. 117 initiatum] uiciatum XT.

[40] T: 8 quod²] *om.* T, not XEb; 14 quod dico] dico quod dico T, not XEb; 21, 23 exercicia XEb, exercia T; 50-51 iurisdictione] interdictione T, not XEb; 58 qui eam] eciam qui T, not XEb; 67 scilicet in] *om.* T, not XEb.

quence of the text in all three witnesses. The text is correct from l. 1-362, the order after that is l. 477-699; 362-477; 699-743, resulting in an incoherent text and fully ungrammatical sentences, a fact which seems not to have bothered the scribes in each of the three manuscripts. In *T*, this garbled version has been messed up even further, as two leaves (f. 244-245), apparently a middle bifolium, have been bound in the wrong order. This leads to a textual sequence: 1-354; 591-699 + 362-364 (f. 244); 354-361 + 477-591 (f. 245); 366-477 + 699-743 (f. 246-247). If nothing else would prove that *T* has been transcribed from *X*, rather than the other way round, this fully jumbled text as transmitted in *T*, but not in *X*, would certainly do this.

In addition, all three manuscripts share in l. 3 the reading "Ad istam questionem respondeo per ea que sequuntur" for "Respondeo que sequuntur" occurring in all other witnesses, and in l. 62 all three of them supply "uel concupiuit" after "ambiuit", whereas they all three also omit 63 "nomen", an obvious error corrected by later hands in *Eb* as well as in *T* (but not in *X*), which supply "nomen" and "exordium" respectively.[41] *Eb* also has variants not occurring in the two other related witnesses.[42] In a few instances *Eb* agrees with the majority of the other witnesses against *XT*, a fact which proves that this manuscript cannot have been transcribed from *X* also. In l. 35, for instance, *Eb* transmits the correct reading "neque" against "uel" shared by *XT*.[43]

Various variants shared by both *X* (representing *XTEb*) and *E* further prove that the text in this latter manuscript is not too far removed from that in the rest of group ξ. I list the following variants: **231** Nam facit] *om. XE*; **302-303** secundum – consequenter]

---

[41] In the first 100 lines, the three manuscripts share the following variants: **16** et magna] *om. XTEb*; **23** sunt² spiritualiores²] *om. XTEb*; **40** in¹] *om. XTEb*, also in *EL*; **42** scientia] sciencie *XTEb*; **50** potest¹] *om. XTEb*; **58** uel] aut *XTEb*; **66** illam potestatem *tr. XTEb*; **82** faciat] faciet *XTEb*; **86** exempli] uerbi *XTEb*; **89** celebrationi] celebratione *XTEb*.

[42] *Eb*: **8** quod dico est] est quod dico *tr. Eb*, not *XT*; **18** in²] *om. Eb*, not *XT*; **72** c.] in ti- *Eb¹*, in c. *corr. Eb²*.

[43] Similarly, *Eb* shares with most other manuscripts the reading **94-95** "spiritualem potestatem" against transposed "potestatem spiritualem" in *XT*; in the same line **95**, *XT* omit "siue ordinis", *Eb* here has an erroneous reading "siue iuris", impossible before directly following "siue iurisdictionis". Precisely this reading, probably reflecting what was present in the common exemplar of *XEb* (and *T*), may have prompted the scribe of *X* to remove the two words altogether.

CHAPTER II 79

om. XE, both resulting in an ungrammatical and incomprehensible text; 375 quam – finem] om. XE; 462 fructus – locatores] om. XE; 510-511 Deo – coram] om. XE;[44] X and E have the best texts, and therefore these manuscripts have been chosen to represent the subgroup in the edition.

II.4.2.2 Group υ (MSS *Kh* V – C – *A L*)

In section II.4.1 attention has been drawn to the fact that manuscripts *Kh* V – C – *AL* have several variant readings in common. In other instances, which are discussed now, *AL* often agree with the majority of other witnesses against variants transmitted in *Kh* V, occasionally supplemented by C also. All of this proves that *AL* together form a separate subgroup, which must be separated from *Kh* V(C).

That *Kh* V belong together closely is immediately clear from a significant variant in l. 721-725 in the second selected passage, where both manuscripts read "Et hic uera penitentia uidetur requirere ut satisfiat lesis et scandalizatis, et ut mala que approbauit, confortauit aut adauxit facto et uerbo reprobet, debilitet et diminuat, et alia que predixi" for "Et uera penitentia in hac parte est satisfacere lesis, scandalizatis et uulneratis per hanc apertam feditatem. Et non uideo quomodo hoc conuenientius fieri potest, nisi ut predixi", transmitted in all other witnesses.[45]

Several admittedly minor variants in the first selected passage suggest that C also belongs in the neighbourhood of these two witnesses, but at a greater distance. Thus, *Kh* V share with C six deviations in the first 100 lines of the text, among them the ungrammatical omission of "eas" in l. 45.[46] None of these variants is

---

[44] Cfr also: 207 sic] sicut XE; 249 Item] om. XE; 277 tunc] om. XE; 370 secundo] ergo XE; 433 equa] econtra XE; 440 quilibet] quibus XE; 473 si] om. XE; 520-521 impensionatis sic XE; 531 absit] absint XE; to these examples can also be added the variants discussed in section II.4.1 above already, 170 regere] M cett., gerere XE; 175-176 absoluendum] M cett., soluendum XE. For the numerous individual variants occurring in either X or E, but not in the other witness, I refer to the *app. crit.*
[45] Cfr also: 697 adextra] om. *Kh* V; 712-713 maxime in illis que] D C X N Z, saltem in hiis quos *Kh* V A L; 718 alia] est *add. Kh* V; 731 correctionem] correctorem *iterum Kh* V; 738 narrantium *Kh* V; 741 quibus] qua *Kh* V; the agreement between C and the majority of the other manuscripts in these instances proves that C is somewhat further removed in the stemma.
[46] The other shared deviations are: 14 est quod dico *tr. Kh* V C; 27 oculus¹] om. *Kh* V C; 49 spiritualioribus] spiritualibus *Kh* V C, also transmitted

convincing in itself, but the relatively large number of them should nevertheless be taken as sufficient proof that all three witnesses together derive from a common exemplar.[47] In the second selected passage, the evidence for a common ancestor is similar; the most significant shared variant reading occurs in l. 733, scientium] sentientium *Kh VC*.[48]

The text in *V*, on the other hand, presents two omissions where *Kh* (and *C*) are correct,[49] proving that neither of these two manuscripts depends on *V*. All in all, the version of the text in *C* (available in print anyway in Clarisse's edition, whatever the worth of his transcript) is the worst of the three, whereas *Kh* has a slightly better text than *V*. *Kh* has therefore been chosen to represent the group in the edition. In *Kh* a single folium containing the text in l. 254-348 has been lost. For this portion of the text *V* has been used as representative of the group.

---

in *L*; 67 scilicet] *om. Kh VC*, also transmitted in $N^1 E^1 L$, but supplemented by the correctors $N^2 E^2$; 74 intentionis] intentio *Kh VC*, cfr elsewhere 139-140 aut – Anchisidorensis] *om. Kh VC*; 156-157 si presbyter, ut oportet, propter episcopatum habendum efficitur] si tunc presbyter, ut oportet, propter episcopatum efficitur *Kh VC*.

[47] Within the group, *Kh C* together share a few deviations where *V* agrees with the other witnesses, 32 illas] *V*, eas *Kh C*; 69 quia] *V*, quod *Kh C*; 97 ait] *om. Kh C* (ait sors *tr. V*). Most of these variants are so minor that any scribe could have substituted one word or abbreviation for another one. Three instances, however, are not as easy to explain, viz. 66 ibidem] ex litera *add. Kh C* (not *V*): the scribe in *V* here probably deleted "ex litera" again, as the Biblical quotation in question is explained allegorically by Grote in what follows, not literally; and 700 de facto illo] *om. Kh C*, de facto illa *V*: the scribe in *V* transcribed the original text, the shared omission in *Kh C* is probably an effort to restitute a grammatically correct text. 701-702 uel magis – inhibet] *hab. V*, *om. Kh C*: the phrase is so unfavourable for German Church officials that it was omitted in both manuscripts independently. 710-711 multe sunt alie differentie] *V*, multas alias differentias *Kh*, secundum multas alias differentias *C* can be explained by suggesting that the scribe in each of the three manuscripts tried to a correct an error in the common exemplar in a different manner.

[48] Cfr also: 701 supra dixi] predixi *Kh VC*.

[49] 44 per – spiritualiter²] *om. V*; 82-83 potestatem – spiritualem] *om. V*.

CHAPTER III

A LETTER ON SIMONIACAL ACQUISITION OF A PASTORAL POSITION (*EP*. 17)

III.1 SUMMARY OF CONTENTS, AND CONTEXT OF *EP*. 17

Grote has written four letters to his fellow townsman Willem Vroede,[1] who had graduated as *magister artium* from Prague University in 1373. He was appointed as schoolmaster in Deventer on 13 September 1378, and served in this function until 5 March 1381.[2] After retiring from the Deventer school he joined the Carthusian order in the convent which was closest to the city of Deventer, Monnikhuizen just to the North of Arnhem. Here he was appointed prior in 1383, and he served in this function until his death on 16 October 1394.[3]

---

[1] *Epp*. 7; 8; 17; 18, cfr VAN DIJK, *Prolegomena*, p. 483-485; 495-497; I confine myself to dating *Ep*. 17 to '1381, before 5 March', and refrain form involving myself in the discussion about the dating of the respective letters here; cfr on this especially H. J. J. SCHOLTENS, 'Hendrik van Eger' (as in the next note), at p. 393-395, with reference to Post's observations.

[2] Official documents from the Deventer council financial administration on his appointment and discharge are printed in J. I. VAN DOORNINCK, J. DE HULLU and J. ACQUOY, *De cameraars-rekeningen van Deventer*, Vol. 5, *1377-1381*, Deventer, 1900, p. 149-151; 355, summarized and supplemented with other sources in MULDER, *Epp*., p. 58 fn. 1. On Vroede's achievements as schoolmaster cfr esp. POST, *Modern Devotion*, p. 91-93.

[3] Cfr Chr. DE BACKER †, 'De kartuize Monichusen bij Arnhem. Prosopografie samen met de regesten van de zopas ontdekte oorkondenschat', in *Amo te, sacer ordo Carthusiensis. Jan de Grauwe, passionné de l'Ordre des Chartreux* – ed. F. Hendrickx – T. Gaens, Leuven, 2012, p. 133-204, at p. 170-171. It was H. J. J. Scholtens who first identified a 'prior Wilhelmus' of Monnikhuizen (mentioned in the lists of Carthusians preserved in two codices from the charterhouse in Trier, and in the minutes of the general chapter of the Order for the year 1395), until then not known by surname, as "Wilhelmus Vroyde", on the basis of an entry in the old *calendarium* of the charterhouse in Koblenz, where he is mentioned with surname on 16 October, the date of his death. Cfr H. J. J. SCHOLTENS, 'Hendrik van Eger uit Kalkar en zijn kring', in *Dr. L. Reypens-album. Opstellen aangeboden aan Prof. Dr. L. Reypens s.j. ter gelegenheid van zijn tachtigste verjaardag op 26 februari 1964* – ed. A. Ampe Antwerpen, 1964, p. 383-408, at p. 393-395. A brief sketch of his career in the Order is given in H. J. J. SCHOLTENS, 'De priors van het kartuizerklooster Monnikhuizen bij Arnhem', *Archief voor de Geschiedenis van het Aartsbisdom*

The subject discussed in *Ep.* 17 involves Vroede's younger brother, who intended to accept a pastoral position despite the fact that he had not yet reached the age of 25 years, which was mandatory for the acceptance of a position on the basis of decisions taken at the Third Ecumenical Council of the Lateran, held in 1179, and reiterated at the Second Ecumenical Council of Lyon in 1274.[4] The contents of this letter are summarized very briefly, but aptly in Post's *Modern Devotion*, from which I quote: "Another, much more serious case, came to Groote's ear. Willem Vroede's brother, who was himself too young to be appointed to pastoral duties, told Groote that William would accept the expected benefice with *cura* in his own name, but in actual fact allow the brother to do the pastoral work. Groote was indignant. This was not only against the law, it was downright deception. Besides, the letters of presentation and collation would be false and unauthentic. [...] He [Grote] will probably have settled this affair with the interested parties."[5]

Despite Grote's indignation, only too clear from the contents of the letter, Willem Vroede's brother had probably devised this ingenious plan together with the patron of the benefice in good faith, and this is undoubtedly the reason why the younger brother had been so frank and outspoken with Grote. For there is jurisprudence in canon law allowing the circumvention of the normal age of 25, consisting in dispensation granted by the local bishop,

---

Utrecht, 56 (1932), p. 1-80, at p. 31-32. The two manuscripts are ms. Trier, Stadtbibliothek, 1669/350, which contains lists of members who have lived or died in the houses in Trier, Köln, Koblenz, Arnhem and Rettel between 1337/1347 and 1682-1668, written in a seventeenth-century hand, mentioning on f. 173rb "Wilhelmus NN. pater, alias prior Geldriae 19 [*leg.* 16] Octobris"; ms. Trier, Stadtbibliothek, 1668/351, f. 27-34, lists of monks who died in Koblenz, Trier, Köln and Monnikhuizen (called 'Gelria' in the ms.) between 1350 and 1521, written in a sixteenth-century hand, mentioning on f. 28r "d. Wilhelmus prior domus gelrie 1394". Cfr on these witnesses also HOFMAN, 'Recipients'. I am most grateful to Mrs. Anja Runkel, photographer of the Stadtbibliothek/Stadtarchiv Trier, who provided excellent digital images of these two documents, and to Prof. Michael Embach, director of the same institution, who was instrumental in making these documents available to me.

[4] The main arguments are enumerated in *Decret.*, X 1.6.7 § 2 (c. II, 52, 9-19, reiterating Conc. Lat. III, can. 3 (a. 1179, *COD*, p. 188, 19-23)) and *Decret.*, VI 1.6.14 (c. II, 953, 42 – 954, 22, reiterating Conc. Lugd. II, const. 13 (a. 1274, *COD*, p. 297-298)), cfr *Clem.* 1.6.3 (c. II, 1140, 21-26). Cfr also the authorities listed in the *app. font.* on *Cura past.*, 8-10.

[5] Quoted from POST, *Modern Devotion*, p. 92. *Ep.* 17 is discussed and summarized in VAN ZIJL, *Groote*, p. 270 also.

CHAPTER III 83

documented in the *Decretals*, in X 1.14.2-3.[6] No new developments regarding the editorial history of this letter have occurred since the publication of van Dijk's *Prolegomena*, and a separate section on this subject is therefore not necessary.

III.2 THE MANUSCRIPTS

H1 Den Haag, Koninklijke Bibliotheek, 78 J 55, s. xvb (1439), f. 1-87 of f. 1-262(-266), Or., Prov.: Liège, Saint-Jacques (Benedictines), cfr VAN DIJK, *Prolegomena*, p. 190-203.

Grote's *Ep.* 17 occurs in a convolute in which three originally distinct codicological units have been bound together at an unknown date in a binding postdating the Middle Ages. The codex was in 1809 acquired for the Dutch Royal Library in The Hague, at an auction organized by the Paris bookseller Renouard. Before that, the codex had belonged to the collection of the Belgian-Spanish bibliophile Cimon de Santander de San Juan, who bequeathed his entire collection to his nephew Charles-Antoine de La Serna y Santander upon his death in 1792.[7] Charles-Antoine published a catalogue of the collection in 1792 already, in which the full contents of our manuscript are carefully described.[8] This description, which also includes the colophon by Pierre Cortoy discussed below, confirms that the three constituent parts had been bound together at least in the eighteenth century already. Owing to the difficult circumstances after the conquest of the Low Countries by the French in 1795, Charles-Antoine was forced to sell the entire collection to Renouard.

---

[6] Formulated as "...mandamus, quatenus clericis idoneis administrationes et custodiam praescriptarum ecclesiarum, donec praedicti pueri ad congruam ueniant aetatem, ... committas", printed in *Decret.*, c. II, 126, 1-47, at 19-24; that such youngsters should hand over the *cura animarum* until they had reached the age of 25 years, is expressly confirmed by BERN. PARM., *Glos. ord. in Decret.* (ed. 1582, super X 1.14.2, comm. sup. 'aetatem' (c. II, 126, 23) (c. 265 (p. 133), gl. b)).

[7] Cfr on Charles Antoine de La Serna Santander e.g. the biography by F. RÉMY, in *Nationaal biografisch woordenboek* – ed. J. Maton et al., Brussel, 1964-, Vol. 2, c. 426-431.

[8] C. DE LA SERNA Y SANTANDER, *Catalogue des livres de la bibliothèque de feu Don Simon de Santander, secrétaire de Sa Maj. Catholique*, Bruxelles, 1792, T. 1, p. 87-88, no. 347 (Ch. 4, art. 2).

84   INTRODUCTION

The first unit of this quarto (205×140, written in single column layout, written space 145-151×81-88) manuscript consists of seven quires, most of them paper sexterniones (1¹⁴, 2-6¹², 7¹⁴), with quire signatures added in a hand differing from the main scribe's hand.⁹ All texts in these quires have been written in a single hand, who finished his last work on 27 September 1439, as is clear from the colophon after the last text, in which he also reveals his identity as Petrus Cortoy.¹⁰ Petrus writes in an expert hand, gradually changing from *cursiua libraria* script in the first quires to *hybrida* alternating with *cursiua* in the third and later ones.¹¹ He was a prolific scribe, from at least 1436 until 1444 active in one of the two Benedictine abbeys in Liège, Saint-Jacques,¹² who also spent some time in or after 1440 in the Benedictine abbey St Paul in Utrecht, where he assisted in attempts to improve the moral standards of the monks in that influential abbey.¹³ He was born in Thorembais-les-Béguines in the modern French-speaking part of Brabant, to the West of Liège and the North of Namur. From a contemporary chronicle of the abbey, which is particularly rich in detail about fifteenth-century events,¹⁴ it can be deduced that the

---

⁹ aI-aVII (f. 1-14), bI-bVI (f. 15-26), cI-cVI (f. 27-38), dI-dVI (f. 39-50), eI-eVI (f. 51-62), fI-fVI (f. 63-74), gI-gVII (f. 75-88), with an error in the signatures of the first septernio: aj (1ˆ14), aij (2ˆ13), aiij (3ˆ12), aiiij (4ˆ11), aiiij [!] (5ˆ10), av (6ˆ9), avj (7ˆ8); I am most grateful to E. van der Vlist, curator of manuscripts, Royal Library, The Hague, for providing me this information.

¹⁰ "...ad honorem sanctorum apostolorum Jacobi et Andree, et ad communem fratrum utilitatem finit regula beatissimi patris Basilii Cappodocie episcopi, scripta in presenti uolumine per fratrem Petrum Cortoy. Orate fratres pro anima eius. a. 1439. 27. Septembris".

¹¹ Examples of his hand on Pl. 186-187 in *CMD-NL* 1.

¹² Cfr S. BALAU, 'La bibliothèque de l'abbaye de Saint-Jacques à Liège', *Compte rendu des séances de la Commission Royale d'histoire ou Receuil de ses bulletins*, 71 (1902), p. 1-61, at p. 24 and fn. 4; 25 and fnn. 2; 5, where at least nine codices or texts signed by him or written in his hand are listed; Balau did not identify our manuscript *H1*, which therefore is the tenth manuscript written in his hand surviving from Saint-Jacques.

¹³ Cfr BALAU, *ibid.*, p. 25 fn. 2, identical with the manuscript mentioned by K. VAN VLIET, 'Bijlage 3. Verloren gegane handschriften en oude drukken van de Paulusabdij', in B. JASKI, 'Een codicologische queeste naar de oudste handschriften en handschriftfragmenten uit de bibliotheek van de Paulusabdij', in *De nalatenschap van de Paulusabdij in Utrecht* – ed. K. van Vliet, H. van Engen, Hilversum, 2012, p. 103-169, at p. 161-162, nos. 3, 4.

¹⁴ *Gesta abbatum monasterii S. Iacobi Leodiensis* – ed. U. Berlière, in U. BERLIÈRE, *Documents inédits pour servir à l'histoire ecclésiastique de la Belgique*, T. 1, Maredsous, 1894, p. 37-57, events in the 1440's including the

abbey was a leading example of austerity and reform until de decease of abbot Reynerus in 1436, but that discipline gradually and in the end sharply diminished under his weak successor Ruthgerus de Bloemendael (1436-1471). An active role in opposition to these developments seems to have been played by Petrus Cortoy, who even went so far as to visit Pope Eugene IV in Rome. From him he obtained a bull in 1444 prescribing measures to improve morals in the abbey, which the abbot flatly refused to carry out. According to the chronicle, Petrus disappointedly left the order after that, and joined a Carthusian monastery in 1444.

The collection assembled by Petrus in the set of seven quires can be characterized as a carefully chosen series of works on two more or less related topics, proprietarism and proper behaviour of monks living a communal life. The collection starts on f. 1-2 with the papal bull "*Ne in uinea*", issued by Pope Urban V (1362-1370) in 1362, in which he attacks proprietarism. After that Petrus has selected four letters by Grote, two of them against proprietarism (*Epp.* 41; 45) followed by two other ones on (acquiescence to) life in a monastery (*Epp.* 16; 62), written on f. 3r-19r in the first two quires. Then follow three letters by Peter of Blois, also chosen "non secundum ordinem, sed secundum huius scriptoris incumbentem necessitatem" (thus Petrus Cortoy, in the *incipit* of the first letter on f. 19r): they discuss similar subjects. The final text in his hand is St Basil's *Regula* in the Latin translation made by Rufinus. This text also deals primarily with the virtues which monks should practice and the vices they should avoid. It seems possible, but cannot be proved of course, that he assembled these texts in preparation of his mission to the abbey in Utrecht.

The collection of the abbey library was sold by auction in 1788, and has for a great part been lost since,[15] but at least three cata-

---

full text of Eugene IV's *bulla* (p. 47-50) at p. 45-52, Petrus mentioned on p. 47; 50.
[15] Paquot (cfr next note) lists 552 manuscripts, of which 194 volumes still survive, listed and localized most recently in *Corpus catalogorum Belgii. The medieval booklists of the Southern Low Countries*, Vol. 7. *The surviving manuscripts and incunables from medieval Belgian libraries* – ed. A. Derolez, with the collab. of Th. Falmagne and L. Otis, Brussel, 2009, p. 194-206, nos. 2456-2650, a list relying heavily on Chr. MORTIAUX-DENOËL, 'Le fonds des manuscrits de l'abbaye [de] Saint-Jacques de Liège', *Revue bénédictine*, 101 (1991), p. 154-191, with localizations of extant manuscripts in *Revue bénédictine*, 107 (1997), p. 352-380 (with the collab. of E. Guillaume); none of the manuscripts con-

logues describing its holdings have been preserved, among them the one prepared for the 1788 auction by J. N. Paquot[16] and another, very detailed and informative one compiled around 1667 by the then abbot Dom Nicolas Bouxhon (1637-1703), arranged by the main subject matter in the individual manuscripts in the form of capital letters, followed by arabic numerals;[17] Petrus Cortoy's collection of texts has been preserved in a manuscript to which Bouxhon accorded the signature F 149.[18] This same signature, entered in a seventeenth-century hand, also occurs in the right hand top margin of f. 1 of the manuscript, an undeniable confirmation of the origin and provenance of this manuscript from the Liège Benedictine abbey.

This seems the proper place to note that the same catalogue also lists a fair number of other works written by Grote (mostly letters) and by other authors belonging to the first generation Modern Devout, such as Gerard Zerbolt and Johannes de Schoonhavia, but also by Thomas a Kempis, testifying to considerable interest in the movement among the Liège Benedictines. Unfortunately, none of these other manuscripts containing texts by Grote seems to have survived.[19]

---

taining texts by Grote (cfr below) is listed as preserved in this latter contribution, as Mrs Mortiaux was not aware that *H1* is identical with Bouxhon's F 149.

[16] J. N. PAQUOT, *Catalogue des livres de la bibliothèque de la célèbre ex-abbaye de Saint-Jacques à Liège dont la vente se fera publiquement au plus offrant, sur les Cloîtres de laditte ex-abbaye, le 3 mars 1788, et jours suivants, à deux heures de relevée*, Liège, 1788, characterized briefly by MORTIAUX-DENOËL, p. 162-163, and by M-R. LAPIÈRE, *La lettre ornée dans les manuscrits mosans d'origine bénédictine (11e-12e siècles)*, Paris, 1981, p. 55.

[17] BOUXHON, *Summa omnium quae in bibliotheca inferiori Sancti Jacobi continentur, ordine quidem alphabetico*, manuscript copy preserved in Brussels, KBR, 13993, characterized briefly by MORTIAUX-DENOËL, p. 159-161.

[18] A summary notice of its contents printed by MORTIAUX-DENOËL, 1991, p. 180.

[19] In what follows, I abbreviate the summary contents from Mortiaux-Denoël's survey, with silent correction of obvious errors against Latin inflection and syntax occurring in her transcripts. Six further manuscripts include works by Grote: E 55 (Joh. de Schoonhavia, *Epp.* 1, 2; Grote, *Epp. et sermones*; Joh. de Schoonhavia, *Collatio de contemplatione*; *Tabula* uen. Bedae; Hier., *Sermo*; Aug., *Sermones*; Bern., *Epp.*) (*Revue bénédictine*, 101 (1991), p. 172); E 79 (Dauid of Augsburg; Ruusbroec/Grote, *Spir. desp.*) (p. 174); E 99 (Grote, *Tract. paup.*; Joh. Schoonh., *Epp.*; Eusebius, *Hom.*) (p. 175-176); F 10 (Anselmus, *Medd.*; Grote, *Epistola qualis debeat esse monachus* (*Ep.* 16?); *Itinerarium anime*; *Definitiones mortis et pacis*) (p. 176); F 41 (Thomas a Kempis, *Disc. claustr.*; Petrus de Alliaco, *Tractatulus*; Grote, *Epp.*; Ruus-

CHAPTER III 87

H2 Den Haag, Koninklijke Bibliotheek, 78 J 55, s. XVa, f. 113-260 of f. 1-262(-266), Prov.: Liège, Saint-Jacques (Benedictines), cfr VAN DIJK, *Prolegomena*, p. 190-203.

The sole contents of the third codicological unit consist in one of the two surviving collections of Grote's collected letters (cfr for a further description of the constituent parts above, *H1*).[20] The text in this quarto (205×140) paper unit has been written in single column layout,[21] on a written space of 150×100 mm. containing 21-30 lines[22] of text within frame ruling, on 13 regular sexterniones (10-22^{12}).[23]

The collection itself has for the most part been written by three main hands, all writing *cursiua libraria* script. The first hand A has written f. 113r-128r. A second hand B has taken over his work in the middle of *Ep.* 8 in mid-sentence,[24] in mid-quire (f. 4 of quire 2), and written the text from f. 128v1 until f. 169v3, ending his work in the middle of *Ep.* 61 in mid-sentence and in mid-quire (f. 9 of q. 5).[25] Mulder further distinguishes this hand B into two different hands, one writing f. 128v1-164r6 (= q. 5 f.3, end of *Ep.* 59) and another one writing f. 164r7 (beginning of *Ep.* 35)-169v3.[26] This is indeed possible, but I find it very difficult to discover really distinguishing traits in the script within these two subparts. The letter forms written by hand B (B1 + B2?) make a slightly more

---

broec, *?De perfecto uirtutum?* (Ps. Ruusbroec-Godeuerd de Wevel/Grote, *Duod. uirt.?*)) (p. 177); F 186 (*Exercitia pia et meditationes de passione Domini*; '*Epp.* magistri Gerardi Magni de Dauentria'; *Breues auctoritates*) (p. 180). For a context of this catalogue cfr GAENS, 'Carthusian influences', p. 94-95.

[20] Cfr on the three 'letter collections' of Grote now primarily VAN DIJK, 'Briefschaften'.

[21] The best description of the manuscript, superior to the one in H. BRUGMANS, *Catalogus codicum manuscriptorum Bibliothecae Regiae*, I. *Libri theologici*, 's-Gravenhage, 1922, p. 212-213, no. 661, still is ACQUOY, *Epistolae*, p. 5-9.

[22] 21 lines per page on e.g. f. 177v (hand A), 30 lines on f. 153v (hand B).

[23] The final quire has not been fully filled with text, the last six folia, of which three have been torn out, have remained empty; in scheme: 257^[268], 258^[267], 259^‹266›, 260^‹265›, 261^‹264›, 262^[263]; I am most grateful to E. van der Vlist, curator of manuscripts, Royal Library, The Hague, for providing me this information and for sharing his thoughts about this manuscript with me.

[24] In the last line on p. 20 ed. Mulder.

[25] In l. 228, 3 ed. Mulder, who duely notes this change of hand on p. 228, fn. a.

[26] GER. MAG., *Epp.* 1-75 – ed. W. MULDER, p. xxii.

pointed impression than those of hands A and C. From f. 169v3 until the last written folium, 262r, the text is in the hand of the third main scribe C, whose script very much resembles that of hand A. Perhaps the two scribes were trained by the same master. The *incipits* introducing the individual letters have been written in another, more careless hand, also writing *cursiua libraria* script, tending somewhat more to ordinary *cursiua* script. This fourth hand D now and then entered corrections also. In addition, he wrote a small portion of text, taking over in mid-sentence and apparently relieving the main scribe for just one verso side (f. 260v).[27] It seems very likely that this hand supervised the work of his fellow scribes. I am not able to follow Mulder in further distinguishing between the scribes writing before and after f. 260v. Occasional corrections and comments[28] have been entered in yet another slightly later hand, writing *cursiua* script. Now and then, as on f. 143r, instructions for the rubricator, in part cut away by the binder, added at the bottom of the lower margin and mainly consisting in the text of titles, are visible. No quire signatures and catchwords have survived.

In section X.4 below it will be argued that Petrus Cortoy, the scribe of the first unit *H1*, copied his text of *Ep.* 41 from this collection. Since he finished the last work in the closely connected set of seven quires *H1* on 27 September 1439, it seems inevitable to escape the conclusion that the letter collection *H2*, which so far has been dated 's. xvbc'[29] or 'around 1450'[30] on the basis of its script, can now be dated before 1439. Since especially hands B and D display clearly early traits, I would even go so far as to date the collection 's. xva'.

Secondly, it seems very likely that Petrus was present in the Benedictine abbey Saint-Jacques in Liège in 1439, which would mean that this abbey can be established as the provenance, though not origin, for this letter collection. Father van Dijk's suggestion that the manuscript may have its origin in the Heer-

---

[27] The contents of his portion of text consist in the greater part of *Ep.* 14, p. 48 ed. Mulder, who notes his intervention in fn. b: "H2. Pergit alia manus".

[28] For one such comment, in a hand datable to s. xvb, cfr the *app. crit.* of *Cura past.*, Tit.

[29] VAN DIJK, *Prolegomena*, p. 190.

[30] VAN DIJK, 'Briefschaften', p. 174; 180, id. ('RvD'), *Moderne Devotie. Figuren en facetten. Tentoonstelling ter herdenking van het sterfjaar van Geert Grote 1384-1984. Catalogus*, Nijmegen, 1984, p. 80-82.

CHAPTER III 89

Florenshuis in Deventer,[31] perhaps proposed on the basis of its contents, is attractive in itself, but cannot be proved unfortunately. Although there are obvious similarities between hands A, C and the hand of Grote's biographer Rudolf Dier as well as hand 7 in *Focar.*,[32] and between hand B and the hand responsible for part of the collection of "Notabilia" of Grote and fellow early Modern Devout compiled in the main house of the Brethren respectively,[33] and although the manner of ruling by frame only and not by a series of lines is characteristic for sober products of the house, I am inclined to state that positive identification of any of the hands writing in *H2* with a hand known to have written in that house is not possible – rather, the similarities are due to the fact that all compared manuscripts are datable to 's XVa'. The proposed provenance of this part of the manuscript from the house of the Tertiary Sisters St Barbara in Delft probably goes back to an unfounded suggestion made by Acquoy in his introduction to his 1857 edition of fourteen of Grote's letters on the basis of *H2*.[34]

---

[31] "Auch editionswissenschaftlich gesehen ist es merkwürdig, dass Mulder nicht schlechthin der Briefsammlung H als Grundlage gefolgt ist, zumal diese aus dem Heer-Florenshuis in Deventer stammt", VAN DIJK, 'Briefschaften', p. 179, cfr p. 174. Quite curiously, van Dijk correctly located the manuscript in the Benedictine abbey in Liège in *Moderne Devotie. Figuren en facetten*, p. 82, most probably following a suggestion made by TIECKE, *Werken*, p. 77, where further argumentation for this in the end correct view is missing.

[32] The parallellism is most conspicuous between hand C in *H2* and hand 7 in *N*, but nevertheless differences occur between the two hands, most notably in -g-, of which I wrote in GER. MAG., *Focar.*, p. 131-132: "hand 7 invariably writes his -g- with a first left curved stroke, followed by a second curved stroke to the right of it, which smoothly proceeds to the descender, at first slightly bending to the right, after that below the line ending in a strongly sketched curve to the left, moving upwards at its end. The upper part of the letter is closed by the two curved strokes. The letter is finished with a final, often slightly curved horizontal stroke to the right." In *H2* the last descender starts directly below the top line. Particularly close also are the two *cursiua* hands D in *H2* and 4 in *N*, but yet there is a marked difference in the descender of -h-, as well as in -v- in initial position, for instance. I also discussed the hands in *N* in GER. MAG., *Turrim*, p. 769-770.

[33] Illustrations and discussion of their hands in e.g. HOFMAN, *Focar.*, p. 130-132 and Pl. 2; 4; early manuscripts having a certain origin in the Heer-Florenshuis listed *ibid.*, fn. 253.

[34] Thus VAN DIJK, *Prolegomena*, p. 190, on the basis of a misunderstood suggestion in ACQUOY, *Epistolae*, p. 11.

L Liège, Bibliothèque de l'Université, 229 (c), a. 1451, Or.: Namur, monastery of the Crutched Friars, Prov.: Liège, monastery of the Crutched Friars, cfr VAN DIJK, *Prolegomena*, p. 270-283.

L is described in greater detail elsewhere, cfr HOFMAN, *Focar.*, p. 135-138; I corrected my mistakes in my earlier description in HOFMAN, 'Crutched Friars', p. 521-529.

*M Magdeburg, Stadtbibliothek, XII 8° 12, s. XVb, 151 f., Prov.: unknown, cfr VAN DIJK, *Prolegomena*, p. 287-300.

In connection with the description of the two closely related letter collections *LH2* a few words seem in place on the lost witness which originally transmitted a slightly diverging collection of Grote's letters. On the basis of the photographs of a few folia preserved in the so-called 'Brandsma Collectie', preserved in two copies in Nijmegen (Titus Brandsma Instituut) and in Boxmeer (Nederlands Carmelitaans Instituut), it can be established that at least two different hands contributed to the collection of letters in this witness. The *cursiua libraria* script of the second hand shows a remarkable similarity to the hand who copied (and probably personally translated) the Middle Dutch version of part of *Focar.*[35] This hand belonged to a Crutched Friar in the house Marienfrede in Dingden just to the North of Wesel in the Niederrhein region. Unfortunately, however, I was not able to identify the two hands as identical – the hand in **M* writes, for instance, 'g' with a third final, horizontal stroke over the two curved lower strokes, while the scribe in Dingden is content with two strokes only.

---

[35] Cfr HOFMAN, *Focar.* p. 225-231.

CHAPTER IV

A *CONSILIVM* ON PASTORAL CARE (*EP.* 73)

IV.1 SUMMARY OF CONTENTS

In this *consilium*, Grote addresses the recommended inner motivation for a prospective parish priest, with special emphasis on simoniacal practices in relation with the acceptance of a position. He further comments on the conditions which an applicant should meet in his view before he can accept such a position when involving pastoral care. In developing his argumentation, he prefers to stick to a strict interpretation of canon law. This has led Post in his summary of contents to pass a negative judgment on this particular *consilium*: "Groote's legal mentality overweighs his sense of charity, pity or magnanimity. He displays a cool, businesslike approach".[1]

Grote had been asked for advice in a specific case, but the ensuing exposition was from the outset meant to have a wider applicability. The case in question concerned a sufficiently educated ("in grammatica imbuto", 2) 24-year old youngster (2), whose primary objective when accepting a position as parish priest had been sustenance for himself (113-122) and for his impoverished parents (3-5; 102). In addition, his sisters had pleaded in favour of their brother with the female (cfr 15) dignitary who was in possession of the right of patronage, and they had offered her manual or other service in return, i.e. they were guilty of the second form of simony as defined by Gregory the Great, "munus ab obsequio"[2] (12-19). Also, the youngster himself had declared that he was not prepared to accept the position without an accompanying benefice (98-101). Grote considers such a motive and attitude as simony on several fronts, and in his *consilium* he explains why. As a constantly returning refrain, he repeats over and over again that proper fulfilment of a pastoral charge implies that concerns for

---

[1] POST, *Modern Devotion*, p. 88; contents summarized *ibid.*, p. 86-88.
[2] Cfr on the three forms of simony as defined by Gregory the Great supra, Ch. I.2.

personal welfare on earth should be made subordinate to a spiritual life in the service of God, having the salvation of souls as its main aim.

After he has dismissed the formal objection that the boy is too young (6-11),[3] Grote states in a section depending on Johannes of Freiburg that he should beware of guiltiness of two of the three main forms of simony, "munus a lingua", implying that he should not acquire his office and benefice through a request resulting in a personal favour, and "munus ab obsequio", implying that he should not acquire it either as compensation for rendered services, by himself or by his relatives (12-41). A person can ask for a pastoral function for himself solely when his intentions are sincere, that is when his single objective is to save souls, and that only in a situation of acute necessity, when no other, more suitable candidate is available (41-45). And even in such precious circumstances sincere persons should not apply voluntarily for such a position according to the leading Church Fathers (46-64). In his day, moreover, applications and assignations are generally afflicted by corrupt practices and bribery, and therefore avoided by sincere people (65-77).

Grote next lists five prerequisites necessary for proper functioning as a good and worthy shepherd. Such a person should have (1) an upright intention to honour God and to guide his flock towards salvation; (2) he should have sufficient knowledge about God and sacred procedure; (3) he should lead an exemplary life, (4) surpassing his flock in care and conduct, and (5) considering earthly possessions as vile and unimportant (78-83). In what follows, he develops the three first requirements mainly, for the structure and argumentation in the first and second ones largely depending on St Thomas.[4]

The longest section of the *consilium* (84-202) deals with the first prerequisite, an upright intention. Proof for this is in Grote's

---

[3] When counting the nine months in his mother's womb (8-11), the boy had reached the required age: during the Council of Vienne (1311-1312), common practice regarding the age required for various positions involving pastoral care was formalized in a decree transmitted in the Clementines (*Clem.* 1.6.3, c. II, 1140, 22-26 ed. Friedberg) and in Mansi, but not in *COD*. The decree specifies the following minimun ages: subdiaconate: 18 years; diaconate: 20 years; priesthood: 25 years.

[4] THOM., *Sent.*, L. 4 d. 24 q. 1 a. 3 qc. 1-2 (T. 7, 2, p. 892-893), a source also used and developed in GER. MAG., *Focar.* 18, p. 418-423 ed. Hofman.

CHAPTER IV 93

view readiness to accept a pastoral office for the sake of exercising pastoral care only, even when it is not accompanied by temporal emoluments in the form of a benefice (84-98), a theme also touched upon in *Locat.* (83-86; 406-419). By refusing to renounce worldly profit, the youngster shows that he subordinates a spiritually oriented life in the service of God (mankind's ultimate goal, 106-112; this argument is based on St Thomas) to temporary gains (92-132). Such a worldly approach to entrance into office is a mortal sin (133-146). When sustenance for himself and his family is his motive for a vocation, he necessarily likewise approaches his position and future functioning as priest, the means to carry out care, with the same goal at the back of his mind (147-168), thus forfeiting eternal reward and absolution, and risking damnation (169-188). He concludes this section with a final appeal to break loose from attachment to material possessions (189-202).

The second prerequisite, sufficient knowledge about matters divine, is a *sine qua non* for proper functioning in office. He adduces a series of apt quotations, thus showing that indignation about insufficiently educated priests dated back a very long time indeed. With their help, he argues that a priest may think that he can come off well with insufficient knowledge, but that God is nevertheless acutely aware of his shortcomings. Precisely because of the holiness and importance of their role as mediators of the divine, priests should imbue themselves with sufficient knowledge of all aspects of their eminent office (203-237).

An exemplary life, the third prerequisite, is an indispensable aspect of vocation, for when his flock looks down on a priest's lifestyle, his teachings will obviously not be taken seriously (238-251). Also, a good shepherd should surpass his flock in conduct, the fourth prerequisite, and unselfishly excel in charity, in order to enhance his authority and to stimulate his flock to imitate his behaviour (252-277). Grote is well aware that this is an arduous demand, for a priest's flock is not easily amenable (278-283), and his ruler and/or patron often puts pressure on him to conspire with him in his earthly intents and purposes (284-296). Nevertheless, a sincere priest should stand firm in all of these circumstances, despite pressure or even persecution. Before accepting a post, the youngster should therefore realize these considerations (297-311). Grote does not dwell any further on the fifth prerequisite, disdain for earthly possessions, as commitment to this principle is more appropriate for experienced priests mainly (312-316).

IV.2 EDITORIAL HISTORY, SUPPLEMENT

Cura past. has been edited twice before already. The *editio princeps* was printed by J. Clarisse as 'Bijlage 3' in 1831, who used the inferior witness *Gr* as basic manuscript, with in the footnotes variants from *A*, which he unfortunately did not use for the establishment of the text.[5] A critical edition was published by Mulder in 1933,[6] who nowhere states which manuscripts he used for the edition. On the basis of his sigla and my own collation, however, I am pretty sure that he used *H2* as basic manuscript, printing variants from *LA* in his notes, with occasional reference to variants transmitted in *H*, apparently only in cases where he did not trust the readings in his other witnesses.

IV.3 THE MANUSCRIPTS

IV.3.1 Manuscripts used for the edition

Some of the manuscripts used for the edition of *Cura past.* (*DDiHLMX*) are described in greater detail elsewhere; cfr, in the sequence of the *conspectus siglorum* below, Ch. II.3.1 above for *D*;[7] HOFMAN, *Focar.*, p. 168-170 for *Di*;[8] p. 132-135 for *H*;[9] p. 135-138 for *L*;[10] Ch. II.3.2 above for *M*;[11] p. 253 for *X*.[12]

---

[5] Cfr CLARISSE, 'Groete', 3 (1831), p. 13-27, cfr on the quality of *Gr* below, section IV.4.2.3; VAN DIJK, *Prolegomena*, p. 462, inadvertently states that Clarisse used ms. Utrecht, UB, 386, but this witness transmits Grote's *Ep.* 70 only, cfr *ibid.*, p. 361-362.

[6] Cfr MULDER, *Epp.*, p. 310-321.

[7] Köln, Historisches Archiv der Stadt Köln, GB 4° 249, a. 1418, Or.: Deventer, most probably Heer-Florenshuis, Prov.: Köln, Crutched Friars, cfr VAN DIJK, *Prolegomena*, p. 229-231; the text of *Cura past.* in this important witness has been written on f. 31v-35r, directly following *Locat.*

[8] Düsseldorf, Universitäts- und Landesbibliothek, B 83, s. xvb, 276 f., Prov.: Dingden bei Wesel, Marienfrede (Crutched Friars), cfr VAN DIJK, *Prolegomena*, p. 173-174; full description of this manuscript by J. Ott in E. OVERGAAUW, J. OTT und G. KARPP, *Die mittelalterlichen Handschriften der Signaturengruppe B in der Universitäts- und Landesbibliothek Düsseldorf*, Teil 1, Ms. B 1 bis B 100, Wiesbaden, 2005, p. 277-281, which was not available to van Dijk. The text of *Cura past.*, written by the same hand, follows after *Focar.* (and a fragment from *Ep.* 70, in a different hand) in a separate quire (6[12-3], f. 61-69) on f. 61r-66r.

[9] Liège, Bibliothèque du Grand Séminaire, Cod. 11 (6 B 17), s. xva, 157 f., Or.: Deventer (?), Prov.: Huy, Clairlieu (Crutched friars), cfr VAN DIJK, *Prolegomena*, p. 250-252; the text of *Cura past.* in this important witness precedes

CHAPTER IV 95

B Brussel, Koninklijke Bibliotheek van België, 4414-24 (2187), s. XVd, cfr VAN DIJK, *Prolegomena*, p. 148.[13]

Cura past. is the last text in this quarto (208×136) paper manuscript, written on f. 126r-130v in unpretentious *cursiua* script datable to the last quarter of the fifteenth century. The manuscript is a convolute, as is clear from several *caesurae* between the various texts transmitted in it.[14] Nothing is known about its origin or provenance, but the manuscript is one of the few witnesses transmitting works written by one of the earliest Louvain theology professors, Joannes Varenacker (*c*. 1413-1475, chairholder 1443/4 until his death on 11 January 1475), on f. 27v-37r and 50r-57r.[15] The presence of these rarely transmitted works may suggest an origin in Leuven for the manuscript.

---

other texts by Grote, *Artic., Ep.* 22, and the extremely rarely transmitted texts *Puncta* and *Obseru.*

[10] Liège, Bibliothèque de l'Université, 229 (c), a. 1451, Or.: Namur, monastery of the Crutched Friars, Prov.: Liège, monastery of the Crutched Friars, cfr VAN DIJK, *Prolegomena*, p. 270-283; I corrected my mistakes in my earlier description in HOFMAN, 'Crutched Friars', p. 521-529.

[11] Mainz, Stadtbibliothek, I 507, *c*. 1450, Prov.: Mainz, St. Jakob (Benedictines), later Mainz, St. Michael (Carthusians), cfr VAN DIJK, *Prolegomena*, p. 315.

[12] Wolfenbüttel, Herzog August Bibliothek, 18. 32 Aug. 4°, Grote part s. XVc, before 1466, Prov.: unknown, cfr VAN DIJK, *Prolegomena*, p. 388-389; this witness (exemplar for *T*) transmits *Cura past.* on f. 266v-271v directly before *Locat.*

[13] In his description, Father van Dijk unfortunately did not attribute the text on f. 70-78, *De contemptu huius mundi, inc. "Nolite diligere mundum..."*, to its author, Johannes de Schoenhauia, although he was aware of this fact, as is clear from autograph personal annotations; cfr on the text GRUIJS, 'Schoonhoven, *De contemptu*', this witness listed *ibid.*, p. 39, another copy of this work is preserved in a manuscript containing Grote's *Epp.* 45; 44, cfr the description of ms. Brussel, Koninklijke Bibliotheek van België, 3672-3690 (1503) below, Ch. XI.3.

[14] Thus, f. 57v-62v; 68v-69v; 83-84 have remained empty. Also, J. VAN DEN GHEYN, *Catalogue des manuscrits de la Bibliothèque Royale de Belgique*, Vol. 3. *Théologie*, Brussel, 1903, p. 335-336, found various different watermarks in the paper used.

[15] The transmission of his literary output is listed in L. BURIE, 'Proeve tot inventarisatie van de in handschrift of in druk bewaarde werken van de Leuvense theologieprofessoren uit de XVᵉ eeuw', in E. J. M. VAN EIJL *et al.* (ed.), *Facultas sacrae theologiae Lovaniensis 1432-1797. Bijdragen tot haar geschiedenis* (= *Bibliotheca ephemeridum theologicarum Lovaniensium*, 45), 1977, p. 215-272, at p. 238-241, our witness mentioned at p. 239; 240, with further references.

IV.3.2 Other manuscript witnesses

Some of the manuscripts not used for the edition of *Cura past.* (*Q Gr H2 Kh V A T*) are described in greater detail elsewhere; cfr, in the alphabetical order of the libraries where these manuscripts are presently kept, HOFMAN, *Focar.*, p. 178-179 for *Q*;[16] p. 181 for *Gr*,[17] Ch. III.2 above for *H2*;[18] HOFMAN, *Focar.*, p. 237-238 for *Kh*;[19] HOFMAN, *Turrim*, p. 767-768 for *V*;[20] HOFMAN, *Focar.*, p. 172-174 for *A*;[21] p. 254 for *T*.[22]

---

[16] Berlin, Staatsbibliothek zu Berlin – Preußischer Kulturbesitz, theol. lat. fol. 194, a. 1471, Or.: Augustinian friary in Lippstadt, Prov.: Augustinian sisters in Lippstadt, cfr VAN DIJK, *Prolegomena*, p. 135-136; contrary to the allegation by van Dijk, p. 135 ("letzter Teil fehlt"), the text of *Cura past.* is complete in this witness; it follows directly after *Focar.* on f. 191ra-193vb. Cfr on the monastery of the Augustinian friars in Lippstadt *Westfälisches Klosterbuch. Lexikon der vor 1815 errichteten Stifte und Klöster von ihrer Gründung bis zur Aufhebung* – ed. K. HENGST, Teil 1. *Ahlen-Mülheim*, Münster, 1992, p. 537-541 (contr. K. Elm, A. Rüther), on the monastery of the female Augustinians *ibid.*, p. 531-537 (contr. C. Kimminus-Schneider), on the 40 surviving manuscripts from the monastery of the male friars KRÄMER, *Handschriftenerbe*, Vol. 2, p. 495.

[17] Groningen, Universiteitsbibliotheek, 21, a. 1459, Or., Prov.: Groningen, cfr VAN DIJK, *Prolegomena*, p. 184-185; the text of *Cura past.* follows after *Matrim.* and *Ep.* 22 on f. 42v-48r.

[18] Den Haag, Koninklijke Bibliotheek, 78 J 55, s. XVa, f. 113-260 of f. 1-262 (-266), Prov.: Liège, Saint-Jacques (Benedictines), cfr VAN DIJK, *Prolegomena*, p. 190-203.

[19] Köln, Diözesan- und Dombibliothek, 1092, s. xvb, Prov.: Hohenbusch, monastery of the Crutched Friars, cfr VAN DIJK, *Prolegomena*, p. 220-222, description and digital images available through http://www.ceec.uni-koeln.de; the text of *Cura past.*, which is acephalous due to loss of several folia, follows after *Locat.* and *Artic.* and before *Ep.* 23 and *Focar.* on p. 251-256.

[20] Köln, Historisches Archiv der Stadt Köln, GB 4° 37, s. xva (before 1419), Or.: Deventer, Heer-Florenshuis (Brethren), Prov.: Vollenhove, Sint-Janskamp (Brethren), later prov.: Cologne, Crutched Friars. The fragmentary text of *Cura past.* transmitted on f. 84r in *V* consists of roughly 27 lines of the text, viz. l. **78-83**, followed, after a transitory sentence "De primo. Notandum quod qui contra rectam intencionem intrat querens temporalia", by l. **134-145** Non – fuisset; **152-155** Quidquid – quero; **203-207** De – prebet.

[21] Utrecht, Bibliotheek der Rijksuniversiteit, 174 (1 L 14), s. xvc, Or. (?), Prov.: Utrecht, Nieuwlicht (Carthusians), cfr VAN DIJK, *Prolegomena*, p. 357-358; the text of *Cura past.* occurs on f. 180r-183v, after *Focar.*, *Ep.* 57, and *Locat.* (interrupted by an intervening text).

[22] Wolfenbüttel, Herzog August Bibliothek, 35. 1 Aug. fol., a. 1466, Prov.: Riddagshausen, St. Maria (Cistercians), cfr VAN DIJK, *Prolegomena*, p. 389-391; this witness (transcribed from *X*) transmits *Cura past.* on f. 238rb-241ra directly before *Locat.*

CHAPTER IV 97

Dk Köln, Historisches Archiv der Stadt Köln, GB 8° 96, c. a. 1400, Or. (?), Prov.: Köln, Crutched Friars, cfr VAN DIJK, *Prolegomena*, p. 236-237.

Manuscript *Dk* transmits on f. 50r a tiny fragment from *Cura past.*, consisting of l. 78-83; after 80 "rectam", the scribe has inserted an adapted version of l. 84-85 "principaliter – intendat". The early part of the manuscript (f. 1-104), dating from *c.* 1400, is a *rapiarium* containing a wide variety of fragments. It has as its provenance the house of the Crutched Friars in Cologne, but where it originated cannot be established anymore.[23] At least nine *rapiaria* were available in this house in the fifteenth century, as is clear from a note on f. 1r which runs as follows: "R_x [= Rapularius] IX^{us} [later erased] quod J, que est litera nona in alphabeto, similiter et 9 cifra. Et pertinet fratribus sancte Crucis in Colonia";[24] six of these *rapiaria* still survived until the collapse of the Historisches Archiv in Cologne in 2009.[25]

Tw Trier, Stadtbibliothek, 771/1350 8°, s. xvc, Prov.: Eberhardsklausen, St. Maria (Windesheim Regular Canons), cfr VAN DIJK, *Prolegomena*, p. 351-352.

This quarto (210×142) paper manuscript is a convolute, consisting of various parts which did not belong together originally. This observation even applies to the three Grote texts transmitted in the codex. Thus, the two Grote letters not edited here (*Epp.* 22; 70) have been written in single col. layout in a regular hand writing *hybrida* script of the C/H variety,[26] datable to s. xvc. *Cura past.*, on the other hand, though datable to the same period, has been penned down in two columns, in a hand writing *cursiua* script which could perhaps better be labelled *currens* than *libraria*. A clear caesura, two empty folia (f. 163-164) between *Ep.* 70 and *Ep.* 73, also points to the fact that the various texts belong to different codicological units. In addition, there is a marked difference in ornamentation. *Epp.* 22; 70 are introduced by a header in *hybrida libraria* script, followed by a single unpretentious lombard letter, whereas *Epp.* 73 is introduced by a header in unpre-

---

[23] Schöler, *Ama nesciri*, suggests a possible origin in Zwolle, but her suggestion cannot be proved beyond doubt, and it is not confirmed by VENNEBUSCH, *Handschriften*, Teil 3, p. 93-99, in his description of this witness.
[24] Cfr VENNEBUSCH, *Handschriften*, Teil 3, p. 93-99, at p. 94.
[25] Cfr Schöler, *Ama nesciri*, p. 73-75.
[26] On the terminology cfr Gumbert's observations in *CMD-NL* 2, 1, p. 29-31.

tentious *hybrida* script. Each section of the treatise starts with an initial ornamented with lavish, sometimes extravagant penwork intermingled with remarkably fine illustrations.[27]

Tc   Trier, Stadtbibliothek, 964/1158 4° (olim 375, D. II. c. 12), s. XVc, Prov.: Trier, St. Alban (Carthusians), cfr VAN DIJK, *Prolegomena*, p. 352-353.

The text of *Cura past.* has in this folio (294×220) paper manuscript been written in an experienced hand writing *hybrida currens* script datable to s. XVc, on folia which had apparently remained empty in this quire at the end of the text of Isidore's *Synonyma*, which has been written in a contemporary hand writing *hybrida libraria* script.

W   Wolfenbüttel, Herzog August Bibliothek, 203 Extravagantes, s. XVbc, Prov.: a Carthusian monastery in the Middle Rhine region, cfr VAN DIJK, *Prolegomena*, p. 379-380.

This quarto (210×155) paper manuscript is a convolute, consisting of five mutually distinguishable parts, written in different main hands.[28] The Grote texts occur on f. 61-69 in a separate quire, a sexternio consisting of f. 61-72, with *Cura past.* on f. 61r-67r, directly followed by a fragments from *Ep.* 45 (end); *Ep.* 46 (beg.) and *Ep.* 65 (beg.). This quire has further been filled with an excerpt from Honorius Augustodunensis' *Speculum ecclesiae*, a text which breaks off in mid-sentence on the last verso side of the quire. The texts in this codicological unit have been written in a hand using C/H script datable to s. XVc.[29]

IV.4.1 Procedure in establishing a stemma – Choosing a basic manuscript

The text of *Cura past.* (*Ep.* 73) is transmitted in 18 manuscripts.[30] As in the case of *Locat.*, therefore, I started the procedure which

---

[27] Cfr for an example the illustration in HOFMAN, 'Functionaliteit', p. 185, ill. 1.

[28] Parts (1), f. 1-20, 1^{10}-2^{10}, hand 1; (2) f. 21-27, 3^{8-1}, hand 2; (3) f. 28-60, 4^{10-1}, 5^{12}-6^{12}, hand 3, the last text breaks off in mid-sentence in the middle of the text; (4) f. 61-72, 7^{12}, Grote part, hand 4; (5) f. 73-92, hand 5; small additions on spaces which had originally remained empty occasionally in yet other hands.

[29] On the terminology cfr Gumbert's observations in *CMD-NL* 2, Texte, p. 29-31.

[30] All witnesses are conveniently listed in VAN DIJK, *Prolegomena*, p. 461. They are described in detail in section IV.3.

CHAPTER IV 99

had to result in the choice of a basic manuscript by collating the first 202 lines of *Cura past.* in two manuscripts having a known or probable origin in Deventer. In this case, I opted for *D* (Köln, HA, GB 4° 249), the witness used as basic manuscript for *Locat.*,[31] and *H* (Liège, BGS, 6 B 17), the witness used as basic manuscript for *Artic*.[32] The preliminary provisional text established on the basis of these two manuscripts was then for the first 101 lines compared to the text as transmitted in most other witnesses.[33] On the basis of this first collation exercise of most extant witnesses (14 full copies and 2 fragments) the provisional text based on *DH* was changed into a definitive text, usually following *H*, but sometimes *D*.[34] In the case of several impossible readings in *H* (and occasionally in some other manuscripts also)[35] as well as of some errors against Latin grammar present in *H*, but not in the

---

[31] An assessment motivating the comparatively good quality of the text of *Locat.* in *D* is provided above, in section II.4.

[32] An assessment motivating the comparatively good quality of the text of *Artic.* in *H* is provided in HOFMAN, *Focar.*, section III.4.1, p. 254-256.

[33] *TW* have not been collated. It has been argued already on the basis of the texts of *Locat.* (cfr above, section II.4.2.1) and *Artic.* (cfr *CC CM* 235, p. 253-254; 258-259) that *T* has been transcribed from *X*; this is true for the text of *Cura past.* also, cfr e.g. 22 Scriptis] Scripto *X T*; 45-46 q. – quota] *om. X T*; 46 qui] quod qui *X T*; 63 declinatur] quam suscipitur *add. X T, sed non sic Greg. Magn.*; 80-81 Secundo tenetur esse illuminatus Dei sciencia] Secundo esse illuminatus de sciencia *X T*; it therefore is not necessary to collate the text in *T*. The text in *W* is extremely bad: in l. 1-32, this witness presents 20 variants, most of them not recurring anywhere else. Since it seems clear on the basis of a shared variant (8 in hoc] *om. X W Gr M*) that *W* belongs in the Eastern German branch of the stemma for which *X* has been chosen as representative (cfr further below), it was decided very early on not to collate this witness any further.

[34] In some instances, a reading in *H* or *D* alone or in *HD* and very few other witnesses has nevertheless been adopted in the text; one such instance occurs in l. 38-40, "Sed uolens sic mitti uel petere ⟨curam⟩ aduertat quod Gwilhelmus uult quod in casu dignus potest pro se petere, sed non semper", where "curam" is omitted in *H L H2 D' Gr*, but present in the other witnesses *A Di B Tw Tc Q M X* (*Kb* defective, later on supplied in *D*). The word is an obvious supplement, gloss or addition, but had probably never been written by Grote, who refers to the object of "petere" as "beneficium curam animarum habens".

[35] 49 in necessitate] necessitate *H Kb L H2*, where it is clear from 42 "tempore necessitatis" that "in" should not be omitted; 58 et] *om. H Kb L H2 Gr*, in a quotation from St Thomas, who writes "et"; 95 creata] *D Di A B Q X Tw Tc M corr. Kb², causata H, tanta Kb¹ L H2, rata Gr*; in this category perhaps also belongs 93 se ipsum] *D Di A B Q X Gr Tw Tc M*, semetipsum *H Kb L H2*.

majority of other manuscripts,[36] the definitive text diverges from the copy in *H*.

It indeed turns out that manuscript *H* transmits a remarkably low number of deviations from the provisional text constituted on the basis of *DH*. This is clear when the number of deviations from the definitive text in all collated witnesses is listed (in the alphabetical order given above in section IV.3):[37]

Q: 20; *B*: 25; *Di*: 19; *Gr*: 50; *H2*: 8; *D*: 9; *H*: 12; *L*: 9; *M*: 30; *Tw*: 19; *Tc*: 27; *A*: 13; *X*: 33

More importantly, however, it also turns out that some manuscripts transmit an even better text than the one in *H*, viz. *D* and *H2L*, the two manuscripts transmitting Grote's 'collected letters'. The text in the letter collections, available in Mulder's 1933 edition, stands apart from the other witnesses by the very nature of the context of its transmission. It seemed inevitable, however, to escape the conclusion that *H* is not the best option to serve as basic manuscript. Credit must therefore be given where it is due, to Conrad's copy available in *D*. The text had to be adapted again, to the version of the text as transmitted in the basic manuscript *D*. In accordance with the regulations set out in section I.5, on editorial principles, readings transmitted in *D* only or in *D* and very few other manuscripts were during a later stage changed in such a way that readings transmitted in the majority of the witnesses, but also in all branches of the stemma, were preferred for the final version of the text, while the reading in *D* was in such cases relegated to the *app. crit.*

On the basis of the collated passage, a few manuscripts could be grouped together, which means that further collation work could be restricted to a single witness, representative of the group as a whole. This primarily applies to a group of manuscripts in the neighbourhood of *H*, most of them having known connections with Crutched Friars, viz. *HKhLH2(V?Dk?)*.[38] For further

---

[36] 52 accesserunt] *D B Q X Gr M*, assenserint *H*, accesserint *H Kh L H2Tw Tc A*, assesserunt *Di*, where after introductory "quod" the mode should be indicative.

[37] Spelling deviations in proper names and book titles, though listed in the *app. cr.*, are not counted. The variants in *Kh* could not be counted, as a missing leaf has resulted in the omission of l. 1-47.

[38] Cfr for argumentation below, section IV.4.2.2. The tiny fragments in *Dk* (transmitting 5(-7) lines of text only) and *V* (transmitting 27 lines of text) have

CHAPTER IV   101

collation work, this group is reduced to two witnesses, *H* as representative for the Crutched Friars copies *HKh*, and *L* as representative for the letter collections in *H2L*. Likewise, *XTWGr*, mostly manuscripts having Eastern German provenances, could conveniently be grouped together.[39] They are represented by *X*.

As a result, the number of manuscripts which had to be collated for a second collation exercise, for which I have chosen a portion of text consisting of l. 102-200, could be reduced from 16 through 14 to 11: *QBDiDHLMTwTcAX*. Unfortunately, some of these manuscripts transmit a rather faulty text containing a significant number of variant readings.

After the second collation exercise had been completed, it proved possible to group two series of manuscripts together on convincing grounds. First, it became obvious that *DiAQ* belong together, discussed below in section IV.4.2.1 as group δ. This grouping is corroborated by negative evidence, consisting in shared deviating readings transmitted in the six manuscripts together constituting group κ, discussed below in section IV.4.2.2. On the whole, the best text is transmitted in *Di*, which was therefore chosen to represent group δ.

Secondly, several other variants, discussed in detail below in section IV.4.2.2, made it abundantly clear that group κ consists of more manuscripts than just *HKhLH2(V?Dk?)*: especially *Tw*, but also *Tc*, belong in the same group. For the rest of the text, these two witnesses were not collated any further.

IV.4.2 Grouping the various manuscripts

IV.4.2.1 Group δ

The most convincing variant suggesting that *DiAQ* should be grouped together occurs in l. 177: inspirante] spirante *DiAQ*. A few other variants, none of them convincing in itself, confirm this grouping.[40] In spite of this week evidence, I have neverthe-

---

hesitantly been grouped here, on the basis of their provenance from the Crutched Friars' house in Cologne mainly.
[39] Cfr for argumentation below, section IV.4.2.3.
[40] 7 aliquid] aliquod *DiAQ*; 173 uel] et *DiAQ* (also in *TwXM*); ungrammatical "audiet" in l. 167 for "audiat" in a list of verbal forms in the subjunctive is ambiguous, as any scribe in any group could have corrected it. The very preservation in manuscripts belonging to various groups in the stemma

less decided to maintain it on the basis of the demonstrable proximity of the text of *Focar.* as transmitted in *DiAQ*.[41] This proximity is further substantiated by the observation that *DiQ* transmit *Focar.* and *Cur. past.*, but none of the other texts written by Grote. A question which also needs to be addressed is whether *Di* has been copied from *D*, as the two manuscripts have as their provenance nearby convents of the Crutched Friars in the Niederrhein region. That this is not the case, is obvious from the fact that the *incipit* of the text is present in the later witness *Di* (XVb), but not in *D* (1418).[42]

Within the group, a somewhat closer relationship between *DiA* is suggested by one variant, the addition of "est" after 151 intentione, impossible in the context in view of the main verb "inficiuntur" in the next line, duely transmitted in *Di*, but corrupted into "conficiuntur" in *A*. A remarkable error in *Q* is the substitution of "inueni(s) (written īueni(s))" for "iuuenis", twice so written (l. 1; 8), and twice corrected. For the edition, *Di* has been chosen to represent the group as a whole. These data lead to branch δ in the stemma below.

IV.4.2.2 Group κ

A group of manuscripts in the neighbourhood of *H*, most of them having known connections with Crutched Friars (whence the siglum κ), viz. *HKhLH2*, shares a few significant variants, among them the correctly missing word "curam" in l. 38, as well as 93 se ipsum] semetipsum *HKhLH2* (both discussed above in section IV.4.1 already).[43] After the collation of l. 102-200, it turned out that *TwTc* derive from the same intermediate exemplar, as is clear from several shared variants, among them the reading

---

(167 audiat] audiet *DiAQ*, but also in groups κ (*HKh L¹ H2, corr. L²*) and ξ (*X*)) suggests that the ungrammatical form goes back to an error or unclear reading in the autograph, for which Grote was responsible himself; another ungrammatical variant transmitted mostly in group δ, but also in representatives of various branches may also go back to a badly legible abbreviation in the autograph: 46 qui] quod *anno 1418 DDiAM*, si *Q*, quod qui *X*, corr. *A²*, cfr also 13 quod] quia *DiA*, not *Q*, also transmitted in *DM*.

[41] Cfr on this further HOFMAN, *Focar.*, p. 204-206.

[42] Also, some variants in *D* are not present in *Di*: 7 aliquid *DHL*; obsteterit *DL*; 70 declinanda] derelinquenda *D*; 81 et¹] om. *D*.

[43] Cfr also the minor variants 22 super] supra *HLH2* (*Kh* defective); 49 in] om. *HKhLH2*; 58 et] om. *HKhLH2 Gr*.

CHAPTER IV 103

"uenis" in l. 198, which makes less sense in the context than "bonis", the reading transmitted in all other witnesses.[44] *Tw*, but especially *Tc*, also transmit a considerable number of distinguishing variants not attested in the other witnesses of the group, thus revealing that more intermediate copies or more careless scribes stand between these two manuscripts from Trier and the common exemplar κ than between the other members of the group and κ.[45] A few variants suggest that the letter collections *LH2* form a separate subgroup within the group as a whole.[46]

It is very difficult to assign the small fragment in *V*, which can be linked to the blind Johannes van Ommen and transmits not more than 27 lines of the text,[47] to its proper place in the stemma, primarily because its variants[48] seldom coincide with those in the other manuscripts. And if they do, there is no consistency in its agreement with manuscripts belonging to other branches in the stemma. On the basis of the close proximity of its text of *Locat.* to the one in *Kh*, the fragment has hesitantly been localized in group κ, in the neighbourhood of *Kh*.

These combined data lead to branch κ in the stemma below.

---

[44] Several other minor variants are not convincing in themselves, but the fact that they are all consistently transmitted in precisely the same group of manuscripts makes it possible to consider them together as convincing evidence: **113** ista] *om.* *H Kh L H2 Tw Tc*, also in *X*, ita *M*; **119** Et¹] *om.* *H Kh L H2 Tw Tc*; **130** interiora] ad *praem.* *H Kh L H2 Tw Tc*; **166** predicet] predictum *H Kh L H2 Tw*; **177** acceperit, siue Deo inspirante] *D X M*, acceperit (accepit *Q*) siue Deo spirante *A Di Q*, siue Deo inspirante acceperit *tr.* *H Kh L H2 Tw Tc*; also in *B*; **184** peccat mortaliter *tr.* *H Kh L H2 Tw Tc*; **186** lucrum subditis *tr.* *H Kh L H2 Tw*.

[45] Cfr, among several other even more minor variants: *Tw*: **38** capitulo] *om.* *Tw Tc*; uolens] uolans *Tw*; mitti] mittere *Tw*; **49** necessitate] inuenti sunt hic ex l. 50 ins. *Tw*; **98** faciendo] faciem deo *Tw*; **113** ad et] *om.* *Tw* (also *X*); **193** uictus totus *tr.* *Tw*; **195** portione] procione *sic Tw*; *Tc*: **5** subueniri] prouideri uel *praem.* *Tc*; **38** mitti uel] *om.* *Tc*; **46** etiam] *om.* *Tc*; **48** prompti] fuerunt *add.* *Tc*; **58** Et sic] Nec *Tc*; **88** necessaria sibi et suis temporalia *tr.* *Tc*; **98** faciendo] facienda *Tc*; **105** sumus et redempti *tr.* *Tc*; **136-137** ad Hebreos Paulus *Tc*; **169** quis] *om.* *Tc*; **173** temporale] materiale (m^ale) *Tc*; **174** cedunt] succedunt *Tc*; **197** pro³ uno²] *om.* *Tc*.

[46] Cfr e.g. **145-146** dici possent *tr.* *L H2*; **147** accepit *L H2* (also in *Di*); **182** eo in] ea *L H2* (also in *Tc M*).

[47] Listed in detail in the fn. 20 (p. 96) accompanying the description of the manuscript in section IV.3.2.

[48] **82** quinto] tenetur *add.* *V Q B L* (logically supplied from its occurrence, four times, in l. 79-82); **137** assumat sibi *tr.* *V M*, sumat sibi *A*; **204** animarum reddatur *tr.* *V Q*.

Maybe κ, which was perhaps copied directly from Grote's autograph in view of the closeness of *HL-H2* to that text, ultimately ended up in Zwolle. In this context it should also be noted that there are reasons to believe that Johannes Cele, the schoolmaster from Zwolle, may possibly have had a hand in the confection of the letter collections,[49] with sigla *LH2* in the *app. cr.* of this edition.

IV.4.2.3 Group ξ

As regards the text of *Artic.* and *Locat.*, *X* served as the exemplar for the slightly later witness *T*. That this is the case for *Cura past.* also, is immediately clear from a few shared significant variants, mentioned in section IV.4.1 above already.[50]

An incredibly bad text is transmitted in *Gr*: As in the case of *Focar.*, many of its variants are unique for *Gr*, not recurring anywhere else, and the majority of them has most probably been caused by haste.[51] Some variants in *Gr* also occur in other witnesses; thus, *GrX* share five admittedly minor variants,[52] and *GrB* two other equally minor ones.[53] Since it seemed a waste of time to collate the text in *Gr* any further, it has been decided to locate it in the neighbourhood of *X* in the stemma on the basis of the observed shared variants in l. 1-100. In view of the great number of unique variants in *X(T)* also occurring nowhere else in the stemma, it can be maintained that both *Gr* and *X* independently derive from the same common exemplar.

Two other witnesses, *BM*, also transmit a great number of unique and/or idiosyncratic readings. Only after the full text had been collated, it turned out to be possible to group them in the neighbourhood of group ξ, on the basis of the following shared variants: **138** ut] tamquam *XMB* (substituting the reading in *Hebr.* 5, 4 for the one in Grote); **248** experientiali] experimentali *XMB*;

---

[49] This is for instance suggested by VAN ENGEN, 'Writings', p. 352-353.

[50] These are: **22** Scriptis] Scripto *X T*; **45-46** q. – quota] *om. X T*; **46** qui] quod qui *X T*; **63** declinatur] quam suscipitur *add. X T, sed non sic Greg. Magn.*; **80-81** Secundo tenetur esse illuminatus Dei sciencia] Secundo esse illuminatus de sciencia *X T*.

[51] Cfr on this further HOFMAN, *Focar.*, p. 181.

[52] **8** in hoc] *om. X Gr W*; **23** Concordant] Concordat *Q X Gr*, syntactically impossible in the context; **81** et¹] *om. D X Gr M*; **90** uel] et *X Gr*.

[53] **17** succedunt] succedit *B Gr*; **37** mitte] mitto *B Gr*.

281 sufficiat] sufficiet *XMB*. Further agreements between *XM*, but missing in *B*,[54] reveal that the latter manuscript occupies the most isolated place in the group. All of this leads to branch ξ in the stemma below.

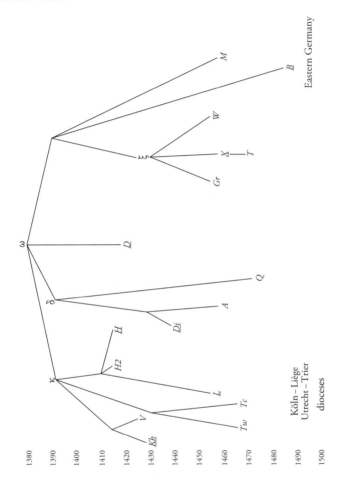

---

[54] **8** in hoc] *om. XM*; **173** uel] et *DiXM*; **174** cedunt] erunt *XM*; **183** personam] persona *XM*; **306** pertransire] transire *DXM*; these readings outweigh a few variants which could have happened to any unobservant scribe: **172** accipit²] *om. BX*; **265** est] et *add. BM*; **309** beatum] *om. BX*; **310** Symonis] et Ihesu *add. BX*, derived from l. **220**.

CHAPTER V

A LETTER (*EP.* 19)
ABOUT PRIEST JOHN AND HENRY FROM SCHOONHOVEN,
EPISCOPAL COMMISSIONER, ON SIMONY

V.1 SUMMARY OF CONTENTS

Two persons figure prominently in this letter, a certain priest John, who wishes to change his worldly lifestyle, and who is very remorseful about the wicked things he has done in his earlier life, and secondly an episcopal commissioner, mentioned at several places in the letter (in l. 5; 6; 52; 54; 60; 83; 90; 98; 103; 106; 107; 109), and identified as Henry only in the last passage where actions of the commisioner are discussed (171). The recipient of the letter is also identified as Henry, namely the priest Henry from Schoonhoven near Gouda,[1] so called in the rubric in both witnesses which transmit its contents, the letter collections *LH2*. While this rubric therefore suggests that Grote wrote the letter to Henry, he nevertheless speaks about him in the third person in the text itself. Grote's actual correspondents therefore may apart from Henry consist of a larger group, most probably his disciples and companions who were about to set up a form of communal life in the vicarage of Florens Radewijns in the Engestraat in Deventer, as will be argued below. Th. van Zijl has aptly summarized the contents of the letter,[2] and although his insistence in con-

---

[1] It should be noted here that this priest had a contemporary namesake: the inventory of official burghers of the small city of Schoonhoven for the years 1386-1504, kept as Archives code 'Ac 1011, Old Archives of Schoonhoven', inventory number 1129, in the Streekarchief Midden-Holland in Gouda, lists for the year 1396 an entry that Heinric Voppenz obtained the official status of burgher of Schoonhoven in that year; since Grote's companion is attested as confessor and manager of a boardinghouse in Zwolle from 1384 until his death in 1410, this namesake cannot be identical with our Henry. I am most grateful to Jan-Willem Klein (Streekarchief Midden-Holland, Gouda), who communicated this information to me.

[2] VAN ZIJL, *Gerard Groote*, p. 272-273 (most footnotes omitted); this letter is summarized in greater detail in POST, *Modern Devotion*, p. 85-86, who condemns Grote's views even more severely than Van Zijl. Post's suggestion that

CHAPTER V

demning Grote's severity in this letter is probably undeserved (as will also be argued below), his summary can nevertheless be taken as a convenient point of departure for further discussion, on the condition that his negative moral comments are disregarded. It is therefore reprinted here, with added references to the line numbers in the edition below.

"There is no case known in which Groote attacked simony with more consistency and rigorism than that dealt with in his letter to Henry van Schoonhoven. The culprit was a certain priest named John who had accumulated wealth by simony, but was ready to change his way of life. There are indications that he had been intimately connected with Groote and his disciples at Deventer. Perhaps he had been one of them. This might explain why Henry van Schoonhoven, appointed by the bishop of Utrecht to arrange John's affairs, sought the advice of Groote, and also why Groote suggested restitution of certain property to his disciples. In his advice Groote insisted in the first place on a sincere and complete conversion and suggested the criteria by which this might be judged. John must be really sorry for his sins, change his intentions [10-28], and even do public penance [39-46] in order to make up for the scandal he had given.

The hardest part of Groote's advice however is his demand of restitution [47-52; 66-84]. Before all other things John must place his possessions entirely at the disposal of the episcopal commissioner and must be willing to accept any decision he might make [4-9; 56-65; 97-98; 102-103]. Though John must not be reduced to poverty, Groote suggested that no more be left him than would satisfy a simple and ascetically minded priest [52-59; 146-154]. His lands should be sold [89-92] and his houses be given away [108-135]; even superfluous clothing and household articles should be disposed of [93-107]. His books were the only property which should be left untouched [85-88]. Against his usual practice Groote did not endeavor to prove all his suggestions from canon law. In this case he let his heart speak. John should be taught a lesson. No restitution of material goods could ever restore the spiritual harm which he had done to the Church. Rigorism and harshness were perhaps the only means to effect a permanent change."

Henry "must be sought among the canons in Utrecht" will be dealt with below.

V.2 ATTEMPT AT IDENTIFICATION, AND EDITORIAL HISTORY

Any attempt to identify this priest John can best depart from the references in the letter to John's place(s) of residence in l. 108-135, and (following Post)[3] from the cursory remarks about "seruitores Dei" or related references in that passage, as well as thereafter until the end of the letter. As regards the first topic, Grote mentions two different houses, a big (cfr **126-127**) one currently inhabited by a further unspecified 'Wolterus', and another one near 'walls' in Deventer. Each of these houses should be handed over for occupation to the 'holy servants of the Church' (**109-110**) or 'of God' (**116**; **128**; **147-150**; **162-164**), a community of 'spiritual men' (**121**), consisting of both clerics and lay people (**128-129**); John may reserve a place for himself in the smaller house. As long as one or both of these houses is being let out, the revenues earned by letting should be earmarked for the same devout community, preferably in Deventer, but for that in Kampen when the community in Deventer does not need the money (**118-123**).

As for the books, household goods, furniture and spare money which John could keep for himself, Grote stipulates that he must consider these as on loan; formally, any item belongs to the devout community of which John intends to become a member, and will have to be returned to it after John's death (**136-156**). Also, the total amount of money left over after the sale of landed or otherwise unnecessary property should flow to the same community (cfr also **89-92**), except for a small allowance for the acquisition of daily necessities and a small sum for additional books – Grote singles out explicitly the *Bible* and Johannes Friburgensis' *Summa confessorum* (**138-139**). In this context it is important also that Grote insists on a change from precious belongings to simple clothing and moveable property, as was customary for the first Brethren also (**93-107**).[4]

---

[3] Cfr POST, *Modern Devotion*, p. 76-77.
[4] Cfr apart from numerous other references e.g. THOM. KEMP., *Dial.*, L. 2 (= *Vita domini Florentii*), ch. 12, *De simplicitate uestimentorum eius*, p. 143-146, esp. p. 143, 12-17 "Vt ergo interiori homini habitus exterior responderet: postquam sacerdos effectus est, non quaesivit molliores vestes quasi prae ceteris sibi magis competentes, sed communibus et simplicibus sicut alii fratres erat contentus".

CHAPTER V 109

There can be little doubt that when Grote mentions a community of 'servants of God', consisting of male clerics and lay people, he indeed refers to the first community of Brethren, which at the moment of the writing of the letter is apparently being established in the vicarage of the altar of St Paul in the Engestraat in Deventer, where Florens Radewijns lived after he had obtained the services connected with this altar.[5] In his discussion of *Ep.* 19, R. Post therefore suggests that the letter has most probably been written in 1383, rather than in 1381, as proposed by Mulder in a note to his edition. Post's main argument to date the letter to 1383 seems to be that Grote mentions a devout community in Kampen, which was founded in that year.[6] *Ep.* 19 is also briefly discussed by Van der Wansem, who accepts Mulder's dating to 1381 and who in part on the basis of this assumption argues that it was written before Florens' ordination to the priesthood, as Florens is not referred to as 'dominus' in the letter (l. 163).[7]

All these arguments remain somewhat speculative in nature, and this is in fact unnecessary. When a dating of this letter to 1383 is linked up with a legal agreement signed and dated on 28 June 1383, for the first time edited properly by Van der Wansem,[8] the 'priest John' in *Ep.* 19 can be identified plausibly. The legal agreement has most recently been analysed by John Van Engen.[9] It concerns an annual income, coming down to the considerable sum of twenty old écus each year, yielded by landed property situated in the polder then and now called Mastenbroek, just to the North-West of Zwolle, and made available by a rich citizen of Deventer and his wife, Henry and Gheze Bierman. The proceeds of this property could support the annual maintenance of "two or three good, inwardly directed poor priests, who separated from the world serve God" (thus formulated in the deed, p. 181, 7-8 ed. Van der Wansem; note the *uerbatim* correspondence with the

---

[5] Cfr for the most detailed substantiation of this supposition VAN DER WANSEM, *Broederschap*, p. 55-58, for a brief survey of Florens' early career *ibid.*, p. 51-54, cfr also – and more recently – WEILER, *Norm*, p. 4-6; WEILER, *Monasticon Fratrum*, Vol. 3, p. 149-151 and VAN ENGEN, *Sisters and Brothers*, p. 86-91.
[6] Cfr POST, *Modern Devotion*, p. 75-77, also WEILER, *Norm*, p. 1-2.
[7] VAN DER WANSEM, *Broederschap*, p. 57-58.
[8] Edited by VAN DER WANSEM, *Broederschap*, p. 179-182, and discussed and analysed *ibid.*, p. 67-73.
[9] Cfr VAN ENGEN, 'Managing the Common Life', p. 116-117, and summarily KRAUß, *Devotio moderna*, p. 304-305.

"seruitores dei" mentioned in *Ep.* 19). The beneficiaries of the annual income had until then been a priest 'John van Vrede, son of Peter', and a citizen and alderman 'John die Hoyer',[10] who apparently willingly agreed to the transfer of this annual income to the community of Brethren *in statu nascendi*. In this connection it is important also that John van Vrede's house was located in the Engestraat in Deventer, just like the vicary in which Florens and his companions lived.[11] Somewhat later on, in 1391, Florens agreed with the noblewoman Zwedera van Runen / van Rechteren to exchange this small house in the Engestraat for her bigger one on the corner of the same street and the Pontsteeg. From the deed ratifying this agreement it can be concluded that priest John had by that time died already.[12] Obviously, the data in this agreement

---

[10] *Lit.* "Johannese Peters zoen van Vrede ende Johanne den Hoyer", ed. VAN DER WANSEM, *Broederschap*, p. 180, 6, cfr p. 181, 3-4, called "Iohannes Petri de Viedam" in a later document from the Heer-Florenshuis, called *Scriptum de bonis et redditibus domus nostre* in ed. VAN ENGEN, 'Managing the Common Life', p. 149-159, at p. 149, no. I.1 (MS described and analysed *ibid.*, p. 133-143, *Scriptum* esp. p. 142). It seems wise to prefer the spelling of the surname as transmitted through the transcript of the original deed ("Vrede") to the spelling in the narrative source as edited by Van Engen ("Viedam"), which was compiled later.

[11] This is clear from a remark in the 1391 deed (cfr next fn.): "...dat huys ende erve dat wyleneer plach toe te horen Johannes Peters soene van Vreden clerc, deen God ghenadigh zy [i.e. thus confirming that he had died by 1391], gheleghen in der stad van Deventer in der Enghestrate..." (ed. VAN DER WANSEM, *Broederschap*, p. 183), and from a reference in the *Scriptum*, I.2: "Fuit alia domus Iohannes [*sic? leg.* Iohannis?] Petri de Viedam quam primum inhabitauerunt fratres in die Engestrate prope _ res inter domum Gerit Berchman et domum Henrick Voetiken..." (ed. VAN ENGEN, 'Managing the Common Life', p. 149 at fn. 112). For a reconstruction of the buildings of the Brethren in the Engestraat and its surroundings, with ill. and map, cfr R. VAN DIJK, T. HENDRIKMAN, *Deventer in het voetspoor van de Moderne Devotie. Stadswandeling door Deventer en fietsroute naar Diepenveen*, Deventer, 2000, p. 42-43, for an ill. in full colour cfr VAN DIJK, *Salome*, p. 61, for a slightly different reconstruction (map), KRAUẞ, *Devotio moderna*, p. 73-74.

[12] This deed has been edited by VAN DER WANSEM, *Broederschap*, p. 183-187, on the basis of a transcript of the lost original charter which was made by Dumbar in the eighteenth century. This transaction has been discussed and analysed by e.g. VAN DER WANSEM, *Broederschap*, p. 86-91; WEILER, *Norm*, p. 5-6; VAN ENGEN, 'Managing the Common Life', p. 116-117; WEILER, *Monasticon Fratrum*, Vol. 3, p. 149-151; VAN ENGEN, *Sisters and Brothers*, p. 86-91; KRAUẞ, *Devotio moderna*, p. 73-75; since this deed nowhere even hints at an eventual departure of John from the Brethren, he cannot be identical with a priest "John" mentioned in the biography compiled by Petrus Horn, proposed by VAN ZIJL, *Gerard Groote*, p. 272, fn. 95, in an attempt to identify our priest John: "One evening during their usual chapter of faults Groote expressed his

fit in very well with the recommendations set out by Grote in his letter to his disciples and companions in Deventer.

Grote's letter, which discusses preparatory actions, evidently preceded the actual passing of the deed on 28 June 1383 before the bailiff of Salland, Wolter Macharis sone.[13] Proof for this is possibly found in the letter itself also, in the passage where Grote discusses the annual disbursement by the actual tenant of the rent due for the larger one of priest John's two houses. This annual payment, writes Grote (l. 118-122), becomes available just after Easter, which fell very early in 1383, on 22 March.[14] On the basis of this small passage, *Ep.* 19 should probably be redated to February or early March 1383. Why Grote communicated with his closest followers about this important matter by letter remains unclear, but an educated guess might be that he was busy with one of his preaching tours when the matter perhaps became acute suddenly.

Some further considerations are in place here, the third one admittedly somewhat more speculative. When it is accepted that the subject matter of our *Ep.* 19 deals with the transfer of an – admittedly considerable – annual income from one private party to another one, there is at the same time no need to look for a high ranking episcopal commissioner from Utrecht as supervisor for the correct settlement of the arrangement on behalf of the Bisshop:[15] such a transfer between two parties in a city in the diocese could as well be supervised by a local representative acting on the authority of the bisshop. There is, in other words, no reason to question the identification of Henry from Schoonhoven mentioned in the rubric of the letter with Hendrik Voppenz from Schoonhoven near Gouda, an early confident of Grote, who moved into Florens' house at a very early stage. This Henry was probably chosen as supervisor of the transfer on the basis of his status as a formerly evidently wealthy secular priest. Additional

---

doubts about John's perseverance. Somewhat later John left the group", with reference to HORN, *Vita Gerardi Magni*, Ch. 13 – ed. Kühler, *Nederlands Archief voor Kerkgeschiedenis*, N.S. 6 (1909), p. 361.

[13] He thus identifies himself in the first sentence of the deed, as edited by Van der Wansem.

[14] As can be calculated easily through the on-line version of GROTEFEND's *Zeitrechnung des deutschen Mittelalters und der Neuzeit*, at: http://www.manuscripta-mediaevalia.de/gaeste/grotefend/grotefend.htm (accessed 4 March 2016).

[15] This is suggested by POST, *Modern Devotion*, p. 85-86 and fn. 1.

evidence suggesting that at least Grote held him in high esteem can be deduced from the fact that Grote sent him to Zwolle somewhat later on, in 1384, in order to function as confessor of the newly established devout community in that city. There he also organized a boardinghouse for young students attending Cele's famous school in his own house, and he established several Sisters' houses, in Zwolle but also in Arnhem, for whom he became confessor.[16]

Secondly, in the passage on John's smaller house (l. 111-113) Grote twice states that this house is situated "apud muros (Dauentrie)". One is tempted to take this as 'situated near the city walls', but another interpretation is possible also. Quoting Dumbar, Weiler remarks that a single house only separated the vicarage from John Vrede's house, but that the two houses bordered on one another in their backyards, and that an opening was made in the wall separating the houses in order to facilitate communications.[17] It could be argued therefore that "muros" in *Ep.* 19 refers to this wall between the two houses, with "Dauentrie" taken as a locative case form in the sense 'in Deventer'.

Thirdly, Grote mentions in the letter a 'Wolterus', who rented the larger one of priest John's two houses (l. 110-111; 126-127). If Grote would have been speaking about a random tenant, further unknown to him, he would surely have identified him more precisely: by just calling him 'Wolter' he betrays that he as well as his correspondents are well acquainted with this tenant. It could therefore be suggested that this Wolter is identical with the bailiff of Salland, the secular administrative district to which Deventer belonged, 'Wolter the son of Macharis', before whom the deed transferring the donated property was passed. In this connection it should also be noted that the tenant could afford to rent a 'large house', which means that he must have fulfilled a position or job involving personal wealth, and that Grote hints at the possibility that the tenant terminates his tenancy in the near future (l. 126-

---

[16] Much of this is set out in his *uita*, edited by SCHOENGEN, *Narratio*, p. lxvi-lxxi, on the basis of the famous ms. Brussel, Koninklijke Bibliotheek van België, 8849-8859, f. 81v-83v [115v-117v], containing the *uitae* of many of the early brothers (or., prov.: Deventer, Heer-Florenshuis). Cfr. on Hendrik Voppenz (d. 1410) WEILER, *Norm*, p. 27-29, and WEILER, *Monasticon Fratrum*, Vol. 3, p. 407; 423, with further references, on Sisters' houses cfr also VAN ENGEN, *Sisters and Brothers*, p. 125-137.

[17] Cfr WEILER, *Norm*, p. 5, and WEILER, *Monasticon Fratrum*, Vol. 3, p. 151.

CHAPTER V 113

130) – is this bailiff, appointed fairly recently in 1381, perhaps still searching for an owner-occupied house?

V.3 THE MANUSCRIPTS

The manuscripts transmitting *Ep.* 19, *LH2*, are described in greater detail elsewhere; cfr Ch. III.2 above for *H2*;[18] HOFMAN, *Focar.*, p. 135-138 for *L*.[19]

---

[18] Den Haag, Koninklijke Bibliotheek, 78 J 55, s. XVa, f. 113-260 of f. 1-262, Prov.: Liège, Saint-Jacques (Benedictines), cfr VAN DIJK, *Prolegomena*, p. 190-203.

[19] Liège, Bibliothèque de l'Université, 229 (c), a. 1451, Or.: Namur, monastery of the Crutched Friars, Prov.: Liège, monastery of the Crutched Friars, cfr VAN DIJK, *Prolegomena*, p. 270-283; I corrected my mistakes in my earlier description in HOFMAN, 'Crutched Friars', p. 521-529.

CHAPTER VI

THE *STATUTES* OF THE MEESTER GEERTSHUIS

(Marinus VAN DEN BERG)

VI.1 INTRODUCTION, WITH AN ANALYSIS OF THE *STATUTES*

Since 21 September 1374, the city of Deventer was the proprietor of the house in the Bagijnenstraat where Geert Grote had been born in 1340.[1] On that date, he sealed and signed a transfer charter, in which he changed the destination of the house into a place of residence for "arme luden die Gode dyenen willen" (poor people who wish to serve God).[2] Grote's intention was that the residents would be women, and this probably, but not certainly, from the beginning.[3]

Almost five years after the original transfer charter the statutes of the house were drawn up, and formally enacted and signed. It was Grote's intention that these would function as a solid legal basis for his foundation. As a jurist, he wished to be confident that after his death also his original intention would be perpetuated unalteredly, as the management and administration of his legacy would pass into the hands of the aldermen in Deventer. In the five years between the transfer of his house and the official confirmation of the statutes, Grote had gone through a process of spiritual growth, not only in relation with his experiences in his own house, but also as a result of his stay as a paying guest in the Carthusian monastery Monnikhuizen near Arnhem. During the three years of his absence from Deventer, the supervision of the

---

[1] This paragraph rests on Ch. 2 and the introductory section in Bijlage 2.1 in VAN DIJK, *Salome*, p. 60-75 and p. 307-309.

[2] On this charter cfr VAN DIJK, *Salome*, p. 60-69. It has been edited by DUMBAR, *Deventer*, I, p. 548, and is quoted in full in v. GINNEKEN, *Levensbeeld*, p. 162-163, cfr also VAN ZIJL, *Gerard Groote*, p. 99-101; an ill. can be found e.g. on the dust-jacket of GOUDRIAAN, *Innigheid*.

[3] Cfr on this aspect, and on the confusion about the originally intended residents, VAN DIJK, *Salome*, p. 65-66, esp. fn. 10.

CHAPTER VI 115

daily affairs in his house probably rested with (one of) the city aldermen.

The statutes of the Meester-Geertshuis have come down to us in two redactions: a longer one, dated 13 July 1379 (= *D*, preserved in the city archives in Deventer), and a shorter one, dated 16 July 1379 (= *L*, preserved in the Leiden University library).[4] Neither of these witnesses is an autograph copy in Grote's hand. The short redaction *L* is chronologically older than the long redaction *D*, although the actual transcript is from a later date. Its text is suggestive of a draft version, probably derived from a standard model kept in a repertory to which the city notaries could have access as often as they had to draw up charters or other official documents.[5] This draft version was most probably submitted to Grote for approval by the city aldermen. Grote inserted a great number of adjustments and modifications in it, preserved in the longer redaction, which he finally signed and sealed personally three times.[6] After this, the statutes were legally valid. The draft version had now lost its function, and it was subsequently stored

---

[4] Cfr for a description of these witnesses below, section VI.4

[5] That this draft version is an edited version of a standardized sample document, seems suggested by the fact that male forms of pronouns have occasionally been preserved in a context on female residents, as e.g. in *L* **177** "hij" (as opposed to *D* **178** "sie", in a passage stretching in *LD* from **160-180**): "Ende weert dat hoer yenighe in desen of in anderen saken die der meistersche bevolen weren, ongehoirsam were, ... of die in den saken daer hij orloff bidden solde, oerlof geweyghert worde...". Note also the use of "hi(j)" for "sij" in *LD* **139** (cfr *app. crit. ad loc.*), and the use of male instead of female possessive pronouns in *L* **32**; **33-34** = *D* **37**; **38** "si(j)ns" and "sinen" for "haren/horen" and "haere/hoere(n)", where male forms again refer to female residents; these male forms probably occurred in the draft version submitted to Grote for approval by the city officials, and were apparently inadvertently taken over by him in unaltered form in the final version. The male forms of pronouns and articles in **451-473**, in a paragraph on the rights and obligations of heirs after a resident has died, conceived by Grote himself and therefore occurring in *D* only, can be explained differently. All male forms here refer to the deceased resident, called "dode(n)" in l. **456**; **458**; **460**; **462**; **467**. This word is masc. even when referring to a female person (cfr VERDAM, *Handwoordenboek*, s.v.), and female forms therefore would be more awkward in this context than the male forms used by Grote; the form "die" preceding "dode" in **462**; **467** must here be taken as a masc. demonstrative pronoun, and male "siere" in **455** can be explained as a case of anticipation, under the influence of directly following "dode".

[6] This is clear from the subscription in *D*, l. **673-677** in the edition below: "In orcunde deser dinc, want dese brief van twe stucken ghemaect is, so heeft her Gherijt die Groet sinen zegel an desen brief drierweghen ghehanghen".

somewhere in the city archives three days later.[7] It must here be noted also that neither redaction of the statutes has come down to us in its original form. The single witness of the shorter draft version survives in an apograph datable to s. xvc, while the single witness transmitting the longer final version can be dated to s. xvb.[8]

The two surviving documents contain many overlapping passages, but there are elsewhere in the texts considerable differences between the two versions also, and even contradictions and inconsistencies, as is immediately clear in the edition below, where the two versions are printed in iuxtaposition. As a consequence, the two redactions can impossibly have had legal validity simultaneously. Thus, the short redaction *L* mentions a single community and a single "meistersche" ('mistress', an official with executive powers) only, whereas *D* knows two communities and two "meysterschen",[9] of which one most probably is in charge of the 'poor, devout women', whereas the other guides the women who wish to form a semi-religious community (the text itself in l. **98-121** is not specific about this; it only states that one of them comes from (and is chosen by?) the community living in the stone house, the other one from the community in the 'achterhuis', the outbuilding erected in the rear garden before the transfer in 1374 already). In short, Grote adopted for the revised second redaction *D* more than once whole phrases or passages taken in (virtually) unaltered form from the draft version *L*, while he entered revisions and added passages or sometimes full paragraphs to it elsewhere. This effectively means that two different parties (in the legal sense) were involved in the final redaction of the statutes: the city government of Deventer (or a notary or delegate representing it, who had prepared the draft version on their behalf), and Geert Grote.

The draft version *L* deals primarily with issues which were important for the city government. Therefore, the responsibilities

---

[7] Cfr for a full argumentation and a convincing exposition on this likely course of events KLAUSMANN, 'Satzungen', p. 31-34, and for a historiography of earlier views and ideas trying to explain the existence of the two mutually inconsistent versions of the statutes VAN DIJK, *Salome*, p. 69-75.

[8] Cfr for a description of the manuscript witnesses further below, Ch. VI.4.

[9] Cfr l. **90-95**; **98-100** below, and also l. **168-169**; **184-189**; **595**; **613-614** (all references to both documents *LD*); the opposition is less clear here, as it consists in use of sg. as opposed to pl. forms only, without added numerals.

and interests of the aldermen get considerable emphasis in it, figuring more prominently than those of the founder, Grote. In line with this, there is special emphasis in this version on regulations and decisions which became relevant only after Grote's death, such as the division of responsibilities between the aldermen and the "meystersche" and hereditary issues. However, this version was not legally valid, as it had not been signed and sealed by Grote.

In the final version *D*, Grote significantly gives a great deal of prominence to the immovable property in the Bagijnenstraat, which he considers as an indivisible, unchangeable and entailed estate. Until the date of his death, he wishes to control the management of this estate and its occupants, without outside involvement, but in accordance and agreement with the city government. He further specifies in *D* that he plays an important role himself in practical and juridical matters concerning the house and its occupants as long as he is alive, while after his death the city government in Deventer, as worldly power, is first of all responsible for its management. In these added paragraphs, he comes to the fore as a conscientious and careful mentor, especially in matters pertaining to spiritual growth and the religious attitude of the residents in the house. Significantly, however, the document contains no regulations concerning the prayer routine in the daily schedule.

VI.2 SUMMARY OF CONTENTS

The statutes are meant as a legal document, regulating the daily routine in the Meester-Geertshuis, the spiritual way of living of its residents, and the safeguarding of the founder's ideas for future times. This intention is reflected in their contents and set-up. The contents of these statutes and the intention(s) of their compiler(s) in drawing them up have been analysed and summarized (or rather: paraphrased) in great detail by VAN DIJK, *Salome*, p. 110-127. The equivalent arrangement in both redactions can therefore be summarized very briefly here, using the paragraph numbers introduced in the text by Post in his 1952-edition, which have been taken over in unaltered form by van Dijk in 2015, followed by the line numbers valid for both redactions:

1-7 (1-97) definition and description of the intended legal status and position of the house.
8-12 (98-208) the function, duties and rights of the "meistersche(n)" ('mistress(es)', an official with executive powers).
13-20 (209-345) behaviour and views leading to expulsion from the house, with in *D* special attention for (supposedly) heretical convictions among residents.
21 (346-376) the obligation to carry out manual labour, and its advantages.
22-23 (377-443) spatial lay-out of the house.
24-28 (444-543) mutual distribution of income, and other practical matters.
29-33 (544-637) allowed and prohibited external contacts.
34 (638-655) annual remembrance of the founder and his family.
35 (656-666) additional observations on the "meisterschen".
36 (667-680) subscription, dating and official sealing.

VI.3 EDITORIAL HISTORY

The short redaction of the statutes,[10] *L*, was in the eighteenth century discovered by G. Dumbar, since 1708 first secretary and archivist in the city of Deventer, and published as one item among many others in his *Kerkelyk en wereltlyk Deventer*.[11] After Dumbar had printed his transcript, this witness disappeared for centuries, until it was rediscovered by Klausmann early in the twenty-first century, in the form of a small quire bound together with related material in the Leiden manuscript BPL 1045.[12] The second, long redaction *D* was also discovered in the archives in Deventer, by the archivist J. De Hullu, who published a diplomatic edition of its text in 1897.[13] The fusion of the two versions in Van Ginneken's 1942 version can best be disregarded for scholarly purposes.[14]

---

[10] This short section is a revised and updated version of the editorial paragraph preceding van Dijk's edited text and rephrasing of the statutes in VAN DIJK, *Salome*, on p. 307-308, and the editorial supplement printed there by the present editors, p. 309.
[11] DUMBAR, *Deventer*, I, p. 549a-550b.
[12] Cfr KLAUSMANN, 'Satzungen', p. 31-34, and the description of this witness below, Ch. VI.4.
[13] Cfr HULLU, 'Statuten'.
[14] Published in J. VAN GINNEKEN, *Geert Groote's Levensbeeld naar de oudste gegevens bewerkt* (*Verhandelingen der Nederlandsche Akademie van Wetenschappen, Afd. Letterkunde*, N.R., 47, Nr. 2), Amsterdam, 1942, p. 206-210. The prominent Jesuit Jacques van Ginneken, Professor of Dutch, Sans-

CHAPTER VI 119

R. Post then published a second diplomatic edition of the two redactions in juxtaposition in 1952, comparable to the one in this volume,[15] which from its publication was considered as the standard edition of the statutes. Due to its alleged standing, van Dijk originally intended to use this edition for his rephrasing of the statutes in Modern Dutch, which he wished to publish in juxtaposition together with a slightly modified version of Post's 1952-edition of the original Middle Dutch text for his 2015 volume on Salome Sticken. However, when I consulted the text of this edition for a different purpose in 2014, I discovered that it contained linguistic forms which were simply not viable or possible in Middle Dutch. I therefore decided to collate the text of the statutes again against *D*, thereby uncovering more than 90 transcription errors in Post's transcript of *D*. I then transformed my new collation in a first critical edition of the statutes as part of van Dijk's monograph on Salome, in a form which integrated the redactions in *L* and *D*. For the present edition, the two redactions were separated from one another again, and not only the text transmitted in *D*, but also that in *L* was collated afresh.

VI.4 THE MANUSCRIPTS

D Deventer, Stadsarchief en Athenaeumbibliotheek, 0690 (olim 1607) Stad Deventer, periode Middeleeuwen, "Olde in papier gescreven copienboick", s. xvb, Or., Prov.: Deventer, city government, cfr VAN DIJK, *Prolegomena*, p. 172.

The version of the statutes preserved in this witness is transmitted in a convolute containing a large collection of official pieces pertaining to the city government and administration in Deventer, all of them copies of original documents, as is suggested by the word "Copienboeck" written on its front flyleaf already. In the codex several parts which originally did not form a coherent whole are bound together. The transcript of the statutes

---

krit, general and comparative Indo-European linguistics at the Catholic University in Nijmegen since its foundation in 1923, was an outstanding linguist by all standards, but as a philologist and historian he had his shortcomings. Cfr further on him the balanced and thoughtful essays in *De taal is kennis van de ziel. Opstellen over Jac. van Ginneken* – ed. A. Foolen – J. Noordegraaf, Münster, 1996, with further references.

[15] Cfr POST, 'Statuten'.

has been written in *littera cursiua libraria*, in a hand that can be dated to s. xvb. This dating is confirmed by the other documents transmitted in the same quire, which are all dated between 1411 and 1446.

L Leiden, BPL 1045, s. xvc, Prov.: unknown, but an origin in Deventer (or Overijssel more generally) seems likely, not mentioned in VAN DIJK, *Prolegomena*, cfr below.

The short redaction of the statutes survives in a small octavo (140×100) paper quire currently consisting of five folia,[16] with plummet ruling of the frame only, which has at some date been bound together with other material also having its origin in the eastern Low Countries, a codex of 171 folia having as its title "Dijkrechten van Salland en Mastenbroek met de Reformatie", dated to 1546. Who combined these diverging codicological units, and why he or she did this, remains unclear. The text of the statutes has been written in a hand writing expert *hybrida* script (C/H variety), datable to s. xvc, in single column layout. This witness was found by Klausmann early in the twenty-first century, and published in 2004, too late to be included in Father van Dijk's *Prolegomena*, published in 2003.

VI.5 TRANSCRIPTION AND EDITORIAL POLICY

The policy adopted for transcription, word division, and similar matters is discussed in greater detail in the general introduction above, in section I.5.2.

---

[16] The most recent description of this witness is J. P. GUMBERT, *Illustrated inventory of medieval manuscripts in Latin script in the Netherlands*, Vol. 2, *Leiden, Universiteitsbibliotheek, BPL*, Hilversum, 2009, p. 104, no. 01466-01467. Here the quire is dated to the turn of the sixteenth century, but Peter Gumbert, whose recent death is much deplored by all who have known him, very kindly confirmed to me that a dating to s. xvc is in fact more probable than the later dating in his *IIMM*. I am most grateful to him for this additional information, and for sharing his views on the transmission of this quire together with other material in a single convolute.

CHAPTER VII

A TREATISE ON SIMONY FOR A COMMUNITY OF BEGUINES
(*DE SIMONIA AD BEGVTTAS*)

(Rijcklof HOFMAN & Marinus VAN DEN BERG)

VII.1 CHARACTER OF THE TREATISE AND SUMMARY OF CONTENTS

This conglomerate of three Parts (or 'chapters', or 'books', as Grote calls them himself in l. **686**), which discuss simony in the vernacular in relation to the acquisition of a place in a religiously oriented community, has most recently been characterized by Koen Goudriaan as a series of three essays approaching simoniacal entry from different perspectives.[1] However, it can in the end also be taken as a single *consilium* consisting of three parts. It provides an answer to queries put to Grote by one (or more?) female communities. Any discussion of the text must now rely heavily on Goudriaan's detailed analysis.

Van Dijk followed Épiney-Burgard when he stated that the three chapters which together form the treatise are loosely connected with each other only (in this edition l. **1-603**; **604-771**; **772-1154**).[2] Goudriaan goes one step further, and holds that the three chapters are in fact three separate 'essays' on the same subject matter, originally destined for different addressees.[3] In his analysis, he contends that Part 1 was directed at a community of female religious, probably living in Kampen (cfr **364-385**, addressed as 'my dear sisters' (**17**), but not forming part of the Third Order of St Francis (cfr **40-63**, esp. **60-62** "Unde des en is gheen noet te scriven up desse tijt, want gij segget dat de Derde Orde daer nicht an en hanget"). For this essay, he suggests the beguinage St Michael's convent, just outside the city walls of Kampen, as addressee, a convent which was influenced by the Modern

---

[1] Cfr GOUDRIAAN, 'Grote on simony', passim.
[2] Cfr VAN DIJK, *Prolegomena*, p. 463, with reference to ÉPINEY-BURGARD, *Lettres*, p. 105 and fn. 4.
[3] Cfr GOUDRIAAN, 'Grote on simony', p. 120-123.

Devout at an early date already, but which never considered transfer to the Third Order.[4]

For Part 2 Goudriaan does not suggest a specific addressee. Since, however, the juridical argumentation in Part 1 is in fact supplemented in Part 2 by a presentation of the same subject matter from a biblical perspective, and since in addition several internal cross-references link Part 1 to Part 2,[5] it might be possible to suggest that this second Part was intended as a clarification, addressed to the same community as Part 1.

The final Part 3 picks up again in greater detail the spiritual dimension of life in a religious community, touched upon briefly already in Part 1, and supplies additional arguments convincingly proving that both beguines and Third Order sisters should be considered as religious women, if not to the letter of the law, then in any case in their manner of life. Goudriaan considers this third Part as a separate 'essay', written for a Third Order community, as the issue of association with the Third Order seems much more relevant here (cfr most notably **916-917**). A Third Order community with which Grote has demonstrably been in touch several times, is the Olde Convent in Zwolle,[6] a community which switched allegiance a few times in the course of the fourteenth century, but which stuck to the Third Order during Grote's lifetime in any case.[7] Goudriaan therefore suggests this community as the addressee of Part 3. The formal conclusion of Part 1 (l. **593-603** below) is one of the strongest arguments adduced by Goudriaan in support of his view that we are here confronted

---

[4] *Ibid.*, with reference to J. GROOTEN, *Niet aan kloostergeloften en regel gebonden gemeenschappen van devote vrouwen te Kampen*, Utrecht, 1981, p. 23-25.

[5] The following references to Part 1 occur in Part 2: **685-688**: cfr **340-363**, esp. **686** "de ic in den anderen boke sprac"; **748-751**: cfr **304-322**, evt. also **433-462**, esp. **749-750** "als vor gescreven is"; another, internal cross-reference links two passages within the same Part 2, **673-675**: cfr **619-625**, esp. **674** "als vor gescreven is".

[6] Goudriaan, *ibid.*, cites his *Epp.* 31 and 32, and points to several narrative historical sources substantiating his involvement as well.

[7] Cfr on the Chapter of Utrecht, the organized form of the Third Order of St Francis in the Diocese of Utrecht (formally established in 1399), most importantly H. VAN ENGEN, *De derde orde van Sint-Franciscus in het middeleeuwse bisdom Utrecht. Een bijdrage tot de institutionele geschiedenis van de Moderne Devotie*, Hilversum, 2006.

with three separate, successive short tracts.[8] However, it can with equal validity be maintained that Grote summarizes in this final paragraph the main conclusion which can be derived from what he has said before.

While this attractive new interpretation is in principle possible, it is yet not necessarily the final word on the treatise. A few objections come to mind. First, the three parts which can be distinguished in the treatise have been fused together loosely with the help of transitory sentences, most probably by Grote himself. Next, the cross-references discussed above in connection with Part 2 suggest a coherence between Parts 1 and 2, while a remark in the introductory paragraph of the third treatise (l. 772-782), where Grote declares in a summarizing sentence among others that he wishes to discuss simony, even though this concept has been explained sufficiently already 'above' ("Wattan weert ghenoch allen guden herten in den dingen de hijrvoer open verclaert sijn"), points to a connection between Parts 1 and 3. The reference to 'good hearts' in this phrase explicitly refers to a passage discussing the choice made by 'good hearts' and 'bad hearts' respectively in Part 1 (l. 171-190). And thirdly, in the passage quoted by Goudriaan as if suggesting that the third Part has been written for a community of Third Order sisters, these sisters are mentioned in one breath with and as equivalent to beguines. Rather than as a *consilium* for Third Order sisters, this third Part should be taken as a defence of *all* communities living a religious life without taking formal vows, including both beguines and Third Order sisters, as well as the communities of Brethren and Sisters of the Common Life, for that matter, which were being established during the last years of Grote's life. This alternative view is substantiated precisely by the equivalent treatment of such communities in a passage in which Grote discusses the differences and correspondences between Third Order communities and beguine ones (l. 1093-1129).

---

[8] *Ibid.*, p. 120, cfr on the layout of a mediaeval letter with its obligatory elements *salutatio, exordium, narratio, petitio* and *conclusio* CONSTABLE, *Letters*, esp. p. 16-20, summarized in R. VAN DIJK, 'Bemoedigende wenken voor een wankelmoedige Kartuizer', in R. VAN DIJK, *Twaalf kapittels over ontstaan, bloei en doorwerking van de Moderne Devotie* – ed. Ch. Caspers, R. Hofman, Hilversum, 2012, p. 45-84, at p. 52.

On the basis of these signs of internal coherence, the treatise can in an alternative interpretation be taken as a unity after all, written in successive stages and displaying in its unorderly composition all traits and typicalities of Grote's mode of operation when he was fully occupied or in haste. The initial occasion would in this interpretation have been a request for a *consilium*, to which he responded by writing the first Part. On second thoughts, he then decided to supplement this by approaching the same subject matter from a different perspective, probably at a later date. The result of this was Part 2. In the end, he then resolved to deal with his original subject matter from a broader perspective, and to set out that communities which formally do not meet the requirements of a proper religious order can yet be considered as gatherings which are equally acceptable to God, and perhaps even more acceptable than religious communities that do not sincerely follow the rules which they have vowed to observe. His intention to demonstrate this is well served by the line of reasoning in Part 2, by putting various *loci* from the Bible to good use to show that beguines and sisters, as well as his own followers, are very well able to open their hearts for God, just as Jezus' followers had done. Grote, therefore, needs Parts 1 and 2 as overtures for his exposition in Part 3. The references to the Third Order, in Part 1 (esp. l. **33-63**) as well as in Part 3 (esp. l. **916-922**; **1093-1135**), are only used to compare different communities of people leading a religiously oriented life without taking vows with each other. In this context it is important to note that all cross-references occur in the second and third Parts only, and that these – except for a single instance – consistently refer back to what has been observed in the first Part already. All the same, this does not necessarily exclude that he has recycled older material in this treatise, as he would demonstrably do in *Leeringhe* (cfr Ch. VIII below), but in this case this supposition cannot be proved beyond doubt.

Since the treatise has been written in Middle Dutch, it seems in the light of its better understanding expedient to provide a detailed summary of its contents.[9]

---

[9] An earlier summary in Dutch of l. **1-568** with interspersed commentary was published by WEILER, 'Grote en begijnen', p. 117-120, a summary in English by GOUDRIAAN, 'Grote on simony', p. 126-136.

CHAPTER VII 125

First Part (1-603)

Following Goudriaan,[10] the first part of the treatise can be subdivided into four smaller sections, comprising l. 1-218, simony is a crime; 219-418, in accordance with distributive justice spiritual commodities should be awarded to the person most fit to receive them; 419-490, preferentiality should be avoided; 491-592, counterarguments against several thin excuses. These four sections are followed by a conclusion (l. 593-603 below) in accordance with the epistolary genre.

'Evidently [Grote] had been asked by a community...', writes Van Zijl,[11] 'whether or not it was simony to buy a cell or a prebend in a convent of their type' (1-2). Grote answers that as soon as spiritual aspects can be associated with a job or assignment, even in a context of hospital service,[12] an offer or requirement of money or of any other form of donation preceding admission to its execution should be considered as simony (3-32). This holds true *a fortiori* when such a function, or a place of residence, is associated with a religious context, even when the monastic vows of poverty, obedience and chastity are not formally taken, as in a beguinage or a Third Order convent (33-39). Followers of the latter one of these two forms of religious life vow obedience to a rule, and they are therefore commonly considered as truly religious women; this implies that simony can in their case be punished in the manner prescribed in several decretals, by transferring the culprit to a more severe religious Order (40-63). Since women choosing for beguine life (forbidden during the Council of Vienne in 1314, but afterwards recognized by Johannes XXII in 1318, 64-73), however, do not observe a rule, they are not formally considered as true religious women. Their final intention is nevertheless to serve God, although without vows, and they should

---

[10] *Ibid.*, p. 126-131.
[11] Van Zijl, *Groote*, p. 228.
[12] LYNCH, *Simoniacal entry*, p. 111 and fn. 18, observes: 'Hospitals were generally structured as groups living under a religious rule', cfr for further discussion of simony in relation to entry as staff in hospitals, with numerous references to contemporary documents, among others from Paris from the thirteenth century, also *ibid.*, p. 168 and fn. 95-97; p. 213-214 and fn. 67-68. Cfr for an example of alleged simony in relation to a hospital also W. J. COURTENAY, K. B. SHOEMAKER, 'The Tears of Nicholas. Simony and Perjury by a Parisian Master of Theology in the Fourteenth Century', *Speculum*, 83:3 (2008), p. 603-628.

therefore yet be grouped among religious women (**64-90**): despite a theoretical possibility to give up religious life, they are bound by conscience to persevere in their chosen form of life (**91-104**). In addition, Grote observes – with reference to the *Decretal* X 5.3.46 – that the official Church often turns a blind eye on the form of simony under discussion. Anyone guilty of it should nevertheless seek absolution, which is in his eyes valid only when the repentant culprit decides never to practice simony again (**105-125**). For in the eyes of God such unpunished behaviour, which anyone would indeed confess to be simony in his own conscience and before God, is no less wicked than prosecuted forms of simony (**126-159**). In his days, however, complains Grote, he has not witnessed anyone convicted for simony (**160-170**). The reason for this is that worldly people unwisely tend to prefer temporary commodities to eternal reward (**171-190**).

Grote then rouses the conscience of his addressees with a concrete example, directly understandable for them. When given the opportunity to fill a vacancy in their house, he asks, would they prefer a devout, industrious, but poor candidate, or a haughty, selfish, but rich one, who is able to reward their preference for her (**191-218**).

Relying on St Thomas (I, q. 21 a. 1 co.), Grote next states that distributive justice (emanating from God in each man's heart by nature and by grace, **233-238**) naturally suggests that spiritual commodities should be awarded to the person most fit to receive them, and that the application of this principle shall surely be weighed during the Last Judgment (**219-253**). Grote applies this proposition to his concrete example, the dilemma whether a community should concede a vacant position in a beguinage to a rich or to a poor candidate (**254-262**). In view of the example set by Christ himself, who consistently favoured the poor, the choice should of course work out in the advantage of the fitting but poor candidate (**263-280**). Poverty best prepares for a life in the service of God (**281-286**), and therefore a place should be bestowed to a poor candidate in accordance with social justice (**287-292**) rather than to a rich one against divine equity (**293-303**). Favouring the rich candidate comes down to excluding the person who has sincerely followed Christ's example, and who even may have given away her former wealth. Moreover, it is in direct conflict with at least one of the three monastic vows (**304-322**).

Approaching the same subject matter from a wider perspective, Grote further holds that a biased choice for a rich candidate is comparable to entrusting the community's common valuables to an unreliable steward (323-339), directly contradicting God's own recommendations for good and honest stewardship (*I Cor.* 4, 1-2; *Luc.* 12, 42-48) (340-363). With reference to a case of nepotism in the city of Kampen (364-376),[13] he also argues that a preference for a rich candidate may be acceptable in filling a vacancy for a city alderman in a secular context, but even then only when he promises to use his wealth to further the common good, and on condition that he does not acquire the position through bribing (377-393). An influential layperson can also be invited to assist in the external management of the convent, provided that his virtue be the criterion for the choice, and not his wealth, influence or family relationship with someone in the convent (394-418). But, as Goudriaan rightly observes with reference to a parallel *locus* in *Cura past.* (284-290), Grote expresses severe doubts about the aptitude and virtuousness of most lay governors of religious institutions or positions.

In the next section, Grote addresses the vice opposed to distributive justice, which is 'acceptio personarum', favouritism or 'partiality towards persons (with reference to God in dealing with sin, dispensation, etc.)'.[14] Following St Thomas and *in extenso* quoting *Iac.* 2, 1-6 from the Bible, Grote takes this in a narrower sense and applies it to a situation in which a person is given preferential treatment for the wrong reasons, because he is rich rather than fit for the task for which he is chosen (**419-466**). Grote bluntly equates such preferentiality with simony (**467-477**), and adds that in a worldly context also a preference for an avaricious ruler rather than a just one can only lead to unseemly government (**478-487**). The inevitable conclusion therefore must be that a poor but worthy candidate should be preferred (**488-490**).

In the fourth and last section Grote retaliates invalid arguments. Thus, many people defend the practice of imposing a charge before admitting a candidate by drawing attention to a seemingly

---

[13] It cannot be established with certainty whether this case had actually occurred recently and/or has had any relevance to the beguines addressed in the treatise, cfr VAN DIJK, *Prolegomena*, p. 463, with further references.

[14] I found this definition in the on-line *German English Dictionary of Religion and Theology* – ed. W. Kunze *et al.*

similar practice, taking place before a secular canon is admitted to a prebend. Grote objects that canons only give a recompense (often funded from their new prebend) after they have been admitted, and that their financial position before their admission does not influence the choice (491-516). Another defence, that regular monks or nuns perpetrate the same practices, is irrelevant, as such obnoxious behaviour is in their case likewise condemned as simony in canon law (517-526). It is sometimes advanced as an excuse, by decretalists also, that the modest resources of a monastery cannot support additional conventuals (527-533), but in the context of many wealthy German and Dutch convents this should be interpreted as simony in disguise (534-540). And since inhabitants in a beguinage earn most of their own subsistence with the work of their hands, this argument is not valid for them anyway (541-556).

In conclusion to this first part of his treatise, Grote once more urges his addressees to bestow the vacancy in their beguinage to the person who is most fit to receive it, and who deserves and needs it most (557-573). No one should be allowed in on the basis of conditions or a contract. Grote compares this procedure to the outsourcing of the management of an altar to a priest on the basis of a contract. He considers this a form of simony, as in this manner revenues meant for the Church are drained away to private parties (574-592). In sum, rather than submit to earthly wickedness, the beguines should focus on divine justice and eternal glory (593-603).

Second Part (604-771)

The second Chapter or 'Book', as Grote calls it himself (l. 686), basically consists of an introductory section on the supremacy of divine law and wisdom, followed by a *catena* or chain of biblical quotations, selected because of their suitability to illustrate the advantages of a life oriented on God, away from worldly preoccupations.

Grote first sets out that all human law and justice flows from God, a section based on *Prou.* 8, 14-16 and *Iac.* 1, 17. It follows that anything that is inequitable or unjust necessarily springs from mankind or the devil, who lie and sin when not inspired by God (604-625). Sincere people distance themselves from any law based on such lies and its compilers, for such laws contradict God's

CHAPTER VII 129

commandments and exclude those in need of justice (626-633), whereas God's distributive justice does not exclude anyone, unless he be born to the flesh (*Gal.* 4, 23) (634-640), i.e. those who are primarily concerned with themselves and their own, temporary profit (641-648) and who do not devote themselves to work in God's vineyard (*Matth.* 20, 1-16), but concentrate on earthly benefit (649-664). Such a preoccupation with personal interests, and preferentiality no less, is injustice and sin towards God (665-675) as well as an intentionally perpetrated sin, both when issued and when obeyed as an order (676-684). Grote then stresses the relevance of such considerations for his conviction that a vacancy in a beguinage should be awarded to the most fitting candidate, as argued in his first Chapter (685-701). People should therefore avoid to act or to legislate against divine law. In this connection, he cites Christ's dispute with the Pharisees (*Matth.* 15, 1-20; *Marc.* 7, 1-23) (and the Church Fathers' exegesis on this topic), who scrupulously observed man-made legislation on ritual hand washing, but failed to observe God's commandments (702-743). With reference to the fulfilment of a vacancy in a beguinage, he further adduces *Is.* 10, 1-2, where the prophet criticizes preferential legislation favouring the rich to the detriment of the poor, poor widows in particular (744-755). In conclusion, Grote finally quotes with approval from St Thomas (I-II, q. 93 a. 3 co; ad 2) that anything that is just in positive law ultimately stems from divine law (756-771).

Third Part (772-1154)

As has been demonstrated convincingly by Goudriaan, this third part of the treatise is meant as a refutation of a *consilium* which Grote calls '*Counterarguments (Wederboec) from Cologne*'.[15]

Grote's line of reasoning in this third part is to explain what he exactly means by spiritual things, and to apply this concept on the virtue 'religion'.[16] Following Guillaume d'Auxerre, he defines spiritual things as those concepts which are imbued by the Holy Spirit, primarily miracles, the sacraments, and virtues (783-795).

---

[15] GOUDRIAAN, 'Grote on simony', p. 132-136.
[16] A full translation in French of l. 783-1154 is available in G. ÉPINEY-BURGARD, *Gérard Grote, fondateur de la Dévotion Moderne, Lettres et traités. Présentation, traduction et notes*, Turnhout, 1998, p. 109-119.

Highest among these are the virtues, especially the theological ones, faith, hope and charity (cfr *I Cor.* 13, 13). Miracles and sacraments are just symbols of divine presence, having as main impact that they can stimulate people to love God. Moreover, they can be administered by both good and bad people. The virtues, on the other hand, in fact have the capacity to bring man closer to God (**796-833**). All virtues are a gift of the Holy Spirit. They are rooted in and lead to the highest one among them, charity, which is the virtue that enables man to come close to and eventually be united with God (**834-847**). Practising and exercising virtues in a spiritually oriented life is to be preferred over performing miracles (**848-854**). Moreover, both acquiring the power to perform miracles by means of money and performing miracles in exchange for money after that, as Simon the magician had done (*Act.* 8, 18-24), are forms of simony (**855-865**). It is on no condition allowed to trade in virtues or anything associated with them for money, as is of course self-evident to virtuous persons (**866-887**), although sacraments and objects associated with them can occasionally be sold and bought (**877-884**).

Whereas the handling of sacraments and miracles can be evaluated by anyone witnessing them, it is most difficult to determine whether a person lives up to the virtues he allegedly practices, as the processes involved take place in the mind and cannot be judged by external standards (**888-898**). And yet, since they potentially help most in bringing people closer to God's grace and glory, trading in them is the worst form of simony, although it is unfortunately also the least punished one (**899-915**).

After this long digression on virtues in general and their mutual hierarchy, Grote focuses on a single virtue, religion, which is in St Thomas's definition man's intention to serve and venerate God (**916-922**). Religion is the most spiritual and Christian one among the moral virtues, directly below the theological ones (**923-935**). Grote next lists the internal exercises and external manifestations that can be associated with this virtue (**936-944**), which all have as their aim to let people serve God better (**944-954**). Precisely because of its spiritual dimensions, this virtue and its proper application bear in themselves great dangers of simony (**954-957**). Again following St Thomas, from whom he also borrows the definition of the figure of speech antonomasia in a special sense as the use of a single concept to designate a group of people or things (**957-969**), he groups together as 'religious persons' all those who do their utmost (in behaviour, intention and thought) to serve God, in other words all those who practice the virtue religion, or better: religious life (970-980). This virtue, which manifests itself as unconditional, all-encompassing love of God, can be practiced either in a formal monastic setting, or alone or in family life, or in a community of kindred brothers or sisters (981-986). What matters is that the intention is and remains sincere and that earthly possessions and preoccupations and one's own free will are renounced and relinquished (987-993). This theoretical exposition ends in an unalloyed eulogy of communal life in the service of God, in poverty, chastity and obedience, whether with or without vows, where mutual support during moments of weakness or despair is the norm (994-1040).

Trading in cells, positions or places in such collective life forms is to be characterized straightforwardly as simony, whether they are formally organized as monastic communities or informally practise communal religious coexistence, precisely because of the religious character of their way of life (1041-1058). But the official Church tends to recognize formal monastic life as the only true religious way of life (1073-1076), despite the fact that informally organized communal groups (1076-1092) and occasionally even temperate ordinary citizens (1059-1072) in fact practice the monastic virtues in a better way than monks. Grote next applies these observations first to communities of tertiaries, and after that to communities of papally recognized beguines, and concludes that their form of life in fact is at least in part and along the lines defined by St Thomas and canon law truly religious and spiritual (1093-1112). And since the Church has condemned the acquisition of a place in a conventional monastery with the help of money as simony, this same verdict also holds true for a similar conduct in relation to a beguinage (1113-1129), if not formally in court, then at least in conscience before God (1130-1135). Grote ends his *consilium* by providing an etymology for the word '*religio*' (1136-1154).

VII.2 EDITORIAL HISTORY, SUPPLEMENT

A recent survey of the editorial history is presented in the first section of Goudriaan's study,[17] which supplements Father van

---

[17] GOUDRIAAN, 'Grote on simony', p. 115-117.

Dijk's *Prolegomena* in *CC CM*, vol. 192, p. 463-464. A few additions to van Dijk's overview, mostly taken from Goudriaan's analysis, follow here. The *editio princeps* of the single surviving witness of *Simonia beg.* was published in 1902 by R. Langenberg under the title "Gerrit de Grootes verlorener Traktat *de Simonia ad beguttas*", as the first text in his *Quellen und Forschungen zur Geschichte der deutschen Mystik*. In the elucidation following on the edited text, he gave no further details about the whereabouts of the manuscript source from which he had transcribed the text. When the eminent palaeographer and authority on Middle Dutch (spiritual) literature Willem de Vreese found the same manuscript source in 1905 in the main convent of the Crutched Friars in St Agatha near Cuyk, he began to compare Langenberg's transcript with the original source. In the introduction to his revised diplomatic transcript of the text, he makes no secret of his scorn for Langenberg's in his eyes utterly despicable achievement. The edition was in principle ready for publication in 1921 already, but De Vreese never saw it through the press, as he hoped to be able to supplement parts of the commentary.[18] Only after his death in 1938, the edition was finally printed, in 1940 thanks to D. de Man, who unfortunately neglected to update the commentary and bibliography.[19]

Several lost copies of *Simonia beg.* are known to have existed. In addition to the copy in the Heer-Florenshuis in Deventer, mentioned by van Dijk on the authority of Grote's biographer Petrus Horn, Goudriaan was able to locate now lost copies originally present in the Carthusian monastery in Ghent as well as in the Windesheim monastery Zevenborren near Brussels and in the beguinage in Hoorn NE of Amsterdam, where Grote personally had deposited "a book... containing much on simony".[20] He also points to the parallels between *Simonia beg.* and *Leeringhe sym.* (cfr next chapter).

---

[18] Cfr G. I. LIEFTINCK, 'Een posthuum werk van Willem de Vreese'. Boekbeoordeling, *Tijdschrift voor Nederlandsche Taal- en Letterkunde*, 60 (1941), p. 311-316.

[19] As is appropriately observed by R. R. POST in a book review published in *Historisch Tijdschrift*, 19 (1940), p. 90-92.

[20] "Een boec... dat veel roert vander symony", quoted from GOUDRIAAN, 'Grote on simony', p. 119.

CHAPTER VII

VII.3 THE MANUSCRIPT

C Cuijk, Kruisherenklooster Sint-Agatha, coll. Frenswegen C 9, s. xvbc (1438, 1455), 2+218+1 f., [Or.], Prov.: I (f. 1-126) Schüttorf, Mariengarten (Sisters of the Common Life).

A very detailed description of the quarto (216×146; 215×150) paper manuscript transmitting *Simonia beg.* precedes De Vreese's transcript of the text.[21] From his analysis it can be deduced that a single scribe wrote f. 1-126 of the manuscript, in a fine *cursiua libraria* hand. He dated his work on f. 3-36; 87-105 in 1455, and reveals his identity in the *explicit* on f. 105r as Hermannus Alen.[22] He has been identified as Hermannus Wersebrockhus aka Bartscher of A(h)len (to the south east of Münster), confessor of the Sisters of the Common Life in Schüttorf (just to the East of the modern Dutch border near Bentheim, between Münster and Enschede) at least from 1428 until his death in 1474.[23] A contemporary entry in a different hand, writing *hybrida libraria* script, just below the *explicit* on f. 105r, "Dyt boeck heft uns gescreven ons leve Eerweerdige vader her herman van Alen den got genedich moet sijn", reveals that their confessor wrote the collection of texts for the Sisters, probably at their request. The script in the next three quires (13^5, followed by 14^8-15$^{10\text{-}2}$ containing *Simonia beg.* on f. 111-126) is in Hermannus' hand also, and contemporaneous, i.e. most probably dating from the 1450's also.

Hermannus has regularly corrected occasional slips in his text, almost invariably during the first stage of the writing process. All of these autocorrections are scrupulously listed by De Vreese in

---

[21] DE VREESE, *Simonia*, p. ii-xix; cfr for a more recent description I. STAHL, *Die Handschriften der Klosterbibliothek Frenswegen*, Wiesbaden, 2004, p. 103-105, with updated references.

[22] On the scribe, cfr DE VREESE, *Simonia*, p. iii-xvii, most notably p. xiii, and VAN DIJK, *Prolegomena*, p. 161 fn. 125. Another surviving manuscript written in his hand, dated 1449, is presently kept in Strasbourg, Bibliothèque municipale, 33, containing Conradus de Brundelsheim (Ps. Soccus), *Sermones de sanctis* (85 sermons), followed by a small fragment from Iordanus de Quedlinburgo (?), *De Dedicatione Ecclesiae*, on the last two folia, cfr STAHL, *Handschriften*, p. 145.

[23] Cfr P. F. J. OBBEMA, *Een Deventer bibliotheekcatalogus van het einde der vijftiende eeuw. Een bijdrage tot de studie van laat-middeleeuwse bibliotheekcatalogi*, 2 vols, Brussel, 1973, p. 167, further references in GOUDRIAAN, 'Grote on simony', p. 118-119, to which should be added *CMD-NL* 2, p. 242, nos. 907-908, with on Pl. 938a; 940a illustrations of his handwriting.

the notes to the edited text. Since they are all available already, I have limited myself to mentioning the most important ones only in the *app. cr.*

The manuscript is presently kept in the convent of the Crutched Friars St Agatha in Cuyk in the modern Dutch province of Brabant, but that it has ultimately arrived there essentially is the consequence of a case of mistaken identity.[24] In the wake of the French Revolution, in 1806, the Windesheim priory Frenswegen, located close to the Dutch border near Enschede in the modern German Bundesland Nordrhein-Westfalen, was finally abolished as a religious community. For several decades thereafter, its sizeable collection of manuscripts and early editions remained there unsupervised, in a library whose holdings became gradually more and more damaged by weather influences. Probably in the 1860's, a local parish priest, Joseph Berning from Remsede, managed to lay hands on at least 47 manuscripts, which therefore owe their survival to his in fact illegal acquisition. Berning kept the manuscripts for himself, but permitted several scholars access to his treasures, among them Langenberg and De Vreese.[25] Perhaps as early as 1877 already, he began to feel remorse for his illegal possessions, but it was not before 1907 that he finally parted with them. On the advice of officials of the diocese Osnabrück, for which he worked, he donated 24 manuscripts and a number of early editions to the Crutched Friars' priory in Cuyk, then the mother house of the Order as a whole, in the mistaken belief that the Windesheim Canons Regular were identical with the Canons Regular of the Order of the Holy Cross (Crutched Friars).

---

[24] This paragraph summarizes the combined data in A. COSANNE, 'Zur Geschichte der Klosterbibliothek Frenswegen', in *Kloster-Leben. Vom Augustinerchorherrenstift zur ökumenischen Begegnungsstätte* – ed. H. Voort (*Das Bentheimer Land*, Bd. 131), Nordhorn, 1994, p. 201-220, esp. p. 208-210, and B. NONTE, 'Untersuchungen über die Handschriften des Augustiner-Chorherren-Stiftes Frenswegen bei Nordhorn', *Westfälische Forschungen*, 14 (1961), p. 133-148, esp. p. 140-144. On the fate and present whereabouts of the surviving manuscripts from Frenswegen cfr esp. I. STAHL, *Die Handschriften der Klosterbibliothek Frenswegen*, Wiesbaden, 2004.

[25] Cfr on their editions section VII.2 above.

VII.4 Transcription and editorial policy

A fresh collation of the single surviving manuscript has revealed that De Vreese's diplomatic transcript is virtually flawless, and that he follows the manuscript text scrupulously, in words as well as in interpunction. Since a fully trustworthy diplomatic transcript is available in print already therefore, it has been decided to present an edited text in this edition, and to help the reader by deviating from the manuscript interpunction scrupulously given by De Vreese.

At several places in the text, someone different from the author Grote, presumably the scribe Hermannus Alen or the scribe of his exemplar, has facilitated an easy consultation of the text by inserting chapter titles, or small indications of the contents of the following section. Whereas De Vreese decided to incorporate these extratextual reading aids in the main body of his diplomatic transcript, I have decided to relegate them to the *app. crit.*[26] Since, however, this extratextual material nevertheless constitutes a sensible attempt at subdividing the main subject matter of the treatise, but also in order to mark typographically the places in the text where these captions had been inserted, I have introduced blank lines at all places where the *codex unicus* transmits subtitles.

Other aspects of the transcription policy of the Middle Dutch text are discussed above, in section I.5.2.

---

[26] Cfr on this topic John Van Engen's critical assesment of my decision to incorporate extratextual subtitles in my edition of *Turrim*, in *Ons geestelijk erf*, 78 (2004), p. 355-368. Such aids occur twice in the text: **569** Van in te laten; **604** Dit capitel bewiset wo quaet unde unrecht is in enich convent in te setten der personen, in te nemen mit ener zeker summen geldes, unde nicht na aller bequemicheit unde noettrufticheit.

CHAPTER VIII

A TREATISE ABOUT AND DESCRIPTION OF THE SIN OF SIMONY

(Marinus VAN DEN BERG)

Two letters written by Grote and addressed at a community of Third Order Franciscan sisters, which had until then gone unnoticed, were discovered early in the twenty-first century by Hildo van Engen.[1] By mutual arrangement and in collaboration with Hildo van Engen, it was decided to replace his diplomatic edition in *Ons geestelijk erf* with a critical edition in this volume. For this new edition, he very kindly made available for us in digital format his original publication and images of the manuscript source.

VIII.1 SUMMARY OF CONTENTS

In an introductory paragraph, Grote refers to his first letter to the same community, in which he had set out how the Third Order rule should best be observed (1-12). After that he continues by stating that he has heard that this community levies an entrance fee from prospective candidates. He condemns this practice as straightforward simony (13-26). Since he wishes to save his correspondent(s)' soul(s), he proposes to write an essay on what precisely should be considered simony in the context of religious life, under which he ranges communities following the Third Rule of St Francis (27-43).

After that follows a long section of text which Grote has taken over from his earlier treatise *Simonia beg*, and which therefore evidently shows considerable overlap with this earlier text.[2] In a

---

[1] Edited in VAN ENGEN, 'Brieven'. Van Dijk was unaware of this witness when he collected the material for his *Prolegomena*. Illustrations of the folia containing the Grote texts are kept in the collection at the Titus Brandsma Institute as no. Photocopies collection 300. I am most grateful to Rijcklof Hofman for critical observations on an earlier version of this Chapter, and for his English translation.

[2] The agreement between the two texts, but especially the differences due to interventions by the revisor Peter Jansz are discussed below, in section

CHAPTER VIII 137

transitory sentence (44-49), Grote imparts his audience to stay clear from simony and not to impose conditions on prospective candidates. He then sets out, as he had done in *Simonia beg.*, that as soon as spiritual aspects can be associated with a job or assignment, even in a context of hospital service,[3] an offer or requirement of money or of any other form of donation preceding admission to its execution should be considered as simony (49-90). This holds true *a fortiori* when such a function, or a place of residence, is associated with a religious context, even when the monastic vows of poverty, obedience and chastity are not formally taken, as in a Third Order convent (91-105). Followers of this form of religious life live in the same manner as members of an officially recognized order, and they vow obedience to a rule. They are therefore commonly considered as truly religious women; this implies that simony can in their case be punished in the manner prescribed in several decretals, by transferring the culprit to a more severe religious Order (105-131). In addition, Grote observes – with reference to the *Decretal* X 5.3.46 – that the official Church often turns a blind eye on the form of simony under discussion. Anyone guilty of it should nevertheless seek absolution, which is in his eyes valid only when the repentant culprit decides never to practice simony again (132-157). Another defence, that regular monks or nuns perpetrate the same practices, is irrelevant, as such obnoxious behaviour is in their case likewise condemned as simony in canon law (158-172). It is sometimes advanced as an excuse, by decretalists also, that the modest resources of a monastery cannot support additional conventuals (173-183), but in the context of many wealthy German and Dutch convents this should be interpreted as simony in disguise (183-190). However, since tertiary sisters earn most of their own subsistence with the work

---

VIII.3. All parallel passages are listed in the *app. fontium* accompanying the edition below.
  [3] As is observed by LYNCH, *Simoniacal entry*, p. 111 and fn. 18: "Hospitals were generally structured as groups living under a religious rule", cfr for further discussion of simony in relation to entry as staff in hospitals, with numerous references to contemporary documents, among others from Paris from the thirteenth century, also *ibid.*, p. 168 and fn. 95-97; p. 213-214 and fn. 67-68. A concrete example is discussed and analyzed in W. J. COURTENAY, K. B. SHOEMAKER, 'The Tears of Nicholas. Simony and Perjury by a Parisian Master of Theology in the Fourteenth Century', *Speculum*, 83:3 (2008), p. 603-628.

of their hands, this argument is not valid for them anyway (191-203). In conclusion Grote once more urges his addressees to bestow the vacancy to the person who is most fit to receive it, and who deserves and needs it most. No one should be allowed in on the basis of conditions or a contract (204-215). Grote finishes his letter with a paragraph which in its wording resembles an oath. He has brought the truth about the sin of simony out into the open as best he could, and this just as if he would die straight away, and as if he had to account for it before the highest Judge (216-223).

VIII.2.1 THE SCRIBE OF *LEERINGHE ENDE ONDERSCHEIT VAN DER SONDEN DER SYMONIEN*

During the months before his death on 12 April 1531, the Third Order Franciscan lay brother Peter Jansz copied two letters written by Geert Grote into a manuscript containing a collection of texts and documents on the Order of St Francis.[4] In the first of Grote's letters, on f. 14r-18r, originally destined at a prioress of a community of Sisters of the Third Order in Zwolle and/or its surroundings,[5] Grote instructs them about "die punten van der Derder Regulen des salighen sinte Franscisci" (aspects of the third rule of blessed St Francis). The second, more personal letter, on f. 18r-21v, was written to an individual Sister, probably the prioress of the Third Order convent, with an abbreviated title *"Leeringhe ende onderscheit van der sonden der symonien"* (An instruction about and description of the sin of simony). Both letters are didactic in character: Grote is concerned with *"merckelijc onderwijs"* (important teaching) and *"leeringhe"* (instruction). The two letters have come down to us in a single witness only.

An anonymous fellow friar has entered a short biography of the scribe Peter Jansz on an unnumbered folium, preceding the actual collection of texts.[6] In this biography he notes that Peter Jansz collected and copied various texts, and that he had been held in high esteem "bij de generaele" (among the superior officials).

---

[4] This section is primarily based on VAN ENGEN, 'Brieven', p. 105-130. On the manuscript cfr further section Ch. VIII.4 below.
[5] Cfr for the identification of the addressees section VIII.2.2 below.
[6] The biography is printed in full in VAN ENGEN, 'Brieven', p. 108-109, fn. 9.

These officials had sent him to various convents of the Order with special commissions. On their authority, he reformed the convent of the friars in Diest in the province Brabant in modern Belgium, and he made an attempt at reform in the convent in Mechelen (Malines). Possibly for the same reason he spent shorter or longer periods of time in the communities of the Third Order in Brussels, Aarschot and Tienen. According to his biographer, he also functioned as procurator and novice master. In one of the houses of the Order, Peter Jansz had had access to the two letters written by Grote. Most probably, this exemplar had been written in Grote's native Eastern Middle Dutch dialect.

Peter Jansz was born in Baarland, a village on the island Zuid-Beveland in the modern Dutch province Zeeland. When he copied the letters written by Grote, he already was "een out vader" (an old friar) in the Third Order convent in Antwerp. Probably much earlier (the biographer does not give information on the age he had reached), he had entered the Order and done his profession in this same convent.

The anonymous fellow friar not only wrote a biography of Peter Jansz, but he also compiled a table of contents for the collection of texts and documents assembled by Jansz, all written in Middle Dutch. This table reveals that all documents are either transcripts or translations of texts dealing with the Order of St Francis, including – apart from various canonical documents and bulls – several treatises. The collection as a whole received the title *Den saligen oorspronc van de Derde Regel s. Franciscus* (*sic*) (The blessed origin of the Third Rule of St Francis), derived from the rubric preceding the first text in the collection. After a short text on St Francis and two bulls issued by Pope Nicholas IV (in 1289) and Pope Clement V (in 1307)[7] follow on f. 14-21 *Een merckelijc onderwijs* and *Een zuverlike leeringhe*, written in quires 4-5 (f. 8-23). Both texts are preceded by programmatic rubrics.[8] In the first letter, Grote concludes that a group of Sisters

---

[7] Cfr for a full list of the contents of the collection VAN ENGEN, 'Brieven', p. 106-107, fn. 4, and for a reference to editions of these bulls ibid., p. 113, fn. 16.

[8] The rubric of the first letter reads: "Een merckelijc onderwijs op die punten van der Derder Regulen des salighen vaders sinte Francisci, diewelke dat meester Gheeraert die Grote ghescreven heeft den susteren van der Derder Ordenen tot Swolle ende den ghestichte daeromtrent, want zi die regule der bruederen van penitencien qualijk ende tonrechte ontfinghen

has undeservedly received the Rule of the Third Order, and that they moreover do not observe it properly. Grote points out clearly which adjustments are necessary. The second letter deals with simony.

VIII.2.2 *Een merckelijc onderwijs* and *Leeringhe*

In *Een merckelijc onderwijs* Grote sets out how the Rule is observed properly. His letter was provoked by the fact that the Sisters "die regule der bruederen van penitencien qualijc ende tonrechte ontfinghen ende oeck qualijck ende ongherechteliken hielden" (undeservedly and wrongly received the Rule of the Friars of penitence, and also wrongly and unjustly observed it; thus in the rubric). He points out to a prioress of a community of Sisters in Zwolle or its surroundings, whom he addresses as "alderliefste in Christo" (most beloved one in Christ), that nothing is wrong with a choice for the Third Order, but that such a choice has its consequences. He then lists the nature of these consequences in a series of precepts and requirements, regarding the proper manner of dressing, permitted food and fasts, and daily prayers.[9] At this point the text of the letter is interrupted by an intrusion, which is in layout exactly equivalent with the layout of the main text, in other words, it is not marked off from the main text by the use of different script, or ink in a different colour. This intrusion shows in part remarkable overlap with the rubric preceding the text of the letter, but it mentions in addition that the Sisters commit a sin, as they live together without the supervision of a "minister" (a supervising spiritual

---

ende oeck qualijc ende ongherechteliken hielden", that of the second one: "Een zuverlike leeringhe ende onderscheit van der sonden der symonien, diewelke ghelegen es in geesteliken husen ofte plaetsen provenden te coepen oft yemande met voerwaerden te ontfangen, in den welken dat oeck openliken wort gheseit ende bewesen dat die bruederen ende susteren van der Derder Oerdenen sinte Francisci † scrijft meester Gheeraert die Grote †"; as noted by VAN ENGEN, 'Brieven', p. 137, fn. b, already, something seems to be missing at the end of this introductory rubric, a fact observed by a later reader of the text also, who entered an obelos-like symbol at the relevant place in the text.

[9] This part of the letter is summarized in greater detail in VAN ENGEN, 'Brieven', p. 113-116.

custodian).[10] The reference to Grote's correspondent(s) here, "den susteren van Swolle" instead of "den susteren van der Derder Ordenen tot Swolle ende den ghestichte daeromtrent" (thus in the rubric), suggests that the person responsible for the intrusion just abbreviated the text of the rubric, but it might perhaps also be taken as an indication that what follows after the intrusion was intended for a single community only (i.e. the Sisters in Zwolle), whereas what preceded was intended for more than one community. The reference to Grote and the use of third ps. personal pronouns clearly shows that this intrusion must have been written by someone else than Grote, but yet someone who was well acquainted with the situation in Zwolle at the end of the fourteenth or the beginning of the fifteenth century,[11] rather than by Peter Jansz in 1531. After this intrusion follows, again in the same layout and script, another series of precepts, on a necessary check of the antecedents of prospective Sisters, on arrangements regarding eventual debts or personal possessions, and on the necessity of a spiritual custodian, all of it attributable to Grote. The final sentence addresses illicit conditions and the levy of an entrance fee for prospective Sisters, introducing the main topic of the second letter: simony.

Grote sends the second letter to the same correspondent. As an answer to a question which he had been asked, he proposes to formulate a well-reasoned and trustworthy *consilium* on simony and to present an enumeration of transgressions which belong in its domain, as Third Order Friars and Sisters tend to breach God's commands, canon law and the precepts of the Church. Whole stretches of the second part of the letter correspond, often almost *uerbatim*, with passages of *Simonia beg.*[12] Where the contents of the two treatises present more important differences, these can in general be ascribed to the fact that *Leeringhe* was written for a community of Third Order Sisters, while *Simonia beg.* was destined for a community of beguines.

---

[10] The full text of this passage, as printed by VAN ENGEN, 'Brieven', p. 135, reads as follows: "Dit screef aldus meester Gheert die Grote den susteren van Swolle, omdat zi die derde regule der bruederen van penitencien tonrechte aennamen ende oeck tonrechte hielden, want aldaer noch doen gheen minister en was oft en woende diewelke dat se na der regulen hadde moghen ontfanghen alst betaemt".

[11] This is suggested also by VAN ENGEN, 'Brieven', p. 118, cfr p. 120.

[12] Cfr. Ch. VII above, Text 6 below, as well as the *app. fontium* of both texts.

VIII.3.1 SCRIBE, TRANSLATOR, REVISOR

In his short biography, the anonymous fellow friar characterizes Peter Jansz not only as an important member of the Third Order, but also as a stylistically gifted scribe. He remarks about the manner in which he operated when copying: "hi was daer seer suptijl ende cloec in om de scrift te cieren ende wel te setten of te dichten; van een cleine sinne maecte hij wel veel woerden met scriven" (he was very ingenious and skilful in embellishing text and in formulating and composing well; he transformed a short sentence into many words when he wrote); in other words: rather than copying faithfully from his exemplar, he had an inclination to expand the text which he found in his source. This mode of operation can clearly be observed in the treatise on simony.

Neither the first nor the second letter transcribed by Peter Jansz has come down to us in its original form. However, as observed already, the contents of the second part of the second letter correspond to a large extent with sections of *Simonia beg.* The single extant copy of this text is presently kept in the convent of the Crutched Friars St Agatha in Cuyk in the modern Dutch province of Brabant, where it arrived in the nineteenth century from the important Windesheim priory Frenswegen, located close to the Dutch border near Enschede in the modern German Bundesland Nordrhein-Westfalen.[13] The manuscript containing the treatise was written in the 1450's in Schüttorf, close to Frenswegen, by Hermannus from Alen, confessor of the Sisters of the Common Life in that village.[14]

In all probability, Geert Grote himself made the first move towards a revision of his older treatise *Simonia beg.*, originally destined for beguines, in order to transform it into a letter for a community of Third Order Sisters. With this revision in mind, he either adapted[15] or omitted passages specifically relevant for

---

[13] Cfr more elaborately Ch. VII.3 above, with further references.
[14] Cfr for further details again Ch. VII.3 above.
[15] For instance, *Simonia beg.*, **99-102** "ende vort alle der beginen verbunde unde er gude ghewonte van binnen... maken dat dese staet off manere van leven geistlic sijn vor Gode" is in *Leeringhe*, **128-130**, rendered as: "Ende want der beghinen ofte der susteren intencie ende meininghe altijt ghedraghet tot geestelijcheiden, zoe sijn sij oeck mede voer Gode geestelijck".

CHAPTER VIII   143

beguines.[16] In *Simonia beg.*, **40-63**, he had briefly mentioned the Third Order already. Here he had characterized such a community of followers of St Francis as being "ghene vulcomene religio" (not a full-fledged religious order), but it is nevertheless similar "mit religien"(to a religious order). As a consequence, its members must observe various rules and precepts. When they are guilty of simony, for instance, they must give up the place which they had obtained in a community and move over to a stricter order.[17] Since Grote is not concerned with the Third Order primarily in *Simonia beg.*, he there writes (**62-63**): "Mer late wi de Derde Orde staen an uwer conscientie" (but let's leave the Third Order to your conscience). Somewhat later on there apparently was sufficient reason for him to compose his first letter for a Third Order community, *Merckelijc onderwijs*.[18] In *Simonia beg.*, he restricts himself after this short passage to a discussion of the life and precepts in a beguinage, with occasional reference to religious orders, addressing the sin of simony exhaustively in ll. **129-515**.[19]

In his second letter to the same Third Order community Grote likewise occasionally mentions beguines in passing, without elaborately discussing topics specifically concerning them. This becomes evident for instance when we compare F, l. **541-549**, with A, l. **191-192**.[20] After this passage where the two texts deviate

---

[16] Now and then, he translated quotations from canon law or decret(al)ists and Church Fathers, adapting the original phrasing in order to make them more easily understandable (compare e.g. *Simonia beg.*, **6-11** = *Leeringhe*, **58-64** *paene ad litt.*; *Simonia beg.*, **17-32** = *Leeringhe*, **74-89** *paene ad litt.*, etc.; cfr further the *app. font.*); these passages are not relevant in the context here, as they are taken over (almost) *uerbatim* in the revised text for the Third Order Sisters.

[17] Grote here follows the prescriptions set out in several decretals, mentioned below in the *app. font.*, **49-59**.

[18] Cfr further the analysis in VAN ENGEN, 'Brieven", p. 113-120, and the edition, ibid., p. 131-136.

[19] Cfr on this subject also the comparable discussion in VAN ENGEN, 'Brieven", p. 120-125.

[20] *Simonia beg.*, **541-549**, reads: "Unde bovenal so en ist oec gheen ghelijc varwe met desen baghinen, want se ghene vulle voedingen noch cledinge en gheven unde em een mensche gheen groet hinder en is te nemen, of altoes den wal nemen moghen unde holden, inden dat daer se de eere inholden unde elc emselven holt uutghenomen wat vordels in potagie, in vieringe of in dranke of in weynich anders coste. Tymmeringe, de solden se holden mit den ghemeynen guede of scheiten daerto elc of bidden daerto. Dat wee beter dat se deden wes se doen mochten", whereas *Leeringhe*, **191-**

the series of parallel passages is continued, until we arrive at a passage in F on priests and altars (l. 574-592), which is not relevant in the context of the Third Order: it is again left out, now in its entirety, in *A* after l. 215. Finally, the concluding paragraph in A (l. 216-223) differs from the one in *F* (l. 593-603). In *Leeringhe*, its wording resembles that of an oath: "Ende ick, meester Gheeraert de Grote, neme hier die ewighe Waerheit te ghetughe" (And I, master Geert Grote, call the eternal Truth as a witness). He has brought the truth about the sin of simony out into the open as best he could, and this "recht alsoft ick tehant sterven soude" (just as if I would die straight away), and as if he had to account for it before the highest Judge. In *Simonia beg.*, on the other hand, an "ic" (I) addresses "Myne lieve zustere in Unsen Leven Heren" (my dear sisters in our Lord) with a message in which he confronts the evil world, which disregards justice, with God's justice, which comes to his people, ending with a prayer formula.

Also, it is clear from a comparison between both texts that Grote has adjusted his views on the Third Order of St Francis in a positive manner since the writing of *Simonia beg.*[21] For this reason, he has gone to great lengths to explain "hoe dat men die heilighe Oerdene van der Derder Regule sinte Francisci van der Penitencien sculdich es te houdene ende die forme ofte maniere des levens te volghene ende den Heere Jhesum Christum met ynnicheiden te dienen om salicheit uwer zielen te verwerven"(in what manner one should observe the regulations of the holy Order of the Third Rule of St Francis of Penitence, and should follow the form or manner of this life, and should serve devoutly Our Lord Jesus Christ in order to obtain salvation of your souls).[22] Earlier on, cases of simony among beguines had become known to him, and now he was confronted with the same offence in relation with the Third Order. He had been told "hoe dat ghi u ontgaende sijt in die onduechdelike sonde der symonien"(how you

---

192, just has: "Ende bovenal soe en eest oeck gheen ghelike verwe met personen: het sijn susteren of andere, et cetera".

[21] Cfr on this also VAN ENGEN, *Derde Orde*, p. 80-81.

[22] *Leeringhe*, 3-7; in l. 35-43, he points out that the Rule has been approved by bishops [i.e. most notably Pope Nicholas IV in 1289] and decretalists ("Church doctors"). Therefore, "beide bruederen ende susteren, die de forme ende maniere van desen leven houden, sijn gheestelike personen"(both Brothers and Sisters are spiritual persons when they observe the form and conventions of this life, l. 40-41).

make a slip in the unvirtuous sin of simony, l. 13-14). The offence was clearly related to the levy or payment of an entrance fee, as it was allowed for Third Order sisters to keep personal possessions after entry in a community.[23] And just like he had written a treatise on the dreadfulness of this offence for beguines, so he had now set out, "van rechter caritaten" (out of sincere commitment, l. 45), to compose a letter on the same subject for the Sisters, recycling older material. However, whereas he had begun *Simonia beg. in medias res* with the remark "Dit is my ghevraghet: oftet symonia sij ene stede of ene provende te copen in ene beghinenconvente" (I have been consulted whether it be simony to acquire a place or a prebend in a beguinage, l. 1-2), he now introduced his disquisition in a pastoral and didactic manner, continuing after that with an almost *uerbatim* quotation from *Simonia beg.*: "Ende opdat ghi dese dinghen te claerlikere verstaen moghet, so sal ic u segghen die vraghe die tot my daeraf es ghedaen, dats oft symonie es een stede oft een provende te coepen in een beghinenconvent" (And in order that you may understand these things more plainly, for this reason I shall tell you the question that I have been asked about this, that is whether it is simony to acquire a place or a prebend in a beguinage (*sic*, while writing at a Third Order community!), l. 49-52).

Not only Geert Grote himself has revised the original text, but Peter Jansz also must undoubtedly be held accountable for at least part of the adjustments and expansions. Hildo van Engen raises this possibility, but dismisses it immediately, since there is no positive proof for this assumption.[24] It is certainly true that extensions in references to canon law are most probably not attributable to him, as he demonstrably was not versed in this subject matter. However, as regards other adjustments, especially linguistic ones, his involvement with Grote's original text is considerable, as it goes way beyond mere copying. The main reason for his interventions is that the Southern Middle Dutch dialect of the new audience differs markedly from the Eastern Middle Dutch of the IJssel region. This aspect and its consequences must be dealt with now.

---

[23] Cfr VAN ENGEN, *Derde Orde*, p. 64.
[24] Cfr VAN ENGEN, 'Brieven', p. 125.

VIII.3.2. FROM IJSSELLANDISH TO BRABANTINE

Geert Grote has undoubtedly written the texts on simony in his mother tongue: the IJssellandish dialect spoken in his native city Deventer. This is true for *Simonia beg.* as well as for the two letters, of which the first one has a rubric mentioning "den susteren van der Derder Ordenen tot Swolle ende den ghestichte daeromtrent" (the Third Order Sisters in Zwolle and the houses in its neighbourhood).[25] The Middle Dutch dialect in the region Salland, where Deventer as well as Zwolle are located, belongs to the Saxon dialects, then and in part now still spoken in a territory stretching uninterruptedly from the river IJssel in the West to the river Elbe in the East, and from the line Groningen – Kiel in the North to the line Bocholt – Werden – Olpe through Münden until Merseburg in the South.[26] The literary output of the Modern Devotion could spread comparatively easily in this vast monolingual territory.[27]

Except for a few relatively small differences, the dialects spoken in the Westfalen village of Schüttorf (where the text of *Simonia beg.* was copied in the 1450's by Herman from Alen),[28] in the nearby Windesheim priory Frenswegen (where it was kept for centuries), and in the city of Deventer display a remarkable

---

[25] The Old Convent in Zwolle was originally founded as a beguinage. Shortly after 1361, the beguines adopted the Third Rule of St Francis; cfr on the community further VAN ENGEN, 'Brieven', p. 125.

[26] Cfr W. KÖNIG, *dtv-Atlas Deutsche Sprache*, München, 2011, p. 56, on the Old Saxon region; from *c.* 1250 onwards, Old Saxon developed into Middle Low German, cfr *ibid.*, p. 60, and p. 77 for a short characteristic of this development. More elaborate information is provided in 'Ergebnisse der Sprachgeschichtsforschung zu den historischen Sprachstufen, IV: Das Mittelniederdeutsche', in *Sprachgeschichte. Ein Handbuch zur Geschichte der deutschen Sprache und ihrer Erforschung* – ed. W. Besch, 2nd rev. edition, Bd. 2.2, Berlin – New York, 2000, p. 1409-1477.

[27] Cfr R. SCHLUSEMANN, 'Von der IJssel bis Ostwestfalen: ein Kulturgebiet?', in *Die Devotio Moderna. Sozialer und kultureller Transfer (1350-1580)*, Bd. 1. *Frömmigkeit, Unterricht und Moral. Einheit und Vielfalt der Devotio Moderna an den Schnittstellen von Kirche und Gesellschaft, vor allem in der deutschniederländischen Grenzregio* – ed. D. E. H. de Boer, I. Kwiatkowski, Münster, 2013, p. 57-83; in her study, the author exemplifies in an innovative manner the distribution of writings of the Modern Devout in the German-Dutch border regions, according equal weight to the respective German and Dutch traditions of given texts.

[28] Cfr in greater detail Ch. VII.3 above.

CHAPTER VIII 147

homogeneity.[29] This becomes clear at once when the linguistic phenomena occurring in the *Statutes of the Meester-Geertshuis*[30] (from now on referred to as: Deventer) are compared to those in *Simonia beg.* (from now on: Frenswegen).[31]

In Deventer, the graphemes -o- and -a- are used alternately in open syllables. This is the case, for instance, in 221 *LD*; 243 *D*; 381 *D*; 392 *D* "boven", 385 *D* "bovenste", 179 *L*; 402-403 *D* "daerboven", 328 *D* "bovenal", 51 *L* "over",[32] 446 *L* "clenode", 339 *D* "oversten" (in the sense 'superior') side by side with 51; 176; 513 *D* "aver", 446 *D* "clenade", 180-181 *D* "daerbaven", 194 *D* "avete" [mod. 'ooft', = 'fruit']. Frenswegen does not have a-forms; here we find words such as – among many other examples – 657; 834 (twice) "boven", 223 "daerboven", 388; 412; 541 "bovenal", 237 "openbaren", 19; 27 "ghenomen", 41; 1041; 1113; 1126 "opene" and 108; 109; 162; 516 (and elsewhere) "over". The vocabulary in Lübben's *Mittelniederdeutsche Grammatik*, on the other hand, has o- and a-forms side by side: "apenbarlike, baven" alongside with "over, overwinnen, boven". The same holds true for Köbler's *Mittelniederdeutsches Wörterbuch* (available on internet); here I found: "open" and "apen", "over" and "aver", "boven" and "baven", "ovet" and "avet" (= 'ooft', 'fruit').[33]

In open syllables, the grapheme -o- also often occurs instead of -oe-. In Deventer, we find words such as 20 *D* "armode", 344 *D*; 447 *LD* "boke", 77 *L* = 78 *D*; 328 *D* "daerto",[34] 649 *D* "mynrebro-

---

[29] I here refrain from an exposition on the various names which have in the course of the history of dialect research been accorded to the common language spoken in this region; I have decided to use the terms IJssellandish, Eastern Middle Dutch, and Western Middle Low German alternately, taking them more or less as synonyms.

[30] The *Statutes* are transmitted in two versions, *L* and *D*; cfr on these Ch. VI.1 above, and KLAUSMANN, 'Satzungen', esp. p. 30-35. The linguistic phenomena listed here occur in both versions.

[31] In my comparison between the respective dialects in the two regions I make no claim to be exhaustive. My single aim here is to stress the close proximity of the dialects in Deventer and in Western Westfalen in connection with the textual changes introduced by Peter Jansz.

[32] *D* here "aver", but compare 55 *D* = 54 *L* "over"; this same word "over" in *D* also in l. 75; 521; 654, in *L* also in l. 651.

[33] Cfr A. LÜBBEN, *Mittelniederdeutsche Grammatik, nebst Chrestomathie und Glossar*, Leipzig, 1882, and G. KÖBLER, *Mittelniederdeutsches Wörterbuch*, 3. Auflage, 2014.

[34] Note also 102 *L* "dairto" = 103 *D* "daertoe".

deren", 589 *D*; 593 *LD*; 607 *D* "nomen",[35] 65 *D* "tobehoerde" = 63-64 *L* "tobehoeren", 415 *D* "tolegghen" side by side with 15-16 *L* = 23-24 *D* "oetmoede" (cfr 67 *L* = 68 *D* "oetmoedeliken"), 265-266 *D*; 337 *D* "boeke(n)", 374 *D* "behoeven", 458 *D* "groeve", 564 *D* "zoeken",[36] 92 *D* "tevoeren" (opposed to 92 *L* "tevoren"). Frenswegen also knows this phenomenon: 268; 308; 310; 388; 502; 535; 537; 1071; 1089 "armode", 71; 124; 222; 476 "boke" (and eight other instances), 91; 141; 228; 510 "daerto" (and six other instances), 289; 632 "behoven", 261; 366; 640 "blode" (cfr 328 "blodes", gen. sg.), 140; 434; 556; 800 "te done" (and two other instances), 275 "gheropen" (cfr "ropinghe" in the same line), 298 "moten", 70 "nomen", 197; 330; 931 "vermoden", 314 "woveer" (note also 28 instances of "wo") side by side with 266; 281; 501; 989; 1049 "armoede", 958 "boeke", 119; 790; 919 "te doene", 373; 580 "moeten", and 339; 342-343 "vermoeden". In Deventer -o- and -oe- balance one another out, whereas in Frenswegen o-forms tip the scales.

The close affinity of the dialects is also exemplified in the use of the Modern Dutch personal pronouns "hij, zij, wij" ('he, she, we'). The Deventer *Statutes* mention both "se" and "si"; in the present-day dialect of this region, Salland, both "he" and "we" still occur next to standard "hij" and "wij", but nowadays "wie" is also used in addition to "we". Frenswegen has not only the -e-forms "he, se, we", but the scribe Herman, originally born in Alen, also knows "sij".

The fem. possessive pronoun has in plural forms an easterly as well as a westerly form: "hoer, hoere, hoeren, hoerre, horen" alongside with "haer, haerre, haere, haeren, haren". In Frenswegen these forms are not attested, probably due to the different genre of the text.

Also noteworthy is the use of a single grapheme -a- instead of a double grapheme -ae- representing /ā/ in closed syllables. The *Statutes* write: 43 *LD* "**a**nhang(h)en", 163 *D* "onhoers**a**m" ("ongehoirsam" *L*), 668 *L(D)* "ghez**a**t", 286 *D* "vrat**a**chtich", 306 *D* "w**a**rt", 382; 388 *D* "z**a**lre", and only rarely: 85 *D* "**ae**nsien" (but: "ansien" *L*); Frenswegen writes: 13; 134; 143; 157 "vorw**a**rde(n)" (and four other instances), 17; 88 "d**a**r... to" (but in this case "daer" is

---

[35] "Noemen" is not attested, the past participles 515-516; *Simonia beg.* 19 (twice); 27; 296; 1071 "ghenoemen/uetghenoemen/aenghenoemen" (two instances in *Leeringhe*, 76, 78, also) have a different etymology.

[36] Cfr *Simonia beg.* 645 "zoken".

much more common), 3-4; 34; 40; 113 "an... hanget" (but 54-55 "aenhanget"), 62; 156 "daeran", 172; 228; 229; 333 "anseyn" [= regard] (and nine other instances), 258; 381; 882; 883 "doghentsam" (and four other instances), 326 "vruchtbarlixt", alongside with many instances of "daer... an", "daerto", "daerumme", 165; 431; 435; 468 "entfaen" (and nine other instances), 291; 525 "entfaet", et cetera.

This same phenomenon can also be observed, although less often, for -o- instead of -oe- representing /ō/. Deventer has 616 *D* "onorbaer" ("onorber *L*) alongside with 86-87; 597 *D* "oerbaer" ("orber" *L* 87), but in the case of this vowel sound the spelling with -e- indicating length is obviously dominant. As regards Frenswegen, here forms missing -e- indicating length occur more often than in Deventer: 17; 641-642 "antwort", 2 "gheantwort", 100; 507; 508; 510; 525 "ghewonte", 169 "orloven", 69 "georloft", 191 "otmodich" and 31 "worden" ('words', alongside with the same spelling for short /ŏ/ in the verbal form "worden"; twice, directly after 30 "woerde"), 21; 319; 780 "antworden". Side by side with these forms we find other ones written with -oe-: 168 "ghewoente", 260 "gheboerte", 185 "oersake", 235; 1153 "oersprunclike" and 30; 146; 234; 355 "woerde" (and fifteen other instances).[37] The grapheme -o- sometimes represents a sound which is pronounced as short /ĕ/ in present-day standard Modern Dutch, while this sound is still pronounced as short /ŏ/ in the contemporary dialect of Salland, as in "oflegghen".

Typically easterly forms are further in Deventer 141 *LD*; 178-179 *LD*; 193 *D*; 222-223 *LD* "solde(n)" (and four other instances), 641 *LD* "oldervaderen", 358 *D* "olderen", 172-173 *LD*; 337-338 *D*; 461 *D*; "wolde(n)", "golt", "molt", in Frenswegen 195; 707; 716; 978 "olde", 52; 58; 133; 150 "solde(n)" (and 22 other instances), 178; 181; 300; 544 "wolde(n)" (and 12 other instances).

An easterly form "unde" is not attested for the coordinating conjunction in the *Statutes*, which consistently write "ende", although on the other hand "nummer(meer)" is written consistently for more westerly "nemmer(meer)" in 39 *D* = 35 *L*; 81 *L D*; 377 *D*; in

---

[37] In the on-line *Mittelniederdeutsches Wörterbuch* I have not encountered any example writing -oe- with -e- indicating length, while in Middle Dutch spelling variants -o-; -oe-, -oi-, -oo- occur, all representing /ō/. Herman from Alen may of course have taken over these spellings from his exemplar.

Frenswegen, "unde" is the common spelling, as well as "nummermeer" in 561.

I nowhere encountered the preposition "umme" (around, about) in Deventer, although "umme" is still acceptable in the contemporary dialect of Salland, both in compounds and independently used. However, **19** *D*; **27** *D* "onghebunden" ("ongebonden **27** *L*), **241** *D* "sunder", **44**; **62**; **518** *D* "sunderlinghe" ("sonderling(h)e" **44**; **61** *L*), **673** *D* "orcunde" do occur in Deventer side by side with **11** *L D*; **33** *L*; **84**=**85** *LD*; **108**=**114** *LD* etc. "sonder", **158** *L*; **228** *L*; **346** *L*; **481** *L* etc. "sonderlinghe", **16** *D*; **258** *D* "onder", **277**-**278** *L* "sonden", as well as **680** *L* "up" (= "op" **674** *L*). Frenswegen very rarely uses forms spelling -o-; the common use there is: "daerum(me)" (ubiquitous, 23 instances), **67** "daerunder", **38**; **67-68** "gebunden", **91** "ghedwungen", **345** "ghevunden", **130**; **135**; **160**; **194** etc. "hundert" (and compounds), **8**; **59**; **94**; **95** etc. "sunder", **18**; **163**; **716** "umdat", **94** "ummekeren", **106-107**; **642**; **647** etc. "sunderlinghe", **107** "bisunderlinghe", **66**; **73** "ungheloven", **147**; **172**; **181**; **201** etc. "unse" (inflected forms also), **27**; **277**; **278**; **279** etc. "updat" (note, however, also **131**; **823** "opdat"), **604**; **622** "verbunt" (cfr **99-100**; **1100** "verbunde"), **44**; **293**; **683**; **983** etc. "vulcomen" (note, however, **19-20**; "Daer... op").

In the more westerly Dutch speaking linguistic regions, original /ē/ has developed into /ie/, as in the verbs "zien", "dienen" and the substantive "zieke". Deventer has **77**; **79** *LD* "sien" (compare several instances of the compound "aensien" in both *L* and *D*), **138** *LD* "siec(k)", **602** *D* "sieken", next to **23** *D* "te deenenne" (gerund) ("to dienen", **15** *D*), the subjunctive form **80** *D* "scee" (will happen, "geschie", **78-79** *L*), and the noun **578-579** *D* "zeken". Frenswegen has, along with **60**; **206** "zele" and the borrowing **472-473**; **781**; **1152** "manere(n)", the forms **273**; **366**; **371** "keisen" (and four other instances), **174**; **1013** "verkeiset", and for instance **202**; **205** "ghi seit", **214** "sei gij" (among many other examples of conjugated forms of the verb 'to see'), next to **19**; **76**; **86**; **267** "te deynen" (and four other instances; cfr also **27**; **250**), **240**; **244**; **386**; **777** "te seyne", **343** "deynre", **344** "deynste", with -i- and -y- indicating length.

VIII.3.3.1 The changes introduced by Peter Jansz

When Peter Jansz was confronted with the easterly Middle Dutch text in his source, which he probably found in one of the

CHAPTER VIII

convents where he spent part of his life, his first impression surely must have been that he was dealing with a text in a foreign language. He may have been born in Zeeland, but he entered the convent of the friars in Antwerp, and he spent much of his adult life in Third Order communities in the Southern Low Countries, for a large part situated in Brabant. Ultimately, he died in Antwerp. His first task had therefore to be to adapt the language in the source text to the Brabantine dialect spoken in the Antwerp convent, in order to make it comprehensible for the intended audience.[38] Since Grote's original text has not come down to us in its original IJssellandic form, I use Herman from Alen's transcript for my analysis of the changes probably attributable to Peter Jansz. As has been demonstrated above, this transcript comes linguistically close to Grote's original. Also, this copy seems not to have undergone significant changes as regards contents.

That Peter Jansz did dispose of an exemplar written in easterly Middle Dutch or westerly Middle Low German, is evident when coinciding passages in both texts are compared to one another. Next to sections which differ from each other in phraseology, we find a considerable number of passages which overlap *uerbatim*. Below, this is demonstrated with the help of a series of examples which have all been taken from the beginning of that part of the text where both versions run parallel. In these examples, the text as copied by Herman from Alen is marked with F (= Frenswegen), that by Peter Jansz with A (= Antwerp):

F (1-2) "oftet symonia sij ene stede oft ene provende te copen in enen beghinenconvente"
A (51-52) "oft symonie es een stede oft een provende te coepen in een beghinenconvent"

F (9-10) "we dat ene kopet, he heitet oec dat ander te copen"
A (62-63) "wie dat eene copet, hy heet oeck dat ander mede te copen"

F (11-12) "Unde elc mensche mach dat voelen in sijns selves consciencie"

---

[38] Herman from Alen transcribed *Simonia beg.* some 80 years after the confection of the text, Peter Jansz worked some 150 years after Grote had composed the two letters. We do not have exact information on the development of West Germanic dialects in this period, but major changes occurred in the language only later, in the course of the sixteenth century simultaneously with the rapid growth of the Reformation.

A (65-66) "Ende elc mensche mach dat in sijn selves consiencie gevoelen"

F (17-18) "oft symonie sij ghelt te gheven"
A (75-76) "oft symonie es gelt te gheven"

F (19-20) "of dat he ghenomen werde in een malaeteschhues"[39]
A (78-79) "oft dat hy aenghenomen wort in een malaetschhuys"

F (34) "wanneer daer enich geistlic ding an hanget"
A (92) "wanneer daer eenich geest·lijck dinck aen hanghet".

Peter Jansz has therefore transcribed many passages just as he found them in his source. However, he also sometimes felt an urge to adapt the source text for his Third Order community, the new audience, in various manners. He feels no urge to justify these adaptations, but they have nevertheless been observed by his biographer.[40] His generally formulated observation makes it clear that Jansz' mode of operation was the same for all texts which he adapted or translated. Jansz' aim undoubtedly was to render Grote's letters faithfully and clearly, but he did not – or could not – always succeed in translating literally. The phrasing in the biography suggests that he discussed his method of translating with his fellow friar, and this (or these) discussion(s) apparently have made such an impression on the biographer that he has decided to insert an explicit remark about it in his biography. In this connection, one of Jansz' interventions is revealing. In the original source text, Grote had written a remark exemplifying his translation technique, directly following after a translated quotation from a canon law text, attributed to 'masters':

> F (30-32) "Dit sijn der meistere woerde van worden te worden vorscreven, daer ander lerers mede concorderen"
> A (87-88) "Siet, dit sijn deser voerseider meesteren woerden ende oeck veel ander leeraren die daermede op accoerderende sijn".

Compared to minor changes such as the added emphatic interjection "Siet" ('see, mark this') and the replacement of the past participle "vorscreven" (written before) by the adjective "voerseider" (aforesaid), the omission of the phrase "van worden te worden" (word by word) is really noteworthy. Herman from Alen

---

[39] Middle Low German knows forms such as "malatzsch, malatch" side by side with forms displaying a grapheme representing /ə/, "malate, malatisch" (leprous), cfr the on-line *Mittelniederdeutsches Wörterbuch*.

[40] Cfr the beginning of section VIII.3 above.

CHAPTER VIII

may probably have agreed with Grote on how to translate properly, and he therefore left Grote's original phrasing unaltered. As for Grote, this approach is typical for him when translating sources conscientiously.[41] He was known as a scrupulous translator, and this attitude is evident from his own introduction to his translation of the *Hours of the Virgin*. Here he writes: "[These] sijn in Duytsche ghesat van woerden te woerden als hi naest konde die sie oversatte, beholden heelheit ende verstandelheit ende waerheit des sinnes. ...in sulken steden daer die slechte Duytsche woerde niet proper en stonden na den sinne of den sin verdonckerden, daer heeft hi ghesat die naeste Duytsche woerde die den rechten ende openstens in gheven."[42] ([These] have been translated into Dutch word for word, as best as the translator was able to do, while at the same time preserving the purity and understanding and truth of the sense... In passages where inadequate Dutch words did not fit in properly in accordance with the sense or obscured the meaning, there he has substituted them for the closest Dutch equivalents (*lit.* words) that render the sense correctly and clearly). On principle, words function for Grote in service of the sense, and therefore he translates as literally as possible ("van woerden te woerden") and as closely to the Latin source text as possible, unless the comprehensibility is affected. In the course of his translating activity, problems arise for Grote – as well as of course for other translators – as soon as the source language Latin differs from (easterly) Middle Dutch in the syntactical, but also in the lexicological and terminological sphere. As a consequence, he had to make explicit the function of the various constituent parts in the sentence, for instance with the help of prepositions replacing the case forms customary in Latin sentences. Also, he was faced with considerable difficulties when he had to render notions from canon law or scholastic theology in the vernacular, as suitable terminology expressing the specific legal and theological jargon was not available for him.

In order to translate adequately and to preserve intelligibility at the same time, Grote was driven back on various methodologies.

---

[41] As opposed to his use of sources when paraphrasing, cfr on this above, Ch. I.4.

[42] Cfr P. WACKERS, 'Latinitas en Middelnederlandse letterkunde: ter inleiding', in *Verraders en bruggenbouwers. Verkenningen naar de relatie tussen Latinitas en de Middelnederlandse letterkunde* – ed. P. Wackers *et al.*, Amsterdam, 1996, p. 23.

Sometimes he retained calques based on technical terminology used in his source texts in unaltered form, but more often he created neologisms, or he used loan translations based on Old French, or he opted for paraphrases. Quite often he decided in favour of doublets, writing a calque on the original term first, but supplementing it with a paraphrase or elaboration, or he used (near) synonyms directly after one another which rendered different aspects of the original term or phrase, often in order to express the emotional connotation.[43] Grote therefore obviously showed great respect for his sources and their contents. This is evidenced also by his apology that he cannot check a passage in a bull issued by Pope John XXII, as he currently does not have his collection of decretals at hand. He knows the contents of the bull, but as a jurist he prefers not to rely on a loose paraphrase.[44]

When presenting direct quotations in translation, cited for the spiritual benefit of beguines and Third Order communities, Grote undoubtedly operated very conscientiously when modifying content or stylistic elements. Only in more loosely formulated paraphrases of source texts he took liberties in the form of extensions or reductions, or by restructuring his sources or adapting them stylistically. He may then also occasionally have simplified or clarified their contents, in order to adapt these to the educational level of his audience.[45]

Essentially, Peter Jansz was confronted with similar problems when he adapted Grote's text on simony to the needs of the community of Friars in Antwerp. The Brabantine dialect with which he was acquainted for the larger part of his life and which he surely must have written (and spoken) fluently himself, differs markedly from the IJssellandic dialect spoken in Salland. These differences can be accounted for by pointing to the divergent linguistic origin of the respective West Germanic dialects. Brabantine evolved from original Old Low German through Old Low Franconian, whereas IJssellandic and the cognate easterly dialects

---

[43] Cfr WACKERS, 'Latinitas', p. 23. In his Latin translations of Middle Dutch source texts, Grote operates in the same manner, cfr below, and HOFMAN, 'Brulocht', p. xxvii-xxx.

[44] Cfr *Simonia beg.*, **63-71**. After "der beghinen staet [had been] wedersproken in *Clementinis*", ... it was by a later pope "georloft, ... mer niet gheconfirmeert, mit enen 'extravagante' de ic (= Grote) up dese tijt nicht nomen en kan, want ic myne boke van rechte nicht bi my en hebbe".

[45] Cfr WACKERS, 'Latinitas', p. 30.

CHAPTER VIII 155

have developed from Old Low German through Old Saxon.[46] For Jansz' intended audience a text written in easterly Middle Dutch or westerly Middle Low German must have presented considerable difficulties,[47] and this is the reason why Jansz must have felt obliged to accommodate his source text. His biographer notes that he did this "uut sonderlinger minnen ende devocien die hy totter oerden hadde" (because of the exceptional love and devotion which he felt for the Order).[48]

Linguistic and spelling conventions in Brabant differed from those in Salland. Neither of these regions knew a generally valid standard for the representation of given sound values in script. Moreover, most individuals adopted highly individualized and all too often not very systematic or consistent practices when they committed to paper (or parchment) what they pronounced. All of this led to graphic liberties, which together with a diverging use of words or notions formed a serious hindrance for a proper understanding of Grote's texts among the new intended audience in Brabant. The following series of examples, derived from the easterly Middle Dutch text on the one hand and the Brabantine one on the other hand, may serve to give insight in the manner in which Peter Jansz clarified the texts on which he had managed to lay hands for his readers.

VIII.3.3.2 Spelling and use of words

Peter Jansz saw himself obliged to modify the spelling of the text with which he was confronted in his source, as various words were in Grote's native Salland dialect pronounced in another manner than in the Brabantine tongue to which Jansz was accus-

---

[46] Cfr W. KÖNIG, *dtv-Atlas Deutsche Sprache*, München, 2011, p. 102, or on the internet the convenient tables on https://www.uni-due.de/SHE/SHE_Germanic_Languages.htm (accessed on 06-04-2016).

[47] It cannot be ruled out that several words, idiomatic phrases and expressions were fairly unclear for Jansz himself. He may therefore occasionally have permitted himself liberties when confronted with unclear phrases. This might be the case, for instance, at the beginning of this sentence: F (113) "ist dat de Derde Orde daer nicht an en hanget", which becomes in A (135-137) "Op alsoe dat die Derde Ordene sinte Francisci daer niet mede aen en hanghet"; another instance is the substitution of "derre" for "wil" in F (116-117) "noch ic en wil dat niet seggen vor den besten of vor den naesten wech", which becomes in A (141-142) "noch ic en derre oeck dit niet segghen als voer dat beste te wesen ende voer den naesten wech".

[48] Cfr VAN ENGEN, 'Brieven', p. 108-109, fn. 9.

tomed. In the following examples, F (= Frenswegen) again denotes *Simonia beg.*, and A (= Antwerp) *Leeringhe*.[49]

– graphic adjustment occurs for instance in the various categories of pronouns. This happens in personal pronouns, e.g. F (25) "he", A (55) "hij"; F (119) "se", A (144) "sij", demonstrative pronouns, e.g. F (4) "de", A (55) "die"; F (49) "an den dat", A (114) "indien dat"; F (52, 61) "desse", A (119) "dieselve"; indefinite pronouns, e.g. F (25) "icht", A (84) "yet"; possessive pronouns, e.g. F (51) "erer", A (119) "hoerder"; relative pronouns combined with personal pronouns, e.g. F (528) "den se", A (179) "die sij", fusions of two different personal pronouns, e.g. F (530) "mochten seene voeden", A (177) "mochten sij hem ghevoeden";
– conjunctions are spelled or combined differently, or replaced by other conjunctions with a different meaning: e.g. F (11) "unde", A (64) "ende"; F (23-24) "Ist dat een mensche, inden dat he dus entfangen wert", A (82-83) "Eest dat enich mensche oft yemant die aldus in deser wijsen ontfangen wort"; F (524-525) "yewer... of", A (168-169) "oft... oft"; F (118-119) "ten rouwe em dat seet ghedaen hebben", A (144) "tensij dat hem ierst berouwe dat sijt gedaen hebben"; F (123-125) "Also spreket dat leste capitel van symonien", A (151-152) "want gheliken dat daer staet ghescreven in den laetsten capittele van der symonien"; F (127-128) "wattan en heit dat nijn symonie vor den gherichte van buten", A (155-156) "alsoft sij van buten in den werken volbracht ware"; F (532-533) "also dat cloester sunder sware last bleve", A (180-182) "want sij se sonder swaren last des convents ende sonder hindere niet ghevoeden en connen, opdat dat convent also onghelast daervan bleve";
– adjectives and adverbs are substituted for different ones by Jansz: F (12) "dat dat waer ‹si›", A (66-67) "dat het waerachtich es"; F (8-9) "nicht", A (61-62) "niet"; F (34) "wo", A (93) "hoe soe"; comparable with this are substitutions with synonyms where the meaning remains the same: F (534) "wisse" is replaced by A (184-185) "zekere",[50] and elsewhere (F (6)) by A (58) "in der waerheit", or (F (521)) by A (164) "rechte", F (116) "ghenoch" by A (140) "ghenoech", F (55; 519; 528; 538) "lude" by A (124; 162; 174; 189) "personen",[51] F (109) "richtet" by A (131-132) "veroerdeelt"; note also the word "weder" (against), which occurs in F twice in l. 553, but which is rendered in A (198-199) by both

---

[49] In what follows I limit myself to a small selection chosen from the overwhelming evidence. Its sole purpose is an elucidation of Peter Jansz' mode of operation.

[50] Cfr also F (115-116), where "vor wisse waer" becomes A (139-140) "voer waer oft voer zekere"; the instances of "wisse" in F, 156; 207; 231; 367; 372, have no parallels in A.

[51] But elsewhere, this word is adapted to the Brabantine dialect, as in F (517) "lude" = A (159) "lieden".

"weder" and "teghens". Perhaps the rendering of F (25) "ding" by A (85) "recht" should be taken as a (deliberate?) change of meaning, or as a misunderstanding, as F (3; 5; 7) "ding" is rendered by Jansz as A (54; 57; 59) "dinck/dinghen" (and elsewhere).
– the preposition F (13) "to" is replaced by A (69) "te" or (94) "tot". In idiomatic expressions, Jansz replaces prepositions in accordance with local usage: F (17) "wat men antwort in der vraghe", A (74-75) "wat men antwoert totter vraghen"; F (113-115) "unde nemen penitencien vor dese symonie", A (137-138) "ende nemen oft ontfanghen penitencie van deser hateliker sonden der symonien";
– the copula "is" is consistently replaced by the Southern form "es", e.g. F (14-15) "dat is al symonia", A (70-71) "dat es al tesamen symonia";
– the Umlaut form (3rd ps. sg. pres. ind.) "steit" in F (10) "Also steit in Decreet" is replaced by "ghescreven staet", in A (63-64) "Also als in dat Decreet ghescreven staet";
– subjunctive forms are almost invariably replaced by their indicative equivalents, as in F (18-19) "ghenomen werde te deynen", A (75) "aenghenomen wort... te dienen"; F (18) "oft symonie sij ghelt te gheven", A (75-76) "oft symonie es ghelt te gheven"; elsewhere, they are replaced by constructions with modal auxiliaries: F (49) "Unde henge desse Derde Orde aldus an", A (113) "Ende daeromme, waert dat die Derde Oerden sinte ·Francisci· voerseit daeraen cleefde oft aenhinghe", note also F (9) "wert", A (61-62) "mach worden"; F (24) "vercrighe", A (83-84) "es vercrigende";
– conjugated forms with easterly Middle Dutch endings are normalized, as in: F (7) "wanner twe dinghe also tegaderhanget" (3rd ps. pl. pres. ind. ends in easterly dialects in -t), A (59-60) "van tween dinghen die alsoe tegaderehangen"; this ending is in F attested elsewhere also, in parts of the text not taken over in A;
– the 3rd ps. pres. ind. of the verb "hebben" (to have) is attested as "heft" in easterly dialects:[52] F (43) "dat een heft", A (105) "dat een mensche hevet".

VIII.3.3.3 Additions

Preliminary observations

For his adaptation for the sake of a Brabantine audience Peter Jansz could almost certainly dispose of a source text which was

---

[52] This may be a hypercorrect form: final -t- is missing in the present-day dialect. On the other hand, in Middle Low German both "heft" and "hef" are attested in the 3rd ps. sg., cfr A. LÜBBEN, *Mittelniederdeutsche Grammatik, nebst Chrestomathie und Glossar*, Leipzig, 1882, p. 94.

close to Grote's autograph. It is essential to note here that Grote's original text is not a derivative product, translated from an original written by someone else in a different language, but that he had composed the text of the letter himself, albeit recycling for it material which he had formulated earlier. At the same time, his text is composite in character. While he had written *Simonia beg.* for an audience which cannot possibly be characterized as juridical specialists, he had nevertheless as a jurist inserted quotations from canon law sources in it, which he had translated into the easterly Middle Dutch / westerly Middle Low German dialect spoken by his audience. No doubt in order to avoid unjust insinuations, he had demonstrably stuck as closely as possible to the contents of his sources. His quotations from renowned Latin sources are the point of departure for the line of reasoning in the treatise on simony. These are used in and for a context of non-specialists, and he was therefore inevitably faced with the necessity to translate comprehensibly. His autograph copy of *Simonia beg.* has not survived, but we can yet dispose of an apograph written in a dialect which hardly differs from that spoken in his native city, as has been set out in section VIII.3.2 above. As a consequence, although we cannot investigate Grote's idiolect, we can yet come very close to it by comparing Jansz' adaptation to the transcript made by Herman from Alen, who wrote (and spoke) in a dialect very similar to that of Grote himself. For him, there was no linguistic need to intervene in Grote's dialect, as this was easily understandable for the Sisters in Schüttorf for whom he wrote.

Peter Jansz, on the other hand, could not be content with merely transcribing his exemplar. He had to adapt it, and to translate it into the dialect of his audience in Antwerp. While it is certainly true that Grote introduced various changes in his Latin translations of Ruusbroec's originally Middle Dutch (Brabantine) mystic treatises,[53] this does not necessarily mean that he did the same when he adapted his original *Simonia beg.* for a new audience in *Leeringhe*. He might have done so in his exposition of quotations from canon law sources, but there is no reason to believe that he did the same when adapting a source text written by himself. It is in this light that I approach Peter Jansz' interventions

---

[53] Cfr on these HOFMAN, 'Brulocht', p. xxvii-xxx.

CHAPTER VIII 159

in the sections of the text that *Simonia beg.* and *Leeringhe* have in common.

Peter Jansz expands his source text in various manners. Some instances have been mentioned in passing already in the section on spelling and use of words (VIII.3.3.2). It is now time to subject these interventions to a more detailed analysis.

(1) The most simple expansions consist in the addition of adverbs (as in **52-53** "aldus", **56** "dan", **62** "mede", **70** "tesamen", **84** "voerwaer"), demonstrative pronoun (as in **68** "dat"), or nouns (as in **69** "ghelts");

(2) More elaborate expansions are for instance added (near) synonyms, resulting in doublets:

F (2) "Ic hebbe gheantwoert", A (52-53) "(dat ic aldus) antwoerde ende segghe";
F (3) "an de stede", A (53) "aen dier plaetse oft stede";
F (18-19) "umdat een mensche ghenomen werde te deynen", A (76-77) "omdat een mensche ontfanghen ende aenghenomen wort... te dienen";
F (23-24) "he dus (entfangen wert)", A (82-83) "die aldus in deser wijsen";

(3) Occasionally Peter Jansz inserts clarifications which may vary from very brief additions to more elaborate ones:

F (40) "de Derde Orde", A (100-101) "die Derde Regule van der Penitencien des salighen vaders sinte Francisci";
F (43) "datselve dat een heft", A (104-105) "datselve dat een mensche hevet";
F (46-47) "Also spreket Johannes Andree in *Clementinis*", A (109-110) "Also spreket Johannes Andree in dat boeck *Clementine*";
F (48) "unde ander lerers", A (111-112) "ende meer ander leeraren die dat proberen ende volghen waer te wesene";
F (49-50) "Unde henge desse Derde Orde aldus an den dat een mensche in enich convent queme", A (113-115) "Ende daeromme, waert dat die Derde Oerden sinte Francisci voerseit daeraen cleefde oft aenhinghe, indien dat een mensche in een van den conventen deser oordenen quame om brueder of sustere te sine".

Sometimes such interventions lead to inevitable change in the sentence structure; thus, the addition of "als" after the adverb "alsoe" in l. **58** results in a change from main sentence into subordinate clause, where the phrase "alsoe als" now functions as a conjunction:

F (6-7) "Want alsoe scrivet dat gheistlike recht", A (58-59) "want alsoe als in den geesteliken rechte gescreven staet".

Another example demonstrates conveniently in which manner Peter Jansz deals with his source. He not only clarifies the text, but also polishes the phrasing in it. This results in a sentence which can be read and understood more easily. In addition, he has also, either consciously or unconsciously, introduced formal changes in the contents of his translated sentence:

> F (12-14) "Unde we in aldusdanen dingen icht lovet of vorwarde maket in to brengen, etsij van ener summen of van denselven dat he hevet, dat is al symonia, want men in al desen dingen entlike nicht gheven en sal um enich tijtlic gheven of brengen".

(And who promises something in such things or posits a condition to bring ‹something› in, either ‹consisting› of a sum or of a thing that one possesses, that is all simony, for one shall in all these things certainly give nothing as a (sort of) temporary form of giving or bringing (in)).

> A (67-71) "Ende daeromme, soe wie dat yetswat van aldusghedanen dinghen ghelovet oft eneghe voerwaerde maket yetswat in te bringhen, hetsij van eenre summen ghelts of anders dat hy heeft, ghelovet in te bringhen, dat es al tesamen symonia, want men in desen dinghen al niet gheven noch geloven en sal, oft dat men om enich tijtlic goet te gheven oft gheloven in te bringhene yemande ontfanghen sal".

(And therefore, whoever promises anything in such things or posits any condition to bring something in, either ‹consisting› of a sum of money or promises to bring in anything else that one possesses, that is all together simony, for one shall in these things certainly not give nor promise, or that one will receive someone through the giving of a temporary good, or through a promising to bring (this) in).

Apart from the substitution of easterly flavoured words such as "we, icht, to" and clarification of the subordinate clause, with the help of causal "daeromme" and announcing "soe", Jansz has expanded "voerwaerde" (condition) by inserting an attributive adjunct "eneghe", supplied an object for the verb phrase "in te bringhen" in the form of an indefinite pronoun "yetswat", supplemented "summen" with an partitive genitive "ghelts", replaced "van denselven" by "anders", and finally clarified "al" by sliding in "tesamen".

Next, Peter Jansz has changed the causal subordinate clause introduced by "want" considerably, both in form and in sense. The replacement of "al" results in an entirely different sense for the word, it now functions as emphatic particle for the negation "niet" rather than for the nouns phrase "desen dingen". Also, he has left out emphatic "entlike" (certainly) before the negation "niet", as well as supplemented "gheven" with "noch gheloven". The final phrase in the clause in F is replaced by an entirely new subordinate clause, introduced by "oft dat", in keeping with other "oft"-clauses elsewhere in the text. In this new clause, "um (om)" has changed in meaning. The original meaning of the phrase in F, 'as a (sort of) temporary form of giving or bringing (in)', has been abandoned. In the new subordinate clause, content has in part been derived from the main clause, but additional content comes through the pen of Jansz, resulting in a change of meaning. 'To give' has been supplemented with 'or to promise to bring in': the act is supplemented with a required promise.

Some other extensions can most probably indeed be ascribed to Grote himself, in view of their juridical context. Thus, following after a passage quoted from the *Decretum*, the text in F continues with a generally formulated phrase (**11**): "unde anderen stede in den rechte" (and other places in the law), referring to other *loci* in canon law manuals. The text in A is much more elaborately formulated (**64-65**): "ende oeck mede in veel anderen steden der heiligher scrifturen van geestelijken rechten" (and also again in many other places in the holy writings of spiritual law). While the added synonym "mede" after "oeck" could stem from Grote as well as from Jansz, the use of the qualifying adjective "heiligher" (holy) grades up the standing of canon law.

VIII.3.3.4 Transpositions

At several places, words or phrases are transposed without change of meaning. Elsewhere, however, the original meaning is affected:

F (**12-13**) "Unde we in aldusdanen dingen icht lovet..." (and who promises something in this kind of things...)

A (67-68) "Ende daeromme, soe wie dat yetswat van aldusghedanen dinghen ghelovet" (and therefore, who promises something of this kind of things...)

In F, "aldusdanen dingen" and "icht" are separate parts of speech, but in A they are fused together into a single part of speech, as "van aldusghedanen dinghen" has been made subordinate to "yetswat". As a consequence, but also because of the substitution of "in" by "van", a change of meaning is the result. Another instance is:

F (50-51) "so dunket my dat de mensche de aldusdane symonie daen hadde" (so it appears to me that the people who have committed this kind of simony...)
A (117-119) "soe dunct my ende ghevoele dat alsodaneghe menschen, die aldus symonie ghedaen hadde" (so it appears to me and I feel that this kind of people, who have thus committed simony...)

Quite apart from the addition of "ende ghevoele" and the replacement of the easterly relative pronoun "de" as well as the easterly unprefixed past participle "daen", the transposition of "aldusdane" (changed into a synonymous form "alsodaneghe") is noteworthy. No longer an attributive adjunct of "symonie", it has come to modify in altered form "menschen", replacing the original article. Its constituent part "aldus-" has now become an independent adverb, with as its overall result a change in meaning.

VIII.3.4 Conclusion and summary

When he decided to advise a community of Tertiary Sisters on simony, Grote turned to an older text which he had written on the same subject as a first step. He therefore adapted part of *Simonia beg.* for this new audience. After that, he inserted this adapted draft text in the second part of his second letter for the community of Third Order Sisters, *Leeringhe*. This letter has survived in a single witness only, copied in 1531 by Peter Jansz, a lay brother in the house of the male Tertiaries in Antwerp. Clear traces of *Simonia beg.* can be found in *Leeringhe*, consisting in many passages taken over *uerbatim* or almost *uerbatim*. The original autograph text of *Simonia beg.*, formulated in Grote's native IJsselandic dialect, has not survived, but we do dispose of an apograph written in an easterly Middle Dutch / westerly Middle Low German dialect for the community of Sisters of the common

CHAPTER VIII 163

life in the Westfalen village of Schüttorf. Due to the close proximity of the respective dialects, there was hardly any need for Herman from Alen, the scribe of this transcript, to insert linguistic changes.

When Peter Jansz prepared his transcript of *Leeringhe*, he accommodated the language which he found in his exemplar, most probably written in an easterly Middle Dutch dialect, to the needs of his Brabantine audience in Antwerp. Either consciously or unconsciously, he introduced minor, but also somewhat more major changes, consisting in additions, replacements, transpositions and omissions. It is more than likely that he misunderstood his source at various places, due to dialect variance. As a consequence of his interventions, his text cannot possibly be considered as a reliable Grote text. For there can on the basis of an analytic comparison between his transcript and *Simonia beg.*, an apograph evidently close to Grote's original text, hardly be any doubt that Peter Jansz' manner of translating and adapting has brought about substantial differences between the target text and the source used for it. This conclusion is confirmed by the anonymous biography written by one of Jansz' fellow Friars. Research on Geert Grote's use of Middle Dutch therefore unfortunately cannot rely on the evidence procured by the letters transmitted in this witness. *Simonia beg.* would then certainly be a much more sensible point of departure, provided that we still reckon with possible Middle Low German colouring of the language in this witness.

However, Peter Jansz has nevertheless sufficiently succeeded in correctly conveying to his Brabantine audience the contents of Grote's main message. In doing this, he has aptly come up to the standards and requirements set by Grote for himself in his own Latin translations of Middle Dutch source texts.

VIII.4 THE MANUSCRIPT

A Antwerpen, FelixArchief Antwerpen, Fonds kerkelijke en caritatieve instellingen, inv. nr. 468, a. 1531), 128 f., Or., Prov.: Antwerpen, Convent of the Third Order Regular Franciscan Friars.

The two letters composed by Grote occur in a paper manuscript put together shortly before his death in 1531 by Peter Jansz, a Third Order Franciscan lay friar who had spent much of his life as procurator, serving in the communities of his order at Brussels,

Aarschot, Tienen, Diest and finally Antwerp, where he died.[54] Peter filled the manuscript with a variety of documents on, by, or about Third Order Franciscans, all written in or translated into Dutch, and included the two letters among them on f. 14r-21v. The text of the letters begins in mid-quire in quaternio 3^8 (f. 8-15), and ends, again in mid-quire, in the next quaternio 4^8 (f. 16-23). Peter wrote in a fine and expert *hybrida libraria* hand, and executed his manuscript in two-column layout, most often but not invariably written on regular quaterniones.

---

[54] Cfr section VIII.2.1 above, and in greater detail VAN ENGEN, 'Brieven', p. 106-108, with ill. of f. 14r; 18r; 17r on p. 110; 111; 117. Since Van Engen provides a detailed description of this witness, the description here can be brief.

CHAPTER IX

A LETTER TO A CORRESPONDENT
WHO HAS DONE PROFESSION (*EP.* 27)

IX.1 SUMMARY OF CONTENTS, AND CONTEXT OF *EP.* 27

This letter has been written as an answer to a correspondent who had shortly before informed Grote that he had taken his monastic vows (1-3). Grote warns him that this decision does not automatically imply that he has now left behind all impediments and temptations (3-10). Coming to the point immediately, Grote advises him that he should not be offended when he discovers that fellow monks have not renounced personal property. Rather than blaming them for it, he should ignore their offensive behaviour, unless he is sure that he can change their ways (11-27). And when he calls someone to account, he must first pray for God's assistance, and then carefully prepare his admonition, in order to avoid that the culprit feels insulted (28-41). Also, he must himself be careful to set aside thoughts about personal possessions at once (42-47). In a short final section, Grote admonishes his correspondent to stay away from worldly preoccupations and small-talk, and to be aware that he cannot do more than his best, that life in accordance with a monastic rule is an attempt at perfection, and that small failure does not really matter in all circumstances (48-60).

IX.2 EDITORIAL HISTORY, SUPPLEMENT, AND THE RECIPIENT OF
EP. 27

Probably on the authority of the *incipit* in the latish (post-1470) and not too trustworthy witness *R*,[1] Mulder posited that Grote

---

[1] MULDER, *Epp.*, p. xxxvi, just writes: "...si, ut opinor, epistola LVII [= *Ep.* 27] ad eundem Matthiam missa est, ..."; 'LVII' here refers to the (adapted) numbering according to the sequence in the The Hague 'letter collection' *H2*, as Mulder explains *ibid.*, p. xxiv. The letters, incidentally, are copied in the same sequence in the Liège 'corpus' *L*.

wrote *Ep.* 27 to his pupil Matthew from Tiel, to whom he certainly addressed *Ep.* 15.[2] In this he was followed by Tiecke, Van Zijl, Rüthing, Épiney and van Dijk. When Rüthing published *Ep.* 85 from the Darmstadt witness *D* in 1966, he hesitantly suggested that this letter might have been written to Matthew also, a suggestion which was taken over with much more confidence by Épiney and van Dijk.[3] Van Dijk further suggests that Matthew did his profession thereafter in the charterhouse Monnikhuizen, just to the north of Arnhem, founded in 1336 and formally active from 1342 onwards,[4] where Grote himself had stayed as a paying guest for at least three years between 1374 and 1379 shortly after his conversion, in order to interioze a more spiritually oriented lifestyle.

However, there is no corroborating evidence at all from Carthusian sources which might confirm the allegation that Matthew spent his novitiate in Monnikhuizen, or even ever lived there: his name does not occur in the reconstructed necrology,[5] and likewise is not listed in the prosopography of the house.[6] Neither is there for the relevant period, up to the second half of the fifteenth century, evidence for a Matthew in any of the other Carthusian houses in the Low Countries or in the Rhine valley.[7]

Secondly, the contents of the letter hardly point to a Carthusian as recipient. Grote discusses except for the first ten lines proprietarism primarily, whereas the Carthusians are the only Order for

---

[2] That Grote wrote *Ep.* 15 to Matthew is confirmed in the *incipit* in three manuscripts; the fact that these manuscripts belong to three different branches in the stemma gives the authenticity of the attribution greater weight. In what follows, I present an abbreviated version of HOFMAN, 'Recipients' (in print), section 3.

[3] Cfr MULDER, *Epp.*, p. xxxi; 119-121; TIECKE, *Werken*, p. 113-114; VAN ZIJL, *Gerard Groote*, p. 220-222; RÜTHING, 'Briefe', p. 400-402; ÉPINEY-BURGARD, *Gérard Grote*, p. 209-210; VAN DIJK, *Prolegomena*, p. 507-508; VAN DIJK, 'Raadgevingen', p. 20-23; 40; POST, *Modern Devotion*, p. 73-74 also seems to take it for granted that Grote wrote *Ep.* 27 to Matthew.

[4] Cfr VAN DIJK, 'Raadgevingen', p. 20-23.

[5] Cfr H. J. J. SCHOLTENS, 'Necrologie van het Kartuizerconvent van Monnikhuizen', in *Archief voor de geschiedenis van het Aartsbisdom Utrecht*, 72.1-2 (1953), p. 90-124.

[6] Cfr Chr. DE BACKER, 'De kartuize Monichusen bij Arnhem. Prosopografie samen met de regesten van de zopas ontdekte oorkondenschat', in *Amo te, sacer ordo Carthusiensis. Jan De Grauwe, passionné de l'Ordre des Chartreux* – ed. F. Hendrickx – T. Gaens, Leuven, 2012, p. 132-204; Matthew cannot be identical with 'Matthias van Amsterdam', *ibid.*, p. 162, no. 199, as this Matthew died in 1479.

[7] Cfr for further substantiation of this allegation HOFMAN, 'Recipients'.

which there is no evidence for the occurrence of this vice in the fourteenth century,[8] precisely the Order also which Grote held in high esteem.[9] When we investigate the other letters written by Grote on proprietarism, all edited in this volume, we find that these are addressed not to Matthew, but to Cistercians, the single Order where proprietarism was especially widespread during the later Middle Ages:[10] *Ep.* 41; 44 have the abbot of the Cistercian monastery in Kamp-Lintfort as recipient, *Ep.* 42 the community under his guidance, *Ep.* 45 the abbess of the Cistercian nunnery Ter Hunnepe near Deventer, hierarchically dependent on Kamp, while finally the garbled collection of notes to a male monastic community which includes at least some individuals possessing private property (*Ep.* 46) seems written to Cistercians too.[11] Moreover, Grote advises his correspondent towards the end of the letter (l. 48-51) not to get involved in futile conversations with fellow monks, for instance during Mass or meals. It is hardly conceivable that he would give such advice to a newly entered Carthusian monk, as this Order was renowned for its strict observance of the oath of silence.[12] All of this suggests that *Ep.* 27 was not meant for a Carthusian at all,[13] and that a Cistercian is a much more likely candidate as recipient. In this context, however, it must be conceded that no Matthew from Tiel is attested or men-

---

[8] Cfr on the strict observance of the monastic vows among the Carthusians especially H. RÜTHING, 'Die Kartäuser und die spätmittelalterlichen Ordensreformen', in *Reformbemühungen und Observanzbestrebungen im spätmittelalterlichen Ordenswesen* – ed. K. Elm, Berlin, 1989, p. 35-58. In 1966 already, RÜTHING, 'Briefe', p. 402, fn. 46, observed that "[d]as Problem des Eigenbesitzes der Mönche ist jedoch in den niederländischen und deutschen Kartausen des 15. Jahrhunderts nie aktuell gewesen".

[9] GAENS, 'Carthusian influences', p. 58 and fn. 29, rightly quotes a remark from Grote's *Ep.* 69 (p. 269, 9 ed. Mulder), where he qualifies the Order as "ordinem tuum, pre ceteris commendatum". Cfr on Grote's esteem for the Carthusians further VAN DIJK, 'Raadgevingen', p. 20-23; ÉPINEY-BURGARD, *Gérard Grote*, p. 51-57.

[10] Cfr on the reluctant attitude towards attempts at reform among Cistercians ELM – FEIGE, 'Verfall'; ELM, 'Westfälisches Zisterziensertum'; ELM, 'Reformbemühungen'.

[11] Cfr for an analysis of these letters further below, Ch. X-XIII, and for the argumentation that *Ep.* 46 is also written to a community of Cistercians Ch. XIII.

[12] Cfr on this topic among many other publications e.g. T. PEETERS, *Gods eenzame zwijgers. De spirituele weg van de kartuizers*, Gent, 2007.

[13] Thus RÜTHING, 'Briefe', p. 402 fn. 46, already; cfr for a more elaborate argumentation HOFMAN, 'Recipients'.

tioned in the preserved *Statuta* of the general chapters of the Order of the Cistercians for the relevant period either.[14]

IX.3.1 MANUSCRIPTS USED FOR THE EDITION

One manuscript used for the edition of *Ep.* 27 (*L*) is described in greater detail in HOFMAN, *Focar.*, p. 135-138.[15]

B Basel, Universitätsbibliothek Basel, A X 92, s. xvb, Prov.: Basel, Margaretental (Carthusians), cfr VAN DIJK, *Prolegomena*, p. 123-125.

This octavo (140×105) paper manuscript seems a convolute, consisting of two parts.[16] The second part, encompassing f. 193-236, penned down in an experienced hand writing *cursiua libraria* script datable to s. xvb, contains on f. 205-221 two letters written by Florens Radewijns and seven letters written by Grote (*Epp.* 16; 8; 70; 62; 15; 27; 10), among them the extremely rare *Ep.* 8, preserved in the letter collections and this witness only.

D Darmstadt, Hessische Landes- und Hochschulbibliothek, 2276, c. a. 1500, Or., Prov.: Köln, St. Barbara (Carthusians), most probably transcribed from an exemplar kept in Koblenz, Beatusberg (Carthusians), cfr VAN DIJK, *Prolegomena*, p. 168-170.

This quarto (216×149) paper manuscript, described several times already,[17] is the *codex unicus* preserving Grote's *Epp.* 82, 83, 84

---

[14] As edited in *Statuta capitulorum generalium Ordinis Cisterciensis ab anno 1116 ad annum 1786* – ed. J. M. Canivez, T. 3. *Ab anno 1262 ad annum 1400*; T. 4. *Ab anno 1401 ad annum 1456*; T. 8. *Indices*, Louvain, 1935; 1936; 1941; for the relevant period, up to 1450, not a single Matthew is attested in the *Statutes*. It seems hardly relevant to consider entries for "Mat(t)heus" in the general index (T. 8, p. 327), as all manuscripts transmitting *Ep.* 15 consistently refer to "Mat(t)hias".

[15] Liège, Bibliothèque de l'Université, 229 (c), a. 1451, Or.: Namur, monastery of the Crutched Friars, Prov.: Liège, monastery of the Crutched Friars; I corrected my mistakes in that description in HOFMAN, 'Crutched Friars', p. 521-529, cfr also VAN DIJK, *Prolegomena*, p. 270-283.

[16] This seems the logical inference from the summary codicological description which was made available to our Institute by Dr. Martin Steinmann (Basel), to whom I am most grateful.

[17] The manuscript has been described by RÜTHING, 'Briefe', p. 393-395 (in the introduction to his *editio princeps* of *Epp.* 82-85), by R. B. MARKS, *The medieval manuscript library of the Charterhouse of St. Barbara in Cologne* (*Analecta cartusiana*, 21-22), Salzburg, 1974, p. 356-357, and by VAN DIJK, p. 168-170; my description here shows overlap with my brief discussion of this

CHAPTER IX 169

(and 85), but the same manuscript also transmits the text of *Epp*. 15 and 27, in a version related to, but somewhat further removed from that in the group of witnesses which can be linked to the Mainz charterhouse. As it turns out from Rüthing's description of the manuscript, its main contents consist in autograph notes and texts, written and collected in the third quarter of the fifteenth century by Henricus Dissen (1415-1485), who entered the Cologne charterhouse in 1437 and ultimately became *vicarius* in this house.[18] Dissen supplemented these autograph texts with transcripts of works of other authors, notably those of Heinrich Egher, who did his profession in the same house and died there in 1408 after a splendid career in the Order. Later on, the five letters written by Grote were together with Heinrich Egher's small *Libellus de continentiis et distinctione scientiarum*[19] inserted on folia which had accidentally remained empty in the original codex, written in somewhat careless *hybrida* (C/H) script in the hand of Gobelinus Laridius (†1556), around 1500, but necessarily after his profession in the Order in 1496.[20] Gobelinus was born at Fischenich near Cologne around 1476, joined the Order at St Barbara's in 1496, and later served as prior in Mainz and Freiburg, but he is especially renowned for his critical edition of the *Vulgate* from 1530.[21] The manuscript itself is one among many witnesses testifying to the efforts to assemble manuscripts for a new library, after a terrible fire had destroyed the entire library of the Cologne charterhouse on 6 November 1451.[22] In view of the attested philological ability of Gobelinus' work on his *Vulgate* edition, admittedly

---

witness in HOFMAN, 'Recipients' (in print); both MARKS, p. 418, and VAN DIJK, p. 417, list the same manuscript among the lost witnesses from the Cologne charterhouse, but neither of them realized that their 'lost' witness is identical with this extant one.

[18] On Dissen cfr further H. KNAUS, 'Dissen, Heinrich von', in *Neue Deutsche Biographie*, 3 (1957), p. 743-744.

[19] Cfr on this work RÜTHING, *Egher*, p. 76-82; it is extant in this witness only, and attested for lost manuscripts originally present in the charterhouses in Koblenz (autograph) and Mainz, and in the house of the religious community at Grüner Wörth in Strasbourg (also known as Gottesfreunde or Knights Hospitaller, cfr the description of *A below) only.

[20] Cfr on the further contents apart from VAN DIJK's *Prolegomena* the description of the manuscript as compiled by MARKS, p. 356-357.

[21] Cfr on Gobelinus and for an evaluation of his critical genius further MARKS (as above), p. 134-137.

[22] Cfr on this disaster and the efforts at quickly assembling an entirely new library collection MARKS, p. 8-12.

later on in his life, it comes somewhat as a surprise that it turns out on the basis of a full collation of *Ep.* 27 that *D* transmits a particularly untrustworthy version of this letter,[23] and that the same is true for the text of *Epp.* 15 and 85[24] as transmitted in *D* also. This sloppiness in texts which are known from other witnesses, combined with his philological talents, might alert us to the fact that Gobelinus may have had access to an inferior transcript of Grote's *Epp.* 82-85.

Very tentatively, an identification for the institution where this idiosyncratic collection originally came from might be suggested. In the *explicit* of Heinrich's *Libellus*, directly preceding the first letter by Grote, Gobelinus has noted that he found this text in an autograph copy in Heinrich's own hand, in his days preserved in the Koblenz charterhouse Beatusberg.[25] In the light of the known relations which Grote maintained with inhabitants of this house,[26] it might therefore perhaps be possible to link the subject matter dealt with in these letters with the house in Koblenz as well.

---

[23] This is apparent from the variants in the *app. crit.* to the edition below.

[24] A photograph of the text of *Ep.* 85, written down on f. 46v in the lost Magdeburg letter collection, is preserved in the so-called 'Brandsma collection' in the Titus Brandsma Instituut, Nijmegen. A comparison between the two witnesses reveals that the quality of the text in the Magdeburg copy (here: **M*) is better than that in *D*. In anticipation of a critical edition of *Ep.* 85 I note the following superior readings (reference is to ed. RÜTHING, 'Briefe', p. 406, with added line numbering): **1** scitis] **M, etiam *C*, sciatis *D*; **4** quod] *sec. Bibl. *M*, quam *D*; **6** meo] in *praem. *M, false*; **9-10** emptans] Rüthing, est potestas *sic D *M*; **10** aliqua nobis *tr. *M* (clearly better, cfr **11** fuerimus); **12** uiriliter] *D*, uniuersaliter **M, false*; **15** desperauerat] *D*, desperauerit **M* (clearly better, cfr **1** estimauerit); **16** loquor] loquar **M*; **16** tamen] *om. *M*. Cfr also the fn. to the description of witness **B* in section IX.3.2 below.

[25] "Iste libellus transcriptus [*sic* Ms., transsscriptus *Rüthing in 1967*] est ex primo originali et diligenter collacionatus ad idem originale quod scriptum erat manu propria huius ter quaterque beati et deuotissimi uiri Henrici Kalkar, et ipsum originale habetur in domo Confluencie", quoted in part by RÜTHING, 'Briefe', p. 396, and in full in RÜTHING, *Egher*, p. 76 fn. 2. When we realize that the *incipit* of the first letter written by Grote occurs in the next line in the manuscript, we might perhaps interpret the words "in tali loco" in this *incipit* ("Epistola magistri Gerardi groett dauentriensis pro duobus juuenibus ad fratres Carthusienses in tali loco") as referring to directly precding "in domo Confluencie".

[26] Cfr on this further HOFMAN, 'Recipients' (in print), and more elaborately H. J. J. SCHOLTENS, 'Hendrik van Eger uit Kalkar en zijn kring', in *Dr. L. Reypens-album. Opstellen aangeboden aan Prof. Dr. L. Reypens s.j. ter gelegenheid van zijn tachtigste verjaardag op 26 februari 1964* – ed. A. Ampe, Antwerpen, 1964, p. 383-408, at p. 391-393.

CHAPTER IX 171

W Hannover, Niedersächsische Landesbibliothek Hannover, XIII 859 (olim Cod. lat. 508), c. a. 1440, Prov.: Wittenburg near Elze, St. Maria (Windesheim Regular Canons), cfr VAN DIJK, *Prolegomena*, p. 211-213.

Manuscript *W* is a convolute, consisting of two parts. The earlier part, f. 1-104; 164-181, contains historical material, in part autograph copies of historical texts and fragments assembled and written by the Windesheim chronicler Theodoricus Engelhus (†1434), in part material assembled at his request by others and annotated by him; this material is dated between 1419 and his death in 1434, in the Windesheim monastery Wittenberg at Elze near Hildesheim to the South of Hannover.

Shortly after the death of Engelhus, his historical work was bound together with five quires (f. 105-163, $1^{14+1}\ 2^{12}\ 3^{8}\ 4^{12+1}\ 5^{12-1}$),[27] containing original, contemporary foliation (f. 16-34) in quires 2-3. This confirms that these five quires, although written by various hands, originally formed a coherent set of texts. The text of the nine letters, or excerpts from letters,[28] by Grote transmitted in the first quire in *W* has been written in a single hand, writing expert *cursiua libraria* (almost *cursiua formata*) script datable to s. xvb, on a quire which can be dated to c. 1440 on the basis of its watermark.

M4 Mainz, Stadtbibliothek, I 349, s. XIVd, Prov.: Mainz, St. Michael (Carthusians), cfr VAN DIJK, *Prolegomena*, p. 312-313.[29]

---

[27] I suggest for the first quire a septernion 1^{14+1}, rather than 1^{16-1}, as in Härtel's description in the catalogue, on the basis of a note in the rubricator's hand in the *explicit* of *Ep.* 57 on f. 119v, the last folium of the quire: "Testimonium Cantoris parysiensis de eodem magistro Gherardo. Require supra proximo in cedula interposita", a reference to the text of *Ep.* 65, written in an empty space after the end of *Ep.* 70 on f. 113r in a different hand, necessarily before the rubricator finished his job.

[28] *Epp.* 66 (excerpt of a few lines, p. 266, 9-18 ed. Mulder); 22 (excerpt of a few lines, p. 98, 16-20 ed. Mulder); 70 (full text); [65, in a different hand on space left empty earlier, cfr previous fn., full text]; 62 (full text); 27 (l. 3-58, introductory and concluding sentences missing); 56 (fragmentary, transmits p. 212, 1-13; 212, 18 – 213, 4; 213, 12 – end, ed. Mulder; the rubric, "Ex epistola ad quendam clericum nomine Bertoldum", reveals that the text was complete in the exemplar); 24 (excerpt, p. 108, 10-29 ed. Mulder); 57 (full text)).

[29] The scientific description of this manuscript by G. LIST, *Die Handschriften der Stadtbibliothek Mainz*, Bd. 3. *Hs I 251 – Hs I 350*, Wiesbaden, 2006, p. 354-358, was not available to Father van Dijk; his observations should therefore be checked against those in this catalogue. Quite inadvertently,

172 INTRODUCTION

This octavo (135×100) manuscript is a convolute, consisting of six codicological units of varying date and antiquity, evidently put together after the confection of the most recent unit, which was written in the first quarter of the sixteenth century by the scribe who also compiled the second catalogue of the Mainz Charterhouse around 1520.[30] It seems plausible to suggest that this librarian put together all six units in their present flexible limp binding, as the contents of the actual manuscript are not listed in the first catalogue compiled c. 1466×1470.

The Grote texts on f. 173r-181v (*Epp.* 15; 27; 41) are the sole contents of the sixth and final unit, a single vellum quinio (15^{10}), of which the last folium (f. 182) has remained empty. They have been written by a single hand, writing somewhat careless *cursiua* script, datable to s. XIVd, necessarily after Grote's death in 1384.

IX.3.2 OTHER MANUSCRIPT WITNESSES

One manuscript not used for the edition of *Ep.* 27 (letter collection *H2*) is described in greater detail above, in Ch. III.2.[31]

B2 Basel, Universitätsbibliothek Basel, A X 47, s. XVd (after 1496), Or., Prov.: Basel, Margaretental (Carthusians), cfr VAN DIJK, *Prolegomena*, p. 122-123.

I had originally devised the sigla *Ma1 Ma2 Ma3* for the witnesses from the Mainz charterhouse preserved in the Stadtbibliothek Mainz with the signatures I 349, I 149 and I 137 respectively. However, after Dr. Annelen Ottermann (Stellvertretende Amtsleiterin, Wissenschaftliche Stadtbibliothek, Mainz, to whom I am most grateful) had observed that I use two different sigla in my description of ms. Mainz, SB, I 454 in HOFMAN, *Focar.*, p. 186-187; 240-241 (cfr p. 247-248) and had very kindly pointed out the inconssitency of using different sigla for the same witness, I decided to distinguish more clearly and consistently in my references to manuscripts preserved in this collection.

[30] Cfr for a description of the two catalogues of the Charterhouse, still preserved in Mss. Mainz, SB, I 577 (the older catalogue, datable to 1466×1470) and I 576 (the younger catalogue, datable to c. 1520) G. LIST – G. POWITZ, *Die Handschriften der Stadtbibliothek Mainz*, Bd. 1. *Hs I 1 – Hs I 150*, Wiesbaden, 1990, p. 10-14. Indispensible for any study of the library is H. SCHREIBER, *Die Bibliothek der ehemaligen Mainzer Kartause. Die Handschriften und ihre Geschichte (Zentralblatt für Bibliothekswesen, Beiheft 60)*, Leipzig, 1927.

[31] Den Haag, Koninklijke Bibliotheek, 78 J 55, s. XVa, f. 113-260 of f. 1-262, Prov.: Liège, Saint-Jacques (Benedictines), cfr VAN DIJK, *Prolegomena*, p. 190-203.

CHAPTER IX 173

The text in this quarto (215×145-150) paper manuscript occurs in a convolute, consisting of seven different parts, in the sixth part (f. 104-128), which has been written in the hand of Jakob Louber (1440-1513), from 1480 until 1501 prior of the Basel Carthusian monastery Margaretental, who also bound the constituent parts of the convolute around 1500. In the quires in which the fragment from Grote has been penned down, Louber has assembled autograph copies of various of the sermons he had preached in the preceding decades. The most recent sermon is dated to 1496, which therefore is the *terminus post quem* for the collection. Louber writes careless *hybrida* script in this undoubtedly personal collection.

The eight manuscript lines of the fragment consist of a few excerpts culled from *Ep.* 27, starting with l. 27 "numquam moneatis" and ending with 37 "rancor suboritur" (for "...rancorem forte accipiunt", *cett. codd.*). In view of the smallness of the excerpt, it is hardly possible to suggest a sensible place in the stemma. The fragment, however, does not share the variants transmitted in l. 27-37 in manuscripts *LM4*,[32] which suggests that neither *L* nor the witnesses in subgroup *Ma* have served as its exemplar. Considering that *B2* shares its provenance from the Basel charterhouse with *B*, it seems reasonable to suggest that the scribe Jac. Louber culled his excerpt from that witness. However, since *B* has not any variant in this section of the text, this cannot be proved beyond doubt.

E Emmerich, Stadtarchiv, 13 (olim 5), s. xvd (after 1470), Or., Prov.: Emmerich, Brethren of the Common Life, cfr VAN DIJK, *Prolegomena*, p. 177-179.

All texts in *E* have been written in a single hand, writing *hybrida formata* script which almost resembles *textualis* in its perfection and layout, and which is therefore very difficult to date. The most recent text penned down by this hand is a letter written by Joh. Brugman to Petrus Horn, inhabitant of the Heer-Florenshuis in Deventer, and written in November 1470. The confection of the manuscript as a whole therefore postdates 1470. On f. 37-51, the manuscript transmits six of Grote's letters (*Epp.* 29; 56; 15; 27; 16; 62), all of them in full, except for *Ep.* 27, of which the first

---

[32] Cfr the *app. crit.* for these variants.

eleven lines only are written down on f. 46v-47r, unfortunately without any variants. The manuscript therefore cannot be accorded a place in the stemma.[33]

K Köln, Historisches Archiv der Stadt Köln, GB 8° 60, s. XVb, cfr VAN DIJK, *Prolegomena*, p. 232-233.

The octavo (145×105) paper manuscript *K* is a convolute, consisting of two parts; both parts are *rapiaria*, assembling excerpts and fragments which struck their collectors as useful for their spiritual growth. The first part (f. 1-126) opens in its first quire (1¹⁰) with three texts from Grote's *Letters*, the full text of *Ep.* 16 preceded by *Ep.* 15 and followed by a small fragment from *Ep.* 27 (l. 3-10 "Sciendum – sunt"), written in *cursiua libraria* script datable to s. XVb, resembling Conrad Scheych's hand, but in details differing from his autographs.[34] The fragment transmits two variants,[35] but unfortunately cannot be assigned a place in the stemma.

M5 Mainz, Stadtbibliothek, I 149 (olim 244), s. XVa (after 1408), Or., Prov.: Mainz, St. Michael (Carthusians), cfr van Dijk, *Prolegomena*, p. 303-305.

This quarto (215×145) paper manuscript, together with *M4* discovered by Mrs. Épiney-Burgard,[36] is a convolute, in which two originally distinct codicological units have been bound together. The first part (f. 1-163) has been written in a single hand writing expert *cursiua libraria* script datable to the first quarter of the fifteenth century. The contents of the codex can best be characterized as a collection of texts and fragments obviously selected because of their usefulness to help its compiler in his spiritual growth. The scribe seems to have exploited various other manuscripts available in the Mainz Carthusian monastery already. Thus,

---

[33] Collation of *Ep.* 15 unfortunately did not help either: the single possible observation is that where there are variants shared with other witnesses, *E* agrees with the independent small collections against the formal *corpora epistolarum*.

[34] Cfr for an analysis of Conrad's script esp. SCHÖLER, "*Ama nesciri*", p. 41-62. Most notably, Conrad invariably writes the abbreviation for "et" as a "ɀ" with a stroke, whereas the hand in *K* writes the same abbreviation "ɀ" without stroke.

[35] 4 trahencia *K*; 9 temptatorum] temptatores *K*.

[36] Cfr ÉPINEY-BURGARD, *Gérard Grote*, p. 317-318.

CHAPTER IX 175

the collection of excerpts on f. 2-71; 73-74 coincides in its entirety exactly with much of the excerpts in the second codicological unit (f. 22-64) of the folio convolute manuscript Mainz, SB, I 23, datable to s. XIV$^{ex.}$, but the scribe of our manuscript has arranged many of the constituent parts in a different order.[37] This fact alone proves beyond doubt that much of our manuscript originated in the Mainz Charterhouse. In addition, our scribe selected other texts (f. 74-163), which include on f. 81v-82v; 97r-120v a fairly great number of letters written by Grote's friend and mentor Heinrich Egher of Kalkar.[38] After that he included at the end of his collection eight letters written by Grote, on the actual f. 152r-159v (*Epp.* 70; 10; 16; 62; 15; 27; 41; 29, interrupted by a selection of quotations from St Bernard between *Epp.* 27 and 41). Several of these letters are at present fragmentary, due to loss of several folia,[39] but since the text is present in *A*, which has been transcribed from *M5*,[40] these missing folia obviously must have been present in our witness in the (early?) fifteenth century. The text of

---

[37] This is clear from the analysis presented in G. LIST – G. POWITZ, *Die Handschriften der Stadtbibliothek Mainz*, Bd. 1. *Hs I 1 – Hs I 150*, Wiesbaden, 1990, p. 55-58; 273-274. The earlier manuscript has an ownership notice "Iste liber pertinet ad domum montis sancti Michaelis prope mogunciam ord. carth.", entered on the first folium (f. 22r) of the codicological unit f. 22-64.

[38] Cfr on Heinrich esp. RÜTHING, *Egher*, on his relationship with Grote also e.g. ÉPINEY-BURGARD, *Gérard Grote*, p. 39-41.

[39] A single folium, 152, contains a small part of *Ep.* 70, acephalous (l. 291, 14-30 + 293, 1-20 ed. Mulder; the text is continuous, Mulder prints a Middle Dutch version on the even pages for this letter), *Ep.* 10 in full, and the beginning of *Ep.* 16 (l. 52, 1 – 53, 15 ed. Mulder). This means that from *Ep.* 70 a portion of text equivalent to three folia in witness *H2*, a quarto manuscript like *M5*, is missing, and that the same amount of text is missing from *Ep.* 16 (53, 15 – 57, 21 ed. Mulder) and *Ep.* 62 (l. 232, 1-10 ed. Mulder), roughly equivalent to 2,5 + 0,5 f. in *H2*. On the basis of this equivalence it seems reasonable to suppose that three folia before f. 152, and three further folia after f. 152, have been lost from *M5* after *A* had been copied from this witness. Unfortunately, the original make-up of the quires of this witness can no longer be reconstructed since its restoration in 1968. Dr. A. Otterman, Stellvertretende Amtsleiterin, Wissenschaftliche Stadtbibliothek, Mainz, to whom I am most grateful, very kindly, but in the end to no avail, checked this make-up for me. In an e-mail message dated 7 April 2016 she observes: "Die Handschrift wurde 1968, zu einer Zeit also, in der man die heute standardisierte minimalinvasive Restaurierung noch nicht kannte, "restauriert". Der Buchblock wurde dabei komplett neu geheftet, erhielt einen neuen Einband und ist so eng gebunden, dass man unmöglich mehr den Verlauf der Heftfäden sehen kann. Zudem müssen diese nicht der originalen Situation entsprechen".

[40] Cfr for this the argumentation in section X.4 below.

Epp. 15; 27; 41 in *M5* has been transcribed from *M4* (described above, in section IX.3.1), as will be substantiated below, in section X.4. The collection ends with an anonymous letter, which its author finished in Heidelberg on 20 October 1408, according to the colophon.[41]

*A Strasbourg, Bibliothèque municipale, olim [660] D 108, Prov. (Or.?): Strasbourg, Grüner Wörth (Knights Hospitaller), cfr VAN DIJK, *Prolegomena*, p. 401-402.

The text of eight letters written by Grote,[42] among them *Epp.* 27 and 41, has been printed by De Ram in 1861 on the basis of a now lost manuscript formerly kept in the municipal library in Strasbourg, which was destroyed in 1870 during hostilities in the Prussian-French war. As De Ram explains in his introduction, he based his edition on a collation made at his request by André Jung (1793-1863), in those days librarian in Strasbourg, or one of his assistants,[43] after he had visited the library in 1829. De Ram's description of the manuscript is not in accordance with modern standards, as he nowhere gives any indication about the material, age, codicology or provenance of his witness. However, he does provide a list of contents of both witnesses used for his edition, which he gave the sigla *A* and *B* (here: **A* and **B*). These contents coincide exactly with the description of two codices in the catalogue of the collection of the religious (or: mystic) community at the Grüner Wörth just inside the main extension to the city walls of Strasbourg, founded in 1366-67. It had taken the form of a commandery of Knights Hospitaller with an extensive body of lay

---

[41] "...Amen. Mementote mei, fratres in Christo, me uestris orationibus inscriptum habete. Scriptum Heidelberge 1408 in uigilia undecim milium uirginum [= 20 October]".

[42] **A* contained Grote's *Epp.* 70; 10; 16; 62; 15; 27; 41; 29, i.e. the same eight letters in the same sequence as in *M5*; cfr for the manuscript and its history also HOFMAN, 'Recipients' (in print).

[43] "...eo tunc tempore [*sc.* in 1829] impetraueram a uiro cl. Jung, bibliothecae praefecto, ut describerentur epistolae illae, quarum quidem exemplar iam ab annis nimium multis in nostris scriniis latitant...", writes F.-X. DE RAM, 'Venerabilis Gerardi Magni de Dauentria epistolae VIII ex duobus codicibus MSS. bibliothecae publicae Argentoracensis', *Compte Rendu des séances de la Commission Royale d'Histoire ou Recueil de ses Bulletins*, 3ᵉ Sér., T. 2, Bruxelles, 1861, p. 66-110, at p. 66. Cfr on Jung *Dictionnaire du monde religieux dans la France contemporaine.* 5. *Les protestants*, Paris, 1993, p. 271-272.

CHAPTER IX 177

associates since 1371, after negotiations between its founding father, the rich banker and lay mystic Rulman Merswin, with Fr. Konrad von Braunsberg, then Prior of the German branch of the Hospitallers.[44] Since autopsy of the manuscript was not possible, variants deduced from De Ram's edition are listed with the asterixed siglum *A.

*B Strasbourg, Bibliothèque municipale, olim D 107, (Or.?), Prov.: Strasbourg, Grüner Wörth (Knights Hospitaller), cfr VAN DIJK, *Prolegomena*, p. 402.

In Strasbourg, De Ram had had access to a second manuscript, transmitting a selection of the letters of Grote as preserved in *A (*Epp.* 15; 62; 27; 16; 70).[45] His description of this second witness, which he gave the siglum B, is even shorter than the one of *A, but from his list of contents it is clear that this witness can be identified with manuscript D 107 in Witter's catalogue of the collection of the religious community at the Grüner Wörth in Strasbourg.[46] From the summary list of contents given by both Witter and De Ram, it seems possible to surmise that the scribe of this second witness combined items which for some reason seemed attractive to him from the texts present in *A with additional material.

---

[44] Cfr J. J. WITTER, *Catalogus Codicum Manuscriptorum, In Bibliotheca Sacri Ordinis Hierosolymitani Argentorati Asservatorum*, Strasbourg, 1746, p. 49-50, available online at the Bayerische Staatsbibliothek, München, through the link http://reader.digitale-sammlungen.de/de/fs1/object/display/bsb11054632_00005.html. Compare De Ram, p. 67-69, with Witter, p. 49-50, where *A = D 108, and *B = D. 107, and cfr further HOFMAN, 'Recipients' (in print). Stephen Mossman is currently preparing a monograph on the Grüner Wörth with as provisional title: *Rulman Merswin and His Age: The Literary Spirituality of the Strasbourg Hospitallers and the Late Medieval Rhineland*; cfr for the moment K. BORCHARDT, 'Hospitallers, mysticism and reform in late-medieval Strasburg', in *The military orders*, Vol. 3. *History and heritage* – ed. V. Mallia-Milanes, Aldershot, 2008, p. 73-79. I am most grateful to Stephen Mossman for information on the community of the Knights Hospitaller in Strasbourg.

[45] In his introductory section, De Ram states that his manuscript *B (D 107) transmits *Epp.* 15; 62; 27; 16 only, but in his footnotes he gives variants from *B for *Ep.* 70 also; since he continuously reiterates the same sequence of letters, both in his introduction and in his first footnote accompanying each letter, we must apparently conclude that *Ep.* 70 was the last Grote text transmitted through *B.

[46] Cfr the description of the preceding witness *A, and further HOFMAN, 'Recipients' (in print).

A third manuscript kept in Strasbourg and containing *Epp.* 70; 15; 85; 27 escaped De Ram's attention in 1829, but in the preface to his 1861 edition he writes that it became known to him later on, as it is mentioned by Acquoy in the preface to his 1857 edition.[47]

R Wien, Österreichische Nationalbibliothek, 15228, s. xvd, Or. (?), Prov.: Roermond, Bethlehem (Carthusians), cfr VAN DIJK, *Prolegomena*, p. 376-378.

This quarto (212×142) paper manuscript is a convolute, in which three different parts have been bound together; the greatest notoriety has befallen the last part, f. 108-220, which contains Hendrik Herp's Middle Dutch *Spieghel der Volcomenheit*. Three of Grote's letters (*Epp.* 16 (fragment); 27; 62) occur on f. 34r-40r, all three written by a single well trained hand in *hybrida* script datable to the earlier part of s. xvd, perhaps to the later half of s. xvc. They have been written in the second codicological unit (f. 5-107), in which three different hands worked together closely and alternated with one another. Another fragment, also culled from *Ep.* 16, occurs in the first codicological unit (f. 1-4) on f. 3r. The quality of

---

[47] In the preface to his edition (*Epistolae*, p. 12), Acquoy writes that he was aware of the existence of a third ms. from Strasbourg thanks to a communication by Delprat, in the mid-nineteenth century a leading expert on the Modern Devotion, who in turn knew about its existence through a letter sent him by Jung: "Sed ecce nouum indicem, cui iuuat per beneuolentiam nostratis Delprat, uiri de omnibus quae ad Gerardum Magnum fratresque uitae communis spectant meritissimi, addere posse epistolas, quas in tribus codicibus habet Bibliotheca publica Argentorati, quasque priuatis litteris ei indicauit V. Cl. Jung, Bibliothecae illius praefectus" (ACQUOY, p. 12). Acquoy may have decided to get in touch with Delprat after he had read a remark occurring in the first edition of G. H. M. DELPRAT, *Verhandeling over de Broederschap van G. Groote, en over den invloed der Fraterhuizen op den wetenschappelijken en godsdienstigen toestand voornamelijk van de Nederlanden, na de XIV. eeuw* (*Nieuwe verhandelingen van het Provinciaal Utrechtsch Genootschap van Kunsten en Wetenschappen*, 7.5), Utrecht, 1830, p. 273: "Onderscheidene Brieven van G. Groote worden in H.S. bewaard in de Bibliotheek te Straatsburg. Vergelijk Biographie univ. l.l. p. 175", a remark which Delprat omitted at the parallel place in his second, 1856 edition, p. 348. The contents of this third codex (viz. *Epp.* 70; 15; 85; 27) are listed in ACQUOY, *Epistolae*, p. 17. The presence of *Ep.* 85 proves that this codex is independent from the two other ones, as this rare letter is missing in *L H2* and is attested twice only, in the lost Magdeburg collected letters (f. 46v, cfr VAN DIJK, *Prolegomena*, p. 293, Werk 36) and in the Darmstadt manuscript used by Rüthing: cfr VAN DIJK, *Prolegomena*, p. 551-553. Cfr also the description of witness *D* in section IX.3.1 above, and HOFMAN, 'Recipients' (in print).

CHAPTER IX   179

Ep. 27 in this witness is definitely inferior, and the manuscript has therefore not been used for the edition.

IX.4 RELATIONS AMONG THE MANUSCRIPTS

Ep. 27 is transmitted in full or almost in full in ten witnesses, of which eight still survive, fragmentarily in three other ones (*B2* (l. 27-37, abbreviated) *K* (l. 3-10) *E* (l. 1-11), cfr also section IX.3.2 above), and attested for the 3rd 'corpus epistolarum' and the 3rd 'Strasbourg codex *C'. Unfortunately, only the witnesses transmitting the full contents of the letter can be assigned a certain place in the stemma, in part with the help of evidence culled from *Ep.* 15 and in a few cases *Ep.* 10.[48]

As in the case of *Ep.* 41, the lost first Strasbourg manuscript *A has all variants present in *M5*, which in its turn has all those transmitted in the earlier witness *M4*; for *Ep.* 27, De Ram also collated the text in the second lost Strasbourg manuscript *B, printing deviations of *B from *A in footnotes. On the basis of his collation, we can conclude that this second witness was copied from *A. Variants shared by all four witnesses prove that they belong together closely.[49] Moreover, *A M5 together have additional variants not present in *M4*,[50] and *A (as well as, presumably, *B) yet more variants, present neither in *M4* nor in *M5*.[51] This observation suggests that *A has been copied from *M5*, which in turn has been copied from *M4*. On the authority of De Ram, we may assume that the copy in the second lost Strasbourg manuscript *B has all variants present in *A as well as some additional ones, among them

---

[48] This evidence is presented more fully in HOFMAN, 'Recipients'.

[49] The most conspicuous ones are 34 et – plurimum] *om. M4 M5 *A *B*; 59-60 Valete – eum] *om. M4 M5 *A *B*.

[50] Cfr among many more minor (and in the case of *A sometimes uncertain) variants e.g. 6 temptaciones non sunt] *M4 cett.*, non sunt temptaciones *tr. M5 *A*; 14 uobis erit] *M4 cett.*, erit uobis *tr. M5 *A*.

[51] A clear example proving this occurs in the very beginning of the letter, where the introductory section has been abbreviated in the same manner in all three witnesses, with two additional variants in *A: 1-2 Frater et socie in Christo Ihesu predilecte, recepi litteras uestras in mense decembri. Valde est secundum cor meum quod estis professus] *cett.*, Recepi litteras ⟨et cetera *add. *A*⟩. Insuper ualde est secundum meum cor (*thus switched in M4 M5, switched again into* cor meum *in *A*) quod estis professus *M4 M5 *A*; other proof for further variants in *A: 3 Sciendum *M4 M5 cett.*, Scientes *A*; 45 miser] *hab. M4 M5 cett., om. *A *B*.

17 superius positus *M4M5cett.*, superus (?) prepositus **A*, supremus prepositus **B*, which proves sufficiently convincingly that **B* depends on **A*.

Several shared variants further prove that other witnesses having their provenance (or origin) in 'Carthusian' monasteries belong in the same branch of the stemma. These include an inferior subj. form "habeant" for "habent" in l. 12, transmitted in *RDBM4* (representing *M5*A*B*), and caused by the preceding subj. form 11 "moueat"; this latter form is adhortative, whereas the phrase containing "habent" relates plain fact: the indicative mode is therefore clearly to be preferred here.[52]

From the *app. cr.* it becomes at once apparent that *L* as well as *W* have many idiosyncratic variants, proving that these witnesses represent separate branches in the stemma. *E* does not transmit any convincing variant for *Ep.* 27, but for *Ep.* 15 this witness as well as *K* (fragmentary for *Ep.* 27) have several variants occuring nowhere else,[53] showing that these witnesses represent separate branches also. This leads to the following full stemma, with underlining for the manuscripts used for the edition:

---

[52] Another variant confirming this interrelationship is: 15 ne] non *RBM4*: "ne" is the proper form in this Biblical quotation.

[53] References are to added line numbers in ed. Mulder, 1933, p. 50-51: 2 tue] *om. K*; 14-15 tamquam] non *add. K*, homines *add. E*; 15 nec] tamen *add. E*; 18 temptacionem] temptaciones *K*; 34 uult hic suos *tr. K*; 35 suggestionibus] tribulari et probare *add. K, om. cett.*

CHAPTER IX

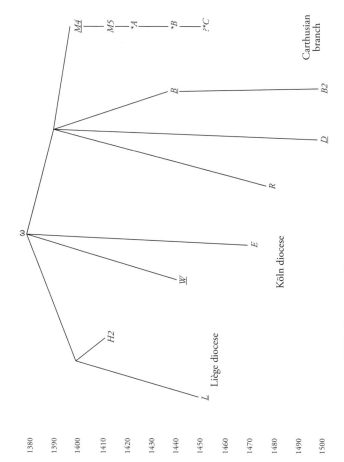

CHAPTER X

A LETTER ABOUT PROPRIETARISM, WRITTEN TO THE ABBOT OF THE CISTERCIAN ABBEY IN KAMP-LINTFORT (*EP.* 41)

X.1 SUMMARY OF CONTENTS

A summary of *Ep.* 41, written in November 1382 by Grote to William II of Cologne, the recently elected new abbot of the Cistercian abbey near Kamp-Lintfort in the Niederrhein region, must necessarily depart from the detailed analysis published by R. van Dijk in 2013.[1] Grote starts his letter by congratulating the abbot with his election by his community (1-3). On the basis of his former acquaintance with him,[2] Grote is sure that William will energetically take in hand the reform in the abbey near Kamp (the 'head') and in the thirty abbeys dependent on the paternity of the main convent Kamp (the 'members') (3-24).[3] The most important abuse, which should get priority in reform attempts as it is so strikingly in contrast with the very essence of one of the main monastic ideals, poverty (43-49), is personal property among conventuals, especially in the female houses, and most notably in the female convent Ter Hunnepe near Deventer (25-62, cfr 182-206 on Ter Hunnepe). William should take firm action against this evil,

---

[1] Cfr VAN DIJK, 'Kartuizers', on *Epp.* 41 and 42. The two letters are summarized *ibid.*, p. 133-139; 143-144, and translated into Dutch on the basis of Mulder's 1933 edition *ibid.*, p. 147-161. Cfr for shorter summaries ÉPINEY-BURGARD, *Gérard Grote*, p. 214-215 and VAN ZIJL, *Gerard Groote*, p. 220-224, as well as from a slightly different perspective POST, *Modern Devotion*, p. 70-72.

[2] The intimate manner of formulating in this section and the allusions to longer acquaintance evidently suggest that Grote and William knew each other well. However, it can yet not be maintained that this friendship dated back to a period of joint studies in Paris, as not a single William from the diocese of Cologne is mentioned anywhere in the indices in COURTENAY, *Rotuli*, Vol. 2, as resident in Paris in the years in which Grote lived there, except possibly for William de Wese, who applied for a prebend in 1353, when Grote had not yet arrived in Paris.

[3] Cfr for an enumeration of the six male and 24 female subordinate abbeys VAN DIJK, 'Tussen kartuizers', p. 132-133 and fnn. 30-32, where van Dijk summarizes M. DICKS, *Die Abtei Camp am Niederrhein. Geschichte des ersten Cistercienserklosters in Deutschland (1123-1802)*, Kempen, 1913, p. 310-313.

CHAPTER X 183

differentiating between *proprietarii* who are willing to mend their ways (who should be approached kindly) and stubbornly persevering ones (who should be persecuted severely) (63-82).

After that Grote sets out that proprietarism should be discouraged for ten different reasons. It leads to disturbed mutual relationships (83-88), whereas lack of personal belongings increases concern for the community (89-105). Also, people who already possess personal property more easily claim joint possessions for themselves (106-111), thus creating mutual jealousy (112-119) and an acute sense of inequality (120-129) among the members of a community.[4] Proprietarists are also prone to reserve external donations to the community for themselves and to negotiate with and in the world, thereby infecting other members of the community (130-143). This leads to diminishing gifts from worldly benefactors, and even to appropriation of monastic property by worldly rulers (144-152). Grote contrasts such developments with the much more sympathetic and benevolent attitude of worldly parties towards several orders which have been reformed already (153-160). As a consequence, families debar their professed relatives from their rightful share in an inheritance, or they place handicapped ones in a monastery (161-181). Grote illustrates this with an example which he had recently encountered in the female abbey Ter Hunnepe near Deventer, against regulations set out in a recent bull issued by Pope Urban V (1362-1370) in 1363 (182-193). Most unfortunately, this has led to the undesirable practice that rich but unsuitable candidates are accepted for entry in a community, whereas suitable ones are refused because they are poor, a subject which Grote has elaborated in greater detail in *Simonia beg.*, 191-490 (194-206).

After this long foundation of his arguments, Grote repeats his plea to William to end proprietarism, pointing out the many ad-

---

[4] I hesitated whether emendation of the text is called for in this section, but finally decided not to intervene in the text as transmitted in all witnesses. In l. 125-129, Grote opposes monks disposing of personal wealth to those lacking such personal property, in a series of six successive characterizations. In accordance with standard use, he starts referring to monks behaving reprehensibly with the deictic demonstrative pronoun "iste", using "ille" for commendable poor monks. In the third element of the series, however, he paraphrases *I Cor.* 11, 21, using "iste" for the commendable monk and "ille" for the reprehensible one; after this, he continues in the next three opposite clauses with such grammatically unsound references.

vantages of such an attitude in this world and hereafter (207-225). In the final section of his letter, he urges William that there is no middle course in this matter (226-231), and that he should focus on God's rewards while coming to his decisions, adding many diverse *loci* from the Bible, God's own word, most notably an apt long quotation from Ezechiel (*Ez.* 34, 2-4) (231-244). Also, he should first seek collaboration among sympathetic members of his monastic family, and take action against defiant ones only after that (245-253).

X.2 EDITORIAL HISTORY, SUPPLEMENT

A small collection of letters, among them *Ep*. 41, was for the first time printed by De Ram in 1861, on the basis of the inferior witness *A, until its destruction in 1870 during the Prussian-French war kept in the municipal library in Strasbourg. For several of the other letters in the collection he had access to another witness also then kept in Strasbourg, which he gave the siglum *B* (here *B, because of its destruction) and from which he culled variants reported in the notes to his *editio princeps*.[5] Mulder re-edited *Ep*. 41 in his 1933 edition, allegedly on the basis of *H2* (*L*).

In the preface to his 1933 edition, Mulder wrote that he had in general followed the text as transmitted by *H2*, but that he had occasionally preferred superior readings from other witnesses, sometimes justified in notes, but sometimes adopted silently.[6] Quite to my surprise, I found in the version transmitted by *A (as well as by *M4M5*) as printed by De Ram a number of variants which Mulder has adopted in his 1933 edition, but which are transmitted neither in *H2H1* nor in *L*. Among these variants are readings which are evidently less accurate than the one's transmitted in *H2L*.[7] Apparently, therefore, Mulder basically reprinted

---

[5] Cfr on the Strasbourg manuscripts further above, section IX.3, sub *A *B.
[6] "Textum haganum [*sc. H2*] imprimendum curaui, cui quae praestantiora in textu leodiensi [*sc. L*] aliisque codicibus quos conferre licebat leguntur, inserui. Ceteroquin, si inscriptiones epistolarum excipias, tantillum inter se textus differunt, ut superfluum iudicarim discrepantiarum semper rationem reddere, ne frusta annotationum cresceret numerus et taedium", GER. MAG., *Epp*., p. xx, cfr on Mulder's own qualms about his editorial work VAN DIJK, *Prolegomena*, p. 103-105.
[7] Especially garbled is Mulder's rendering of manuscript readings in l. 39, where he prints a reading disputauerunt] '*Ita H1, H2 et LU1. An legendum cum*

De Ram's text, modifying it without too much care on the basis of *H2*, and occasionally *L* also, when confronted with impossible sentences or constructions transmitted in **A*. His deviations from De Ram's text are sometimes accounted for in the notes, but more often this is not the case. Further, I failed to see a connection between *Epp.* 41 and 42, cfr for a motivation below, section XI.2

X.3 THE MANUSCRIPTS

Except for *Z*, all manuscripts transmitting *Ep.* 41 are described in greater detail elsewhere; cfr HOFMAN, *Focar.*, p. 135-138 for *L*,[8] Ch. III.2 above for *H2H1*,[9] Ch. IX.3.1 above for *M4*,[10] Ch. IX.3.2 above for *M5*[11] **A*[12] **B*.[13]

Z Wolfenbüttel, Herzog August Bibliothek, 314 Gud. Lat. 4°, s. XVa, 35 f., Prov.: unknown, cfr VAN DIJK, *Prolegomena*, p. 381.

The text of *Ep.* 41 in this small quarto (185×130) vellum manuscript, on f. 32-35, occurs in a small collection consisting of 35 folia, written in three hands, all of them writing *cursiua libraria* script datable to s. XVa. It transmits as its main contents three treatises by Grote, supplemented by short notes mostly: *Paup.* occurs

---

de Ram "deputauerunt" ', which is not extant in any of the codd.: **39** disputarunt] *sic L H2 H1*, deputauerunt *M4 M5 *A*, deputarunt *Z*; another case of misrepresentation of most manuscript readings is **78** ducibilibus *L Z*, dulcibilibus *H2 M4*, du[l]cibilibus *corr. c. punct. del. M5*, dulcibus *H1 *A*; where Mulder has as comment: "ducibilibus] *'Ita LU1.; H1 et H2 de Ram: "dulcibilibus"* '; cfr also Mulder's unfortunate preference for "nam" where "iam" is much more elegant: **50** iam] *sic L H2 H1 M4 Z*, nam *M5 *A*.

[8] Liège, Bibliothèque de l'Université, 229 (c), a. 1451, Or.: Namur, monastery of the Crutched Friars, Prov.: Liège, monastery of the Crutched Friars, cfr VAN DIJK, *Prolegomena*, p. 270-283; I corrected the mistakes in my description in HOFMAN, 'Crutched Friars', p. 521-529.

[9] Den Haag, Koninklijke Bibliotheek, 78 J 55, a. 1439 (part 1, f. 1-88 of f. 1-262(-266)) and s. XVa (part 2, f. 113-260 of f. 1-262(-266)), Prov.: Liège, Saint-Jacques (Benedictines), cfr VAN DIJK, *Prolegomena*, p. 190-203.

[10] Mainz, Stadtbibliothek, I 349, s. XIVd, Prov.: Mainz, St. Michael (Carthusians), cfr VAN DIJK, *Prolegomena*, p. 312-313.

[11] Mainz, Stadtbibliothek, I 149, s. XVa (after 1408), Or., Prov.: Mainz, St. Michael (Carthusians), cfr VAN DIJK, *Prolegomena*, p. 303-305.

[12] Strasbourg, Bibliothèque municipale, olim [660] D 108, Prov. (Or.?): Strasbourg, Grüner Wörth (Knights Hospitaller), cfr VAN DIJK, *Prolegomena*, p. 401-402.

[13] Strasbourg, Bibliothèque municipale, olim D 107, (Or.?), Prov.: Strasbourg, Grüner Wörth (Knights Hospitaller), cfr VAN DIJK, *Prolegomena*, p. 402.

on f. 1-20r (written by hand 1), after some short texts and excerpts followed by *Artic.* on f. 26v-29v (written by hand 2, who succeeds hand 1 in mid-quire on f. 20r and is responsible for f. 20-31). The text of *Ep.* 41 is in a different but related third hand, perhaps written on a separate binio. That the scribe probably was not familiar with the local context in the Low Countries, is suggested by a spelling variant "Dauantria" for more usual "Dauentria" in l. 182-183 and by the omission of "in Honepe" in 184.

X.4 Relations among the manuscripts

Ep. 41 survives in six extant witnesses, $LH_2H_1M_4M_5Z$. In addition, its text has been printed by De Ram in 1861 on the basis of a now lost manuscript *A formerly kept in the municipal library in Strasbourg, but destroyed in 1870 during hostilities between Prussia and France. The close proximity of the two collections of Grote's letters (LH_2) had been established during the collation of *Ep.* 73 already, and it is confirmed by a remarkable agreement of variants for *Ep.* 41 also. Although the most sensible text is generally transmitted in L (H_2H_1), a significant wrong reading which proves this proximity occurs in l. **150-153**, where LH_2 (as well as H_1) read: "principes et iudices terre, qui totaliter patrimonia et uberrima cum monasteriis ex communibus uixerunt. Et religiose fundabant et ne hoc (non)..."; this is impossible as regards sense, with in addition an omission caused by homoioteleuton and on top of that an incomprehensible too early start of the next sentence,[14] with (in L only) improper omission of "non". ZM_4 (and M_5*A) read here more correctly "principes et iudices terre, qui tota patrimonia et uberrima, cum monasteria ex communibus uixerunt, et religiose fundebant et effundebant. Et ne hoc non...". H_1 is transmitted in the same convolute as H_2. This witness transmits all variants present in H_2 after the corrector of this codex H_2^2 had finished his activity,[15] but it has additional variants not pres-

---

[14] By a later hand correct interpunction restorend in H_1.
[15] Most shared variants occur in L also, but that H_1 was not copied from L is proved by the false reading 77 ablacionis] oblacionis, present in H_1H_2 (and in M_4M_5*A also), but not in L (and Z), and also by 83 "Ostendendum et puto", where L reads "Ostendendum est et puta", but H_1H_2 read "Ostendendum et puta"; the most conspicuous variants shared by all three witnesses are: 11 iam] *om.* LH_2H_1; 17 fideli] filii LH_2H_1; 18 Christo] Christus LH_2H_1;

CHAPTER X 187

ent in *H2* also.[16] It seems reasonable to suppose therefore that its scribe Petrus Cortoy used *H2* as his exemplar.[17]

After the collation of the first 96 lines already, it turned out that all variants transmitted in *M4* are present in *M5* also, but that *M5* has additional variants not occurring in *M4*. This circumstance, combined with the known shared provenance of both witnesses from the Carthusian monastery in Mainz, proves that for *Ep.* 41[18] *M4* served as exemplar for *M5*. The text printed by De Ram from **A* contains all variants present in *M4 M5*, supplemented by still other ones present nowhere else.[19] One variant in particular proves the dependence of **A* on *M4* through *M5*: in l. 93-94, the noun "tenuitas" is specified by an attributive clause "in bonis temporalibus tam in diuiciis quam in fama". In *M4*, this clause is written in two consecutive lines, with abbreviated "tpa^bus^" occupying the last position in the first line. Since superscript "-bus" has been written in fairly high position, almost touching the letters in the previous line, it was apparently overlooked by the scribe in *M5* and after that necessarily by the one of **A* also: the scribe in *M5* combined the two successive words "tempora tam" and wrote the in the context impossible form "temporatam", which was by a later hand corrected into "temporalibus", thus leading to the omission of

---

[19] sancte] *om. L H2 H1*; a reading which proves that Petrus Cortoy copied *H1* after *H2* had been corrected occurs in l. 60: per quem] *sic L H1 M4 *A Z, marg. H2²*, que per quem *ex* que que quem *'corr.' ipse H2¹*.

[16] Some instances are: 4 graue onus *tr. H1*; 63 dilecte] *L H2 cett.*, predilecte *H1*; 68 salutem] *L H2 cett.*, falsum *H1*.

[17] Cfr further section III.2 above, where I demonstrate that Petrus Cortoy transcribed *H1* from *H2* in the Liège Benedictine abbey Saint-Jacques in 1439.

[18] *M4* served as exemplar for *M5* for *Epp.* 15 and 27 also, as is substantiated in section IX.4 above; cfr for *Ep.* 15 also HOFMAN, 'Recipients'.

[19] A good example is the impossible reading in 30-31, with attempt at correction in **A*: maximos et grandissimos ydolatras] maximis et grandissimis ydolatris (idolatriis **A*) *M4 M5 *A*; other significant examples are: 7-8 commisso] *L H2 H1*, 9īsso *abbr. M4*, communissimo *emend. falso M5 *A*; 42 potest] *sic L H2 H1 Z*, possunt *falso pro H2 adnotauit Mulder*, possint *M4 M5 *A*; cases where *M4* is correct, and *M5 *A* are together wrong: 58 apparentis] *M4 cett.*, apparentes *M5 *A*; 64 scilicet] *M4 cett., om. M5 *A*; 74 restriccionis] *M4 cett.*, refectionis *M5 *A*; variants in **A*, where the other witnesses are correct: 21 ambulante] ambulanti **A*; 23 ut Abraham ipsos] Abraham impios **A*; conversely, in l. 108 De Ram prints for correct "deputare, ad propriam utilitatem (*L cett.*)" an in part correct reading "deputari, ad propriam uidelicet" from **A* against a further error in *M4*: "deputari, aliud propriam uidelicet", on the basis of a fortuitous emendation by the corrector of *M5*, who changed "aliud" originally present in his manuscript into "ad".

"tam". In *A we find a correction "temporaneis tam", either proposed by the original scribe of the manuscript or by De Ram. This overlap in variants establishes not only that *A was copied from M5, but also that De Ram's reproduction in print of the collation made by the Strasbourg librarian Jung is remarkably accurate. External confirmation of the close proximity of M5 *A consists in the fact that the two codices transmit the same small collection of letters in the same order (*Epp.* 70; 10; 16; 62; 15; 27; 41; 29).

As compared to these subgroups, the variants transmitted uniquely in Z are comparatively independent.[20] This witness therefore obviously represents a separate tradition. These combined data lead to the following stemma for *Ep.* 41 (MSS used for the edition are underlined):

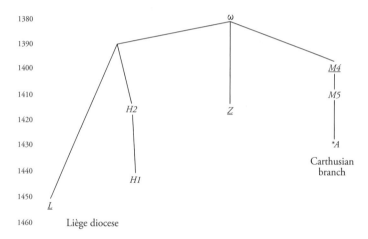

In view of these observations, I have decided to use three witnesses for the edition, *LM4Z*. As is immediately apparent from the *app. crit.*, the text as transmitted in *L* is obviously superior to that in the other witnesses used for the edition. For this reason I follow in general the text as transmitted in *L* (representing *LH2H1*), but I prefer readings from the other subgroups when they together agree against *L(H2H1)*.[21] Readings transmitted in *L* only,

---

[20] Significant examples are: **7** iam] *om.* Z; **24** pungiendo Z; **81** seu ueritatis Z; **84** respectu] conspectu Z.

[21] A fine example of the combined superiority of *M4Z* (representing *M4 M5 *A Z*) against the impossible, garbled text in *L* (representing *L H2 H1*)

CHAPTER X

and not even in the other witnesses belonging to the same subgroup (*H2 H1*), are not adopted in the edition.[22]

---

occurs in l. **17-18**, where the allusion to *Gal.* 4, 28; 3, 16 confirms the correctness of these other witnesses: **17-18** fideli Abrahe, id est Christo] *M4 M5 *A Z*, filii Abrahe, id est Christus *L H2 H1*; In view of the parallel text in l. **98-99**, the reading in *Ma Z* should be preferred in l. **96** plus amat et curat quam aliena uel communia] *M4 M5 *A Z*, plus amat uel curat quam aliena, quam communia *L H2 H1*; cfr also the perseveration error **76** ammonicionis, uinum comminacionis *M4 M5 *A Z*, uinum comminacionis *om. L H2 H1*; other examples are: **11** iam] *sic M4 M5 *A Z, om. L H2 H1*; **19** sancte] *hab. M4 M5 *A Z, om. L H2 H1*; **34-35** ammonicione *L H2 H1*; **55** et] *M4 M5 *A Z* (confirmed by the Psalm text), *om. L H2 H1*; **83** et puto] *sic M4 M5 *A*, et puta *L H1 H2*, puto etiam *Z*; cfr also the superior readings in **172** simonie] *M4 Z*, simonia *L H2 H1*; **173** maxima] *M4 Z*, maxime *L H2 H1*; **218** sint] *M4 Z*, sunt *L H2*, where the subj. form after "quamuis" is supported by parallels in l. **41**; **70**; **193**.

[22] Examples are the impossible readings **8** ministerio] monasterio *L*; **57** peccatoris] peccatorum *L*; **83** Ostendendum] est *add. L.*, and the transposition **135** hoc clare *tr. L*, occurring in *L* only.

CHAPTER XI

TWO LETTERS ON SIMONY AMONG THE CISTERCIAN SISTERS
IN TER HUNNEPE NEAR DEVENTER

XI.1 SUMMARY OF CONTENTS

In this second letter to William II of Cologne, the recently elected new abbot of the Cistercian abbey near Kamp-Lintfort in the Niederrhein region, written at the end of 1382, Grote denounces the simoniacal routines openly practiced by the nuns in the female abbey Ter Hunnepe near Deventer, which was dependent on the paternity of the main convent near Kamp.[1] After an introductory paragraph in which he laments deteriorating moral standards in the contemporary world at large (1-15), Grote urges his old friend to come to grips with the abuses which he has detected in Ter Hunnepe, as even lay people mend their ways and consequently take offence at them (16-32). Focusing on a single, recent concrete example concerning a young girl who had arranged to pay a fee of 60 Old Écus upon entrance into the abbey,[2] he remarks that both the entrant and the community in the abbey risk excommunication for their offence, on the basis of a recent bull issued by Pope Urban V (1362-1370) in 1363 (*Sane, ne in uinea*), and that he himself as well as their priest and curate consider them as excommunicated already (33-42). Abbot William is therefore confronted with the same dilemma (43-54). Also, he has warned their confessor Johannes already that he risks formal irregularity when he closes his eyes for their prohibited behaviour (55-60). In conclusion, Grote states that William should therefore also condemn them (61-72).

---

[1] Cfr on the relation between Ter Hunnepe and Kamp most recently VAN DIJK, 'Kartuizers', and also above, section X.1, with further references. This letter is also summarized in ÉPINEY-BURGARD, *Gérard Grote*, p. 216.

[2] This transaction is the focus of attention in POST, *Modern Devotion*, p. 70-72. Grote's intervention did not really help, corruption continued to be the normal practice in Ter Hunnepe for centuries, cfr on this P. A. A. M. WUBBE, *Het archief der Abdij St. Mariënhorst te Ter Hunnepe*, 's-Gravenhage, 1931, esp. p. 15, as quoted by ÉPINEY-BURGARD, *Gérard Grote*, p. 216, fn. 67.

Concurrently with the letter to abbot William Grote wrote a short letter (*Ep.* 42) to the full monastic community (monks and lay brothers), to which he added a copy of the letter to their abbot. He urged them to support their new abbot, and pointed out that reform, in subordinate female houses also, could only be successful when the abbot was backed up by his community (1-12). This holds true for the resident confessor in Ter Hunnepe, father Johannes, also (12-14), who should resist requests from the sisters to continue with their old habits (15-20). The community should therefore defend the truth, support their abbot, and even prompt him (21-24), for those who defend the truth despite much resistance from worldly oriented dissidents shall be rewarded in future (25-37).

XI.2 EDITORIAL HISTORY, SUPPLEMENT

In the introduction to his edition of Grote's collected letters Mulder convincingly argues that Grote's letters to the abbot (*Epp.* 41; 43; 44) and community (*Ep.* 42) of the Cistercian abbey near Kamp-Lintfort should be linked to the election of William of Cologne, who took up his office on 7 November 1382.[3] He further associates *Ep.* 42 to the community with the first letter to the abbot (*Ep.* 41),[4] in which Grote congratulates him with his election and gives him advice about proper behaviour when confronted with proprietarism (cfr further above, section X.1). This association, however, is not motivated, and it is also inconsistent with the sequence of the letters in all three collections, in which *Ep.* 42 precedes *Ep.* 44. Moreover, the recently discovered witness from Koblenz only transmits *Epp.* 45; 42; 44. If *Ep.* 42 should indeed really be associated with *Ep.* 41, it cannot be explained why that letter is missing in the Koblenz codex. In addition, there are strong parallels between the contents of *Epp.* 42 and 44. It seems inevitable to escape the conclusion, therefore, that Grote wrote to the community in Kamp to ask them to support their abbot in

---

[3] Cfr MULDER, *Epp.*, p. xli-xlii.
[4] Most clearly so in a note to his edition of *Ep.* 42, at p. 170, fn. 2, but also in his introduction, p. xli-xlii; on p. xlii, l. 3, 'XIII' is a typographical mistake for 'LIII'. In this association, Mulder is followed by ÉPINEY-BURGARD, *Gérard Grote*, p. 215 and fn. 66, by VAN ZIJL, *Gerard Groote*, p. 224 and fn. 58, and by POST, *Modern Devotion*, p. 70 and fn. 2.

his attempts to tackle simony in relation with entry into religious life in Ter Hunnepe.

Grote's *Epp.* 44; 45 had been printed by Hyma already in 1930, and after that by Mulder, who in fact just printed a transcript of *H2* with occasional, but in no way systematically collected variants from *L* in the notes. In his analysis of *Ep.* 44, van Dijk also includes, although hesitantly, MS Köln, HA, GB 8° 70 among the witnesses, but this small excerpt has a few words with *Ep.* 44 in common only, as van Dijk observes elsewhere.[5] For this edition, all five extant witnesses have been collated; the text as transmitted in *L* is followed, except for those instances in which the text in the other witnesses is clearly superior,[6] or in which the text in *L* deviates from that in all other witnesses.[7]

XI.3 THE MANUSCRIPTS

Ep. 44 is transmitted in the two letter collections *LH2*, which have been described in greater detail in section III.2 above (*H2*) and in HOFMAN, *Focar.*, p. 135-138 (*L*), and apart from that independently in three other witnesses, *K O B*, which are described here. *Ep.* 42 is transmitted in *L H2 K* only.

B Brussel, Koninklijke Bibliotheek van België, 3672-90 (1503), s. XVc, Prov.: Leuven, Bethlehem (Windesheim Regular Canons), cfr VAN DIJK, *Prolegomena*, p. 147-148.

This folio (290×205) paper manuscript is a convolute, consisting of several codicological units.[8] Grote's *Epp.* 44; 45, on f. 167ra-168ra, occur in the third unit (f. 128-172), which has been written in

---

[5] Cfr VAN DIJK, *Prolegomena*, p. 521; 234.
[6] E.g. 41 in elemosynam] O B, et alia *L H2*.
[7] The single instance is **68** et²] *om. L.*
[8] Clear caesurae in the form of empty folia (f. 67-68; 126-127; 171-172; 188) suggest that at least five different units have been bound together in the actual manuscript. Note that the first part, dated 1388 in its *explicit*, consists of f. 1-68 (not 1-65, thus VAN DIJK, p. 147), and that the date '*c.* 1450', as suggested in *CMD-B*, 2, p. 84-85, no. A 154, is valid for the fourth unit only, which mainly consists of papal bulls probably written on two regular quaterniones on f. 173-188. The entries on this witness in E. PERSOONS, 'Het intellectuele leven in het klooster Bethlehem in de 15de eeuw', *Archief- en Bibliotheekwezen in België / Archives et Bibliothèques de Belgique*, 43 (1972), p. 47-84; 44 (1973), p. 85-143, at p. 126-127, with fn. 530; 533; 546, and on another codicological unit in fn. 547, are not really helpful for our purposes.

two-column layout in a hand writing *cursiua currens* script, tending to *libraria*, and datable to s. xvc.[9] The provenance from the priory Bethlehem of the Windesheim Regular Canons in Herent, just to the North of Louvain, is confirmed by ownership notices on the first (f. 1r) and final (f. 154v) folia of the manuscript.[10]

K Koblenz, Landeshauptarchiv, Best. 701:165 (olim D IIII), s. xvb, Or.: possibly Köln or its surroundings, Prov.: Niederwerth, S. Maria in Insula (Windesheim Regular Canons), cfr VAN DIJK, *Prolegomena*, p. 217

This octavo (140×105) manuscript is a convolute consisting of several parts, written in at least seven hands.[11] The codicological units together forming the manuscript have been bound together in the fifteenth century already, in a binding containing a charter drawn up in Bergheim near Cologne, suggesting that the constituent parts originated there or in this neighbourhood. A later ownership notice proves that the manuscript was later preserved in the priory of the Windesheim Regular Canons in Niederwerth on an island in the Rhine just to the North of Koblenz.

The three letters written by Grote (*Epp.* 45; 42; 44), all of them dealing with simony in relation to entry into religious life in the Cistercian nunnery Ter Hunnepe near Deventer, combined with the full text of the papal bull '*Sane, ne in uinea*', issued by Pope Urban V (1362-1370) in 1363 and referred to by Grote in his letter (l. 33-42), are the sole contents of a single quire 5⁸ (f. 35-42), written by hand 3. This hand writes an expert *cursiua libraria* hand, datable to s. xvb, and confirmed by the various watermarks, which are all datable between 1421 and 1448.

---

[9] In his description, van Dijk unfortunately did not attribute the first text in this codicological unit, on f. 128-132, here called *Epistola de fuga mundi*, inc. "*Nolite diligere mundum...*", to its author, Johannes de Schoenhauia, although he was aware of this fact, as is clear from autograph personal annotations; cfr on the text GRUIJS, 'Schoonhoven, *De contemptu*', this witness listed *ibid.*, p. 39, another copy of this work is preserved in a manuscript containing Grote's *Cura past.*, cfr the description of ms. Brussel, Koninklijke Bibliotheek van België, 4414-4424 (2187) above, Ch. IV.3.1.

[10] Cfr the notice on f. 154v, "Pertinet monasterio b. Marie in Bethleem prope Louanium".

[11] Listed by C. MECKELNBORG, *Die nichtarchivischen Handschriften der Signaturengruppe Best. 701 Nr. 1-190*, Wiesbaden, 1998, p. 348 (manuscript described in full *ibid.*, p. 348-351).

O Leuven, Maurits Sabbe Bibliotheek (formerly Bibliotheek Faculteit Godgeleerdheid), Collectie Grootseminarie Mechelen 30, s. xvb, Prov.: Ophain, Heer-Isaaks-Bosch (Windesheim Regular Canons), cfr VAN DIJK, *Prolegomena*, p. 249-250.

This quarto (188×140) paper manuscript has in its entirety been written in *cursiua libraria* script in the hand of Johannes Bellens in the second quarter of the fifteenth century.[12] The scribe did his profession in the priory of the Windesheim Canons Heer-Isaaks-Bosch in Ophain to the South of Brussels between 1424 and 1442, and became later on in his career (1450-1458) prior of the house. The contents of this small codex of 54 f., mainly ascetical treatises intended to guide its owner on his spiritual journey, reflect the personal interests of its compiler, and they include on f. 25r-28v Grote's *Epp.* 44; 45. The manuscript transmits the full text of *Ep.* 45 on f. 25r-27v, and a small fragment (l. **136-151** in the edition below) further down in the same manuscript, on f. 31 among a series of excerpts. Perhaps not surprisingly, this fragment transmits the same variants that are found in the full text, as well as a single additional one. These observations inevitably imply that Joh. Bellens used his own full copy when preparing the excerpt. The full copies of *Epp.* 44; 45 are transmitted anonymously, whereas the fragment is preceded and followed by introductory sentences ("Magister gerardus magnus dicit"; "Hec magister gerardus magnus"), which reveal that Joh. Bellens was nevertheless well aware of the identity of the author of the letters.

XI.4 RELATIONS AMONG THE MANUSCRIPTS

A full collation of all extant manuscripts corroborates that the best text of *Ep.* 44 is transmitted in the closely related witnesses *LH2*. *K* stands apart from all other witnesses, the text in *OB* shows much overlap.[13] On the basis of the date of its confection, the later

---

[12] The manuscript is analyzed in greater detail in HOFMAN, 'Functionaliteit', p. 184-185, with ill. VI.

[13] Significant deviations in *OB* from the superior readings in *LH2* are among others: **19** fetidissimam] fedicissimam *sic OB*; **66-67** impediueritis] iuueritis *iterum OB*; in one instance the scribes of *OB* were clearly stupefied by the reading in their common exemplar; the one in *O* simply opted for a blank space in his text, whereas the one in *B* apparently faithfully transcribed

CHAPTER XI

manuscript *B* (s xvc) cannot have been transcribed from the earlier witness *O* (s xvb). Since at some places *B* shares a reading with *LH2* against an equally possible variant in *O*, as in **27** antiquati] *LH2B*, antiqui *O*, the inevitable conclusion must be that both manuscripts derive independently from the same exemplar.

In some instances the reading transmitted in *KOB* deserves to be preferred. This is the case, for instance, in l. **41-42**, where the reading of *KOB*, "sexaginta antiqua scuta in elemosynam (et alia *LH2*) abbatisse et sororibus optulit", is clearly superior, as is proved by many parallels listed in *Lexicon Nederl.*, E, c. 108-109.[14] These observations lead to the following stemma:

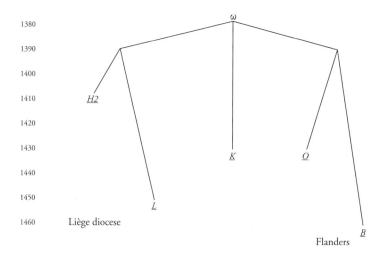

---

what he found in the exemplar: **69** reddat] rdada *B*, *om. spatio uacuo relicto O*; cfr for further instances the *app. cr.*

[14] Another superior reading, **54** "columpna et firmamentum", is discussed above, in section I.1.

CHAPTER XII

A LETTER TO THE ABBESS OF THE CISTERCIAN ABBEY TER HUNNEPE NEAR DEVENTER ON PROPRIETARISM (*EP.* 45)

XII.1 SUMMARY OF CONTENTS

In the introductory paragraph (1-11), Grote writes that the topic of this letter is proprietarism among nuns, which he qualifies as the greatest danger for their spiritual well-being. Personal property among nuns is inconsistent with an essential element of monastic life, the vow of poverty (12-26). Quoting *Luc.* 14, 28-30; 33 on the cost of being a disciple, he points out that the choice for monastic life implies renunciation of all personal belongings (27-42). Through a further long quotation from Cassian he then stresses that when the ideal of communal property preached by Christ was no longer feasible for the majority of the newly converted Christians, this superior life form with shared property continued to be practiced by members of religious orders (43-74).

After that he counters objections which could possibly be put forward by nuns. If a sister cannot live without personal belongings, why has she then opted for religious life so inconsiderately (75-79)? If she adduces ignorance, then she has not weighed the pros and cons of her choice (80-86). If she points to permission granted by her abbess or superior abbot, she forgets that several *Decretals* state that not even the pope can grant such permission (X 3.35.6) and that canon law is quite clear about the prohibition of personal belongings and even prescribes excommunication for unrepentant culprits (X 3.35.2) (87-108). Also, dispensation is out of the question in the case of unequivocally bad behaviour (109-119). The purpose of religious life is contemplation and the pursuit of charity, which are both hindered by concern for temporal belongings (120-135). Of course, some monasteries have insufficient means and profits to support the entire community. Only in the case of such an emergency can voluntary offerings be accepted, provided that these are immediately handed over to the abbess or prioress for common usufruct (136-151).

CHAPTER XII

The consistent use of feminine references[1] makes it abundantly clear that this letter (or *consilium*, cfr 136) was intended for a community of nuns, and the use of "soror" in the address line (1) further suggests that it was directed at their abbess. The letter itself does not contain any reference to a specific addressee, and the contents are indeed of general applicability.[2] Nevertheless the text should in all probability be associated with the community of decadently living Cistercian nuns in Ter Hunnepe and their abbess, in 1382 Mechtild van Bylandt, a noblewoman originating from the Niederrhein region between Nijmegen and Kleve.[3] Ter Hunnepe was situated at a half hour's walking distance to the South-East of Deventer,[4] and it is mentioned in all of the letters to the abbot of the male house in Kamp (*Epp.* 41, **182-206**; 44, esp. **16-60**, cfr 42, esp. **8-20**). An external argument supporting this identification can be found in the *incipit* of two witnesses, one of them now lost.[5]

The tone of this letter is evidently more polite and detached than Grote's straightforward condemnation of the Sisters' corrupt behaviour in his letters to their superior abbot (*Epp.* 44; 42, discussed above in Ch. X; XI). This difference in tone has led Mrs Épiney to suggest that *Ep.* 45 predates his letters to the recently

---

[1] Cfr e.g. 2; 10 filias; 8 filiabus; 43; 87 religiosa; 75; 136; 148 monialis (-ibus; -li); **139-140** prelatarum.

[2] And it was so used: outside the letter collections copies can with certainty be located among Benedictinesses (*M*), Crutched Friars (*Kk*); male Windesheim Regular Canons (*B*, *O*).

[3] This is not the proper place to delve deep in archival records on this influential family; Mechtild was the daughter of Johan van Bylandt (1330-1412), "Geldernscher und Klevischer Rat und Amtmann", and Jutta van Halt van Spaen (1340-?), cfr http://genealogy.richardremme.com/tng/getperson.php?personID=I3377&tree=tree01 (accessed 19-10-15). Mechtild is documented as abbess in Ter Hunnepe in 1390, cfr P. A. A. M. WUBBE, *Het archief der Abdij St. Mariënhorst te Ter Hunnepe*, 's-Gravenhage, 1931, p. 197, no. 209; her predecessor Hermanne van Wije is documented as abbess in 1375 for the last time, cfr *ibid.*, p. 187, no. 181.

[4] Cfr on Ter Hunnepe most recently *Zusters tussen twee beken. Graven naar klooster Ter Hunnepe* – ed. N. Herweijer – H. Lubberding – J. de Vries (*Archeologische Werkgemeenschap voor Nederland, AWN-reeks*, no. 1), [Deventer, 1998], with further references.

[5] "Incipit epistola magistri Gerardi Groten ad abbatissam monasterii in Hoenepe ordinis Cisterciensis Traiectensis dyocesis, pro exhortatione animarum salutari" *tit. in M*, "Epistola eiusdem ad abbatissa in Honepe", *tit. in the lost Magdeburg codex*, cfr Tiecke, p. 118; VAN DIJK, *Prolegomena*, p. 289, Werk 6.

elected abbot William II of Cologne of Kamp.[6] However, I see no need to follow her in this. Grote quite naturally addressed an exceedingly wellborn noblewoman, perhaps not even known to him personally, more politely than an abbot with whom he had most probably been acquainted well for a longer period of time already. I therefore suggest that Grote wrote this letter either concurrently with *Epp.* 41 and 44 (as well as 42), or shortly after these.

XII.2 EDITORIAL HISTORY, SUPPLEMENT

After l. 135, Mulder inserted a few paragraphs totalling just over 40 lines in the lay-out of the present edition, which occur in virtually the same words in *Ep.* 46. As he pointed out in his footnotes,[7] he decided to insert this passage in *Ep.* 45 also, despite the fact that it is transmitted in the context of *Ep.* 45 (rather than in that of *Ep.* 46) in one of the six manuscripts known to him only. This decision is clearly contestable, on various grounds. First, this portion of text occurs not in a full copy of *Ep.* 45, but in a fragmentary one; secondly, the single witness transmitting these contents in this manner can best be characterized as part of an elaborate *rapiarium* or commonplace book (a type of journal in which people wrote poems, songs, Latin sayings, religious prayers, recipes, etc.) about proprietarism, consisting of excerpts and fragments culled from a variety of sources, transmitted in a separate codicological unit in a Cologne manuscript, which is, thirdly, an autograph product written in the hand of Conrad Scheych of Grünberg, the librarian of the house of the Crutched Friars in Cologne, who had a reputation to lose when it comes to the combining of excerpts from various sources into new textual amalgams;[8] and fourthly, Conrad hints himself that his version of

---

[6] Cfr ÉPINEY-BURGARD, *Gérard Grote*, p. 216 and fn. 72. Also, Mrs Épiney's suggestion in the same footnote that this letter consists of separate parts which are loosely connected with each other only, should not be followed in the light of what follows in section XII.2.

[7] Cfr esp. MULDER, *Epp.*, p. 181, fn. d; 2; p. 183, fn. b; p. 184, fn. 1.

[8] Cfr on Conrad Scheych HOFMAN, 'Functionaliteit', p. 173-180, and SCHÖLER, "*Ama nesciri*", on his methods when combining material from different sources esp. p. 68-75; illustrations of autographs of Conrad *ibid.*, p. 43-61, Abb. 3-16; on *rapiaria* in general cfr esp. N. STAUBACH, '*Diuersa raptim undique collecta*: Das Rapiarium im geistlichen Reformprogramm der Deuotio moderna', in *Florilegien, Kompilationen, Kollektionen. Litera-*

'*Ep.* 45' should be considered as a compilation in several transitional sentences.[9] Since there is moreover no textual evidence in any of the eight other known witnesses of *Ep.* 45 supporting the inclusion of this fragment in *Ep.* 45 rather than in *Ep.* 46, it seems wise to omit it from the text of *Ep.* 45.

XII.3 THE MANUSCRIPTS

Witnesses $H1^{10}$ and $H2^{11}$ have been described in greater detail in section III.2 above, W^{12} in section IV.3.2 above, $B^{13} K^{14} O^{15}$ in section XI.3 above, and L^{16} in HOFMAN, *Focar.*, p. 135-138.

---

rische Formen des Mittelalters – ed. K. Elm, Wiesbaden, 2000, p. 115-147, esp. 118-121.

[9] Cfr e.g. the transitional sentence published in ed. Mulder, p. 181, fn. g: "Prosequitur magister gerardus magnus de ista materia", a phrase indicating that the preceding paragraph (ed. Mulder, p. 181, 15-22) has been culled not from GER. MAG., but directly from GREG. MAGN., *Dial.* 4, 57, 11 (p. 190, 81-86): Conrad gives here more details than can be found in the paraphrase in *Decret.*, X 3.35.6 § 2 (c. II, 599, 35-38), quoted by GER. MAG., *Ep.* 41, **35-39**, which can in turn be compared to the quotation from *Decret.*, X 3.35.2 in *Ep.* 45, 97-104.

[10] Den Haag, Koninklijke Bibliotheek, 78 J 55, a. 1439, f. 1-87 of f. 1-262, Or., Prov.: Liège, Saint-Jacques (Benedictines), cfr VAN DIJK, *Prolegomena*, p. 190-203.

[11] Den Haag, Koninklijke Bibliotheek, 78 J 55, s. xva, f. 113-260 of f. 1-262, Prov.: Liège, Saint-Jacques (Benedictines), cfr VAN DIJK, *Prolegomena*, p. 190-203 (letter collection).

[12] Wolfenbüttel, Herzog August Bibliothek, 203 Extravagantes, s. xvc, Prov.: a Carthusian monastery in the Middle Rhine region, cfr VAN DIJK, *Prolegomena*, p. 379-380.

[13] Brussel, Koninklijke Bibliotheek van België, 3672-90 (1503), s. xvc, Prov.: Leuven, Bethlehem (Windesheim Regular Canons), cfr VAN DIJK, *Prolegomena*, p. 147-148.

[14] Koblenz, Landeshauptarchiv, Best. 701:165, s. xvb, Or.: possibly Köln or its surroundings, Prov.: Niederwerth, S. Maria in Insula (Windesheim Regular Canons), cfr VAN DIJK, *Prolegomena*, p. 217.

[15] Leuven, Maurits Sabbe Bibliotheek (formerly Bibliotheek Faculteit Godgeleerdheid), Collectie Grootseminarie Mechelen, 30, s. xvb, Prov.: Ophain, Heer-Isaaks-Bosch (Windesheim Regular Canons), cfr VAN DIJK, *Prolegomena*, p. 249-250. This witness transmits a full copy of *Ep.* 45 on f. 25r-27v, and a small fragment (l. **136-151** in the edition below) further down in the same manuscript, on f. 31 among a series of excerpts.

[16] Liège, Bibliothèque de l'Université, 229 (c), a. 1451, Or.: Namur, monastery of the Crutched Friars, Prov.: Liège, monastery of the Crutched Friars, cfr VAN DIJK, *Prolegomena*, p. 270-283 (letter collection). I corrected the mistakes in my description in HOFMAN, 'Crutched Friars', p. 521-529.

M København, Det Kongelige Bibliotek, NKS 2741 4°, a. 1476, 1477, cfr VAN DIJK, *Prolegomena*, p. 244.

This quarto (202×140) paper manuscript of unknown origin and provenance, but preserved later in the Benedictine abbey Marienmünster near Höxter to the South of Hannover, transmits a collection of texts mostly criticizing proprietarism, among which the greater part of *Ep.* 45, up to l. **135**. Most texts are dated to 1476 or 1477 (thus *Ep.* 45 at the end of the text), and have been written in an expert hand writing *hybrida* script.

Kk Köln, Historisches Archiv der Stadt Köln, GB 8° 152, a. 1438, 1448, Or., Prov.: Köln, priory of the Crutched Friars, cfr VAN DIJK, *Prolegomena*, p. 240-241.

This octavo (145×110) paper manuscript is a convolute, consisting of three or four parts,[17] written in several hands. All identified ones belong to brothers living in the Crutched Friars' monastery in Cologne, where the constituent parts were bound together and received an ownership notice ("Liber fratrum sancte Crucis in Colonia Agrippina, f. 1r) in the fifteenth century already. This makes it pretty sure that the manuscript as a whole originated there.

The fragments of *Epp.* 45; 46 have been written on f. 42v-45r in the hand of the librarian of the house, Conrad Scheych, in a clearly coherent codicological unit (quires 4^8 5^8 6^{8+5}, f. 27-55, cfr further above, section XII.2) dated 1438 by Conrad on f. 52v. Another one of Grote's letters, *Ep.* 72, is transmitted on f. 82v-86v (= f. 3-7, numbered c3^⟨7⟩ – c6 of quire 9^{12} = f. 80-91) in another, undated codicological unit, also written by Conrad in the second quarter of the fifteenth century.

P Paris, Bibliothèque de l'Arsenal, 532, a. 1458, Or., Prov.: Korsendonck, St. Maria (Windesheim Regular Canons), scr. Walter van de Vliet, cfr VAN DIJK, *Prolegomena*, p. 332-333, HOFMAN, 'Functionaliteit', p. 185, *CMD-F* I, p. 95 with Pl. 102.

---

[17] The facts in this description are derived from VENNEBUSCH, *Handschriften*, Teil 3, p. 143-148. The manuscript contains quire signatures 'a1 – ⟨e6⟩' on f. 56-118, and 'a1 – ⟨b6⟩' on f. 119-143; moreover, these codicological units are built up in the form of sexterniones, whereas the preceding quires are usually quaterniones. These facts prove that the various parts were originally not intended as constituent elements for a single codex, and that they were bound together only after they had been finished.

CHAPTER XII   201

This folio (300×214) manuscript with mixed paper/parchment quires has in its entirety been copied in a fine *hybrida* hand in two-col. lay-out by Walter van de Vliet from Rethie (†1483). Among its contents, Walter copied on f. 94r-99v an anonymous *Epistola contra proprietates religiosorum*, which is also transmitted in *O*, which he finished on 12 May 1458 according to the *explicit*.[18]

XII.4 RELATIONS AMONG THE MANUSCRIPTS

The text of *Ep.* 45 is transmitted in full in six witnesses (*LH2H1KOB*), in part in three other ones (*KkMW*), and indirectly and again fragmentarily in yet two other ones (*O2P*). The extant witnesses can on the basis of their variants be split up in four mutually independent groups, two of them consisting of more than one witness (subgroups λ and π), two other ones consisting of a single witness only: manuscripts *KM* and the extracts in *Kk* contain a number of idiosyncratic readings not transmitted elsewhere,[19] on the basis of which they cannot be linked easily to either of the two subgroups. For this reason *KMKk* have all three been collated for the edition.

Subgroup λ consists of the copies in the two letter collections *LH2*, supplied by *H1*, which is as in the case of *Ep.* 41 an apograph of *H2* (cfr above, section X.4),[20] after that manuscript had been corrected.[21] In general, the text transmitted in this subgroup stands out because of its quality, confirming the conclusion reached after the collation of other letters transmitted both in the

---

[18] "Explicit epistola contra proprietarios et euagantes de monasteriis suis, scripta per fratrem Walterum Vliet de Rethy anno Domini .MCCCCLVIII. in festo Nerei et Achillei et cetera. Orate pro se et suis omnibus", f. 99vb.

[19] These are all documented in the *app. crit.*

[20] This is clear from the fact that *H1* transmits all variants present in *H2*; among the more notable ones I list: 34 esse meus *tr. contra Luc. H2 H1*(also *KOB*); 67 ut] *om. H2 H1*; 79 meus] Christi *H2 H1* (also *OB*); the obvious error 8 "filialibus" in *H2* is corrected into "filiabus" in accordance with the other witnesses rather than into more classical "filiis" in *H1*; cfr also below, where I have listed all instances in which I have preferred readings in *KMO*.

[21] Thus, the following corrected variants are not adopted in *H1*: 62 tempore] sequente *add. H2¹, sed postea del. H2¹ uel ²*; 104 nullum] nullus *praem., sed exp. H2*; similarly, *H1* takes over a supplement in the hand of *H2 ²* in 116 idem] *om. H2¹, suppl. H2 ²*, where the directly preceding omission of "Nam" in *H1* but not in *H2* provides additional proof that (the earlier) *H2* cannot have been copied from (the later) *H1*.

202 INTRODUCTION

letter collections and independently (*Epp.* 73 (cfr section IV.4); 44; 41).

Subgroup π, consisting of the full copies *OB* and the fragmentary ones *O2P*, transmits a less reliable text, but must nevertheless be discussed here. As has been concluded already in the discussion of the witnesses transmitting *Ep.* 44 (cfr above, section XI.4), the later manuscript *B* (s xvc) cannot have been transcribed from the earlier witness *O* (s xvb): at some places *B* shares a reading with witnesses belonging to other subgroups against the reading transmitted in *O*, and vice versa.[22] The two witnesses must derive independently from one another from the same exemplar. Apart from these witnesses transmitting a complete text, a section of the letter[23] occurs indirectly as a quotation in an anonymous treatise (or rather a series of consecutive excerpts in the form of a letter) on proprietarism, preceded in the two extant witnesses (*O2P*) by the title *Epistola contra proprietates religiosorum*,[24] also collated for this edition. The earlier (s xvb) witness *O2* has been penned down in the same manuscript which also transmits the full text *O*, and it would therefore seem attractive to designate its scribe Joh. Bellens,[25] at one time a member of

---

[22] That the two manuscripts belong together closely, but yet derive independently from a common exemplar is strikingly clear from a single short fragment, l. **111-114**: "ut (*sic B cett.*, Vnde *O*) dicit beatus (*sic OB, om. cett.*) Bernardus in libro *De* (*hab. O, om. B*) [*precepto et* (*hab. cett., om OB*)] *dispensacione* et *Epistola ad Adam monachum*, que est *septima*. Sed habere proprium (propria *OB*) est per se malum, ut (*sic B cett.*, Vnde *O*) dicit Bernardus in eadem *Epistola*.". A few other exx. testifying to the close proximity of *OB*, chosen from the more significant ones, are: **35** sunt – ex] *om. OB*; **89** per] *om. O* (not *B*); pape et] *om. OB*; **94** licenciam] *om. contra Decret. OB*.

[23] L. **120-135**, followed by l. **136-151** after a section from *Ep.* 41 (**85-87**) separating the two fragments, followed by "magister gerardus magnus dicit" *after* the first, but *before* the second fragment!

[24] Transmitted in *O*, f. 28v-38r and in *P*, f. 94r-99v, *inc*. "In domino dominorum continuam consciencie pacem et regnum secum optinere sempiternum...", *expl*. "Vale (Valete *P*) iugiter cum fratribus uestris in domino Ihesu Christo saluatore nostro". This *incipit* therefore differs from the *Tractatus de uitio proprietatis* compiled by Johannes Fabri ('Smits') during his years in Korsendonk, *inc*. "Sicut modicum fermentum totam massam corrumpit...", mentioned by GAENS, 'Carthusian influences', p. 89 and fn. 183.

[25] This monk did his profession in the Windesheim Canons priory Heer-Isaaks-Bosch in Ophain to the South of Brussels between 1424 and 1442, and he became later on in his career (1450-1458) prior of the same house; cfr further above, p. 194, and HOFMAN, 'Functionaliteit', p. 184-185, with Pl. VI. *O* is a

CHAPTER XII 203

the Windesheim priory Heer-Isaaks-Bosch in Ophain, as the author of the anonymous treatise. However, while both *O2* and *P* have several variants in common with *O*,[26] the slightly later (a. 1458) witness *P*, penned down by Walter Vliet in the Windesheim priory Korsendonk, nevertheless transmits at several places a significantly better text than *O2*, as in 136 Si queratur quale dem] *POcett.*, quale dem *O2*. These superior readings in *P* inevitably lead to the conclusion that both indirect witnesses together derive from a common exemplar probably containing the archetype of this collection of excerpts on proprietarism. Since in addition *O2P* together transmit correct readings at several other places where *OB* have incorrect readings,[27] this exemplar cannot have been copied from either *O* or *B*, or their common exemplar. These combined observations lead to the stemma under the hypothetical common ancestor π for this subgroup of manuscripts all originating in modern day Flanders.

The fragment in *W* transmits a portion of text totalling 16 lines (l. 136-151) which diverges so much from the text in the other witnesses that it can better be characterized as a free adaptation than as a faithful transcript. Where it has variants in common with other witnesses, it is closest to the version transcribed by Conrad Scheych in Cologne (*Kk*). The fragment has with some hesitation got a place in its neighbourhood in the stemma.

The observations made so far imply that the text as transmitted in *L* must serve as basic text for the edition. When, however, the mutually independent witnesses *KMO* agree collectively with one another against a reading transmitted in *L*(*H2H1*),[28] their reading

---

small manuscript which can best be characterized as a personal notebook, which Bellens bequeathed to his priory after his death.

[26] At some places *O* is correct, whereas *O2P* together transmit a variant: 120 inspicienti] *Ocett.*, Aspicienti *O2P*; 122-123 huiusmodi] *hab. O*, om. *O2P*; 123 finem] *hab. O*, om. *O2P*; note also 141 fictione cordis] *Pcett.*, cordis ficcione *tr. KO*, fictione *O2*.

[27] Cfr e.g. 121 quomodo] *O2P cett.*, quod *OB*; 137 uestes] *O2Pcett.*, uestis *O*; 140 ponerent ea] *O2Pcett.*, ponerentur *OB*.

[28] This is the case in 17 oportet] *KMOB*, eius *LH2H1*; 18 singulis] *KMOB*, simul *LH2H1*; 19 apostolicam regulam *tr. LH2H1*; 47 exstitit] *KMOB*, existit *LH2H1*; 53 ceperunt propria *tr. LH2H1*; 75-76 propria habuerit *tr. LH2H1*; 116 ait] *KMOB*, dicit *LH2H1*; 129 teneantur] *marg. corr. L²*, *cett.*, tenentur *L¹H1KkO2P*; 132 fini] *add. KMOBO2PKk*, om. *LH2H1*; 150-151 singularitatibus] *KOBO2P*, singularibus bonis *LH2H1* (*MKk W* not present here).

is preferred for the edition, and the one in *L* is then considered as a variant.

These combined data lead to the following stemma for *Ep.* 45 (MSS used for the edition are underlined):

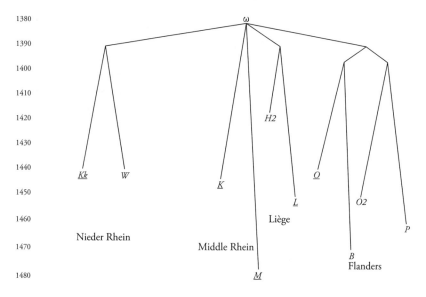

CHAPTER XIII

A LETTER TO A MONASTIC COMMUNITY (*EP.* 46)

XIII.1 SUMMARY OF CONTENTS

In the first part of the letter to a monastic community,[1] l. 1-19, Grote distinguishes between three different types of monks who have personal property at their disposal, elaborating a line of reasoning also found in St Thomas' *Summa theologiae* (II-II, q. 186 a. 9 co.). Depending on their willingness to hand it in, their degree of guilt and sinfulness, and in line with this their capacity to absolve others, differs. Monks who possess immaterial property only, specifically ordination in a function involving pastoral duties, retain their right to absolve, and they cannot be suspended or excommunicated, whether they agree or refuse to hand in their spiritual tasks at the request of their abbot (1-4). Monks possessing material property can again be subdived (5-7). One group among them consists of monks who are willing to hand in their personal property at the request of their abbot (8-12 and 42-44). Such monks can absolve others, although it is perhaps wise to confess to another priest in case this is a feasible opportunity (12-19). To the second group belong monks who refuse to hand in their personal property, even at the request of their abbot. Such monks live in mortal sin, and they pile sin upon sin whenever they deal with sacred things, a view expressed in *Focar.* (*Dictum* 18) also (20-26 and 45-56).

After that, the subject matter is changed without any transitory remark. In the next section (27-35), which is repeated further down (57-60), Grote's advice for monks who have to work in monastery gardens together with women is that they should return to their monastery immediately, even when this involves insubordination to their superiors. This section is concluded with a valedictory formula, occurring in the middle of the letter (35-36).

---

[1] That a community is addressed rather than its abbot is clear from the use of plur. forms in address and concluding section, in l. 1 and 35.

Then follows advice for young monks of good will. When these observe irregularities in their monastery, they should at first just await their superiors' reaction (37-41). After some reformulated items discussed already (cfr above), Grote gives all monks the advice to stay away from nuns, because of the combined dangers of sexual contact and association with simony or proprietarism (61-73).

In a final section, he sets out that the vow of poverty taken during profession can be confirmed at a later date by an oath or promise not to possess personal property and to exclude prospective candidates who are not prepared to promise or vow this, which is less solemn, but nevertheless valid also, again formulated twice (74-90; 91-105).

When considered in its entirety, *Ep.* 46 is a problematic letter. Both Épiney-Burgard[2] and Rüthing[3] observed already that its contents do not form a coherent sequence of interrelated topics. First, the concluding valedictory section occurs halfway in the actual extant letter (in l. 35-36). Secondly, subtitles without verbal form and introducing a new topic (in l. 27; 91) seem intrusions, originally present in the margin, and probably inserted within the main text in the actual apographs for the first time. Thirdly, on three occasions paragraphs further down in the actual letter repeat subject matter which has been discussed already. Thus, the pointedly formulated text in l. 20-25 is also found in l. 45-56, in a much more repetitive form, and the subjects discussed in l. 28-32 and 74-90 respectively are touched upon in less well-chosen words in l. 57-60 and 91-105. These second discussions seem draft versions of the finally written text. And finally, one of the two independent witnesses (*W*) transmits the main body of the letter (up to l. 35) only, whereas the other one (*Kk*) contains that part, supplemented by the single most apt excursus or draft version (42-56). All of this suggests that the additional sections originally did not form part of the letter, but were instead culled from a *rapiarium* or collection of *dicta* composed by Grote, and were inserted in

---

[2] ÉPINEY-BURGARD, *Gérard Grote*, p. 209, fn. 24, writes: "Dans cette lettre sur la pauvreté monastique qui est une compilation de plusieurs déclarations sur le sujet...".

[3] RÜTHING, 'Briefe', p. 398, fn. 25, writes: "...des aus mehreren Schreiben kompilierten Briefes...".

CHAPTER XIII 207

the letter collection at this place by its compiler because they fitted here best.

In addition, Épiney-Burgard and Rüthing identify the "iuuenes" mentioned in l. 37-41 with two young lads Euerwinus and Iohannes, who had presented themselves as novices at the abbey Kamp in October 1382 on the advice of Grote, with an introductory letter written by him (*Ep.* 43), following a suggestion tentatively put forward by Mulder.[4] On the basis of correspondences between elements in *Ep.* 46 with subject matter dealt with in the focarist dossier, however, it remains to be seen whether this latter identification can indeed stand the test of criticism. The contents of *Ep.* 46 must therefore first be analyzed scrupulously.

In l. 76 Grote writes that sincere monks should follow the Rule of St Benedict. This reveals that the letter was most probably intended as a series of recommendations for proper behaviour for Cistercian monks. A Cistercian milieu as recipients of the letter is further supported by Grote's warning about the dangers of outlying "grangiae", (monastic) granges or farm buildings complexes, which were typical for the Cistercian way of organizing their monastic economy.[5]

In conclusion, it seems wise to redate *Ep.* 46 to the end of 1383 or to 1384, rather than to the end of 1382, as has been proposed by Mulder. This is clear from a reference to earlier work inserted by Grote himself. The reference occurs in a context in which Grote addresses the topic of perseverance in mortal sin. If someone deliberately refuses to end this sinful state, thereby piling sin on sin, he should automatically be excommunicated, as he had set out elsewhere already (l. **23-26**, "De excommunicacione talis uiri alias scripsi"). No other *locus* on the same topic can be traced in the

---

[4] *Ibid.*, with reference to MULDER, *Epp.*, p. 185 fn. 7; ÉPINEY-BURGARD, *ibid.*, fn. 21, further suggests to identify this Euerwinus with an Euerardus mentioned by Grote in *Ep.* 14 to Johan Cele.
[5] Cfr on Cistercian monastic economy most recently J. BURTON – J. KERR, *Cistercians*, Ch. 7, 'Conuersi, granges and the Cistercian economy' (p. 149-188, mostly on the earlier period), Woodbridge, 2011, as well as W. RÖSENER, 'Grangienwirtschaft und Grundbesitzorganisation südwestdeutscher Zisterzienserklöster vom 12. bis 14. Jahrhundert', in *Die Zisterzienser. Ordensleben zwischen Ideal und Wirklichkeit, Ergänzungsband* – ed. K. Elm, P. Joerißen, Bonn, Köln, 1982, p. 137-193.

208   INTRODUCTION

Letters,[6] but an exact parallel, even including the same reference to both St Thomas and Albertus Magnus, can be found in *Focar.* 23 (and 18).[7] That excommunication is the logical consequence of such perseverance in sin is set out in *Focar.* 18 (2539-2549). This casual remark therefore proves that *Ep.* 46 should be dated after *Focar.*, i.e. after August 1383.

XIII.2 THE MANUSCRIPTS

All manuscripts transmitting *Ep.* 46 (*LH2KkW*) also transmit *Ep.* 45, and they are described in greater detail in section XII.3

XIII.3 RELATIONS AMONG THE MANUSCRIPTS

The text of *Ep.* 46 is transmitted in full in the two extant letter collections only, and it seems sensible therefore to choose one of these as basic manuscript for the edition. Since the text in *H2* is available in a more or less reliable transcript in Mulder's edition already,[8] I have opted for the one in *L* for the present edition. I have departed from *L* only when its reading is demonstrably inferior to the differing readings in other manuscripts.[9]

Apart from the full text in *LH2*, fragments or excerpts are culled from the letter in two other witnesses. In *Kk* Conrad Scheych,

---

[6] Mulder, p. 185 fn. 3, refers to a passage in *Ep.* 45, but it has been set out above (section XII.2) that he has mistakenly included this passage, occurring in exactly the same words in *Ep.* 46, in *Ep.* 45 also.

[7] The precise references, mentioned in the *app. font.* at 23-26, are GER. MAG., *Focar.* 23 (3190-3251); *Focar.* 18 (2519-2531); *Artic.* 10 (77-84); *Artic.* 2 (25-29); *Obseru.* (10-22).

[8] For the part of the text for which *Kk* is available (l. **8-26**; **42-56**), Mulder occasionally, but not systematically prefers variants transmitted in *Kk* only, cfr his *app. crit.* For variants in *H2* not or not correctly documented by Mulder cfr my *app. crit.* below at l. **21**; **23**; **43**; **55** ("solam" correctly in *LH2*); it is clear from superior readings present in *L*, but not in *H2* (cfr e.g. the *app. crit.* at **84**), that Mulder did not collate *L* for the constitution of the text of *Ep.* 46.

[9] This is the case in: **21** nullo modo] *sic WKk*, a nullo *L*, nullo *H2*: the variants in *LH2* point to a misread abbreviation "nllo°" representing "nullo modo" in their common exemplar, with attempt at emendation in *L*, but not in *H2*; the variant "persona ecclesie" in *WKk* in l. **23** against "personam ecclesie" in *LH2* is supported by "persona ecclesie" in *Focar.* and *Artic.* in a comparable context; finally, **51** "minister" in *Kk* is obviously better than "ministri" in *LH2*.

CHAPTER XIII

librarian in the house of the Crutched Friars in Cologne, has inserted two small excerpts (l. **8-25**; **42-56**) in the middle of part of *Ep.* 45;[10] these excerpts prove that a full copy of both letters must have been present in Cologne in his day. *W* transmits an extremely faulty version of l. **1-35**, which nevertheless has some merits: despite its numerous errors,[11] this witness supports in l. **15** the *lectio difficilior* "et pro parte" against "et pace" in *Kk*, and reads in l. **21** "nullo modo" together with *Kk* against "(a) nullo" in *LH2*.

An interesting deviation, with subsequent attempt at restoring a text which was at least sensible and readable, occurs in *L* in l. **13-15**. The text transmitted in all other manuscripts reads: "Tamen in confessione facienda, in quantum bono modo caritate mutua seruata, et pro parte mallem alteri confiteri". The original variant in *L* consisted in a reading "fugienda" for "facienda", which resulted in a sentence which is senseless in the context. The corrector *L²* therefore emended this into "Sunt tamen in confessione fugiendi", without further intervention in the second half of the sentence. For the third hand *L³* this was apparently still not satisfactory, for he emended the second half also, into: "Sunt tamen in confessione fugiendi, in quantum bono modo caritate mutua seruata ‹hoc fieri possit›, et propterea mallem alteri confiteri". These subsequent emendations at the same time prove that *L³* worked after *L²*. Since *L³* should almost certainly be identified with the main scribe Willem van Tongeren, who acted as supervisor for the confection of the manuscript as a whole and who checked the text in *L* against that in the exemplar, this means that the error was present in that manuscript also.

The fragments *WKk* overlap for not more than 27 lines (**8-35**), and in this small portion of text they do not have errors in common. From other texts in this volume it is clear that *LH2* derive from a common exemplar. As a result, no better sensible stemma than this can be produced:

---

[10] Cfr on his mode of operation further above, section XII.2.

[11] In view of the paucity of extant witnesses, the numerous variants in *W* have all been documented in the *app. crit.*

INTRODUCTION

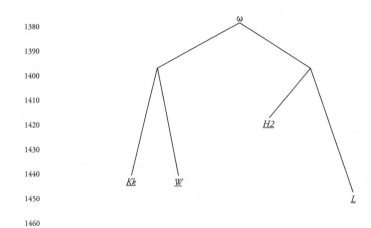

CHAPTER XIV

A SERMON ON THE OCCASION OF PALM SUNDAY
ABOUT VOLUNTARY POVERTY

XIV.1 POSSIBLE OCCASION AND DATE OF THE TEXT, COMPOSITION,
SOURCES AND SUMMARY OF CONTENTS

XIV.1.1 Possible occasion and date of the text

The title transmitted in the *incipit* of this text in the basic manuscript *A* indicates exactly what Grote wishes to communicate: *A sermon on the occasion of Palm Sunday about ⟨voluntary⟩ poverty*.[1] None of the manuscripts specifies when or where Grote delivered this sermon, but the contents in general, as well as cursory remarks and instances of direct address at several places in the text reveal that the intended audience was a religious community.[2] One instance in particular provides a clue which may enable us to track down this audience, an instance aptly quoted by Van Zijl:[3]

> Quapropter – et nonne aptissime? – in hac die paupertatis, secundum sanctorum patrum pauperum iusta et congrua instituta, in monasteriis religiosorum, qui omnes paupertati sine proprietate ex solempni uoto sunt asstricti, quicunque inter eos cum quarumcunque rerum proprietate fuerint inuenti, a templo Dei, id est ecclesia sancta et fidelium participatione, excommunicationis sentencia seu mucrone anime expelluntur, ceterosque ad eam quam promiserant paupertatem sermone paupertatis in hac die adhortantur (l. **228-236**).

---

[1] Cfr the *app. crit.* (**tit.**); virtually the same *incipit* occurs in the related Ms *L* (in expanded form also in *G*), and the same title is mentioned in the *explicit* of *L*, as well as of *El* (at 1180), which belongs to the other branch in the stemma. The occurrence in both branches probably means that the title in this form is original.

[2] I list the following remarks: **125** "Hunc pauperes religiosi modum in rebus uideant acquirendi", with in the next lines (**126-130**) a hardly veiled allusion to BENED., *Reg.*, c. 33, 1-6 (p. 562); **253-254** "maxime tamen religiosis, ad quos est sermo"; "religiosi" or "religiose" are directly addressed in a vocative case form in commands in l. **469** and **551** (cfr a comparable reference in **481**); a less clear allusion occurs in l. **613-614**.

[3] Cfr VAN ZIJL, *Gerard Groote*, p. 229-230 fn. 34, unfortunately with wrong page reference (430: *leg.* 439).

Grote is quite explicit in this fragment, quoted from the very end of the *exordium* of the sermon, about the message which he wishes to convey: professed monks (note the masc. forms "religiosorum"; "asstricti"; "inuenti" in 230-232) have vowed to remain poor, and when they yet avail of personal property in a monastic community, they should be excommunicated in accordance with canon law.[4] This briefly formulated viewpoint, which is further worked out in the development of the first aspect of the main theme of the sermon (l. 242-568), shows considerable overlap with the contents of Grote's *Ep.* 41, written in November 1382 to William II of Cologne, the recently elected new abbot of the Cistercian abbey near Kamp-Lintfort in the Niederrhein region, which is also edited in this volume (cfr Ch. X). Since this letter is the only known example written by Grote of straightforward repudiation of personal property of male monks,[5] G. Épiney is probably clearly right when she suggests that Grote intended this sermon for the religious community in Kamp.[6] He perhaps also delivered the sermon there in person. Some caution is in place here, however, as textbooks on prayer composition prescribe a prayer at the end of the *prothema*.[7] One paragraph at the end of the *prothema* can indeed be interpreted as prayer (l. 210-219; note the repeated use of 'o' and the 2nd ps. sg. pers. pron. 'tu'), but this fragment nevertheless is not a straightforward address of, for example, Christ or Mary.

Cistercians form part of the Benedictine branch in monasticism, and references in the sermon to customs or institutions in that branch would therefore support the thesis that it was intended for

---

[4] 229-230 "secundum – instituta" refers to GRAT., *Decr.*, C.12 q.1 c.5 (c. I, 678, 1-3); C.12 q.1 c.9 § 1 (c. I, 679, 28-37); C.12 q.1 c.10 § 3-4 (c. I, 680, 12-28); *Decret.*, X 3.35.2 (c. II, 596, 59-61); *Decret.*, X 3.35.6 § 2 (c. II, 599, 31-42), cfr further the *app. font. ad loc.*, where parallels between *Tract. paup.* and *Ep.* 41 are listed also.

[5] A letter with similar contents, *Ep.* 45 (to the abbess of the Cistercian nunnery Ter Hunnepe near Deventer, a daughter house of Kamp, cfr Ch. XII above), is less relevant here, as it was intended for a female religious community.

[6] Cfr ÉPINEY-BURGARD, *Lettres*, p. 137 and fn. 2, an assumption also surmised without further substantiation in ÉPINEY-BURGARD, *Gérard Grote*, p. 220.

[7] Cfr CHARLAND, *Artes praedicandi*, p. 125-135. My colleague Charles Caspers yet remarks on the basis of his long acquaintance with late Medieval liturgical practices that such perscriptions in textbooks should not be interpreted too strictly. The structure of the sermon is analysed in the next section.

CHAPTER XIV 213

the community in Kamp-Lintfort. Such clues indeed occur in the text of the sermon. Thus, Grote inserts two, albeit veiled, references to the rule of St Benedict.[8] Also, the main official in Benedictine monasteries is referred to as 'abbot' (unlike the branch following the rule of St Augustine, where this official is called 'prior'), and the members are called 'monachi', rather than 'fratres', the word used to refer to members of the mendicant orders, or 'canonici (regulares)', the reference for Augustinians. In his sermon, Grote occasionally refers to the main official of the audience as 'abbot' and to the community as 'monks'.[9] There is support for this assumption in another way also, viz. a casual remark in l. 1016-1018 in the text which portrays the mendicant orders in a very negative manner.[10] Grote surely would not have formulated in such a spiteful manner if his audience had belonged to the mendicant branch of religious life.

Corroborative evidence for this supposition seems to be present in *Ep*. 41, **208**, where Grote suggests that he can deliver a sermon on (voluntary) poverty.[11]

If this assumption is taken as correct, we can further assume that the sermon postdates November 1382, when *Ep*. 41 was written, and was commissioned by the abbot. We must then date the delivery to 15 March 1383, the day on which Palm Sunday fell in 1383.[12]

---

[8] Cfr the *app. font.* ad **126-130**; **315**; less relevant are the references in **265-272**.

[9] The most convincing example occurs in l. **357-359**, cfr **349**, where Grote supplements a Biblical quotation (*Luc.* 12, 42) with references adapted to the audience of the sermon: "ut *fidelis et prudens dispensator, quem constituit dominus* abbas *super familiam suam* monachorum, *non querens que sua sunt*"; another example occurs in l. **315-319**; the references elsewhere in the text to 'abbot' and 'monks' are less convincing, as Grote here uses them in quotations from the *Decretales* (X 3.35.2, **337-343**; X 3.35.6 § 2, **284-293**; **321-325**) or in their context (e.g. **296**; **327**; **334-337**). The reference to "monasterium" in the fragment quoted above also substantiates my allegation.

[10] This remark was noticed by ÉPINEY-BURGARD, *Lettres*, p. 183, fn. 43, already.

[11] "Hec, pater peramande, respicientes si conamine uestro proficieritis, de quibus grandior et interpretabilior fieri possit sermo, *pariter cum hiis inestimabilia* uobis *bona uenient* simul et dona Altissimi", where "hec" can be taken to refer to the preceding text in l. **194-206**, where Grote complains that the vow of poverty is not taken seriously in many monasteries, and especially nunneries.

[12] Easter fell very early that year, on 22 March 1383, retrieved on 4 September 2015 from http://www.manuscripta-mediaevalia.de/gaeste/grotefend/grotefend.htm.

An alternative date is 3 April 1384, Palm Sunday the next year. This date, however, seems less attractive, as Grote had various other projects at hand that year, among which the composition of his focarist dossier and the translation project involving a *Book of Hours* in Dutch.

XIV.1.2 Composition of the text

It is now time to turn to the structure and composition of the sermon. Both in her biography of Grote and in the introductory section of her translation of the sermon, G. Épiney qualifies this sermon as one of Grote's best written and best composed achievements.[13] In her words, the sermon shows up to advantage when compared to many of his other works, most notably his letters, which were often written in great haste.[14] This is indeed the case, but does this conclusion really come as a surprise? As a sermon, the text belongs to a well-defined genre, and by Grote's days there were plenty of textbooks in circulation elaborating on the intricacies of sermon composition.[15] That Grote used such a textbook, emerges for instance from his use of technical terminology in the body of his text.[16]

A standard fourteenth-century sermon is built up following a fixed structure. It begins with a biblical or liturgical lection or *thema*, followed by an *exordium* or *prothema*, often but not invariably introduced by a second lection. One or more key words from the main lection are used as structuring elements, and the contents of the sermon are often subdivided in several parts announced in the *diuisio(nes)* of the lection. The sermon ends with a final prayer and/or a doxology. The basic structure of a twelfth-century sermon is conveniently presented in a scheme by

---

[13] Cfr ÉPINEY-BURGARD, *Lettres*, p. 137, and ÉPINEY-BURGARD, *Gérard Grote*, p. 223.

[14] Grote himself is the last to deny this reproach, cfr e.g. the last words of *Ep.* 17, which was (l. 87) "Scriptum festinanter Dauentrie".

[15] The essential study and reference work on fourteenth-century sermon composition still is CHARLAND, *Artes praedicandi*, who lists a great number of treatises, attributed as well as anonymous ones (p. 21-106), and provides a detailed analysis of the required or favoured structure of an average sermon (p. 107-226). Also, I used with great profit the various contributions in KIENZLE, *Sermon*.

[16] E.g. **568** diuisio; **241** thema.

CHAPTER XIV 215

Kienzle.[17] Some alterations to this scheme are necessary since Grote composed his sermon roughly two centuries later, but it can nevertheless *mutatis mutandis* be applied to Grote's text:

(1) Lection: a biblical or liturgical lection: *Videant pauperes et letentur* (Ps. 8 (69), 33) (1)
(2) Identification of the liturgical feast: Christ's triumphal entry in Jerusalem on Palm Sunday (1-10)
(3) Development of the theme of the *Exordium* or *Prothema*: Christ's entry is marked both by poverty and dignity: "Hic summus ornatus inornatus est" (106) (11-209)
A short prayer (210-219)
Exhortation to implement the scriptural message (220-241)
(4) Recollection of the lection (237-241)
Diuisio (242-248)
(5) Development of the first aspect of the main theme: *Videant*: Christ's example must be imitated by actions (249-450)
Exhortation to implement the scriptural message (451-550)
(6) Transitory passage, anticipating the second aspect (551-568)
(7) Development of the second aspect of the main theme: *Letentur*: the worthiness of poverty deserves to be praised
Introduction of the second aspect of the theme (569-575)
(7a) First subdivision of the second aspect of the main theme: the connection between poverty and man's relationship with God (576-770)
Exhortation to implement the scriptural message
(7b) Second subdivision of the second aspect of the main theme: the advantages of poverty in the natural world (771-1163)
Exhortation to implement the scriptural message
Conclusion instead of final prayer (1164-1180)

XIV.1.3 Sources used in the text

The sermon is unusual and atypical for another reason also, namely the secular sources Grote has used in it. From the inventory of sources used by Grote as compiled by De Beer, it would

---

[17] Cfr B. M. KIENZLE, 'The twelfth-century sermon', esp. § II 'Development of the genre: its structure and style', p. 281-285, at p. 285, in KIENZLE, *Sermon*, p. 271-323; the continuity of this development starting in the twelfth century is demonstrated by the fact that later sermons follow the same basic structure, cfr N. BÉRIOU, 'Les sermons latins', § I.A 'Un art de construire', p. 370-382, at p. 370-372, in KIENZLE, *Sermon*, p. 363-447. This observation is confirmed for the fourteenth century by CHARLAND, *Artes praedicandi*, where even the chapter titles as listed in the 'Table des matières' (p. 421) follow the same order as the scheme in KIENZLE.

seem at first sight that Grote uses pagan authorities regularly.[18] In fact, however, he usually limits himself to quotations from biblical, ecclesiastical and canonistic authorities. This becomes clear in a next inventory, where De Beer diversifies which sources Grote used on which topics in which of his treatises.[19] It must be noted in advance that this second inventory is very defective and full of lacunae and gaps, and that De Beer moreover makes no differentiation between sources which Grote quotes directly and indirect quotations.[20] When bearing this in mind, we can yet deduce from this inventory that quotations from secular sources occur especially in *Tract. paup.* and in *Matrim.*, and to a much lesser extent in the letters. What is more, these sources are in general attributed. The attributed passages from Seneca's Stoically flavoured *Letters to Lucilius* perfectly fit in with the line of argumentation developed in the sermon,[21] but attributed quotations from Roman (pseudo-)historians and pagan philosophers such as Pliny, Valerius Maximus and Apuleius, let alone a reference to the utterly pagan Acheron *uerbatim* attributed to Vergil, are frankly speaking fairly unprecedented in his oeuvre. It comes as no surprise that Grote was acquainted with the work of Vergil, the me-

---

[18] DE BEER, *Spiritualiteit*, p. 254-257, lists attributed quotations in Grote's oeuvre from 35 Christian and 16 secular authorities. A *caueat* is in place, as de Beer's enumeration is not exhaustive at all, not even as regards attributed quotations. Missing among Christian authorities, for instance, are the many decretists and decretalists quoted frequently in all of Grote's works, and among secular ones e.g. Vergil, quoted *uerbatim* in *Focar.* 17 (p. 415, 2445-2450) and in *Tract. paup.*, 420-421, below.

[19] DE BEER, *Spiritualiteit*, p. 258-267. He introduces this inventory as follows: "Een andere lijst kunnen wij opmaken van de onderdeelen van zijn leer, waarin hij van genoemde auteurs gebruikt heeft gemaakt".

[20] Thus, in the section on Grote's views on the priestly office (XIV, 1, p. 265), De Beer lists a quotation from Ps. Bernard of Clairvaux (*rectius* GAUFR. (PS. BERN. CLAR.), *Coll. Sim.* 21, 24 (*PL*, 184, c. 451C)) for *Cura past.* (cfr *app. font.* below, 220-223), but he fails to observe that the same quotation also occurs in *Focar.* 18 (p. 421, 2563-2567); also, in section XIII.1, p. 264, attributed quotations from the rules of St Augustine and St Benedict are noted for *Ep.* 45, but not for *Tract. paup.* (l. 265-272 below). All of this underlines the urgent need for an adequate list of Grote's sources.

[21] Not only the attributed quotations, but also many more anonymous references and reminiscences (in l. 776-808; 812-831; 855-904; 964-975; 1006-1071, cfr *app. font. ad loc.*) are enumerated and analysed by Father MEERSSEMAN, *Seneca*, p. 122-128; some of his identifications, however, are superseded by more appropriate (mainly biblical) parallels in the *app. fontium* of the edition below.

diaeval school author *par excellence*, and Grote was sufficiently well educated of course to know other pagan authorities, but in general he tends to omit references to this pagan education in his written legacy, and if he quotes them, it is most often indirectly through the Church Fathers.[22] I cannot provide an explanation why Grote decided to expose his acquaintance with pagan culture in a sermon for monks, in a context where he exhorts them to give up personal property.

XIV.1.4 Summary of contents

Immediately following the lection, taken from *Ps.* 68 (69), 33 and according to the Vulgate text to be translated as 'Let the poor see, and be glad',[23] and the identification of the liturgical feast (1-10),[24] Grote extols the dignity of Christ's triumphal entry in Jerusalem on Palm Sunday in the *exordium* or *prothema*. That he rides on the back of a young ass, as described in *Matth.* 21, 1-9; *Marc.* 11, 1-10; *Luc.* 19, 29-44; *Ioh.* 12, 12-16,[25] symbolizes at the same time his poverty and his majesty. At the same time, the warm reception by the assembled joyful crowd and their display of reverence reveal the nobility and dignity of a life in poverty (**1-49**). The worthiness of poverty is further confirmed by his disciples and followers, who were as poor as Christ himself (**50-66**). Christ's appearance and clothing looked poor (**67-73**), while he rode on the colt of an ass, the poor men's animal (**74-93**). Further typical features of utter poverty were that this colt had neither saddle, nor reins, nor stirrups (**94-108**). Christ therefore entered Jerusalem unadornedly on that triumphal journey, humble, and satisfied with the barest essentials (**109-124**).

---

[22] The most unbiased evaluation of non-Christian and philosophical influences on Grote is ÉPINEY-BURGARD, *Gérard Grote*, p. 32-35, where she observes among others: "Certains passages de son œuvre trahissent en tout cas une admiration spontanée pour les Anciens", with reference to *Locat.*, [now:] l. 537-543. But as is clear from de *app. font. ad loc.*, even this passage goes back to LACT., *Diu. inst.* 6, 6, 24-28 (p. 504, 2 – 505, 7).
[23] On the basis of the original Hebrew text, the *King James Bible* translates this as Ps. 68 (69), 32 'The humble shall see this, and be glad'.
[24] The contents of the sermon are also briefly discussed and summarized in ÉPINEY-BURGARD, *Lettres*, p. 138-140; ÉPINEY-BURGARD, *Gérard Grote*, p. 220-223 and VAN ZIJL, *Gerard Groote*, p. 229-232.
[25] Further biblical references can be found in the *app. bibl.* accompanying the edition below.

Grote then urges his contemporary religious audience to follow this example of modesty, announced by the prophet Zechariah (138-148) and by Christ himself (148-154), and to be content with what is at hand (125-137). Had not Christ himself during that triumphal journey condemned all those who despise poverty and in its wake peace: the rich, the powerful, and the inconsiderate intellectual elite (155-176)?

This is also the day on which the ancient Jews in the Old Testament selected a lamb without blemish, to be kept for four days until it was finally killed. In line with traditional typological exegesis (starting with *I Cor.* 5, 7; *Ioh.* 1, 29), Grote takes this lamb of God as a prefiguration of the killing of Jesus five days later (177-193). Before salvation is possible, all religious need to practice a life in poverty, following the example of Christ (194-219), during which Christ purified the temple of God (220-228). Grote concludes the *prothema* with a short prayer exalting this day of poverty (210-219), and he exhorts all religious to observe their vow of poverty (220-241).

In accordance with traditional sermon composition, Grote then briefly repeats the lection (237-241), after which he presents the *diuisio* of the sermon (242-248), summarizing the two subjects which he wishes to develop in its two parts. These are, firstly: Christ's life in poverty must be imitated by his followers, summarized in *Videant* and elaborated in l. 249-568, and secondly: the dignity of poverty deserves to be praised, summarized in *Letentur* and elaborated in two subdivisions in l. 569-1163.

In the elaboration of the first aspect, that Christ's life in poverty must be imitated, Grote focuses quickly on its relevance for his intended audience in particular. While a life in poverty is recommended for all Christians, it is an obligation for religious people (249-258). For poverty, in practice shared property of common possessions in imitation of the way of life of the earliest Christian communities, is prescribed together with chastity and obedience in the rules composed by the founders of monastic life (259-283). Consequently, personal belongings were strictly prohibited for monks in canon law (Grote quotes X 3.35.6, cfr the *app. font.* accompanying the edition below) (284-293), and burial in the dung pit was prescribed for offenders on the authority of a decision taken by Gregory the Great (*Dial.* 4, 55) (294-317). Another decretal (X 3.35.6 § 2) confirms this ban on private property, restricting a *peculium* (in a technical sense, control over financial

CHAPTER XIV

resources) to monastic officials having specific administrative tasks only. These must administer such resources scrupulously, in accordance with the common interest (318-363). Unfortunately, many officials misuse their privileged position and appropriate the entrusted resources as their own personal possessions (364-376).

In a digression, based in part on St Thomas (II-II, 61, 2), Grote states that man as a member of society, pagan or Christian, should not consider possessions as inalienable personal property, which he has at his disposal without limitation. Rather, he must be aware that he just has the use of them, that he can administer them, but that they never belong to him exclusively. Since it is man's nature to look better after his own goods than after common property, society as a whole functions better when goods are given out on loan in this manner. Monks, on the other hand, possess nothing personally, in their case all goods belong to the community, and they are distributed according to necessity (377-425).

When property is in this way understood as goods on loan, it is only fair that anything that is not essentially necessary to survive should be handed over to others. This view was aired by pagan philosophers already, but Christ's example teaches us that it is the natural and obvious behaviour for Christians (426-450).

In line with the precepts of the genre, Grote ends this first part of the sermon with a flamboyant exhortation to the audience. While the use of necessary amenities for personal purposes is defendable for lay people, religious have with their vow promised to distance themselves from personal property. In an impressive and skilful example of the stylistic device of anaphora,[26] Grote summons his audience to observe their vow of poverty, summarizing at the same time the entire contents of what had preceded in his sermon (451-468),[27] and he urges them to imitate the example of Christ and his first followers in their poverty and mutual solidarity (469-486). He then states in a section that culminates in a second powerful anaphora that anything that exceeds the essential living conditions is not really necessary, as Christ has shown on this very day (487-504) and as is confirmed by St Ber-

---

[26] Grote was probably aware of the impact that this figure of speech could have through the basic textbook teching the essentials of Latin grammar still in common use in his days, DON., *Mai.* 3, 5 (p. 664, 14 – 665, 2 ed. Holtz).

[27] Precise references are incorporated in the *app. font.*

nard (505-514). In a final appeal he then calls on the audience to stick to the essentials and to give away generously anything that is superfluous, for God looks after all who show charity (515-550). In a transitory paragraph, anticipating the contents of the second aspect of the main theme, he sets out that life becomes easier when one values in poverty the little and the small for what it is worth, and when one stays away from redundancies (551-568).

In the second part of the sermon, Grote discusses the worthiness of poverty, which deserves to be praised, on the basis of the second element in the lection or *thema* of the sermon, *Letentur*. This second part is essentially subdivided in two sections, one discussing the connection between poverty and man's relationship with God (576-770), the other one dealing with the advantages of poverty in the natural world (771-1163).

Grote starts the first section with the observation that it is evident from many remarks as made by Christ in *Scripture* that the reward of poverty in this life will be eternal blessedness in the Kingdom of Heaven, as formulated in the Beatitudes (*Luc.* 6, 20-23), and that there will be no room there for the rich (576-598). But voluntary poverty has many advantages in this world also. It is the only sure course to come closer to God (an allegation which Grote substantiates with many biblical quotations), and a basic prerequisite for religious life (599-625). The poor's orientation on God is neither diverted by other people, who take no notice of him (626-634), nor by worldly possessions or preoccupations (635-649). Poverty teaches the poor tribulation and humiliation, as he feels despised by worldly companions (650-675), but in the end these experiences strengthen the poor man's capacity to enjoy and practice the theological virtues belief, hope and charity (676-689). Because he possesses nothing, the poor man is well aware that his hope and trust are in the Lord, who provides much more safety and stability than any man can offer (690-719). He knows that God will always care for him, a certainty again substantiated with a wealth of biblical *loci* (720-738). Grote then turns to the cardinal virtues, in his case justice, prudence, temperance and humility (which he substitutes for the more traditional fortitude).[28]

---

[28] Grote calls them "uirtutes morales" in 739-740. The fundamental study on the cardinal virtues in the Netherlands is PANSTERS, *Deugden*.

CHAPTER XIV 221

These seem to derive in an almost natural manner from poverty, as Grote states in a chiastic construction, "humilitas et paupertas sicut causa et effectus connectuntur" (739-770).[29]

Grote next focuses his attention on the advantages of voluntary poverty in the natural world, in a section which owes much to Seneca's observations in his *Letters to Lucilius* and his *De moribus*.[30] A state of poverty is much more natural than wealth or riches, as is clear from the penurious circumstances accompanying our birth and death (771-784). Inbetween, during our lifetime, we need food, drink, clothing and accommodation, but the most simple form of it protects us as well as a lavish one (785-802). It is a natural inclination to satisfy immediate necessities, but in a moderate manner, and it is against natural law to store anything for future needs (803-820), as is clear from animal behaviour (837-857). Anything that exceeds such provision for immediate needs is born from avarice or cupidity, and it only leads to an always increasing but essentially unnatural wish to assemble ever more commodities (821-836).

In a long development of his argumentation based largely on various sections in Seneca's *Letters to Lucilius*, Grote then focuses on the moral advantages of voluntary poverty. From a moral perspective someone is and feels rich when he is content with available property, and in line with this, poverty should be termed true wealth, an idea derived through Seneca from Stoic philosophy (855-873). Excessive possessions become an obsession (874-889), and it is better to be good or to possess the good than goods, as the good cannot be taken away by enemies (890-909). While the poor is free from worries as he possesses nothing to worry about (910-923; 964-975), the rich is always concerned about what he may loose (924-932) or may not obtain (950-963), and distressed and dissatisfied about what he has lost (933-944).

Voluntary poverty also results in peace: peace with others as there never is 'mine' or 'yours' to quarrel about (976-990),[31] and

---

[29] Grote found this figure of speech in his grammar as "hysterologia", cfr DON., *Mai.* 3, 6 (p. 670, 8-9 ed. Holtz).

[30] Cfr the analysis in MEERSSEMAN, *Seneca*, p. 122-128, quoted in the previous section already.

[31] Grote uses this same wording in *Ep.* 41, 112-114. ÉPINEY-BURGARD, *Gérard Grote*, p. 223, fn. 43, notes that Zerbolt attributes a similar passage to Ps. SEN., *De moribus*, and in ÉPINEY-BURGARD, *Lettres*, p. 183, fn. 40, she traces it in the edition in *PL*, 72, c. 31A. On the text, which is a compilation of fragments on

peace of mind as there is no reason to worry about losses (991-1023). For this reason many prudent pagan rulers and philosophers voluntarily gave up their influence or possessions (997-1005, cfr 890-909). Poverty is also full of joy and pleasure (1024-1025). Even Epicurus and his followers, whose philosophy consisted in maximalization of pleasure, held that this goal is achieved more easily through abstinence than through the acquisition of wealth (1025-1053). Poverty is a source of joy also, as it is essentially stable and predictable, unlike wealth, which is by its very nature insecure and therefore unstable (1054-1066). Since a poor man is satisfied with modest amenities, he can truly enjoy what he has now (1067-1075), and a Christian poor can in addition look forward at ease to eternal joy in afterlife (1076-1086).

Elaborating a second main topic, Grote holds that the poor live more healthily also, as immoderate food ruins the rich man's bodily health (1087-1097), concerns about his possessions continuously affect his mental health (1098-1105), and risks prompted by greed as well as jealous fellow men augment the chance of an untimely death (1106-1115).

The final paragraphs (1116-1163) can be interpreted as the exhortation concluding the second part of the sermon, an element required by the genre. In Grote's sermon, this exhortation takes the form of an enumeration of examples worthy of imitation, taken mostly from pagan history, by presenting famous Romans who either played a decisive role in the constitution of the Roman Empire despite a life in poverty, or who voluntarily gave up their wealth (1120-1140), or who lived in poverty voluntarily, in accordance with their philosophical principles (1141-1163).

The sermon ends with a short conclusion (1164-1180). It really comes as a surprise that we still do not perceive the advantages of poverty (1165-1173), especially on this festive day, Palm Sunday, on which Christ set the example of a life in poverty yet dignity (1174-1180), which 'the poor see, and they are glad about it' (*Ps.* 68 (69), 33).

---

morality selected from various, mainly Stoic authorities, cfr MEERSSEMAN, *Seneca*, p. 49-58.

CHAPTER XIV   223

XIV.2 EDITORIAL HISTORY, SUPPLEMENT

In the introduction to his *editio princeps*,[32] Moll sets out that his edition is primarily based on the text in the Brussels manuscript *A*.[33] He was well aware that the text in this codex was not flawless, and adds that his contemporary H. Nolte kindly and carefully[34] checked his transcript against the text in *L* (for which he uses the siglum *B*). In his edition, he therefore replaced inferior readings in *A* by better ones in *L*, all of them documented in footnotes to the edition. Variants in *L* which were inferior in his view to the ones in *A* are listed in the footnotes too. However, a fresh collation of the text in *L* reveals that Nolte did a good job in general, but nevertheless overlooked many of the variants in *L*, especially words and phrases erroneously omitted in Moll's basic manuscript *A*.[35] Nolte's inaccuracies are silently supplemented in the *app. crit.* to my edition. Moll himself was much more precise, I have found but a very small number of flaws in his transcript, which I have corrected silently also.[36] In other instances, the testimony of the majority of the collated manuscripts now and then shows that Moll was occasionally wrong when he decided to prefer variants from *A* against the readings in *L*; when readings sup-

---

[32] cfr MOLL, 'Sermoen', p. 430-431.
[33] On the basis of a fresh collation of *A*, it can be established that Moll's transcript very adequately represents the text in the manuscript; in the two passages initially chosen for collation (l. **1-96**; **484-578**, cfr section XIV.4 below), I note the following minor slips only: **32** plausibus] *om. Moll, hab. A*; **61** Quomodoue] *sic A*, Quomodo *Moll*; **510** fraternis *A*, fratris *Moll* (this variant is attested for *L*); **530** habere] Moll lists this reading for *A*, but it is again attested for *L* (correctly, it is the reading in St Bernard, who is here quoted), not *A*: habete *A cett.*; **549** magis quod] *thus A cett.*, magisque quod *L*, magisque *Moll and Nolte*; **576** sunt] *sic cett., om. A*, sint *L*.
[34] Nolte, he writes, did this "met eene naauwkeurigheid, waarvoor ik niet genoeg dankbaar kan wezen".
[35] Variants present in *L*, which were not recorded by Nolte, include for l. **1-96**; **484-578** e.g. **16** in – Christi²] *hab. L, om. A*; **47-48** Domini¹ – gloria] *om. L*; **528** Bernardum] beatum *praem. L*; **536** .I. Iohannis .III.] *thus correctly L*; Iohannis .II. *according to Nolte in L just as in A*; **564** te] *om. L*; **562** ista nec (non *L*) uult nec potest *tr. Ek Z G El L*; **570** presentis uite *tr. Ek Z G El L*; **574** qui] quia *L*; **565** ista nec uult nec potest *tr. L with all other witnesses against A*; **573** presentis uite] *thus L with all other witnesses against A*.
[36] Thus, apart from the slips listed in the previous notes, Moll forgot to print e.g. **334** de facto; **377** uel proprietarii: present in *A*, but not in *L*; also, he misprinted **128** prepositiorum discretioni] *codd.*, prepositioni discretiorum *Moll*; **439** precipit] *codd.*, precepit *Moll*.

porting *L* against *A* occur in both branches of the stemma, I have regularly decided to prefer such readings, relegating the reading in *A* to the *app. crit.* Such instances only prove that Moll was indeed right in pointing out that *A*, despite its superiority to the other witnesses, cannot be qualified as an excellent transcript from Grote's autograph.

Misprints (or misreadings?) from Moll's edition occasionally found their way into the *Dictionary of Medieval Latin from Dutch sources*, as in the case of 302 "abhominatum", for which Moll printed "abhobinatum". Fuchs and Weyers adopted this typo as a *hapax legomenon* in the first fascicle of their *Lexicon* in 1970 (*Lexicon Nederl.*, A 40, 33, cfr 19) despite the fact that none of the extant manuscripts actually transmits this ghost form.[37] Similarly, Moll unnecessarily suggests an ireggular passive meaning for "adhortantur" in 234-236 "ceterosque ad eam quam promiserant paupertatem sermone paupertatis in hac die adhortantur", by adopting the variant "ceterique", transmitted in *A*, rather than "ceterosque", with understood subject "sancti patres pauperes", to be supplied from 229.

XIV.3 THE MANUSCRIPTS

Ek Berlin, Staatsbibliothek zu Berlin – Preußischer Kulturbesitz, lat. fol. 690, a. 1397-1402, Or.: Erfurt, University milieu, Prov.: Erfurt, Salvatorberg (Carthusians), cfr VAN DIJK, *Prolegomena*, p. 131-132, HOFMAN, *Focar.*, p. 148; 177-178.

This folio (*c.* 300×200) paper/vellum manuscript, which contains two texts from Grote written shortly after one another (*Focar.* (f. 312r-349v) and *Tract. Paup.* (f. 353v-364v)), has been described in greater detail in my introduction to *Focar.* already. The data presented there are summarized in this description. The manuscript can on the basis of the paper used be dated *c.* 1400.[38]

---

[37] Similar examples of false *hapax legomena* are: 234 mucrone] *sic codd.*, microne *false* Moll, *Lexicon Nederl.*; 435 dispositores] *sic codd.*, disponitores *false* Moll, *Lexicon Nederl.* (but it may be that Moll here wrongly expanded the abbreviation "dispo͞itores" in *A*).

[38] This description of the manuscript depends on information most kindly and generously supplied by E. Overgaauw, Leiter der Handschriftenabteilung, Staatsbibliothek zu Berlin – Preußischer Kulturbesitz. The watermark

It has as its provenance the Carthusian monastery Salvatorberg in Erfurt, where it arrived before the third quarter of the fifteenth century, as it is mentioned in the great catalogue compiled there in or shortly after 1475.[39] Before it arrived there, it belonged to the personal library of Johannes Ryman (†1408), secular canon of the Marienkirche in Erfurt and one of the scholars who played a decisive role in the establishment of the University of Erfurt, founded in 1392.[40] The Grote texts have been written on irregular quaterniones, which have outer parchment bifolia or single leaves.[41] *Tract. paup.* has been written in two hands B and C, starting in the middle of quire (6) and finished in the middle of quire (7). Transitions from one text to the next occur in several instances in mid-quire throughout the manuscript. It seems therefore reasonable to suppose that its contents were meant as a homogeneous collection from the outset. Many texts have associations with Ryman or his circle.

El Berlin, Staatsbibliothek zu Berlin – Preußischer Kulturbesitz, lat. fol. 704, s. XVc (1454-1460), 327 f., Prov.: Erfurt, Salvatorberg (Carthusians), cfr VAN DIJK, *Prolegomena*, p. 132-133.

The part of this folio manuscript containing Grote's *Tract. paup.*, of which no description is in print so far,[42] has been written in expert, somewhat hastily executed *cursiua libraria* script

---

of f. 313 resembles MOŠIN-TRALJIČ, no. 2234-2235, produced in 1397-1398, the one of f. 359 PICCARD, O XII 239, produced 1395-1399.

[39] Published by P. LEHMANN, *Mittelalterliche Bibliothekscataloge Deutschlands und der Schweiz.* II. *Bistum Mainz, Erfurt*, München, 1928, p. 239-593; manuscript *Ek* is listed as 'codex C 75' ibid., p. 290.

[40] On Ryman, cfr KLEINEIDAM, *Universitas studii Erffordensis. Überblick über die Geschichte der Universität Erfurt im Mittelalter*, Teil I: 1392-1460, Leipzig, 1964, p. 41f.; 301-302, and F. P. SONNTAG, *Das Kollegiatstift St. Marien zu Erfurt von 1117-1400*, Leipzig, 1962, p. 132-134.

[41] *Focar.* has been written on five quaterniones, $1^{8\text{-}1}$ (f. 312-318, first leaf parchment, last leaf missing without loss of text), 2^8 (f. 319-326, 1^8 parchment, catchword on f. 326v), $3^{8\text{-}1}$ (f. 327-33, layout as quire 1), 4^8 (f. 334-341, 1^8 parchment), 5^8 (f. 342-349, 1^8 parchment); *Tract. paup.* begins on f. 353v = f. 4v of the sixth quire and ends in the middle of f. 364v = f. 8v of the seventh quire: $6^{8\text{-}1}$ (f. 350-356, first leaf missing, eighth leaf parchment), 7^8 (f. 357-364, 1^8 parchment).

[42] The reference by van Dijk to V. ROSE, *Verzeichniss der Lateinischen Handschriften der Königlichen Bibliothek zu Berlin*, Bd. 2 *Die Handschriften der Kurfürstlichen Bibliothek und der Kurfürstlichen Lande*, Abt. 2, Berlin, 1903, p. 188-190, is an error, Rose here describes ms. Berlin, SBB, lat. qu. 704, not lat. fol. 704.

datable to s. xvc. In the introduction to his edition of the great medieval catalogue of the Carthusian monastery Salvatorberg in Erfurt, Lehmann states that several manuscripts with a known provenance from this charterhouse are not listed in the 1475 catalogue. Among them he mentions *El*, which should or could have been included, as the date of its confection (1454-1460) predates the date of the catalogue.[43] That the manuscript was donated to the monastery after its confection is confirmed by the fact that our witness *El* has not been transcribed from *Ek*, which was present in the same house probably for several decades already when *El* was written. Details about its origin or provenance are difficult to establish, as no proper full description of the manuscript exists to date.

A Brussel, Koninklijke Bibliotheek van België, 1216-34 (1129), s. xvb, Prov.: Rooclooster, St. Paul (Windesheim Regular Canons), cfr VAN DIJK, *Prolegomena*, p. 141-142.

This folio (290×210) vellum manuscript from the Windesheim priory Rooklooster[44] is a convolute, consisting of different parts, as is shown by several clear caesurae in the form of empty folia at the end of quires and by changes in hands and in layout.[45] The text of *Tract. paup.* occurs in the first codicological unit, on f. 47va-58vb, and forms in this manuscript part of a collection of theological treatises, many of them written by Church Fathers. It has been written in two column layout in carefully executed *hybrida* script, datable to s. xvb, for the most part but not systematically on regular quaterniones (catchwords on f. 44v; 52v; 68v).

---

[43] Cfr P. LEHMANN, *Mittelalterliche Bibliothekscataloge Deutschlands und der Schweiz*. II. *Bistum Mainz, Erfurt*, München, 1928, p. 228-229.

[44] An ownership notice "Liber monasterii rubee uallis in zonia prope Bruxellam" occurs on the last f. 202v.

[45] The manuscript, for the most part written in two-col. layout, consists of units (1-2) (f. 1-60, with a clear caesura formed by the empty f. 59-60 at the end of a quire; apparently regular quaterniones, catchword on f. 52v); (f. 61-92, f. 92 empty, written in the same hand, transitions from one text to the next in mid-folio on f. 72v; 79r); (3) (f. 93-116, transitions from one text to the next in mid-folio on f. 102v; 112v); (4) (f. 117-198, written in long lines, transitions from one text to the next in mid-folio on f. 150r; 162v; 174v; 183r; 194r); (5) (f. 199-202). The various hands are listed in *Catalogus codicum hagiographicorum Bibliothecæ Regiæ Bruxellensis*, ediderunt hagiographi Bollandiani, Vol. 1 (*Subsidia hagiographica*, 1; *Analecta Bollandiana*, 2), Bruxellis, 1886, p. 287.

CHAPTER XIV 227

Contemporary foliation (not in the main scribe's hand, as it occurs throughout the manuscript) has been entered in the middle of the top margin of the recto sides. The manuscript has been used as basic manuscript for his *editio princeps* by Moll.

G Gent, Universiteitsbibliotheek, 1745, a. 1420, cfr VAN DIJK, *Prolegomena*, p. 181-182.

This small[46] octavo (132×87) vellum manuscript contains three texts, two of them by Grote. All texts have been written in carefully executed *cursiua libraria* (almost *formata*) script, which the main scribe dates to 1420 on f. 36v, directly preceding the beginning of *Tract. paup.*, and in the *explicit* of Grote's *Gener. medit.*, on f. 72r. The provenance of the manuscript cannot be retrieved unfortunately, as two words only of an erased ownership notice on f. 1r are legible, "Pertinet monasterii...".[47] Due to the inferior quality of the text of *Tract. paup.* as transmitted in this manuscript, this witness has not been used for the edition.

K Köln, Historisches Archiv der Stadt Köln, GB 4° 85, c. a. 1424, Or., Prov.: Köln, Crutched Friars, cfr VAN DIJK, *Prolegomena*, p. 225-226.

This quarto (215×145) paper manuscript is a convolute, consisting of two main parts,[48] as is clear from the diverging sets of quire signatures. The two parts were bound together in the Cologne Crutched Friars' house in the fifteenth century. The second part, containing on f. 79-100 Grote's *Tract. paup.*, was written on regular sexterniones (8¹²-12¹²) in single col. layout in expert *cursiua* script datable very early in s. xvb. This date is confirmed by the paper used, which contains exactly the same watermarks as an-

---

[46] The margins were reduced only after the manuscript had been completed, as is clear from marginal entries: on f. 75r, for instance, a corrector supplied "bestie" as subject (instead of correct 77 "fere" 'wild animals', which proves that he did not have access to the exemplar), of which only the first letters "best-" have been preserved. The manuscript is mostly composed of regular quaterniones (1-13⁸ 14¹²⁻²).

[47] I am most grateful to F. Vanlangenhove and H. Defoort, collaborator and keeper of the manuscripts, Gent University library, who very kindly checked this once again for me, unfortunately to no avail.

[48] (1) f. 1-78, probable or. Köln, Crutched Friars, quire signatures: b; c; d; d; e; (2) f. 79-139, or., prov. *ibid.*, quire signatures r-x. These and other codicological data are summarized from J. VENNEBUSCH, *Die homiletischen und hagiographischen Handschriften des Stadtarchivs Köln*, Teil 1. *Handschriften der Gymnasialbibliothek* (= Vol. 6, 1), Köln etc., 1993, p. 120-122.

other product of the same house (MS Köln, HA, GB f° 20), which is dated and localized by its main scribe to 1424 in an *explicit* on f. 141r,[49] thus establishing our manuscript's origin also. Unfortunately, and in view of the manuscript's origin also quite remarkably, the bad quality of the text transmitted in this witness should not be trusted. Due to its inferior quality, this witness has not been used for the edition.

L Liège, Bibliothèque du Grand Séminaire, 6 G 28, a. 1466, Or., Prov.: Liège, Crutched Friars, cfr VAN DIJK, *Prolegomena*, p. 256-257.

Grote's *Tract. paup.* is the first text in this quarto (212×145) manuscript, written on f. 6-30 in expert *hybrida* script by Godefridus Wythus de Kamen, one of the most prolific scribes of the Crutched Friars' house in Liège, who wrote the larger part of the texts in this manuscript (up to f. 209) in 1466. They include among much else several other *Deuotio moderna* texts written by Johannes de Schoonhavia, as well as texts by Carthusian authors who were either contemporaries or even friends of Grote. Godefridus was very well acquainted with the Bible, as is clear from a peculiarity in his copy of *Tract. paup.*: on many occasions, he abbreviates biblical quotations (attributed as well as anonymous ones) in Grote's text by writing a few letters of the individual quoted words only, as in e.g. 713-714 "Tribulationes cordis m . multi . st, de neces . m . e . m ." for "Tribulationes cordis mei multiplicate sunt, de necessitatibus meis erue me" (*Ps.* 24 (25), 17, summarily attributed in l. 710 as "Talis dicat cum Dauid").[50] Just like *K* and its apograph *T*, *L* transmits subtitles at major transitions from one section of the sermon to the next. In section XIV.4 it will be argued that these subtitles cannot stem from Grote. After its confection by Godefridus, the manuscript remained in the Liège

---

[49] "Expliciunt sermones et omelie de sanctis Deo gracias per manus fratris Theodrici professi huius domus A.D. .MCCCCXXIIII." (Köln, HA, GB f° 20, f. 141r, cfr VENNEBUSCH, Vol. 6, 1, p. 6; 9).

[50] Another example is 727-730 "quia non uidit iustum derelictum, nec se . eius que . pa . Cuius oculi in pau . resp . , e . propter miseriam inopum et gemitum pauperum" for "quia non uidit iustum derelictum, nec semen eius querens panem. Cuius oculi in pauperem respiciunt, exsurget propter miseriam inopum et gemitum pauperum" (*Ps.* 36 (37), 25; *Ps.* 10, 8; *Ps.* 11 (12), 6).

house until its shutdown in 1804, when it was transferred to the (later) seminary library.[51]

T Trier, Stadtbibliothek, 687/249 8°, s. xvd, Prov.: Trier, St. Eucherius und St. Matthias (Benedictines), cfr VAN DIJK, *Prolegomena*, p. 350-351.

The particularly bad copy of *Tract. paup.* on f. 100v-125v in the quarto (210×144) manuscript T was transcribed from the almost equally bad one transmitted in K, as is clear from the overlap in variants documented below, in section XIV.4. The text has been written in *cursiua* script in a careless hand datable to s. xvd,[52] in a quarto (210×144) manuscript having the Benedictine abbey in Trier as its provenance. The attribution to 'Johannes' rather than to 'Gerardus' Groet in both *incipit* and *explicit* reveals that the scribe was not familiar with the author. Due to the inferior quality of the text, this witness has not been used for the edition.

Z Wolfenbüttel, Herzog August Bibliothek, 314 Gud. Lat. 4°, s. xva, cfr VAN DIJK, *Prolegomena*, p. 381.

This manuscript has been described in greater detail in section X.3 above, and also in HOFMAN, *Focar.*, p. 242. Hand 1, who wrote *Tract. paup.* in fine and slightly pointed *cursiua libraria* script, can certainly be dated to s. xva.

XIV.4 RELATIONS AMONG THE MANUSCRIPTS

In order to get a first impression of the relations among the manuscripts and also with the choice of a basic manuscript in mind, I started with a collation of the first 42 lines of the text in all eight extant witnesses. After this short collation exercise I was

---

[51] This is clear from ownership notices on f. 1r ("Fratrum Sancte Crucis conuentus Leodiensis. Pertinet fratribus Cruciferis in Leodio. Pertinet cruciferis in Leodio. Cruciferis per·tinet·") and 5r ("Liber conuentus fratrum Sancte Crucis Leodiensis"). Cfr for the quarto format of the codex the exposition catalogue [anon.], *Les manuscrits des Croisiers de Huy, Liège et Cuyk au XV*e *siècle. Exposition-Catalogue* Liège, 1951, p. 76 no. 53.

[52] The date 1479, mentioned by van Dijk, occurs in the *explicit* of another text further down in the manuscript, on f. 219r, in a part of the codex that may belong to a different codicological unit, as is suggested by the empty f. 183, which may reveal a caesura.

able to single out three witnesses which at this stage transmit a relatively low number of deviations when compared to the variant readings transmitted in some or all of the other witnesses, viz. *ZGEk*. Also, I was able to eliminate one of the witnesses from further collation work at this stage already: *T* (s xvd) transmits all variants also present in *K* (c. a. 1424),[53] and moreover has additional variants not present in *K*.[54] It seems obvious therefore that *T* has been transcribed from *K*.

In addition, *T* transmits subtitles at major transitions from one section of the sermon to the next, just like *K* and *L*. These shared subtitles, often but not invariably similar or the same, suggest that these three witnesses belong in each other's proximity, a suggestion corroborated by a great number of shared variants which will be discussed in a moment. In one instance (l. 1124), such a subtitle occurs in the middle of a quotation from Apuleius. This awkward position proves that the subtitles cannot stem from Grote himself, but must go back to the scribe of the common exemplar of *LK(T)*, as Grote himself would surely never have inserted a subtitle within a fragment quoted from one of his direct sources. That the subtitles are not always the same, and moreover vary in number in each of the three witnesses, further proves that the scribes of the individual manuscripts each of them inserted additional subtitles at their own initiative.

Since no suitable basic manuscript emerged so far, I decided to collate two random sections of the text next, l. 42-96 and l. 484-578. After some hesitation, I chose *G* as my tentative basic manuscript for the first section, basically but not exclusively modifying

---

[53] Cfr, apart from the shared subtitles discussed below, among many other variants these more notable ones: 9 pauperem] ipsum *praem*. *KT*; 10 obtutibus] nucibus *KT*; 13 amicissima] uidentur et *add*. *KT*; 14 irradiant et resplendent *tr*. *KT*; 18 e regione] *om*. *KT*; 37 Regem¹] proclamabant *hic add*. *KT*; Regem²] *om*. *KT*; for the second collated section these variants can be supplemented by the following more important deviations in *K* (*T* no longer collated): For 499-502 "Quid in hac Christus habuit uel magnum uel multum, quid preciosum, quid curiosum, quid exquisitum, quid difficile parabile, quid ornatum uel pulchrum, quid uoluptuosum uel commodosum?" *K* reads: "Quid in hac Christus habuit uel magnum uel multum et quid preciosum seu quid curiosum, quid ornatum, quid exquisitum, quid difficile, quid habile, quid pulchrum, quid uoluptuosum uel commodum?"; 520 hos] habeas *K*; 521 uiuunt] *om. K*; 538-539 Sed cottidie in oculis nostris tot occurrunt egeni nutriendi, tot nudi uestiendi] Sed tamen cottidie in oculis nostris tot occurrunt egeni nutriendi, nudi tegendi *K*.

[54] Cfr 21 fuerit] *hab. K, om. T*; 38 Israhel] et *add. T, om. K*.

CHAPTER XIV   231

the provisional text according to the version in this witness.[55] The second collation exercise is therefore based upon seven witnesses: *AZLKEkGEl*, with *G* serving as provisional basic manuscript. After the completion of the collation, it became at once clear that *G* has many more idiosyncratic readings, which do not occur in any of the other witnesses, than *Ek*. For the third section I therefore chose *Ek* as basic manuscript. Several idiosyncratic readings and errors in this next portion of the text,[56] as well as some grammatical flaws, which are not at all necessary or logical,[57] confirmed that *G* is not an ideal choice as basic manuscript.

After this second portion, I was able to eliminate *K* from further collation work also, not reluctantly, as this manuscript (together with *T*) transmits a particularly faulty version of the text,[58] full of idiosyncratic variants, which do not recur anywhere else. Where there is agreement with variants in other witnesses, the ones in *K* coincide most often with those in *L*, and occasionally with those in *AZ*, thus suggesting a division into two main branches *AZLKT* and *EkGEl*.[59] The variants shared by *K* and *L*, such as 523 habundantiarum] ab *praem. LK*,[60] are sufficiently convincing to justify the conclusion that these two manuscripts belong in the same branch of the stemma. Their textual agreement is supported by the fact that both manuscripts originated in

---

[55] External and admittedly weak arguments prompted this choice, namely the fact that the versions of *Ep.* 41; *Artic.* and *Focar.* in respectively *Z* and *Ek* are less trustworty or less easy to group than the versions in other witnesses for these other works by Grote.

[56] Cfr e.g. 488 imperat] dominatur *G*; 493 cognoscit] concupiscit *G*; 503 genera] quam *G*.

[57] Cfr 516 earum] eorum *G*, referring to fem. "diuiciarum et possessionum".

[58] In the two collated sections 1-96 and 484-578 I counted 110 deviations in *K* (excluding subtitles and instances of deviating spelling), many of them not recurring in any other witness than *T*.

[59] Cfr e.g. 85 Dominus etiam *EkGEl*, etiam Dominus *AZLK(T)*.

[60] Cfr also: 522 tegamur] tegimur *LK*; 528 Bernardum] beatum *praem. LK* (also in *ZEl*); 530 habere *correctly LK*, habete *cett.*; 578 qui] quia *LK*. Some inversions and minor flaws in other manuscripts of the group *AZLK* which are missing in *L* are less convincing, but they have nevertheless some weight in view of the enormous amount of slips and inversions in *K*, whose scribe seems to have had a habit to switch consecutive words: 68 nudam cum tibiis nudis *tr. ZL*; 92 quelibet] quibus *AL*; et] *om. AL*; 511 rebus] *om. AK*; 533 suam] *om. ZK* (also *El*); cfr finally also 534 si salutifera tibi] si tibi salutifera *tr.* Z, tibi si salutifera *tr. K*; si salutaria tibi *L*; 536 in canonica *.I. Iohannis .III.*] ut in canonica *.I. Iohannis .III. AZL*, in canonica *Iohannis .III. K*.

houses of the Crutched Friars which demonstrably had close contacts anyway,[61] and that these are the only manuscripts to insert subtitles, often (but not invariably) the same or very similar.[62]

Nevertheless, I still had not found one single manuscript transmitting a text significantly superior in quality to that in the other witnesses, nor was I able to group the manuscripts on convincing grounds, and the collation of a third randomly chosen fragment was therefore inevitable. I decided to collate l. **842-962** in the six remaining witnesses *AZL – EkGEl*, again opting for *Ek* as provisional basic manuscript. First, this led in any case to confirmation of the validity of postulating two branches in the stemma: in fourteen instances[63] the readings transmitted in *AZL* together differed from those in *EkGEl* together; also, the variant in *AZL* was most often clearly superior. The four most conspicuous examples substantiating this claim are discussed in the body of my text here.

In **906** the reading "cui", transmitted in *AZL(K)*, must be preferred to "ymmo" in *EkGEl*: in a sentence "Et sicut uere diues est pauper, cuius omnia bona inseparabilia sunt, sic [sicud *GEl, clearly wrong*] fortunatus et felix, cui nichil de suis auferri potest, cui [ymmo *EkGEl*] omnia que in motu fortune uult, succedunt prospere. Quomodo non felix? Ymmo, quicquid optat, habet." "Ymmo" in *EkGEl* may have been triggered by the occurrence of the same word in the next sentence, but it is less appropriate. The sentence as a whole functions as a parallel construction, in which the first element has been made subordinate to the second one by the formula "sicut... sic"; in the main clause "sic fortunatus et felix [*sc.* est pauper]", both "felix" and "fortunatus" are elucidated by a second degree subordinate clause, in zeugmatic arrange-

---

[61] Cfr on this topic e.g. HOFMAN, 'Crutched Friars', with further references.
[62] In l. **1-96**; **484-578** the following subtitles are found: **11** Quod paupertas et maiestas Christi simul resplenduerunt *ut subtitulum interposuit KT*; **29** De regali aduentu *ut subtitulum interposuit KT, marg. adnot. L*; **67** Apparatus] De apparatu Christi *ut subtitulum interposuit KTL*; **74** De iumento *ut subtitulum interposuit L*; **85** Asinaturus] De asino Christi *ut subtitulum interposuit L*; **94** Talis] De phalera Christi *ut subtitulum interposuit KT*, De faleris *L*; **505** Nam] De communicando fratri temporalia *ut subtitulum interposuit L*, De modo communicandi sine temporalia *K*; **569** Dixi] secundum membrum *ut subtitulum interposuit L*.
[63] Convincing diverging readings occur (cfr the *app. crit.*) in l. **842**; **851**; **910**; **911**; **914**; **920**; **921**; **927**; **930** (twice); **949** (here *EkGEl* superior); **954** (twice); **957**.

ment, parallel to the first second degree subordinate clause exemplifying "uere diues".

Although 914 "ante" (*EkGEl*) might at first sight seem more attractive than "antea" (*AZLK*) in "crastinam famem..., forte numquam, si ante moriatur..., futuram", 'when he dies before', the variant in *AZLK* should nevertheless be preferred: it is the *lectio difficilior*, and "antea" is in general to be preferred when there is an opposition between 'before' and 'afterwards' ("post(ea)"), here implied in "crastinam".[64]

In 921 "Deus" is omitted in *EkGEl* in "Si hiis omnibus naturali rerum prouidentia Deus sollicitus est". However, a subject 'God' is clearly needed in this sentence, as a created human being was the subject in the preceding sentences.

In 957, "diminuendi" is omitted in *EkGEl*, in a sequence "non accipiendi, diminuendi uel perdendi", incorrectly, as is shown by the parallel sequence 954 "attingendi, augendi et retinendi".[65]

These superior variants are surely not counterbalanced by the more attractive readings in *EkGEl* in the following instances: 85 "Asinaturus Dominus etiam (etiam Dominus *tr. AZL*) in hoc impreciato iumentorum genere elegit uel sexu fragile et ad inseden-

---

[64] Similarly, the deviating readings 910 "Hinc] *AZL*, Eciam *EkGEl*" in the two groups seem equivalent at first sight; however, on closer inspection the argumentation after 910 is a further development of what had been argued before (as implied by "hinc") rather than an argument of equal value (as implied by "etiam").

[65] The remaining instances are: 9 totis] hodie *iterum praem*. *EkGEl*, in a sentence "ut pauperem regem Christum hodie aduentantem totis spiritualium oculorum obtutibus *uideant et letentur*", where the second 'hodie' is clearly superfluous; 77 Numquid] non *add. EkGEl* in a sentence "Numquid tui fuerunt et sunt omnes fere siluarum, iumenta in montibus et boues?", where 'non' is again clearly superfluous; 575 propheticis] *AZK*, et prophetis *Ek*, et prophetarum *GElL*: that poverty is rewarded in afterlife, is more a topic in the New Testament than in the Prophets in the Old Testament; 920 ita] *om*. *EkGEl*: an adverb introducing the subordinate clause with consecutive flavour (despite ind. "fuit" for "fuerit"!) in what follows seems preferable here; 930-931 "ad ulteriora et ad plura adipiscenda astutior" (*AZL*) seems more attractive than "ad ulteriora et adipiscenda plura astutior" (*EkGEl*), but the choice is admittedly subjective and influenced by acquaintance with Grote's style of writing; 932-933 in fortuitorum inconstantia perspicacior] *AZ*, in fortuitorum inconstantior perspicacior *Ek*, in fortuitorum inconstantior et perspicacior *LGEl*: "in", introducing the attributive clause, proves that the reading in *AZ* must be correct; the original, but impossible sequence "inconstantior perspicacior" (*Ek*) was awkwardly emended in *LGEl*; 954 sicut] *AZL*, *fortasse delendum*, sic *certe false hab. EkGEl*.

dum fedum, ...". In **949**, the reading in *EkGEl* "(que [*sc.* desiderium et spes] nullo modo) pauperem molestant" is superior to "pauperi (pauperem *L*) molesta sunt" (thus *AZL*), on the basis of parallel phrases in **1020** "(pauper cupidini) non molestatur" and **1035-1036** "(desideria naturalia) quiescunt nec amplius molestant". Similarly, **959** qua] *ZEkGEl* is supported by one witness from the other branch, *Z* (quo (*AL*) is triggered by preceding "eo").[66]

Group *AZL(KT)*

The comparatively close proximity of *LKT* could be established after the collation of l. **1-96** already. It remains to be sorted out in which manner *AZ* are related to these three witnesses. It turns out that neither of these two witnesses agrees significantly with any of the other ones in a consistent manner. Thus, we sometimes find agreement between *ZA*, as in **946** dirimunt] *LEkGEl*, diminuunt *AZ*,[67] at other times agreement between *AL*, as in **92** quibus inepta quelibet et fragilia] *ZEkGEl*, quibus inepta, quibus fragilia *AL*.[68] This means that each of the three witnesses *AZL* independently derives from the common exemplar. Combined with the established interrelationship between *L* and *K (T)* this leads to the proposed representation in the stemma below.

Group *Ek G El*

The third collation also enabled me to group the various manuscripts in group *EkGEl* more precisely. First, a longer omission in *Ek* proves that the (later) manuscripts *G* (a. 1420) and *El* (a. 1454-1460) cannot have been copied from *Ek* (c. a. 1400): **557** bonum[1] – proprium] *om. Ek, hab. GEl*. Secondly, several variants shared by *GEl*, but not present in *Ek*, suggest a closer proximitity between these two witnesses. Apart from **906** sic] sicud *GEl* and **932-933** inconstantia] inconstantior *Ek*, inconstantior et *GEl* (also in *L*),

---

[66] Cfr also: **535** in] ut *praem. AZL*; **954** et] *EkGEl*, uel *AZL* (to be preferred on the basis of parallel **956-957** desideratarum et habitarum); cfr elsewhere in the text e.g. **975** cantet *EkEl*, cantat *ALZ*, to be preferred on the basis of the parallel subjunctive form **973** sit (in all witnesses).

[67] Cfr also **861** minime] *LEkEl*, minimis *AZ*, nec minimis *G*; **862** pauper] est *add. AZG*.

[68] Cfr also **889** eas] *om. AL*; **901** Stilbon] *sec. Sen. legendum est, sic Z (etiam K) Ek*, Stibbon *A*, Scibbon *L*, Stilben *G*, Salbon *El*.

CHAPTER XIV

I note: **4** allegoricis] allegoriter *GEl*; **934** Adest] Atque *GEl*.[69] These combined data lead to the proposed representation in the stemma below, with manuscripts used for the edition underlined:

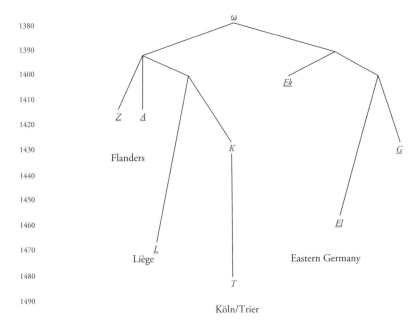

On the basis of the superior readings in *AZL*,[70] as revealed after the third collation exercise, I decided to opt for a basic manuscript from this group. The best choice, obviously, would be the

---

[69] Cfr also the less convincing variants: **850** docuit] docet *GEl*; **870** est plenus *tr*. *GEl*; et] sed *GEl*; **880** nos suis *tr*. *ZGEl*; **965** tenebit *GEl* (interestingly, the scribe of *Ek* here shows greater acumen: he corrected an error present in the common archetype: tenebit timebit *corr. se ipsum Ek'*).

[70] In a few instances there are no external grounds to prefer the variant in either of the two branches. The superiority of branch *AZL(K)* in other instances has led me to tip the scale in favour of the reading transmitted in this group: **842** comes plenus *tr*. *EkGEl*; **851** acquirenda] *AZL*, acquirendum *EkGEl*; In the phrase **911** "qui nichil uult, nichil cupit", both variants, "nichil[2]] *AZL(K)*, uel *EkGEl*", can be defended. The alternatives can both be explained as a misread abbreviation: either "n[l—"] for "ul-", or the other way round. Both variants are possible also in: **927** que[2]] *om. EkGEl*. Another example clearly showing that *AZL* should be distinguished from *EkEl* is **747-749** Sic paupertas edificat *turrim fortitudinis a facie inimici*, que turris sicut alta in profectu et utilis in refugio, sic in Christo et humilitate firmiter fundata est] *AZL*, Sic paupertas efficit *turrim fortitudinis a facie inimici*, que turris sicut alta est in profectu et utilis in refugio, sic in Christi humilitate firmiter fundata est *EkEl*.

manuscript containing the smallest number of distinguishing variants. When unimportant spelling variations are left out, the number of distinguishing variants, both those present in a single manuscript only and those shared by several manuscripts, are for the respective manuscripts in the three collated sections: *Z*: 54; *A*: 48; *L*: 52; *Ek*: 60; *G*: 110; *El*: 79. This count reveals in the first place that Moll had been very lucky when he prepared his *editio princeps*: he could dispose of two manuscripts which now turn out to be the best extant witnesses. Since *A* contains the smallest number of distinguishing variants, and also since the variants in *L* are in general of a slightly more serious nature than those in *A*, I have decided to use *A* again as basic manuscript. However, Moll observed already that the text transmitted in *A* cannot be qualified as a flawless transcript.[71] For this reason, I follow in general the text in *A*, but where this copy transmits deviating readings occurring in none of the other witnesses, or where readings in other witnesses are clearly superior – provided that these occur in both branches of the stemma –,[72] I follow the majority of other witnesses. This ultimate choice for *A* also meant that the provisional text of the collated sections had to be adapted to the text as transmitted in *A* again. In view of the great number of variants occurring in *G*, which are in addition often unique to this codex, I also decided to exclude *G* from further collation work; the edition is therefore based on five witnesses belonging to two groups, viz. *A Z L – Ek El*.

Two manuscripts transmitting *Tract. paup.* have their origin in centres with close associations with Grote or his earliest disciples, *K* and *L* (written in the Crutched Friars' houses in Cologne and Liège). Many excellent copies of other works by Grote are transmitted through these centres, and it turns out that one of the best witnesses for *Tract. paup.*, *L*, has its origin in the Liège Crutched Friars' convent. It may therefore come as a surprise that the quality of the copy from the Cologne house, *K*, is somewhat inferior.

---

[71] In the Preface to his edition, Moll writes: "Dat de afschrijvers van geen van beide Hss. een volkomen zuiveren tekst ten voorbeelde gehad hebben, blijkt vooral aan het einde van het sermoen", with an example elucidating this observation (p. 431).

[72] Apart from the examples listed above, I departed from this principle in a few instances, following the clearly superior reading in *Ek El* in e.g. **792 sit]** *Ek El*, sic *A Z L*, with notable consequences for the division of sentences in this case.

GERARDI MAGNI

SCRIPTA CONTRA SIMONIAM ET PROPRIETARIOS

CONSILIVM DE LOCATIONE
CVRE PASTORALIS

CONSPECTVS SIGLORVM

codex principalis

D KÖLN, Historisches Archiv der Stadt Köln, GB 4° 249, a. 1418

codices

N DEN HAAG, Koninklijke Bibliotheek, 79 K 22, s. XIVd-XVa

Familia υ

A UTRECHT, Bibliotheek der Rijksuniversiteit, 174 (1 L 14), s. XVc
Kh KÖLN, Diözesan- und Dombibliothek, 1092, s. XVb

Familia ζ-ξ

E ERLANGEN, Universitätsbibliothek, 543, a. 1456
X WOLFENBÜTTEL, Herzog August Bibliothek, 18. 32 Aug. 4°, s. XVc
Z PADERBORN, Erzbischöfliche Akademische Bibliothek, Ba 12, a. 1407

Hos codices in plagulis phototypice expressis contulimus.

⟨CONSILIVM DE LOCATIONE CVRE PASTORALIS⟩

Queritur an quis possit locare sub annuo censu curam animarum aut regimen una cum prouentibus et redditibus ipsi cure debitis. Respondeo que sequuntur.
Primum quod obuentiones, oblationes et redditus alicuius cure
5 possunt locari sub annuo censu, si sine regimine locentur, id est, si regimen non locetur, ut patet Extra, *Ne prelati uices*, c. *Querelam* cum suis concordantiis.
Secundum quod dico est quod regimen animarum nullo modo per se locari potest sine symonia sub annuo censu uel pro pretio
10 uel ad annum uel annos. Patet ex titulo rubrice, qua dicitur "ne prelati uices suas uel ecclesias sub annuo censu concedent", | et eodem t., c. *Quoniam enormis*, et per Bernardum et Innocentium in eodem c., et .i., q. .iii., c. *Saluator* cum suis concordantiis.

22ra 119

120

4/7 cfr *Decret.*, X 5.4.4 (c. II, 768, 31-43), de prohibitione regiminis praesertim X 5.4.3 (c. II, 768, 22-27)   10/11 *Decret.*, X 5.4.1 (c. II, 767, 52-53)   12 cfr *Decret.*, X 5.4.3 (c. II, 768, 22-27)   12/13 cfr BERN. PARM., *Glos. ord. in Decret.*, super X 5.4.3, comm. sup. 'regimen statuantur'; 'sacerdotium' (c. II, 768, 24; 25) (c. 1648 (p. 38), gl. g; i); in prima glosa Bern. ad locum ex *Decr.* a Ger. etiam allegatum se refert   cfr INNOC., *Comm. Decretal.*, super X 5.4.3, comm. sup. 'regimen' (c. II, 768, 24) (ed. 1570, p. 602, c. 1, sub num. 3, 22-27)   13 cfr GER. MAG., *Simonia beg.*, 6-11; hoc caput infra, 71-73, partim uerbatim allegatur   cfr GRAT., *Decr.*, C.1 q.3 c.8 (c. I, 413-415), praesertim § 1 (c. I, 414, 12-34), ubi allegatur epistula Vrbani II (*JL* 5743 (4308), T. 1, p. 697), prius prelo data a MANSI, *Sacrorum conciliorum*, T. 20, c. 660-663, reiterata in *PL*, 151, c. 529C-533B   concordantiis] cfr BRIX., *Glos. ord. in* GRAT., *Decr.*, super C.1 q.3 c.8, in duobus partibus expositionis casus (c. 758 (p. 447), ante gl. o) et comm sup. 'Quisquis' (c. I, 414, 12) (c. 759 (p. 448), gl. d)

Tit. De locatione cure animarum sub annuo censu cum redditibus eius *inc. in Kb*, Explicit tractatulus magistri Gherardi Groed de periculo pastoralis cure. Et incipit tractatus eiusdem magistri de locacione ecclesiarum *inc. in X*, *inc. om. DNAZE*   3 Responde o] Ad istam questionem *praem. X*   que] per ea *praem. X*   4 Primum] primum dictum *marg. clarificat N²*, primum *marg. clarificat Kb A² E²*   oblationes] *om. N¹, marg. suppl. N²*   6 c.] *corr. N², § N¹*   8 Secundum] secundum dictum *marg. clarificat N²*, secundum *marg. clarificat Kb A² E²*   10 annos] *add. praem. ZE*   11 concedant *melius X E sec. Decret.*   et¹] *om. A*   12 eodem] eo *Kb*   c.] *om. Kb, corr. N², § N¹*   13 et] *om. N¹, suppl. N²*   .i., q.] prima questione circa *A*   c.²] *om. N¹ Kb, suppl. N²*   concordantiis] Extra, De symonia, c. Cum querelam *add. Kb*

Tertium quod dico est quod sic regimen animarum accipere et locare pro pretio uel annuo censu cum pacto interposito est horribilis et magna symonia, quod patet ex predictis et per multa iura probari possit. Sed clarius uidetur si res inspiciatur. Nam in tribus horribilior est symonia, scilicet in ordine, in dignitatibus et in curis animarum. Potestas ordinis et potestas iurisdictionis, que est in | dignitatibus ecclesiasticis, et potestas regiminis animarum sunt res ualde spirituales et habent exercitia ualde spiritualia et actus et executiones ualde spirituales. Et quanto res sunt spiritualiores in se et earum executiones et exercitia sunt spiritualiores, tanto eas uel locare uel emere pro re temporali uel exercere uel exequi propter temporale lucrum uel propter questum est turpior symonia et magis diabolica. Et tanto magis requiritur quod intentionis nostre oculus et affectus nostri oculus, quo intendimus eis et afficimur ad eas, sit sincerior et purior, et tanto magis requiritur quod cognitionis nostre oculus sit in eis perspicacior et prudentior et subtilior quanto res sunt magis spirituales, | magis mystice, aut magis diuine. Alias namque neque affectus neque intellectus neque intentionis oculus recte in illas res spirituales ire et transire potest, neque aliter ualet eas recte penetrare uel attingere neque recte eas ad opus explicare et exponere. Non est enim conuenientia neque proportio grosse, impure et imprudentis mentis et intentionis ad subtilia et spiritualia et diuina mysteria capienda et exercenda.

Ideo primum et maximum quod requiritur ad has potestates utiliter capiendas et exercendas est congrua dispositio hominis in

---

14/26 cfr infra, 333-344 ; 620-622   14/19 cfr *Decret.*, X 5.3.15 (c. II, 753, 32-55)

14 Tertium] tertium dictum *marg. clarificat* N^2, tertium *marg. clarificat* $Kh\,A^2\,E^2$ est quod dico *tr. Kh*   suscipere *Kh*   et] ac *L*   16 et magna] *om. X*   patet – et²] *om. N¹ Kh, marg. suppl. ipse N¹*   17 posset *X*   possit] Extra, De simonia, c. Querelam cum suis concordantiis *add. C, marg. suppl.* N^2 Nam] de tribus horribilibus symoniis in tribus potestatibus ualde spiritualibus *marg. clarificat* $N^2\,A\,Kh$ 22 exequuciones *sic N*   22/23 sunt¹ spiritualiores¹ – exercitia] *om. E*   23 executiones] actiones *Z*   23 sunt spiritualiores] *om. X*   24 uel⁴] *om. Kh¹, suppl. Kh²*   27 oculus¹] *om. Kh*   oculus¹ – nostri] *om. E*   31 magis] *om. E*   neque¹] *om. N¹, suppl. N²*   32 illas] eas *Kh*   33 aliter] *om. Kh*, alter *E*   neque²] uel *X*   34 explicare] D^1, applicare *corr. marg.* D^2 36 et spiritualia] *om., sed add. ipse N¹*   capienda et] *om., sed add. ipse N¹*   38 Ideo] quomodo ante omnia oportet hominem spiritualem esse in uita et (uel *Kh*) scientia *marg. clarificat* $N^2\,Kh\,A$

40 scientia et in actione et in | ordine circa illas potestates aut circa illud officium uel ordinem, quia, ut ait Dionysius in libro *De angelica ierarchia*, "Ierarchia est ordo, scientia et actio". Et ergo oportet accedentem ad has esse spiritualem in actione et in uita et spiritualiter per scientiam intelligere, ut possit ad has spiritua-
45 liter accedere et eas spiritualiter exercere. Qui enim in se non percepit ea que Dei sunt nec spiritualiter examinatur carnalis et animalis existens, quomodo circa alta mysteria et profunda Dei sacramenta et ecclesie, qualia sunt in executione ordinum, que ceteris spiritualioribus profundiora et secretiora sunt, spiritualiter
50 percipere uel examinari potest? Aut quomodo potest talis in iurisdictione aut in cura animarum aliis spiritualiter preesse aut iudicare spiritualiter, qui nec sibi ipsi preesse nec se spiritualiter regere aut diiudicare ualet?

Caracter ordinis cuiuscumque a Deo et Spiritu san|cto est,
55 etiam quamuis sit in malo homine ordinato et a malo ordinante. Similiter potestas omnis spiritualis, siue in regimine animarum siue in iurisdictione, spiritualis est a Deo et a Spiritu Sancto, siue qui eam habuerit uel dederit malus fuerit siue bonus. Talis potestas est a Spiritu sancto et est ad opera Spiritus sancti et ad spiri-
60 tualia finaliter ex natura sua ordinata. Vnde in se et in uirtute sua et in effectu est tota spiritualis.

41/42 cfr GER. MAG., *Cura past.*, 204-206   cfr THOM., I, Q. 108 a. 1 arg. 2 (T. 5, p. 494, c. 1, l. 28-29), ubi allegatur DION., *Cael. Hier.* 3, 1 (p. 785, c. 4 (l. 3)), sed **43** ordo] Ger. hic Thom., secundum me ordo diuinus et *Dion. sec. transl. Ioh. Scot. Eriug.*; quae uaria lectio (sicut et uocabulum 'angelica' pro 'caelesti' adhibitum) demonstrat allegationem sec. Thom. uel ex memoria factam esse   **50/53** cfr GER. MAG., *Cura past.*, 92-98   cfr THOM., *Perf.*, c. 27 co. (T. 41, p. B 106, 289-301)   **54/61** cfr GER. MAG., *Cura past.*, 161-168 cfr THOM., *Sent.*, L. 4 d. 24 q. 1 a. 1 qc. 1 arg. 1; qc. 1 co.; qc. 2 co.; ad 1 (T. 7,2, p. 887, c. 2; p. 888, c. 2); de malis ministris L. 4 d. 24 q.1 a.3 qc. 1 arg. 1; co.; ad 1 (T. 7,2, p. 892, c. 1; p. 893, c. 1), sed praesertim THOM., III, Q. 64 a. 5 co. (T. 12, p. 46, c. 1 – c. 2), etiam GRAT., *Decr.*, C.1 q.1 c.30-33 (c. I, 371, 28 – 372, 12); C.1 q.1 c.77-78, praesertim C.1 q.1 c.84 § 4 (c. I, 388, 15-29)

---

40 in¹] *om. XE*   **42** gerarchia *bis DZ, secundo uice V*   sciencie *X*
45 eas] *om. KbVC*   Quod *E*   **48** sunt] sicut *sic N*   **49** spiritualibus *Kb*   securiora *E*   **50** potest¹] *om. X*, possit *E*   potest²] possit *E* in] ex *E*   **51/52** iudicare – nec] *om. E*   **52** qui] quia *N*   ipsi] *om. N¹*, *suppl. N²*   **53** aut] *corr. N²*, ne *N¹*   ualet] *corr. Kb²*, ualeat *Kb¹*   **54** Caracter] quod hee potestates semper a Spiritu Sancto sunt et (uel *Kb*) ad spiritualia operanda *marg. clarificat N² Kb A*   Spiritu] a *praem. NA Z*
55 etiam] et *Kb*   sit] *om. E*   **57** spirituali *N*   **58** uel] aut *X*
59 est¹] tamen *Kb¹*, tam *em. Kb²*   et est²] quam est *Kb*   **61** in] *om. Z*

Nec fuit aliud | quam potestas spiritualis quam Symon ambiuit et petiit, a qua omnis symonia nomen accepit. Dixit enim Petro: "*Da michi hanc potestatem, ut cuicumque manus imposuero, accipiat Spiritum sanctum,*" ut dicitur *Actuum* .VIII. Et intelligitur ibidem quod potestatem illam uoluit habere dandi Spiritum sanctum, id est donum Spiritus sancti, scilicet in signo uisibili per uirtutem signorum. Et in hoc duplex fuit Symonis symoniaca prauitas, primo quia illam potestatem emere uoluit estimans *per pecuniam donum Dei possidere*, secundo propter pecunias eam uoluit exercere, "ut ex uenditione signorum, que per eundem fierent, multiplicatam pecuniam lucraretur", ut dicitur c. *Saluator*, .I., q. .III. Et sic fuit prauitas in mente eius tam accipiendi quam dandi spiritualia symoniace. Et fuit intentionis eius tam potestatem habere symoniacam quam executiones facere symoniacas. Et ista est plenissima symonia, precipue | quando simul potestas et executio eius sunt spirituales et consistunt in conferendis mere spiritualibus.

Inde est quod, si potestas, que est annexa ordini sacro, si ematur uel cum aliquo temporali acquiratur, est symonia maxima, quia presumendum est quod talis tales symoniacas ordinis executiones faciat qualem recepit potestatem. Et hoc est quod communiter accidit, uidelicet quod ille qui emit spiritualem potestatem | per temporalia, quod ipsam propter auaritiam uel propter

---

63/65 Act. 8, 19   65/68 cfr Act. 8, 20   69/70 Act. 8, 20 paene ad litt., allegatum sec. GRAT., *Decr.*, C. 1 q. 3 c. 8 (c. I, 414, 1)

62/63 GER. MAG., *Sim. beg.*, 860 paene ad litt.   66/72 GER. MAG., *Sim. beg.*, 860-863 paene ad litt.   69/73 GER. MAG., *Sim. beg.*, 863-865 paene ad litt.   GRAT., *Decr.*, C.1 q.3 c.8 (c. I, 414, 6-8), hic partim uerbatim allegatus, cfr supra, *Locat.*, 13

---

62 Nec] quod symon magus non peciit nisi (*om. Kh*) potestatem *marg. clarificat* $N^2 Kh A$ ambiuit] uel concupiuit *add.* X   63 qua] quo E nomen] *om.* X   64 potestatem hanc *tr. a.c.* D   66 ibidem] ex litera *add. Kh*   illam potestatem *tr.* X   dando E   67 scilicet] *om.* $N^1 Kh E^1$, *suppl.* $N^2 E^2$ 68 Et] duplex fuit symonia symonis *marg. clarificat* $N^2 Kh A$ fuit duplex *tr.* Z   69 quia] quod *Kh*   73 sic] si Z   74 intentio *Kh* 75 Et] in quo consistit plena symonia *marg. clarificat* $N^2 Kh A$ 76/77 executio] *corr.* E^2, persecutio E^1 77 sunt eius *tr. a.c.* D   79 Inde] quomodo communiter symoniacus in potestate acquisita symoniace eam exercet *marg. clarificat* $N^2 Kh A$ annexa est *tr.* D   82 faciet X   recipit D   84 propter] *om.* N^1, *suppl.* N^2

inanem gloriam uel aliud huiusmodi temporale exercet et exequitur, prout a radice mala omnes fructus mali pullulant, ut, exempli gratia, non uideo quomodo sciens, potens et uolens spiritualiter missam celebrare possit pecuniam pro sacerdotio dare, cum spirituali celebrationi huiusmodi symonia est tota contraria. Nam hoc uitium symonie carnalissimum est, ymmo a fide alienum, et contrarium fidei formate, que per dilectionem operatur.

Et ergo ille nullatenus potest pro tunc spiritualis esse uel spiritualiter ex caritate operari, qui contra fidem formatam uel contra fidem ex dilectione operantem symoniace sibi huiusmodi spiritualem potestatem acquirit, siue ordinis siue iurisdictionis siue cure animarum. Et hoc est quod dixit Petrus Symoni mago: "*Non est sors*", ait, "*neque pars tibi in sermone isto. Cor enim tuum non est rectum coram Deo. In felle amaritudinis et obligatione iniquitatis uideo te esse.*" 'Fel amaritudinis' est in|trinseca fellica malitia, congesta in bursa conscientie, id est in intentione mala, effectiua amaritudinis culpe et pene, qua intendit quis usurpare sibi potestatem ad quam non est dispositus, et pecunia sibi eam comparare. Et consequenter est in *obligatione iniquitatis*, qua obligatur | et constringitur, inclinatur aut intendit ipsam potestatem inique exercere propter pecuniam. Fel fuit in intentione cum amaritudine, et obligatio consequenter uenit in operatione per iniquitatem.

Inde patet causa cur in ordine accepto symoniace magis punitur in iure accipiens symoniace ordinem quam symoniace dans eundem ordinem, cum tamen superior dans, maxime ex magnitudine status et quia principalis est in actione, forte magis pec-

---

96/99 Act. 8, 21 ; 23   103 Act. 8, 23

---

86 Rvp. Tvit., *Apoc.* 2, 2 (c. 879, 19), cfr etiam supra, intr., cap. 1   107/123 cfr Grat., *Decr.*, C.1 q.1 c.8 (c. I, 359, 37 – 360, 14)

---

85 temporale] *om. A¹, marg. suppl. A¹ uel A²*   86 exempli] uerbi *X*   89 celebratione *X*   91 formate] *om. D¹, suppl. D²*   delectationem *Z*   92 pro tunc potest *tr. E*   94 sibi] *om. E*   94/95 potestatem spiritualem *tr. X*   95 siue ordinis] *om. X*   96/97 ait non est sors *tr. E*   97 ait] *om. Kb*   sermone] *cett. sec. Bibl.*, symone *D*   99 fel] *ex* uel *corr. ipse A¹*   fellicita *E*   100 in²] *om. Kb E*   affectiua *N*   101 potestatem sibi *tr. E*   103 communiter] consequenter *D*   105 fel] uel *Z E*   in] *om. Kb E*   107 Inde] Cur magis punitur in iure simoniace accipiens quam dans *marg. clarificat N² Kb A*   in] ex *Kb*   108 accipiens simoniace accipiens *sic N*   109 dans tamen superior *tr. E*

246 CONSILIVM DE LOCATIONE CVRE PASTORALIS

cauerit. Sed intentio malitie accipientis in sola acceptione symoniaca non quiescit nec stat, ymmo magis incipit accipiendo, et consequenter ad futuram nequitiam in exequendo ordinatur, crescit et multiplicatur. Sed dando dans non iubet symoniace exe-
115 qui ordinem datum, et suam in hoc compleuit malitiam. Vnde per penas magis iura nituntur principiis obstare, que ad multas malas disponunt executiones, initiatum magis quam unam superioris potestatis executionem ualde prauam punire, licet utrisque, secundum quod possunt iura, penas imponunt, et iudicio Dei et
120 iudicio conscientiarum in multis et pro maiori parte penas iustas committunt. | Similiter punitur magis eadem ratione dignitatem aut curam animarum symoniace procurans quam symoniace concedens aut quam committens alicui | easdem symoniace.

125

23va

Sciendum quod in istis tribus potestatibus caracter presbyterii,
125 in quantum presbyter, requiritur et presupponitur, tam ad plenam dignitatem, ut est episcopalis, quam ad curam animarum executiue regendam, uelut abbatias, prioratus et parochiales ecclesias. Licet enim diaconus possit habere curam animarum, tamen infra annum tenetur promoueri nisi secum dispensetur, et tenetur in-
130 tendere fieri presbyter et intendere exequi officium cure, alias fructus non faceret suos ex cura prouenientes, nec bona fide curam possideret. Et ergo ad potestatem regiminis animarum habendam in foro conscientie bona fide et ad fructus iuste tollendos requiritur uoluntas executionis, et sine ordine presbyterii eam
135 exequi non ualet. Et ergo ista presupponunt caracterem presbyterii in executione earum.

118/119 cfr GRAT., *Decr.*, C.1 q.1 c.6 (c. I, 359, 5-9)   121/123 cfr GRAT., *Decr.*, C.1 q.1 c.7 (c. I, 359, 13-33)   128/132 cfr *Decret.*, VI 1.6.14 (c. II, 953, 42 – 954, 22, praesertim 954, 13-20, reiterantem Conc. Lugd. II, const. 13 (a. 1274, *COD*, p. 297-298)); VI 1.6.22 (c. II, 961, 8-15) uel BERN. PARM., *Glos. ord. in Decret.*, super X 1.14.5, comm. sup. 'breue tempus' (c. II, 457, 7) (c. 267 (p. 134), gl. b, l. 12-20 in gl.)

---

111 malitie] male *X*   113/114 multiplicatur, in exequendo ordinatur, et crescit *tr. E*   114 dans] dando *tr. a.c. D*   non] *om. N¹, suppl. N²*   116 magis] *om. Kh*   obstare principiis *tr. X*   117 initiatum] uiciatum *X*   122/123 concedens] aut quam concedens *iterum add. E*   123 quam] *om. Kh*   simoniace] *om. Kh*   124 Sciendum] Notandum eciam *X*   125 requiritur] *corr. Kh²*, inquiritur *Kh¹*   128 tamen] cum *Kh*   130 officium] beneficium *E*   cure] turbe *sic Z*   136 eorum *X*

CONSILIVM DE LOCATIONE CVRE PASTORALIS   247

Archidiaconi uero et similes licet habeant dignitatem et iurisdictionem sine presbyterio, hoc magis ex consuetudine et usurpando prouenit quam ex ordine rei in se aut ex commissione et
140 in uirtute episcopi, ut dicit ⟨Archidiaconus⟩. Iurisdictio enim spiritualis cure animarum ab initio coniungebatur, et ergo plenam iurisdictionem non habent archidiaconi huiusmodi.

Et si bene inspiciatur, tunc | cura animarum | superior et plenior est in episcopo, et similiter plena iurisdictio et spiritualior et
145 altior est in eo. Et ergo ista episcopalis dignitas est maior potestas et spiritualior, et executiones eius sunt maiores et spirituasliores, quia non solum episcopi possunt consulere uel precipere, sed etiam coartare et compellere subditos ad bonum. Item, quia dant potestates alias tamquam ab ipsis deriuatas, scilicet potestatem

23vb
126

137/138 cfr de necessaria ordinatione in decanum, sed non in presbyterum *Decret.*, X 1.6.7 § 2 (c. II, 52, 15-19), locum ex conc. oecum. Lateran. III, can. 3 (ed. *COD*, p. 188, 23-26) sumptum; etiam X 1.14.1 (c. II, 125, 45-46); GRAT., *Decr.*, D.60 c.1-3 (c. I, 226, 30-44); loci alii, qui neque a GRAT., neque in *Libro X* assumpti sunt, in *DDC* 1 (1935), c. 977-978, enumerantur   137/142 cfr ARCH., *Comm. Decr.*, super C.16 q.7 c.11, comm. sup. 'prebendas ecclesiae' (c. I, 804, 6-7) (f. 271r[1], c. 2, 10-31), ubi Arch. praesertim se refert ad *Decret.*, X 1.23.4 (c. II, 150, 53-61) et BERN. PARM., *Glos. ord. in Decret.*, super X 1.23.4, comm. sup. 'consuetudinis' (c. II, 150, 57) (c. 313 (p. 157), gl. c); ambo eandem materiam tractant, sed minus cum Ger. concordant quam Arch.; eandem materiam etiam tractant statuta synod. Leodiens. Iohannis IV episc. (a. 1288), tit. 16, n. 4 (p. 158, 7-8 ed. Avril), allegata ab A. AMANIAV, *DDC* 1 (1935), c. 969, sub uoce 'archidiaconus', 3.3.2; cfr generaliter super archidiaconos inde a saeculo duodecimo ibid., c. 962-976; minus uerisimiliter Gerardus hic in paraphrasi GVIL. ALT., *Summa*, L. 4 tract. 14 (de clauibus), c. 3 (que persone habeant claues) (4, 344, 65 – 345, 3) citasse uidetur, ubi Guilh. de munere archidiaconi in loco episcopi operantis tractat   140/145 cfr THOM., II-II, Q. 184 a. 6 ad 2; ad 3 (T. 10, p. 458, c. 2 – 459, c. 2)   143/145 cfr *Decret.*, X 1.23.1 (c. II, 149, 60 – 150, 6); X 1.23.7 § 2-3 (c. II, 151, 41-58); BERN. PARM., *Glos. ord. in Decret.*, super X 1.23.4, comm. sup. 'consuetudinis' (c. II, 150, 57) (c. 313 (p. 157), gl. c)   145/154 cfr THOM., II-II, Q. 184-185 (T. 10, p. 456-485), de statu perfectionis, specialiter (q. 184, a. 5-8) in praelatis ecclesiae et (q. 185) in episcopis   145/152 cfr THOM., II-II, Q. 184 a. 6 co. (T. 10, p. 458, c. 1-2)

---

137 Archidiaconus *X*   139/140 aut – Anchisidorensis] *om. Kh*   140 Archidiaconus] *sic legendum, cfr app. font.*, Ancisidorensis *N*, Archisidorensis *ZX*, Archisideren- *E*, Antesidorensis *A*   141 coniungebantur *X*   142 non habent] *om. E*   144/145 et[1] – ista] *marg. inf. prius oblitus suppl. ipse N[1]*   145 eo] *sic E[1]*, episcopo *corr. E[2]*   ergo] *om. D*, igitur *N*   dignitas episcopalis *tr. E*   est[2]] et *Kh*   maior] magis *E*   146 spiritualior] *corr. N[2]*, spiritualis *N[1]*   et[2]] *om. Kh*   147 uel] et *Z*   percipere *N*   148 coartare] *corr. Kh[2]*, coercere *Kh[1]*   149 ipsis (*sc.* ip̄is)] episcopis (*sc.* epīs) *Z*

248   CONSILIVM DE LOCATIONE CVRE PASTORALIS

150 ordinis et particularis cure animarum, et ideo executiones eius sunt uehementiores et altiores, et consequenter debent esse spiritualiores et puriores, quia eorum status, ut ait Dionysius in multis locis *Ecclesiastice ierarchie*, est alias potestates non solum purgare aut illuminare, sed purgatas et illuminatas perficere.

155 Et ideo hec est pessima symonia episcopatus dignitatem symoniace acquirere, et eo plenius, si presbyter, ut oportet, propter episcopatum habendum efficitur. Tunc currit in mente hominis in eundem alueum presbyteratus ad quem currit episcopatus, quia consequitur presbyteratus in mente et in intentione hominis cur-
160 sum et uoluntatem ad episcopatum. Sic similiter in eo qui propter beneficium presbyter efficitur, sequitur ut communiter ut talis sit in intentione et affectu presbyteratus qualis est in affectu et in intentione, in beneficio | optando uel acquirendo.   24ra

Illi uero qui habent iurisdictionis potestatem sine presbyterii
165 ordine, ut archidiaconi, certum est quod archidiaconi curam habent aliqualem animarum, saltem in exterioribus defectibus animarum de consuetudine | in curatis et in curam animarum ha-   127
bentibus. Et ergo officium eius est altius in hoc, et quasi architectonicum respectu curatorum et respectu defectuum quos curati
170 regere non ualent. Sed aliunde habent presbyteri curati executiones magis spirituales quam archidiaconi, maxime in foro conscientie.

152/154 cfr THOM., II-II, Q. 184 a. 5 co. (T. 10, p. 457, c. 1, 3-11), ubi allegat DION., *Eccl. Hier.* 5 (p. 1369, c. 1 (l.3)), sec. transl. Ioh. Scot. Eriug.; q. 184 a. 6 s.c. (T. 10, p. 458, c. 1, 18-22), ubi allegat DION., *Eccl. Hier.* 5 (p. 1345, c. 4 – p. 1346, c. 2 (l. 3)), sec. transl. Ioh. Scot. Eriug.   **164/165** cfr locos supra, 137-138, collectos, sed praesertim *Decret.*, X 1.23.7 § 1-5 (c. II, 151, 35-59), elucidatum in *DDC* 1 (1935), c. 969-974

---

151 consequenter] per consequens X   **152** quia] quam N   **153** gerarchie DZ, irarchie A   potestates] *om.* Kh   **154** aut] uel E   **156** si] tunc *add.* Kh   **157** habendum] *om.* Kh   **159** in²] *om.* XE   **160** Sic] Nota de eo qui propter beneficium presbyter efficitur *marg. clarificat* Kh   Sic] *om.* X   similiter] est *add.* Kh   **161** ut¹] *om.* D   ut²] quod NKh   **162** in¹] *om.* Kh   in³] *om.* NZXE   **165** quod] ad *add.* E   **166** aliqualem] aliquarum Kh   defectibus] *ex* effectibus *corr* A¹ ᵘᵉˡ ²   **168** ergo] igitur N   **169** curati] sicut etiam *praem.* Kh   **170** regere] gerere XE

CONSILIVM DE LOCATIONE CVRE PASTORALIS 249

Vnde notandum quod ad tria opera et ad tres executiones principales finales potestas caracteris ordinis presbyterii ordinatur, scilicet ad consecrandum sacramentum eucaristie, et ad absoluendum et ligandum, et tertio ad predicandum et informandum. Ista tria principalia sunt in potestate ex officio presbyteri. Et consequenter multa alia adiunguntur, scilicet baptizare, benedicere, matrymonia coniungere et inungere et cetera. Sed hec omnia excepta consecratione sacramentali non habet simplex presbyter executiue nisi in casu necessitatis, nec potest ea exequi nisi sibi materia detur in quam ualeat ea exequi. |

24rb

Et ideo symoniacus presbyter simplex in ordine non habet tam multas executiones et intentiones symoniacas, sicut incipit habere iam presbyter simplex existens et curam animarum symoniace acquirens. Nam talis et ordinem et potestatem, quam iam habet in ordine et quam acquirit in cura, ad eundem finem exercendo retorquet. Nam accipiendo curam obligatur iam ad omnia hec exequenda.

Et qui curam accipit per pecuniam uel propter pecuniam, ille etiam celebrat missam, sicut simplex presbyter ex | ordine, propter pecunias secundum quod cura requirit, et consequenter predicat et absoluit propter pecunias, quia, ut ait Ambrosius, primo libro *De officiis*, "affectus nomen operi tuo imponit", et "intentio

128

173/177 cfr infra, 364-365; GER. MAG., *Ep.* 19, 24-25; 32-34   cfr THOM., *Sent.*, L. 4 d. 24 q. 2 a. 2 co.; ad 1; ad 4-5; ad 8; ibid., a. 3 co.; ad 2 (p. 897, c. 2 – 899, c. 1); etiam L. 4 d. 24 q. 1 a. 2 qc. 2 arg. 2 (p. 890, c. 1); qc. 3 ad 2 (p. 891, c. 2), prope locum supra (54-61) allegatum; insuper summatim officia sacerdotis describuntur a HVG., *Comp.* 6, 36 (p. 233, c. 2, 14-20; 37-40)   180/181 cfr inter fontes e.g. IOH. FRIB., *Summa Conf.*, L. 3, t. 27, q. 10 (f. 194r, c. 1-2)   186/193 cfr infra, 368-370; GER. MAG., *Cura past.*, 164-168   193/196 cfr THOM., *Sent.*, L. 2 d. 40 q. 1 a. 2 arg. 2-3 (T. 2, p. 1013), ubi allegat AMBR., *Off.* 1, 30, 147 (p. 53, 31-32); ARIST., *Metaph. Lat.*, 3, ut demonstret bonitatem uel malitiam uoluntatis sufficere ad hoc quod actus exteriores siue bonos, siue malos dicantur

---

173 Vnde] Nota tres casus finales ordinis presbyterii *marg. clarificat Kh*, Nota que requiruntur ad dignitatem presbyteratus *marg. clarificat A²*, de potestate caracteris ordinis presbiterii quam habet presbiter *marg. clarificat E²* ad¹] *om. Kh*   174 potestates *X*   175 eukaristie *N A E*, eucharistie *X* ad²] *om. Kh*   175/176 soluendum *X E*   176 et¹] *om. E*   177 presbyterii *X*   178 adiunguntur] *corr. Kh² X²*, coniunguntur *Kh¹ X¹*   179 et inungere] *om. N¹, suppl. N²*   et cetera] *om. X*   excepta] *om. A*, accepta *marg. inf. suppl. A²*   180 habent *X*   180/181 execucione *Kh*   183 Et] *om. X*   in ordine] *om. Kh*   184/185 iam habere *tr. Kh*   193 absoluat *Kh*

et finis operis formam dat operi" (ut qui fornicatur propter pecunias, magis est auarus quam luxuriosus), ut ait philosophus. Ideo secundum quod homo afficitur ex intentione ad rem et quod querit sibi in re et placet sibi in ea, hoc dicitur facere in ea.

Et ergo symoniacus symoniace celebrans uel absoluens propter pecunias magis querit pecunias quam missam uel absolutionem. Volo hoc ex istis inferre quod quis accipiens curam animarum particularem post ordinem presbyteratus potestatem iam accipit maiorem et ampliorem potestatem et materiam in exequendis illis que ex ordine presbyterii potuit exercere, et potestatem talem | accipit executiuam cui executiones immediate coniunguntur.

Vnde sic Christus, cum post auctoritatem quam habuit ab instanti conceptionis executionem in resurrectione accepisset, ait: *"Data est michi omnis potestas in celo et in terra"*. Sic etiam ait curam acceptans: "Nunc datur michi executiue potestas exequendi fere omnia que ordinis mei sunt". Vnde patet quod in cura animarum data uel commissa magna datur potestas spiritualis, et dantur executiones libere et currentes, quasi daretur potentia propinqua ad suum actum uel ad actus completos, et maxime ad actus qui exercentur respectu aliorum, unde lucrum et questus pro|ueniunt.

Nam presbyter per se potest celebrare, sed non absoluere nec predicare. Et in istis includitur preesse et potestas quibus aliis preest in comparatione salutis eterne. Vnde ista est spiritualissima negotiatio. Nam soluendo aperit presbyter celum, et repellendo claudit. Numquid longe maioris potestatis est absoluere in anima

---

209 Matth. 28, 18

220/221 cfr GER. MAG., *Focar.* o (p. 304, 135-136)

---

195 ut] Vnde *Z*   **196** philosophus] in ethicis *add. X*   **199** symoniacus] sacerdos *praem. X*   **200** pecunias²] pecuniam *E*   **203** ampliacionem *Z*   potestatem et materiam] *hab. E¹, sed postea del. E¹ ᵘᵉˡ ²*   materiam] iurisdictionem *X*   **203/204** exquendis *A*   **204** presbyteri *DNKhAZ*   **207** si *Z*, sicut *XE*   **208** accepisset] *om. Kh¹, suppl. Kh²*   **209** Sic] quomodo in acceptione cure datur potestas exequendi que sunt ordinis *marg. clarificat Kh²*   **209/210** curam] *om. D*   **211** Vnde] *om. E*   **212** datur potestas spiritualis magna *tr. Kh*   **217** Nam] que potest simplex presbyter *marg. clarificat Kh²*   posset *E*

et coram Deo quam in foro contentioso aut coram hominibus? Quanto maior est liga et spiritualior et uerior in anima quam que adextra est. Et absoluit presbyter curatus de maximis peccatis, licet non possit absoluere aliquando de maxime apparentibus adextra. Nam absoluit fere ab omni quo in sola conscientia sine opere exteriore peccatur. Et plura talia sunt peccata grauiora in conscientia quam sepe que adextra | apparent.

Et est etiam maxima potestas potestas celebrandi, unde a pluribus dicitur quod papa est potentior quia presbyter quam quia papa. Nam facit de creatura Creatorem in consecrando quia presbyter. Hec et plura alia in cura acceptata executiue presbyter accipit, et ipsas celebrationes missarum, quarum executionem antea habuit, una cum aliis ea mente quali alias suas cure executiones siue pure siue impure exequitur.

Et ideo ecclesie est meo uidere maius periculum in eo qui curam animarum accipit symoniace quam qui presbyterium accipit sy|moniace. Et plus sibi et ecclesie nocet, eo quod latius et liberius tunc patet executio officii sui symoniace, et plures uel inficit uel negligit. Et accipit potestatem preessendi pluribus, quos magis abducit quam ducit, quos magis creberrime inficit et uulnerat quam curat, quia *fur* et mercenarius est *ueniens ut mactet et furetur.*

Item ex alio est spiritualior potestas meo uidere regimen animarum in foro conscientie quam in iurisdictione tantum coram

---

242/243 Ioh. 10, 10 paene ad litt., cfr Ioh. 10, 12-13

230/231 cfr GER. MAG., *Focar.* o (p. 307, 195-196)   231/232 cfr GER. MAG., *Focar.* o (p. 304, 130-131)   242/243 locus biblicus etiam allegatur in GER. MAG., *Focar.* 21 (p. 433, 2858)

---

223 liga] *sic ex* ligo *corr. D¹*   225 possit absoluere] *om. Kh*   maxime] *corr. N²*, maximis *N¹*   226 uere *E*   228 que] *om. Kh*   229 potestas²] *om. KhXE*   unde] nota de presbytero et papa *marg. clarificat Kh²*   230 quam] *om. Kh¹*, *suppl. Kh²*   231 Nam facit] *om. XE*   in consecrando] *om. Kh*   232 accepta *DXE*   presbyter] *om. Kh*   233 et] *om. E*   233/234 antea] anima *D*   235 exequuntur *Z*   236 meo uidere ecclesie est *tr. X*   meo uidere] *om. Kh*   eo] eorum *Z*   238 sibi plus *tr. a.c. A¹*   239 uel] *om. X*   240 preeundi *Kh*   241 abducit] et seducit *add. X*   inficit] *praem. A*   242 est] et *E*   ueniens] et *add. E*   244 Item] Nota quod maior est potestas in regimine animarum quam in iurisdictione *marg. clarificat hoc uice ipse Kh¹*, etiam *A²*   regimen] in regimine *Kh*   245 foro *Z*

hominibus iure fori. Nam ibi est cura anime secundum quod in ueritate existit, in iurisdictione uero solum secundum quod apparet.

250 Item in regimine anime consulitur uere saluti et uere uirtutibus ad uitam eternam, in iurisdictione maxime paci et concordie hominum per constitutiones humanas consulitur. | Et illa dumtaxat puniuntur sine quibus societas christiana humana non ualet stare uel non bene stare, quibus, secundum Augustinum in ⟨.I.⟩ libro *De libero arbitrio*, canonica et humana iura aptantur.

255 Regimen animarum mundat conscientiam et aperit homini ecclesiam triumphantem et celum, et unit hominem corpori Christi mistico. Sed iurisdictio mundat in exterioribus ecclesiam militantem de bonis et malis congregatam a quibusdam apparentibus et enormibus scandalis et excessibus aliquorum, quia *nondum ue-*
260 *nit tempus* ut omnia scandala auferantur ab ea. Vnde patet longe potestatem maiorem et spiritua|liorem esse in regimine animarum, et ergo uere coram Deo enormior est symonia, si ematur uel locetur.

Sepius tamen ecclesia repetit et crebrius monet ad uitandam et
265 prohibendam emptionem uel locationem iurisdictionis spiritualis fori contentiosi quam ad prohibendam eandem in cura animarum. Hoc ideo non est quia minus est peccatum emere uel locare curam animarum in foro conscientie, sed quia ecclesia magis potest exteriora, que contingunt in foro exteriore, cognoscere, arguere
270 et iudicare et reformare. In reliquis autem, que tangunt conscien-

---

259/260 cfr Ioh. 6, 7

249/253 cfr THOM., I-II, Q. 96 a. 2 CO. (T. 7, p. 181, c. 2, 3-12)   253/254 cfr THOM., I-II, Q. 96 a. 2 ad 3 (T. 7, p. 181, c. 2), qui allegat AVG., *Lib. arb.* I, 5, 13 (p. 219, 73-77), et cui Ger. in argumentatione concordat

---

246 secundum] *om. A¹, suppl. A²*   247 solum] *om. Z*, solam *Kh*
249 Item] *om. XE*   redicione *E*   250 iurisdictione] uero *add. E²*
252 christiana] seu *add. X*   252/253 stare – bene] *om. Kh*   253 quibus] quia *X*   .I.] *sic legendum, om. codd.*   254/348 canonica – aliis mi-] *om. uno folio deperdito Kh*   255 mundat] *om. D¹, suppl. D²*   et] *om. X*
256 unit hominem] unionem *E*   259 nondum] non *D*, nundum *NA*
262 uero *Z*   264 Sepius] Nota quare ecclesia sepius prohibet emptionem iurisdictionis spiritualis et cetera *marg. clarificat A²*   recipit *E*
267 non] *om. D¹E, suppl. D²*   268 potest] *om. D*   269 cognoscere] *om. V*   270 et] uel *bis X*

CONSILIVM DE LOCATIONE CVRE PASTORALIS 253

tias hominum et forum conscientie in ualde multis, etiam grauissimis peccatis latentibus, ecclesia homines | Deo et diuinis preceptis et euangelicis, que scribuntur in tabulis cordis hominum, reliquit, Deo et iudici confessionis illorum iudicia reseruans et committens. 25rb

Ymmo aliquando est contrarium iudicium ecclesie in foro iudicio ecclesie in conscientia. Et tunc tenetur quis magis sequi iudicium conscientie quam iudicium fori, et hoc plus pertimescere, ut habetur Extra, *De sententia excommunicationis, Inquisitioni*. Ex hoc est quod crebrius admonet ecclesia et scribit et punit de symonia iurisdictionis fori quam de symonia in cura animarum, licet utrumque prohibeat ecclesia, quamuis longe sit anime grauius et periculosius curam animarum locare quam temporalem iurisdictionem in foro causarum.

Et etiam grauior meo ui|dere est ambitio et enormior ingerere se cure animarum aut petere eam pro se sine hoc quod pecunia interueniat quam iurisdictioni causarum se ingerere non symoniace, sed ambitiose, licet in utroque turpis et nimis sit ambitio. Vnde Gregorius, primo *Pastoralium*: "uirtutibus pollens tractus ad regimen ueniat, uirtutibus uacuus nec tractus accedat". Et Augustinus, .XIX. *De ciuitate Dei*: "locus superior, et si teneatur ut de- 132

276/279 cfr *Decret.*, X 5.39.44 (c. II, 908, 12-14), et cfr specialiter BERN. PARM., *Glos. ord. in Decret.*, super X 5.39.44, in expositione casus uersus finem (c. 1916 (p. 172), 65-68), et ibid., comm. sup. 'humiliter sustinere' (c. II, 908, 13) (c. 1916 (p. 172), gl. h, 69-71), ubi in commento super consilium super debito coniugali dicit: "et potius debet sequi conscientiam quam sententiam ecclesiae, cum quis certus est in hoc casu"   289/304 cfr GER. MAG., *Cura past.*, 52-59   289/290 HENR. GAND., *Quodl.* 2, q. 18 (p. 139, 83-85), qui allegat GREG. MAG., *Reg. past.* 1, 9 (p. 160, 38-39, cfr *PL*, 77, 22C)   290/292 HENR. GAND., *Quodl.* 2, q. 18 (p. 136, 7-8), qui allegat AVG., *Ciu. Dei*, 19, 19 (p. 687, 31-33), cfr etiam GRAT., *Decr.*, C.8 q.1 c.11 (c. I, 594, 9-12); THOM., II-II, Q. 185 a. 1 s.c. (T. 10, p. 466, c. 1 – 467, c. 2) paene ad litt., ubi allegatur AVG., *Ciu. Dei*, 19, 19 (p. 686, 22 – 687, 40, uerba allegata ibid., p. 687, 31-33)

---

271 et forum] in foris *Z*   271/272 grauissimis] eciam *iterum add. E*   272 peccatis] *om. V*   ecclesia] eciam *V*, ecclesie *E*   omnes *E*   273 cordis] *om. A*   274 relinquit *V*   iudici] iudicii *N*   276 Ymmo] Nota iudicium ecclesie ⟨in foro⟩ est aliquando contrarium iudicio ecclesie in conscientia *marg. clarificat A²*   277 tunc] *om. XE*   279 inquisioni *V*   280 et¹] *om. V*   282 quam *X*   sit longe grauius anime *tr. V*   286 cura *D*   pro] per *X*   288 ambicione *D*   nimis] *om. spatio uacuo relicto Z*, nimia *V*   289 tractus¹] coactus *V*   291 . XIX.] . IX. *E*   Dei] *om. A*

ceat, indecenter tamen appetitur". Et, ut dicit Gregorius, .VIII., q. .I., c. *In scripturis*, "locus regiminis desiderantibus negandus, fugientibus offerendus est".

295 Vnde certum est | quod, si quis precibus fusis pro se ipso, si indignus fuerit cura, [et] propter preces proprias curam obtinuerit, siue ad tempus siue ad uitam suam, [certum est quod] ipso facto est symoniacus a lingua, prout tenent iuriste et theologi. Et patet per Thomam in *Secunda Secunde*, q. .C., art. .V., in respon-
300 sione ad tertium argumentum. Ymmo secundum Thomam ibidem, "si quis pro se rogat ut obtineat curam animarum, ex ipsa presumptione redditur indignus. Et sic secundum presumptionem preces sunt pro indigno", et consequenter secundum presumptionem iuris symoniace.

305 Est tamen casus dabilis, in quo quis potest curam pro se petere intentione subeundi onus et seruitium, non propter honorem nec propter lucrum temporale. Et tunc, si non propria uoluntate et desiderio, sed necessitate et utilitate publica compulsus, et si nullus alius dignior inuenitur, potest cum timore et quasi | coactus
310 pro utilitate publica et necessitate curam petere, si non generetur species mali ex facto suo, qua ambitiosus uideatur, et aliis si ambitionis exemplum non dederit.

Hec dico ut uideatur quanta sit in cura appetenda ambitio et malitia, et quod quis solis precibus fusis pro se digno facit symo-

---

292/294 HENR. GAND., *Quodl.* 2, q. 18 (p. 139, 66-68), qui allegat GRAT., *Decr.*, C.8 q.1 c.9; uerba allegata cum in titulo (c. I, 592, 22-23), tum in textu capitis (c. I, 592, 28-29) inueniuntur   295/300 cfr THOM., II-II, Q. 100 a. 5 co. (T. 9, p. 362, c. 2, 13-20)   298 iuriste] sc. Vrbanus Papa secundus, decerptus a GRAT., *Decr.*, C.1 q.3 c.8, partim (sc. c. I, 414, 12-19) allegatus a THOM., II-II, Q. 100 a. 5 s.c. (T. 9, p. 362, c. 1, 41-45)   300/304 THOM., II-II, Q. 100 a. 5 ad 3 (T. 9, p. 363, c. 1, 4-7)   305/312 cfr GER. MAG., *Cura past.*, 42-46   cfr HENR. GAND., *Quodl.* 2, q. 18 (p. 139, 88 – 141, (1)26), cfr etiam THOM., II-II, Q. 100 a. 5 ad 3 (T. 9, p. 362, c. 2, 53 – 363, c. 1, 2)

---

292 ut] *om. E*   294 fugientibus] *corr. N²*, fugiendus *N¹*   est] *om. E*
295 quod] *om. X*   297 certum est quod] *quia haec uerba supra*, 295, *etiam scripta sunt, hic delenda censeo*   quod] *om. DZXE*   298 Et²] Etiam *A*, ut *E*   299 patet] *om. X*   per] *om. A*   in¹] *om. X*   in²] *om. Z*
300 secundum] *om. D¹*, *suppl. D²*   302 secundum presumptionem] *om.V*   302/303 secundum – consequenter] *om. XE*   305 potest quis *tr. a.c. N*   306 nec] aut *V*   307 propter] *om. V*   308 sed] de *add., sed postea del., ut uidetur, A*   si] *om. X*   310 publica] *om. D*   311 qua] quo *X*   313 petenda *spatio in fronte uacuo relicto E*

CONSILIVM DE LOCATIONE CVRE PASTORALIS 255

315 niam in cura animarum querenda ⟨secundum⟩ presumptionem iuris, licet aliquando in casu et rarissime, ut dixi, posset peti cum multis circumstantiis predictis, ut ex | hiis quis uideat quantum malum et quam horribilis symonia sit indigno aut digno, si locet precibus et pro pretio curas animarum. 25vb

320 Nec multum differt siue perpetue ad uitam siue ad tempus uel ad annos huiusmodi cura locetur, uel si committatur pro pretio uel annuo censu. Nam diuturnitas regiminis non uariat genus malitie nec ambitionis, licet diutius esse malum peius est quam breuius. Manet enim peccatum adulterii, siue proponat per annum siue
325 semper adulterari. Et illi qui obligant se ad tres uel quattuor annos ad regimen animarum, aliquando fortius obligati sunt uinculo exteriori ad preesse quam qui illud semper obtinendum recepit. Nam omnem curam animarum curatus quilibet citra episcopatum propter ingressum religionis uel aliam iustam causam potest licite
330 resignare, sed mercenarius obligatus cogitur sepe secundum iudicium fori tenere in quo se obligauit, | quasi sub pretextu locationis prouentuum quos uidetur locasse. 134

Quarto dico quod, si quis curam et regimen animarum sibi acquirit sub annuo censu, pacto interposito de certo dando annua-
335 tim sine locatione reddituum et prouentuum, et qui in hoc intendit lucrum pecuniarum et appetit alias non accepturus regimen si lucrum pecuniarum non speraret, | quod talis omnia que acquirit et lucratur in cura, tenetur restituere ecclesie, maxime illa que utiliter in utilitatem ecclesie non ponit aut consumit. De utiliter con- 26ra
340 sumptis in expensis et uestibus necessariis pro nunc nichil dicere

---

328/330 cfr GRAT., Decr., C.19 q.1 c.1; q.2 c.1-2 (c. I, 839, 17 – 840, 18)
334/338 cfr infra, 507-510; GER. MAG., Cura past., 97-102; Ep. 17, 68-73
337/342 cfr GER. MAG., Ep. 19, 81-103

---

315 querendo E   secundum] sec. 302/303 supplendum uidetur, om. codd.   315/316 presumptionem iuris] om. V   318 si locet] locari X   318/319 precibus et precio locare V   319 precibus] om. Z   320 perpetuo A   perpetue] siue add. X   uel] siue X   323 est] om. A   325 quattuor] ad praem. NE   326 ad] om. E   sunt obligati tr. V   327 qui illud] qui ille E, ille qui corr. E²   semper] ad praem. V   obtinendum] ad praem. E   330 sed] si X   331 quasi] sed praem. V   332 quas DNA   quos – locasse] om. V   333 Quarto] quartum dictum marg. clarificat N, habens regimen sub annuo censu tenetur omnia restituere marg. clarificat A²   et] sed V   335/336 intendit in hoc tr. E   336 recepturus X   337 quod] om. X   338 restituere tenetur tr. E   340 in] et Z   dicere nichil tr. E

uolo, sed de superlucratis uidetur omnino quod restituenda sunt in hoc casu. Nam hoc est apertissima symonia, quia pactum et pecunia interuenit cum intentione corruptissima in periculosa et maxima symonia, ut supra dictum est.

345 Et ergo maxime isti debent puniri magis pre ceteris symoniacis. Nam symoniaci omnes puniuntur priuatione fructuum acceptorum, quando scienter symoniam cum pacto interposito fecerunt etiam in beneficio simplici et in aliis minoribus symoniis.

Quinto dico quod qui sola uoluntate principaliter lucrandi in 350 officio regiminis ipsum regimen locat, locat etiam sine pacto interposito uel conuentione de certo censu dando, turpissime acquirit, quia ex specie ambitionis et ex intentione mala, ymmo pessima, eo quod ordinat res spirituales ad finem rerum temporalium, tamquam res uiles ad res meliores, res quibus magis | fruen-
355 dum est, ad res quibus utendum. Vnde in se ipso plus amat et plus reputat et estimat pluris ipsum | temporale quam ipsum spirituale, quia "propter ⟨quod⟩ unumquodque tale, et illud magis". Et hoc est infidelitas quedam et heresis et diuisio a corpore Christi mystico, ymmo ydolatria quedam est et peccatum maximum, et 360 contemptus maximus Dei et spiritualium rerum et sacrorum sacramentorum.

Sexto dico quod longe maius peccatum facit et maior symoniacus est coram Deo qui sic sine pacto interposito finaliter prop-

---

344/345 cfr supra, 14-26   353/357 cfr Ger. Mag., *Cura past.*, 114-117; *Ep.* 19, 15-18   cfr Thom., *Sent.*, L. 4 d. 24 q. 1 a. 1 qc. 3 s.c. (T. 7,2, p. 888, c. 1, 3-7), ubi Thomas a Ger. citata uerba allegat ex Arist., *Post. Lat.* 1, 2, in uersione latina a Iac. Venetico confecta et a Guil. de Moerbeka reuisa (p. 287, 29-30, cfr p. 9, 13-14 (Arist., *Post.* 1, 2, 72a29-30 Bekker))

---

342 hec *X*   343 pecunia] *om. D¹, marg. suppl. D²*   interuentione *V* in] et *Z*   in periculosa] *om. X*   345 isti maxime *tr. E*   347 symoniace *N*   348 -noribus] *textus iterum transmittitur in Kh*   349 Quinto] quintum dictum *marg. clarificat N Kh*   qui] *corr. Kh², que Kh¹*   350 locat] *secundo uice om. Kh Z X E*   etiam] et *Kh*   351 dando censu *tr. a.c. N*   354 tamquam] *om. D*   355 est] *om. X*   ad res] *om. E,* rebus *corr. E²*   utendum] est *add. Kh*   357 quod] *hab. X, om. cett., sed sec. Thom. supplendum uidetur, ut ex app. font. et loc. simillimo in* Cura past., 116/117, *euidenter patet*   illud] ipsum *X*   magis] tale *add. E*   Et²] etiam *Kh* 360 rerum spiritualium *tr. E*   360/361 sacramentorum] contemptus *add. X*   362 Sexto] sextum dictum *marg. clarificat N Kh*   maius] magis *D* 362/477 Sexto – continet] *sequuntur post* 705 *in X, cfr praefationem, Cap. II.3*   363 est] *om. Kh*

CONSILIVM DE LOCATIONE CVRE PASTORALIS 257

ter et ad auaritiam exercet curam animarum in predicando, ab-
365 soluendo et in sacramenta ministrando et celebrando quam si quis
animo proficiendi subditis et subeundi oneris curam animarum,
pecunia etiam cum pacto data collatori, sibi usurparet.
Patet, quia malitia que est ex fine auaritie, coinquinat omnes
actus subsequentes et multiplicat symoniacas actiones et inten-
370 tiones per totum tempus regiminis. Et secundo, quia nociuior est
subditis oues excorians et tondens et tondendo et ad auaritiam
singula retorquendo. Et negligit curam et spiritualem profectum
ouium, quas non amat nec intendit, et suo exemplo oues occidit
nec murum opponit lupis. Tertio, plus capit actus malitiam ex fine
375 quam ex | medio ad finem, quia finis actioni nomen imponit, ut 136
supra dixi.
Et licet intendat quis proficere et onera subire, | tamen per sy- 26va
moniam ad hoc peruenire non est medium, quo debeat et possit
pertingere ad ipsam curam. Ymmo est simpliciter malum et inex-
380 cusabile, quia propter bonitatem cuiuscumque finis intenti non
sunt facienda mala ut ueniant bona, et maxime mala simpliciter,
sicut est pacisci de regimine animarum in certo dando.

372/374 cfr Ioh. 10, 11-14

364/365 cfr supra, 173-177; GER. MAG., *Ep.* 19, 24-25; 32-34   cfr THOM.,
Sent., L. 4 d. 24 q. 2 a. 2 co; ad 1; ad 4-5; ad 8; ibid., a. 3 co.; ad 2 (p. 897,
c. 2 – 899, c. 1); etiam L. 4 d. 24 q. 1 a. 2 qc. 2 arg. 2 (p. 890, c. 1); qc. 3 ad 2
(p. 891, c. 2), prope locum supra, 54-61, allegatum; summatim officia sacerdotis describuntur a HVG., *Comp.* 6, 36 (p. 233, c. 2, 14-20; 37-40)   368/
370 cfr supra, 111-114; 186-193; GER. MAG., *Cura past.*, 164-168   370/374 cfr
GER. MAG., *Ep.* 17, 26-29; *Cura past.*, 265   374/376 cfr supra, 193-198   cfr
THOM., *Sent.*, L. 2 d. 40 q. 1 a. 2 arg. 2-3 (T. 2, p. 1013), ubi allegat AMBR., *Off.*
1, 30, 147 (p. 53, 31-32); ARIST., *Metaph. Lat.*, 3, ut demonstret bonitatem uel
malitiam uoluntatis sufficere ad hoc quod actus exteriores siue bonos, siue
malos dicantur   377/385 cfr infra, 565-573   382/405 cfr GER. MAG., *Simonia beg.*, 888-898

364 et ad] *sic hab. A¹, cum punctis del. A²*   365 et celebrando] *om. D¹,
marg. suppl. D¹ uel D²*   quis] *om. D*   367 eciam pecunia *tr. E*   colla-
tori] collocari *D*   368 coinquinet *N Kh A Z*   369 actiones] et *praem. A¹,
del. A²*   370 totam *sic A*   secundo] ergo *X E*   nociuior] *sic corr. N²*,
nocior *N¹*, ..s *praem. A*   371 excoriens *X*   et³] *om. X*   372 retor-
quenda *Kh*   negligerit *Kh*   373 quas] quam *N A Z E*   374 nec – lupis]
om. X   malitiam] *om. Kh*   375 quam – finem] *om. X E*   377 Et] *nota
malum non est faciendum propter bonum marg. clarificat A²*   Et] *om. Kh*

Verumtamen plus punitur in iure in ecclesia militante qui pactum interposuit de certo, quamquam ad bonum finem ordinauerit beneficium acquirendum, quam qui ipsum propter lucrum temporale locat uel exercet sine pacto symoniaco precedente, quia iura humana et ecclesia militans adextra non iudicat de intentionibus hominum latentibus, sed de apparentibus. Et ergo in symonia mentali sola, qua quis solo affectu coram Deo symoniacus dicitur et non coram hominibus, in illo etiam remittit hominem "suo Creatori per penitentiam satisfacere", ut Extra, *De symonia*, c. finali cum suis concordantiis.

Sed reuera in iudicio conscientie per confessionem longe aliter debet confessor transire in beneficio curato et aliter in non curato. Non curatum potest quis retinere, si ipsum per symoniam mentalem acquisiuit, et hoc si mutato proposito officium et actus, qui sibi incumbunt ex beneficio, non | propter temporale, sed | propter salutem suam eternam uelit exercere et exerceat, et ipsum beneficium sibi proficuum fuerit ad salutem, et non impediuerit eum a salute. Tunc potest remanere in eo, alias non. Nam si ad temporale lucrum finaliter retorserit exercitia spiritualia, tota conscientia manet infecta et intentio hominis, que est oculus hominis et lumen, quo existente tenebroso tota uita hominis redditur tenebrosa. Et ideo absolui non potest nec debet in foro conscientie, quamdiu tales intentiones habuerit, nisi resignauerit.

De eo qui symonia mentali acquisiuit sibi curam, aut propter questum uel lucrum eam acceperit uel locauerit, uel ad questum uel ad lucrum eam exercet, non potest absolui nisi mutato pro-

---

383/388 cfr GER. MAG., *Cura past.*, 123-130   hic locus melius cum loco in *Cura past.* concordat quam locus (565-573) a uiro docto Mulder in comm. suo sup. *Cura past.* propositus   388/392 cfr *Decret.*, X 5.3.46 (c. II, 767, 44-50) 393/419 cfr infra, 706-725   406/419 cfr GER. MAG., *Cura past.*, 178-188 408/410 cfr GER. MAG., *Cura past.*, 85-98

385/386 temporale] *om. E*   386 locet *X*   symoniaco] symoniace prauitatis *E*   387 iudicant *A*   388 in] de *A*   389 solo] *om. E*   393 aliter longe *tr. Kh*   394 in²] *om. Kh*   395 Non] *D Kh C*, Nam *N A Z X E* 396/406 et hoc – De eo] *suppl. uel rest. in ras.* $A^{2\ uel\ 3}$ 398 suam] *om. Kh*   400 manere *A*   in eo] *om. Kh*   402 que] qui *Kh*   403 existente] *om. Kh*   405/406 resignauerit. De eo qui ...] *sic sententiae sec. codd. contra Clarissem diuidendae sunt, cfr* Lexicon Nederl., R, 370, 30-38   407 uel¹] aut *N A*   accepit *Kh Z*   408 ad] *om. X*   exercit *sic E* nisi] sine *E*

CONSILIVM DE LOCATIONE CVRE PASTORALIS   259

posito, ut finaliter ad salutem animarum et ad propriam salutem
410   curam regiminis uelit exercere et exerceat. Et nisi dignus sit talem
curam habere, non potest absolui ut maneat, etiam si nichil obstet aliud nisi indignitas aut nichil preter hoc obstiterit, uidelicet
quod sit ignarus aut seculariter uiuens. Et meo uidere oportet
etiam quod sit in tali intentione quod curam illam uelit exercere
415   et regere, etiam si nullum emolimentum temporale ab ea deriuaretur, | si ipse aliunde uictum et uestitum habeat uel haberet. Hec   27ra
et multa alia in iudicio anime perpendenda sunt in penitente sacerdote curato, antequam curam possit cum pura conscientia obtinere.
420   Quod quidam superficiales iuriste non perpendentes, obmissis
diuinis et naturalibus legibus, iudicium ecclesie adextra dumtaxat
attendentes, sepissime omnes indifferenter | huiusmodi symonia-   138
cos mentales in confessionis iudicio permittunt in suis curatis uel
non curatis beneficiis.
425   Ex istis septimo dico quod quis bona intentione ad lucrum animarum dumtaxat sine locatione fructuum et prouentuum curam
animarum cum precedente pacto symoniaco de annuo censu sibi
usurpans tenetur restituere que lucratus est, maxime in quibus ditior factus est. Patet, nam sicut non nocet mentalis symonia in fine
430   uel intentione hominis quo magis puniatur adextra, sic nec iuuat
mentalis bonitas in intentione quo minus puniatur manifestum
pactum symoniacum de certo dando. Nec ecclesia uult latens punire nec ex latenti iuuare. Equa est huiusmodi conditio ecclesie,
ut nec condempnet ex latentibus nec | absoluit in iudicio exte-   27rb
435   riori ex latentibus.

410/413 cfr GER. MAG., Cura past., 203-251   413/416 cfr GER. MAG., Cura
past., 84-88   429/430 cfr supra, 386-392   430/432 cfr supra, 383-385

410/411 habere talem curam tr. NKhA   411/412 obstat D   412 aut]
et Kh   obstiterit XE   415 ea] eo KhAZ   417 sunt] om. DZXE   in²]
et Kh   420 Quod] nota de superficialibus iuristis marg. clarificat A²
quidem Kh   421 adextra eciam E   422 huiusmodi indifferenter tr.
a.c. N   422/423 symoniacas DNKhAZ   423 uel] et X   425 Ex istis]
septimum dictum marg. clarificat NKh, dictum septimum de restitutione
marg. clarificat A²   quod] quia E   quis] qui Kh   426 et] uel X   426/
427 curam animarum] ante dumtaxat pos. Kh   428 que] quod E
429 est] om. A   430 intentione] in praem. KhX   430/431 hominis –
intentione] om. E¹, marg. suppl. E²   431 puniantur Kh   432 ecclesia]
eciam ZXE   433 ex latente DZX, exaltante E   equa] econtra XE

Et maxime hoc patet quia pactum hoc exterius est exemplum pessimum et nociuum ualde ecclesie. Et est commune malum, quo ecclesie et anime horribilissime, latissime et frequentissime leduntur et corrumpuntur. Vnde conuenit uniuersaliter hoc puniri et nullius secreti pretensione excusari, cum quilibet posset dicere se talem habere intentionem. Nec deberet bonus uir uelle ut impunitum hoc peccatum in se maneret, sed potius, in quo peccauit, quod in illo puniretur secundum penam statutam a canone, que utilis esse ualeret exemplariter aliis, ne similia attemptarent. Et sicut probauit et approbauit facto suo, quantum in eo est, quod talis pactio interposita est licita exterius, sic et exterius eam reprobet per penam, maxime quia mani|festa et quasi notoria solet esse huiusmodi symonia.

Octauo dico quod absque dubio in nullo liberatur quoad Deum uel excusatur mercenarius (qui intentione lucrandi temporalia, alias non facturus, conueniendo et paciscendo de certo locat uel accipit sub annuo censu simul fructus siue prouentus una cum regimine simul), ut uideatur solum prouentus locasse et accepisse sub censu, et non regimen. Nam, ut ait | Pascalis papa, .I., q. .III., c. *Si quis obiecerit* et c. *Saluator*, "si quis alterum eorum, sine quo alterum non prouenit, uendiderit, neutrum eorum inuenditum derelinquit".

Vnde quia non prouenit nec solet prouenire communiter ut fructus ⟨concedantur⟩ sub annuo censu sine regimine, tamen id ipsum fieri potest. Tum, quia sic non fit alicubi et quasi publicum est quod sine commissione regiminis non uolunt alicui locare

---

442/443 cfr GRAT., *Decr.*, C.1 q.3 c.15 (c. I, 418, 11-22)   449/454 cfr infra, 517-525   454/457 GRAT., *Decr.*, C.1 q.3 c.7 (c. I, 413, 16-18) paene ad litt., reiteratum in GRAT., *Decr.*, C.1 q.3 c.8 (c. I, 414, 30-33), ubi Grat. citat ex epistula Vrbani II (*JL* 5743 (4308), T. 1, p. 697), prius prelo data a MANSI, *Sacrorum conciliorum*, T. 20, c. 660-663, reiterata in *PL*, 151, c. 529C-533B

---

436 Et] nota de malo exemplo *marg. clarificat A²*   est] in *D*   438 latissime] *om. X*   439 et corrumpuntur] *om. E*   440 quilibet] quibus *XE*   441 Nec] nota bonus uult malum puniri *marg. clarificat A²*   443 que] si *E*   444 ne] *corr. Kh²*, nec *Kh¹*   448 symonia] miserabilis *praem. X*   449 Octauo] octauum dictum *marg. clarificat NKh*, octauum *marg. clarificat A²*   dubio] quod *iterum add. Kh*   452 siue] uel *X*   453 et] uel *E*   455 obiecit *XE*   456 alterum²] eorum *iterum add. X*   uenditum *Kh*   458 quia] *om. Kh*   459 concedantur] *scripsi*, concedentur *codd.*, concederetur *X*   id] *om. E*   460 tum] tamen *X*   sic] *om. E*   quasi] *om. XE*

fructus sine regimine, alias et ipsi locatores fructus non locaturi, tunc sciens hoc scit quod unum sine alio non prouenit. Et ergo locando unum locat et reliquum, tam in facto quam ex intentione utriusque. Vnde patet ex facto quod accipiendo uel locando prouentus statim gerit officia curati spiritualia in ecclesia.

Miror, si sic possit fieri in cura animarum, ubi tot sunt spiritualia officia et tot pericula oriuntur, ⟨cur⟩ non possit hoc fieri in prebenda, ut quis simul locet prebendam illi qui gerat pro se officia et capiat redditus pro certo. Item, si possit sic locari cura ad aliquos annos indifferenter secundum iurium placitum, cur non possit tunc dari ab aliquo collegio quod quasi perpetuus est curatus ad uitam ipsius locantis. Et si hoc concedatur posse fieri, rogo a quo differt talis locatus a uero curato aliquo, cum ipse uerus curatus | non nisi ad uitam curam huiusmodi habeat? Et michi non uidetur multum differre nisi in hoc quod unus sine censu eam habet quam alius sub censu continet. Item, si sic fieri potest, cur non possit collator sub annuo censu huiusmodi curas alicui conferre sine symonia, ex quo locatio predicta finalem habet uigorem in spiritualibus sicut locatio. |

Verum quia ex regimine proueniunt prouentus, maxime ubi nulla sunt certa, talis commissio digniori fieri debet, et aptitudo

---

481/494 cfr GER. MAG., *Cura past.*, 123-128

---

462 fructus – locatores] *om.* XE   463 alio] reliquo E   ergo] igitur N
464 ex] est Z, in X   467/481 Miror – Verum] *sic praebet A contra assertionem uiri docti Clarisse in app. suo, om.* C, *et cantat, et celebret, et predicat et absoluit*; *cur non possit locari, ut uidetur, ad uitam hominis, si potest ad aliquos annos locari? Et, si ad uitam locetur, non uidetur differre in effectu ab eo, si ei conferretur sub annuo censu. Et si sic, cur non prebenda possit sic locari ad uitam uel ad annos, in qua minora longe eunt complenda spiritualia, non uideo. Et praebet hic non A, sed C*   467 Miror] nota quare prebenda non possit locari *marg. clarificat Kh*   sunt tot *tr.* XE   468 cur] *scripsi sec.* KhE, *cfr* 471, 477, cum DNAZX   470 Item] nota quare locacione non sit perpetuus curatus *marg. clarificat Kh*   sic possit sic X, possit sic *corr. c. punct. del.* X²ʾ   cura] animarum *add.* X, *del. c. punct. del.* X²ʾ
471 iurium] numerum ZXE   472 quod] *sic* A, *postea del. cum punct. delentibus* A¹ ᵘᵉˡ ²   473 si] *om.* XE   fieri posse *tr.* N   a] in Kh
474 uerus] *om.* E   475 non] *om.* Kh   habet] non *praem.* E
477 alia Kh   continet] *om.* X, *etiam* TEb, *quorum ordo textualis confusus est:* 477/699 Item – uidetur] *ante* 362/477 *posita sunt, cfr praefationem, Cap. II.3 et adnot. ad* 362, continent Kh   Item] nota si sic possit quare collator sub annuo censu curas ⟨possit⟩ conferre *marg. clarificat Kh*   posset E
478 posset E   479 finalem] secundum *praem.* Kh   habet] que Z
480 collocacio Kh   481 Verum] Et Kh

persone debet attendi principaliter et profectus salutis animarum, quantumcumque et cum quocumque quo annexo prouenit, etiam si nichil ueniret ad bursam committentis. Lucrum enim animarum omnis qui fideliter Christum amat, lucro omni temporali anteponit, et non illi qui magis dat committit, sed qui magis proficere potest committendum est.

Et est recte sicut si uenderem equum meum uel concederem sub annuo censu simul cum regimine ecclesie, alias | equum meum non concessurus nisi simul regimen accipiat, et maxime si accipiens, nisi locaret prouentus, curam non acciperet per se. In illa concessione et locatione simul spirituale locatur cum temporali, et est plena symonia, si pactum de certo dando interponitur. Nec differt si dimitto | tibi pecunias michi a te debitas, ut des michi regimen uel beneficium semper uel ad annos, uel si do tibi tantas pecunias propter id ipsum: equalis est symonia utrobique. Sic et equalis symonia, si tibi loco uel concedo pro minori pecunia fructus et prouentus una cum regimine animarum, quam ualeant fructus estimatione communi, ac si non locarem tibi prouentus et darem tibi pecuniam ut regeres. Similiter uenit in idem, si locem tibi fructus ecclesie una cum regimine cure cum pacto pro tanto censu annuo quantus census ex fructibus ecclesie prouenire potest secundum arbitrium et estimationem communem, demptis expensis in uictu et uestitu regentis, ac si concederetur tibi sola ecclesia cum pacto dandi uictum et uestitum.

Et ergo, qui regimen ecclesie sine locatione prouentuum et sine lucro temporali sperato non uellet sibi committi nec uelit subire, si haberet unde uiueret, si cum pacto, ut supra dictum est, locat curam et regimen, est plene symoniacus meo uidere coram Deo –

507/515 cfr supra, 334-338, et GER. MAG., *Cura past.*, 97-102; *Ep.* 17, 68-73

---

484 et] *om. Kb*   quo] *om. Kb*   annexio *Z*   etiam] et *Kb*   485 uenire *Z*   enim] eciam *X*   486 omni] enim *E*   487 sed] *om. N¹, suppl. N²*   489 Et] nota exemplum consimile *marg. clarificat A²*   Et est] *om. E*   491 accipiam *A*   maxime] *corr. A²*, magis *A¹*   493 et locatione] *om. A*   495 Nec] exemplum *marg. clarificat Kb*   michi] *om. N¹, suppl. N²*   496 semper – annos] *om. Kb*   tibi do *tr. Kb*   497 tantas] *om. Kb*   equalis] est *add. Kb*   500 ualebant *N*   tibi] *om. NX*   503 annuo censu *tr. E*   504 posset *E*   506 tibi] *om. D¹, marg. suppl. D²*   dando *DX*   507 Et] nota symonia est fetidissima coram deo *marg. clarificat A²*   regimen] *marg. corr. D²*, requiem *D¹*   509 haberet – est] *om. Z*   510 coram] cum *ZXE*   510/511 Deo – coram] *om. XE*

CONSILIVM DE LOCATIONE CVRE PASTORALIS 263

et fetidissima coram Deo et omnibus sanctis est symonia, quamquam, proch dolor, est ualde | communis, regnante auaritie spiritu in clericis | multis, qui non querunt nisi perapsidem exterius mundare, nullo modo ueritatem adintra curantes, licet nec in hac
515 parte perapsidem exterius mundant. Ymmo, undique eam coinquinant et maculant exterius ad oculos non solum spiritualium, sed etiam communium hominum, quamuis sub pretextu locationis reddituum et prouentuum, ex quibus emolimenta et lucra querunt et proueniunt, palliare nituntur et excusare, quasi regimen et
520 curam ipsis annexam non locarent, et quasi uoluntarie in pensionatis reddittibus aut locatis se de cura intromitterent, aut quasi gratis sine commodo temporali essent curam et regimen accepturi, etiam si redditus non locassent uel si nullum emolimentum lucri ex reddittibus sperassent, maxime si haberent aliunde unde
525 uiuerent.

Heu, male mundata est perapsidis adextra, quando ex immunditia et auaritia turpiter apparente et specie symoniaca scandalizentur plurimi et pene communis populus, uidentes locari animarum regimina more aliorum regiminum temporalium habentium
530 redditus annexos.

Sed absit in uillis bene rectis sic temporales consulatus uel scabinatus uel magistratus quoscumque, quibus homines socialiter et politice secundum seculum | reguntur, etiam apud paganos taliter pro annuo censu locari uel conduci. Si sic alicubi fit, ue ciuitati
535 illi, non solum de scandalo, sed etiam de dampno intollerabili. Et uere tale non potest dici regimen, sed tyrannides pecunia usur-

142
28rb

28va

513/515 cfr Matth. 23, 25-26   526 cfr Matth. 23, 25-26

513/515 GER. MAG., *Cura past.*, 131-132, eundem locum biblicum citat
517/525 cfr supra, 449-454   531/543 cfr GER. MAG., *Simonia beg.*, 377-393

---

511 est] et Z   512 auaricia E   513 non] *om.* E   parapsidem Z X
519 proueniunt] *om.* X   520/521 impencionatis sic Kh, impensionatis
sic X E   521 se] Si Kh   de cura] *om.* E   quasi] q (qui?) sic X E   522/
523 acceptaturi E   523 si²] *om.* E   526 Heu] nota quomodo populus
scandalizatur *marg. clarificat* A²   perapsis Kh   527 et²] ut N   527/
528 scandalizantur Kh   530 annexus E   531 Sed] nota de temporalibus
regiminibus sub annuo censu conductis *marg. clarificat* Kh   absint X E
uel] et N   532 socialiter] *corr.* Kh², sociatur Kh¹   et] uel E   533 pollitice N Kh A X E   536 tyrannidis Kh   536/537 usurpata] est *add.* E

264   CONSILIVM DE LOCATIONE CVRE PASTORALIS

pata et questus tur|pissimus. O, si sederet hic iudex, non dico 143
quisquam sanctorum, sed quisquam gentilium rationabilis, aut
Tulius aut Seneca aut Catho aut Fabricius aut Socrates aut Plato
540 aut Aristides aut quisquis gentilium philosophorum aut consulum
prudentium, quantum abhorrerent has abhominationes fieri etiam
in secularibus rebus aut etiam in templo Dyane aut Appollinis aut
cuiuscumque alterius deorum, seu potius demoniorum.
   Heu, heu, et quis non ⟨uidet⟩ quales propter hec fiunt raptores
545 de pastoribus, et quales sunt qui ascendunt cathedras, indocti, inexperti, animales, bestiales, ambitiosi, luxuriosi, auarissimi et con-
cubinarii apertissimi, negotiatores callidissimi, curiarum sectatores
stolidissimi. Et hii locatores et rectores tui sunt, popule christiane,
in locis plurimis. Cur? Quia non qui plurimum sciunt uel sanctius
550 uiuunt tibi ⟨presunt⟩, sed qui plus dant uel auarius appetunt, aut
qui questuosius sciunt trahere aurum seu | pecunias a barbaris,   28vb
uel subtilius fictis uerbis negotiari norunt.
   Sed heu, nescio si hec euidentius et apertius et fetidius et crebrius et dampnosius in aliquibus rebus fiunt apud christianos
555 quam in huiusmodi locatione curarum siue regiminum simul cum
redditibus aut prouentibus. Considera et circumspice undique si
aliquod periculosius negotium pro populo christiano et abhomi-
nabilius rationi recte possit inueniri, quod tam generale est in

---

537/543 plerasque auctoritates hic allegatas, inter quas etiam raras (sc. praeter M. Tullium Ciceronem et Catonem, etiam Fabricium et Aristidem) in contextu fere simili, sed minus fauorabili etiam nominat LACT., *Diu. inst.* 6, 6, 24-28 (p. 504, 2 – 505, 7), partim in allegatione ex CIC., *Off.* 3, 4, 16-17 (p. 90, 7-14)

537 O] nota locans regimen animarum peius est gentilibus *marg. clarificat A²*   539 aut¹, aut⁵] *om. X*   Thulius *E*   Fabricius aut Catho *tr. X*   Frabricius *A*   540/541 aut Aristides – prudentium] *om. X*   540 Arisdides *A*, Aristotiles *Z*   541 abhorrent *N A Z*   542 aut²] uel *N*   Appollonis *Kh*, Apollinis *A*   Appollinis aut] *om. E*   542/543 aut³ – demoniorum] *om. X*   544 Heu] nota quales sunt qui pro nunc regunt *marg. clarificat A²*   uidet] *scripsi sec. Z X E*, uidit *cett.*   545 et] *om. X*   cathedras] Petri *add. X*   545/546 inexperti, indocti *tr. X*   547/548 curiarum – stolidissimi] *om. X*   547 sectatores] et *add. Z*   549 in] nec *Kh*   550 uiuunt] tendere *add. Kh*   presunt] *scripsi sec. Kh*, prosunt *cett.*   551 ab arboribus *E*   552 uel – norunt] *om. X*   subtilibus *Z*   uerbis fictis *tr. E*   553 Sed] nota comparationem regiminis temporalis ad regimen animarum *marg. clarificat Kh*   553/554 crebrius et] *om. X*   555 in] *om. X E*   siue] seu *X*   556 radicibus *sic A*   aut] et *X*   558 ratione *Z*

CONSILIVM DE LOCATIONE CVRE PASTORALIS 265

Almania, aut si quid Sancto Spiritui | et sanctis doctrinis genera-
560 lius et uehementius contrarietur diabolica sua feditate quam hoc
commune malum et latissimum locationis regiminum. Nec uere
palliari potest, nec apud Deum nec apud homines. Et quis est,
rogo, hominum, qui has feditates diabolicas ignoret, in cuius na-
ribus aliquid est de Dei Spiritu?
565   Si diceres: "possit inueniri qui non turpis lucri gratia, sed forte
ut prodesset populo, locaret regimen simul cum redditibus sub
annuo censu pacto interposito", respondeo: imaginor hoc esse
possibile, sed numquam hoc a sancto uel bono uel laudato uiro
uel in uitis sanctorum uel in historiis legi peractum nec laudatum.
570 Absit a bono uiro longissime, quorum | nullus nisi coactus ad cu-
ram animarum solet peruenire, ut uelit per pactum symoniacum
ad curam ascendere uel ab eo curam accipere qui eam non daret
nisi temporalia pacto interposito de quantitate certa sibi redderet.
     Ymmo, si nichil esset nisi species hec mala et pessima locatio-
575 nis adextra apparens, ex hoc solo uehementissime uir bonus hanc
abhorreret nequitiam, ne suo exemplo hec turpissima et fetidissima negotiatio et periculosissima populo uel confirmaretur uel
augeretur uel approbaretur uel magis defenderetur. Nam si hoc
faceret, hoc esset magnum scandalum actiuum. Et scandalizaret
580 non solum bonos, qui hanc speciem abhorrent, sed etiam questo-
res auaros et pessimos, qui iam ceciderunt, ut profundius aut
audacius caderent aut | impingerent, et imbecilles et fatuos, qui

144

29ra

145

565/573 cfr supra, 377-385   hic locus a uiro docto Mulder in comm. suo
cum GER. MAG., *Cura past.*, 123-130, aequiperatur, sed minus apte quam locus
supra (383-388; 481-494) propositus   570/571 cfr GER. MAG., *Cura past.*, 52-59
cfr HENR. GAND., *Quodl.* 2, q. 18 (p. 139, 83-85), qui allegat GREG. MAG., *Reg.
past.* 1, 9 (p. 160, 38-39, cfr *PL*, 77, 22C), supra (289-290) allegatum   574/
578 cfr THOM., II-II, Q. 43 a. 1 ad 4 (T. 8, p. 323, c. 1-2)

---

559 Alamannia *Kh*   aut] et uide *D*   Spiritui Sancto *tr. Kh*   559/
560 generalibus *X*   561 regimen *X*   Nec] nota istud malum non potest
palliari *marg. clarificat A²*   uere] *om. N¹, suppl. N²*   562 possit *E*
563 rogo] ergo *Z*   564 est aliquid *tr. X*   spiritu dei *tr. a.c. N*
565 Si] nota dicit si quis non gratia lucri, sed ut prodesset locaret *marg.
clarificat Kh*   forte] *om. Kh*   567 imaginare *X*   568 uel bono] *om. X*
uel²] aut a *X*   uiro] *om. N*   569 legi] *om. E*, lego *A*   570 uiro bono
tr. a.c. N   572 eo] illo *Kh*   573 nisi] *om. N*   temporalia] per *praem. E*
temporali *Z*   certa] *om. Kh¹, suppl. Kh²*   575 hoc] *om. E*   578 des-
cenderetur *E*   579 faceret] *marg. ex* faciunt *corr. ipse N¹*   hoc] *om. E*
580 abhorrerent *E*   582 et¹] aut *N*

similia attemptandi pronitatem acciperent, et quarto totum populum, qui per consequentiam per hos mercenarios symoniacos apud Deum in anima negliguntur uel demerguntur. Melius illi esset, quia non *unum pusillum*, sed sine numero plurimos, etiam qui nesciunt quid intersit inter dextrum et sinistrum, *scandalizaret*, quod mille *mole | asinarie suspenderentur in collum suum et mergeretur in profundissimum omnium marium.*
De pecunia acquisita per hunc modum in octauo dicto expressum nescio quid dicere certi. Forte possit aliquibus uideri, ex quo palliari potest et uideri potest, quod non nisi redditus sint locati, uelut ab illo qui curam uoluntarie accepisset, etiam si lucrum non sperasset. Ideo ecclesia adextra hanc non uidetur iudicare sibi fore manifestam symoniam. Et hoc uidetur exterior ecclesia, a qua sunt multa scandala Dei iudicio auferenda, hic scienter pati et dissimulare, que intentiones hominum, que sibi occultantur, non iudicat et que permittit *zizania crescere*, ne *simul eradicetur et triticum*. Et ideo uidetur sola esse symonia mentalis secundum presumptionem ecclesie hic in hoc exilio iudicantis, de qua in confessione "per penitentiam suo Creatori satisfacere" uidetur et "sufficere", Extra, *De sententia excommunicationis*, c. finali, maxime quia nullus potest cuiquam ad | faciem ecclesie manifeste probare ipsum aliam intentionem habuisse, nisi quod solos red-

---

585/589 Matth. 18, 6 paene ad litt.   598/599 cfr Matth. 13, 29-30

590/591 cfr supra, 449-454; 517-525   599/602 *Decret.*, X 5.3.46 (c. II, 767, 44-50), partim paene ad litt., supra et infra, 388-392; 625-627, etiam allegatum; Ger. in allegatione tituli et capituli errare uidetur, quippe quia in ultimo cap. tit. 39 (X 5.39.60, c. II, 912-913) nihil de confessione per penitentiam inuenitur

---

584 sequentiam *N*   585 uel] et *E*   586 non unum] unum *Kb¹*, unum non *suppl. Kb²*   587 intersit] iuris sit *X*   587/588 scandalizarent *A*   589 mergerentur *A*   profundum *X*   590 De] nota de pecunia symoniace acquisita *marg. clarificat A²*   592 possit *bis E*   sint] *marg. corr. N², sunt N¹*   593 uelut] *om. Kb*   uoluntarie curam *tr. a.c. Z*   594 ecclesia] *marg. corr. N²*, eciam *N¹ Kb Z*   abextra *E*   non] ecclesia *praem. N¹ Kb, del. N²*   596 hic] hoc *Z*   598 iudicant *Kb*   ne] *om. Z*   599 esse sola *tr. E*   602 et] *om. Kb*   Extra] *om. Kb*   sententia excommunicationis] symonia *recte X E forte sec.* 625/627 *infra*

ditus locasse uideatur. Et inde forte dici potest quod ecclesia sepe pro redditibus uel prouentibus ecclesie accipiatur, | ut in *Decretali*, Extra, *Ne prelati uices*, c. *Querelam*. Et isto modo uidetur iam transire ecclesia, et in foro iudicii presentis temporis hec symonia toleratur, utrum bene uel non bene, uideant sibi qui presunt. Hoc tamen magis estimo quod magis toleret hanc nequitiam quasi non potens eam undique exstirpare, uel timens peiorem scissuram fieri uel *eradicari et triticum* sanctorum antecessorum nostrorum. Vel quis, si iudex sederet, patrum sustinuisset uel sustineret tam lamentabile malum et tam putridum uulnus in ecclesia, ex quo tot mala et scandala et fetores toti mundo oriuntur etiam data intentione bona secundum modum predictum, si potuisset uel posset per iudicium remedium apponere? Nec ecclesia de secretis tunc iudicaret, sed de manifestissimis nequitiis et scandalis intolerabilibus. Numquid hic manifestum pactum interponitur? Numquid pecunia interuenit de certo in re multum spirituali, uidelicet in regimine animarum, ut supra dixi? Et quid deficit hic ad manifestam symoniam, si factum est publicum et manifestum? Et quid est hic non plenum malo, aut specie mali?

Longe secus est in c. finali, Extra, *De symonia*, | quia ibi "sine pacto uel conuentione, sed affectu animi precedente" res ageba-

---

612 cfr Matth. 13, 29-30

605/607 sc. *Decret.*, X 5.4.4 (c. II, 768, 44-50), cfr specialiter BERN. PARM., *Glos. ord. in Decret.*, super X 5.4.4, comm. sup. 'praefatam ecclesiam' (c. II, 768, 40) (c. 1649 (p. 39), gl. c), ubi Bern. Parm. de uaria significatione nominis 'ecclesia' distinguit, inter alia (l. 16-17 in glosa) sexta et ultima significatione dicens "Item dicitur ecclesia ipsae obuentiones ecclesiasticae prouenientes occasione ecclesiae, ut hic", cfr etiam summarium decretalis (c. 1648 (p. 38), l. 80-81)   608/613 cfr infra, 654-666; 699-705   cfr GER. MAG., *Simonia beg.*, 108-109; 160-166; *Leeringhe*, 131-132   615/617 cfr supra, 425-429, etiam 305-312   620/622 cfr supra, 17-26; 79-91   625/627 *Decret.*, X 5.3.46 (c. II, 767, 44-50), partim paene ad litt., supra, 388-392; 599-602, etiam allegatum

---

605 quod] *om. E*   608 et²] *om. E*   612 et] *om. X*, uel *Kh*   612/613 Quis, si iudex sederet, sanctorum (*om. N*) antecessorum uel nostrorum *tr. NKh*   613 nostrorum] *om. E*   614 sustinuisset] si *praem. Kh*   malum] uerbum *praem. X*   et] uel *E*   616 bona] uana *E*   617 posset] si *praem. X E*   618 ecclesia] eciam *E*   619 Non quid *N*

tur. Nec ibi tot pericula aut scandala aut fetores | necessarie se- 29vb
quebantur. Et ideo non uidetur hoc capitulum eos iuuare, quo
magis "sufficit eis Creatori satisfacere" et pecuniam retinere.
630 Adiunge doctrinam Innocentii in c. *Quoniam enormis*, qua docet
debere contractus separari, quando cura uel regimen, que nullo
modo locari possunt, aliis locandis uel uendendis coniunguntur,
ut quando pro mora hominis in tali uilla uel dampno absentie ab
alio loco lucroso locat uel accipit eis pecunias et gratis curam ac-
635 ceptat. "Debent", inquit Innocentius, "contractus tam in pactis
quam in intentione esse segregati, ut mercedem quam accipit pro
diuinis non accipiat".

Sic similiter est quando mercenarius locat et contrahit de dando
pro prouentibus ecclesie, quia idem est, ut supra dixi, si pacisca-
640 tur sibi dari certum, et si pro minori quam estimatiue prouentus
ualeant spe lucri eos locet. Pacta debent separari, ut aliud sit pactum de redditibus locandis et aliud uel alio tempore fiat de regimine, sed maxime intentiones debent separari.

Sed heu, hec miscentur omnia et simul fiunt uno contextu, tam
645 in corde contrahentium quam in pactis exterius. Et ideo, si ad
iudicium ueniret, estimo quod | patres sancti iudicarent hanc fore 30ra
ecclesie manifestam symoniam, si simul contractus uno contextu
facti probarentur. Et ergo c. *Quoniam enormis* dicit hanc "enormem consuetudinem contra sanctorum patrum institutiones",
650 dicit et "sacerdotium sub huius|modi mercede uenale disponi". 148
Et clarum est secundum intellectum et glosas ueras illius *Decre-*
talis tam regimina quam lucra ex regimine prouenientia secundum
illam enormem consuetudinem locari solere.

630/637 INNOC., *Comm. Decret.*, super X 5.4.3, comm. sup. 'regimen' (c. II, 768, 24) (ed. 1570, p. 602, c. 1, sub num. 3, 27-36), partim (635-637 = l. 31-33) uerbatim   638/641 cfr supra, 495-506   648/650 *Decret.*, X 5.4.3 (c. II, 768, 22-23; 25-26) paene ad litt.

---

627 Nec] *ex* Nunc *corr. ipse Kb¹, ut E*   629 eis] *om. E*   facere satis *E*
630 enormis] in *praem. N²A Z*   632 modo] *om. X*   aliis] quando
praem. X   633 ut] unde *Z,* uel *E*   pro] *om. Kb*   dampno] pro *praem. N*
dampnum *Kb*   634 eis] pro *praem. Kb*   634/635 acceptam *Z*
636 ut] et *E*   638 mercenarius quando *tr. E*   639 pro] et *praem. E*
640 estimacionem *E*   641 eos] *om. Kb*   debent] *om. Kb,* debet *E*
ut] et *E*   aliud sit] *om. E*   643 sed] et *Kb*   644 uno] una *A*
645 ad] *om. A¹, suppl. A²*   648 ergo] igitur *Kb*

Si dixeris: "cur suffert hec ecclesia?", respondeo, ut estimo, quod inuita hoc patitur propter causas supra dictas. Et considera, dilecte, quod ecclesia uidens crescere malitias hominum et multiplicari tergiuersationes et calumpnias malorum et maxime potentium raro condempnat iam aliquem de symonia. Non uidi ego quemquam symoniacum temporibus meis condempnatum, sed hoc non laudo.

Attendo tamen quod aut rarissime aut non admittit ecclesia articulos aliquos obiectiuos, et maxime de symoniaca prauitate obicientes, uidens, ut estimo, pronitatem falsorum testium et periurorum et falsitatem accusantium potentium non curantium siue uera siue falsa obiciant, dummodo lites clericis, precipue pauperibus uel eis | contrariis, moueant et ad uexationes et expensas perducant, et pondere diuitiarum suarum et longitudine temporis in litibus et expensis eos opprimant, maxime per falsa testimonia.

Et uere, si sine differentia articuli obiectiui admitterentur, omnia litibus implerentur, et uix pauperes et bassi homines uel minus callidi uel impotentes in beneficiis remanerent. Sic ecclesia in medio malorum posita multos patitur inuita symoniacos, Deo et iudicibus conscientiarum iudicia hec committens. Et quando sic inuita ecclesia patitur multos symoniacos, quos ta|men patitur, non ideo est minus peccatum nec minus tenetur restituere pecunias symoniace acquisitas, ut uidetur.

Ceterum, si factum tale esset ut ecclesia potens esset iudicare hec et sine scissura peiore, nollet tamen iudicare propter latens iudicium in conscientia, ut in c. finali, Extra, *De symonia*, cum aliis concordantiis. Tunc adhuc, si mala et scandala fuissent exorta ex illo facto aut aliqua publica et enormis consuetudo aut malitia fuisset per actum huiusmodi alicuius probi uel docti uel potentis

---

654/660 cfr supra, 608-613, infra, 699-705   cfr GER. MAG., *Simonia beg.*, 108-109 ; 160-166 ; *Leeringhe*, 131-132   678/679 sc. *Decret.*, X 5.3.46 (c. II, 767, 44-50)

---

654 Si] nota dicit cur suffert hec ecclesia *marg. clarificat Kh*   Si] Sed praem. *X*   cur] cum *Z*   **655** inuite *X*   hoc] hec *NXE*   **657/658** potentum *NZXE*   **659** meis] magis *E*   **661** Attende *N*   **663/664** periuriorum *ZXE*   **665** dummodo] dum tales *Z*   precipue] et *praem. X*   **666** eis] eciam *E*   **668** in] *om. Kh*   eas *Kh*   **670** lassi *D*   **672** inuita] *om. D*, inuite *X*   **674** inuite *X*   tamen] cum *Kh*   **675** minus est *tr. Kh*   **677** factum] illud *add. Kh*   ut] in *Kh Z*   **678** peiori *X*   **681** aut²] et *ZXE*   **682** fuissent *E*   uel potentis] *om. E*

uiri magis | confirmata, aucta aut colorata, talis in foro penitentie penitens de huiusmodi facto teneretur, si possit, huiusmodi consuetudinem uel malitiam, saltem in quantum eam confirmauit, auxit aut colorauit, factis et dictis infirmare, diminuere et detegere et reprobare. Et sic restituitur uere ecclesie sua sanitas et iustitia, quam abstulit, et sic leuat uel leuabit uel sanabit, si potest, quos deiecit, scandalizauit uel uulnerauit. Et michi uidetur non dimitti hoc peccatum, nisi restituatur ablatum, si potest restituere. Et nescio quibus modis hoc euidentius et exemplarius et uiuacius facere potest quam ut pecunias illas lucratas in laudabiles et publicos usus sanctitatis ipsi ecclesie sancte posuerit uel restituerit, facto et dicto reprobando quod tam enormi facto etiam corde approbauit, ut in illo puniatur in quo deliquit, et ratione cuius acquirendi hanc enormitatem turpem aggressus est.

Et istud uidetur dicendum in factis illis, que adextra ecclesia in genere suo uoluntarie sustinet, quia de occultis non iudicat. Quanto ma|gis hoc dicendum uidetur in hiis que ecclesia inuitissime | patitur! Patitur tamen de facto illo ne peior scissura fiat, ut supra dixi, uel magis ex incuria et negligentia prelatorum in Almania, que uniuersalis ecclesia inhibet, et que sanctis patribus ecclesia iudicat esse contraria, et maxime in illis rebus uel in illis locationibus, ubi nec sufficit intentio bona, et ubi manifesta pacta interponuntur.

Rogo te, si etiam ecclesia adextra hec patitur propter predicta, debet ergo iudex conscientie hec pati? Et est magna diuersitas symoniacorum uolentium satisfacere ecclesie in iudicio conscientie,

---

689/696 cfr GER. MAG., *Ep.* 17, 49-65; *Ep.* 19, 47-52   689/693 cfr *Decret.*, VI 1.6.35 § 4 (c. II, 965, 45-53)   699/705 cfr supra, 608-613; 654-660 cfr GER. MAG., *Simonia beg.*, 108-109; 160-166; *Leeringhe*, 131-132   706/725 cfr supra, 393-419

---

683 uiri] *om. Kh*   aut] et *Z*   tollerata *NZ*   686 tolerauit *NZ*, accolorauit *E*   687 sua] *om. N¹, marg. suppl. N²*   688 leuat uel] *om. X* uel¹] et *Z*   saluabit *D X E*   690 hoc] hic *Kh*   691 ueracius *E*   693 sancte] *om. Z*   694 corde] *om. Kh*   696 est aggressus *tr. X* congressus *E*   697 istis *D*   adextra] *om. Kh*   699 in hiis] *textus in X (etiam TEb) interruptus in* 477*, iterum praebetur, cfr praefationem, Cap. II.3 et adnot. ad* 362, 477   700 de facto illo] *om. Kh*   701 supra dixi] predixi *Kh*   et] uel *X*   701/702 uel magis – inhibet] *om. Kh*   702 sanctis] *om. X*   704 nec] non *X E*   sufficit] sic *Kh¹*, sufficiat *marg. corr. Kh²*   705 imponuntur *Kh*   707 ergo] igitur *Kh*   hoc *X*   Et] *om. NAXE*

etiam ubi sola symonia est mentalis, ut dixi supra secundum diffe-
710 rentiam beneficii curati uel non curati in dicto sexto, et sunt multe
alie differentie. Si dixeris: "c. finale, Extra, *De symonia*, dicit 'sufficere per solam penitentiam satisfacere Creatori', maxime in illis
que ecclesia uoluntarie pretextu propter occultationem interiorum sustinet", respondeo quod uerum est, sed in ueris peniten-
715 tibus. Magna est diuersitas requisitarum penitentiarum. Satisfactio
enim, que pars magna est penitentie, ualde diuersa est in diuersis
negotiis, et alia in | hiis et alia in istis, alia in manifestis, alia in
occultis, et alia in restituendis bonis temporalibus uel spirituali-
bus Deo, ecclesie uel ho|minibus, alia in reformandis et sanandis
720 uulneratis uel lesis uel scandalizatis temporaliter aut spiritualiter,
alia in reuocandis falsis doctrinis siue uerbo uel facto ostensis uel
approbatis, alia in fama et fauore per nos infectis restituendis. Et
uera penitentia in hac parte est satisfacere lesis, scandalizatis et
uulneratis per hanc apertam feditatem. Et non uideo quomodo
725 hoc conuenientius fieri potest, nisi ut predixi.

Nescio plus dicere. Consilium meum est restituere has pecunias
in publicos pios sanctos usus, et facto et uerbo prius gesta repro-
bare. Si quis sciuerit sanius uel melius consilium, det et propinet
et doceat me et uos: libenter accipio. Dico que michi uidentur,
730 libenter correctorem suffero. Ymmo, si in aliquo deuiaui, opto inuenire correctionem. Et si necesse fuerit, spero me uel multa horum uel omnia sanctorum auctoritatibus posse roborare, semper

31ra

151

711/714 *Decret.*, X 5.3.46 (c. II, 767, 44-50)

---

710 sexto] capitulo *add.* E   710/711 sunt – differentie] multas alias differentias *Kh C*   711 Si] nota diuersitatem penitentie *marg.* clarificat *Kh*
finale] *scripsi sec.* N, *hab.* etiam *V C*, finali *ut titulum praebent D Kh A Z X E*
712/713 maxime in illis que] *D N C Z X E M*, saltem in hiis quos *Kh V A L*
713 pretextu] *om.* N¹, *corr.* N²   pretextu occultationis *sic* D¹ *Kh V A L*,
pretextu propter occultationis *corr.* D²   713/714 interiorum] *om.* N C, interioris *Kh V A L*   714/715 in ueris penitentibus, respondeo quod uerum est,
si N   716 enim] etenim N   717 alia¹] est *add.* N   718 alia] est *add. Kh*
719 Deo] uel *add.* N   720 aut] uel X   721 uel¹] siue X E   723 uera]
hic *praem. Kh*   in hac parte] *om. Kh*   est satisfacere] uidetur requirere
ut satisfiat *Kh*   lesis] et *add. Kh*   et¹] uel N   724 et uulneratis] *om. Kh*
724/725 per – predixi] et ut mala que approbauit, confortauit aut adauxit
facto et uerbo reprobet, debilitet et diminuat, et alia que predixi *Kh*
727 pios] et *add.* X   uerbo et facto *tr.* E   729 uos] *om.* X   730 correctionem *A X*   Ymmo] *om.* A¹, *suppl.* A²   730/731 inueniri X   731 cor-
rectionem] *om.* N¹, *marg. suppl.* N², correctorem *iterum Kh E*

sub correctione sancte matris | ecclesie et melius scientium. Dixi consilium, adiunxi rationes. Quantum rationes mee bone menti concludunt, tantum faciat, consulo, querat in hoc consilio Dei homines quibus illuminata est sancta mens et uita concordat. Recedat a mundantibus exterius tantum perapsidem, secundum hominum traditiones narrantes fabulationes, sed non ut lex Dei.

Ego immundus sum et infimus peccatorum. Malo ista a talibus audire quam aliis uulneratis hec proloqui. Gaudeo tamen ad uocem | Sponsi et sanctorum, quibus michi hec uel horum exemplaria uisa sunt. Quam recte, Deus et alii uideant, quem rogo ut uideamus et uiuamus. Amen.

736/737 cfr Matth. 23, 25-26   737/738 cfr Col. 2, 8

---

733 scientium] sentientium *Kh*   736 concordet *NKh A*   738 narrantium *Kh*   Dei] in mundo *add. X*   739 Ego] Sic et *praem. X*   immundus sum et ego *tr. E*   immundus sum et] *om. Kh A X*   a] *om. X E*   a talibus] ab aliis *Kh A*   741 quibus] qua *Kh*   michi] nichil *E*   743 uideamus et] *om. E*   et uiuamus] post hanc uitam in eterna patria *X*   amen] et sic est finis istius compendii ualde boni *add. A*   Explicit opusculum uenerabilis uiri magistri Gherardi (Gherhardi *E*) dicti (*om. X*) Groet (Groed *X*, Grot *E*) de Dauentria (Dauantria *XE*) dyaconi de locacione (locacionibus *ZXE*) cure pastoralis *expl. in DNZXE, post quod sequuntur in E nomen scriptoris, locus, dies et annus in introductione, cap. II.3 inuestigati*, Explicit hoc opus d⟨iaconi⟩ G⟨erardi⟩ Magni m⟨agistri⟩, breue et multum utile copulatum Dauentrie et cetera *expl. in A, expl. def. in Kh*

EPISTOLA (17) AD WILHELMVM VROEDE
DE CVRA PASTORALI RECVSANDA A MINORIBVS AETATE

CONSPECTVS SIGLORVM

codices

H2 DEN HAAG, Koninklijke Bibliotheek, 78 J 55, s. XVa
L   LIÈGE, Bibliothèque de l'Université, 229 (c), a. 1451

Hos codices in plagulis phototypice expressis contulimus.

⟨EPISTOLA AD WILHELMVM VROEDE
DE CVRA PASTORALI RECVSANDA A MINORIBVS AETATE⟩

Domine et cetera in Christo dilecte, narrauit michi frater uester   199va 58
quod quidam uolens et intendens sibi quandam curam conferre
in persona uestra litteras presentacionis aut collacionis iussit con-
scribi, ut, quia frater uester minor annis curam habere non potuit,
5 uos ad suam utilitatem et ad suum commodum curam teneretis,
et ut, cum ad debitam etatem a canonibus cure deputatam frater
uester peruenerit, eandem fratri uestro resignaretis.

   Hec res est plena fraudibus, circumuencionibus et collusioni-
bus, in ecclesie sancte non modicum grauamen, in animarum
10 uestrarum grande periculum, in iuris diuini et humani fraudem et
detrimentum, nec non in scandalum plurimorum, qui hoc facto

---

   1 hanc epistulam Gerardus ineunte anno 1381 Wilhelmo Vroede, magistro
scholarum Dauentriae a. 1378 (13 sept.) – 1381 (5 mart.), misit, cfr de cetero
supra, in introductione   3 presentacionis] "i.e. quibus ad munus illud ecclesiasticum habendum praesentaris siue commendaris", Acquoy   colla-
cionis] "i.e. quibus munus illud tibi confertur, in te transfertur, tibi conceditur uel donatur", Acquoy   4/7 cfr GER. MAG., *Cura past.*, 8-10   cfr
Decret., VI 1.6.14 (c. II, 953, 42 – 954, 22, reiterantem Conc. Lugd. II, const. 13
(a. 1274, *COD*, p. 297-298)) et *Clem.* 1.6.3 (c. II, 1140, 21-26), ubi Clemens
terminat ut clerici in .xxv. aetatis suae anno regulariter ad presbyteratus ordines promoueantur, confirmans consuetudinem et ea quae determinata
erant in Conc. Lat. III, can. 3 (a. 1179, *COD*, p. 188, 19-23) et reiterata in Conc.
Lugd. II, const. 13 (iam cit.), contra aetatem annorum .xxx. praescriptam a
GRAT., *Decr.*, D.77 c.1-7; D.78 c.1-5 (c. I, 272, 1 – 276, 19), sicut legitur in IOH.
ANDR., *Glos. ord. in Clem.*, super *Clem.* 1.6.3, comm. sup. 'Generalem' (c. II,
1140, 21) (c. 65 (p. 474), gl. e), ubi '77' pro '87' legendum est; fortasse etiam
Decret., X 1.6.7 § 2 (c. II, 52, 9-19) sic interpretanda est, sicut admonet IOH.
FRIB., *Summa Conf.*, L. 3, t. 22, q. 12 (f. 162r, c. 2 in fine, 54-58); sed possibi-
litas haud neganda est Ger. statutis diocesanis synodalibus usum esse, sicut
Stat. synod. Leod., tit. 16, c. 4 (p. 158, 7-17 ed. Avril; Stat. synod. Trai. comparabilia tradita non sunt)   quamuis dispensatiue tales pueri iusso episcopi
tolerari possunt, generaliter .xxv. aetatis annum praescribit etiam BERN. PARM.,
Glos. ord. in Decret., super X 1.14.2, comm. sup. 'aetatem' (c. II, 126, 23) (c. 265
(p. 133), gl. b); super X 1.14.3, comm. sup. 'aetatem' (c. II, 126, 42) (c. 266
(p. 133), gl. d)

   Tit. ad eundem *praem. rubricator ut tit. in L*, ad eundem / nota de falsis
pastoribus *marg. exponit L²*   2 conferre] *sic L H2*, conferri *Mulder*

audito ad simile faciendum possunt stimulari, aut si abhorruerint factum hoc, prout omnes bene docti faciunt, in personas uestras fetorem scandali et nequiciam notabunt.

15 Falsus pastor omnino est cuius non sunt oues proprie, sed falsissimus cuius non est cura uere sua aut propria, sed solum simulata sua uel simulata propria. Falsum habet nomen curati qui nec curat nec pascit nisi simulate, sed falsissimus est curatus qui nec curat nomine proprio nec ton|det nomine proprio nisi simulate. 20 Aut enim nomine proprio tondetis et pascitis, aut nomine alieno. Non nomine proprio, ut patet, nec nomine alieno, nam si nomine alieno, aut ille est pastor, aut non pastor. Si ille est pastor, non est frater uester, quia frater uester pastor et curatus esse non potest, ut canunt iura. Aut ille est non pastor, et nomine non pastoris 25 *intrare in ouile* est *furis uel latronis*; et nomine non pastoris pascere est ewangelisare sine missione, et nomine non pastoris tondere est lanas, id est emolimenta temporalia, ab ouibus, id est a subditis, iniuste rapere, et non pastori, id est fratri uestro, tradere. Rursus, uel uos estis pastor ouium, uel frater uester. Non 30 frater uester, quia etas sibi repugnat. Et si uos estis pastor, cur res ecclesie et emolimenta non in utilitatem ecclesie, sed in sanguinem et carnem, scilicet fratrem uestrum, funditis? Cur alius et non uos de stipendiis ecclesie uiuit, cur curam ad annos fratris uestri reseruatis? Et si uere curam haberetis, quomodo eam fratri uestro, 35 qui nec scienciam nec uitam ueri pastoris habet nec adhuc habere potest, possitis resignare et cecas oues ceco committere?

Aliud est quod agitis, aliud est quod littere canunt uos egisse. Littere canunt uelut testes mortui uos esse pastorem, quibus curam tamquam uestram ab impetrantibus uel impetentibus defen-40 ditis. Veritas actionis pretense est, cui et fama concordat, fratrem uestrum esse pastorem. Hoc collator aut presentator intendebat,

---

25 cfr Ioh. 10, 1   27/29 cfr Ez. 34, 8   36 cfr Matth. 15, 14

23/24 cfr *Decret.*, VI 1.6.14 (c. II, 953, 42 – 954, 22); *Clem.* 1.6.3 (c. II, 1140, 21-26) supra, 4-7, iam cum comm. allegatos   26/29 cfr GER. MAG., *Locat.*, 370-374; *Cura past.*, 265   34/36 cfr GER. MAG., *Cura past.*, 206-209

---

32 scilicet] siue *falso Mulder*   34 si] *prius om., sed marg. suppl. ipse* L[1]
35 uitam] *sic* L   37 agitis] uos *prius praem., sed eras. ipse* H2[1]
40 pretense] *sic codd.*, pretente *emend. sec.*   45 contra *codd. Mulder*

hoc et uos eandem curam acceptantes pretendebatis, quamquam frustra, quia nec coram Deo nec coram hominibus ex defectu etatis frater uester est uel dici potest curatus, nec fructus suos facere.
45 Ergo cum littere omnino contrarie sunt accioni pretente, constat eas manifeste fore falsas tam in re quam in iure quam ex intencione uestra et conferentis. Et ergo uigore talium litterarum falsarum undique non potest frater uester fructus suos facere aut futuram curam acceptare. Et quia accio pretensa in mente confe-
50 rentis nullum ius fratri uestro conferre potest, ymmo aufert, quia contraria est iuri, ergo nec | sibi nec uobis coram Deo aut in iure licet fructus tollere aut curam reseruare. Et quidquid tuleritis de cura uel uos uel frater uester, tenemini ecclesie restituere. Et si frater uester non restituerit adhuc illa que frater uester per manus
55 uestras aut per uestras litteras uel earum uirtute acceperit, antequam rite absolui potestis, tenemini restituere.

†In omnibus enim talibus casibus†, ubi indirecte contra intencionem iuris agitur retentis uerbis iuris, ut hic supponitur persona habilis ad beneficium curatum, cui uidetur dari, cum tamen mi-
60 nori annis et inepte realiter datur, hoc est "legis sentenciam saluis uerbis legis circumuenire", ut FF, *De legibus* ⟨*senatusque consultis*⟩, *Contra legem* et sequenti. Et clarum est quod omnis taliter rem acquirens uel fructus percipiens est fraudulentus et male fidei possessor, qui tenetur de omnibus perceptis, ymmo et de omni-
65 bus que percipi potuissent, restitucionem facere.

Sunt multa alia pericula illis qui uoluntarie se ingerunt curis animarum, et maxime illis qui non ualent et preualent scientia

200ra
60

49/65 cfr GER. MAG., *Locat.*, 689-696; *Ep.* 19, 47-52   cfr *Decret.*, VI 1.6.35 § 4 (c. II, 965, 45-53)   57/62 IVST., *Dig.* 1.3.29-30 (p. 34, c. 2 [13, 22-28]), partim paene ad litt.; quia fontem secundarium hunc locum citantem inuenire nequiui, Ger. Iust. directe citat – neque enim gloss. ord., neque Innoc., neque Bohic, neque Arch. istum locum in comm. suis supra, 4-7, allegatis citat; fortasse autem Ger. locum inueuit per ARCH., *Comm. vium*, super *Decret.*, VI 1.6.14, comm. sup. 'alii' (c. II, 954, 6, quem decretalem Ger. supra, 4-7, allegat) (f. 25v, c. 1, 9-11), ubi Arch. se ad commentum proprium refert in *Decret.*, VI 1.6.5; ibi, in comm. sup. 'procurant' (c. II, 950, 1) (f. 21r, c. 1, 66-71), Arch. locum Iustiniani allegat, tamen sine uerbis a Ger. citatis   67/68 cfr *Decret.*, X 1.6.7 § 2 (c. II, 52, 14); *Decret.*, VI 1.6.14 (c. II, 954, 1-2)

---

50 uestro] suo *L*   57 *hic clausula supplenda est, sicut et uiro docto Acquoy uidetur, e.g.* ⟨sic fieri oportet⟩   61/62 senatusque consultis] *sic sec. Iust. legendum*, et constil- *L*   66 alie *sic L*

spirituali et moribus. Sed propter lucrum temporale principaliter alias non ⟨accepturus⟩ curam accipere, est uicium diabolicum et
70 maximum, licet iam diabolo in mundo dominante ualde commune est. Quis est iam rarissimus curatorum, qui curam animarum, si haberet aliunde uiuere et si nichil temporalis curam sequeretur, diligeret? Maledicti pastores, qui pascunt se et sua querunt; non operantur in uinea Domini, secundum Gregorium
75 in *omilia*. Maledicti et ducentes in malediccionem, luent penas omnium malorum | suorum subditorum; requiretur ab eis omne 61 infirmum, omne confractum, omne dispersum secundum Ezechielem prophetam, de quo grandis posset fieri sermo et uerissimus, tamen multis nostrorum temporum ualde horribilis.
80 Supersedeo de presenti, quia resignari omnino oportet, ut predicitur.

Valete, dilecte, et agite sapienter in malicia temporum presencium et non sequamini multitudinem curancium, secundum doctrinam Salomonis, ymmo pocius Christi, ueri Salomonis, quem
85 opto uos induere et renouari spiritualiter et huic mundo non configurari, sed crucifigi.

Scriptum festinanter Dauentrie.

73/74 cfr Ez. 34, 8   76/78 cfr Ez. 34, 4   85/86 cfr Phil. 3, 10

68/73 cfr GER. MAG., *Locat.*, 334-338; 507-510; *Cura past.*, 97-102   73/75 cfr GREG. MAG., *Hom.* 19, 2 (p. 145, 57-65)

---

69 accepturus] *sic legendum, cfr Locat.*, 336, accepturos *codd.*   84 Psalomonis *bis* H2

CONSILIVM DE CVRA PASTORALI
(EPISTOLA 73)

CONSPECTVS SIGLORVM

codex principalis
D   KÖLN, Historisches Archiv der Stadt Köln, GB 4° 249, a. 1418

Familia δ
Di   DÜSSELDORF, Universitäts- und Landesbibliothek, B 83, s. XVb

Familia κ
H   LIÈGE, Bibliothèque du Grand Séminaire, Cod. 11 (6 B 17), s. XVa
L   LIÈGE, Bibliothèque de l'Université, 229 (c), a. 1451

Familia ξ
B   BRUSSEL, Koninklijke Bibliotheek van België, 4414-24 (2187), c. a. 1480-1490
M   MAINZ, Stadtbibliothek, I 507, c. a. 1450
X   WOLFENBÜTTEL, Herzog August Bibliothek, 18. 32 Aug. 4°, s. XVc

Hos codices in plagulis phototypice expressis contulimus.

⟨CONSILIVM DE CVRA PASTORALI⟩

Queritur a me cur dissuadeam cuidam iuueni circa uicesimum quartum annum constituto, in gramatica imbuto, ut curam animarum non acceptet, cum parentes sui sint adeo tenues in temporalibus quod bene indigeant per predictum iuuenem sibi in temporalibus subueniri.
5 Respondeo quod curam uolens acceptare primo debet uidere si aliquid canonicum obstiterit, quo magis non possit sine sua perditione curam accipere. Et in hoc, in hac parte iuuenis uideat ut sit tempore collacionis beneficii sibi facte in uicesimo quinto

D 31va, 310

8/10 cfr GER. MAG., *Ep.* 17, 4-7   cfr *Decret.*, VI 1.6.14 (c. II, 953, 42 – 954, 22, reiterantem Conc. Lugd. II, const. 13 (a. 1274, *COD*, p. 297-298)) et *Clem.* 1.6.3 (c. II, 1140, 21-26), ubi Clemens determinat ut clerici in .xxv. aetatis suae anno regulariter ad presbyteratus ordines promoueantur, confirmans consuetudinem et ea quae determinata erant in Conc. Lat. III, can. 3 (a. 1179, *COD*, p. 188, 19-23) et reiterata in Conc. Lugd. II, const. 13 (iam cit.), contra aetatem annorum .xxx. praescriptam a GRAT., *Decr.*, D.77 c.1-7; D.78 c.1-5 (c. I, 272, 1 – 276, 19), sicut legitur in IOH. ANDR., *Glos. ord. in Clem.*, super *Clem.* 1.6.3, comm. sup. 'Generalem' (c. II, 1140, 21) (c. 65 (p. 474), gl. e), ubi '77' pro '87' legendum est; uerisimiliter etiam *Decret.*, X 1.6.7 § 2 (c. II, 52, 9-19) sic interpretanda est, sicut admonet IOH. FRIB., *Summa Conf.*, L. 3, t. 22, q. 12 (f. 162r, c. 2 in fine, 54-58); sed possibilitas haud neganda est Ger. statutis diocesanis synodalibus usum esse, sicut *Stat. synod. Leod.*, tit. 16, c. 4 (p. 158, 7-17 ed. Avril; *Stat. synod. Trai.* comparabilia tradita non sunt)

Tit. Consilium (est *add. B*) siue responsio (*om. Di*, uenerabilis uiri *add. A*) magistri (*om. HB*) Gherardi (Gerardi *HDiB*) Groot (Magni *HB*, Magni dicti Groet *Di*, de Dauentria dicti Groet dyaconi *A*) cognominati (*om. HDiBA*, siue mensio *add. Di*) cuidam iuueni data, cui collata fuit ecclesia quedam curata ad instantiam sororum suarum (*tr. B*) *tit. in DiHL* rubricator *in H2B*, Incipit tractatus magistri Gerardi Groot de cura animarum non acceptanda *tit. in W*, Sequitur tractatus de cura animarum non acceptanda magistri Gherardi Magni *tit. in Tc*, Incipit magister Gherardus dictus Magnus de cura non acceptanda. et cetera *tit. in Tw*, Incipit tractatulus magistri Gherardi groed de periculo pastoralis cure *tit. in X*, Alia epistola eiusdem quam scripsit cuidam iuueni uolenti accipere beneficium curatum ob paupertatem suorum parentum *tit. in Gr, tit. om. DQM*, Lege istam epistolam, quisquis ad curam animarum festinas, et quod periculosum sit anhelare ad prebendam uel officium cui annexa est cura animarum perpende. *marg. sup. suppl. alia manus in H2*   5 subeniri *sic B*   7 aliquod *Di*   obsteterit *DLX*   magis] *marg. corr. M², minus M¹*   8 in hoc] *om. XM*
9 collocacionis *Di*

anno, saltem quod eum attigisset, nouem mensibus, quos habuit in utero, secundum quosdam sibi in subsidium computatis. Secundo uideat ne symoniace intret per preces carnales. Preces enim, quas sorores pro fratre fundunt, ex eo quod frater est, sunt nate de carne et sine dubio carnales. Et si fundunt eas intuitu seruicii, quod fecerunt uel facture sunt, presentatrici aut collatrici, adhuc preces ille sunt carnaliores. Ymmo tunc seruicium non loco precum carnalium tantum, sed loco precii succedunt. Et si intuitu seruicii sororum aut precum earum intuitu principaliter | detur cura animarum, manifesta est symonia, maxime quando fiunt pro indigno, prout timeo de hoc iuuene: tunc factum est symo|niacum. Patet per Thomam in *Secunda Secunde*, q. .c., art. .v., et in *Scriptis super Sententiarum*, di. .xxv., cui concordat Hostiensis in *Summa*, libro .v., rubrica *De symonia*. Concordant Raymundus et Gofredus, doctores theologie et iuris canonici.

Et si fiant carnales preces pro digno non intuitu dignitatis aut meriti principaliter, nec datur quod precatur nisi carnali intuitu et non respectu dignitatis: tunc coram Deo est sic inter petentem et dantem ac si indignus esset, quia dignitas persone non respicitur et utriusque mentes secundum proprias intentiones sunt immundissime et symoniace. Sed in foro contentioso presumitur, quando dignus est, ad dignitatem eos respexisse, hoc est secundum iuris presumptionem, licet aliud sit in ueritate.

10/11 locum inuenire non potui   12/30 cfr IOH. FRIB., *Summa Conf.*, L. I, t. I, q. 14 (f. 6r, c. I, 17-46), ubi allegat omnes auctoritates a Ger. citatos, sc. THOM., II-II, Q. 100 a. 5 co.; ad 3 (T. 9, p. 362, a. 5, c. I, 33 – c. 2, 8; 32-40 – uerbatim); THOM., *Sent.*, L. 4 d. 25 q. 3 a.3 ad 4 (T. 7,2, p. 915, c. 1); RAYM., *Summa de paen.*, L. I t. I § 7 (c. 284-285 ed. Ochoa; uerbatim); HOST., *Summa*, L. 5 t. 8 §?, sub uoc. 'sin autem' (ed. 1537, f.?); Goffredus; duo posteriores sicut a Ger., ita et a Ioh. sine locis allegantur   14/17 cfr IOH. FRIB., *Summa Conf.*, L. I, t. I, q. 7 (f. 5r, c. I, 18-22)

---

10 anno] *om. B*   attingisset *X*   12 uideat] ipse *praem. X*   13 fatre *sic Di*   quod] quia *D Di M*   14 carnaliter *B*   fundant *D Di B*   15 presentanti *sic M*   16 carnales *X*   tunc] sunt *X*   17 succendunt *Di*, succedit *B*   si] *om. Di*   18 sororum] *om. Di*   intuitu precum earum *tr. B*   intuitu] *om. M*   19 cura] *om. H*   est manifesta *tr. X*   20 de] in *X*   hoc] *om. Di*   est] *om. B*   .c.] .I. *M*   22 Scripto *X*   supra *H L*   di.] q. *B*   cui] et *X*   22/23 Hostiensis – concordant] *om. B*   22 hostis *sic Di*   23 Summa] sua *marg. add. L²*   Concordat *X*   24 Gotfridus *H*, Goff- *X*, Goffre- *M*, Gaufridus *B*   doctores] et *praem. X*   25 preces carnales *tr. X*   25/27 aut – dignitatis] *om. B*

Item quis petere pro se non potest beneficium curam animarum habens, etiam si dignus esset, secundum Hugonem, Raymundum, Thomam, Hostiensem et Gofridum, licet glosa Wilhelmi in Raymundo dicat quod quis dignus existens potest pro se beneficium curatum petere exemplo Ysaye dicentis: *Ecce ego, mitte me*, *Ysaye* .VI. capitulo. Sed uolens sic mitti uel petere aduertat quod Gwilhelmus uult quod in casu dignus potest pro se | petere, sed non semper. Talis enim modus loquendi iuris doctoribus est consuetus.

Vnde tempore necessitatis, quando alius non inuenitur melior et quando species mali non adest et salus animarum dumtaxat queritur, potest forte petere pro se beneficium curatum, ut determinat Henricus de Gandauo in *Quodlibeto* secundo, q. nescio quota. Aduertat etiam qui sequitur Gwilhelmum quod curam et sacerdotium Ysayas non | petiit, sed prophetiam et predicationem. Multi enim sanctorum ad predicandum se mitti prompti aliquando in necessitate, ut de Gregorio et Equicio et aliis legitur, inuenti sunt.

37/38 Is. 6, 8, allegatum sec. HENR. GAND.

33/40 cfr denuo IOH. FRIB., *Summa Conf.*, L. 1, t. 1, q. 14 (f. 6r, c. 1, 46 – c. 2, 7), ubi allegat omnes et easdem auctoritates a Ger. citatas, etiam sine locis specificis praeter locum a Gwil. allegatum, sicut nec Ger. locos allegat   37/38 loc. ex Is. 6, 8 allegatur non solum a IOH. FRIB., sed etiam in HENR. GAND., *Quodl.* 2, q. 18 (p. 140, 8-10) infra citato et a GREG. MAG., *Reg. Past.* 1, 7 (p. 150, 9-11, cfr *PL*, 77, 20B)   42/46 cfr GER. MAG., *Locat.*, 305-312   HENR. GAND., *Quodl.* 2, q. 18 (p. 139, 88 – 141, (1)26), cfr etiam THOM., II-II, Q. 100 a. 5 ad 3 (T. 9, p. 362, c. 2, 53 – 363, c. 1, 2)   48/50 cfr GREG. MAG., *Dial.*, 1, 4, 8 (T. 2, p. 44, 84-99)

---

33 quis] aliquis *X*   34 hu^oes *D*, Hugonem *HX*, Hugo- *M*, Hugucionem *DiLB*   35 Hostiensem, Thomam *tr. B*   Gafredum *Di*, Gaufridum *B*, Goff- *X*, Gofredum *M*   Gwylhelmi *DDi*, Guillermi *B*   37 mitto *B*   me] *om. L*   38 petere] curam *add. DiXMB, postea suppl. D*   39 Wilhelmus *LX*, Wil- *M*, Guillermus *B*   42 melior] et *praem. M*   44 potest] *om. D*   45 Henricus] *om. X*   Gandeno *Di*   Quotlibeto *HX*, Quolibeto *DiLB*   45/46 q. – quota] *om. X*   46 qui] *postea (fere anno 1455) corr. D*, quod anno *1418 D, DiM*, quod qui *X*   Wilhelmum *LX*, Guillermum *B*, sc. *M*   49 in] *om. HL*   inniti uel necessitati *M*   et Equicio] *om. M*   Equicio] de *praem. B*

Ad curam autem animarum aut regiminis non lego quod recti et boni accesserunt nisi coacti. Vnde primo *Pastoralium* Gregorius ait: "uirtutibus pollens coactus ad regimen ueniat, uirtutibus uacuus nec coactus accedat". Et Augustinus, .XIX. *De ciuitate Dei*:
55 "locus superior, et si teneatur ut deceat, indecenter tamen appetitur". Vnde Thomas, q. .C., art. .V., in responsione ad tertium argumentum: "si quis pro se rogat ut habeat curam animarum, ex ipsa presumptione redditur indignus. Et sic preces sunt pro indigno". Eciam aduertendum est secundum Gregorium, primo *Pas-*
60 *toralium*, quod Ysaias, | "qui mitti uoluit, per altaris calculum 32rb prius purgatum se uidit, ne quis non purgatus ministeria sacra adire audeat. Quia ergo ualde difficile est purgatum se quemlibet posse cognoscere, predicacionis officium tucius declinatur." Hec Gregorius.
65 Item, ut quis canonice introeat istis temporibus in prouisione et institucione, que communiter in hac terra cum quibusdam pactis pecuniarum dandarum fiunt cum institutoribus et prouisoribus, qui alias, nisi darent uel promitterent tantum se daturos, institutionem et prouisionem non obtinerent. Hec et huiusmodi peri-
70 culosa est symonia, bonis uiris omnino declinanda, propter quas solas declinandas multi bonorum istis temporibus beneficia de-

---

52/59 cfr GER. MAG., *Locat.*, 290-304; 570-571   52/54 HENR. GAND., *Quodl.* 2, q. 18 (p. 139, 83-85), qui allegat GREG. MAG., *Reg. Past.* 1, 9 (p. 160, 38-39, cfr *PL*, 77, 22C)   54/56 HENR. GAND., *Quodl.* 2, q. 18 (p. 136, 7-8), qui allegat AVG., *Ciu. Dei*, 19, 19 (p. 687, 31-33), cfr etiam GRAT., *Decr.*, C.8 q.1 c.11 (c. I, 594, 9-12) paene ad litt., ubi allegatur AVG., *Ciu. Dei*, 19, 19 (p. 686, 22 – 687, 40, uerba allegata ibid., p. 687, 31-33)   56/59 cfr THOM., II-II, Q. 100 a. 5 ad 3 (T. 9, p. 363, c. 1, 4-7)   59/64 GREG. MAG., *Reg. Past.* 1, 7 (p. 152, 25-31, cfr *PL*, 77, 20C) paene ad litteram

---

51 autem] *om. M*   legi *X*   52 boni] beati *B*   assenserint *H*, accesserint *L*, assesserunt *Di*   53 uirtutibus²] autem *add. X*   54 uacans *Di* .XIX.] *post* Dei *pos. M*, .IX. *X*   Dei] dicit *add. X*   56 Thomas] Secunda Secunde *add. M*   art.] c. *X*   .V.] . VI. *M*., VIII. *B*   57 ex] et *Di*   58 et] *om. HL*   59/60 postoralium *Di*   60 quod] *om. X*   calculum altaris *tr. B*   62 diffi^ue (*sc.* diffinitiue) *Di*   purgatum] *om. M*   63 cognoscere posse *tr. M*   declinatur] quam suscipitur *add. X, sed non sic Greg. Magn.*
65 intret *M*   65/66 institutionibus et prouisionibus *M*, prouisiones et instituciones *B*   66 communiter que *tr. a.c. D*   67 pecuniarum] *marg. corr. Di²*, pniārum (*sc.* penitenciarum) *Di¹*   68 qui] quas *M*   68/69 institutionem et prouisionem] *om. M*   70 bonis] et *praem. Di²*   declinanda] derelinquenda *D*

clinant, ne in limite et in introitu ad beneficium cum dyabolicis
symoniacis sy|moniace se commisceant et dyaboli laqueis se in-
uoluant cum illis periculosissimis hominibus, qui omnes institu-
75 tiones et prouisiones ad questum pecuniarum retorquent. Hec de
canonicis uel contra canonicas sanctiones ⟨periculis⟩ dicta sufficiant.

Item omnis uolens digne intrare curam animarum iudicio consciencie ex diuinis et naturalibus legibus tenetur primo habere in-
80 tencionem rectam. Secundo tenetur esse illuminatus | Dei scien-
cia, tercio tenetur et uixisse et uiuere uita bona et exemplari,
quarto tenetur amore interno et uita alios precellere, quinto ter-
rena et mundana contempnere.

De primo. Ad intentionem rectam requiritur ut principaliter ho-
85 norem Dei et lucrum animarum intendat. Et hoc per hoc cognos-
citur, si ipsam curam animarum, si nullum emolimentum temporale esset ei annexum, acceptaret propter animas curandas, si
alias haberet temporalia sibi et suis necessaria. Hoc enim est prin-
cipale in intentione alicuius in actu aut officio quocumque, quo
90 dato uoluntas fertur in rem, et quo remoto auertit se uoluntas uel
non curat.

Zelus enim animarum quis possit esse in eo qui proprie salutis
immemor se ipsum non zelauit, cum tamen omnis rectus zelus
caritatis a se ipso incipiat. Vnde non est caritas uera proximi que
95 a se ipsa non incepit. Non est creata res carens principio. Item
Sapiens dicit: *Miserere tui placens Deo.* Ista est prima miseri-

---

73/74 cfr I Tim. 6, 9   95/96 Eccli. 30, 24

79/82 cfr Thom., *Sent.*, L. 4 d. 24 q. 1 a. 3 qc. 1-2 (T. 7,2, p. 892-893)   85/
91 cfr infra, 178-188, et Ger. Mag., *Locat.*, 406-419   92/98 cfr Ger. Mag.,
Locat., 50-53; 406-410   cfr Thom., *Perf.*, c. 27 co. (T. 41, p. B 106, 289-301)

---

72 limite] sic codd., limine *M, sic emend.* Mulder, *sed cfr* Lexicon Nederl.,
L, 176, 38-41, *ubi alius locus datur, ubi* limes *poniturpro* limen   in²] *om. B*
73 se] *om. H*   73/74 se inuoluant se *sic H*   76 periculis] *sic M, sic
emend.* Mulder, pericula *codd.*, dicta pericula *tr. H*   79/80 rectam intencionem *tr. M*   80 tenetur] *om. X*   Dei] de *X*   81 et¹] *om. D X M*   uiuere et uixisse *tr. M*   bona uita *tr. M*   82 interno] eterno *H*   83 quinto]
tenetur *add. L B*   85 hoc¹] *om. X*   88 est enim *tr. X*   90 auertat *D X*
uel] et *X*   93 semetipsum *H L*   95 ipsa] ipso *Di*   incipit *X*   cre-
ata] causata *H*, tanta *L*

cordia. Vere immisericors est qui se interficit, maxime in anima. Quomodo creditur sibi de zelo et misericordia aliis faciendo? Quid plura? Vt met iuuenis confitetur, non est zelus tantus in
100 eo quod sine emolimento temporali curam acceptaret propter lucrum animarum, si haberet tamen | unde posset in cura se sustentare. Sed heu, ipse ut suos parentes sustentet, uult curam accipere. Heu, heu, quanta ista est impietas coram Deo, et quanta mentalis symonia! Seruire uult Deo et animabus, ut uiuat ipse uel sui, cum
105 propter hoc ab Eterna Sapientia creati et redempti sumus et uiuimus ut Deo seruiamus. Est enim racionalis creatura instituta a Deo, ut dicitur primo *Sententiarum*, ut Deo seruiat et ipsum amet et laudet. Sed hunc ordinem iste iuuenis totum peruertit, ut finem institutionis humane, in Dei laude et seruitio constitutum, ad se et
110 suam uitam retorqueat. Et hec est auersio ab | ultimo fine et eterna felicitate, ymmo a spiritualibus et finalibus bonis humanis et diuinis.

Et ista ad et propter uilissimum questum pecuniarum querit et ordinat immediate, ut illis mediantibus uiuat, hoc est facto suo,
115 mente sua, opere suo temporalia diuinis et corporalia spiritualibus preponere in dignitate et bonitate, quia "propter quod

---

97/102 cfr Ger. Mag., *Locat.*, 334-338 ; 507-510 ; *Ep.* 17, 68-73   106/108 cfr Petrvs Lomb., *Sent.*, L. 2 d. 1 c. 4 qc. 4 (T. 1.2, p. 332, 26-28), partim, sed quibusdam uerbis a Ger. allegatis omissis citatum a Thom., *Sent.*, L. 2 d. 1 q. 2 pr. (p. 44, 22-23)   113/122 cfr infra, 147-157, et Ger. Mag., *Locat.*, 353-357 ; *Ep.* 19, 15-18   116/117 eundem locum Ger. allegat in Ger. Mag., *Locat.*, 357 cfr Thom., *Sent.*, L. 4 d. 24 q. 1 a. 1 qc. 3 s.c. (T. 7,2, p. 888, c. 1, 3-7), prope locum a Ger. supra, 79-82, allegatum, ubi Thomas a Ger. citata uerba allegat ex Arist., *Post. Lat.* 1, 2, in uersione latina a Iac. Venetico confecta et a Guil. de Moerbeka reuisa (p. 287, 29-30, cfr p. 9, 13-14 (Arist., *Post.* 1, 2, 72a29-30 Bekker)), sed sine mentione auctoritatis et loci, qui autem in codice a Ger. adhibito in forma glossae praesentes esse potuerint, de quibus praesertim Thom. etiam alibi una cum eadem citatione mentionem facit, e.g. Thom., I, Q. 16 a. 1 arg. 3 (T. 4, p. 206, c. 1, art. 1, 22-23), cfr etiam L. 2 d. 1 q. 2 a. 2 s.c. 1 (p. 47, 30), sed Thomas hic ipsissima Aristotelis uerba non allegat

---

97 se] se ipsum *B*   98 sibi] *om. M*   faciendum *B*   99 met] *sic anno 1418 D*, ipse met *corr. anno fere 1455 D*   100 quod] ut *B*   101 tamen] *sic codd.*, *om. B*, tantum *M*, *sic ed.* Mulder   in cura posset *tr. M*   in] sine *B*   possit *D*   102 ut] ipse *iterum add. B*   sustentet parentes *tr. H* sustentaret *X*   103 est ista *tr. X*   mentalis] inde talis *B*   103/104 Deo – uult] *om. H*   105 propter] ab *B*   106 ut] sicut *X*   Deo – a] *om. X*   107 Scienciarum *sic B*   Deo²] sibi *B*   seruiet *M*   108 laudat *H*   110 suam] ad *praem. M*   113 ista] *om. HLX*, ita *M*   ad et] *om. X*   115 sua] *om. M¹*, *suppl. M²*   opere] et *praem. B*   116 quod] *om. B*

unumquodque tale, et illud magis", primo *Posteriorum*. Et "in omnibus fines sunt desiderabiliores" et meliores "hiis que" ordinata sunt ad finem, primo *Ethicorum*. Et sic maternus uictus et tempo-
120 ralia lucra sacra | mentis et sacramentalibus executionibus et actibus,   33ra
Dei laudibus et seruitiis uidentur tali menti meliores, secundum ordinationem qua eas ordinat.

Et ego soleo dicere, prout scripsi eciam in quadam questione, quod minus malum esset emere curatum beneficium, sicut emitur
125 uacca uel bos, ab eo qui non intenderet temporale lucrum, sed animarum salutem, quam qui canonice quoad extra ad curam ueniret et lucrum principaliter intenderet uel lucrari uel temporalia emolimenta. Hec probaui in eadem questione. Et quamuis ius canonicum non iudicet secundum, sed primum, hoc est quia ma-
130 gis respicit ad exteriora quam interiora, *Deus* tamen *intuetur cor* et scrutator est cordium et uult perapsidem intus precipue mundari.

Item, quando sic temporalia querit iuuenis et ad beneficium sic accedit, non est dubium eum mortaliter peccare ipso ingressu et
135 a Deo separari. Vnde istius introitus pocius dyabolus est agitator quam Deus, cum tamen *Sacra scriptura* dicat, in *Epistola Pauli ad*

---

130 cfr I Reg. 16, 7, fortasse allegatum sec. THOM. (cfr app. font.)   131/
132 cfr Matth. 23, 26   136/138 Hebr. 5, 4

117/119 cfr THOM., *Sent.*, L. 4 d. 49 q. 3 (de delectatione) a. 4 qc. 3 arg. 1 (T. 7,2, p. 1221, c. 1, 6-8), cum expositione, ibid., L. 4 d. 49 q. 3 a. 4 qc. 3 co. (T. 7,2, p. 1222, c. 1, 47-58), ubi allegat ARIST., *Ethic. Lat.* (fasc. 4, p. 141, 18-19 (ARIST., *Ethic.*, A, 1, 4 (1094a13-15 Bekker)); sed in editione a. 1858 Parmae prelo data prima clausula tantum Arist. uerborum ("in ... desiderabiliores") sec. uersionem latinam a Grosseteste factam et a Guil. de Moerbeka reuisam allegatur   123/130 cfr GER. MAG., *Locat.*, 383-388; praesertim 481-494; locus a uiro docto Mulder propositus (565-573) dissimilior esse uidetur   129/
132 cfr THOM., *Sent.*, L. 4 d. 25 q. 3 a. 1 qc. 1 ad 1 (T. 7,2, p. 910, c. 2, 57 – p. 911, c. 1, 9)   131/132 GER. MAG., *Locat.*, 513-515 eundem locum biblicum citat

---

117 magis] *sec. Arist. D cett.*, maius *HL*   Postriorum *B*   118 finis *sic Di*   119 primo] ut dicitur *praem. X*   Et] *om. HL*   121 menti] iuueni *X*, mente *B*   122 eos *X*   123 eciam] *om. X*   126 salutem animarum *tr. B*   127 et] ut *X*   lucrari] lucrum *iterum B*   uel²] *om. H*   128 Hoc *X* Et] *om. L*   ius] *om. B*   129 quia] quod *X*   130 respicit] *om. DB, sed postea suppl. anno fere 1455 D*   interiora] ad *praem. HL*   cor] *om. B* 133 iuuenis sic temporalia querit *tr. DXM*   134/135 et – separari] *om. X* 136 scriptura sacra *tr. B*

Hebreos, quod *nemo sibi assumat honorem, nisi qui uocatur a Deo, ut Aaron*. Vnde secundum Dyonisium, .v. capitulo *Ecclesiastice ierarchie*, "Ihesus *non se ipsum glorificauit, sed qui locutus est ad eum:* | '*Tu es sacerdos in eternum secundum ordinem Melchisedech*'". Qui ergo ex se et ex propriis agitatur, mendacium loqui|tur et uanitatem agit, et a dyabolo conducitur, maxime in hoc opere acceptionis cure, in quo mortale peccatum committit, mortem anime ingrediendo sibi procurans, eciam si antea mortuus non fuisset. Multa hic de capitulo eodem Dyonisii possent dici, sed sufficiunt hec intelligenti.

Item, quando quis taliter curam accipit, propter finem predictum temporalium in proprium uictum aut parentum suorum ordinatum, quando tunc accedit ad ordines propter curam eandem, tunc ordines et acceptio ordinum secundum intentionem accipientis eadem intentione symoniaca qua curam querit, inficiuntur. Quidquid enim est medium ad aliquid ordinatum ad finem, est medium ad ipsum finem. Et quacunque ratione et intentione feror ad finem, tali ratione et intentione feror ad medium, quod ad ipsum finem ordino et quero. Ideo talis est intentio et intentionis macula in ordinibus qualis est in cura animarum propter quam ordines accipio. Si enim *lumen quod in te est* et *oculus*

139/140 Hebr. 5, 5, allegatum sec. DION. (cfr app. font.)   140/141 Hebr. 7, 17 ; Ps. 109 (110), 4, allegatum sec. DION.   141/142 cfr Ioh. 8, 44   157/159 Matth. 6, 23

138/141 DION., *Eccl. Hier.* 5 (p. 1361, c. 7 (l. 3 uel 4) – p. 1362, c. 1 (l. 3 uel 4)), sec. transl. Ioh. Eriug. uel Ioh. Sar., hic sine auctoritatibus interuenientibus allegatum sicut patet ex l. 145-146, sed **139** glorificauit] *Ger. Mag., Dion.*, clarificauit *Bibl., Hebr.* 5, 5   147/157 cfr supra, 113-122

---

137 quod] quia *L*   assumat sibi *tr. M sec. Hebr.* 5, 5   **138** ut] tamquam *XMB sec. Hebr.* 5, 5   **139** se ipsum non *tr. M*   **140** in eternum] *om. B*   **141** Melchizedech *Di*   **143** acceptionis] *sic L¹*, acceptationis *corr. L²*   peccatum mortale *tr. B*   **144** procreans *Di*   ante *X*   **145** hic de] de hoc *Di*   hic] *post* possent *pos. B*   eodem c. *tr. B*   **145/146** dici possent *tr. L*   **146** sufficiant *DX*   **147** curam taliter *tr. B*   curam] animarum *add. L²*   accepit *Di L*   **147/148** temporalium predictum *tr. a.c. D*   **148** uictum] *om. B*   aut] in *add. B*   **149** propter – eandem] *om. B*   **151** intentione] est *add. Di*   **152** aliquid] *om. B*, aliquod *D*   **153/154** ratione – tali] *om. X*   **154** intencione uel (et *corr. M²*) racione *tr. M*   **156** in²] *om. B*   **157** lumen] *corr. anno fere 1455 D*, lucrum *anno 1418 D*

CONSILIVM DE CVRA PASTORALI 289

intentionis hominis malum et *nequam fuerit, totum corpus* nequam et *tenebrosum erit* secundum doctrinam Christi. | 33va
160 Item et omnis qui hoc modo quesiuit sibi ordinem aliquem, habet coram Deo caracterem infectum quoad eius initium. Vnde timentur mala multa secutura, non quod substantia caracteris, que deiforme signum est et Dei instrumentum, in se sit infectum, quia sacramenta non maculantur a malis, sed quia timendum est quod
165 talis tales faciat ordinis executiones qualiter eosdem accepit, ut eodem modo et propter eundem finem predictum confessionem audiat, absoluat, inungat uel celebret, propter quem curam accepit.

Omnia uestigia pedum cuiuscumque Romam euntis diurnam
170 mercedem uel penam accipiunt, secundum eam intentionem qua quis Romam proficiscitur. Si bene et propter Deum accipit, Deum accipit in premium et eternam retribucionem in quolibet gressu suo. Si male et propter temporale, dyabolus uel temporalia sibi cedunt in mercedem. Sic longe profundius et magis in quolibet
175 actu sacerdotali et cure intrat intentio, siue bona siue mala fuerit, qua quis curam principaliter, siue propter | temporalia dyabolo   316
instigante, siue Deo inspirante acceperit propter salutem animarum principaliter. Et hic est infinita abyssus, quia numquam talis curatus uictum aut temporalia | principaliter querens potest a quo-   33vb

---

162 alludit ad Hebr. 1, 3

161/168 cfr GER. MAG., *Locat.*, 54-61   162/163 cfr THOM., III, Q. 63, fere passim, sed praesertim a. 4 co. (T. 12, p. 36, c. 1 – c. 2) et q. 64 a. 1 co. 2 (T. 12, p. 41, c. 2, co. 14-20)   163/164 cfr e.g. THOM., *Sent.*, L. 4 d. 24 q. 1 a.3 qc. 1 arg. 1 (T. 7,2, p. 892, c. 1), sed praesertim THOM., III, Q. 64 a. 5 co. (T. 12, p. 46, c. 1 – c. 2)   164/168 cfr GER. MAG., *Locat.*, 186-193   178/188 cfr supra, 85-91, et GER. MAG., *Locat.*, 406-419

---

158 hominis] *om. B*   corpus totum *tr. Di*   158/159 fuerit – nequam] *om. L¹, marg. suppl. L²*   160 et] *om. X*   hoc] in *praem. Di*   presumit *Di*   163 infectum] *sic codd.,* infecta *fortasse legendum*   164 est] *om. X*   165 faciet *DiHLXB*   166 eodem] in *praem. B*   finem eundem *tr. B*   predictum] predicet *HL*   confessionem] et *praem. B*   167 audiat] *corr. L², audiet HL¹DiX*   170 accipiunt uel penam *tr. B*   accipient *X*   171 proficitur *sic Di*   Deum²] *om. X,* in *praem. Di*   172 accipit] *om. XB*   173 suo] *om. B*   Si] autem *add. X*   temporale] lucrum *add. D²*   uel] et *DiXM*   174 cedunt] erunt *XM*   175 intret *X*   177 acceperit siue Deo inspirante *tr. DDiXM*   accepit *H*   inspirante] spirante *Di*   178 est] *om. B*

180 cumque absolui, nisi propositum et mentem et intentionem mutauerit. Nulla potestas in celo nec in terra potest hominem absoluere eo in intentione spiritualiter mala permanente. Ymmo in quolibet actu quem exercet in personam ecclesie quasi officio suo utens, mortaliter peccat, nisi quis ad hoc deueniat ut permutet in-
185 tentionem, ut mallet cura cum temporalibus carere, si hoc esset subditis lucrum spirituale, et etiam ut in tantum crescat intentio recta, si haberet aliunde uiuere, quod uellet curam sine emolimento regere.

Item, si quem sciret melius oues recturum, quod illum mallet
190 eas pocius quam se ipsum regere, rexisse et recturum. Si enim homo uellet opposita horum, tunc quereret *que sua sunt*, unde ex caritate non moueretur. Possumus enim considerare quanto amoris glutino illi rei, ex qua totus noster honor, status et totus uictus et uestitus noster pendet, simus incorporati et conglutinati, quando
195 manifeste uidemus quod pro modica possessionis nostre portione uel glorie uel nominis, uidelicet pro una tunica, pro uno equo, pro uno iniuriarum uerbo, totus cordis nostri status euertitur, tota mens nostra inquietatur, toti nos animo et corpore et bonis ad uindicandum | uel ad defendendum nisu indicibili nitimur et la- 34ra
200 boramus. Ex hoc uidemus quod res nobis quasi cordi nostro ui-

---

191 cfr Phil. 2, 21

182/184 cfr GER. MAG., *Focar.* 18 (p. 418-419, 2519-2527)   cfr THOM., *Sent.*, L. 4 d. 24 q. 1 a. 3 qc. 5 co. (p. 894, c. 1, 63-66); cfr ibid., qc. 5 ad 4 (p. 894, c. 2, 16-19) sec. IOH. FRIB., *Summa Conf.*, L. 3 t. 22 q. 25 (f. 163v, c. 2, 19-35)
192/201 cfr GAVFR. (PS. BERN. CLAR.), *Coll. Sim.* 2, 2 (*PL*, 184, c. 438C)

---

180 et[1]] *om. B*   et mentem] *om. X*   181 nec] et *M*   182 eo in] ea *L M*   Ymmo] et *add. B*   183 persona *X M*   184 peccat mortaliter *tr. H L*   185 ut] scilicet *add. anno fere 1455 D*   curam *Di*   cum] a *B*   esset] dum *add. X*   186 lucrum subditis *tr. H L*   speciale *B*   187 quod] *om. B*   189 illi *X*   190 pocius eas per talem regere, rexisse et recturum quam per se ipsum *sic M*   eas] *om. B*   pocius] committere *add. X*   et] uel *X*   recturum] esse *add. anno fere 1455 D*   homo] sic merito *D Di H B*; scribae nonnulli abbreuiaturam h° interpretati sunt quasi esset hoc, atque emendationes uarias proponunt: hic *L*, hoc *X*, postea exp. *X[1 uel 2]*, pro hoc uellet *scribit* hoc nollet sed *M*   191 quereretur *Di*   191/192 unde – moueretur] sic sine caritate non meretur *M*   192 non] *om. Di*   possimus *D* enim] tamen *M*   193 honor noster *tr. B*   194 dependet *B*   198 et[2]] *om. M*   bonis] uenis *H L*   199 nisi *B*

CONSILIVM DE CVRA PASTORALI   291

dentur colligate, et ideo uere pauci exeunt a questu temporalium,
qui curas propter temporalia inuadunt.
   De secundo, quod scientia diuina requiritur ad hoc quod quis
dignus ad curam reddatur animarum, patet quia omnis "ierarchia",
205 siue angelica siue humana, uidelicet ecclesiastica, "est ordo, scientia et actio", et ex illis consistit. Quomodo quis cecus aliis ducatum prebet? Si cecos ceci ducent, ceci et duces cecorum omnes
in precipicium cadunt. Quomodo curabit scientia non habens
scientiam? Nonne "ars artium", secundum Gregorium in primo
210 *Pastoralium*, "est regimen animarum?" Et quomodo quis docere
potest quod nunquam didicit? Vnde secundum Gregorium, ubi
supra, sunt plures "qui dum metiri se ipsos nesciunt, que non di-
dicerunt docere concupiscunt; qui pondus magisterii tanto leuius
estimant, quanto uim magnitudinis eius igno|rant". Et infra: "Sepe   317
215 qui nequaquam precepta spiritualia cognouerunt, cordis se medicos profiteri non metuunt, dum qui pigmentorum uim nesciunt,
carnis se medicos profiteri erubescunt". Hec Gregorius.

   206/208 Matth. 15, 14 paene ad litt., uerbatim allegatum a GAVFR. (Ps. BERN.
CLAR.), *Coll. Sim.* 15, 18 (*PL*, 184, c. 447C-448B) (infra, 297-306, in paraphrasi allegatum) et GRAT., *Decr.*, D.38 c.5 (c. I, 142, 2-3)

   203/237 latet me cur Ger. nec GRAT., *Decr.*, D.36 c.1-3 nec D.38 c.1-15, ubi
de eadem re tractat, usus sit, cum hic (ibid., D.36 p.c.2 § 4 (c. I, 134, 28-31)
inter plurimos alteros locos e Biblia sumptos etiam locus e Mal. 2, 7 allegatus
sit   203/251 cfr GER. MAG., *Locat.*, 410-413   204/206 cfr GER. MAG.,
Locat., 41-42   cfr THOM., I, Q. 108 a. 1 arg. 2 (T. 5, p. 494, c. 1, l. 28-29),
ubi allegatur DION., *Cael. Hier.* 3, 1 (p. 785, c. 5-6 (l. 3)), sec. transl. Ioh. Eriug.
   206/209 cfr GER. MAG., *Ep.* 17, 34-36   209/210 GREG. MAG., *Reg. Past.*,
Pars 1, c. 1 (p. 128, 4-5)   211/214 GREG. MAG., *Reg. Past.*, Prol. (p. 126,
27-30)   214/217 GREG. MAG., *Reg. Past.*, Pars 1, c. 1 (p. 128, 6-9) paene ad
litt.

---

   201 collegiate *H*   exiunt *Di*, exuunt *B*   202 propter temporalia curas *tr. B*   inuadunt] et cetera *add. M*   203 requiratur *X*   205 uidelicet]
ualet *Di L*   206 hiis *X*   Quomodo] Et *praem. Di H L*   alius *M*   206/
207 prebet ducatum *tr. B*   207 prebeat *M*   ducant *B*   cecorum]
eorum *M*   208 scientia] et *add. Di*   209 Nonne] Nam *B*   primo]
principio *praem. M*   210 est regimen animarum *post* 209 artium *pos. X*
   211 quod] qui *M*   211/212 unde – supra] sicut enim ibidem dicit *X*
   212 que] qui *B*   213 magistrorum *M*   216/217 profiteri – medi-
cos] *om. Di*   217 erubescant *X*   Hec Gregorius] *om. X*   Gregorius]
ille *B*

Vnde Dominus ait, *Malachie* .II. capitulo: *labia sacerdotis custodiunt scientiam, et legem requirent de ore eius, quia angelus | Domini exercituum est.* Et uere, secundum beatum Bernardum in libro *De colloquio Symonis et Ihesu*, sacerdos et clericus angelus est aut bonus aut malus, et prauitas inuenta in angelis maior est quam humana. Vnde de scientia et illuminatione sic ait Dyonisius *Ad Demophilum*: "Si ergo sacerdotum ornatus est illuminatiuus, perfecte cecidit a sacerdotali ordine et uirtute qui non est illuminatiuus, magis autem qui non est illuminatus. Et audax michi uidetur sacerdotio manum apponens, et non timet neque uerecundatur diuina, preter dignitatem exequens et putans Deum ignorare que ipse in se ipso cognouit, et decipere estimat ab ipso falso nomine Patrem appellatum, et audet ipsius immundas diffamias, non dicam orationes, supra diuina signa christiformiter enuntiare. Non est iste sacerdos, sed inimicus dolosus, delusor sui ipsius, et lupus super diuinum populum pelle agnina armatus." Hec Dyonisius. Et ideo speculatores positi sunt curati, qui tenentur omnia scire que ad eorum officium pertinent, tamquam mundiores oculos ad omnia et longiora et densiora discernenda et ad premuniendum et defendendum habentes.

34rb

218/220 Mal. 2, 7, partim ("quia – exercituum") in loco a GAVFR. citato allegatum

---

218/220 cfr GER. MAG., *Focar.* o (p. 305, 148-150); 18 (p. 421, 2565), ubi idem locus biblicus in extenso (*Focar.* o) et partim una cum loco ex Gaufr. (*Focar.* 18) allegatur   220/223 cfr GAVFR. (PS. BERN. CLAR.), *Coll. Sim.* 21, 24 (*PL*, 184, c. 451C), in GER. MAG., *Focar.* 18 (p. 421, 2563-2567) etiam, sed ibi paene ad litt. allegatum   223/234 DION., *Ep.* 8, sec. transl. Ioh. Sar. (p. 1533, c. 3 (l. 4) – p. 1535, c. 3 (l. 4)), partim allegatum a THOM., *Sent.*, L. 4 d. 24 q. 1 a. 3 qc. 5 s.c. 1 (T. 7.2, p. 893, c. 1), unde fortasse Ger. ad locum ipsum directus est; THOM., III, Q. 64 a. 6 s.c. (T. 12, p. 47, c. 1 – c. 2) minus probabilis locus uidetur, quia hic Thom. eundem locum etiam partim allegat, sed uocabulo 'illuminatus' non utitur

---

220 uere] *om. B*   beatum] *om. DX*   220/221 in libro] *om. Di*   222 aut¹] *om. B*   magis *Di*   223 humanis *Di*   et] de *add. B*   sic] sicut *D*   ait sic *tr. M*   224 Domophilum *B*   ergo] *om. B*   225 perfecte] sic *codd.*, profecto *sec.* Dion. H2   et uirtute] *om. B*   225/226 illuminaturus *bis Di*, illuminatus *bis M*   226 autem] aut *H*   Et] *om. B*   michi] *om. M*   229 cognouerit *L*   et] *om. Di*   230 immundans *B*   232 delusor] et *add. L*   233 supra *B*   237 habentes] et cetera *add. M*

CONSILIVM DE CVRA PASTORALI 293

De tertio. De uita non est dubium quod quis debet uite exem|plum suis subditis dare, quia sicut doctrine, ita et uite plenitudo in ierarchia | debent reperiri, ut sicut precedit doctrina, ita et uita. Presbiter quasi prebens iter uerbo et exemplo, quia illius predicatio despicitur, cuius uita contempnitur. Vnde omnium, que post eum sunt, plenitudo in ⟨ierarcha⟩, ut dicit Dyonisius, primo *Ecclesiastice ierarchie,* debent reperiri. Et secundum philosophum, nescio in quoto *Pollitice,* naturaliter princeps omnium subditorum in se uirtutem debet continere. Et ideo scribitur de Christo, *Actuum* .I., quod incepit *facere et docere,* maxime quia scientia perfecta non habetur sine experientiali gustu, que illuminata perficit, ut solet tractari circa idem primum capitulum *Ecclesiastice ierarchie.* Et uere sine experientia diuinorum nec quis sui ipsius nec aliorum aptus est iudex aut reformator.

De quarto et quinto, quia tempus non adest, facilius transcurro. Non enim sufficit bona uita curato nisi excellat, ut ex predictis patet, uitam subditorum. Quomodo leuabo alium nisi alcius ste-

318
34va

246/247 Act. 1, 1 paene ad litt.

---

241 cfr GER. MAG., *Focar.* o (p. 305, 152)   241/242 cfr GRAT., *Decr.,* C.3 q.7 p.c.2 § 3 (c. I, 526, 41) uel THOM., *Sent.,* L. 4 d. 24 q. 1 a. 3 qc. 4 s.c. 2 (T. 7,2, p. 893, c. 1, 3-5), ubi GREG. MAG., *Hom.* 12, 1 (p. 82, 36-37) allegatur, a Ger. ordine uerborum permutato allegatum   242/244 cfr DION., *Eccl. Hier.* 1 (p. 1080, c. 3 (l. 4) – p. 1081, c. 4 (l. 4)), sec. transl. Ioh. Sar.   244/246 cfr THOM., I-II, Q. 105 a. 1 co. (T. 7, p. 262, c. 2, co., l. 9-16), ubi allegatur ARIST., *Pol. Lat.* 3, 5, 5, in uersione latina a Guil. de Moerbeka facta (p. 171, 4-6); locus a Mulder propositus, sc. ARIST., *Pol. Lat.* 1, 13 (p. 54, 2-5 (1260a17 Bekker)) etiam possibilis est, sed non uideo ubi Ger. istum locum inuenire potuisset   247/250 cfr DION., *Eccl. Hier.* 1 (p. 1074, c. 7 (l. 4) – p. 1077, c. 7 (l. 4)), sec. transl. Ioh. Sar.   250/251 cfr DION., *Eccl. Hier.* 1 (p. 1087, c. 13 (l. 4) – p. 1088, c. 10 (l. 4)), sec. transl. Ioh. Sar.

---

238 tertio] scilicet *add. X*   De uita] *om. B*   quis] curatus *add. B* uite] *om. M*   238/239 suis subditis uite exemplum *tr. B*   239 doctrina *B*   240 iherarchia *Di*   debent] *sic H,* debet *XB, corr. ipse H¹*   sicut] *om. B*   precedit] semper *add. M*   243/246 omnium – ideo] *om. X* 243 post eum] opus *M*   ierarcha] *sic legendum sec.* DION., *Eccl. Hier.* 1 (p. 1080, c. 5 (l. 4)), *sec. transl. Ioh. Sar.,* ierarchia *codd.*   244 debet *B* 245 quoto] quo *M*   Pollicie *sic Di,* Pollicite *sic H,* Policite *sic L* 246 scribit *B*   247 cepit *M*   248/249 perfecta – perficit] *om. Di* 248 perfecte *HLB*   experimentali *XMB*   249 ut] et *M*   249/ 250 ut – ierarchie] *om. X*   250 experigencia *sic X*   251 nec²] aut *M* actus *B*   253 ex] in *X*   254 uitam subditorum] *om. X*

255 tero, quomodo succurram nisi potentior fuero? Quomodo in me uirtutes speculantur subditi, quas non habuero? Ideo *super montem excelsum Syon adscendet qui ewangelizabit Syon.* Et non sufficit curato ut amet Deum, nisi plus aliis et nisi eminencior in eo caritas fuerit. Et ideo Christus, cum uellet Petro | 260 oues suas committere, dixit: Si amas *me | plus hiis*, id est quam alii, tunc *pasce oues meas* et aggredere onus regiminis spirituale. Vere, uere, magna caritas requiritur ad bonum pastorem, si bonus pastor ponit animam suam pro ouibus suis, quia maiorem caritatem nemo habet, ut animam suam ponat quis pro amicis suis. 265 Vere, uere, mercennarius est, non pastor, qui querit oues tondere.

Et uere debet curatus et qui preest, secundum beatum Bernardum in quodam *Sermone super Cantica*, de pleno fundere, non ut canale, quod sumens refundit non retinens, sed debet esse uelut amphora stans, que non prius refundit in propinqua nisi 270 plena et superfusa fuerit.

Sunt etiam alia perpendenda in curis habendis, inter que est unum, ut subditi sint abiles ad informandum et susceptiui uerbi Dei. Alias ex magnis demeritis prelatorum contingit ut illis pre-

319
34vb

256/257 Is. 40, 9 paene ad litt.   259/261 cfr Ioh. 21, 15-17

259/264 cfr GAVFR. (PS. BERN. CLAR.), *Coll. Sim.* 11, 12 (*PL*, 184, c. 444C-D), ubi locus e Ioh. 21, 15-17 eodem modo allegatur, sc. 260 amas] *Gaufr. Ger.*, diligis *Ioh.*   265 cfr GER. MAG., *Locat.*, 370-372; *Ep.* 17, 26-29   266/270 cfr BERN., *Serm. Cant.*, 18, 1, 2-3 (Vol. 1, p. 104, 8-28, praesertim 19-25); locus in ed. Mulder, p. 319, nota 3, allegatum minus apte ualet, qui est BERN., *Serm. Cant.*, 54, 5, 12 (Vol. 2, p. 110, 10-26)   273/277 cfr GREG. MAG., *Reg. Past.* 2, 7 (p. 222, 56-70); *Moral.* 24, 25, 53 (p. 1227, 32-38), loci a Mulder in ed. sua uerbatim praesentati, prouenientes ex operibus a Gerardo ipso in *Conclusis et propositis* suis, p. 98, 5-8 ed. Pohl, inter praesertim fautos imprimis enuntiatis et approbatis; obseruandum tamen etiam est quod alii loci ex eisdem operibus Gregorii consilio Gerardi aeque apti allegantur in GRAT., *Decr.*, D.47 c.3 (c. I, 170, 8-36); D.49 a.c.1 (c. I, 175, 5-15), sc. in D.47 locus e GREG. MAG., *Moral.* 19, 27 (p. 995-996, 46-74), in D.49 e GREG. MAG., *Reg. Past.* 1, 10-11 (p. 164, 33-39; 1-5)

---

256 uirtutes speculantur] *om. X*   subditi] *om. M*   supra *HLXM*
257 ewangelizabit qui ascendet Syon *tr. B*   Syon²] *om. B*   258 Et non sufficit] et cetera. Sufficit *H*   259 Et] *om. X*   260 dixit] sic *praem. B*
261 tunc] *om. B*   spiritualis *B*   262 uere²] *om. B*   263 imponat *B* quia] et *Di*   264 suis] et cetera *X*   265 est] et *add. MB*   266 beatum] *om. H*   267 supra *B*   268 ut] est *H*   sed] et *M*   269 nisi] quam *B*
271 eciam] *om. B*   aliis *H*   273/274 preferant *B*

ferantur, quibus prodesse ex duritia et malitia non possunt, ut dicit Gregorius, tam in *Pastoralibus* quam in *Moralibus*. | Correspondent enim analogice merita subditorum cum prelati habitu et e conuerso. Inutilibus occupari ad quid ualet?

O, quam fatuum est fatuis uirginibus oleum dare, cum uix nobis sufficiat ad bone conscientie testimonium! O, quam difficile est regere iam senescente mundo | secundum caritatem duodecim oues uel duodecim monachos! Quis ergo sufficiat ad mille uel ad duo millia, et non dico ouium, ymmo leonum et ursarum pro parte et insensibilium quorundam animalium curam regendam?

Rursus principes temporales uolunt esse supra sacerdotes, et uolunt curam eo modo regi per curatos quo temporalibus et eorum dominio expediat, uoluntque celebrari cum ipsi iusserint, similiter et absolui uel ligari et sacramenta ministrari. Quod si quis fecerit, cadet in abyssum malorum contra Deum et canonicas sanctiones. Et si facere recusauerit, numquam pacem habebit, semper turbabitur, semper inueniet impugnantes.

Similiter difficilimum est, si curatus etiam nichil aliud obseruare deberet quam debite excommunicatos, interdictos et suspensos a canone uel iudice in diuinis et in conuersatione euitare. Quod si non fecerit, ut excommunicatorum presentiam in celebrando non

---

278/279 cfr Matth. 25, 1-12

284/290 cfr GER. MAG., *Simonia beg.*, 407-418   291/295 cfr INNOC., *App. in vium*, super VI 5.II.I, comm. sup. 'irregularitatem' (c. II, 1094, 13) (f. 213v, c. 1 in fine, sub num. 4), in GER. MAG., *Focar.* 4 (p. 334, 708-720), in extenso a Ger. citatum   294/295 cfr *Decret.*, VI 2.14.1 (c. II, 1007, 39-43); VI 5.II.I (c. II, 1094, 12-15)   cfr GER. MAG., *Focar.* 4 (p. 330-345, 646-902); *Artic.* 18 (p. 531, 156-162)

---

274 malitia et duritia *tr. B*   275 Gregorius] beatus *praem. X*   tam – Moralibus] *om. X*   in²] *om. L*   276 analogyce *Di corr. M²*, anoloyce *L*, analoyce *HM¹*   prelato *M*   277 Inutilibus] enim *add. B*   278 dari *M*   281 uel] *om. M*   sufficeret *Di*, sufficiet *XMB*   ad²] *om. M*   282 ouium] hominum *M*   ursorum *X*   282/283 pro parte] porcorum *M*   283 quorundam] *om. M*   animarum *H*   285 quo] que *M*   286 dominio] ieiunio *praem. H*   dominio] *corr. anno fere 1455 D*, domino *anno 1418 D*   287 et¹] *om. X*   uel] et *X*   288 cadit *X*   289 facere] sancte *M*   290 turbulabitur *B*   rupugnantes *sic Di*, impugnacionem *B*   291 etiam] si *add. Di M*, scilicet *add. X*   293 iudice] a *praem. L X*   in²] *om. B*   euiptare *sic Di*   294 ut] si *add. anno fere 1455 D*   non] *om. M*

295 strictissime uitauerit, statim suspenditur ipso iure. Et si postea suspensus celebrauerit, statim irregularis efficitur.

Et uere, si quis recte istis temporibus curam regere uelit, non est dubium eum multas per|secutiones habiturum, non solum a principibus, sed a multis quibus preest, quia pauci | uolunt regi. 300 Nam secundum *Ecclesiasten, peruersi difficile corriguntur, et stultorum infinitus est numerus*. Et si malis et persecutionibus incumbentibus a cura et a iustitia seruanda cessauerit, est de illis qui *uidet lupum uenientem et fugit, quia mercenarius est* et sua querit, *et non pertinet ad eum de ouibus*. Si restiterit uiriliter et fortiter 305 permanserit, uere per artam uiam Christi et angustam eum oportet pertransire, difficiliorem quam credit iuuenis. Et multo leuius esset ut parentibus suis mendicaret quam tribulationes et angustias, quas istis temporibus ueros curatos et rectos sustinere oportet, pateretur. Vnde secundum beatum Bernardum, in libro *De* 310 *colloquio Symonis* supradicto, uix angelicis humeris cura animarum sustentatur.

De quinto, scilicet mutabilium et temporalium contemptu, dicere que dicenda sunt supersedeo, ne durus uidear, et quia hoc magis est pro proficientibus quam pro incipiente iuuene, cui res-315 pondi in Christo per predicta. Cui laus, gloria et imperium in secula seculorum. Amen.

300/301 Eccle. 1, 15   302/304 Ioh. 10, 12-13, allegatum sec. GAVFR.

297/306 cfr GAVFR. (PS. BERN. CLAR.), *Coll. Sim.* 15, 18 (*PL*, 184, c. 447C-448B)   309/311 cfr supra, 220-222   cfr GAVFR. (PS. BERN. CLAR.), *Coll. Sim.* 16, 19 (*PL*, 184, c. 448B-D)

---

295 euitauerit *X*   296 efficitur] erit *M*   297 recte] racione *B*   298 persecutiones] turbulaciones *Di*   299 quia] nam *B*   300 Nam] quia *B*   secundum] quod dicit *add. X*   Ecclesias^tem *H*, Ecclesiasticus *X*   301 malis et] *om. X*   302 a²] *om. X*   303 uident *B*   fugiunt *B*   est] *om. M*   304 ad] *om. Di*   Si] Sed *Di*, uero *add. B*, autem *add. X*   resisterit *M*   305 remanserit *M*   angustiam *Di*   306 transire *D X M*   iuuenis] inueniet *M*   leuius] melius *M*   308 et rectos] *om. X*   rectores *B*   309 beatum] *om. X B*   de in libro *tr. a.c. D*   310 Symonis] et Ihesu *add. X B*   supradicto] *om. X*   311 sustendatur *Di*   sustentatur] et cetera *add. M*   313 quia] *om. X*   314 pro¹] *om. X*   pro²] *om. M*   insipiente *B*   315/316 Cui – Amen] *om. Di*   315 laus] et *add. L X*   et imperium] *om. X*   315/316 in secula seculorum] per infinita secula *X*   316 Amen] *om. M*, Explicit Responsio Magistri Gerardi dicti groet, de pluralitate beneficiorum *add. D*, Explicit tractatulus magistri Gherardi groed de periculo pastoralis cure *add. X*

EPISTOLA (19)
SVPER IOHANNEM PRESBYTERVM
ET DOMINVM HENRICVM DE SCOENHOVE DE GOVDA
DE SIMONIA EVITANDA IN CVRA PASTORALI

CONSPECTVS SIGLORVM

codices

H2   Den Haag, Koninklijke Bibliotheek, 78 J 55, s. XVa
L   Liège, Bibliothèque de l'Université, 229 (c), a. 1451

Hos codices in plagulis phototypice expressis contulimus.

EPISTOLA
SVPER IOHANNEM PRESBYTERVM
ET DOMINVM HENRICVM DE SCOENHOVE DE GOVDA
⟨DE SIMONIA EVITANDA IN CVRA PASTORALI⟩

Alpha et o., a quo omnia ueniunt, ad quem omnia tam naturaliter quam per gratiam reducuntur, dirigat que inchoauit, compleat que direxit, in Christo Ihesu Domino nostro.
Primo queratur ab eo si omnia sua libere resignauerit ad manus commissarii episcopalis, ut secundum dictamen iuris diuini et humani et secundum arbitrium uiri boni ipse commissarius omnia libere disponat, habito respectu ad ea que secundum exigenciam malorum preteritorum requirit equitas diuina et sancta Dei ecclesie constitucio.
Secundo quod doleat quod ita uilipendit spiritualia et sacramenta Christi, et maxime trinitatis misteria et ministe|ria sancta, que omne precium et omnia temporalia excedunt et que ducunt ad uitam gracie et glorie, ad que temporalia omnia ordinantur, respectu quorum temporalia nullam omnino proporcionem nec ualorem habent. Doleat quod ista ita uilipendit et pre eis temporalia

231va 65

231vb

1/2 cfr Apoc. 1, 8; 21, 6; 22, 13

---

1 hanc epistulam Gerardus anno 1383 ignotae destinationi, uerisimiliter fratribus uitam communem incipientibus, misit super actiones domini Henrici de Schoenhove prope Goudam, commissarii ab epispopo Traiectensi constituti, cuius actus patent infra, praesertim 169-172, sed etiam 4-7; 52-56; 59-61; 105-106; 109-115; 155-156; 160-161; cfr de cetero supra, in introductione
4 eo] sc. Iohannes, presbyter paenitens de quo tota epistola agit, infra (60; 112; 139; 159; 166-167) nominatim praesentatus   15/18 cfr GER. MAG., *Locat.*, 353-357; *Cur. past.*, 113-122   cfr THOM., *Sent.*, L. 4 d. 24 q. 1 a. 1 qc. 3 s.c. (T. 7,2, p. 888, c. 1, 3-7), ubi Thomas a Ger. in *Locat.*; *Cura past.* citata uerba allegat ex ARIST., *Post. Lat.* 1, 2, in uersione latina a Iac. Venetico confecta et a Guil. de Moerbeka reuisa (p. 287, 29-30, cfr p. 9, 13-14 (ARIST., *Post.* 1, 2, 72a29-30 Bekker))

Tit. Ad dominum henricum de scoenhoue (schoenhoue *marg. inf. in manu procuratoris scriptorio superuidentis in L*) de gouda *tit. in L H2*
1 nota de restitutione et de redditibus ad uitam non emendis *marg. exponit L³*   7 respectu] *sic marg. se ipsum corr. L*, illud *H2, a.c. L*   15 eis] *sic a.c. L, postea exp. L¹ ᵘᵉˡ ²*

elegit et preelegit, et posuit ista quasi media et organa et instrumenta sua finaliter ad temporalia, ut ad finem suum ad temporalia acquirenda. Et hoc ita manifeste fecit ut omnibus suus questus turpissimus manifeste appareret. Vnde procul dubio plurima
20 scan|dala sunt exorta et plures oues spiritualiter sunt neglecte uel   66
occise uel infirmate.

Deinde ante omnia imponatur sibi ut de cetero tale nephas mercenaritus et questus coram Deo symoniaci nullatenus committat, et ut in suis ecclesiasticis ministeriis – in celebracionibus,
25 predicationibus et sacramentorum amministrationibus – pre oculis gloriam Dei et Deum habeat, et intendat ecclesie sancte construccionem, et lucrum spirituale in eis querat principaliter et pretendat. Hec enim contricio cordis requirit.

Quarto consulatur sibi ut causas et occasiones quibus posset
30 appropinquare aut relabi ad pristina mala, longius fugiat, ab eis se remoueat. Et hoc est satisfaccionis | magna pars.   232ra

Quinto consulatur sibi ut in sui officii execucionibus, siue in missis siue in predicacionibus siue in amministracione sacramentorum, quolibet tempore, et maxime in componendo nouo statu
35 aut in capiendo aliquod beneficium aut aliquod spirituale officium, perpendat et perspiciat medullitus cur et propter quid hoc faciat aut attemptet, et quid moueat ipsum in hoc et imperet sibi ad hoc.

Sexto consulatur sibi ut omnem speciem mali in istis fugiat, et
40 exibeat iam se organum et membrum execucionis spiritualis ad iusticiam spiritualem publice et aperte, suaque mala preterita, que manifesta fuerunt et sunt, publice condempnans et dolendo manifestans, ut sit *odor suauitatis Domino* apud alios mercennarios questuosos. Sed occulta sua non nisi secretis amicis aut medicis
45 suis reuelet, maxime illa que alios scandalizare ualerent, occultet. Iste sunt satisfactionis legitime et salubres partes.

---

43 cfr e.g. Ex. 29, 41; Leu. 2, 9; 4, 31; 17, 6; Num. 15, 3; 15, 7; Eph. 5, 2

24/25; 32/34 cfr GER. MAG., Locat., 173-177; 364-365   cfr THOM., Sent., L. 4 d. 24 q. 2 a. 2 co; ad 1; ad 4-5; ad 8; ibid., a. 3 co.; ad 2 (p. 897, c. 2 – 899, c. 1); etiam L. 4 d. 24 q. 1 a. 2 qc. 2 arg. 2 (p. 890, c. 1); qc. 3 ad 2 (p. 891, c. 2)

---

32 sui] *sic p.c.* L, suis H2 *a.c.* L   42/43 manistestans *sic* H2   43 mercenarios H2   46 satisfactionis] *sic p. c. ipse* H2, satisfactiones *a.c.* H2

EPISTOLA DE SIMONIA EVITANDA IN CVRA PASTORALI 301

Deinde dicatur sibi quod, si sederent sancti patres iudices – tale enim iudicium requirit conscientia, qui et ipsi nos cum Christo iudicabunt –, ipsi iudicarent quod omnia que ita turpiter acquisi-
50 uisset, sancte ecclesie, in cuius preiudicium symoniam commisit, restituere deberet, et multa plura quam iam habuerit uel quod iam resignauerit. De | quibus pluralioribus commissarius eum pro nunc supportet, quia paupertas et inopia possibilitatem exclu|dunt, et hic, in quantum potest et debet, commissarius secun-
55 dum potestatem clauium et commissionem sibi factam remittat et ⟨indulgeat⟩, si in proposito suo sancto permanserit. Sed si ad pinguiorem et uberiorem exteriorum bonorum fortunam perueniret, ut ampliora quam *uictum et uestitum* simplicem, quibus apostolici presbiteri *contenti sunt*, haberet uel acquireret, tunc consulat
60 commissarius quod ipse dominus Iohannes pro tunc consulat sanctos uiros, qui considerata ista indulgencia et remissione tunc iudicent aut arbitrentur quid et quantum et in quo et quomodo ipse tunc ecclesie refundere debeat aut satisfacere. Et in hoc tunc consultores illi, quos ipse sibi bona consciencia dictante elegerit,
65 habeant omnimodam arbitrandi potestatem.

Rursus ante omnia doceat eum quod uideat quod ecclesie materiali non directe satisfit aut refunditur, si redditus suos ad uitam resignauerit, quia nichil lucratur adextra ecclesia. Sed sancte militanti ecclesie secundum spiritualem saporem et direccionem Spi-
70 ritus in hoc aliqualiter | applauditur quod ipse acquisitis uult carere. Et in hoc ecclesia spiritualis letatur quod suo facto suadet

232rb
67

232va

58/59 I Tim. 6, 8 sec. uersionem Hieronymi (cfr app. font.) paene ad litt.

47/51 iudicium patrum, quamquam in contextu diuerso, Ger. etiam minatur in *Locat.*, 650-652   47/52 cfr GER. MAG., *Locat.*, 689-696; *Ep.* 17, 49-65 cfr *Decret.*, VI 1.6.35 § 4 (c. II, 965, 45-53)   52/54 sic commissarius faciat sec. praeceptum datum in *Decret.*, X 3.5.4 (c. II, 465, 26-31), ut patet ex fontibus a Ger. infra, 72-75, partim nominatim allegatos   54/56 cfr THOM., *Sent.*, L. 4 d. 18 q. 1 a. 3 qc. 1 co.   56/59 cfr infra, 104-106 et GER. MAG., *Stat.*, 64-80   58/59 cfr HIER., *In Matth.* 1 (sup. Matth. 6, 11, p. 37, 783-786), cuius uersionem uersus biblici (I Tim. 6, 8) Ger. hic paene uerbatim allegat; fere eandem locutionem adhibet primo capitulo *De prima congregatione clericorum in Dauentria* THOM. KEMP., *Dial.*, 4, 1 (p. 216, 20-25 ed. Pohl, uerbatim citata uerba ibid., 23-24)

---

56 indulgeat] sic sec. *Acquoy legendum*, indulget *L H2*   63 debeat] et uel aut *praem., sed postea eras.* ipse *H2ʳ*   71 swadet *sic L*

redditus ad uitam non emendos, qui ab aliquibus magnis doctoribus illiciti iudicantur. Et sunt procul dubio secundum sanum concilium, ut Innocentius, lucerna iuris, testatur, cunctis christianis dissuadendi. Et uere huic concilio moralis, naturalis et diuina racio michi uidetur consonare.

Et quid amplius? Scio sanctissimam regulam esse Au|gustini in tam periculosis negociis: "dimitte incertum, tene certum", maxime quando accusat et repugnat temporale contra spirituale. Et si hoc cunctis christianis concilium est sanum, quid tunc in presbitero, cui et licite et iustissime negociaciones sunt prohibite. Hoc ergo ponat sibi in satisfaccionem, quod resignet omnes redditus in termino sibi a commissario prefigendo, et quod dicat in resignacione quod non audeat ea in consciencia retinere.

Deinde libri sui sicut pauperi ad uitam concedantur, ex ea racione quia ecclesie et sibi sunt utiliores in sua persona quam in alia uel alteri. Sic etenim ecclesia triumphans cuilibet utilissima sibi tribuit, quia *omne datum | de sursum optimum est* cuilibet.

Item, uendat agrum uel agros illos, ut cicius congrue poterit, et pecunias secundum commissarii arbitrium in aliquam notabilem et manifestam construccionem spiritualis ecclesie refundat et ponat, ut inferius dicetur.

Item, domestica instrumenta, superlectilia et utensilia teneat non superflua nec pulcra nec preciosa ad quantitatem illam ut sufficiant tribus personis, uidelicet sibi et uni presbitero et uni ancille, pro lectisterniis et utensilibus secundum sufficienciam christianam et humilem. Quecunque autem plura sunt quam ad hec sufficiant, uendantur, et pecunia ponatur ad manus commissarii.

---

88 Iac. 1, 17

72/73 Iohannem (Andreae?), Gaufredum, Innocentium et Hostiensem inter doctores qui sic iudicant enumerat HENR. BOIC, *Dist. sup. Decret.*, X 3.5.4 (c. II, 465, 26-31) (Pars 1, p. 386, c. 1, 15-25; 47-54 sub num. 1; 4)   73/75 cfr INNOC., *Comm. Decret.*, super X 3.5.4, comm. sup. gl. 'consideratis facultatibus' (= BERN. PARM., *Glos. ord. in Decret.*, super X 3.5.4, comm. sup. 'necessaria' (c. II, 465, 28) (c. 1026 (L. 3, p. 18), gl. g) (ed. 1570, f. 355r, c.2), allegatum sec. HENR. BOIC, *Dist.*, in adnotatione priore citatum   74 eodem epitheto utitur GER. MAG., *Focar.* 1 (p. 315, 366)   77/78 PS. AVG., *Serm.* 393 (*PL*, 39, c. 1715, 18), etiam allegatum a GRAT., *Decr.*, C.2 q.33 c.3 (De pen., D.7 c.4) (c. I, 1245, 33-34), qui autem clausulas in ordine mutato citat   81/103 cfr GER. MAG., *Locat.*, 337-342

EPISTOLA DE SIMONIA EVITANDA IN CVRA PASTORALI   303

Item, si que curiosa aut pulcra sint aut pretiosa aut inordinata,
100 que non decent sanctitatem domesticam, et alia instrumenta, si
indigencia requirat eiusdem generis instrumentorum uel superlectilium, emantur uiliora aut simpliciora, et pecunia, si superfue-
rit emptis uilioribus, ad manus commissarii ponatur.
   Ceterum et uestimenta, si qua sint curiosa aut superflua aut
105 preciosa, in simplicem uestitum mutentur secundum arbitrium
commissarii, et in commutacione si superfluxerit pecunia, ad ma-
nus | ponatur commissarii.   233ra
   De domo Dauantriensi sic se habeat ut nullatenus illam suam
credat, sed commissarius assignet et adiudicet eam sanctis eccle-
110 sie seruitoribus, tam proprietatem et dominium illius domus quam
Wolterus inhabitat, quam usum et usufructum illius | domus apud   69
muros Dauentrie. Sed ipsi domino Iohanni inhabitacionem istius
domus, apud muros scilicet, et quando, et non alias, uoluerit
Dauantrie morari, assignet, quousque uixerit, sicut pauperi et
115 indigenti presbitero Deo seruienti. Et quando Dauentrie esse
noluerit, tunc seruitoribus Dei et plene conuersis eam ad in-
habitandum concedet, immo uerius, ut in propriam admittat, salua
locacione istorum †qua† de presenti eam conduxerunt. Durante
autem locacione presencialiter inhabitancium, pensionem pecu-
120 niarum, post festum Pasche deinceps deriuantem, in subsidium
locacionis uel acquisicionis habitacionis hominum spiritualium
Dauentrie ponet. Vel si ibi opus non fuerit, ad easdem res in
Campen ponatur. Et manifestus in hoc sit quod hoc de eis ordinatum sit, uel quod hoc sic ordinauit ex causis conductionis ec-
125 clesie sub annuo censu, ut gloria Dei et sanctitatis in eo mani-
festetur. Proprietatem et dominium domus sue mag|ne, in qua   233rb
Wolterus habitat, quanto utilius poterit in commoditates hominum
presencium et futurorum Deo seruiencium, laycorum aut clericorum, ponet et ordinabit, siue ad illum usum resignando siue uen-
130 dendo et precium in tales usus reponendo. Et ut breuiter conclu-

---

104/106 cfr supra, 56-59 et GER. MAG., *Stat.*, 64-80

---

99 sint] *sic etiam H2*, sunt *Mulder*   aut pretiosa] *marg. suppl. H2²,
om. H2¹*   **112** iħoi *sic abbr. H2*   **113** et¹] *uiro Acquoy delendum uidetur*
   114 Dauentrie *H2*   **114/115** *clausula fortasse sic:* [et] quando uoluerit
Dauantrie morari et non alias *legendum est*   **118** qua] qui *sec. Acquoy legendum*   **125** annuo] *corr. H2², anno H2¹*

dam, in hiis debet esse dumtaxat Christi dispensator et procurator fidelis spiritualium pauperum Christi, prout per hoc possunt dirigi in uiam salutis uel ad conuenientem modum secundum Deum uiuendi. Hec est realis ecclesie spiritualis constructio per temporalia, et ad hoc sunt omnia temporalia sicut ad finem ordinata.

Item, de pecuniis que ueniunt de terra uendita aut de rebus uenditis, triginta uel quadraginta antiqua scuta accipiantur et ponan|tur ad unam *Bibliam* et ad unam *Summam confessorum* et ad alios libros, et in istis emptis libris habebit dominus Iohannes tantum usufructum, quamdiu uixerit, sicut pauper presbiter indigens huiusmodi libris, et proprietas et dominium istorum librorum erit seruitorum Dei et manifeste ad Deum conuersorum, sicut aliorum librorum suorum presentium proprietas et dominium erit | apud eosdem. Sed in iam habitis libris habeat potestatem permutandi, sic quod eorum non diminuat ualorem.

Similiter et utensilia retinenda et superlectilia. Quoad usum duarum partium, utatur eis sicut sibi a seruitoribus Dei concessis ad uitam, et quoad terciam partem, teneat ⟨eam⟩ pro uno socio uel pro alio seruitore Dei, si socium non habuerit, et tamquam ad eundem finem sibi a seruitoribus Dei mutuatis aut ut apud eum depositis. Proprietas autem et dominium omnium predictorum utensilium et superlectilium apud predictos erit Dei seruitores in Dauentria et in Campen, nec habebit posse, eciam in testamento, predicta omnia aut domus aut eciam libros a predictis alienare.

Item residua pecunia a terra et ab aliis accepta dominus Heinricus disponet ad utilitatem seruitorum Dei. Et in hoc accipiet Celiam consciam et accessorem. Et secundum quod uidebitur eis expedire, possunt ad presentem annum transeundum ipsi domino Iohanni aliquam quantitatem largiri sicut pauperi presbitero, si aliunde non possit haberi conueniencius unde sustenetur. Et residuum summe reseruetur ad dictamen domini Heynrici et Celie, si debeat ad utilitatem seruitorum Campensium distribui, uel ad

---

131/132 cfr Luc. 12, 42

162 cfr WEILER, *Norm*, p. 1

147 concess- *H2*, concessum *emend. Mulder*   148 eam] *sic sec. Acquoy legendum*, ea *L H2*   159 presbitro *sic L*

EPISTOLA DE SIMONIA EVITANDA IN CVRA PASTORALI 305

dictamen Florencii et Gerardi, si debeat ad utilitatem Da|uentrie
Dei seruitorum deputari. Et in hoc prospiciatur indigencia maior
165 seruitorum, et in cuius ecclesie lesionem maiorem questus | symoniacus ⟨sit⟩ commissus, quod ipsi domino Iohanni melius constare poterit. Et forte bonum esset quod dominus Iohannes illam porcionem pecunie, que sibi pro uictu anni presentis traderetur, ignoraret de suis uenisse pecuniis. Et si hoc sit congruum, iudicet
170 dominus Heynricus. Omnia et singula que non plene hic determinata sunt uel specificata, iudicio domini Heinrici commissarii reseruentur et illorum quos uoluerit ut accessores ⟨consilii⟩ assumere.

Deus, qui est super omnia in omnibus, et qui solus omnibus
175 sufficit, et in quo omnia habentur, sit cum omnibus nobis per omnia secula seculorum. Amen.

233vb

71

---

163 sc. Fl. Radewijns et Ger. Magnus, cfr supra in introductione

---

163 Gherardi *H2*   165 seruitorum] *sic L H2*, seruitorem *error preli in ed. Mulder*   in] *sic L H2, om. Mulder*   166 sit] *sec. Acquoy legendum*, sibi *L H2*   domini *Mulder*   170 Heinricus *H2*   172 concilii *L H2*

STATVTA DOMVS A MAGISTRO GERARDO
FEMINIS DEVOTIS DESTINATAE

cura et studio

Marinus Van Den Berg

CONSPECTVS SIGLORVM

D   DEVENTER, Stadsarchief en Athenaeumbibliotheek, 0690 (olim 1607) Stad Deventer, periode Middeleeuwen, "Olde in papier gescreven copienboick", s. XVb
L   LEIDEN, Bibliotheek der Rijksuniversiteit, BPL 1045, s. XVc

Hos codices in plagulis phototypice expressis contulimus.

L

172r Dit is die satinge ende ordinancie van den huyse ende erve dat heer Gherit die Grote in die ere Godes ghegheven hevet

1. Int irste so is to weten dat hy huse ende erve mit horen begripe niet en ghevet noch ghegheven hevet om ienighen nyen gheistliken staet of nye religie te maken, want dat en mach niemant doen sonder orlof des pawes, mer tot eenre herberghe joncvrouwen die der herberghen begheren om God ende om Gode te bet to dienen mit oetmoede ende penitencie.

2. Ende wat lude men daerin setten sal, die sullen ongebonden wesen van mannen noch mit gheenre orden of religien. Ende oec en sal men van nieman die daerin comet lofnisse of verbont eischen of nemen. Wie mit sins

D

Dit is die satinghe ende ordinancie van den husen ende erve dat heer Gherijt die Groet in die ere Gods ghegeven hevet

1. Int ijrste so ist to weten dat hi huse ende erve mit horen | begrijpe niet en ghevet noch ghegeven hevet om ienighen nyen gheesteliken stat of nye religio te maken, want dat en mach nieman doen sonder oerlof des pawes, noch om beghinenstaet te maken, want die baghinen mit namen van den pawes ende van der ghemener Kerken verboden sijn onder den banne in den gheesteliken rechte, meer tot eenre herberghen joncvrouwen ende vrouwen onghebunden die van armoden der herberghen noet is, of die der herberghen begheren om God ende om Gode te beet te deenenne mit oetmoede ende penitencie in der herberghen mitten armen luden.

2. Ende wat lude dat men daerin setten sal, die soelen onghebunden wesen van mannen, noch mit gheenre oerden, noch van religien. Ende oec en sal men van enghenen menschen die daerin coemt, lofnisse noch ver|bunt

192r
3 Post 65 Hullu

66 H.

4 P.

10/12 ut praescribitur in *Decret.*, VI 3.17.1 § o (c. II, 1054, 74 – 1055, 13)
12/17 (*D* tantummodo): cfr infra, 228-255, et GER. MAG., *Simonia beg.*, 64-68   cfr *Clem.* 3.11.1 (c. II, 1169, 30-52); Ger. hic de mitigatione a Ioh. .XXII. proposita mentionem non facit, quam alibi, *Simonia beg.*, 68-73, sec. *Extrauag. comm.* 3.9.1 (c. II, 1279, 33 – 1280, 17) disputat

Tit. Copia der ordinancien van meister Geerds des Groten huys *marg. sup. ut tit. scr. man. al. (D³) in D*

L

willen eens uytgaet of sonder sinen willen uytgesat woert, die en sal nummer|meer weder incomen.

3. Sie sullen all lekelude bliven ende heyten, ende ghien doen hebben of anhangen an ienighe religiose lude sonderlinge.

4. Si sullen to rechte staen voer den schepenen int ⟨weerltlike⟩ recht ende gelike ander lekelude daer geven ende nemen. Ende die scepene na heren Gherides dode sullen over dat huys macht hebben insettens ende uytsettens te ordinieren ende berichten, gelijc als sij hebben over heren Stappenhuys na der formen die hijr bescreven is.

6. Item, hoere gheen en sall ommermeer enighe sonderlinghe manier van cleder draghen die enighe religiosen luden allene tobehoeren. Hoer cleder ende hoer

D

eyschen of nemen, want si sullen vri bliven weder uet te waren ende hem to verbeteren waer ende waen sie willen. Ende wie mit sijns willen eens uetgheet of weder sinen willen uetghezadt werdet, die en sal nummermeer weder incomen.

3. Si soelen ael lekelude bliven ende hieten, ende gheen doen hebben noch anhanghen an ienighe religiose lude sunderlinghe.

4. Se solen toe rechte staen voer den schepenen int ⟨weerltlike⟩ recht ende ghelijc anders gheleken luden daer gheven ende nemen. Ende die schepene na heren Gherides dode soelen allene aver dat huys macht hebben insittens ende uetsettens tot ordiniren ende berichte, ghelijc als se hebben over heren Stappenhues, na der formen die hier bescreven is.

5. Item soelen sie onderdanich wesen hoeren curaet ghelijc anders sijn kerspellude.

6. Ende haere gheen en sal emmermeer falighen draghen of gheen sunderlinghe manire draghen die den baghinen allene of ieghnighen religiosen luden al-

---

64/80 cfr I Tim. 6, 8

53/56 Ger. se hic ad statuta deperdita domus a Henrico Stappen fundatae refert, quorum forma autem in statutus hic editis, in ea parte quae litteris romanis imprimata est, reconstitui potest   64/80 cfr GER. MAG., *Ep.* 19, 56-59 ; 104-106

---

47 weerltlike] *sic emendaui*, weertlike L

---

47 weerltlike] *sic emendaui*, weerlike D

STATVTA DOMVS FEMINIS DEVOTIS DESTINATAE

L

173r schoen sullen sij sniden ende draghen gelijc ander goeden, vroeden, oetmoedeliken lekenludenvrouwen ende joncvouwen: wit, doncker van verwen. Gheen gesnebbede schoen | sullen sij draghen, noch ghene selsene, of hoverdighe ende uytwendighe maniere hebben in cledere noch om oer hovet, want dese den armen contrarie sijn ende des duvels ende der onkuisheit teykene. Ende daerto sal sien die meistersche dat dit niet en geschie.

7. Item, nummermeer en sal men ghelt opt huys setten int incomen, mer men sal die men innemen wil, puer om God nemen sonder gave, noch niet ansien, myede noch vrentscap dan die ere Godes, ende orber des huses ende nootdrufte der lude. Ende wanneer die schepene yenighe dair in- of uutsetten willen of orloff gheven te tymmeren, so sullen sij tevoren raet nemen mitter meistersche ende mit vijr den vroetsten. Ende wan sij die gehoert hebben, so moghen sij doen na hoere bescheidenheit.

D

lene tobehoerde. Haer cledere ende scoen solen sie sniden ende draghen ghelijc anders goe|den, 5 P. vroeden, oetmoedeliken lekenvrouwen ende joncvrouwen: wiet, doncker van verwen. Gheen ghenebed scoen soelen sie draghen, noch ghene selsene, of hoverdighe ende uetwendighe maniere hebben in cledere noch over hoer hovet, want dese den armen contrarie sin ende des duvels ende der oncuescheit teykene sijn. Ende daerto soelen sien die meysterschen dat dit niet en scee. | 67 H.

7. Nummer en sal men ghelt opt hues setten in incomen. Men sal die men nemen wil, puer om God nemen sonder gave, noch niet aensien, noch mede, noch vrentscap dan die ere Gods, oerbaer des hues ⟨ende⟩ noetrufte der lude. Ende waen her Gherijt bi sinen tiden of die scepene na siere doet ienighe daer in- of uetzetten willen of oerlof gheven to tymmeren, so soelen sie tevoeren raet nemen mitten tween meysterschen ende mit vier den vroedesten. Ende wan sie die ghehoert hebben, soe moghen se doen na haere beschedenheit.

81/83 cfr GER. MAG., *Simonia beg.*, 1-39; *Leeringhe*, 51-96   82/88 cfr GER. MAG., *Simonia beg.*, 419-490

---

94 vroetsten] *sic legendum*, vroeˈsten *L*

---

71 ghenebed] Ger. *hic calceorum formam in suis diebus ubique a feminis gestorum intendit, uulgari lingua* snavelschoen *(.i. calceamentum rostratum) nuncupatam; Post ergo falso contra cod. et contra De Hullu emendationem* 'ghesnebed' *proponit*   81 en] *sic merito sec. L em. Post*, ende *D*   87 ende] *sic legendum*, 7 *D¹*, ende *clarificauit D²*

L

173v 8. Die meistersche sal men alle | jair kiesen op sunte Gregoriusdach of -avont, na den meisten hoep der stemmen, daer ellic die nutste dairto kiesen sal, ende niet na lieve, noch na lede, noch om bede wille.

9. Ende wen die meeste hoep kiest ende die schepene confirmeert, die salt wesen sonder croenen, wil sij op die wer bliven. Ende wan die meistersche van den schepene confirmeert worden, so sal men dese teghenwordige ordinancie om ene ewelike huechnisse voer hem allen lesen.

10. Welke meistersche sal al ding die ten huse comen, bueren, uytgheven ende opnemen. Ende sij sal alle ghemeene ding verwaren ende sal macht hebben to setten na oer bescheit dat volck van den huse ten ghemeene werke, of een deel van den volke na behoerlicheit des werkes. Ende daer en sal niemant weder croenen in hebben.

D

8. Twe meysterschen sal men alle jaer kiesen op sunte Gregorisdach of -avont, na den meesten hoep der stemmen, daer ellic op ende na sine consciencie die nuttesten daertoe kiesen sal, ende niet na leven, noch nae lede, noch om beden willen. | 6 P.

9. Die ene van den meysterschen sal altoes wesen ute der vergaderinghe van den steenhues ende die ander ute der vergaderinghe des achterhues. Ende wen die meeste hoep hier uutkiest, die her Gherijt bi sinen tiden of die schepene na sinen tiden confirmiert, die sal dat wesen sonder kronen, wil se op der weren bliven. Ende wan die meysterschen van den scepene of van heren Gheride confirmiert werden, soe sal men dese tieghenwoerdighe ordinancie om een ewelike huchnisse daervoer om allen lesen.

10. Welike meysterschen soelen alle dinc die ton hues comen, boeren, uetgheven ende opnemen, ende alle dinghe die men deilen sal, deilen. Ende se soelen heren Gheride ende den schepene nae heren Gherides dode, wans se begheren, rekeninghe doen. Sie soelen alle ghemene dinc verwaren ende soelen macht hebben to setten nae haeren bescheyde dat volc van den hues tot ghemenen werke, of een deel van den volke na behoerlicheit des werkes. Ende daer en sal nieman weder cronen in hebben.

122/126 cfr Act. 2, 44-45; Act. 4, 32; 35

122/126 cfr infra, 512-523, etiam GER. MAG., *Tract. paup.*, 986-990; *Ep.* 41, 83-88; 106-119; *Ep.* 46, 16-21   cfr AVG., *Reg.* 5, 2 (p. 428-430, 153-157)

L

174r 11. | Wie sieck were of bescheiden red[d]en hadde dat ⟨sij⟩ op die tijt niet wercken en mochte, die solde die saeck ende hoer noit toenen der meistersche. Ende duncket dan der meistersche dat redene te wesen, soe mach sijs oer dan verdraghen, op ene ander tijt dat te vervullen, opdat die burdene gelijc werden. Die meistersche sal berichten onmanierlike cledinge ende onmanierlike wanderinge van binnen ende van buten. Ende all twijnge ende onvrede sal sij to rusten maken van bynnen ende van buten. Ende alles onvredes van bynnen ende twijnge sal men an hoer blyven.

12. Ende weert dat hoer yenighe in desen of in anderen saken die der meistersche bevolen weren, ongehoirsam were, of teghen hoer harde verkierde woerde hadde, of die groten onvrede macte, of onmanierlike haer cleder snede of droghe, ende des by der meistersche rade niet afleggen en wolde, of die quade gheselschap helde, of wan sij gebo‑
174v den worde to des ghemeyns | huses werke niet ghaen en wol‑

D

11. Wie siec waer of bescheyden reden hadde dat ⟨si⟩ op die tijt
140 niet werken en | mochte, die 7 P. solde die sake ende hoeren noet toenen den meysterschen. Ende duncket dan den meysterschen dat reden wesen, soe moghen
145 sies hoer dan op die tyt verdraghen op ene ander tijt dat te vervullene, opdat bordenen ghelijc werden. Ende si soelen berichten onmanierlike cledinghe
150 ende onmanierlike wandelinghe van binnen ende van | buten. 68 H. Ende alle twijnghe ende onvrede soelen sie toe rosten maken van binnen ende van buten. Ende alles onvredes van binnen ende
155 twijnghe sal men an hem bliven, tenwaer dat scepene of her Gherith dat | sonderlinghe berichten wolden. 192v

160 12. Ende waert dat haerre ienich in desen of in anderen saken die den meysterschen bevoelen waeren, onhoersam waere, of weder hem herde verkierde woerde
165 hadde, of die groeten onvrede maecte van binnen, of onmanierlike hoer cleder snede of droghe, ende des bi der meysterschen rade niet oflegghen en wolde, of
170 die quaet gheselscap helde buten of binnen, of niet, wan se gheboden worde, to des ghemenes

---

139 reden] *sic legendum, cfr D,* redden *L*   sij] *sic legendum, quia Ger. de feminis loquitur, hij L*   155 men] *al add., sed postea del. L*

---

139 si] *sic emendaui,* hi *D; Gerardus (uel fortasse scriba qui postea copiam fecit) hic formam pronominis personalis in masculino genere scripti ex exemplari a moderamine Dauentriensis ciuitatis praeparato transcripsit, sed alibi Ger. genus pronominis mutauit, sc. in l.* ***178*** *"sie" Ger. in D, contra* ***177*** *"hij" in L*

L

de, off die ienighe van hoer ge-
sellynnen onschuldelike quade
worde overseghede, daer hoer
geruchte mede gekrenket woerde, of die in den saken daer ⟨sij⟩
orloff bidden solde, oerlof geweyghert worde, ende daerboven
mit een crighe dat dede, of die
versmade orlof te bidden, off
enich ander grote sake dede te-
gen dat huys of des huses ordinancie ende die meistersche. In
allen desen ende desen geliken
punten, omdat men vrede te bet
bynnen holde, sal die meistersche macht hebben aldusdanigen
verkierden luden dat af te nemen
mit scharper vermaninge voer
twee ander vroeder van bynnen.
Vort alle merre saken daer men
yenighen om uytsetthen mochte,
die sal men an die schepene
brengen.

13. Dit sijn saken daer men yemande om uytsetten sal: om on-

D

hueswerke gaen en wolde, of
die ienighen van hoeren ghesellinne onsculdelike quade woerde averseghede, daer haer ghe-
ruchte mede ghekranckt worde,
| of die in dien zaken daer sie
oerlof bidden solde, oerlof ghe-
weyghert worde, ende daerbaven mit een crighe dat dade, of
die versmade oerlof to bidden, of
ienighe ander grote sake dade
weder dat huys of des huses ordinancie ende die meysterschen;
omdat men vrede de bat binnen
halde mit wat bedwanghen, solen die meysterschen macht hebben aldusdanen verkierden luden of te nemen ende niet te gheven tot eenre tijt, na behoerlicheit
der broke, van den dinghen die
men ghemene deilen solde,
iewer van avete, of van enighen
dinghen dat daer inghegeven
worde. Ende dat soelen die
meysterschen doen mit rade allene twier ander vroeder van binnen. Ende bliven sie daernae
nochtan hart ende verkeert, soe
mochten die meysterschen mit
consente der twier vroede een
jaer of twe hem nemen hoer deel
haves. Voert alle meerre saken
daer men ienighe om uetsetten
mochte, die sal men an die scepene brenghen na heren Gheri-
des dode. |

13. Dit sijn saken daer men ieghe-
welken om uetzetten sal: om on-

8 P.

9 P.

---

177 sij] *sic legendum, quia Ger. de feminis loquitur,* hij *L*

---

177 ghekranckt] *sic em. Post,* ghekranck *D, cfr **176** gekrenket *L*
178 sie] *sic em. Post,* hie *D* 197 meysterschen] in allen desen ende in
desen gheliken punten *add., sed postea del. D¹ (uel D²)*

STATVTA DOMVS FEMINIS DEVOTIS DESTINATAE

L

175r cuys|cheit van lichame, of geve hoer yenich manne trouwe, of helde besprokene geselscap mit yenighe manne, of helde hoerre ienich die visevase, die mynnerscap heyt, daer men oncuysheit mede verwet voer oghen der simpelre lude, of die stele ofte vochte, of temael hart in onvreden waer ende ongehoirsame, of die boven orlof lange uit weer. Dese mocht men ende sold men uytsetten, of om anders ienighe grote sake of misdaet, dat den schepene dochte dat sij es verdient hadden.

D

cuysheit van lichame, of gheve hoere ienich iemanne trouwe, of helde besproken ghezelscap mit ienighen manne, of helde hoere
215 een die visevase, die mynnerscap heet, daer men oncuyscheit mede varwit voer oghen der simpelre lude, of die stele of vochte, of temael hart in onvre-
220 den ende in hoersumme bleve, of die boven oerlof langhe uyt waer. Dese | mocht men ende 69 H. solde men uetzetten, of om anders enighe groete sake of misdaet, dat heren Gheride of den
225 schepene duchte dat sies verdient hadden.

14. Ende sonderlinghe en sal nieman binnen bliven die ienich
230 punt, daer die beghinen om verboeden sijn in den ghemenen rade der heiligher Kerken to Viennen, of ienich punt weder den heilighen ghelove helde of
235 leerde, ende wie van der hogher Triniteit ende van den simpel wesen Gods of van den sacramente Christi ende der heiligher Kerken om onderwonne to disputieren
240 of mit enen wille na sinen dunckene sunder soburheit van dien of van anders hoghen saken boven syns selves mate onderwonne te sprekene of te lerenne,
245 of die pleghe te spreken of te | 10 P.

228/261 cfr supra, 12-17, et GER. MAG., *Simonia beg.*, 64-73   cfr *Clem.* 3.II.1 (c. II, 1169, 30-52); Ger. hic flagitia singula beguinabus in Conc. Vien. a Clemente Papa obiecta enumerat

---

212 hoer] *ex* hoere *corr.* L²

215/216 mynnerscap] *sic emendaui, cfr* 215/216 mynnerscap L, mynuerscap D

leren vremde leren, of worde of prophane lere ende worde onghelijc of contrarie der leren ende den woerden Christi ende den heilighen luden ende der heiligher Scripturen, of in vreemden manieren wandelde ende levede onghelijc ende contrarie Christo, den heilighen ende den scrifturen,

15. of heelde of leerde enich van den achten boesen articulen, die de heilighe Kerke onder den bagharden ende den baghinen ghevonden hevet als in *Clementinis* staet,

16. of ienich van den achtentwintich articulen Eckards, die de heilighe Kerke wederseghet hevet ende verdoempt, of bi wen boeken ghevonden worden daer ienich van desen articulen in stonde of ienich ander onghelove, ende zonderlinghe of ienich ghevonden worde, die men dickewile in Duesche land vindet,

17. die weende, heelde of seghede hem God scouwenden nae siner hogher Triniteit of nae sinen sempelen wesen, die men nochtan bevonde in groten sonden sonder dogheden, alsof sie nochtan waren onlidende ende onghelaten in weerliken saken, hoverdich dunckende van hoers-

---

262/272 sc. articuli .XXVIII. condempnati a Iohanne .XXII. Papa in bulla 'In agro dominico', data Auinione die 27 mens. Mart. a. 1329 – ed. L. Sturlese, 'Acta Echardiana', in : *Meister Eckhart. Die deutschen und lateinischen Werke. Die lateinischen Werke.* Bd. 5. *Acta Echardiana*, p. 597-600, et missa Archiepiscopo Coloniensi die 15 mens. Apr. a. 1329 – ed. L. Sturlese, *ibid.*, p. 601-605

---

269 of] *suppl. sup. lin. ipse D*

selves goetheit, wijsheit of hoe-
cheit, of dat se bevonden worden
sonder mynne tot horen even-
kersten ende sonder werke van
mynnen, vratach|tig, mit bliven- 11 P.
den toren, hatich ende achter-
sprakich, want dese lude na lere
Christi ende der heiligen sijn al in
duysternisse ende in dwalinghe,
ende en moghen niet scouwen in
den lichte noch in der waerheit.
18. Item, wie leerde of helde dat
hem gheen dinc binnen spreken
en mochte dan God of die heilighe Gheest, of die waende dat
al goed ware ende waer, dat hem
quame binnen, dat ware een be-
dwalen ongheoffent gheest, want
nieman op orden levet, den die
bose gheest ende sijn vleysch
niet inspreken ende niet indra-
ghen en | moghen. 70 H.
19. Item, we heelde of leerde dien
wech die hoere salic heten, dien
lichten wech to Gode wart, in
bloter ledicheit, uetwendich of
inwendich, sonder van binnen in
zedeliken dogheden ende sonder uetwendich doghetliken werken van buten ende sonder penitencie of sonder gheren ende
staen Christus weghe ende der
heylighen nae te gaene in haeren
levene, in doghene ende sonder
mynnenwerke ende warke der
barmherticheit, want dusdane
ledicheit ende scouwen is een
beghin, na der heiligen lere, van
al-
len onghelove.
20. Dese dinghe noemt her
Gherijt daerom, want men vint
lude | hieromtrint in Duschen 193r

---

293 leerde] ende *add., sed postea ipse del.* D

L

21. Item om ledighe bloetheit te schuwene ende den wech ende lere der hilligen te holden, soe sall een iegelic die machtich ende gesont is sinre lede ende arbeiden kan, van arbeide hoerre hande leven op dat tot den huse hoert. Ende die en sal om oer | broet niet gaen, noch bidden in kercken, noch stede maeltijt uyt eten.

175v

D

lande, die groten sca|den hem- 12 P.
325 melike in desen punten doen. Ende hierom bidt hi den scepene ende den meysterschen, dat men bovenal daerto sie nae siere doet ende dat men die uutsette, die
330 daer ienich ghelijc mede hebben bi rade wiser, gheestliker lude, of wie mit aldusdanen luden omghenge ende hemelic ghezelscap mit bagharden helde, of die dese
335 voerscreven articule ende puncte ende alle die sie hielden, lude of boeke, niet versweren en wolden, wan dat ienich van horen oversten in gheestlicheit: bis-
340 scop, archidiaken, kettermeyster, kerspelpape of die scepen of her Gherijt van hem begheerden, dat se verswoeren ende versekerden beide die articule, punte, boke
345 ende lude al vorseghet.

21. Ende sonderlinghe om dese lediche bloetheit to scuwene ende den wech ende lere der heilighen to holde, so sal een iewe-
350 lic die machtich ende ghesont is siner lede ende arbeiden can, van arbeide hoere hande leven, opdat se hevet ende dat int hues ghegeven wordt. Ende die en sal
355 om hoer broet niet gaen, noch bidden in kerken, noch stede maeltiden uet eten. Mer wie van krancheden of van olderen of van | anderen kenliken redeliken 13 P.
360 zaken niet arbeiden en conde, of die in der waerheit so voele niet

---

348/352 cfr II Thes. 3, 6-12

---

333 ghezelscap] ghezes praem., sed postea exp. ipse D   335 voerscreven] sic legendum, voersc'. in abbr. scr. D   337 versweren] sic emendaui, versueren D   345 vorseghet] sic legendum, vorsz3 D

L D

winnen en conde, dat hi noe-
dorfte hadde, die mochte bidden
of stade maeltijt nemen, na der
365 manieren dat hem voert na sinen
vermoghen ende pinen dan on-
brake. Ende hoerre gheen sal
bidden noch stede maeltijt eten
sonder oerlof der scepene ende
370 heren Gherides. Ende her Gherijt
bidt ende bevelt elken op haere
consciencie, dat sie nieuwer hem
noch hiernae die scepenen en
bidden meer dan sie behoeven
375 nae pinen ende nae vermoeghen
hoers arbeids. | 71 H.
22. Voert en zolen nummermeer
in den ⟨achtersten huse⟩ meer
dan achte cameren ende achte
380 bedden wesen, ende in den
steenhuse boven op den nedersten zalre zeven bedden ende zeven personen, ende een bedde of
een persoen beneden in der ko-
385 kene. Die bovenste salre daer
zoelen beide vergaderinghe, of
die buten sitten ende ghenen
zalre hebben, haer zaet op leg-
ghen.
390 23. Die twe cameren die her
Gherijt nu hevet, daer solen op
elken een mensche boven wesen. Ende twe persone soelen
haer bedde hebben in dier steen-
395 cameren: een, daer her Gherijt nu
slaept, ende | een daerbi in sijnre 14 P.
studorij. Heren Gherides koke-
neken ende kelreken ende sijn
zaellekijn daervoer, ende daer
400 sine borninghe leghet, dat zal
hoerre drier ghemene wesen, die
twe beneden sijn ende ene daerboven, die op den cleynen huse-

---

378 achtersten huse] *sic marg. corr.* D^2, achterhusen D^1

L

24. Vortmeer, so wie in den huyse stervet, die sal daerynne laten alsodane cledere, bedde, clenode, reetscap, boke, saet als sij bynnen den huys of buten, of byn-

D

ken wonen sal. Die vierde, die
405 op dier steencameren wonen sal,
die sal to haerde gaen mit denghenen die op den zale wonen,
want men sal die dore tusschen
den sale ende der steencameren
410 opbreken, opdat alle die in den
groten steenhues sijn, op die hemelicheit gaen moghen. Ende die
ander doer tusschen der steencamer ende den cleynen huseken
415 sal men weder tolegghen. Ende
die doer die nu gaet op die beide
cameren ende die steet to Johans
have wert ter Hurnen, die sal
men na heren Gherides dode
420 ommesetten an die noertsche
zide, als die de anderen doren ingaen. Wat daerbuten ghetimmert
is of jummermeer op die hofstede ghetymmert wordt, dat sal
425 alinghe den huse bliven ende in
heren Gherides ordinancie ende
der scepene. Ende daer en mach
nieman ienighe menschen mit
hem te wonen nemen sonder der
430 scepen oerlof na heren Gherides
dode. Nieman en sal men weder
sinen wille sonder quaet verdienst uet siner camer stoten.
| Swene van Vreden of hor doch- 15 P.
435 ter storve, daer en mach men
ghiene ghezellinne setten sonder
haren willen, noch sie ende
mochte nieman nemen die heren
Gheride of den schepene mis-
440 haghede of den meysterschen.
Meer of sie storve, soe mocht
men haere dochter ene ghesellinne setten.
24. Voertmeer, so wie daerinne
445 stervet, die sal daerin laten alsodane cleder, bedde, clenade,
reetscap, boke, saet ende doet
vleysch, als sie binnen den hues

L

nen der stat of buten hadde, waer ment vint.

D

450 of buten, binnen der stat of buten hadden, waer ment vint, uetghenamen silver ende golt. Ende wie rente hevet, erflike of ewelike, of van coen, scapen, ymen, die sal een jaer renten daerinne laten na
455 siere doet. | Ende dat solen des 72 H. doden erfgenamen uten, of sie sijn erve boren willen, ende die groeve ende die schult des doden betaelen. Ende waer dat
460 nieman des doden erve boren wolde, soe solde dat hues al alsodaen goet nemen, als die dode achterghelaten hadden, ende bestaden hem ter eerden ende voert
465 alle scolt betalen, alse verre alst reken kunde, dat men daervan boerde, die die dode ghemaect hadde in sijnre suecte bi den meysterschen of anders enighe
470 scult, die kenlic ende apenbaer scult waer, die men bewisen moch|te dat in der waerheit on- 16 P. visiert ende onbedacht waer.

25. Ende wat dinghen dat van den
475 doden ⟨comen⟩, die soelen toe den hues ende to der tymmeringhen comen ende niet an | die de- 193v lenghe. Item, wat dinghe in den testamente ghegeven werden ie-
480 wer in der delinghe of der tymmeringhe sonderlinghe, die sal men alle om rosten wille deilen an tween: die ene helfte ter tymmeringhe, die ander helfte in der
485 deilinghe. Also sal altoes die tymmeringhe deilen mitten luden ende die lude mitter timmeringhen.

---

465 scolt] des doden *sic add. D, postea exp. D¹ (uel D²?)*   betalen] ende waer dat niem *add., sed postea del. D¹*   467 die] die *suppl. Post, om. D*
475 comen] *suppl. Post, om. D*

L *D*

26. Des ghelikes sal men deylen
490 half ende half wat daer in ienigher formen van ieman bi sinen levendighen live ghegheven wordt, uutghenamen bernynghe ende molt, visch ende doet
495 vleysch, worden sie buten testament daer inghegheven, ende uetghenamen timmerholt, steen, callic, yser, die buten testament daer inghegeven worden. Daer
500 sal men mede tymmeren. Die soelen der tymmeringhe bliven, alse die berninghe ende dat molt der deilinghe. ⟨Mer wat buten testament gegeven wart sonder
505 uetnemen, dat sal men al half ende half deylen. Dat solen die meysterschen gheliken, of sij | op   17 P. ene tijt in die deilinghe⟩ meer comen lieten dan die helfte, dat sie
510 dat op een ander tijt der tymmeringhen vervolleden.

27. Voert, alle dinghe die men deylen sal, die sal men al aver al ghelike deylen wie binnen der
515 hofsteden woent, nieman uetghenomen. Ende wordt oec der ener vergaderinghen of der ander sunderlinghe of in ienigherhande manieren ghegeven,
520 dat solden al die meysterschen nae haerre bescheydenheit over al deylen om rosten ende mynnen wille, tenwere dat yet tween

---

512/523 cfr Act. 2, 44-45; Act. 4, 32; 35

512/523 cfr supra, 122-126, etiam GER. MAG., *Sim. beg.*, 290-291; *Tract. paup.*, 986-990; *Ep.* 41, 83-88; 106-119; *Ep.* 45, 17-19; *Ep.* 46, 16-21   cfr AVG., *Reg.* 5, 2 (p. 428-430, 153-157)

503/508 mer – deilinghe] *homoeoteleutou causa om. D¹, marg. sup. suppl. D²*   522 ende] om *add. D¹, del. D¹ uel D²*

STATVTA DOMVS FEMINIS DEVOTIS DESTINATAE 323

L

29. Item, om wiltheyt ende oersake der oncuyscheit ende quader geselscap te myden en sal hoerre engheen ienighen man herberghen bynnen der weer, noch manne to gaste laden, noch mit hem werscapen of eten gheven, tenwere recht noot, als tymmerlude ende arbeidende lude, wan men hoers wercs te doen hadde.

D

of drien bi namen sonderlinghe
525 ghegheven of ghezandt worde, of dat men yet den syeken die op den bedden laghen, gave, dat solden sie allene hebben.
28. Die ghemene tune alomme
530 ende die twee hues der twier vergaderinghen mitten tween cameren die sal men tovoren tym|me- 73 H.
ren ende hoelden van den goede des hues. Ende nieman die buten
535 desen woent op der waere, sal moeghen eyschen dat men sijn hues tymmerde of heelde. Mer waer een temael een arem mensch die kenliken noet hadde an sin-
540 en tymmer, die mochte men om God ende om goedertierenheit ende niet van rechte helpen an sinen tymmer.
29. Item, voert so is gesadt | om 18 P.
545 wiltheit ende oersake der onkuescheit ende quader gheselscap te miden, dat haerre engheen sal herberghen ienighen man binnen der were, noch manne te
550 gaste laden, noch mit hem werscopen binnen der were. Noch haerre en gheen en sal manne eten gheven in oren huys noch in hoer hues leiden, tenwaere recht
555 noot, als van tymmerluden ende arbeidende luden, wan men hoers werkes te doen hadde, of die priesters mitten sacramente ende om biecht te hoeren toen
560 zieken quamen, of dat scepene of her Gherijt om te ordinieren daer inghenghe. Ellic sal mitten mannen buten spreken, die sie toehues zoeken, tenwaer dat ie-
565 nich leec bade of man, die hem

---

551 tymmerlude] *ex* tymmerluden *corr.* L²

L

30. Ende niemant en sal wijff in kindelbedde waren, noch hoer engheen sal buten der weer slapen sonder orlof der meistersche.

31. Wye uyter stadt ghaen sal of varen, die sal die stadt nomen ende en sal nerghen buten ghaen sonder orlof der meistersche.

D

enen brief of anders yet brachte. Den mochten sie eens ende niet meer teten gheven mit der meysterschen oerlove ende an- 570 ders niet.

30. Ghenen dans en soelen sie binnen der ware maken, noch groete werscope. Noch hoeren gheen en sal ienich wijf herber- 575 ghen of bi hoer nemen to slapen sonder oerlof der meysterschen. Haeren engheen en sal wijf in kindelbedde waren. Ander zeken, maghe, vrende of vreemde 580 moghen sie waren om God, vrienscap of om ghelt, mer niet sonder oerlof der meysterschen. Noch hoe|re engheen en sal buten der waere slapen sonder oer- 585 lof der meysterschen. Ende wie jonc is ende daert die meysterschen bescheit of duncket, die en sal nerghen buten eten sonder haren oerlof ende die sal nomen 590 die stat daer sie eten sal of slapen.

31. Wie uet der staet gaen sal of varen, die sal die stat nomen ende en sal nerghen buten gaen 595 sonder oerlof der meysterschen. Ende die meysterschen moghen in noetzaken of in oerbaer die kenlic is, of bedevaerde, oerlof gheven hint tot tien milen veer 600 ende niet veere ende tot achte daghe uyt te wesen ende niet langher. Wie noet hadde veerre of langher uet te wesen, die en mochten niet langher of niet 605 veerre varen sonder oerlof heren Gherides of der scepene nae sier doet. Ende sie solde nomen waer sie vuere ende niet langher uet-

19 P.

---

568 gheven] bede *add., sed postea del.* D

L

32. In desen dinghen beswaert heer Gherijt der scepene ende der meistersche consci|encie, dat men niemant orlof gheven en wille to lopen of onnutlike, of daer oneere of onorber den armen luden off comen mochte, sonder nootsaken. Ende sonderlinge en sal hoer engheen tot enighen capittelen varen.

34. Voertmeer sal men doen jairtijt ende beghencnisse Werners, heren Gherdes vader, ende heren Gherdes oldevaderen, ende Heilewich, sinre moder, ende beide sinre oldermoderen, Bestikens van der Basselen ende Swenen, sins wyves, ende all dergheenre die voer den oghen Gods van rechte loen hebben solen op sunte Clarendach. Ende desgelikes begheert her Gherit dat men sine beghencnisse doe op den dach daer God over hem gebiet.

D

wesen dan hoer dan termijn gheghenen worde.

32. Ende in desen dinghe beswaert her Gherijt de scepene ende der meysterschen conscien|cie, dat men nieman oerlof en gheve wilde te lopen of onnuttelike, of daer onere of onorbaer den armen luden of comen mochte, sonder in noetzaken. Ende sonderlinghe en zal hoerre gheen tot ienighen capitelen varen.

33. Die sieken sal men waren na der ordina|ncien dat men nu pleghet. Ende her Gherijt of die scepene na hem moghen die have die hoere ienich nu hevet, mynren of vermeeren of verwandelen naedien dat hem goet dencket. Ende wie in der vergaderinghen woent, die en sal gheen scoel hoelden, mer die buten der vergaderinghen wonen, die mochten die meysterschen oerlof gheven een kint of twe te leren sonder onruste der anderen | ende sonder scade des huses.

34. Voertmeer sal men doen jaertijt ende begancnisse Werners, heren Gherijds vader, ende her Gerijts oldervaderen, ende Heilewich, sijnre moeder, ende beide sijnre aldermoederen, Bestikens van der Basselen ende Swenen, sijns wijfs, ende alle derghener dies voer den oghen Gods van rechte loen eghen op sunte Clarendach in Onser Vrouwenkerke ende niet ten mynrebroderen, tenwaer dat men niet of gheen ghelt en offerde. Ende desghe-

74 H.

20 P.

194ra

---

650 men] sic D¹, et sic emendaui, mei corr. D²

L	D
	likes begheert her Gerijt dat men sine begencnisse doe op den dach daer God over hem ghebiedet.

35. Item dat voerghezeghet is, dat men die meysterschen | uyt dien tween vergaderinghen kiesen sal, dats to verstaen alsoe verre als daer ienighe bequeme persone inne sint. Mer her Gerijt of die scepene van hoers selves wille, ende niet van ghemenen kiesen, moghen die buten der vergaderinghe woende meysterschen maken daers noet waer.

21 P.

L	D
36. Alle dese saken vorseghet sijn gesat mit wetene ende todoen der schepene ende sint hem gelesen ende apenbaert in hoeren raet, daers hem wal behagede sonder wederseggen, doe men schreyff dusent drijhondert ende neghenendetseventich op saterdach nae sunte Margaretendach.	36. Alle dese saken voerseghet sijn ghezat mit wetene ende toedoen der scepene ende sint hem ghelezen ende apenbaert in haren rade, daer hem wal behaghede zonder wederzegghen. In orcunde deser dinc, want dese brief van twe stucken ghemaect is, so heeft her Gherijt die Groet sinen zegel an desen brief drierweghen ghehanghen. Ghegeven int jaer ons Heren dusent driehondert ende neghenendetseventich up sunte Margaritendach.

---

667 voerseghet] *sic legendum*, voers3 D, cfr L

DE SIMONIA AD BEGVTTAS

cura et studio

Marinus VAN DEN BERG

fontes collegit

Rijcklof HOFMAN

CONSPECTVS SIGLORVM

H   Cuijk, Kruisherenklooster Sint-Agatha, coll. Frenswegen C 9, c. a. 1455, scr. Herman van Alen

Hunc codicem in plagulis phototypice expressis contulimus.

⟨DE SIMONIA AD BEGVTTAS⟩

Dit is my ghevraghet: oftet symonia sij ene stede of ene provende te copen in enen beghinenconvente. Ic hebbe gheantwort: ist dat an de stede of an de provende enich geistlic ding anhanget, of ist dat de mensche, inden dat he de stede vercrighet of de
5 provende, oec mede verkrighet enich geistlic ding dat daerna volghet, so ist wisse symonia. Want also scrivet dat gheistlike recht: wanner twe dinghe also tegaderhanget of sick so vervolghen dat dat ene sunder den anderen nicht en coemt of nicht vercreghen en wert, we dat ene kopet, he heitet oec dat ander te
10 copen. Also steit in *Decreet*, .I., q. .III., c. *Saluator, cum concordanciis*, unde anderen steden in den rechte. Unde elc mensche mach dat voelen in sijns selves consciencie dat dat waer ⟨si⟩. Unde we in aldusdanen dingen icht lovet of vorwarde maket in to brengen, etsij van ener summen of van denselven dat he hevet, dat is
15 al symonia, want men in al desen dingen entlike nicht gheven en sal um enich tijtlic gheven of brengen.

Hoert, myne leven zusteren, wat men antwort in der vraghe dar men vraghet oft symonie sij ghelt te gheven, "umdat een mensche ghenomen werde te deynen den armen int spitael, of dat he gheno-

---

1/16 Ger. Mag., *Leeringhe*, 51-73 paene ad litt.   1/39 cfr Ger. Mag., *Stat.*, 81-83   3/6 cfr *Decret.*, X 5.3.8 (c. II, 750, 45 – 751, 11, praesertim 750, 48-49; 751, 3-6)   6/11 cfr Ger. Mag., *Locat.*, 13   cfr Grat., *Decr.*, C.1 q.3 c.8 (c. I, 413-415), ubi allegatur epistula Vrbani II (*JL* 5743 (4308), T. 1, p. 697), prius prelo data a Mansi, *Sacrorum conciliorum*, T. 20, c. 660-663, reiterata in *PL*, 151, c. 529C-533B   17/32 Ger. Mag., *Leeringhe*, 74-89 paene ad litt. cfr Ioh. Frib., *Summa Conf.*, L. 1 t. 1 q. 75 (f. 13v, c. 1, 47 – c. 2, 1), qui allegat Gvil. Rhed., *App. ad Sum. Raym.*, L. 1 t. 1 § 26, comm. sup. 'mancipatus' (ed. 1603, p. 27, c. 2, 42-59) sed **19** te deynen den armen int spitael *Ger.*, ad seruiendum pauperibus in hospitale *Ioh., colon hoc hic om. Guilh.*; **23/24** in den dat he dus entfangen wert *Ger.*, in tali receptione *Ioh. Frib.*, quando recipitur ad hospitale uel leprosariam uel aliquid tale *Guilh.*; **27** deyne *Ger.*, seruiat *Ioh.*, uiuat *Guilh.*

Tit. Gherd de groet *marg. sup. scr. prima man. (H = Herman van Alen)*   1/2 provende] of *add., sed ipse exp.* H   5 daerna] *ex* dar na *corr. sup. lin. ipse* H   12 si] *om.* H, *suppl. de Vreese*   17 zusteren] vrende *praem., sed exp.* H

men werde in een malaeteschhues of in een aelmissenhues". Daer so antworden op Gwilhelmus in *Glosa Raymundi* unde Johannes in *Summa confessorum* unde spreken dat in dusdanen ghevallen unde | in ersgheliken: "Ist dat een mensche, inden dat he dus entfangen wert, vercrighe enich gheistlic recht, so ist symonie, lovet he of ghevet he icht. Unde ist dat he gheen geistlic ding vercrighet inden dat he aldus entfangen wert, mer wert allene daerum ghenomen, updat he daer deyne, ywer in der kokene of in enen anderen ampte, ter tijt of al sijn leven, so en ist gheen symonie daer wat voer te gheven, wattan al ist anders vuel daervoer icht te gheven of te nemene." Dit sijn der meistere woerde van worden te worden vorscreven, daer ander lerers mede concorderen.

Nu merket: ist symonie in dusdanen leyenlevene unde werliken state, wanneer daer enich geistlic ding an hanget, wo isset dan van den levene dat to Gode al ghesat is unde to geistliken schine unde van der werlt. Vortmeer seit int eerste of an u convent of an de stede in den conventen enighe andere gheistlike dinge ghebunden sijn of sic vervolghen, daerna ist merer of mynre symonie. |

Int eerste ist dat de Derde Orde daeran hanget, dat elc de daerin comet, moet werden van der Derden Orden. So ist opene symonie to ghevene off to verdreghene van ener summen of van in to brengene datselve dat een heft. Want de [de] Derde Orde, wattan en is se ghene vulcomene religio, se is nochtan ene maneer van levene de wat ghelikes hevet mit religien, unde de hilghe kerke entfeet se unde probeert se. Also spreket Johannes Andree in *Clementinis* unde sante Thomas in *Secunda secunde,* unde ander lerers.

33/48 GER. MAG., *Leeringhe,* 89-112 paene ad litt.   43/47 cfr IOH. ANDR., *Glos. ord. in Clem.*, super 3.11.1, comm. in expositione casus (c. II, 1169, 30) (c. 216 (p. 549), exp. cas., l. 14-36); comm. sup. 'obedientiam' (c. II, 1169, 31) (c. 216-217 (p. 549-550), gl. u), infra (1095-1098) fusius allegatum   43/48 locus dictis Gerardi optime conueniens uidetur THOM., II-II, Q. 188 a. 6 co.; ad 3 (T. 10, p. 529, c. 2)

---

39 symonie] *ex* symonien *corr. ipse H*   43 de de] *sic H, de legendum*
43/44 wattan] al ist *praem., sed exp. ipse H*

Unde henge desse Derde Orde aldus an den dat een mensche
in enich convent queme unde dusdane symonie dede, so dunket
my dat de mensche de aldusdane symonie daen hadde, erer weren
vele of weynich of altemale, solden desse stede overgheven
unde nemen in penitencie an een ander, harder orden of een ander,
harder maneer van levene. Also spreken de *Decretael* van
den religiosen luden, *Extra, De symonia*, in den capitel *Quoniam
symoniacum, Dilectus et †Constitutus†*, unde desgheliken Thomas
unde de ghemenen lerers. Unde dese spreken vort andere dinge
mit underscheide: wat men doen solde, off gheen harder orde en
weer, ofte dat men des nicht doen en kunde sunder groten anxt
der zele, oft de menschen wilt werden mochten. Unde des en is
gheen noet te scriven up desse tijt, want gij segget dat de Derde
Orde daer nicht an en hanget. Mer late wi de | Derde Orde staen
an uwer conscientie.

Mer laet uns vort seyn der beghinen staet int ghemeyne. Unde
wattan was der beghinen staet wedersproken in *Clementinis* in
den leste rade der kerken to Vyenne um ungheloven unde um to
hoghe willen te smaken dan er mate was de daerunder ghebunden
waren, nochtan is na een ander pawes gekomen unde heft
se georloft, *Extra, Recta ratio*, mer niet gheconfirmeert, mit enen
'extravagante' de ic up dese tijt nicht nomen en kan, want ic myne
boke van den rechte nicht bi my en hebbe. Want men vele guder
menschen under den beghinen vant, de reyne weren van allen
ungheloven unde van allen unghelovighen smaken.

Nu dan, want baghinen- unde conventenleven is daer|umme
entlike um van der werlt wat te scheiden to wesen in clederen
unde in leven unde Gode te deynen, is dat nicht geistlic ding.
Want dat waerumme unde de entlike ende der dinge, dat settet
unde ghevet den zedeliken dingen eren namen unde ere formen.

49/57 Ger. Mag., *Leeringhe*, 113-127 paene ad litt.   cfr *Decret.*, X 5.3.40;
5.3.30; 5.3.38 (c. II, 765, 47-66, praesertim l. 47-54; 759, 39-57, praesertim l. 54-57; 765, 15-20)   cfr Thom., II-II, Q. 100 a. 6 ad 5 (T. 9, p. 365, c. 1, 19-26)
59/60 compassionem cum talibus uictimis in fontibus inuenire non potui
64/68 cfr Ger. Mag., *Stat.*, 12-17; 228-255   cfr *Clem.* 3.11.1 (c. II, 1169, 30-52)   **68/69** cfr *Extrauag. comm.* 3.9.1 (c. II, 1279, 33 – 1280, 17)   **71/73** cfr *Extrauag. comm.* 3.9.1 (c. II, 1279, 46-61)

---

56 symoniacum] symoniaca *legendum*   Constitutus] *sic* H, Consulere *legendum*

Is dan dat waerumme unde de eynde God unde geistlic leven, so is de stede unde maneer van leven oec geistlic vor den oghen Godes unde in den gerichte der consciencien. Wattan en holt de kerke van buten de lude vor ghene religiose lude, unde wattan en hebben se ghene privilegie geistliker lude, unde wattan zolen se staen vor den werliken rechte, nochtan is de maneer van leven afghescheiden, unde in eren insate unde eer waerumme sal wesen in upsate to geistliken leven unde Gode te deynen. Unde dit sijn alle geistlike eynde unde draghen alle to Gode in der consciencien unde vor den gherichte Godes, wattan en sijn se dar nicht langer to verbunden dan se willen na den geistliken rechten van buten.

Doch sijn se van bynnen daerto ghedwungen daerynne to bliven, dat se ter werlt niet wedergaen en soelen, also vele als de up den besten unde up den wissesten weghe to Gode is, en sal niet willen des noch en mach niet ummekeren sunder groete sunde, noch en mach des begheren sunder sunde. *Want nymant*, sprect Christus, *de syne hant an de ploech ⟨slaet⟩ unde ummeseit, is bequame ten rike Godes*. Unde oec en mach er ghene beghine ter werlt keren mit guder consciencien um scande der werlt unde erer evenkersten. Dese dinge – unde vort alle der beghinen verbunde unde er gude ghewonte van bynnen: se lesen, vasten of andere dinge, – | maken dat dese staet off manere van leven geistlic sijn vor Gode unde in der consciencien, unde daerna meer of myn geistlic, naden dat dese dinge meer off myn volghen na den convente.

Wattan en ist gheen vast ghebunt na den uutwendighen geistliken gherichte, daerum en scrivet de kerke van buten niet sunderlinge weder dese symonie bisunderlinge, unde en doet van buten over dese symonie gheen gherichte. Want wunderlike selden richtet nu de kerke over enighe symonie, welc | dat se sij. Unde daerumme, hope ic, moghen se bliven in eren state, ist dat

---

95/97 Luc. 9, 62

99/113 cfr Ger. Mag., *Leeringhe*, 128-132   108/109 cfr infra, 160-166, et
Ger. Mag., *Locat.*, 608-613; 654-660; 699-705   110/129 Ger. Mag., *Leeringhe*,
132-156 paene ad litt.

---

96 slaet] *sic legendum*, staet H

se em absolveren laten unde mit em dispenseren laten van den bisscope, also veer als em dunket dat em de staet nutte is to erer salicheit – ist dat de Derde Orde daer nicht an en hanget –, unde nemen penitencie vor dese symonie in der consciencie unde in den danken. Dit hope ic, mer ic en wil dat niet seggen vor wisse waer dattes daeran ghenoch sij vor Gode, noch ic en wil dat niet seggen vor den besten of vor den naesten wech. Mer se en mach nymant absolveren up der eerden, ten rouwe em dat seet ghedaen hebben, unde se hebben willen gans dat niet meer te doene, anders en ist ghene penitencie, noch rouwe, noch gheen vuldoen vor Gode. Unde de penitencie unde vuldoen vor Gode is noet in aller sodaner symonien de de kerke nicht en richtet, ofte de allene in der consciencien unde in den danken steet. Also spreket dat leste capitel van symonien in den vijften boke van *Decretael*.

Symonia de in den herten steet unde in der consciencien of in aldusdanen dingen, wattan en heit dat nijn symonie vor den gherichte van buten, nochtan sijn se dickewijl merer, off ghelijc, of weynich mynre vor den oghen Godes. Wat ist mynre vor den oghen Gods: dat ic vijfhundert punt den capitel gheve sunder vorworde, doch daerumme opdat se my ene provende gheven, unde ic heb in mynen herten dat ic em anders nicht en gheve, wist ic dat se my de provende nicht gheven solden? Unde se my dan sunder vorwarde gheven ene provende de se my anders nicht te gheven en dachten, ic en had em de vijfhundert punt gegheven? Wanner dit steit sunder vorworde, so en richtet dit de kerke ghene symonie to wesen in den gerichte van buten, unde men mach de provende holden, ist dat se helpet unde draghet den menschen to syner salicheit unde doen vul gode mit berounisse in der bijcht in vullen willen te wesen dat nicht meer te done. Nochtan sijn de herten al vul symonien unde is daerto een quaet schijn.

Mer waer men datselve mit vorwarde dede, so richtet dat de kerke vor symonie. Unde want de kerke er | underwint dat to richten na heite des geistliken rechtes, so moet ment overgheven in der bicht. De herten sijn hijr al een, mer de woerde sijn under|scheiden: God, de seit in de herte, hijrbi provet oec in unser

---

121/125 cfr *Decret.*, X 5.3.46 (c. II, 767, 41-50, praesertim l. 48-50)

saken, wattan en richtede de kerke niet vor geistlike symonien van buten.

150 Dat ic nochtan nicht seggen en wil wat se doen solde, quame dat to nouwen rechte unde of dit na bescrevenen rechte de kerke nicht richten en solde, dat mochte helpen dat men daerynne bliven mochte van buten. Mer de herten sijn al effen vuel vor Gode, unde dat is veel meer dat in der waerheit is vor Gode, dan daerna
155 dat de dinge in der rekeninge sint.

Unde wo cleyne geistlicheit dat daeran hanget, et is wisse groet quaet aldus de lude te nemen mit vorwarden of mit meyninge werliker winninge, want Christus secht alse steit gescreven in *Luca*: *We in enen cleynen bose is, he is oec bose in enen meerre.*
160 Vort ist nu te weten dat under hundertdusent symonien de nu scheyn in kerken of in provenden, ⟨nicht een⟩ gerichtet en wert: ic en sach myne daghe nye van buten richten over symonien, unde dat komet umdat de kerke in eren gherichten de artikele weder de symonischen selden unde al te selden wil horen unde
165 entfaen um een merer quaet te myden, daer to lange of te scriven weer. Unde daerumme blijft ellic menschen in syner symonien unde de symonie wert seer ghemeyn overal. Unde wetet dat ghene ghewoente of pleghen, al dede dat al de werlt, en mach orloven to enigher symonien of to enigher quader meyninge van
170 bynnen.

Vortan, off gheen uutwendich recht en weer, laet uns de ewe anseyn de in unse herte gescreven is mit naturen unde mit gracien. Dat fundament alre vuelheit unde alre symonien int herte is, dat een mensche tijtlic unde uutwendich guet verkeiset vor geist-
175 lic gued, of vor ewich guet, of vor dinghe de loen inbrengen in ewicheit. We is de mensche de recht ghelovich is unde de in warer hopen staet, de ewich loen eens pater nosters of ener guder begherten derven wolde um enich tijtlic guet, ja um dusentdusent marc. Alle rechte herten solen spreken dat se des nicht en daden
180 van bynnen sunder uutwendighe lere, want dat wiset de ewighe

---

158/159 Luc. 16, 10

160/166 cfr supra, 108-109, et Ger. Mag., *Locat.*, 608-613; 654-660; 699-705

---

161 nicht een] *sic emendaui*, een nicht *H*

ewe Godes unde dat tughet unse herte. Unde we wolde enighen menschen hinderen enich ewich loen mit willen | unde mit voer- 6 113v rade, oft enighe werken hinderen den anderen, daer he wiste daer de mensche ewich loen of crighen mochte, of wesen sake of
185 oersake willens, daer een mensche mynre loen verdeynde of mynre eer Gode dade, of tot mynre eer of tot nederen lone quame. Dat tughen alle gude consciencien, dat se dat mit ghenen berade unde willendes doen en mochten um enich gelt, want dat weer em te setten willendes weder de mynne unde ere Godes
190 unde de mynne in ghewichte weder tijtlic guet.

Nu seit to, dat sijn twe meghede, de ene is otmodich unde wal ghesatet te Gode unde to guden zeden, unde is noetdruftich uwes conventes unde en kan erselven nicht wal in de werlt doen. Ghi en nemet der nicht, daerum allene, want se gheen hundert of
195 viftich olde schilde en heft. Unde ghi nemet een ander, de hoverdigher unde unghezater is unde unnoetdruftigher, um des geldes willen, de na menschliken vermoden ghene ghelike geistlike vrucht brengen kan noch draghen, noch de u oec niet en helpet tot geistliker vrucht, noch gij see. See ghi dan niet wat vruchte,
200 wat lone, wat eren, wat love Godes ghi benemet willendes na vermode unde na moghelicheit unses kennens, unde dit al um cleyne vergenclike dinge, alse ghi seit dat dat arme gude menschekijn moet in de werlt dwelen, dat so nutte unde so vruchtbar hadde ghewest unde uwe staet em so nutte weer, dat nu dicke
205 ghehindert wert, unde ghi seit den riken menschen werlic bliven in der zele oft achterbliven?

Heb ghi hijr gheen oghe, so sijn ghij wisse blint of untruwe. Och, wo cleyne mynne gij Gode unde sijn ere, de des nicht en achtet of versumet willens. We sal en absolveren, also lange alse
210 he in dessen groten versmane steit der eren Godes? Daer en is macht up eerden, de en absolveren mach sunder tokeren ter eren Godes unde keren van den verganclikken gude. Wat is anders wortel alre sunde dan een afkeren van der eren Godes unde een tokeren to tijtliken dingen? Item, sei gij oec niet dat gij hinderen den
215 armen menschen van sinen naesten weghe to Gode mit | un- 114r rechte, want em boert na der gherechticheit Godes de ledighe stede? Ist dat ju nymant bequemer en comet unde de daer doechtsamer is?

191/206 cfr infra, 254-262   191/490 cfr Ger. Mag., *Ep.* 41, 194-206

De gherechticheit Godes, de men heit in Latine *iustitia distri-*
butiua Dei, de na gherechticheit loent unde pijnt alle creaturen
na eren verdensten, de sprect in allen reynen herten, ya natuerlic,
als Aristotiles bewiset in den vijften boke *Van guden zeden*, unde
daerboven | noch zoetliker unde claerliker in de kerstene herten, 7
dat men alle weerdicheit, alle geistlike dingen de men delen sal,
etsij ere etsij ampt, dat men de gheven sal na weerdicheit der personen, naden dat de persone bequemer unde hebliker unde
Gode eerliker sijn to den ampte of to der ere of to den dingen,
unde dat men ghene andere dingen anseyn en sal de daerto nicht
en helpen noch en draghen, unde dat men meest anseyn sal dat
daer meer to draghet unde helpt. Unde na der mate der bequemelicheit unde heblichheit to den dingen so sal men gheven unde
dispenseren de dinge.

Dese gherechticheit leeft eentlike in de herte van naturen unde
van gracien, unde is gheformet in den ewighen woerde Godes
oersprunclike, unde daeruut entspringet se in allen gherechten
rechten beide bi naturen unde bi gracien, unde daeruut comet alle
gherechte gerichte. Se sal er werdelike openbaren in den lesten
gherichte.

Ach arme, we mach sick verhuden vor eer in den lesten daghe?
Och, wo zoete sal se an te seyne wesen na erer ewigher redene
denghenen den se in eren levene ghemynt hebben unde de bi
eer ghebleven sijn in den dingen de se to ghevene, to delene of
to dispenserne gehad hebben? Och, wo weerdichlike zoete unde
schone is se nu oec te seyne enen gherechten herten de se kent
unde mynt unde beleeft nu up der erden. Unde we mach em excuseren of bescudden van den dat he nicht en kande? Want se in
alle redelike herte van naturen ghescreven staet de synne unde
redene hebben, de em willendes selven niet verdoven unde verblinden, ofte de em willendes niet van er en keren. Unde och,
wo gruwelic is se an te seyne na redene den van ghekeerden. Nu

---

219/232 cfr infra, 634-637   cfr Thom., I, Q. 21 a. 1 co. (T. 4, p. 258, c. 2, 1-4), ubi Thomas uerba a Ger. in paraphrasi data citat sec. Dion., *Diu. nom.*, sec. transl. Ioh. Sar. (p. 437, c. 2 – p. 438, c. 1 (l. 4)); in eadem quaestione et eodem articulo, sed in loco superiori Thom. definitionem iustitiae commutatiuae sec. Arist. et iustitiae distributiuae in enuntiatione propria praebet, sc. ibid. (T. 4, p. 258, c. 1, 24-31); cfr etiam II-II, Q. 63 a. 1 co. (T. 9, p. 62, c. 1, 26 – c. 2, 28); II-II, Q. 63 a. 2 co. (T. 9, p. 63, c. 2, 3-30)   **224/238** cfr Thom., I, Q. 21 a. 1 ad 3 (T. 4, p. 259, c. 1, 14 – c. 2, 7)   **233/238** cfr infra, 604-625   cfr Thom., I-II, Q. 93 a. 3 co. (T. 7, p. 164, c. 1, 16 – c. 2, 5)

weset des vor Gode unde vor alle gheiste wisse, dat ghi willendes weder unde teghen eer doet unde spyet er in er oghen, gheistlike to verstane.

Alse ghi aldus de stede de tot Gode unde to Gode te deynen
255 ghesat sijn, gheven na rijcheit, na uwen plech|zeden, dat is duvelic unde aling contrarie der gherechticheit, dat se in u nicht schinen noch bliven en mach, inden dat ghi gheen mensche so bequeme of zo doghentsam of sodane weerdicheit hebben en mach. Na deser gherechticheit vorscreven heft he gheen gelt of is
260 he van snoder gheboerte, ghi en setten em van uwer delingen unde van uwer stede, unde voert ghevet ghi se na den blode; dat is na den maghen unde na den ghelde.

Wat hevet een arm mensche misdaen of he doechtlike dinge hevet bet dan een ander unde ghi en ghevet em nicht? Item, ghi
265 slutet den armen daerum uut daer he Cristo | mede gheliker is; dat is armoede. Item, ghi slutet em daerum uut daer he saligher van is unde bereder is unde bequemer Gode te deynen na der vorscrevenen rechticheit; dat is armode unde neder ghebuert.

Item, gij slutet em daerum uut daer Cristus na koes de syne de he
270 alreleifst hadde, syne apostele unde discipulen, unde daer He uns ynne gaf de rechte forme alre keisinge unde delinge. Unde also leert uns to syne de gude sante Pauwel in der *Epistelen to den van Corinthen*, daer he uns bewiset wo wi keisen soelen na gherechticheit in Cristo, unde spreket aldus: *Seit, broders, uwe ro-*
275 *pinge, want niet vele sint er gheropen wise menschen na den vleische, niet vele mechtigher, niet vele edele. Mer God verkoes de dwase na der werlt, updat he confues makede de wisen; unde de crancken van der werlt vercoes God unde de niet en sijn, updat he de sint verdervede, updat gheen vleschs glorieren en mochte vor*
280 *den angesichte Godes.*

Item, we daer twivelt dat armoede ghene grote bereidinge unde satinge si to Gode te gaen, int ghemene te spreken, de en kande ny dat ewangelium Cristi. Unde daerumme van der gherechticheit vorscreven boerdet bet ene stede enen armen dan
285 enen riken, en weren oec alle ander dinge ghelijc de an bequemelicheit roert.

271/280 I Cor. 1, 26-29   281/282 cfr Luc. 6, 20-21; Matth. 5, 3; 5, 6

254/262 cfr supra, 191-206

Item, al weren alle bequemelicheit ghelijc, want een arm mensche des bet behovet, so solde ment em daerumme meer gheven na der vorgescrevenen gerechticheit, want behoven unde noet anseit oec de gherechticheit, inden dat men enich ding delen sal na behoef der lude deet entfaet. Also steit gescreven in *Actibus apostolorum,* dat *men elken deelde na sijn behoef.*

Item, seit, myne leven zusteren, an, wo gi vulcomen menschen uutslutet de alle dinge unde alle werlic guet overgheghven hadden. | Seit, daerum solen se uwe stede derven, want se vullencomen staet anghenomen hebben. Daer se alre eren unde alles gudes na der ⟨vorscrevenen⟩ gherechticheit umme weert sijn, daerumme moten se des enberen. Recht of gi enen menschen sculdich weren van rechten gheleenden gelde een hundert punt, dat gy em darumme ander hundert punt nicht gheven en wolden, de ju God em to gheven bevoelen hadde unde bede to gheven, so untgulde he unde ontbaer jemerlike sijns rechtes um clare duecht.

Item, wat is dat, dat daer een mensche um uutghesloten wert, want he Cristus raet gevolget heft, unde *al sijn guet heeft vorcoft unde den armen ghegeven.* Unde ach, wat is dat, daerumme van to wisene | in uwen begripe, dat alle religien hebben als een derde strang der vulcomenheit, dat is armode mit underdanicheit unde reynicheit. Item, leve menschen, of sante Clare of sante Lijsbeth queme in armoden na uwen ghesate, weren se uutgesloten. Unde och, also ist vor Gode al uutgesloten dat wi na unsen upsate unde na unsen zaten uutsluten willen of se quemen, dat is al in den herten unde vor Gode gedaen, ghelijc als van der unkuscheit Cristus sprect. Nu provet dan woveer al armen hilghen veer van u sijn, ya, unde alle rike hilghen in den willen, want hadden se niet, ghi en nemen der niet. Neme ghi se, ghi en nemen

---

291/292 Act. 2, 45   305/306 Matth. 19, 21; Marc. 10, 21; Luc. 18, 22 paene ad litt.   311/314 cfr Matth. 15, 1-20; Marc. 7, 1-23

304/322 cfr infra, 748-751, fortasse etiam 433-462   307/309 cfr GER. MAG., *Tract. paup.*, 228-234; *Ep.* 41, 44-47; *Ep.* 45, 12-15; 122-127   cfr infra, 987-993, ubi Ger. allegat THOM., II-II, Q. 186 a. 7 co. (T. 10, p. 497, c. 2, a. 7, 4-37), etiam THOM., II-II, Q. 186 a. 3; 4; 5

---

297 vorscrevenen] *sic legendum,* vorscrevemen H

DE SIMONIA AD BEGVTTAS 339

se niet in den hilghen namen, of inden dat se discipele Cristi weren of hilich, mer inden dat se guet gheven mochten. Waerlike, warlike, de name sal u antworden in ewicheit in den wederghe-
320 ven, daer God den ghirighen betalen sal. Unde we mach u hijraf absolveren up eerden? Ghi en keren aling van desen dingen, ic neme uwes selves consciencie te tughe.

Item, seit an of u een guet gheheel vrent, de u al ere unde erdesch unde tijtlike dingen ghegeven hadde, oec satte up een
325 stucke gudes, dat gij em dat bewaren solden unde doen bewaren, denghenen de em dat alre-eerlixt unde vruchtbarlixt bewaerde, wo mochte gij dat mit enigher guder consciencien enen menschen um sijns blodes willen of um sijns guden willen bevelen to bouwen ofte bewaren? Dat were hues of erve, dat ghi na
330 uwen vermoden of na der vroder lere unde na ghemeyner ghewoente nicht en pleghe so wal te bouwene, of dat hues so wal to bewaerne, noch so eerlike | als een ander, beter mensche, mochte 115v gy dat anseyn in der bevelinge, dat weer bloet off rijcheit dat meer hinderde an der [an der] verwaringhe dan bate, off weert wal dat
335 niet en hinderde, so en mochte ghi des nochtan niet anseyn dan inden dat di bate dede. Aldus ist mit uwer stede of provende, de u God bevolen hevet entlike te ghevene denghenen de se eerliker, duechtliker unde vruchtbarliker besit to Gode, te gane na vermoeden uwer consciencien unde na vermoede der lere Cristi.
340 Item, hijrynne steit de trouwe, solde ghi Gode in desen dinge trouwe wesen. Sunte Pauwel spreect, *To den van Corinthen*, van em unde van den sinen: *Also*, spreket he, *sal men van uns vermoeden dat wi sijn deynre Godes unde scheffeners of delers der deynste Godes. Dat eisschet men nu*, sprect he, *under den scheffe-*
345 *ners, dat een juwelic trouwe ghevunden werde.* Unde Cristus spreket, in *sante Lucas ewangelio: We is*, sprect he, *een truwe scheffener unde | wijs, den de here settet up sijn ghesinde, updat he em* 10

318/320 cfr Matth. 25, 31-46   341/345 I Cor. 4, 1-2, *sed uaria lectio* 344 deynste *lectionem* ministeriorum *pro* mysteriorum *in codice biblico a Gerardo adhibito indicat*   345/351 Luc. 12, 42-44

340/363 cfr infra, 685-688

---

334 an der] *falso bis a H scriptum, et ideo eadem uerba iterum scripta delenda sunt*

gheve mate des weites in der tijt, dat is tijtlike na behoren unde na mate der gerechticheit vorgescreven. *Salich is de knecht den de here vint also doende, wanner he comet. He sal en setten up alle ding de he besittet.* Wat he den quaden doen sal, dat spreket he oec daerna. Unde voert spreket Cristus up datselve: *Al den den he vele ghegeven hevet, daer sal he vele of eischen, unde den se vele bevolen hebben, van den sal men vele bidden.* Dat sijn Cristus woerde van den untrouwen scheffener of van den bozen verwarer. Unde we mach em absolveren, he en worde Gode een ghetruwe scheffener? *Unde wo solde men em an beloven dat waer is, als he aldus ontruwe Gode is in der boser rijcheit?* Also spreect Cristus, in *sante Lucas ewangelio* up een ander ⟨stede⟩. Unde oec, sprect he, *sijt ghi untruwe in enen vremden,* dat is dat uwe nicht en is, alse dese ledighe stede uwes conventes, *we sal u gheven dat uwe is,* dat is weertguet van bynnen: in kennisse, in smake oft in lone.

Voert, mijn leven menschen, ic sette dat een mensche bynnen Campen sij of een scepen, de wanneer [de wanneer] men den keisen sal, keiset na den blode syner maechscap unde let de nuttesten uute bliven, dat is wisse weder de gherechticheit vorgescreven. Dat moghe ghi proven, dat em nymant absolveren en mach, em en berouwe de sunde unde kere em daervan dat he dat niet meer doen en wille, des ghelikes | in allen ampten unde gherichten to keisen.

Is dat aldus alst wisse waer is, so moghe gi proven wo ju desse dinge berouwen moeten de aldus rechte van Gode draghen. Want gheen unrechticheit is quader unde hinderliker unde bozer dan de hinderlic is unde ungherecht in den weghe Godes, want dat draghet in ewighen scaden.

So mochte men spreken dat men keisen mochte enen riken man unde mechtich vor enen anderen to scepene. Dat is waer wanner rijcheit unde macht is ene medezake unde ene berei-

---

352 cfr Luc. 12, 45-47   352/355 Luc. 12, 48   358/360 Luc. 16, 11 paene ad litt.   360/362 Luc. 16, 12

377/393 cfr GER. MAG., *Locat.*, 531-543

---

360 stede] *sic legendum,* stedo H   365 de wanneer de wanneer] *sic H, eadem uerba iterum scripta ut dittographia delenda sunt*

380 dicheit scepen te wesen in den steden daer men behoeft dat men den scepen entseit unde entvruchtet, ist dat he anders doghentsam sij unde truwe, want men werlikes entseyns unde entvruchtens behovet. In alsodanen werliken dingen mach men entseyn, inden dat sake is waerbi dat he de stat de bet regeren mach. Unde
385 anders sal men niet anseyn, dat daer nicht to en helpet. Unde desse dinge en behoeft men nicht an te seyne in aldusdanen beghinen in de per|sonen in te nemen, ya, meer contrarie dinge: armode unde otmoedicheit als vorgescreven is. Unde bovenal seit wo gruwelike unde ungheoerdet dattet weer dat men scepen-
390 doem kopen solde ofte stede, de men na der doecht solde gheven na bereidelicheit to den dingen, unde de also vele geldes nicht en hadde to entberen als hundert schilde, dat he uutghesloten solde bliven.

Unde ic sette dat men nemen mochte up ene tijt of men seghe
395 enen wissen mechtighen menschen duechtsam, dat de nutter underwilen weer umme dat regiment van buten to voerne int convent um dat ghemeyne gued mit macht des gheslechtes unde mit doechden to regeren. Dat mochte men up sulke tijt anseyn daer men des up ene tijt behoefde daers noet weer um dat regiment
400 van buten. Mer ummer in de ghemeynen entfangnisse sal men anseyn doecht to voeren; unde in den regimente solde men de doecht tovoeren anseyn, want doghet mach baten sunder maghe. Unde dicwijl in dusdanighen oetmodighen nederen state, als in religien unde in nederen clerken unde in conventen, ist nutter
405 sunder maghe te wesen, dicwile beide den conventen unde den menschen selven.

Unde daerumme sal men tovoeren anseyn de doecht unde den guden geistliken willen, want macht van maghen, | wanneer se koemt sunder doecht of sunder geistlic leven, so is se wunderli-
410 ken schedeliker dan of de mensche sunder macht weer, want "ungherechticheit de wapen heft, is alrequadest", scrivet Aristoteles, primo *Pollitice*. Unde bovenal, wanneer des noet weer al-

---

407/418 cfr GER. MAG., *Cura past.*, 284-290   411/412 locum inuenire non potui

---

394 men] nymant *add. H, postea del. uel H uel alia man.*   397 macht] *ex* machte *corr. ipse H*   405 beide] *sic merito in textu de Vreese, ex* beiden *corr. ipse H, qui error ex articulo* den *statim sequenti exortus est,* beyden *in app. suo falso scripsit de Vreese*

dusdanen mechtighen menschen te nemen, so solde men den niet laten staen um enich gelt, noch nemen um geldes willen, mer um de bequemelicheit de he hadde to den ghemenen gude to regeren; unde dit valt selden. Unde in den nemene solde alle vorwarde van gelde na gherechticheit unde moste beide uut den herten unde uut den munde bliven.

Item, wil ghi seyn wo cleyne dat men de rijcheit anseyn sal in allen ere unde wo unrecht dat dat is puer de rijcheit an te seene na der rijcheit, so wetet dat dese sunde in den scrifturen heit *acceptio personarum*. Dat is een entfangen der personen, dat men den personen nemet of dat men ghevet werdicheit um dingen de em nicht weerdich en maken ter weerdicheit, of um dinghe de ghene gherechte zake en sijn, dat he bequemer unde be-| reider unde beter sij to den dingen of to der weerdicheit. Dat is to entfane of to ghevene de dinge nicht na weerdicheit der personen, mer na anderen dingen, naden dat uns de personen entfanclic sijn. Unde dese sunde, de entfangnisse der personen, is weder de delende rechtverdicheit Godes, als alle lerers spreken. Unde dit *entfaen der personen is nicht bi Gode*, alse sunte Pauwel sprect, *to den van Rome* unde oec *den van Ephesien*.

Unde is so quaet dit uutnemen der personen, wo ist dat nicht merer quaet dit te done umme bate willen. Mer hoert sunte Jacob spreken: *Mine broders*, secht he, *up entfaen der personen en wilt nicht hebben den gheloven uns Heren Jhesu Cristi der glorien. Ist dat vor uwe aensichte ingheit of comet een man de heeft een gulden vingerlijn in der hant, mit blenkenden clederen, unde ist dat ingheit of komet mede een arm mensche mit vuelen clederen, unde ghi anseit an den riken mit den schonen clederen unde segget: "Sittet hijr wal", unde segt ghi den armen: "Sta du daer" of:*

430/432 Eph. 6, 9, allegatum sec. THOM., II-II, Q. 63 a. 1 co. (T. 9, p. 62, c. 1, 47-48); Rom. 2, 11   **434/447** Iac. 2, 1-6; Iac. 2, 1 allegatum sec. THOM., II-II, Q. 63 a. 2 co. (T. 9, p. 63, c. 1, 51-53)

419/451 cfr THOM., II-II, Q. 63 a. 1-2 co. (T. 9, p. 62-63)   **419/432** cfr infra, 667-671; 693-695   **419/422** cfr THOM., II-II, Q. 63 a. 1 co. (T. 9, p. 62, art. 1, c. 2, 10-15)   **422/429** THOM., II-II, Q. 63 a. 1 co. (T. 9, p. 62, art. 1, c. 2, 2-9) paene ad litt.   **429/432** THOM., II-II, Q. 63 a. 1 co. (T. 9, p. 62, art. 1, c. 2, 24-28) paene ad litt.   **433/462** cfr supra, 304-322, infra, 748-751

---

414 noch] *ex of corr. ipse* H

DE SIMONIA AD BEGVTTAS 343

"*Sitte up den schemel myner voete*", | *so richte ghi bi uselven, unde sijt richter der bozen ghedachten. Hoert, myne levesten brodere, en heft God nicht verkoren de armen, de rike sijn in den gheloven, tot erfghenamen des rikes dat God ghelovet heft synen ghemynden? Unde ghi hebt den armen enteert.* Dit sint sante Jacobs woerde.

Unde hijrmede concordeeren de lerers sante Augustijn, up dit woert, unde sante Gregorius unde ander lerers, dat men den riken allene um sijnre rijcheit willen gheen ere doen en sal noch teiken der doecht. So sal men em vele myn gheven um syne rijcheit dingen unde stede de to der doecht draghen unde ghesat sijn, unde enteer ghi den armen na sante Jacobs woerde, inden dat gij den armen nedersetten jeghen den riken up ene stede, daer he to handes van upstaen sal, unde daer gheen doechtlike dinge an en hangen noch blivende dinge, unde sijn ghi daermede *een richter in bosen ghedachten*. O, wat richter is he dan in boesheiden unde wo enteert he dan den armen unde de doecht, de den armen duechtsamen menschen nedersettet unde en wechwerpet, unde den riken verhevet in de durende stat, daer een mensche gheheel in blivet al sijn leven, unde in der stat de to der doghet unde to Gode ghesat is.

Elc sei hijrin sijns selves consciencie de wat geistlikes verstaens heeft. Unde och, wem entfarmede des niet | of dit nedersitten des armen hem ghedaen worde um tijtlic ghewyn, dat deghene daeraf neme de em aldus nederde, so weert noch vuelre.

Item, so ist to weten so desse dinge meer ghesat sijn to der doecht unde to Gode te deynen, unde daerna naket dit entfaen

---

456/457 Iac. 2, 4

448/451 cfr THOM., II-II, Q. 63 a. 2 sed c. (T. 9, p. 63, art. 2, c. 1, 34 – c. 2, 2); q. 63 a. 3 arg. 3. (T. 9, p. 65, art. 3, c. 1, 8-11), ubi bis allegat *Glos. ord. in Bibl. sup.* Iac. 2, 1 (T. 4, p. 514, c. 1, gl. sup. 'Tu sede; tu sta' (= Iac. 2, 3), ubi citantur AVG., *Ep.* 167 (p. 605, 13-17) et GREG. MAG., *Hom., Lib.* 1, *Hom.* 28, 2 (p. 241, 31-33); quia Aug. in loco a Thom. ex *Glos. ord.* allegato minus euidenter uerba a Ger. in uulgari lingua in paraphrasi data exprimit quam Greg. Mag., qui a Thom. etiam allegatur, uerisimile uidetur Ger. locum in *Glos. ord.* non quaesiuisse

---

446 armen] *ex* arm *corr. ipse* H   **456** en] *suppl. ipse* H1

der personen sunder eer weerdicheit der symonien, unde entfaen
470 der personen sunder eer weerdicheit in enighen dingen de to
Gode draghen, unde de symonie staen up enen grunde unde
werden uut enen quade gheboern unde entspruten na eenre ma‑
neren vor den oghen Godes. Unde daerbi ist dat oec naket de sy‑
monie: dat men werlike macht als keiserscop of regerer te wesen
475 in den steden copet um gelt. Unde Ostiensis seghet in siner *Sum‑
men* in den vijften boke dat dat symonie sij, want he sprect dat
de macht geistlic sij.

Unde ic spreke dat nyman en sal wesen regerer | of en mach   117v
wesen regerer mit guder consciencien, noch men mach em nicht
480 keisen to regeren stede of lande mit guder consciencien den men
weet dat gelt soeket of sijns selves ere van buten, want dat sijn
alle tyrannen. Mer men sal keisen de den ghemeynen lande of
stede nutte is to regeren unde de Gode vor oghen heft unde sijn
regiment to Gode keret, anders en is he nicht recht regerer of
485 copet he dat mit gelde. Gheen mensche up eerden en mach den
tyrannen of den regerer absolveren, he en kere sijn herte to Gode
unde to den ghemenen gude.

Hijrby leert, wo men dan gheistlike stede gheven sal, de uut
der werlt wat ghesat sijn unde al um Gode te deynen, als men in
490 ⟨werltliken⟩ dingen dus doen moet.

Nu vinden Adams kindere menighe woerde de nicht en
draghen in gherechticheit, daer se em mede bescudden of ver‑
weren willen. Se spreken int eerste wo dat canonike gheven wat
geldes of ene cappen int eerste alse se canonike werden. Seit, dat
495 en hevet gheen ghelijc, want gheen arm mensche noch gheen
weerdich mensche of den canonikscap van rechte boert en wort
daerumme verworpen of uutghesloten als ghi doet, want dit ghe‑
ven also cleyne is weder de provende unde he dat lichtlike ne‑
men mach van der provende. Unde | daerumme en is dat nemen   14
500 also niet jeghen de gerechticheit Godes of weder de weerdicheit
der personen of weder armoede als der baghinen ding, want

473/477 Host., *Summa*, L. 5 t. 1 (Quid sit simonia) § 1 (ed. 1537, f. 231v, c. 2, l. 61-68)

469/470 unde entfaen der personen sunder eer weerdicheit] *delenda uidentur, quia iam scripta inutiliter reiterant*   490 werltliken] *sic em. de Vreese*, werliken H

DE SIMONIA AD BEGVTTAS 345

nymant van armoden uutghesloten wert. Unde ghescheide dat erghen, dat were grote, michel sunde. Oec so ist van buten in den rechte so, dat men van rechte de canonike eerst nemen sal sun-
505 der vorwarde of lofnisse enighes gheldes um claer niet.
Unde ist dat se dan ene cappe nagheven off een weynich geldes, willendes na guder ghewonte, dat en is nicht unbyllic dat men de ghewonte holt, want hijr nymant mede buten blivet de arm is. Unde of se naden dat se enen entfangen hadden, daerna
510 enighen daerto dwingen mochten dat he de ghewonte helde, daer spreken de meisters van rechte mit underscheide up, dat gheen noet en is to spreken, want men open seyn mach dat gheen ghelijc en is, noch dat dit en is gheen entfaen der personen teghen weerdicheit, noch en is weder de ere Godes noch weder de ghe-
515 rechticheit. Doch wert daer dicke ynne ghesundighet, want men over de mate des geistliken | rechtes tret. 118r
Anderwerve willen se em bedecken mit ander lude zunden: mit den moniken unde nunnen de gelt nemen, ene verdraghene summen, of verdraghen datselve te nemen dat de lude hebt dat
520 se dat brengen, se weten wal dat se rike sijn. Dit is in der waerheit wisse symonie, alse *Decretael* spreket, *Cum extra uagante*. Unde de vijfte pawes Urbanus heft se alle ghebannet met synen banne, ⟨de⟩ icht gheven of nemen in monikecloester of nonnen-, gelt of cleynode ofte eten, yewer mit vorwoerden of sunder vor-
525 worden, umme der ghewonte willen wan men se entfaet, van welken bullen wi copie af hebben.

503/511 cfr Grat., *Decr.*, C.1 q.2 c.2 (c. I, 408, 12-38); *Decret.*, X 5.3.34 (c. II, 763, 21-45, etiam allegatum a Ioh. Frib., *Summa Conf.*, L. 1 t. 1 q. 48 (f. 11r, c. 2, 46 – 11v, c. 1, 7) sec. Vlricum magistrum suum, sed Ioh. se etiam refert ad Bern. Parm.; Hostiensem et Goffredum); Bern. Parm., *Glos. ord. in Decret.*, super X 5.3.34, comm. sup. 'pure consentiant' (c. II, 763, 35) (c. 1637 (p. 33), gl. d); Ioh. Frib., *Summa Conf.*, L. 1 t. 1 q. 32 (f. 9v, c. 1, 18-27), qui allegat Host., *Summa*, L. 5 t. 8 § 3 sub uoc. 'quid ergo si de consuetudine' (ed. 1537, f. 232r, c. 2, 51-61)   517/533 Ger. Mag., *Leeringhe*, 157-183 paene ad litt.
518/521 cfr *Extrauag. comm.* 5.1.1 (c. II, 1287, 40-52), infra cum nomine Papae Vrbani allegatum, praesertim clausula a praepositione 'cum' incipienti (ibid., 1287, 45-52)   522/526 cfr *Extrauag. comm.* 5.1.1 (c. II, 1287-1288, praesertim 1287, 58 – 1288, 47)

---

523 de] *sic in sermone uulgari regionum orientalium legendum*, die *sic em. de Vreese, dit H*

Mer dit sijn lerers de seggen wal ofte een cloester niet meer lude, monike of nunnen, voeden kunde dan se hadden unde dan een weerdich mensche queme den se gherne nemen solden sun-
530 der gelt, mochten seene voeden van den ghemeynen sunder groten hinder, dat he dan medebrochte. Want se des niet voeden kunnen, daer he bi levede, also dat dat cloester sunder sware last bleve, dunket sulken lerers dat se verdraghen moghen tovoeren.

Sulke spreken daer anders to unde seggen dattet niet wisse
535 en sij also te doen. Unde under desser varwe der armode so ⟨schuelt⟩ manighe symonie under den moniken unde nunnen in Dueschen lande, daer de armode meer | ghevarwet is unde gheen stat en hevet, unde daer se wal meer lude voeden moghen, of daer se den personen niet en nemen, en brochte he niet, weert
540 oec dat se nochtan em voeden kunden.

Unde bovenal so en ist oec gheen ghelijc varwe mit desen baghinen, want se ghene vulle voedinge noch cledinge en gheven unde em een mensche gheen groet hinder en is to nemen, of altoes den wal nemen moghen unde holden, inden daer se de eere
545 inholden unde elc emselven holt, uutghenomen wat vordels in potagie, in vueringe of in dranke of in weynich anders coste. Tymmeringe, de solden se holden mit den ghemeynen guede of scheiten daerto elc of bidden daerto. Dat weer beter dat se deden wes se doen mochten; ya, alle swaerheit to liden, ya, wech te lo-
550 pen of broet te bidden weer beter te doen dan se vulbart gheven to alsulken quaden dinge als vorgescreven is, unde elc in sijns selves consciencien lesen mach. Unde dede dusdane dinge al de

---

527/533 cfr IOH. FRIB., *Summa Conf.*, L. 1 t. 1 q. 49 (f. IIV, c. 1, 8 – c. 2, 15), ubi citat RAYM., *Summa de paen.*, L. 1 t. 1 § 22 (c. 299-300 ed. Ochoa ; ed. 1603, p. 23, c. 2, 22 – p. 24, c. 1, 22) et GVIL. RHED., *App. ad Sum. Raym.*, L. 1 t. 1 § 22, comm. sup. 'offerat se' (ed. 1603, p. 23, gl. x), et in extenso allegat THOM., II-II, Q. 100 a. 3 ad 4 (T. 9, p. 359, c. 2, 30-46) 534/540 GER. MAG., *Leeringhe*, 183-190 paene ad litt. 534/535 cfr *Decret.*, X 5.3.40 (c. II, 765, 47-66, praesertim l. 47-49); BERN. PARM., *Glos. ord. in Decret.*, super X 5.3.40, comm. sup. 'paupertatis' (c. II, 765, 48-49) (c. 1641-1642 (p. 35), gl. c); INNOC., *Comm. Decret.*, super X 5.3.34, comm. sup. 'consentiant' (c. II, 763, 35) (ed. 1570, p. 599, c. 1, 21-24, uide etiam 24-27, a Ioh. non allegatum), locos etiam a IOH. FRIB., *Summa Conf.*, L. 1 t. 1 q. 49 (f. IIV, c. 1, 38-60) allegatos 548/568 GER. MAG., *Leeringhe*, 192-215 paene ad litt.

---

535 armode] *ex* armoet *corr. ipse H* 536 schuelt] *sic em. de Vreese*, schult *H*

werlt weder de gherechticheit, dat en weer gheen bescudt weder gotlike unde na|tuerlike reden. Waerumme en is gheen ander raet dan dese dinge tomale of te latene, unde berouwenisse daeraf te hebben unde een waer opsaet unde vast dat niet meer te done.

Unde waren mit u enighe verkeerde menschen de dat niet doen en wolden, so moghe gij de u pynen willen mit uwen consente altoes wederspreken. Wanner men vorwarde maket yewer van ener summen ofte van denselven dat se hebben te brengen, unde nummermeer en ghevet de provende umme guet, noch en seit gheen guet an noch dat bloet. Mer ghevet se denghenen, also veer alst in uwer macht is, de der bet behovet unde de der best werdich is van duechden unde beter is to den denste Godes unde u nutter is to Godes denste, unde den de provende oec nutter is Gode te deynen. Unde hoet u in den herten unde in woerden vor aldusdane dinge als vor geroert sijn, dat ghi daer niet teghen en doen.

Men mochte wal maken van dingen daerin te laten, ene ghemeyne mate van denselven dat een hadde wenich ofte vele to der tymmeringe behoeff ofte ter cost, ⟨mer⟩ dan en mochte men daer nymanne umme nemen of dat anseyn dat he vele daerynne laten solde.

Item, so spreken see dat de presters mit vorwarden | loven eer altaer to beteren, dre punt des jares ofte veir, of men en gheve em des altaers nicht. Dit en is gheen bescudt, want de presters de dus loven dat altaer te beteren of vorworde daervan maken, de doen grote symonie. Also doen oec deghene de em dat altaer in vorworden gheven. De presters sijn daer quelike an, want se moeten dat altaer overgheven unde vort al de vrucht der kerken gheven de se ie gheboerden ofte de se mochten gheboert hebben. Dat is allen menschen kunt de de waerheit spreken willen uut den gheistliken rechte. Mer ghescheden desse dinge sunder lofnissen in den altaer unde sunder vorworden, mer dat deghene deet altaer gheve, hopede dat he dat beteren solde und wiste he dat he des niet en beterde, dat he em dan des niet en gheve. Unde de prester des altaers niet en beterde, ten worde hem ghegeven,

---

574/592 locum inuenire non potui

---

569 Men] Van in te laten *ut tit. suppl.* H   571 mer] *sic em. de Vreese,* men H

so ist al effen vuel unde quaet vor Gode, doch he mach daerynne bliven, ist dat em dat altaer | even komet to syner salicheit unde sal vor Gode unde vor synen bichter vuldoen vor de sunde in rechter pinen, want he gheen overdracht, noch vorworde, noch lofnisse, noch ghemaect, noch ghelovet en hevet.

Myne lieve zustere in Unsen Leven Heren, ic heb u de warheit um eer [de warheit] unde in mynnen ghesproken. De ghemene werlt is quaet unde des quades is vele. De gherechticheit leghet ghemeynlike under de voete. Elc sei vor em, elc sal sijns selves boerden draghen, niet na den gherichte dat em nu ghehenget wort op der eerden, mer na der waerheit unde der gherechticheit Godes. De tijt is nu kort, de pine is groet unde unmetelic. De glorie Godes is wunderlic in eer unde up syne ghemynde. Alle guet comet uns mit syner gherechticheit, de regneert unde levet mit ghewolde in den Vader unde in den Zoene unde in den Hilghen Geiste in den nu der ewicheit. Amen. |

Alle recht unde menschlike ewe dat verbunt maect, als de hilghen unde oec ander philosophen leren, vloiet unde moet vleiten, salt cracht der ewen hebben, uut de alreoversten, hoechsten unde ewigher reden de Got is. Also spreket de ewighe wijsheit Godes in den .VIII. capitel in *Salomons Proverbien*: *Mijn is*, sprect he, *beide de raet unde de ghelijcheit, mijn is de wijsheit unde starcheit, bi my regneert de coninge, by my so settet de insater der ewe gherechte dinge, bi my so ghebeden de princen, by my so bescheiden de mechtighen de gherechtvindicheit*. Is dan dat waer dat van der oversten, ewighen rede all recht unde lijcheit komet, wo mochtan dat van Gode komen of van der ewigher wijsheit dat beter weer unghesat dan ghesat, off dat unghelijc weer, off verre

---

607/612 Prou. 8, 14-16

604/625 cfr supra, 233-238   604/612 GER. MAG., *Turrim*, 57-62, partim uerbatim in linguam uulgarem traductus allegatione biblica excepta, cfr GER. MAG., *Focar.*, 85-90   cfr THOM., I-II, Q. 93 a. 3 sed c, co. (T. 7, p. 164, c. 1-2)

---

594 de warheit] *haec uerba falso bis scripta merito ut dittographia considerauit et consequenter del. de Vreese*   604 Alle] Dit capitel bewiset wo quaet unde unrecht is in enich convent in te setten der personen, in te nemen mit ener zeker summen geldes, unde nicht na aller bequemicheit unde noettrufticheit *ut tit. suppl.* H

van der ghelijcheit unde van der redene? Van den ewighen gude en coemt niet, noch gifte noch gave, dan de alrebeste unde alrevullencoemste, als sante Jacob sprect int eerste capitel syner *Epistolen*. Waerbi ist openbaer dat in dat herte dat int erste anders insette dan na alre bequamelicheit to geven oft so hadde gewest, dan dat van Gode niet gheboren en was, noch dat em dat niet in en quam uut Gode. Waerumme en ist gheen ewe of verbunt, mer dat is uut den menschen oft uut den duvel gheboren, de beide, wanneer se uut emselven spreken, leighen unde sunden | unde missen des gudes unde der ewe.

119v

Item, mocht men mit sodaner loghene unde missen yenich recht maken of daermede dat ghemene gued breken ofte solde men daerumme breken de gotliken regulen, dat is al te veer van allen guden herten. Item, solde men desen sundighen insetter in deser loghene der zatinghe navolghen unde den duvel, dat weer al te jamerlic; dat is, dat daerumme de uutghesloten weerden de es anders na gherechticheit bet behoven, unde de bequemer na alre bequemelicheit weren daerto.

Item, de delende gherechticheit Godes en slutet nymande uut uut ghenen guden um nymans willen de nicht en wil na eren willen. Item, se is gherecht in erselven unde se en sluet nyman uut dan mit gherechticheit unde denghenen de er uutsluett. Item, se en sluet nyman uut um nymandes satinge willen de uut eer nicht gheboren is, noch um anders satinghe uut den vlesche gheboren unde uut den blode.

'

Unde we is *uut den vlesche gheboren* unde vleislic, daer antwort sante Augustijn dicke up, sunderlinge up sante Pauwels *Epistelen ad Ga|latas*. De is, sprect he, *uut den vleische gheboren*, de emselven suect in tijtliken ghewinne of eren, als de baghinen doen, of deghene de em dat satte of em ghesat weer, de zoken al er proper tijtlic ghewijn. Unde daerbi vallet alle state, als de hilghen spreken, unde sunderlinge, want gheleerde lude dat dicke sterken.

18

616/619 cfr Iac. 1, 17   641 Gal. 4, 23   643 Gal. 4, 23

619/625 cfr infra, 673-675   cfr THOM., I-II, Q. 93 a. 3 co., ad 1, ad 2 (T. 7, p. 164, c. 2)   634/637 cfr THOM., I, Q. 21 a. 1 co. (T. 4, p. 258, c. 2, 1-4); II-II, Q. 63 a. 2 co. (T. 9, p. 63, c. 2, 3-30), supra (219-232) etiam allegatum   641/644 cfr AVG., *Exp. Gal.* 40 (= *in Gal.* 4, 21-24) (p. 109, 2-9)

Item, sante Gregorius up dat ewangelium van den manne de de werclude huerde in den wijngarden, dat is in syner .XIX. *Omelien*, spreket aldus: "Broders", spreket he, "beseit uselven, unde seit of ghi werclude Godes sijn. Elc pense wat he doet unde merke of he arbeit in den wijngarden Godes, want de in desen leven de dinghe de sijn sint soeket, de en quam noch nicht in den wijngarden Gods." De sijn sante Gregorius woerde.

Daerbi ist dat ghi proven moghet, dat juselven to soeken neder of boven andere bequemelicheit en is gheen werc in Godes wijngarden, noch de u dat insatte juselven aldus to soeken. Van yemans ghesette dat dat ghesette uut Gode nicht en is, unde dat en kan nicht dwingen noch vermynren ghemene barmherticheit of ghemene gherechticheit of uut der ghemeente te sluten van node den de gherechticheit nicht uut en sluten. Item, dat juwe te soeken, dat is | na der werlt. Want *de werlt soeket dat eer*, sprect Cristus in sunte Johans *Ewangeli*, in den †.XIII.† capitel.

Daerbi is dit werlike wijsheit unde vleischlike, unde de en is Godes ewe nicht underdaen, unde de is dwaesheit unde unewe vor Gode. Item, seit mit ener corten redene de mensche de dat satte of hadde, heet ghedaen of gegheven na uutnemen der personen, of na rijcheit unde nicht na alre bequemelicheit, dat was unde hadde ghewesen sunde also te doen, eert ghesat was do he verdroech. Unde daerbi ist na merer sunde daer ander lude willen to trecken of to verbinden. Unde wat is sunde na Augustinus leer dan begherte of werc of daet weder de ewe Godes; unde dat weder de ewe Godes is, als vor gescreven is, en mach ghene ewe maken.

Item, dat dit nemen der personen unde ungherecht weder de ewe des Heren is sunde unde unrecht inden de dat so wolde ghescheyn, want alle sunde is meest in den willen, unde noch meerc deet so verbinden wolde an der lude daerto, unde dit ver-

---

649/650 sc. Matth. 20, 1-16   662/664 Ioh. 15, 19

649/655 GREG. MAG., *Hom.*, *Lib.* 1, *Hom.* 19, 2 (= *sup. Matth.* 20, 1-16) (p. 145, 57-60) paene ad litt.   667/671 cfr supra, 419-432   672/675 cfr AVG., *Contra Faustum*, *Lib.* 22, c. 27 (p. 621, 12-13), forte allegatum sec. THOM., I-II, Q. 19 a. 4 s.c. (T. 6, p. 144, c. 1, art. 4, 19-22)   673/675 cfr supra, 619-625

---

656 neder] *ex* weder *corr. ipse* H   664 XIII.] *sic* H, .XV. *legendum*

680 bint willen to vervolghen unde willen anverghen. Wat ist anders dan to consentiren unde to volghen den quaden? Unde de wert ghelijc den verbunden, als de Salm spreket, beide de se maket unde de daerin gheloven. Want vulcomen vulbaert ten quaden is | of heit dade, als men uut Cristus woerde dicwijl proven mach. 19
685 Unde daerum staen al myne redene vast unde bliven staende, de ic in den anderen boke sprac, uut delender gherechticheit unde uut truwheit des sceffeners, unde uut den dat men ghene personen annemen sal sunder sake. Want men dese dinge so nicht breken en mach mit alsodanen insetten, noch dat men
690 daermede den armen unde de es na gherechte noetdruftich sijn off de daer na alre bequemicheit beter to sijn, nicht uutsluten en mach.

Item, dat annemen der personen, dat men heit *accepcio personarum*, dat underscheit men, unde seghet men weder annemen
695 der saken unde weder annemen des waerummes na alre bequemicheit to den dinge, dat men deilen sal; dat heit men *acceptionem causarum*, de men altoes anseyn sal. Unde um enen sundighen willen des insettes in conventen in provende en is een mensche in emselven nywer bequemer noch unbequemer ter
700 provende, of den convente off um dat gelt, wattan al is he gheliker den quaden willen des insates de den personen uutnam.

Item, aldus weder Godes ewe en mach gheen mensche weder insetten, dusentwerve myn dan de bisscop weder den pawes. Unde wat | weder de ewe Godes ghesat weer mit sunden, dat is 120v
705 bose unde quaet, unde dat en verbint nicht. Daerumme versprac Unse Leve Here Jhesus Cristus de Joeden seer, do se vragheden waerumme sine discipele nicht en helden der olden ghebot van den hantwasschen. Do vraghede he em unde versprac se dat se Godes ghebot overgengen um der menschen ghebot willen, als
710 steit in den .XV. capitel in *Matheo* unde in den .VII. capitel in

---

681/683 cfr Ps. 82 (83), 6   683/684 cfr e.g. Ioh. 3, 9-20; 8, 34   705/711 cfr Matth. 15, 1-3; Marc. 7, 5-9

685/688 cfr supra, 340-363   693/695 cfr supra, 419-432; 667-671   cfr THOM., II-II, Q. 63 a. 1 co. (T. 9, p. 62, art. 1, c. 1, 30 – 2, 9)

696/697 acceptionem] personarum *add., sed statim exp. ipse* H

Marco. Unde up *Matheum* Jeronimus unde na em Beda up *Marcum* spreken mit enen woerde dat Cristus "dat valsche begripen der Joden mit warer antworde verwarp, of He secgen wolde: 'Als ghi um ghesate der lude versumet de ghebode Godes, waerumme berispe ghi myne discipele dat se cleyne rekenen of heiten ghebode der olden, umdat se myne ghebode holden?'" Dit sijn Jeronimus unde Beden woerde.

Mer Crisostimus in *Opere perfecto*, in der omeliën up Matheus int originael, spreket dat dat "in der tijt was dat de Joeden em solden van alrehande holdinge unde satinge meer entbinden na vortgange der tijt. So bunden se em so lang so meer mit merer observancien. Unde daerto quam er boesheit dat men ere ghe|bode helt, unde dat se leden dat men Godes gheboede nicht en helt. Daerum was em schult, beide dat se nye dinge makeden, unde dat se wraken op deghene de se nicht en helden. Unde was em twivoldighe sunde, dat se Gode nicht en loveden unde dat se dat deden um der lude willen", of he secgen wolde: "Dat verdoemt u, dat ghi alle dinghe loven den olderen unde den dinge de Gode tohoren ghene roeke en hebt." Dit sijn Crisostimus woerde.

Unde daerum sprect Cristus daerna: wo, *alle plantinge of plantacie, de van den Vader nicht en sijn*, dat sijn de allene insatinge der menschen sijn, alse Crisostimus secht, *de solen al uutgheroedet werden*, unde alle de em volghen. Unde Cristus heitet se *blinden unde leiders der blinden*, want se waren *de scriben unde de pharizeen* geheiten, de wijssten unde de hoghesten des volkes.

Unde Cristus brenget op em de Hilgen Scrift, de Ysaias scrivet in den .XXIX. capitel, unde secht aldus in *Marco*: *Wal heft Ysaias van u ypocriten ghepropheteert, als gescreven is: Dit volc eert my*

731/734 Matth. 15, 13   734/735 Matth. 15, 14   735/736 Matth. 15, 1
737/743 Marc. 7, 5-9   739/740 Is. 29, 13

711/717 HIER., *In Matth.* 2 (p. 127, 1407-1411); BED., *In Marc.* 2, 7 (p. 520, 1246-1250)   718/730 IOH. CHRYS., *Opus imperf.*, Hom. 51, 1 (in Matth. 15, 1-20) (*PG*, 58, c. 510, 1-10) paene ad litt.   732/734 cfr IOH. CHRYS., *Opus imperf.*, Hom. 51, 3 (in Matth. 15, 1-20) (*PG*, 58, c. 514, 35-36; 43-47)   734/736 cfr IOH. CHRYS., *Opus imperf.*, Hom. 51, 4 (in Matth. 15, 1-20) (*PG*, 58, c. 514, 48-56)

---

718 perfecto] imperfecto *legendum*, cfr Focar., 1857, 2061, 2160
721 meer] *ex* merer *corr. ipse* H

DE SIMONIA AD BEGVTTAS 353

740 *mit den lippen, mer er herte is veer van my. Dat is um nicht dat se my oefenen, de leren leringe | unde ghebode der menschen, unde achterlaten de ghebode Godes unde holden satinge der menschen.* Dit sijn Cristus worde uut Ysaias.
Unde oec spreket de Here in den .x. capitel des propheten
745 *Ysaias: We den de stichten unrechte ewe unde de scrivende screven hebt ungherechticheit, updat de drucken den armen int gherichte, unde ghewelt deden den weduen in eren saken unde den nedersten van mynen volke.* Dit sijn Godes worde in *Ysaias,* unde och, wo seer sijn de waerin den insetten der baghinen als vor ge-
750 screven is, daer de nederen unde de armen mede nederlicgen, unde de riken unde de mechtigen mede verhoghet werden. Unde sullic unrecht is gheboren seer unghelijc den groten we des viandes, daer uns allen God voer bescudden moet. Want *salich is he,* sprect de *Psalme, de* inwendelike *versteit up den behovighen unde*
755 *up den armen, want in den quaden daghe sal em God verlozen.*
Mer wo men holden sal Godes ewe tovoren, als *rechten, geloven unde barmherticheit,* unde daerna der menschen ewe de gherecht sijn nicht achter te laten, als *teynden gheven van dillen unde camijne* unde van cleynen dingen, als Cristus secht, worde
760 my te lang te spreken.
Mer dat is in menschen satinge allene seker | unde gherecht unde anders nicht dan dat uut Gode gheboren is; unde daer vloiet uut der fonteyne alre ewe unde satinghe, dat is de overste redene Godes. Item, seit dat menschen satinge en is anders nicht dan een
765 *determinacio;* dat is een underschedende bewisinge des natuerlikes unde des ewighen rechtes in underschedenen saken unde der dinge. Unde we de gherechte menschlike satinge to rechte kent unde to vullen holt, de vint dat naturlike rechte unde redene, unde ewich recht unde Godes, unde rechte redene in menschen,

---

744/748 Is. 10, 1-2   **753/755** Ps. 40, 1   **756/760** Matth. 23, 23 paene ad litt.

748/751 cfr supra, 304-322, fortasse etiam 433-462   **761/770** cfr THOM., I-II, Q. 93 a. 3 co, ad 2 (T. 7, p. 164, c. 1-2), etiam allegatum in GER. MAG., *Turr.* (57-62; 388-391); *Focar.* o (85-92); in posteriore loco aliqua uerba hic (**761-762**) in theutonica lingua allegata latine uersa (88-90) inueniuntur   **764/767** cfr THOM., I-II, Q. 95 a. 2 co. (T. 7, p. 175, c. 2)

---

769 unde³] ewighe *add., sed postea del. ipse* H   redene rechte *tr. ipse* H

rechte een sijn. Salich is de den sijn herte open is. Entfarme dy unser, Heer.

Hijrna wil ic spreken van der symonien. Wattan weert ghenoch allen guden herten in den dingen de hijrvoer open verclaert sijn, inden dat men alsodane insatinge of insetten noch holden en mach noch en sal, unde noch meer daerto dat so nicht ghesat en sij van beghinne, doch dat unghelerde menschen de symonie unde dat daer wedergesproken is, de bet verstaen um dit to seyne claerlike unde to kennen | underscheit der dinge daer symonie ynne is, off meer of myn, in herte of van buten in de kerke, unde up de vraghe to antworden daert *Wederboec van Colene* vraghet waerynne unde in wat manere dat symonie sij stede unde provende te copen.

So sole gij weten int erste, alse sprect Antisiodorensis in synen *Summen* in den derden boke van der symonien in der eersten questien, dat men pleghet aldus mit underscheide to bewisen wat geistlic ding is. "Dat geistlic ding", dat properlike geistlic ding, "dat is daer men ynne heeft den Hilghen Geist, als alle duechde, of daer men in gheeft den Hilghen Geist, als de sacramente, of daer men mede teikent den Hilghen Geist, alse gave der prophetien unde mirakele te doene. Unde men mach waerlike spreken", sprect deselve lerer, "dat geistlic ding sij daer men ynne heeft den Hilghen Geist.

Want men hevet den Hilgen Geist warlike in den duechden unde in den sacrament unde in den werken der mirakele unde in der prophetien mit underscheidenheit."

Unde | de under desen dreen is dat hoechste geistlike guet, doechde unde mynne. Unde de is vele geistliker dan de andere,

---

796/797 cfr I Cor. 13, 13

776/779 cfr supra, praesertim 3-6; 33-39   780/782 locum inuenire non potui; consilium consimile a. 1456 a iuristis etiam Coloniensibus datum quod a De Vreese repertum est, post editionem suam, p. 72-85, prelo dedit   783/795 GVIL. ALT., *Summa* 3, 49, 1 (T. 3.2, p. 940, 35-42) paene ad litt.

---

772 Hijr] Dit capitel bewiset dat geistlike dinge sijn manigherhande mit underscheide daer symonie ynne wesen mach, unde wat dinge den menschen alre geistlics maken unde daer de meeste symonie ynne is *ut tit. suppl. H*   779 buten] bynnen *praem., sed postea del. ipse H*   786 ding²] is *add., sed postea del. ipse H*

want se den menschen geistliker maken in emselven unde Gode naer verenen in den geiste dan de tekene der sacramente of de
800 mirakele te done off de prophetie. Want beide gude unde quade, alst kenlic is, moghen de sacramente nemen unde gheven, of oec gave hebben iewer te propheteerne off mirakele te doene, alst dicwile gheseyn unde ghescheyn is, als Cristus secht unde ghescreven is, *Mathaeus* .VII. Unde de sacramente unde de mirakele
805 unde prophetien, de sijn gheordineert van Gode unde van den hilghen um de doecht te krighen unde um de sele naerre in der mynne unde mit doechden Gode unde mit geistliken levene unde werken to verenen unde an te hangen.

Unde nicht allene gotlike doechde, als *ghelove, hope unde*
810 *mynne,* de den menschen in den geiste geistlic unde verheven maket, zijn geistliker dan ghaven der mirakele off prophetien, mer oec zedelike duechden in Gode sijn geistliker dan mirakele te done. Dat bewiset sunte Augustijn, *Up Paulus epistele ad Galatas,* unde sprect aldus: "De Here en sprac nicht: '*boert up mijn jock*
815 *unde leert van my dat ic dode lichame van veir daghen doet opverwecke unde alle viande van der lude lichame unde zeicheit verdrive*', unde andere dinge des ghelikes, mer he sprect: '*boert | op mijn jock, unde leert, want ick byn sachtmodich unde oetmodich van herten*'. De eerste dinge", dat is mirakele, "dat sijn tei-
820 ken der geistliker dinge, mer to wesen *sachtmodich unde oetmodich van herten* unde een behoeder der gotliken mynne, dat sijn selven geistlike dinge." Dat ander dat sijn tekene, sprect Augustinus, opdat "to den doechden moghen komen vermids mirakele deghene de ghegeven sijn den lichamliken oghen. De den ghe-
825 loven der unseynliken dinge van bekanden unde ghewonliken dingen nicht crighen en kunnen, de soeken den gheloven der dinge in nyen unde seynliken dingen als in mirakele." Dit sijn sunte Augustinus woerde, daer gy uut proven moghen wo geistlike dinge de doechde sijn.

122r

800/804 cfr Matth. 7, 22   809/810 I Cor. 13, 13   814/815 Matth. 11, 29
817/821 Matth. 11, 29

809/811 cfr etiam THOM., II-II, Q. 81 a. 5 ad 1 (T. 9, p. 182, C. 1, 21 – 2, 4), infra (923-924) paene uerbatim allegatum   813/828 AVG., *Exp. Gal.* 15 (= *in Gal.* 2, 11-16) (p. 70, 24 – 71, 8)

815/816 opverwecke] *sic legendum*, opvervecke H

830　Unde so hogher doghet unde inwendigher unde gotliker, so se geistliker is, als *ghelove, hope unde mynne*. De sijn alre geistlixt, de uns sunder ander [ander] middel Gode tovoeghen unde anhangen.

　　Item, de doechde sijn boven doechden, de ene boven den an-
835　deren, na eren grade unde eren ambochten. Unde al sijn se um de | mynne; unde in der mynne verenighen se uns mit Gode unde mit den Hilghen Geiste. So sprect Gregorius, in der *Omeliën*, up dat woert: *Hoc est preceptum meum*: "Als vele telghen komen uut eenre wortelen, also werden gheboren vele duechden uut eenre
840　mynnen. Nicht groenes en heft de telghe gudes werkes, en blijft he nicht in der wortelen der mynnen." Unde daerin draghet alle duechde, um verenighet te werden mit Gode unde um Gode an te hangen unde één gheist mit em te werden. Unde dat is de naeste unde meeste geistlicheit de een mensche hijr hebben
845　mach. Alle duechde is gave unde werc des Hilghen Geistes, unde maket den menschen geistlic. Unde mit elker doghet woent de Hilghe Geist in den geistliken menschen.

　　Daerbi proevet dat alle werke unde oefeninge der doechde sijn geistlike werke unde oefeninge, want *dat gheboren is uut den*
850　*geiste, dat is gheist, unde wat gheboren is uut den vlesche, dat is vlesch*, sprect Cristus. Ya, werke unde oefeninge der doechden sijn geistliker na mynen duncken dan werke der mirakele, wanneer se uut merer unde geistliker herten komen unde uut geistliken grunde unde naere to den gheiste draghen.

855　Nochtan werke der mirakele to vercopen is symonie, unde daer eirste de symonie uut ghenoemt is unde eerst bescreven in der *Scrifturen*, als Gezi dede; de nam van Naaman, de malaetsch was, cleder, want he van synen meister Helizeus ghesunt | ghemaket was, als steit in der *Coninge* boke.

---

831 I Cor. 13, 13　　838 Ioh. 15, 12　　849/851 Ioh. 3, 6　　855/859 cfr IV Reg. 5, 20-27, partim allegatum sec. THOM.

830/837 cfr THOM., II-II, Q. 23 a. 6 CO. (T. 8, p. 170, c. 1, 32 – 2, 3)　　837/841 GREG. MAG., *Hom., Lib.* 2, *Hom.* 27, 1 (= *sup. Joh.* 15, 12) (p. 229, 6-9)
841/847 cfr THOM., I-II, Q. 62 a. 1 co. (T. 6, p. 401, a. 1, c. 1, 29 – 2, 17)
855/859 cfr THOM., II-II, Q. 100 a. 1 ad 4 (T. 9, p. 353, c. 2, 13-17), GRAT., *Decr.*, C.1 q.1 c.11 (c. I, 361, 1-3)

---

832 ander²] *hoc uocabulum bis scriptum delendum est*

860 Unde Symon magus, daer heeft symonie eren namen van. In em was twiërhande boesheit in te begheren werke unde macht der mirakele, als de lerers spreken, unde dat he de macht wolde hebben umme gelt den gheist te gheven in seynliken teken, een ander, updat he dan vercopen mochte de mirakele unde daeruut 865 gelt crighen.

Nu en mach men de duecht noch duechtlike werke noch doghentlike oefeninge ofte doghentlic leven, inden dat se doghentlic bliven of loenlic, nicht vercopen, noch van rechte noch mit der daet. Nochtan mochte de wille wal so wesen se to copen 870 of to vercopen, want unmoghelike dinge mach eens menschen willen, iewer dat he waent dat se moghelic sijn, off dat he wolde dat se moghelic waren. Unde dat he se dan copen of vercopen wolde, also vercopet de ene dwase mensche den anderen syne seile of syne waldaet of syne sunde. Unde we willen hadde 875 syne doghet te vercopen, de en hadde in Gode ghene gherechte doeghet noch loenlic werc.

Mer de sacramente mach men vercopen mitter|daet unde nicht van rechte, unde de dingen de daer hangen an de sacramente. Unde van dese sacramenten unde sacramentalen dingen, unde 880 van den de daer anhangen, sprect meest unde sunderlinge de hilge kerke in den rechte ⟨wan⟩ se van symonien sprect. Want de gherechte doghentsame mensche en vercopet ghene ⟨doeghet⟩ noch doghentsame werke noch oefeninge noch leven, of men se vercopen mochte. Unde oec so en kan men nicht wal doghent-885 same werke off oefenisse vercopen, inden dat see doghentsam bliven, unde oec so syn de doghede in eren grunde verholen unde ere werke unde oefenisse, naden dat se doghentlic sijn.

---

860 GER. MAG., *Locat.*, 62-63 paene ad litt.   860/863 GER. MAG., *Locat.*, 66-72 paene ad litt.   860/865 cfr GRAT., *Decr.*, C.1 q.3 c.8 § 1 (c. I, 413, 35 – 414, 11); uocabulum 'lerers' ad Vrbanum a Grat. allegatum spectat, non ad ISID., *Etym.*, et AVG., *Haer.*, sicut De Vreese, p. 38, asserit, quia hii doctores de haeretica inclinatione a Symone praebita loquuntur, Ger. autem de prauitate emendi donum Spiritus sancti   863/865 GER. MAG., *Locat.*, 69-73 paene ad litt.   866/887 locum inuenire non potui   877/878 cfr IOH. FRIB., *Summa Conf.*, L. 1 t. 1 q. 10, primus casus (f. 5r, c. 2, (49-) 54 – 5v, c. 1, 3), qui allegat GVIL. RHED., *App. ad Sum. Raym.*, L. 1 t. 1 § 5, comm. sup. 'pro spirituali' (ed. 1603, p. 6, c. 1, gl. x, 29 – c. 2, l. 9)

---

873 mensche] *ex* menschen *corr. ipse H*   874 hadde] *ex* hadden *corr. ipse H*   881 wan] *sic legendum*, van *H*   882 doeghet] *sic legendum*, dogh^cet *H*

De sacramente unde wiinghe, unde de presterscop unde de daer anhangen, ambochte unde dade unde oefeninge, unde de provende unde oec de mirakele, de seit men unde kent men bet van buten dat se waer sijn dan men werke of oefenisse der doeghet ⟨kent⟩ dat see uut doechden ghewracht sijn. Want vele guder werke unde oefenisse in eren gheslechte sijn de guet schinen, de nicht wal noch doghentlike ghewracht en werden, de van buten unde na den schine den doghentliken werken unde oefenissen unde levene tomale ghelijc sijn. Unde daerbi en spreket de kerke nicht so vele van deser symonien de hijrin staet als van den anderen symonien. |

Nochtan ist quader symonie unde merer unghelove unde ungheliker den rechten gheloven. Unde dat is meer weder mynne, yenich graet der doghede unde doghentsamen werkes, oefenisse unde levens willen to vercopen dan ienighe wiinghe of sacramente des hiwelics of mirakel te kopen. Want wo wenich dat de graet rechter mynnentliker doghet off doghentliker werke is, off doghentlikes levens of oefenisse, naden dat uut den Hilghen Gheiste gheboren is, so volghet daer na annemicheit Godes gracie unde glorie in loen. Unde dat is beter unde den menschen beter dan te hebben alle de wiinghe of sacramente te nemene off alle mirakele te done sunder de gratie unde annemicheit Godes. Och, wat groter symonien is dan in den herten, de waent of pijnt em de gratie Godes te kopen, off ander lude doghet oec to vergeldene mit ghelde, of te kopen deelachtich te werden, der nu vele sijn up der eerden. Ya, alse sprect Antisiodorensis, dat de Gode ofcopen wolde mit almissen als mit gheweerde, dat he sijn herte verluchte, dat weer de alreboseste symonie. |

Nu um voert te gane ter Derden Orden unde to beghinen state, proevende, stede unde convente, so soele ghi weten dat ene doeghet heit *religio*, dat is daer een mensche mede steit unde mede neighet unde vestet em Gode te deynen, unde em te doene

---

888/898 cfr GER. MAG., *Locat.*, 382-405   905/907 cfr supra, 841-847 cfr THOM., I-II, Q. 62 a. I CO. (T. 6, p. 401, a. 1, c. 1, 29 – 2, 17)   **913/915** cfr GVIL. ALT., *Summa* 3, 49, 2, 3 (T. 3.2, p. 954, 57-59)   **917/922** cfr THOM., II-II, Q. 81 a. 2 CO. (T. 9, p. 179, c. 2, 6-8); Q. 81 a. 4 CO., ad 1-3 (T. 9, p. 181, c. 1, 2 – c. 2, 15)

---

892 kent] *suppl.* De Vreese, *om.* H

DE SIMONIA AD BEGVTTAS 359

920 unde te ghevene gherechte ere, reverencie, denst unde oefenisse. Also sprect Thomas in *Secunda secunde*, in der .LXXXI. questien, in vele artikelen.

Dese doeghet *religio* is seer geistlic unde na den gotliken doechden ghelove, hope unde mynne een de geistlixste doecht.
925 Unde se ghebeidet unde heeft ghewoelt over al den zedeliken doechden, unde ere dade unde werke oerbart se unde offert ten gotliken denste unde ere, unde se regeert unde ordineert unde satet de andere doechden unde alle ding ter glorien Godes.

Dese doeghet en hadden de heidene nicht recht, mer se spre-
930 ken daeraff, unde waenden unde bagheden em de to hebben na eren vermoden. Mer se en is nerghen ghewaerliker unde rechter dan in den kersten menschen. Unde dat bewiset sunte Augustijn, in den boke *Van der stat Godes*, unde in den boke dat men heit ghemeynlike, alst zunte Augustijn selven noemt, *Van der waren*
935 *religiën*.

Dese doghet de *religio* ghenoemt is, hevet werke unde dade de men inwendelike unde uutwendelike hillicheden heit, als Thomas sprect in der vorgescrevenen questien, in den ⟨.VII.⟩ artikel. Ere inwendighe werke unde oefenisse sijn als inwendighe
940 devocie unde | ynnicheit, ghebet unde bidden unde eischen, 123v unde aenbeden inwendelike unde Gode underworpenheit. Er uutwendighe werke unde oefnissen syn aenbeden van buten, knylinge unde nedervallen unde offeren unde desghelijc, to loven Gode van buten unde to danken mit den munde. Unde voert
945 sint werke deser duecht dat se alle werke unde alle dinge, inwendich unde uutwendich, ordineert unde satet to den denste Godes. Unde so een mensche in synen werken, oefnisse, levene unde state dese dinge meer unde meer, vaster unde puerliker unde be-

---

923/924 cfr THOM., II-II, Q. 81 a. 5 ad 1 (T. 9, p. 182, c. 1, 21 – 2, 4); cfr etiam supra (809-811)   923/928 cfr THOM., II-II, Q. 81 a. 6 co. (T. 9, p. 183, c. 2, 4-13), partim paene ad litt.   929/935 cfr THOM., II-II, Q. 81 a. 1 arg. 2 (T. 9, p. 177, c. 1, a. 1, 13-22); a. 1 co. (T. 9, p. 177, c. 2, a. 1, 23-29), infra (1136-1145) etiam allegatum; a. 1 ad 2 (T. 9, p. 178, c. 1, a. 1, 27-33), ubi allegatur AVG., *Ciu. Dei*, 10, 1 (p. 273, 67-75); AVG., *Vera rel.* 55, 113 (p. 259, 122)   936/939 cfr THOM., II-II, Q. 81 a. 7 (T. 9, p. 184, c. 1, 1 – c. 2, 36), in a. 8 (*sic Ms., cfr app. cr.*) materia a Ger. in paraphrasi data non exponitur   944/946 cfr THOM., II-II, Q. 81 a. 5 co. (T. 9, p. 182, c. 1, 8-14)

---

938 .VII.] *sic legendum, cfr app. font.*, .VIII. H   940 bidden] bynnen *praem., sed statim del. ipse* H

redeliker doet, so he meer heft de doghet der religien unde so he vor Gode religioser unde geistliker is. Unde so eens menschen ambocht of graet unde staet meer draghet in unde to desen dingen, sodat ambocht, graet unde staet of leven merer unde religioser is.

Unde in deser doeghet der religien is meer unde properliker symonie ynne unde in eren werken unde oefnissen dan in anderen dogheden, of dan in anderen zedeliken, doghentsamen werken unde oefnissen unde ambochten. Nu spreect sunte Thomas in den | vorgescrevenen boeke, in der .C. unde .LXXXVI. questien, dat "wanneer een name vele dinge tobehoert unde in vele dinge is, so secht men den namen up sulke tijt na der menschen heiten sunderlinge to den dinge de dat hoechliker unde meest hebben dat dat woert beteikent. Also noemt men mit namen der 'starcheit' de doeghet sunderlinge de vasticheit is in den alrezwaersten dinghe, unde so heit men *temperancia* maticheit, de is in den alremeesten lusten." Nochtan is de doghet der starcheit unde der maticheit in vele anderen dingen. Des ghelikes so meent men 'sunte Pauwel' wanneer men spreect int ghemeyne 'de apostel', unde 'Aristotilem' wan men secht 'de meister van naturen', wattan sijn daer vele andere apostele unde philosophen gheweest.

Aldus spreect sunte Thomas: "so heit ⟨anthonomastice⟩" '*religio*' sunderlinge, vulkomen unde hoghe doghet der religien, "unde sunderlinge so heiten religiose lude", van hoecheit unde van vullencomenheit der doghet de *religio* heit in den menschen, "inden dat se sick altomale overgheven unde gheven in den denst Godes. Also spreect sunte Gregorius, *Op den propheten Ezechiel*: 'Dat sijn sulke menschen de nicht in emselven en beholden, mer sijn tunghe, leven unde all tijtlic gued dat se van Gode hebben entfangen, dat offeren se em.' | Unde se werden als in der olden ewe de offerhande de men tomale verbrande, de men *holocaustum* noemt."

957/965 THOM., II-II, Q. 186 a. 1 CO. (T. 10, p. 486, c. 2, a. 1, 17-22) paene ad litt.   970/980 THOM., II-II, Q. 186 a. 1 CO. (T. 10, p. 486, c. 2, a. 1, 22 – p. 487, c. 1, 1) partim paene ad litt.   975/978 GREG. MAG., *Hom. Ez.*, 2, 8 (p. 348, 465-468), allegatum sec. Thom.

---

970 anthonomastice] *sic legendum*, anthonomatice H

Unde dit mach men wal hebben alse vullencomelike buten ghemeynte unde buten cloesteren unde buten cappen als sulke in den cloesteren. Want vulcomen mynne unde vulkomen anhangen an Gode na unser moghelicheit hijr in der ellende, dat is de
985 alremeeste geistlicheit. Unde de mach men hebben unde de vint men manichwerve buten beghevenen cloesteren.

Nochtan hoert daer ummer to een versmaen tijtliker dinge unde tijtliker lust in den lychame unde tijtlikes willen. Unde de dese dree ghevet over – mit willigher armoede dat tijtlike guet, mit
990 willigher reynicheit de meeste unde de vuelste lust des lives, mit willigher underdanicheit den tijtliken willen eens menschen –, de offert tijtlic guet, lijff unde wille den Heren als een *holocaustum*, dat men tomale verbrant, etsij buten orden of bynnen orden.

Unde so woert de doecht vulcomen de *religio* heit unde puere,
995 unde ere werke reyner unde hogher als inwendighe devocie unde inwendich ghebet, dancken unde loven Gode. Unde voert andere uutwendighe unde inwendighe dade unde werke der religien werden puerer unde geistliker, naden dat em de menschen, inwendich unde uutwendich, meer unde meer afdoet, unde meer
1000 verbrant de tijtlike dinge | de verganclic sijn. Also spreket de 27 prophete: *Doestu van dat snode, van den costelen of van den duerbaren, so werstu alse mijn munt.* Unde sunte Augustijn, in den †derden† boke *Van der drevoldicheit*, spreket aldus: "De schoenheit, de alle redelike zelen trect, dan is God, de trecket se
1005 also vele bernender alse reyner is, unde so vele is se reyner als se meer upsteit unde richtet eer meer to geistliken dingen, alse meer sterft den vleisliken dingen." Dit sint sunte Augustinus woerde, de

---

1000/1002 Ier. 15, 19 paene ad litt.

983/985 cfr THOM., II-II, Q. 186 a. 1 co. (T. 10, p. 487, c. 1, 1-5)   987/993 i.e. tria uota monastica, quae Thom. exponit ibid., sc. THOM., II-II, Q. 186 a. 3; 4; 5, quorum summarium a Ger. hic in paraphrasi datum praestat ibid., THOM., II-II, Q. 186 a. 7 co. (T. 10, p. 497, c. 2, a. 7, 4-37), cfr etiam supra, 307-309, infra, 1048-1051, et GER. MAG., *Tract. paup.*, 228-234; *Ep.* 41, 44-47; *Ep.* 45, 12-15; 122-127   1002/1007 AVG., *Trin.* 2, 17 (28) (p. 119, 37-41) sed 1006 'tanto autem ad spiritualia resurgentem' (p. 119, 40) in fonte a Ger. uso homoeoteleutou causa omissa uidentur; error in numero libri exhibitus ('3' pro '2') usum fontis secundarii, sed non inuenti, significare uidetur

---

1003 derden] *sic H*, tweden *legendum*

een advocaet was des gheistes unde nicht des vleschs, alse men nu vele meisters vint advocaet der werlt unde des vleischs; daer uns God voer bescherme.

Unde want een mensche op menighe tijt emselven nicht ghenoech en is in deser doghet der religien to vercrighene unde to oefenen em in eer unde in den denste Godes, so verkeiset een mensche ghesellen unde gheselscop of gheselynnen um te helpen, de ene den anderen in der doghet de *religio* heit, unde eren oefnissen unde werken in den denste Godes. *Och, woe guet unde wo blidelic ist de brodere to wonen in een*, sprect de Psal|me. De hulpe is manichvoldich, gheistlic unde wunderlike, gotlike, nutte, de ene den anderen to entstekene, to lerene, to berispene, to waerne, to troestene, to verblidene mit levene, mit woerden unde mit herten. Unde de gheselscop is so blide togader to biddene of um een ding off de ene vor den anderen unde des ghelikes, togader to levene unde danckene Gode, wanneer se tosamene sijn of wan de ene van den anderen is, unde eens to voelen, eens to smakene unde eens to willen in Gode. Wo blidelic unde geistlic sijn alle dese dinge. Dese geselscop, dese bruderscap of zusterscap, dese ghemeynscap, dese vrentscap, dese *communicatio* unde hulpscap, dese levene, dese state, dese ambochte, dese oefenisse, dat sijn geistlike dinge, daer en twivelt gheen gherecht mensche inne. Want als Antisiodorensis sprect: "De Hilghe Geist wert in der broderscap ghegeven". Unde Cristus sprac: *Waer uwer twe off dree in mynen namen vergadert, daer byn ic inmiddes u.*

Wo vullencomelike off wo unvullencomelike dat men de doghet der religien in desen oefent, des de werke unde doghet gherechte werke sijn der religien unde rechte doecht in mynnen, so sijn de ghesellicheden unde †der† broederlicheden gheistlic. Want van den gheiste en wert nicht gheboren dan geist, unde gheist unde geist vergadert in den geiste en es nicht dan geist, unde dat vermeert unde | puert alle geistlicheit. Hijrum ist open-

---

1016/1017 Ps. 132, 1   1031/1033 Matth. 18, 20

1030/1031 Gvil. Alt., *Summa* 3, 49, 2, 4 (T. 3.2, p. 960, 179-180) paene ad litt.

1037 der] H, de *legendum*

baer dat dese dinge willen te copen off vercopen, dat is opene symonie, ten mynsten int herte, al en weer oec dat nicht verboden in der kerken. Want dit sijn na den gherichte Godes na der rechter doghet religiose, geistlike gheselscap of bruderscap unde
1045 religiose ghemeynscap of religiose levene, of religiose lude of oefenissen. Se sijn in state der vulkomener religioser menschen na der orden, off van buten den state unde gheselscope unde broderscape. De dan vullencomeliker Gode anhangen unde meer versmaen de tijtlike dinge, in armoede, in reynicheit unde in un-
1050 derdanicheit, de heiten vor den gerichte Godes ⟨antonomastice⟩, dat is hoechliker, religiose lude.

Unde want men bet suct overgheven der tijtliker dinge, alse overgheven gudes lives unde willen, dan dat tokeren van bynnen ten geiste, so ist dat men na menschliken seyne suct meer na den
1055 uutwendighen overgheven dan na den inwendigen | tokeren, 125r in den dat de menschen van buten merken unde to nemene pleghen de vulcomenheit der doechde der religien of erer bruderscop off zusterscop.

Nochtan ist moghelic dat een mensche de buten gheselscap
1060 were off de proper guet unde wijf hadde, purliker unde vulcomeliker mit herten weren ghesceyden van tijtliken gude unde tijtliker lust unde van sijns selves willen dan sulke de in der ghemeynte weer off in der geselscap, de alle dese uutwendighen dinge overghegeven hadde, off ⟨dan⟩ sulk de by emselven van
1065 buten dese dinge ⟨overghegeven⟩ hadde. Unde de mensche de se meer van bynnen overghegeven hadde, de weer vulcomenre religioser mensche na den gerichte Gods, mer van buten na den gerichte der kerken unde na erer uutwendighen schoenheit so en heit dat gheen religiose mensche. Noch bruderscop noch gesel-
1070 scap en heiten hoechlike religiose menschen na der kerken dat deghene de dese anghenomen hebben, dat is: armode weder proper guet, kuescheit unde underdanicheit.

1048/1051 cfr supra, 987-993, ubi Ger. in paraphrasi citat THOM., II-II, Q. 186 a. 7 co. (T. 10, p. 497, c. 2, a. 7, 4-37)   1071/1072 i.e. tria uota monastica, cfr e.g. THOM., II-II, Q. 186 a. 7 co. (T. 10, p. 497, c. 2, a. 7, 4-37), supra, 987-993, etiam allegatum

---

1050 anthonomastice] *sic legendum*, anthonomatice H   1064 dan] *sic legendum*, dat H   1065 overghegeven] *sic emend. sec.* 1064; 1066 overghegeven *De Vreese*, overgheven *hic falso* H

Unde de kerke heit de allene religiose menschen na eren gerichte de to deser vullencomenheit em verbinden mit ener solempniteet, dat is mit hoecheit, vor den luden unde in underdanicheit na ener regulen. Nochtan ist moghelic dat een gheselscap weer de dat under em bet holden vor Gode dan bi tyden de lude doen van ghesette | unde van state, van buten, in cloesteren, als men seit in den valle manigher religioser menschen unde in valle der cloesteren. Vele lude moghen vulcomen wesen de nicht en sijn van buten in der kerken in den staten der vulcomenheit, alse leert Thomas in den vorgescrevenen boke, in der .c. unde .LXXXIIII. questien, in den .IIII. artikel, als Cristus sprect, in den †.XXXI.† capitel in *Matheo*, van den vader, de synen twen zoenen sprac, dat se *gaen solden in synen wijngarden*. De ene, ⟨de⟩ segde dat he daerin gaen wolde, *de en genc daer nicht in*. Unde de ander, de sprac dat he daer nicht in gaen en wolde, *de genc daerin*. Aldus en heit de kerke ghene religiose menschen proper na der uutwendigher kerken to spreken dan de armode, reynicheit unde gehorsamheit ghelovet hebbet na ener geproveden regulen. Also spreket Thomas unde de lerer gemeynlike van religiosen menschen.

Unde also sprect dat geistlike recht properlike van religiosen menschen. Unde also en is de Derde Orde | of ander orde de proper guet hebben of hiwelic ghene religio mer na een deel: In alsovele, sprect he, syn se religio alse se deilachtich sijn unde hebben wat dinge de tobehoren den state der religioser menschen. Unde desghelijcs mach men voert secghen van baghinenstate, inden dat se ⟨de⟩ pawes henget. Mer de en hebbet so vele gelics nicht na der kerken verbunde alse de Derde Orde uutwendelike, want se ghene professie en doen unde nicht gheproevet en sijn van der kerken. Mer dat se de kerke henget, wattan hebbe

---

1083/1087 cfr Matth. 21, 28-31, allegatum sec. THOM., in app. font. citatum

---

1073/1092 cfr THOM., II-II, Q. 184 a. 4 co. (T. 10, p. 455, c. 2, a. 4, 15-32)
1095/1098 cfr IOH. ANDR., *Glos. ord. in Clem.*, super *Clem.* 3.11.1, in expositione casus (c. II, 1169, 30) (c. 216 (p. 549), 14-36); comm. sup. 'obedientiam' (c. II, 1169, 31) (c. 216-217 (p. 549-550), gl. u), supra, 43-47, etiam allegatum

---

1083 .XXXI.] *sic* H, .XXI. *legendum sec. Matth.*   1085, 1099 de] *suppl. De Vreese sec. 1086* de, *om.* H

se dicwile of moeghen heb⟨be⟩n meer geistlicheit in em unde under em na den gherichte Godes in gherechter broderscap off zusterscap dan manighe van der Derden Orden. Unde oec underwilen sijn se armer unde in ers willen meer uutghegaen vor Gode dan sulke vervallene religiose menschen in cloesteren. Want als *Horalogium* [in] *der ewighen wijsheit* sprect: "Daer vint men den wundere veel in vele cloesteren, daer se van buten in cappen unde in uutwendighen dingen schinen menschen te wesen unde draghen geistlike teikene, de van bynnen lewen unde beren unde beisten sijn".

Unde daerbi yst vor der kerken opene symonie inganc in cloesteren to kopen of oec inganc in den Derden Orden. Unde oec ist symonie in herte inganc te copene in enich ander gheselscap of broderscap daer gude lude na der doecht de religio heit vor Gode tegader leven. Men moet ghene nyge vulcomen religio, dat is ghene nye regulen maken sunder orlof des pawes. Mer twe, dree of veir of meer tegader te leven na | enigher gheproveden regulen of een deel derna, of na der regulen aller regulen, dat is na den hilghen gebenediden ewangelie, dat en is nicht verboden na mynen duncken. Unde weert dat lude so leveden in broderliker geselscap na den ewangelie in der doecht de religio heit, des de pawes nicht en wiste, of de de pawes wiste unde hengede, of de he wiste unde confirmerde, daer iemant in te nemen um gelt, dat is opene symonie vor Gode in der consciencie. Dese ghemeynscap is geistlic, unde menichwerve geistlic dan sullick de na regulen leven solden unde niet en leven na der regulen, der nu vele sijn.

Mijn | ghelove is dat de kerke richten solde vor symonie, quemet to gerichte in den staten de se gheprovet unde confirmert hevet, als in de inganghe der Derden Orden. Mer wat se doen solden van buten int gerichte van ingaen in baghijnscap, dat en

---

1107/1112 cfr Svso, *Hor.* 1, 5 (p. 408, 21-26); textu circiter a. 1350-1400 in uulgari Brabantina lingua conuerso (p. 37, 13-23 ed. van de Wijnpersse) Ger. usus non est, quia uocabula latina 'monstruosis animalibus' (p. 408, 24-25) ibi in 'leeleken zeebeesten' (p. 37, 19) translata sunt, Ger. autem in paraphrasi (1111-1112) 'lewen unde beren unde beisten' scribit

---

1103 hebben] *scripsi,* hebn H   1108 in] *sic* H, *sed delendum censeo*
1117 religio] maket *add., sed statim del.* H

wil ic nicht spreken, nochtan dat se in der consciencie symonie
doen. Dat dunket my openbaer wesen.

Unde um dit woert religio te verstaen waert affkomet, mach men seyn uut Ysidorum, *Ethimologiarum*, unde oec uut sunte ⟨Augustijn⟩, in den derden capitel des teynden bokes der *Stat Godes*, unde in den lesten capitel van der *Waren religien*, unde als Thomas spreket in *Secunda secunde*, dat religio off religiose lude heiten van *religere* off *religare* of *relegere*, dat is inden dat yewereen al den dach wederleset unde overleset unde kuset de dinge de Gode behaghelic sijn unde wentelt de in synen herten, off yewer dat he weder verkeset dat he versumet unde verloren hevet, of yewer dat he weder of nyes off meer em verbynt. Al dese interpretacien gaen up alle de teikenisse int ghemeyne, want uut der interpretacien en komet gheen underscheit der dinge. Men sal de namen ten dingen trecken, unde niet de dinge to den namen; also spreket dat werlike recht. Mer dat boec van Colen wil de religien scheiden unde de dinge by den namen. Nochtan komet al uut der doecht de religio heit, als vorscreven is, unde hebben al enen oersprung in den namen, also als alle maneren van religiosen menschen uut ener doghet oersprunclike comen, unde daerbi is *religio* een *nomen anologum, et sic est finis huius*.

1136/1145 cfr THOM., II-II, Q. 81 a. 1 co (T. 9, p. 177, c. 2, a. 1, 16-29), ubi allegat ISID., *Etym.*, 10, 234 (1140/1143); AVG., *Ciu. Dei* 10, 3 (p. 275, 27-28) (1144/1145); *Vera rel.* 55, 113 (p. 259, 122) (1145), supra (929-935) etiam allegatum

---

1138 Augustijn] *sic legendum*, Augustijns H

TRACTATVS DE SIMONIACA RECEPTIONE SORORVM
IN CONVENTIBVS TERTII ORDINIS,
VVLGARI LINGVA
'LEERINGHE ENDE ONDERSCHEIT
VAN DER SONDEN DER SYMONIEN' NVNCVPATVS

cura et studio Marinus VAN DEN BERG

adhibita editione a Hildo VAN ENGEN prelo data

fontes collegit

Rijcklof HOFMAN

CONSPECTVS SIGLORVM

A   ANTWERPEN, FelixArchief Antwerpen, Fonds kerkelijke en caritatieve instellingen, inv. nr. 468, a. 1531, scr. Peter Jansz.

Hunc codicem in plagulis phototypice expressis contulimus.

TRACTATVS DE SIMONIACA RECEPTIONE SORORVM IN CONVENTIBVS TERTII ORDINIS, VVLGARI LINGVA 'LEERINGHE ENDE ONDERSCHEIT VAN DER SONDEN DER SYMONIEN' NVNCVPATVS

Gheminde in Christo Jhesu, Onsen Lieven Heere, want wy u na der cleynheit ons verstants ende na onsen besten vermoghen ghepijnt hebben te leerne ende te onderwijsen, hoe dat men die heilige Oerdene van der Derder Regulen sinte Francisci van der
5 Penitencien | sculdich es te houdene ende die forme ofte maniere des levens te volghene ende den Heere Jhesum Christum met ynnicheiden te dienen om salicheit uwer zielen te verwerven, want anders en soude ic u niet raden dat ghij die regule aennemen soudet oft ontfanghen, oft uselven met eeneghen beloften daertoe
10 soudet verbinden, als ghi die niet en meynde te houdene in der waerheit, gheliken alst van rechte behoert, etcetera, alsoe voren gheseit es.

Ende want wy nu ghehoert hebben, hoe dat ghi u ontgaende sijt in die onduechdelike sonde der symonien mits der hatelikere
15 ende verdoemeliker ghewoenten die ghi onder u hebt, indien dat ghi voerwaerden ende composicien ende oec giften nemet oft ontfanct van denghenen die ghi totter oerdenen in uwen husen ende vergaderingen ontfanghen wilt, – dat welke gheheellijck ende altemale es teghen | God ende teghens alle geestelike rech-
20 ten ende oeck mede contrarie allen goeden ghewoenten, institucien ende statuten der heiligher kerken, dat men van yemande giften sal nemen oft ghelt ontfangen, oft enich compact maken metten ghenen die | hemselven begheert te geven tot eeneghen staet van oerdenen oft religien, ende in een geestelike plaetse
25 Gode devoteliken wil dienen ende sijn leven offeren in peniten-

---

1/7; 11/12 cfr GER. MAG., *Merckelijc onderwijs*, praesertim 7-177 (p. 131 – 135)   11/12 scriba Peter Jansz uel scriba exemplaris hic textum in exemplari traditum abbreuiasse uidetur

---

9 ontfanghen] sult *add., sed postea del. ipse P[etrus Jansz]*

cien voer sijn sonden — hieromme, mijn alreliefste, want ic u zielen begheere te behouden ende te verlossen uuten saicke deser quader ghewoenten, soe willic u daeraf een onderwijs doen uuter heiliger scrifturen, opdat ghi moget weten ende bekennen den val
30 ofte den behendighen saick deser anxsteliker sonden der symonien, opdat ghij se dan alsoe moghet vlyen ende scuwen. Want dat sult ghi weten, dat negheen geestelike personen eeneghe compactten oft voerwaerden en moghen maken metten ghenen die sij in horen gheselscappe ontfanghen willen.
35 Ende daeromme, want die Derde Regule des saligen vaders sinte Francisci van der Penitencien ghenoemt een gheapprobeerde regule es ende van veel overste bisscoppen es gheconfirmeert ende vasteghemaect. Ende na die sentencie veelre doctoren soe eest een vaste redene dat die personen deser voerseider
40 oerdenen, beide bruederen ende susteren, die de forme ende maniere van desen leven hou|den, sijn gheestelike personen, *19ra* hem verblijdende van den geesteliken privilegien, bysondere ende oeck int ghemeyne.

Ende want ghi dan alle geestelike personen sijt, zoe eest dat ic
45 u van rechter caritaten gherne soude leeren van deser hateliker beesten der symonien te wachten, ende bidde u van den binnensten mijns herten, dat ghi ymmers gheen compacten ofte voerwaerden met yemande maken en wilt die ghi in uwen gheselscappe by u ontfanghen wilt. Ende opdat ghi dese dinghen te
50 claerlikere verstaen moghet, soe sal ic u segghen die vraghe die tot my daeraf es ghedaen, | dats oft symonie es een stede oft een *139* provende te coepen in een beghinenconvent. Daertoe dat ic aldus antwoerde ende segghe: eest dat aen dier plaetse oft stede, oft aen die provende die men copet, eenich geestelijc dinck aen-
55 hanget ende ghecnopet es, oft eest dat die persoen, indien dat hij die stede ofte die plaetse ghecrighet ende die provende dan oeck

---

35/38 cfr *Reg. ord. tert.* (p. 90-95), a. 1289 a Nicolao .IV. papa approbata 38/43 cfr infra, 105-112, ubi allegantur IOH. ANDR., *Glos. ord. in Clem.*, super 3.11.1, comm. in expositione casus (c. II, 1169, 30) (c. 216 (p. 549), exp. cas., l. 14-36); comm. sup. 'obedientiam' (c. II, 1169, 31) (c. 216-217 (p. 549-550), gl. u), etiam *Reg. ord. tert.*, praesertim c. 8; 13 (p. 92; 93) 51/73 GER. MAG., *Simonia beg.*, 1-16 paene ad litt. 51/96 cfr GER. MAG., *Stat.*, 81-83 53/58 cfr *Decret.*, X 5.3.8 (c. II, 750, 45 — 751, 11, praesertim 750, 48-49; 751, 3-6)

---

44 dan] *marg. suppl.* P   56 oeck] *marg. suppl.* P

medeghecrighet ende enich geestelijc dinck daerna volghet, zoe isset in der waerheit symonie, want, alsoe als in den geesteliken rechte ghescreven staet: van tween dinghen die alsoe tega-
60 dere|hangen, oft die hem soe vervolghen van denwelken dat eene sonder dat ander niet en comt ofte niet vercreghen en mach worden, ende wie dat eene copet, hy heet oeck dat ander mede te copen, alsoe als in dat *Decreet* ghescreven staet, ⟨.I., q. .III., c.⟩ *Saluator cum cordanciis*, ende oeck mede in veel anderen ste-
65 den der heiligher scrifturen van geesteliken rechten. Ende elc mensche mach dat in sijn selves consiencie gevoelen ende verstaen dat het waerachtich es. Ende daeromme, soe wie dat yetswat van aldusghedanen dinghen ghelovet oft eneghe voerwaerde maket yetswat in te bringhen, hetsij van eenre summen ghelts oft
70 anders dat hy heeft, ghelovet in te bringhen, dat es al tesamen symonia, want men in desen dinghen al niet gheven noch geloven en sal, oft dat men om enich tijtelijck goet te gheven oft gheloven in te bringhene yemande ontfanghen sal.

Hoert nu voert, alderliefste in Christo, wat men antwoert totter
75 vraghen die daer noch gevraghet wort, aldus: oft symonie es gelt te gheven, "omdat een men|sche ontfanghen ende aenghenomen wort in eenen hospitale ofte gasthuse om den armen te dienen, oft dat hy aenghenomen wort in een malaetschhuys oft in een ander godshuys". Daerop soe antwoerdet aldus Wilhelmus in
80 *Glosa Raymundi* ende oeck Johannes | in *Summa confessorum*, ende spreken dat in aldusdaneghen ghevalle ende hoers ghelike: "Eest dat enich mensche oft yemant die aldus in deser wijsen ont-

---

58/64 cfr Ger. Mag., *Locat.*, 13   cfr Grat., *Decr.*, C.1 q.3 c.8 (c. I, 413-415), ubi allegatur epistula Vrbani II (*JL* 5743 (4308), T. 1, p. 697), prius prelo data a Mansi, *Sacrorum conciliorum*, T. 20, c. 660-663, reiterata in *PL*, 151, c. 529C-533B   74/89 Ger. Mag., *Simonia beg.*, 17-32 paene ad litt. cfr Ioh. Frib., *Summa Conf.*, L. 1 t. 1 q. 75 (f. 13v, c. 1, 47 – c. 2, 1), qui allegat Gvil. Rhed., *App. ad Sum. Raym.*, L. 1 t. 1 § 26, comm. sup. 'mancipatus' (ed. 1603, p. 27, c. 2, 42-59) sed 77 in eenen hospitale ofte gasthuse om den armen te dienen *Ger.*, ad seruiendum pauperibus in hospitale *Ioh.*, colon *hoc hic om. Guilh.*; 82/83 die aldus in deser wijsen ontfanghen wort *Ger.*, in tali receptione *Ioh. Frib.*, quando recipitur ad hospitale uel leprosariam uel aliquid tale *Guilh.*; 86 sal dienen *Ger.*, seruiat *Ioh.*, uiuat *Guilh.*

---

63 .I., q. .III., c.] *scripsi sec. Simonia beg.*, 10, Questione capittulo tercio *P*
64 cordanciis] *sic cod.*, concordanciis *legendum, sicut ex Simonia beg.*, 11, *patet*

fanghen wort ende dan daermede es vercrigende eenich geestelijck recht, beloeft hy yet oft ghevet hi yet, voerwaer soe eest symonia. Mer eest dat hy negheen geestelijck recht en vercrighet, dan dat hi alleene sal dienen in die cokene oft anders waer daer men hem settet, zoe en eest negheen symonie." Siet, dit sijn deser voerseider meesteren woerden ende oeck veel ander leeraren die daermede op acccoerderende sijn. Daeromme, alreliefste, wilt dit wel merken ende verstaen.

Eest dan symonie dat men in aldusghedanen leekenleven ende weerliken staet gelt ghevet oft gheloeft, soe wanneer daer eenich gees⟨t⟩lijc dinck aenhanghet ende toeghevoecht wort, hoe soe | eest dan van den leven dergheenre die altemale tot Gode gheset worden ende met eenen gheesteliken schine gheheel van der werelt afghescheiden sijn.

Voert meer, zoe merct ende besiet oft aen u convent oft aen die stede in den convente eeneghe andere gheestelike dinghen gebonden sijn oft hem daerin vervolgen, daerna soe eest meerdere of minre symonia. Ende eest dat die Derde Regule van der Penitencien des salighen vaders sinte Francisci daer aenhanghet ende dat elck die daerin comt, wesen moet van der Derder Regulen, soe eest openbaer symonie yet te gheven oft te overdraghen van eenegher summen van ghelde ende van in te bringhene datselve dat een mensche hevet. Want dese heilige Oerden van der Derder Regulen sinte Francisci voerghenoemt es een forme ende een maniere eens godliken levens ende hevet een ghelikenisse metter geestelijcheit oft religioene, ende die heilige kerke ontfaet se ende approbeert se, alsoe als Johannes Andree spreket in dat boeck *Clementine*, ende oeck die heilige man sinte Thomaes in *Secunda | secunde* ende meer ander leeraren die dat proberen ende volghen waer te | wesene.

89/112 GER. MAG., *Simonia beg.*, 33-48 paene ad litt.   105/110 cfr IOH. ANDR., *Glos. ord. in Clem.*, super 3.II.1, comm. in expositione casus (c. II, 1169, 30) (c. 216 (p. 549), exp. cas., l. 14-36); comm. sup. 'obedientiam' (c. II, 1169, 31) (c. 216-217 (p. 549-550), gl. u)   105/111 locus dictis Gerardi optime conueniens uidetur THOM., II-II, Q. 188 a. 6 co.; ad 3 (T. 10, p. 529, c. 2)

---

88 voerseider] *marg. suppl.* P   93 geestlijc] *scripsi*, geeslijc P

TRACTATVS DE SIMONIACA RECEPTIONE SORORVM 373

Ende daeromme, waert dat die Derde Oerden sinte ⟨Francisci⟩ voerseit daeraen cleefde oft aenhinghe, indien dat een men-
115 sche in een van den conventen deser oordenen quame om brueder oft sustere te sine ende alsoedaneghe symonie dede, want sij religiose personen sijn overmits privilegien, soe dunct my ende ghevoele dat [dat] ⟨alsodaneghe⟩ menschen, die aldus symonie ghedaen hadde, hoerder waer vele oft luttele oft altemale, dat sij
120 dieselve stede oft plaetse souden laten ende overgheven ende nemen in penitencien een ander, herder oft strengher oerden ane oft een ander herder maniere van leven vore, ghelijck als spreken die decretalen ende die geestelike rechten van den religiosen oft geestelike personen, Extra, *De symonia,* in den capittele *Quo-*
125 *niam symoniacum, Dilicto, cum Constitutus,* ende oeck desgeliken sinte Thomaes van Aquinen ende int ghemeyne die ander leeraren der heiliger kerken.

Ende want der beghinen ofte der susteren intencie ende meyninghe altijt ghedraghet tot geestelijcheiden, zoe sijn sij oeck
130 mede voer Gode geestelijck. Ende | daeromme soe vallen sij in 20rb deser sonden der symonien. Mer die heilighe kerke en veroerdeelt dese niet. Ende daerby zoe hope ic dat sij mogen bliven in horen, eest sake dat sij hem laten absolveren ende met hem doen dispenseren van den bisscoppen, alsoe verre als hem dunct dat
135 die plaetse hem nutte ende bequame es tot hoerder salicheit. Op alsoe dat die Derde Ordene sinte Francisci daer niet mede aen en hanghet, ende nemen oft ontfanghen penitencie van deser hateliker sonden der symonien in der consiencien ende in den danck, dit hope ick. Mer ick en wil dat niet segghen voer waer oft voer
140 zekere te wesen, dat daermede oft daeraen ghenoech soude ghedaen wesen | voer Gode, noch ic en derre oeck dit niet segghen 142 als voer dat beste te wesen ende voer den naesten wech. Die

---

113/127 Ger. Mag., *Simonia beg.,* 49-57 paene ad litt. cfr *Decret.,* X 5.3.40; 5.3.30; 5.3.38 (c. II, 765, 47-66, praesertim l. 47-54; 759, 39-57, praesertim l. 54-57; 765, 15-20) cfr Thom., II-II, Q. 100 a. 6 ad 5 (T. 9, p. 365, c. 1, 19-26) **128/132** cfr Ger. Mag., *Simonia beg.,* 99-113 **131/132** cfr Ger. Mag., *Simonia beg.,* 160-166; *Locat.,* 608-613; 654-660; 699-705 **132/156** Ger. Mag., *Simonia beg.,* 110-129 paene ad litt.

113/114 Francisci *scripsi,* Franciscus P 118 dat²] *delendum censeo* alsodaneghe] *sic emend. van Engen,* also dageghe P 122 maniere] *emend. van Engen,* lemaniere P 132 ic] *marg. suppl.* P

bisscoppen, sy en moghen nyemande absolveren opter eerden, tensij dat hem ierst berouwe dat sijt gedaen hebben, ende sij en
145 hebben oeck eenen ganssen wille in hem dat niet meer te doene, oft anders soe en eest gheen penitencie, noch gheenen rouwe, noch gheen voldoen der | sonden voer Gode. 20va

Ende die penitencie ende dat voldoen es nochtan zeer van noode voer den almoghenden God in aldusghedanegher sonden
150 van symonien die de kerke niet en veroerdeelt ende die alleen staet in der consiencien ende in den dancke, want gheliken dat daer staet ghescreven in den laetsten capittele van der symonien in dat vijfste boeck van den *Decretale* ende es aldus sprekende. Voer Gode soe es die symonie in der herten ofte in der consien-
155 cien ghelijc even quaet, alsoft sij van buten in den werken volbracht ware, welke woerden zeer te ontsiene ende te vreesen sijn, als zi te rechte aenghesien worden.

Mer nu willen sij hem bedecken ofte ontsculdigen met ander lieden sonden, als metten monnicken ende metten nonnen, die-
160 welke dat gelt nemen, wanneer sy yemande sullen ontfanghen oft aennemen als van eenre overdraghender summen oft te overdraghene datselve te nemen dat die personen hebben dat sij weten, oft sij weten se by te bringhen dieghene die sij weten oft wel kennen dat rijke sijn. Dit es seker in der waerheit rechte symo-
165 nie, | alsoe als dat in den decreete ofte *Decretale* ghescreven staet. 20vb
Ende oeck die vijfde paeus Urbanus die heeft se alle te banne ghedaen van sijnre autoriteyt ende pauslikere macht, die yet gheven of nemen in moncken- oft in nonnencloesteren, hetzi gelt of cleynoden oft yetswat met voerwaerden oft sonder voerwaerden
170 om der ghewoenten wille ontfanghen soe, wanneer dat men die personen aennemet, van welker bullen der excomunicacien dat wy copie by | ons hebben. 143

148/153 cfr *Decret.*, X 5.3.46 (c. II, 767, 41-50, praesertim l. 48-50) **158/172** Ger. Mag., *Simonia beg.*, 517-526 paene ad litt. **159/165** cfr *Extrauag. comm.* 5.1.1 (c. II, 1287, 40-52), infra cum nomine Papae Vrbani allegatum, praesertim clausula a praepositione 'cum' incipienti (ibid., 1287, 45-52)
166/172 cfr *Extrauag. comm.* 5.1.1 (c. II, 1287-1288, praesertim 1287, 58 – 1288, 47)

---

164 rechte] *marg. inf. suppl.* P

TRACTATVS DE SIMONIACA RECEPTIONE SORORVM 375

Mer nu daer ⟨sijn⟩ summeghe leeraren die segghen willen oft een cloestere niet meer personen ghevoeden en conste van mon-
175 cken oft van nonnen dan sij hadden, ende dat daer een goet ende vaerdich persoen toequame om God te dienen, den welken die sij oeck gherne ontfangen ende aennemen souden, mochten sij hem ghevoeden van den gemeynen goede sonder hindere oft last van den cloestere, dat sij dan met hem brachten, dat zi hadden
180 oft daer sij van leven mochten, want sij se sonder swaren last des convents ende sonder hindere niet ghevoeden en connen, opdat dat convent alsoe onghelast daervan bleve. Dit duncket den | 21ra summeghen dat sij dit wel moghen overdraghen tevoren. Ende sulke andere spreken hierteghens ende segghen dat het niet se-
185 kere en es alsoe te doene, want onder desen schijn oft verwe der armoeden soe soude wel veel symonien ghedaen worden oft gheschien onder moncken ende nonnen, ende namelijc in den Duytschen lande, daer die armoede meer gheverwet es ende gheen stat en hevet, ende daer sij wel meer personen voeden moghen
190 oft sij se innemen wouden al en brachten sij niet.

Ende bovenal soe en eest oeck gheen ghelike verwe met personen; het sijn susteren oft andere, etcetera, die hoer broot moghen winnen ende allen arbeit oft swaerheit lijden. Daeromme weghen te loepen ende broot te bidden waer beter te doene
195 dan volboert of consent te gheven tot alsulken quaden dinghen ghelijc dat voerscreven es, alsoe als elc mensche in sijn selves consiencie lesen ende vinden mach. Ende al dede alle die werelt aldusdanege dinghen weder die gherechticheit, dat en waer

---

173/183 GER. MAG., *Simonia beg.*, 527-533 paene ad litt.   cfr IOH. FRIB., *Summa Conf.*, L. 1 t. 1 q. 49 (f. IIV, c. 1, 8 – c. 2, 15), ubi citat RAYM., *Summa de paen.*, L. 1 t. 1 § 22 (c. 299-300 ed. Ochoa; ed. 1603, p. 23, c. 2, 22 – p. 24, c. 1, 22) et GVIL. RHED., *App. ad Sum. Raym.*, L. 1 t. 1 § 22, comm. sup. 'offerat se' (ed. 1603, p. 23, gl. x), et in extenso allegat THOM., II-II, Q. 100 a. 3 ad 4 (T. 9, p. 359, c. 2, 30-46)   **183/190** GER. MAG., *Simonia beg.*, 534-540 paene ad litt.   **183/185** cfr *Decret.*, X 5.3.40 (c. II, 765, 47-66, praesertim l. 47-49); BERN. PARM., *Glos. ord. in Decret.*, super X 5.3.40, comm. sup. 'paupertatis' (c. II, 765, 48-49) (c. 1641-1642 (p. 35), gl. c); INNOC., *Comm. Decret.*, super X 5.3.34, comm. sup. 'consentiant' (c. II, 763, 35) (ed. 1570, p. 599, c. 1, 21-24, uide etiam 24-27, a Ioh. non allegatum), locos etiam a IOH. FRIB., *Summa Conf.*, L. 1 t. 1 q. 49 (f. IIV, c. 1, 38-60) allegatos   **192/215** GER. MAG., *Simonia beg.*, 548-568 paene ad litt.

---

173 sijn] *suppleui, om.* P

nochtan gheen bescudden voer ons te doene teghens godlike
ende naturelike redenen, waeromme datter gheenen anderen |
raet en es dan dese dingen temale af te snyden ende berouwenisse daeraf te hebben ende een ghewarich vast opset te nemen
dat niet meer te doene.

Ende waren met u eeneghe verkeerde menschen die dit niet
doen en wouden, soe moechdij uselven purgeren ende suveren
met uwen consente dat | altoes te wederspreken, wanneer dat
men met yemande voerwaerden maken wille van eenre summen
te gheven oft van in te bringhen dat sij hebben, ende nummermeer soe en ghevet yemant stede of plaetse of eneghe provende
om ghelts wille, noch en siet gheen goet ane noch dat bloet, maer
gheeft se denghenen die se best behoeft ende dier werdich es van
duechden ende bequamelijcste es totter dienste Gods. Ende hoedet uwe herte dattet niet en consentere in aldusdaneghen dingen
als hiervoren gheseit sijn, noch dat ghi in woerden oft in werken
gheensins daerteghens en doet, wilt ghi u ziele behouden.

Ende ick, meester Gheeraert de Grote, neme hier die ewighe
waerheit te ghetughe dat ic in desen dinghen die ic geseit hebbe
van der sonden der symonien, na mynen besten gevoelen die
waerheit daeraf gesproken hebbe | sonder eeneghe neyghinghe
tot u ofte oeck tegens u, mer recht alsoft ick tehant sterven soude
ende alsof my die ziele rechtevoert van den lichame soude verscheiden ende den Oversten Rechter daeraf redene soude moeten gheven.

EPISTOLA (27) DE PROPRIETATE MONACHORVM AD QVENDAM PROFESSVM

CONSPECTVS SIGLORVM

codex principalis

L   Liège, Bibliothèque de l'Université, 229 (c), a. 1451

codices

W   Hannover, Niedersächsische Landesbibliothek, XIII 859, s. XVb (c. a. 1440)

Familia κ

D   Darmstadt, Hessische Landes- und Hochschulbibliothek, 2276, c. a. 1500
B   Basel, Universitätsbibliothek, A X 92, s. XVa
Ma1 = *M4*   Mainz, Stadtbibliothek, I 349, s. XIVd

Hos codices in plagulis phototypice expressis contulimus

EPISTOLA (27) DE PROPRIETATE MONACHORVM AD QVENDAM PROFESSVM

Frater et socie in Christo Ihesu predilecte, recepi litteras uestras in mense decembri. Valde est secundum cor meum quod estis professus. Sciendum quod, ubicumque homo in mundo fuerit, impedimenta habebit, quedam uel a bono retrahencia uel impediencia bonum uel diminuencia bonum inuenit. Non est locus in terris cui temptaciones non sunt coniuncte. Non est locus siue religio qui uel que permittit hominem sine pugna militare et uiuere. Numquid tota *uita hominis milicia est super terram*? Numquid sicut temptator spiritus, ita et temptaciones et temptatorum comites, scilicet mali homines, ubique sunt?

Assumite ergo uobis *gladium, scutum et bellum*, et non moueat uos quod aliqui habent propria. Non uos coinquinat aliorum malum, cui nec consentitis, nec facere proponitis. Ymmo, tanto magis uobis erit premium quod aliis propria habentibus uos *immundum ne tetigeritis.* | Quid ad uos quod alii habeant propria? Hoc non ledit uos nec uobis fit iniuria, nec uestrum interest iudicare proprietarium, quia non estis speculator seu superius positus ad

---

8 Iob 7, 1   11 Ps. 75 (76), 4, cfr Eph. 6, 16-17   14/15 II Cor. 6, 17

---

15 cfr GER. MAG., *Ep.* 15, 13-14   eodem loco biblico ut themate Ger. in *Focar.* utitur, cfr GER. MAG., *Focar.* (299, 11-12) et conclusiones plurimorum dictorum in hoc sermone   15/17 infra, 22-28, Ger. disertius eandem rem disputat   17/18 cfr GER. MAG., *Ep.* 41, 230-231

Tit. Item epistola ad quendam professum *inc. in W*, Epistola magistri Gerardi Groet ad fratrem Mathiam de Tyla *inc. in R*, Epistola magistri Gerardi Groett *tit. in D, tit. om. LB Mai*   1 Frater – predilecte] *om. Mai*   Christo] in Christo *iterum scr. B*   1/3 Frater – professus] *om. W*   1/2 uestras – decembri] insuper *Mai*   2 est] *om. D*   meum cor *tr. Mai*   estis] est *sic D*   5 minuencia *W*   6/7 temptaciones – religio] *om. Mai¹, marg. suppl. Mai²*   7 que] qua *Mai*   promittit *B*   11 Assumite] de proprietate *marg. ut subtit. scr. L³*   et non] nec *D*   12 habeant *DB Mai*   12/13 malum aliorum *tr. L*   13 nec¹] non *D*   14 propria] bona *Mai*   habent *Mai*   15 ne] non *B Mai*   16 interest] est *W*   17 estis] est *sic D*   ad] *om. Mai*

corrigendum. Si ipsi melius uestiantur quam uos, propter hoc non magis frigus patimini; si melius comederint, propter hoc non magis esuritis, et sic de aliis. Quale ergo nocumentum eorum habundancia? Certe nullum, dummodo uos sine proprietate manseritis. | 120

Et illos qui habent propria non debetis contempnere, nec acriter uel dure increpare uel in eos inuehere, quia non interest uestra, nisi cum magno moderamine et gemitu et beniuolencia possitis illis aliquando dicere quos crederetis posse emendare, et non aliis, quia fraterna correpcio locum non habet ubi emendacio non speratur. Habeatis ergo pro regula ut numquam moneatis aliquem proprietarium ut derelinquat propria, nisi prius precogitaueritis in cubiculo uestro modum et formam uerborum quibus uelitis eum informare, et nisi premissa oracione, quia solus Deus conuertit corda hominum. "Frustra sonus ad aurem uenit nisi Deus in corde loquatur". Et scire debetis quod ille moniciones improuise, non precogitate ut plurimum secundum carnem sunt et non meritorie, ymmo, aliquando et ut plurimum cum impetu uel aliqua mentis perturbacione, uel saltem non in pace.

Item ad illos qui non beniuole accipiunt, caritas ad uos diminuitur, quia rancorem forte accipiunt aliquando contra uos. Et hoc multum debetis cauere, ne caritas | alicuius erga uos uel erga 250rb quemcumque alium corrumpatur uel diminuatur, quia non magis spolium uel dampnum quam in caritatis ablacione uel diminucione fit.

Et suaderem uobis quod quocienscumque in mente uestra ueniret cogitacio de proprietate, quod eam remoueretis sicut temp-

---

18/20 cfr GER. MAG., *Tract. paup.*, 786-797, ubi Ger. allegat SEN., *Ep.* 4, 10 (p. 9, 7-8)   22/23 cfr supra, 15-17   30/31 cfr GER. MAG., *Ep.* 23 (p. 101, 15 ed. Mulder)   31/32 hoc prouerbium neque in SINGER, *Thesaurus prouerbiorum*, neque in WALTHER, *Prouerbia*, inuenire potui; cfr tamen WALTHER, *Prouerbia*, 10046a "frustra lingua laborat, si cor non simul orat", fortasse etiam 10042 "frustra conatur, cui non Deus auxiliatur", quamquam locus uere improbabilis optime conuenit, sc. SINGER, *Thesaurus*, s.u. 'Hören 67' (Vol. 6, p. 188), e Hartmann v. Aue, *Iwein*, 249

---

20 Quale] hoc *add.* D   23 uel¹] nec D   inuehi D   24 gemitu et] ingenita D   25 aliquando illis *tr.* L   27 ut] quod D   28 aliquem] aliquo modo D   30 uelletis L   32 loquitur Ma1   ammoniciones W   33 impreuise Ma1   33/34 secundum – aliquando] *om.* Ma1¹, *marg. suppl.* Ma1²   34 et – plurimum] *om.* Ma1   37 accipiunt] correpcionem uestram *add.* D   39 magis] *sic* L¹, maius WD *marg. corr.* L²   40 oblacione B   42 suaderemus B   quocienscumque] *corr.* Ma1², quociensque Ma1¹

tacionem, semper cogitando defectus uestros proprios, dicendo in
uobis: "Quid, miser, de illis te intromittis que Deus non expetit
a te", et cetera. *Miserere anime tue*, non, dicit Sapiens, *aliene, placens Deo*.
Ceterum secularia colloquia fugiatis, quia illa non sunt in locis
ubi necesse est uos esse cum eis, scilicet nec in choro, mensa, et
cetera. Quod rigor ordinis non tenetur ab aliis, de illis non intromittatis uos, sed de uobis uideatis.
Sed scire debetis quod non omnia que ponuntur in regula,
precepta sunt, et quod in multis eciam potest prelatus dispensare, et precipue in omnibus pene corporalibus excerciciis, sicut
ieiuniis, | uigiliis, leccionibus, et cetera. Non enim profitentur et
uouent regulam, sed secundum regulam uiuere. Et non sitis nimis
rigorosus, si aliquando non compleuerint omnia, dummodo uos
bonus emulator et discretus fueritis.
Valete in Christo Ihesu, et excerceatis uos in promissione Christi
ad imitandum eum.

46/47 Eccli. 30, 24

52/56 cfr THOM., II-II, q. 186 a. 2 co. (T. 10, p. 488, a. 2, c. 1, 31 – c. 2, 24);
a. 9 co. (T. 10, p. 500, a. 9, c. 2, 6-20)

45 non] *om. Ma1¹, suppl. Ma1²*   46 dicit Sapiens non *tr. W, sic Mulder*
48/50 Ceterum – cetera] *om. W*   49 nec] *om. D*   choro] nec in *sic
add. Mulder, sec. W tantummodo, om. cett.*   50 ab aliis non tenetur *tr. L*
53 sunt precepta *tr. D*   54 pene in omnibus *tr. W*   55/56 ut uoueant *D*   56 nimis] *corr. Ma1², nimium Ma1¹*   59/60 Valete – eum] *om.
W Ma1*   Magister Gerardus Groitt composuit doctor decretorum et cetera
licenciatus in decretalibus   *expl. in D*, prescripta hec quidam magister
Gerhardus (Gerhardus *Ma2*) Magnus scripsit *expl. in Ma1, expl. om. L W B*

EPISTOLA (41) AD ABBATEM IN CAMP
DE PROPRIETARIIS VITANDIS

CONSPECTVS SIGLORVM

L LIÈGE, Bibliothèque de l'Université, 229 (c), a. 1451
Ma1 = M4 MAINZ, Stadtbibliothek, I 349, s. XIVd
Z WOLFENBÜTTEL, Herzog August Bibliothek, 314 Gud. Lat. 4°, s. XVb

Hos codices in plagulis phototypice expressis contulimus.

⟨EPISTOLA AD ABBATEM IN CAMP
DE PROPRIETARIIS VITANDIS⟩

Humiliori mea in Christo Ihesu recommendacione premissa, pater et domine reuerende, gaudium fuit cordi meo in Domino, cum uos monasterio Campensi prelatum perceperim. Non quod ignorauerim quod onus graue humeris uestris impositum sit, non
5 quod non sciuerim quia pro diuersis et monasteriis et personis ad Dei gloriam et ad animarum salutem principaliter et ad temporalium conseruationem secundario uobis iam ex debito et commisso ministerio incumbat cotidiana sollicitudo et continua instancia. Sed hinc cum Sara leto rideo spiritu, et omnis qui hec
10 audierit mecum et ipse spiritualiter rideat, quia contra spem, id est contra communem multorum iam episcoporum et abbatum processum et consuetudinem, non prodesse sed preesse, non ministrare sed ministrari appetencium, se quoque et sua querencium, non Deum et animarum salutem emulancium, secundum
15 *mundum et rectores tenebrarum* ambulancium. Confido in eam spem, qua uos singulariter preter alteram ⟨uestram⟩ consuetudinem dico *filium promissionis*, ueluti alterum *Ysaac* | fideli Abrahe, id est Christo in fine temporum, id est beatissimo Bernardo in generacione filiorum spiritualium iam uetulo, | id est sancte Cister-

242ra 161

162

242rb

---

9 cfr Gen. 18, 10-15   14/15 Eph. 6, 12 paene ad litt.   16/17 Gal. 4, 28 paene ad litt.   17/18 cfr Gal. 3, 16

2/4 Ger. hanc epistulam anno 1382 mense nouembri misit Guilelmo de Colonia, abbati uicesimo secundo (1382-1402) nuper electo in abbatem abbatiae cisterciensis ordinis Kamp-Lintfort ad Rhenum prope Duisburg, cfr GER. MAG., *Ep.* 44, 2   17/21 cfr infra, 212-216

Tit. ad abbatem campensem *marg. inf. prima man. L, ante textum rubric. L H2,* de proprietariis *add. L³,* M⟨agister⟩ G⟨erardus⟩ Groot abbati campensi *tit in H1,* Epistola magistri Gerardi Groyt ad abbatem Campensem *tit. add. rubr. in Z*   1 Ihesu] *om. Z*   4 quod] quia *Ma1 Z*   5 non] *om. L¹, marg. suppl. L²*   7 iam] *om. Z*   8 monasterio L*   11 iam] *sic Ma1 Z, om. L*   16 uobis *Ma1* uestram] *emend. De Ram,* naturam *codd.*   17 fideli] filii *L*   18 Christus *L*   19 uetulo] seculo *Z*   sancte] *om. L*

ciensi religioni uersus senium magno iam lapsu declinanti, nasciturum. Ex quo per Iacob, Esau secundum sanguinem ambulante supplantato, spirituales patriarchas confido processuros, si tamen ut Abraham ipsos ydolatras non corpore sed animo dissenciendo, reprobando et puniendo fugeritis et fugaueritis.

Miramini forte quos fugandos et fugiendos putem ydolatras? Respondeo: proprietarios monachos uel religiosos magnos et pergrandes fore ydolatras. Nam si secundum apostolum uerissimum est *auariciam esse ydolorum seruitutem*, numquid rectissime sequitur auaros esse ydolatras, et maxime et inexcusabiliter et indispensabiliter et impalliabiliter auaros fore maximos et grandissimos ydolatras? Quales sunt proprietarii inter religiosos, quos nec abbatis nec episcopi nec summi pontificis licencia uel auctoritas nec aliqua potestas super terram ualet excusare, quos sicut ethnicos ydolatras habendos frequentissima et creberrima monicione et excommunicacione sentit ecclesia. Et ut horum horror cunctos uiuentes inuadat, ipsorum corporibus sepulturam non

---

21/22 cfr Gen. 25, 27-34; 27, 1-40, praesertim 27, 36   cfr Gal. 4, 23; 4, 29; etiam Rom. 8, 1; 8, 4, ubi pro 'sanguine' 'carnem' legitur   23/24 cfr Gen. 21, 8-13 sec. Gal. 4, 22-31   28 Col. 3, 5 paene ad litt.

20/21 cfr infra, 153-158, ubi Ger. probitatem nonnullarum aliarum ordinum contra deminutionem ordinis Cisterciensis eminere facit   31/33 cfr GER. MAG., *Ep.* 45, 89-94; *Tract. paup.*, 318-325   cfr *Decret.*, X 3.35.6 § 2 (c. II, 600, 15-19)   33/35 cfr GER. MAG., *Ep.* 42, 12-13; *Ep.* 45, 97-103; *Tract. paup.*, 231-234; 334-343   cfr praesertim *Decret.*, X 3.35.2 (c. II, 596, 59-61), ubi legitur: "Qui uero peculium habuerit, ... a communione remoueatur altaris", etiam GRAT., *Decr.*, C.12 q.1 c.5 (c. I, 678, 1-3); C.12 q.1 c.9 § 1 (c. I, 679, 28-37); C.12 q.1 c.10 § 3-4 (c. I, 680, 12-28); *Decret.*, X 3.35.6 § 2 (c. II, 599, 31-42); in locos a BERN. PARM., *ibid.* (c. 1291 (L. 3, p. 150), gl. f, l. 70-72) collectos (sc. GRAT., *Decr.*, C.12 q.1 c.11; C.18. q.1 c.1; C.27 q.1 c.32) excommunicatio transgredientibus non minatur   35/39 cfr GER. MAG., *Tract. paup.*, 284-309   cfr *Decret.*, X 3.35.6 § 2 (c. II, 599, 35-38), ubi Innoc. .III. sepulturam extra monasterium in sterquilinio praescribit, auctoritatem Gregorii .I. (GREG. MAG., *Dial.*, 4, 57, 11, p. 190, 81-86) nominatim in paraphrasi loco Gerardi nostri simili allegans; sepultura extra monasterium tantum praescribitur ibid., *Decret.*, X 3.35.2 (c. II, 597, 1-2); X 3.35.4 (c. II, 598, 18-32, ubi de canonico regulari agitur), sicut BERN. PARM., *Glos. ord. in Decret.*, super X 3.35.2, comm. sup. 'sepulturam' (c. II, 597, 2) (L. 3, c. 1292 (p. 151), gl. g, l. 4-5) adnotauit

---

20 lapso *Ma1*   24 pungiendo *Z*   fugieritis *sic Ma1*   27 pregrandes *Ma1 Z*   30/31 maximis et grandissimis ydolatris *Ma1*   grauissimos *Z*   34/35 ammonicione *L*   35 exercitacionem *Ma1*   Et] Eciam *Ma1*

EPIST. AD ABBATEM IN CAMP DE PROPRIETARIIS VITANDIS 387

tantum extra sacra loca, sed eciam in horrendo sterquilinio superaddita maledictione tam iura canonica quam sancti patres debitam disputarunt. Horribile est hec audire, sed | horribilius est hec 242va
40 uidere, sed horribilissimum est hec pati. A quibus qualia proprietariis in futura preparantur uita, quamuis inestimabilia sint, aliquatenus potest coniecturari.
O proprietas in monacho, quam terribilis es! O monstruosa | 163
auaricia in eo, cuius esse est pauperem esse! Nam monachum uel
45 religiosum esse est pauperem esse. Paupertas enim essencialis est religioni et monachatui. Inde est quod habere obulum proprium non solum in monacho auaricia est, sed esse et ualorem monachi dirimit. Inde est hoc frequens inter patres prouerbium: "Monachus habens obulum non ualet obulum".
50 Sed heu, iam multi inueniuntur scienciam Dei non habentes, terminos quos posuerunt patres nostri transgredientes, qui proprietarios ex sciencia uel licencia abbatis uel superioris et aliis quesitis coloribus excusare et palliare nituntur, querentes *excusaciones in peccatis*, non precauentes se *a sagitta uolante in die, a*
55 *negocio perambulante in tenebris, ab incursu* multorum, *et a meridiano demonio*, quod est *angelus sathane* et nequicie *transfigurans* se per *oleum* quod *impinguat caput* peccatoris *in angelum* ueritatis et *lucis* apparentis uel apparenter excusantis. Ve mundo, ue monasteriis, *a scandalo* hoc! Sed duplex *ue*, ymmo

---

54/55 Ps. 140 (141), 4   55/56 Ps. 90 (91), 6   56 II Cor. 12, 17   56/
58 II Cor. 11, 14   57 cfr Ps. 140 (141), 5   58/60 Matth. 18, 7

44/47 cfr GER. MAG., *Simonia beg.*, 307-309; 987-993; *Tract. paup.*, 228-234; *Ep.* 45, 12-15; 122-127   cfr THOM., II-II, Q. 186 a. 3 CO. (T. 10, p. 490, c. 2 – 491, c. 1)   48/49 cfr GER. MAG., *Tract. paup.*, 315-317   prouerbium ab HELIN., *Serm.* 13 (*PL*, 212, 589C) originem ducit, cfr SINGER, *Thesaurus prouerbiorum*, Bd. 8, p. 227, sect. 1, 2 (der Mönch darf nicht nach Weltlichem streben), n. 25; hoc prouerbium neque in WALTHER, *Prouerbia*, T. 2 (p. 914-915, n. 15025-15029) uel T. 8 (p. 447, n. 38311-38326; cfr etiam numeros in indice, T. 6, p. 134, s.u. 'obolus' citatos), nec in WERNER, *Sprichwörter*, inuenire potui; in medio quod uocatur aeuo uarie, sed false HIER. (e.g. ab ARN. GHEYL., *Gnot.* 1, 3, 3 (p. 226, 50-51)) uel GREG. MAG. (e.g. in *Homil. Vadst.*, p. 17, 138-140) attribuitur

---

38 tam] secundum *L*   39 disputarunt] sic *L*, deputauerunt *Ma1*, deputarunt *Z*   40 qualia] om. *L¹*, qualia tormenta *marg. suppl. L³*   42 potest] possint *Ma1*   43 est *Z*   O²] O, o *Z*   44 esse pauperum *tr. Z*
45 enim] autem *Ma1*   55 et] om. *L*   57 inpignat *Ma1*   peccatorum *L*

multiplex *ue* illi *per quem scandalum* hoc monasteria ingreditur, uel hec iniquitas prolongatur uel augetur, licenciatur uel roboratur, palliatur uel excusatur!

Quapropter, pater dilecte, uos hortor in Domino ut ad expellendam hanc ydolatriam a capite, scilicet Campensi monasterio, tota mente prudenter et discrete et proinde prout fratrum et multitudinis requirit infirmitas, nitamini et insistatis, ut deinde paulatim in cetera que capiti subsunt membra ordinate et congrue fluat seu descendat hoc ad salutem omnino necessarium, ineuitabile et inestimabile bonum. Et quamuis quibusdam hoc difficulter parabile propter inolitam consuetudinem uideatur, Deus tamen scit, ut sapio, quam facillimum sit prelato *fideli et prudenti dispensatori, non que sua sunt sed que* multorum cum apostolo *querenti*. | Infundendum puto oleum infirmis, sed non sine uino. Oleum dico largioris ministracionis in communibus, oleum restriccionis in propriis uestris expensis et comitiua, oleum mansuete et dulcis ammonicionis, uinum comminacionis, uinum resecacionis imparis uictus et uestitus, uinum ablacionis pecuniarum propriarum et reddituum, uinum excommunicacionis. Oleum ducibilibus et informabilibus, uinum duris et induratis. Oleum amoris, amicicie, honoracionis et promocionis in singulis uel pauperibus | uel obedientibus, uinum coartacionis, seueritatis et depressionis proprietariis resistentibus.

Ostendendum et puto eis non solum quam periculosum sit habere propria in respectu uirtutum et salutis eterne, sed eciam quanta mala temporalia, discordie, rixe, scissure, inobediencie,

---

71/72 Luc. 12, 42   72 Phil. 2, 4; 2, 21 a Ger. conflantur   73 cfr Luc. 10, 34; Cant. 1, 1-2   73/82 cfr Luc. 10, 25-37

68/69 cfr GER. MAG., *Tract. paup.*, 576-586; 1079-1086; 1171-1173 super gaudium regni celorum   71/72 cfr GER. MAG., *Tract. paup.*, 357-359, ubi Ger. in contextu dissimili eosdem locos biblicos coniunctim citat   83/88 cfr infra, 106-119; etiam GER. MAG., *Stat.*, 122-126; 512-523; *Tract. paup.*, 986-990; *Ep.* 46, 16-21

---

60 ue] ue ue *Z*   66 deinde] sic *L1*, demum *Ma1 Z*   69/70 parabile] *Ma1 Z*, probabile *L*   71 facilimum *L Z*   74 amministracionis *Z*   oleum] uinum *marg. falso corr. L²*   75 comitatiua *Z*   76 uinum comminacionis] *om. L*   77 oblacionis *Ma1*   78 et¹] uel *Ma1*   dulcibilibus *Ma1*   79 et] uel *Ma1 Z*   81 seu ueritatis *Z*   83 Ostendendum] est *add. L*   et puta *L*, puto etiam *Z*   quam] quod *Z*   84 conspectu *Z*

EPIST. AD ABBATEM IN CAMP DE PROPRIETARIIS VITANDIS 389

euagaciones et dissoluciones, commessaciones, ebrietates, detracciones et similia sine numero, maxime tamen ipsa paupertas communis, ex proprietatibus oriantur. Declarandum quoque est quomodo, si omnia ad communia 90 ponerentur et redigerentur, multa et grandia bona et uita religiosa et pacifica, tranquillitas et omnium necessariorum habundancia prouenirent. Notum michi estimo quod ex proprietate et proprietariis omnia mala, et maxime depauperacio et tenuitas in bonis temporalibus tam in diuiciis quam in fama, proueniant. Cuius pro- 95 bacio, prout de presenti occurrit, hec est: nam quilibet sua uel propria plus amat et curat quam aliena uel communia. Hoc dico secundum naturam infectam et non secundum caritatem (que "non *querit que sua sunt*", sed communia plus curat et amat quam propria, ut Augustinus dicit in *Regula*), ⟨quia⟩ natura infecta sem- 100 per ad se ipsam sit recurua, cum sue potestati dimittitur. Inde, ut docet Philosophus, primo *Politice*, communia minus curantur et crebrius negliguntur. Sic propriarum et priuatarum rerum admissio communes | res et communium rerum sollicitudinem, curam, 243rb custodiam et prouidenciam dirimit, postponit, negligit et confun- 105 dit.

98 Phil. 2, 21 paene ad lit., sec. Aug. allegatum

89/119 cfr infra, 203-204   89/91 cfr GER. MAG., *Tract. paup.*, 976-978, etiam 163-164; 211-212   cfr THOM., II-II, Q. 29 a. 1 co., ad 1 (T. 8, p. 236, a. 1, c. 2, 7-26), ubi allegat AVG., *Ciu. Dei* 19, 13 (p. 679, 10-11)   95/102 cfr GER. MAG., *Tract. paup.*, 377-407   cfr THOM., II-II, Q. 66 a. 2 CO. (T. 9, p. 85, c. 1-2); Ger. hic in attributione opinionis allegatae ad Arist. errat, quia haec opinio a Thom. tantum defenditur (ibid., T. 9, p. 85, art. 2, c. 1, 40 – c. 2, 2); Thom. ibi in uicinitate Arist. re uera allegat (sc. ARIST., *Pol. Lat.* 1, 3 § 6, in uersione latina a Guil. de Moerbeka facta (p. 31, 9-10 = 1256b7-8 Bekker), ibid., THOM., II-II, Q. 66 a. 1 CO. (T. 9, p. 84, art. 1, c. 2, 5-7)), cuius sententia tantummodo est quod "possessio rerum exteriorum est homini naturalis"; haec omnia luce clarius in loco infra ex *Tract. paup.*, sc. 388-390, citato patent
97/99 cfr GER. MAG., *Stat.*, 122-126; 512-523   cfr AVG., *Reg.* 5, 2 (p. 428-430, 153-157), partim paene ad litt.

86 commessaciones] et *add. L*   89 quoniam (qm-) *Z*   92/93 proprietariis] ex *praem. Z*   94 perueniant *Ma1 Ma2*   96 et] uel *L*   uel] quam *L*   98 curat] *om. L¹, marg. suppl. L²*   99 sicut *Z*   quia] *scripsi*, quamuis *Ma1 Z, De Ram sec. *A*, quam *L*   100 incurua *Z*   tamen *Z*   sue] *sic L*, suo *falso Mulder*   102 Sic propriarum] *om. Ma1*   propriarum] *sic L*, propriam *falso Mulder*

390 EPIST. AD ABBATEM IN CAMP DE PROPRIETARIIS VITANDIS

Et sepe, quod lamentabilius est, ea que communia sunt et communi cure subsunt, cum potuerit dispensator quidquid si|bi priuate deputare, ad propriam utilitatem et suorum infideli dispensacione et inequali retorquentur et frequenter inutiliter expenduntur, non ut decet nec ut debet quis, sed ut libet profusius largiuntur et uariis modis dilapidantur et extenuantur. Hinc paupertas uenit monasteriis cum multorum malorum comitiua. Vnde rixe, scissure et discordie, non solum in monasteriis sed in toto mundo, nisi a pronominibus 'meum' et 'tuum' nasci notum est. Et quot rancores et odia et lites et dampna, et quot murmuraciones et oblocuciones, quotque torui oculi et terribiles aspectus, *absque eo quod intrinsecus latet* ⟨malo⟩, ueniunt inter patres et inter fratres ex impari cultu, uestitu et uictu, uos ipsi sepius estis experti.

Quantam enim mencium et uocum dissonanciam et separacionem faciat hoc, quod, cum monachi fratres seu pares sint seu pariter pauperes, quod eorum tunice, cappe et scutelle sorores non sunt, sed tam dispares et inequa|les, inestimabile est. Hinc ex scutellis et uestibus et ex propriis inequalibus diuiciis tam discors, tam uaria uita et conuersacio in monasteriis: iste diues, ille pauper; iste pinguis, ille macer; *iste esurit, ille ebrius est*; iste angelus, ille dyabolus; iste ⟨Israelita⟩, ille Babilonius; iste corpore de filiis Israhel, mente manens Egiptius et semper secularis, ille Iudeus reuersus in Egiptum contra prohibicionem Altissimi.

Ad seculum et ad consanguineos pendunt monachi. Census annuos et bona ad proprios et non ad communes usus uel crebrius uel annuatim accipiunt. Euagantur, uendunt, emunt, permutant

---

116/117 Cant. 4, 1; 4, 3   126 I Cor. 11, 21 paene ad litt.   126/129 cfr Ex. 16, 2-3; 17, 3

106/119 cfr supra, 83-88, etiam GER. MAG., *Stat.*, 122-126; 512-523; *Tract. paup.*, 986-990; *Ep.* 46, 16-21   112/114 cfr GER. MAG., *Tract. paup.*, 986-990 cfr PS. SEN., *Mor.* 5 (p. 466 ed. Haase = *PL*, 72, 31A)

---

107 quidquam *L*   107/108 priuate sibi *tr. Z*   108 deputari, aliud propriam uidelicet *Ma1* et] uel *Z*   110 profundius *Ma1*   113 et] *om. Z*   115/116 quod, quodque *ter Z*   117 ea, quia *Ma1*   malo] *scripsi*, mala *codd.*   ueniant *potius legendum*   inter] *om. Z*   118 estis] *om. Z*   120 Quanta *Z*   121 hoc quod] *om. Ma1*   priores sunt *Ma1*   122 ac *Z*   125 tam²] *om. Ma1*   127 Israelita] *sic emend. De Ram*, Isra(h)el *codd.*

EPIST. AD ABBATEM IN CAMP DE PROPRIETARIIS VITANDIS   391

res per se, non habentes respectum ad id quod prodest toti monasterio et multis, sed sibi et suis dumtaxat utilitatibus inseruiunt.
135 Nonne hoc clare reuerti in Egiptum est? Inde mores egypcii et tenebrosi. Numquid digne talibus lumen diuine gracie subtrahitur, ut palpent in tenebris tamquam in meridie, *ut uidentes non uideant et* intelligentes *non intelligant*, cum dimittat eos Deus *secundum desideria cordium* ipsorum, ut uadant et non ulciscantur *in*
140 *adinuencionibus* ipsorum? Tunc turpis uita proximos inficit, nec intra est sanctitas nec extra in eis lucet uel | boni exemplum uel gloria Domini. Sed dumtaxat monstruosa animalia sunt, adextra pelle oui|um, scilicet ueste religiosa, cooperti dumtaxat.

Cumque *a fructibus eorum* a principibus terrarum et communi
145 populo *cognoscuntur*, manus ab olim largas in monasteria atque elemosinas uberiores, securitates et defensiones retrahunt. Vtinam solum manus retraherent, et non uariis angariis et perangariis, exaccionibus et talliis monasteria et res monasteriorum constringerent. Vtinam ui et armata manu atque fraudulenciis bona
150 monasteriorum nec raperent nec attraherent principes et iudices terre, qui tota patrimonia et uberrima, cum monasteria ex communibus uixerunt, et religiose fundebant et effundebant.

Et ne hoc non proprietariis et malis que ex eis sequuntur, sed malicie temporum et mundi senio imputetur: uideant qualiter
155 Cartusiensium et aliarum religionum et Cisterciensium et Premonstratensium et Regularium Canonicorum monasteria proprietarios non habencia uiuant, qualiter et in hoc tempore et amantur et

166

243vb

135/136 cfr Ex. 16, 2-3   136/137 cfr Iob 5, 14   137/138 cfr Mc. 4, 12;
Is. 6, 9-10   138/140 Ps. 80 (81), 13, partim paene ad litt.   142/143 cfr
Matth. 7, 15   144/145 Matth. 7, 16; 20 paene ad litt.

153/158 cfr supra, 20-21, ubi Ger. deminutionem ordinis Cisterciensis lamentatur

---

135 hoc clare *tr. L*   137 ut] et *Z*   139 cordis *fortasse merito, sec. Ps. 80, 13 Z*   uideant *Z*   ulciscatur *Z*   in] scilicet *Z*   140 uita] *om. Z*
142 adextra] ad exempla *Z*   144 Cumque] tamquam *Ma1*   145 cognoscuntur] *sic sec. Matth. 7, 16; 20 Z*, agnoscuntur *L Ma1*   146 detrahunt *Z*
149 Vtinam] nec *Z*   150 nec¹] *om. Z*   151 terrestres *Z*   tota] *Ma1 Z*, totaliter *L*   monasteriis *L*   152 fundabant *L*   et effundebant] *om. L*
153 non] *false om. L*   154 nundi *sic L*   deputetur] uideat *Z*
155 Cartusienses *sic Z*   Cistercen- *sic L*   et³] *om. L*   156 Canonicorum] et Teutonicorum *Z*   157 et³] *om. Z*

dotantur et defenduntur a malis et a terrarum principibus. Inde est quod tam pauperes sunt diuites proprietarii respectu patrum
160 pauperum antiquorum in communibus tam diuitum.

Accedit ad depauperacionem monasteriorum quod in pluribus terris iam layci non permittunt suas hereditates ad filios suos uel filias, monachos uel moniales, uel ad eorum diuolui monasteria, ut et diuina equitas et iura dictant, sed deputantes uel in ingressu
165 religionis uel in | eorum testamento non ad communem monas- 244ra terii usum sed ad filiorum suorum et filiarum commodum certum quid in prompto uel anime perpetue uel ad uitam. Per hoc ab omni futura successione et parentum et propinquorum eos resecant.
170 Ad que accipienda et attrahenda si illi uel ille qui presunt pro tempore non starent nec laborarent, plus modicum et presens lu|crum, quamuis creberrime cum simonie et proprietatis mix- 167 tura inquinatum, estimantes quam maxima temporalia et iuste et secundum Deum deriuancia in futuro, numquam consuetudo non
175 succedendi tantum inoluisset et preualuisset, sed nec illa corruptela, qua omnes de seculo uel corpore difformes uel inhabiles uel in anime uiribus destitutos uel destitutas non tanquam Deo sacrificium beneplacitum offerentes, sed se onere proprio subleuantes, monasteria non honorant sed onerant, quasi ille uel illa, qui
180 uel que nec matrimonio aptus uel apta sit uel patrimonio indignus uel indigna, in monasterio retrudenda sit.

Et unum in Dauentria inter multa alia ubilibet contingencia, exempli causa in medium ueniat. Nam est quedam Dauentriensis

---

162/164 cfr I Reg. 1, 24-28; Act. 2, 44; 4, 32; I Cor. 9, 13-14

---

160 cfr GER. MAG., *Tract. paup.*, 859-865   cfr SEN., *Ep.* 14, 17 (p. 44, 3-6)
161/162 Ger. hic ad GRAT., *Decr.*, C.1 q.2 a.c. 1 (c. I, 407, 16-40, praesertim I, 407, 19-28); c.8-9 (c. I, 410, 9 – 411, 10, praesertim 411, 13-19; 39-51) alludere uidetur, ubi in canonibus citatis etiam loci biblici (cfr 164 "diuina equitas") (sc. I Reg. 1, 24-28; Act. 4, 32; I Cor. 9, 13-14) allegantur

---

161 ad] *om. Ma1*   163 uel²] seu *Z*   164 et¹] *om. Z*   166 suorum filiorum *tr. Z*   170 trahenda *Z*, sunt *add. Z*   qui] uel que *add. Z*   prosunt *Ma1*   172 simonia *L*   173 maxime *L*   175 sed] sicut *Z*   176 que *L*   homines *Z*   179 onorant *Ma1*   180 uel³] *om. Z*   182 Dauantria *Z*   contingenda *Z*   183 exempla *Ma1*   causa] scilicet *add. Z*   Dauantrie *Z*

EPIST. AD ABBATEM IN CAMP DE PROPRIETARIIS VITANDIS 393

sanctimonialis in Honepe, cui certa a suis deputata sunt, meo
iudicio non sine magno eius periculo. Que si nomine monasterii
ad successiones suorum fuisset admissa, maiorem ex ea dumtaxat
tempora|lium utilitatem monasterium recepisset quam forte ex
omnibus datis non sine periculo in ingressu et ex omnibus proprietariis infra triginta annos accepit, quamuis secundum nouellam
constitucionem Vrbani .v. extrauagantem omnes religiosi et religiose qui in ingressu religionis ante professionem uel post aliqua
clenodia, iocalia, pecunias, prandia, et cetera pretextu consuetudinis accipiunt, ipso facto excommunicati sint.

Quid ergo dicendum de illis monasteriis monialium, ubi numquam nisi filie uel diuitum uel nobilium recipiuntur, ubi numquam nisi certum quid largiantur, acceptantur? Excluduntur pru-
dentes, excluduntur deuote, excluduntur habiles, dum tamen sint
pauperes. Paupertas in culpa est, paupertas spernitur | ab eis qui-
bus amor paupertatis in precepto est. Et cur sic? Certe quia diuites esse uolunt, et receptas propriis uel in parte uel in toto uolunt
sustentari. Et cum iam recipiunt ingressuras, ipsas proprietarias
efficiunt.

Vnde communi monasterio tam enormis, ut predictum est, paupertas oritur et tenuitas. Que omnia meo uidere in predicto monasterio facilime reparabilia sunt, dum tamen a capite, ut leges
uolunt ciuiles, edatur racio et a sanctuario incipiatur.

Hec, pater peramande, respicientes si conamine uestro profi-
ceritis, de quibus grandior et interpretabilior fieri possit sermo,
pariter cum hiis inestimabilia uobis *bona uenient* simul et dona
Altissimi. Deo eritis carus, et bonis hominibus et principibus pla-
cebitis, et nomen uestrum requiretur in generacione et genera-

---

209 cfr Sap. 7, 11

189/193 cfr *Extrau. comm.*, 5.1.1 "Ne in uinea" (c. II, 1287-1288, praesertim
1288, 2-20), hic in paraphrasi allegata   194/206 cfr Ger. Mag., *Simonia beg.*,
191-490   203/204 cfr supra, 89-119

---

184 monialis Z   in Honepe] *om. Z*   186 maiora Z   189 annos]
om. L   quam Z   191 que L   192 prandia] *om. Z*   et cetera] *sic Ma1 Z*,
marg. corr. L², eciam L¹ (H2 H1)   193 facto] *om. L¹*, marg. add. L²
195 uel¹] *om. Z*   196 largiatur Z   199 est] *om. Ma1*   207/208 per-
ficeritis L   210 hominibus] et *praem. Ma1*   211/212 generacione²] gene-
racionem Z

cione. Et generacio spiritualis in filiis et multiplicacio bonorum et honoris uestri erunt cum semine Abrahe benedicte et multiplices *sicut arena maris* et *sicut stelle celi*, que numerari non possunt, absque eo quod tunc *intrinsecus latebit*, scilicet gaudium permanens, pax inconcussa, *caritas* que *nunquam excidet*. Nam *omnis gloria* anime, que figura *Regis* eterni et communissimi et generalissimi boni est, *abintus* est, quamuis et eius *fimbrie* sint *auree*, omni aggregacione uere bonorum exterius *circumamicte*, absque quoque et illa infinita dulcedine et gloria, quas *nec oculus uidit nec auris audiuit*, et que abscondite sunt a timentibus Deum, quas *preparauit Deus diligentibus se* et precipue renunciantibus omnibus, sequentibus Christum in paupertate, pauperes scilicet pauperem, nudi nudum, quibus *omnia* secundum apostolicam regulam sunt *communia*, et ubi *suum nullus aliquid dicit*.

Iam uobis, pater, uita precellens et mors dura, eterna benedictio et indeficiens malediccio, dextera Excelsi et sinistra dyaboli preponuntur. Non potestis, ut prius, medius stare uel indifferens. Necesse est iam uos uel frigidum fore uel calidum, uel lucem uel tenebras. | Omnium iam onera portatis, speculator positus estis, ut edificetis, plantetis, euelletis et dissipetis. | Quod si, quod absit, non feceritis, uobis quod *pastoribus Israhel* per Ezechielem Dominus dixit, iuste minatur: *Ve pastori, qui pascebat semetipsum. Lac* de grege *commedebatis, et lanis operiebamini, et quod crassum erat occidebatis, gregem autem meum non pascebatis. Quod infirmum fuit non consolidastis, et quod egrotum fuit non sanastis, quod fractum est non alligastis, et quod abiectum fuit non reduxistis, et quod perierat non quesistis, sed cum austeritate*

213/214 cfr Gen. 22, 17, partim (paene) ad litt.   215 Cant. 4, 1; 4, 3
216 I Cor. 13, 8   216/219 cfr Ps. 44 (45), 14-15   220/222 Is. 64, 4 sec.
I Cor. 2, 9   224/225 cfr Act. 4, 32   231 cfr Ier. 1, 10   232/239 Ez. 34, 2-4

212/216 cfr supra, 17-21   230/231 cfr Ger. Mag., *Ep.* 27, 17-18

---

212 in filiis] *om. L, etiam H2 sed etiam (contra Mulder) H1*   218 est²] *om. Z*   fimbree *Mai*   sunt *L*   221 abscondita *Z*   225 nullus suum *tr. Z*   226 diuina *Z¹*, dira *corr. Z²*   227 inefficiens *Z*   229 fore] stare *Z*   231 euelletis] *sic codd.*, euellatis *legendum*   233 dixit Dominus *tr. Z*   233/234 pascebant semetipsos *Z*   236 solidastis *Z*   237 est] *om. Mai*   238 et – quesistis] *om. Z*

imperabitis eis et cum potencia. In quibus uerbis Domini manifeste, ut idem subdit propheta, ostenduntur que Deus in hoc tempore et in futuro iudicio a uobis requiret. Det Deus altissimus conari uos et inuenire uitam, calorem et benediccionem, lucem et dexteram, ut uestra in singulis reformacio possit dici *mutacio dextre Excelsi.*

Et si Deus dederit uobis cor ad reformandos proprietarios, in principio non reseretis cor uestrum ipsis, sed illis dumtaxat qui ad hoc possunt et libentes uolunt adiuuare, attrahentes primo suasionibus et dulcedinibus, primo et facilius reparabiliores, deinceps et alios oportunis momentis et occasionibus.

Parcatis, pater precare, si quid durum uobis uisum protuli. Deus scit quam uera sunt et quam utilia uobis, et amor ad uos cogit ueritatem confidenter effundere. Parcatis et de scriptura, quia | tedebat rescribere uilem scriptorem et turpem pictorem.

239/241 cfr Ez. 34, 10-11   243/244 Ps. 76 (77), 11

241/243 spectat ad dicta supra, 226-230, pronuntiata

---

239 In] Iam *Z*   246 ipsis] in *praem. Z*   illis] uel *Z*   249 aliis *Z*
253 Amen. Finitur epistola et cetera *expl. in Z, expl. om. L Ma1*

EPISTOLAE DVAE
AD ABBATEM (44) ET FRATRES (42) IN CAMP
DE SORORIBVS CISTERCIENSIBVS IN TER HVNNEPE

CONSPECTVS SIGLORVM

B	BRUSSEL, Koninklijke Bibliotheek van België, 3672-90 (1503), s. XVc (*Ep.* 44 tantum)
H2	DEN HAAG, Koninklijke Bibliotheek, 78 J 55, s. XVa
K	KOBLENZ, Landeshauptarchiv, Best. 701:165 (olim D IIII), s. XVb
L	LIÈGE, Bibliothèque de l'Université, 229 (c), a. 1451
O	LEUVEN, Maurits Sabbe Bibliotheek (formerly Bibliotheek Faculteit Godgeleerdheid), Collectie Grootseminarie Mechelen 30, s. XVb (*Ep.* 44 tantum)

Hos codices in plagulis phototypice expressis contulimus.

⟨EPISTOLA AD ABBATEM IN CAMP
DE SORORIBVS CISTERCIENSIBVS IN TER HVNNEPE⟩

Humili mea in Christo Ihesu recommendacione premissa, uenerabilis pater multorum et multarum, scitis [quod] uergente mundo in senium recto iusticie Dei ordine sancta et bona in carnalia mala et mala in pessima uerti et declinari, necnon animales homines secundum *ueterem hominem* uiuentes, quibus pene nichil de uera Dei agnicione et sanctorum imitacione constat, consuetudines et corruptelas et inuenciones sathane quasi priuilegia et iura pretendere. A quorum consorcio et consensu et consilio omnis renouata anima omnisque spiritus Dei bonus recedit longissime, et cogitur ueritate imperante et communione sanctorum constringente mente et actu recedere. *Odiui*, inquit propheta, *ecclesiam malignancium, et cum impiis non sedebo*, maxime tunc omniquaque necessarium est recedere, quando humana iura exteriora discernencia et potestates sublimiores id ipsum facere precipiunt.

Hinc est, pater et pater nostrarum sororum monialium in Honepe, hinc est, dux earum ad terram uiuencium, quod uestram paternitatem secundum Dei emulacionem piissime exhortor ut consuetudinem, ymmo uerissime corruptelam fetidissimam et diabolicam presumptionem, qua notorie et publice infecte sunt

___

5 cfr Eph. 4, 22 ; Col. 3, 9   11/12 Ps. 25 (26), 5

___

1 Ger. hanc epistulam anno 1382 exeunti misit Guilemo de Colonia, abbati uicesimo secundo (1382-1402) in abbatia cisterciensis ordinis Kamp-Lintfort ad Rhenum prope Duisburg, cfr Ger. Mag., *Ep.* 41, 2-4 ; in hac epistula sorores in abbatia Ter Hunnepe prope Dauentriam, quae Guilelmi curae demandatae erant, de proprietate priuata reas fecit

___

Tit. Secunda epistola (*om.* H2) ad abbatem in Campen *tit. in* LH2, nota, contra symoniam *marg. exponit* L², Ad abbatem in Camp *tit. in* K, Epistole due magistri Gerardi Groot doctoris *tit. in* B, *tit. om.* O   2 quod] *sic codd.*, *om.* Mulder   4 mala²] *om.* OB   7/8 preuilegia *sic* L   8 A] De B et²] *om.* OB   9 renouata] remota O, renonota *sic* B   Domini K bonos B   13 omniquaque] KOB, omni quam (qᵃ₃ *in abbr. scribunt*) LH2   19 fedicissimam OB

moniales in Honepe, non iuuetis aut fortificetis, sed pocius, ut decet uerum patrem, non nomine tantum sed re et paterne procurantem secundum canonica statuta, ad eius abolicionem dignemini laborare et laborantes confortare.

25 Non est ydoneum, non est possibile ut sine nota diffamie et rerum discrimine iam moniales suas conseruent symoniacas prauitates in terra illa, in qua usurarii antiquati et aliorum multorum malorum homines suas usuras et alia consueta, licet simonia minores, | undique post|ponunt. Laici uicia deponentes religiosas
30 eadem uel maiora retinentes habent opprobrio. Estimo, nisi deposuerint, quod ipse dominis terrarum et seculari milicie erunt ludibrio et contemptui.

Nos autem et curatus Dauentriensis necnon ceteri Deum pre oculis habentes aut iura scientes sicut excommunicatas et eas
35 reiectas ab ecclesia habebimus et uitabimus et uitandas propalabimus. Capellanus earum, deuotus uir, earum excommunicacionem uerens et suam irregularitatem timens iam recessit, ex quo iam coram et manifesto dicant se illam uelle retinere iuuenculam de Campen, quam contra constitucionem domini Vrbani quinti in
40 extrauagante *Ne in uinea*, et cetera, acceperunt, quia pretextu consuetudinis sexaginta antiqua scuta in elemosynam abbatisse et sororibus optulit.

Vos pater earum non potestis eas eximere a potestate summi pontificis. Nichil eas excusat, sed accusat maledicta pocius cor-
45 ruptela quam pretensa consuetudo. Si bonus pastor sitis, ut spero, hic animam uestram, si necesse esset, poneretis. Longe magis bonus pastor animarum quam exteriorum bonorum timet detrimenta. Econtra tirannus et terrenus: *Qui de terra est, de terra lo-*

48/49 Ioh. 3, 31

33/42; 55/60 cfr *Extrau. comm.*, 5.1.1 "Sane, ne in uinea" (c. II, 1287-1288, praesertim 1288, 2-20)   33 certe non Petrus de Noertmersche, sicut Mulder existimat, quippe qui a. 1368 obiit

---

22 non] *om.* K   25/26 et rerum] rerumque O B   27 antiquati] *sic* L H2 K B, antiqui O, antiquanti *Mulder*   29 postponant O B   31/32 ludibrie (lidubrio B) et contemptu *sic* O B   34 scientes iura *tr.* O B   37 iam] iamiam K   38 et] *om.* O B   39 Vrbani] pape *add.* O B   40 pretextu] in *praem.* O B   41 in elemosynam] O B, merito, *cfr loci paralleli in* Lexicon Nederl., E, 108-109, et alia L H2 K   46 sit O B   posueritis O B   magis] *marg. suppl.* L², *om.* L¹   48 Econtra] quam O B

quitur et curat. Det nobis Deus Spiritum suum. Vos estis qui iam
potestis iam saluti animarum uel obesse uel prodesse. Si uero et
bono consentitis et adhereatis, sequetur fructus Deo gratus, sanctis conformis, letificans supernam ciuitatem. Si terga uertitis, si
oculum clauditis, diabolice corrupcionis eritis – quod longissime
absit – non dicam adiutor, sed columpna et firmamentum.

Dominus et frater Iohannes, confessor ibidem, periculo irregularitatis sue cogitur recedere uel *organa* cum ipsis *suspendere*,
quam ipsum celebrantem coram excommunicatis ex constitucione predicta timemus et premuniuimus incurrere. Necesse fuit
omnimo, si uellet sine periculo irregularitatis esse, ut recederet.
Sciunt hoc qui uere iura sciunt et intelli|gunt.

Non potest hec res dissimulacione | palliari, non potest hic ferrea consuetudo subuenire, nulla antiquata prauitas excusacionem
nisi frontosam defert. In uobis, pater, stat: si uos abolicioni malorum consentitis et depulsioni, symoniaca prauitas pro magna
parte recedet. In uos referunt partes aduerse et eciam conuerse
uota sua. Si iuueritis ut recedat, ueniet pax et concordia, si impediueritis ne recedat, omnis iniquitas in uerticem uestram descendet, et exteriores ignominie tamen non recedent et infamie. Confido omnino quod ueri patris facietis imitaciones, et reddat uobis
summus Pater cum benedictionibus in secula, qui in uobis et in
uestris operibus et in omnibus nobis sit benedictus et gloriosus in
secula. Parcatis de dictamine et scriptura satis malis.

---

56 cfr Ps. 136 (137), 2   71/72 cfr Rom. 9, 5; Dan. 3, 26; 3, 52

---

55 cfr Ger. Mag., *Ep.* 42, 12   55/59 cfr supra, 33-42

---

50 uel¹] iam *O B*   prodesse uel obesse *tr. K O B*   51 sequetur] *sic*
L H2 K O, sequitur *B, Mulder*   54 dicam] enim *praem. O B*   firmamentum] *sic K O B*, firma fundamentum *corr. ipse L¹*, fundamentum *H2¹*, firma inter lineas add. H2²*   57/58 consuetudine *O*   58 timemus et premunimus
sic p.c. O¹, premunimus timemus et *a.c. O¹*   59 irregularitatis esse periculo
tr. O B   60 sciuerunt *O B*   61 potest] *om., sed marg. suppl. ipse L¹*   61/
62 non² – subuenire] *om. O B*   62 antiquata] *sic corr. H2²*, antiqua
H2¹   66 tua *sic O B*   66/67 impediueritis] iuueritis *iterum O B*
67 uestram uerticem *tr. O B*   67/68 descendet] *sic corr. H2²*, descendat
H2¹ O B   68 recedant *K O B*   et²] *om. L*   69 reddat] rdada *B, om. spatio uacuo relicto O*   72 mala *O B*   Expliciunt due epistole magistri
Gerardi dicti teutonice Groet pie recordationis *expl. in O B, expl. om. L H2 K*

⟨EPISTOLA AD FRATRES IN CAMP
DE SORORIBVS CISTERCIENSIBVS IN TER HVNNEPE⟩

Amabiles in Christo domini et fratres, copiam litterarum per me missarum ad | abbatem cupio uos legere et perspicere, ac intencionem nostram, ymmo uero Christi procul dubio legacionem promouere.

5 Vos membra confortetis caput uestrum, ut ex eo spiritualis uita et sincerus sensus ad inueterata quedam sicca membra effluat. Iam punctus est ut uinum uel fex uini aut pocius ab eo pix descendit. Sicut se iam determinat abbas uestro consilio, sic res nostris temporibus, timeo, permanebit, non tamen, si – quod absit a bono uiro – fuerit contrarius ueritati: sine scandalo, sine nota diffamie, sine rerum discrimine moniales in antiquis malis possunt perdurare. Dominus Iohannes necessitate constrictus, consciencia permotus et irregularitatis periculo perpulsus est ad standum ueritati.

15 Maledicta allegacio uelle in antiquis malis permanere, supplicare ut permittantur in malis in quibus inuente sunt. Heu, odium fraternum est quod huic allegacioni consentit, furor est pertinax *ueteris hominis,* uetustatem suam nolens deponere aut deponen-

---

6/7 cfr Ps. 74 (75), 9; fortasse Eph. 5, 18   18 cfr Eph. 4, 22; Col. 3, 9

1/2 sc. *Ep.* 44, in hac editione praecedentem; Ger. hanc epistulam anno 1382 exeunti misit monachis in abbatia cisterciensis ordinis Kamp-Lintfort ad Rhenum prope Duisburg, cfr GER. MAG., *Ep.* 41, 2-4   12 Iohannes, monachus Cisterciensis e monasterio Campensi, confessor monialium in Ter Hunnepe fuit, ut ex *Ep.* 44, 55-59, patet   12/13 cfr GER. MAG., *Ep.* 41, 33-35; *Ep.* 45, 97-103; *Tract. paup.*, 231-234; 334-343   cfr praesertim *Decret.*, X 3.35.2 (c. II, 596, 59-61), ubi legitur: "Qui uero peculium habuerit, ... a communione remoueatur altaris", etiam GRAT., *Decr.*, C.12 q.1 c.5 (c. I, 678, 1-3); C.12 q.1 c.9 § 1 (c. I, 679, 28-37); C.12 q.1 c.10 § 3-4 (c. I, 680, 12-28); *Decret.*, X 3.35.6 § 2 (c. II, 599, 31-42)   15/16 cfr THOM. KEMP., *Chron.*, c. 1 (p. 337, 23-30), ubi Thom. describit quomodo Ger. aliquem similia dicentem reprehendat

---

Tit., Epistola ad fratres eiusdem monasterii in Campen *ante textum rubric. L H2,* ad fratres in camp *tit. in K*   7 uinum] uel *praem. K*   9 timeo temporibus *tr. K*   11 possunt] (non) *praem. contra codd. Mulder*

tem uel deponere uolentem non admittere. O, durissima frons uetustissimi et insensibilis hominis in pessimum pertinaciter!

Vos domini non sic, quia *renouamini spiritu mentis uestre*. State | uiriliter pro ueritate et permanete fortiter et abbatem uestrum in bonis iuuate, et ut bene faciat commonete et confortate.

Valete, dilectissimi in Dilecto, ualete in gaudio futurorum, quando *iusticia conuertetur in iudicium*. Dulcissima nobis dies illa et pre gaudio totis uisceribus amplexanda, quam nisi desideremus futuram, perdemus, ut dicit Augustinus in libro *De ouibus*. Tunc omnis propalata ueritas clare patebit, clare confitetur nos, qui eam iam multis a nequicia diaboli deceptis resistentibus confitemur. Tunc confirmabuntur omnes nostre sentencie uere, tunc testabitur nobis omnis creatura. Non sit nobis durum quod a malis sentencie nostre accepte non fuerint, a quibus si accepte essent, sanctis et Deo essent despecte. Tunc faciet ueritas ueritatem omnibus uel in uerbo uel in corde uel in opere iniuriam pacientibus. Valete in die illa, et tunc ualere appetamus et procuremus et gaudeamus.

---

21 Eph. 4, 23   26 Ps. 93 (94), 15

27/28 cfr Avg., *Serm.* 47, 8 (De ouibus) (p. 579, 221-222)

---

20 pertinaciter *L H2*   25 dilecti *K*   26 uobis *K*   32 a] *om. K*

EPISTOLA (45) AD RECTRICEM MONIALIVM DE PROPRIETARIIS

CONSPECTVS SIGLORVM

codex principalis (familia λ)

L   Liège, Bibliothèque de l'Université, 229 (c), a. 1451

codices

K   Koblenz, Landeshauptarchiv, Best. 701:165 (olim D IIII), s. XVb
Kk   Köln, Historisches Archiv der Stadt Köln, GB 8° 152, a. 1438
M   København, Det Kongelige Bibliotek, NKS 2741 4°, a. 1477
O   Leuven, Maurits Sabbe Bibliotheek (formerly Bibliotheek Faculteit Godgeleerdheid), Collectie Grootseminarie Mechelen 30, s. XVb (familia π)

Hos codices in plagulis phototypice expressis contulimus.

⟨EPISTOLA⟩ AD RECTRICEM MONIALIVM
DE PROPRIETARIIS

Tibi, in Christo soror, ut secundum Christum scias et ut secundum scienciam Dei filias tuas dirigas, scribo quedam que forte ignoras.

Iam in monasteriis quibusdam pericula, inter que capitale et
5 quasi omnium uiciorum fomentum et fundamentum est hoc uicium, quod, heu, iam in pluribus monialium monasteriis sorores singule singulares habent redditus, eis a parentibus uel consanguineis deputatos. Quod tuis filiabus ne facias exhortor et quantum ualeo dissuadeo. Si feceris, procul dubio erras et non
10 modice peccas, filiasque tuas ad grande ducis meo uidere periculum.

Certum et uerum est omni religioni tria substancialia esse et inseparabilia, a quibus nullus religiosorum potest excusari uel liberari eo manente in statu religioso, obediencia uidelicet, castitas et
15 paupertas.

245ra 177

1/2 Ger. hanc epistulam anno 1382 exeunti misit Mechtildae de Bylandt, abbatissae in abbatia sororum Ter Hunnepe prope Dauentriam, tractans de modo uiuendi sororum ibidem commorantium, quae demandatae erant curae Guilemi de Colonia, abbatis in abbatia cisterciensis ordinis Kamp-Lintfort ad Rhenum prope Duisburg, super quem cfr GER. MAG., *Ep.* 41, 2-4   12/15 cfr infra, 122-127, et GER. MAG., *Simonia beg.*, 307-309 ; 987-993 ; *Tract. paup.*, 228-234 ; *Ep.* 41, 44-47   i.e. tria uota monastica, cfr THOM., II-II, Q. 186 a. 3 ; 4 ; 5, quorum summarium a Ger. hic in paraphrasi datum praestat ibid., THOM., II-II, Q. 186 a. 7 co. (T. 10, p. 497, c. 2, a. 7, 4-37)

Tit. Ad rectricem monialium in monasterio constitutam *ante textum rubric. L*, nota, de proprietariis *marg. exponit L³*, Incipit epistola magistri Gerardi Groten ad abbatissam monasterii in Hoenepe ordinis Cisterciensis Traiectensis dyocesis, pro exhortatione animarum salutari *tit. in M*, Item de proprietate siue peculio monachorum ac monialium Magister Gerardus Magnus Dauentriensis sic scribit in loco quodam sentenciarum suarum, et est notabile *ut tit. ante excerptum 120/147 praebet Kk*, Epistole due magistri Gerardi Groot doctoris *tit. in B*, Ex scriptis magistri Gerardi Groot de proprietate religiosorum. Magister Gerardus Magnus inter alia dicit *ut tit. ante excerptum* 136/147 *praebet W*, magister Gerardus Magnus dicit *inter duo excerpta scr. O2 P, tit. om. H2 H1 K O*   **5** fomentum uiciorum *tr. M*   **7** eis] *post* consanguineis *pos. O B*   **8** filialibus *sic H2*   facias] seu permittas *add. M*   **9** erras] permaxime *praem. M*   **10** meo uidere] secundum sanctos doctores *M*

Paupertatem dico que nichil proprii habere permittit, ut nullus suum quidquam esse dicat. Sed oportet omnia esse communia et distribui singulis, *prout cuiquam opus est*, a prepositis secundum regulam apostolicam. Hec paupertas de substancia omnis religio-
20 nis est, hec in uoto cuiuslibet religiosi includitur. Quecumque ergo religiosa aliquid proprii habet, a status sui substancia et ordine cecidit et sui uoti immemor est et transgressor. Ideo, ut ait *Ecclesiastes, melius | est non uouere quam post uotum uotum non implere. Displicet enim*, ait, *Deo infidelis et stulta promissio*. Si uo-
25 tum paupertatis implere non curauerit, *infidelis* est, si implere non uoluerit *stulta* fuit *promissio*.

245rb

Audiat omnis religiosus de hac materia premunientem se Christum et dicentem, *Luce* .XIIII.: *Quis enim ex uobis uolens turrim edificare nonne prius sedens computat sumptus, qui neces|sarii*
30 *sunt, si habeat ad perficiendum, ne, posteaquam posuerit fundamentum et non potuerit perficere, omnes qui uiderint incipiant illudere ei, dicentes: Quia hic incepit edificare et non potuit consummare*. Et post pauca subiungit: *Sic ergo omnis ex uobis qui non renunciauerit omnibus que possidet, non potest meus esse*
35 *discipulus*. Hec sunt uerba Christi, ex quibus patet quod turris hec edificanda est disciplinatus suus, et sumptuum preparacio

178

17/18 cfr Act. 4, 32; 4, 35, ad quem locum Ger. in *Tract. paup.*, 262-265, se refert, etiam Act. 2, 44-45   22/23 Eccle. 5, 4 paene ad litt.   24; 25/26 Eccle. 5, 3 paene ad litt.   27/33 Luc. 14, 28-30, uerisimiliter allegatum sec. Thom., cfr app. fontium   33/35 Luc. 14, 33

16/20 cfr infra, 43-52, et Ger. Mag., *Tract. paup.*, 259-265   cfr Cass., *Coll.* 18, 5 (p. 509, 19 – 510, 5; 510, 23 – 511, 8)   27/35 cfr infra, 76-79   35/37 cfr Thom., II-II, Q. 189 a. 10 arg. 3; ad 3 (T. 10, p. 552, c. 1, a. 10, 20-36; p. 553, c. 2, 3-17, praesertim l. 13-17, ubi Thom. dicit: "Sed hoc cadit sub deliberatione, utrum hoc quod facit, sit abrenuntiare omnibus quae possidet, quia nisi abrenuntiauerit, quod est sumptus habere, non potest, ut ibidem subditur, Christi esse discipulus, quod est turrim aedificare"

---

16 proprium *O*   17 dicat] *corr*. H2¹ ᵘᵉˡ ², dicit H2¹   oportet] eius *L H2 H1*   18 simul *L H2 H1*   19 apostolicam regulam *tr. L H2 H1*   21 religiosa] persona *praem. M*   22 est] *om. O*   24 promissa *O*   25 adimplere *M*   28 enim] *om. O B*   30 postea quando *O B*, postea postquam *M*   32 hic] homo *sec. Luc. add.rubric. L²*   incipit *K*   34 esse meus *tr.* contra Luc. *H2 H1 K O B*   35 sunt – ex] *om. O B*   36 edificata *L*   disciplinatus] *sic L¹ K O B*, loci paralleli infra 70 exhibiti causa hic quoque defendendum censeo, quamuis hoc nomen substantiue adhibitum in hoc sensu hapax legomenon est, *cfr* Lexicon Nederl., D, 523, 46-51, discipulatus *M corr. L¹ uel L²*   suus] finis *O B*

est renunciacio omnium que quis possidet. Nec dubium est cuiquam religionum regulas inspicienti aut patrum monimenta, quin religiosi, quoad paupertatem et communitatem bonorum tem-
40 poralium, habeant statum discipulorum Christi, qui *non posse quemquam suum esse discipulum*, nisi *omnibus renunciauerit*, affirmauit.

Quis tante auctoritati potest contradicere? Audiat religiosa religionis exordium, non mea uerba, sed abba|tis Paymon, *Colla-*
45 *cione* .XVIII. Inquit enim idem abbas: "Itaque cenobitarum disciplina a tempore predicacionis apostolice sumpsit exordium. Nam talis exstitit in Iherosolimis omnis illa credencium multitudo, que in *Actibus apostolorum* ita describitur: *Multitudinis autem credencium erat cor unum et anima una, nec quisquam eorum que*
50 *possidebat aliquid suum esse dicebat, sed erant illis omnia communia*. Possessiones et substancias uendebant, et diuidebant ea omnibus *prout cuique opus erat*." Deinde postquam declarauit qualiter multi gentilium et Iudeorum postea propria ceperunt habere, subiungit de origine religiosorum, dicens: "Hii autem qui-
55 bus adhuc inerat apostolicus feruor, memores illius pristine perfeccionis, descendentes a ciuitatibus suis et ab illorum consorcio qui sibi uel ecclesie Dei remissioris uite negligenciam licitam esse credebant, in locis suburbanis et secrecioribus commanere et ea, que ab apostolis per uniuersum corpus ecclesie generaliter me-
60 minerant instituta, priuatim et peculiariter excercere ceperunt. Atque ita coaluit ista disciplina, quam diximus discipulorum, qui se ab eorum contagione sequestrauerunt. Qui paulatim tempore

245va

40/41 cfr Luc. 14, 33   48/51 Act. 4, 32, allegatum sec. Cass., ad quem locum Ger. in *Tract. paup.*, 262-265, se refert   51/52 Act. 4, 34 partim paene ad litt., allegatum sec. Cass.

43/52 cfr supra, 16-20, et GER. MAG., *Tract. paup.*, 259-265   43/68 CASS., *Coll.* 18, 5 (p. 509, 19 – 510, 5; 510, 23 – 511, 8)

---

38 monumenta *OB*, monita *M*   39 ad *M*   41 discipulum suum esse *tr. M*   renunciauit *L*   44 Pyamon *M*   44/45 Collacionem *L*   45 inquit – abbas] ubi sic inquit *M*   47 existit *L H2 H1*   Iherozolimis *L M*   51 possiones *sic B*   52 cuiquam *OB*   53 ceperunt propria *tr. L H2 H1*   57 uel] *om. H2*   58 secrecioribus] et *add. OB*   commanare *OB*   59 que] *om. L¹, suppl. L²*   ab] *om. OB*   60 peculiarriter *B*, peculialiter *M*   61 Itaque *OB*   62 tempore] sequente *add. H2¹, sed postea del. H2¹ uel 2*

procedente segregati a credencium turbis, ab eo quod se a coniugiis abstinerent et a parentum se consorcio mundique istius conuersacione se secernerent, monachi seu monozantes singularis ac soli|tarie uite districtione nominati sunt. Vnde consequens fuit | ut ex communione consorcii cenobite, et celle et diuersoria eorum cenobia uocarentur." Hec Paymon.

Ex quibus tam religiosorum paupertas quam status eorum iuxta formam disciplinatus Christi manifeste apparet, quamuis postea per regulas conditas et professionis uota ad paupertatem forcius et strictius religiosi obligantur: quis contra regulas et uota et professiones, nisi forte propter bonum aliquod tocius christianitatis uel simile, potest dispensare?

Si dixerit monialis non posse se aliter uiuere, nisi habuerit propria, respondeo cum Christo: "Quare turrim edificare cepisti, quam perficere non potuisti? Quare sumptus tuos tue renunciacionis antea non computasti? Nescisti quia nisi quis *omnibus renunciauerit, non potest esse meus discipulus?"*

Si dixeris: "nesciui", "ignorancia tua", inquam, "ignorancia iuris est, non facti, nec iuris humani tantum, sed diuini precepti, et precipui precepti ad statum tuum pertinentis: ideo te non excusat. Attende quod tua ignorancia uincibilis sit, et scire potuisti et scire debuisti. Audisti continue regulam tuam et euangelium meum et sanctos patres una uoce contra proprietarios pronunciantes, exclamantes".

Si dixerit religiosa: "abbas et abbatissa dederunt michi licenciam habendi ea que habeo", respondeo non uerba mea, sed

---

76/78 alludit ad Luc. 14, 28-29, supra (27-33) uerbatim allegatum   78/79 Luc. 14, 33 paene ad litt., supra (33-35) etiam allegatum

---

76/79 cfr supra, 27-35

---

65 cernerent *OB*, disiungerent *M*   monayzantes *M*   66 discretione *M*   67 ut] *om. H2 H1 L¹, marg. suppl. L²*   68 Paymon] abbas *add. M*   69 paupertatis *K*   70 disciplinatus] *cfr commentum, ad l.* 36 *supra,* discipulatus *M*   72 quis] enim *add. M*   75/76 propria habuerit *tr. L H2 H1*   78 ante *OB*   nesciuisti *OB*   78/79 renunciauerit omnibus que possidet *sec. Luc. M*   79 meus] Christi *H2 H1 OB*   80 numquam *OB*   81 non] non *iterum false add. K*   tantum] *om. O*   precipue *M*   83 inexcusabilis *M*   scire enim *M*   84 scire] *om. OB*   regulam tuam continentie *M*   85/86 pronunciantes] *om. OBM*   87 abbas, prior, abbatissa uel priorissa *M*

per | uerba pape et iuris canonici, Extra, *De statu monachorum,* c. *Cum ad monasterium,* sic dicentis: "Nec estimet abbas quod super habenda proprietate possit cum aliquo monacho dispensare, quia abdicacio proprietatis, sicut et custodia castitatis adeo est annexa regule monachali ut contra eam nec summus pontifex possit licenciam indulgere". Ex quibus uerbis patet quod licencia abbatis modicum liberat proprietarium, ex quo papa hoc se confitetur non posse, qui plenitudinem habet potestatis.

Ymmo, ut habetur in c. *Monachi,* nec peculium quodcumque monachus habere poterit. Quod si "habuerit peculium, nisi sibi pro iniuncta amministracione fuerit permissum, a communione remouetur altaris. Et qui in extremo cum peculio inuentus fuerit, et digne non penituerit, nec oblacio fiat pro eo nec inter fratres accipiat sepulturam." Et infra in *Decretali* dicitur: "Abbas | autem qui diligenter ista non cauerit, officii sui iacturam se nouerit incursurum". Ex quibus patet quod nullum liberat, eciam si dicat sub potestate abbatis se habere que habet, et quod abbas, si uellet, posset auferre. Nam hoc est de natura peculii, ut sit in superioris potestate. Patet eciam quod sola amministracio excusat peculium, et in hoc concordat Innocencius in *Glosa,* et saniores canoniste.

89/94 cfr Ger. Mag., *Ep.* 41, 31-33; *Tract. paup.,* 318-325   *Decret.,* X 3.35.6 § 2 (c. II, 600, 15-19)   95/96 cfr *Decret.,* X 3.35.2 (c. II, 596, 50-51)   97/104 cfr Ger. Mag., *Ep.* 41, 33-35; *Ep.* 42, 12-13; *Tract. paup.,* 231-234; 334-343   *Decret.,* X 3.35.2 (c. II, 596, 59 – 597, 4) paene ad litt.   104/106 cfr supra, 90-95   cfr *Decret.,* X 3.35.6 § 2 (c. II, 599, 40-42) et (c. II, 600, 16-18), supra, 90-93, allegatum   107/108 cfr supra, 98-99   cfr Innoc., *Comm. Decret.,* super X 3.35.2, comm. sup. 'peculium' (c. II, 596, 50-51) (ed. 1570, p. 516, c. 2, 64-65 = sup. X. 3.35.2, 1-2) "'peculium': nisi pro iniuncta administratione, ut infra, § sequen.", et sup. 'administratione' (c. II, 596, 59) (ed. 1570, p. 516, c. 2, 68-69 = sup. X. 3.35.2, 5-6), cfr etiam super X 3.35.6 § 2, comm. sup. 'Summus' (c. II, 600, 18) (ed. 1570, p. 517, c. 2, 17-22)

---

89 per] *om. O*   pape et] *om. OB*   90 estimat *K,* existimet *M*   92 castatis *sic K*   94 licenciam] *om.* contra *Decret. OB*   94/95 patet – abbatis] *om. L¹, marg. suppl. L²*   96 se] *om. M*   97 quodquam *OB*   98 habere monachus *tr. OB*   sibi] *om. O*   100 remoueatur *M*   altaris] *om. L¹, marg. suppl. L²*   qui] *om. L*   extremis *M*   fuerit] cum peculio *iterum add. B*   101 non digne *tr. O*   103 iacturam] priuacionem *KM*   104 nullum] nullus *praem., sed exp. H2*   105 que] ea *praem. OB*   habeat *OB*   106 posset] illa *add. M*   sit] *om. L¹, marg. suppl. L²,* si *O*   107 ministracio *OB*   108 in¹] cum *OB*   Innocencius] quartus *add. M*

Patet eciam ex natura rei in hiis rebus dispensacionem non cadere. Nam in illis que sunt per se mala, que non possunt bene fieri, | non cadit dispensacio, ut dicit Bernardus in libro *De precepto et dispensacione* et *Epistola ad Adam monachum*, que est septima. Sed habere proprium est per se malum, ut dicit Bernardus in eadem *Epistola*: "Propria", inquit, "habere seculari homini medium est, quem et possidere et non possidere licet; monacho, quia possidere iam non licet, purum malum est". Nam ut idem ait in *Epistola ⟨undecima⟩ ad Carthusiensem*: "Vbi proprietas, ibi singularitas; ubi singularitas, ibi angulus; ubi angulus, ibi sine dubio sordes et rubigo". Hec Bernardus.

Sed adhuc inspicienti finem religionis secundum regulam Augustini uel Benedicti uiuencium patet quomodo habere | propria sit fini religionis contrarium. Est enim finis religionis huiusmodi contemplacio seu perfeccio caritatis, ad quem finem obtinendum necessaria est bonorum temporalium resignacio siue renunciacio, ut ex multis locis *Ewangelii* patet, ut possit libere sine sollicitudine et pressura temporalium soli Deo inherere et uacare. Quicumque ergo intrans religionem secum portans et retinens bona sibi deputata precludit sibi possibilitatem finis in reli-

---

124/125 cfr Luc. 14, 33; Act. 2, 44-45; 4, 32

109/113 cfr BERN., *Ep.* 7, 4 (p. 34, 6-9), ubi Bernardus de puris malis agit, "quae utique nec uel bene praecipi uel perfici possunt, nec male prohiberi uel non fieri", etiam BERN., *Praec.*, 3, 6 (p. 257, 25 – 258, 2)   113/116 BERN., *Ep.* 7, 4 (p. 34, 16-17)   116/119 BERN., *Ep.* 11, 3 (p. 55, 10-11) paene ad litt.   120/122 cfr GER. MAG., *Tract. paup.*, 265-272   cfr BENED., *Reg.*, c. 33 (p. 562); AVG., *Reg.*, c. 1 (p. 418, 5-14)   122/127 cfr supra, 12-15, et GER. MAG., *Simonia beg.*, 307-309; 987-993; *Tract. paup.*, 228-234; *Ep.* 41, 44-47   cfr THOM., II-II, Q. 186 a. 2 CO. (T. 10, p. 488, a. 2, c. 2, 3-24); Q. 184 a. 5 CO. (T. 10, p. 456, a. 5, c. 2, 9-24)

---

109 rebus] uerbis *OB*   110 his *M*   possint *B*   111 ut] Vnde *O*   Bernardus] beatus *praem. OBM*   De] *om. B*   111/112 precepto et] *om. OB*   113 propria *OB*   ut] Vnde *O*   Bernardus] idem *praem. M*   115 quem] quoniam *M*   licet] ei *praem. M*   monacho] autem *add. M*   116 idem] *om. H2¹, suppl. H2²*   117 dicit *LH2H1*   undecima] *hic potius sec. Bern. legendum est*, decima *codd.*   120/135 inspicienti – licenciare] *hanc partem textus praebent Kk O2 P*   121 Augustini] beati *praem. KkM*   Augustini *sic K*   Bernardi] sancti *praem. M*   quomodo] quod *OB*   122/123 huiusmodi] *om. Kk*   126 et pressura] *om. Kk*   128 deputata] *om. L¹, marg. suppl. L²*

gione intenti. Quamuis enim non omnes religiosi teneantur esse
perfecte caritatis nec contemplatiui, tamen tenentur se ad hoc
extendere et laborare secundum potenciam et modum cuiuslibet
ut | illi quantum possint fini appropinquent, nec sine grandi pec- 246va
cato et periculo obicem uoluntarie ponere possunt perfeccioni
caritatis. Et hec est radix cur impedimentum per propria bona nec
papa possit religiosis prestare nec licenciare.

Si queratur quale dem consilium monialibus iam professis,
quibus nec uestes nec uictus competens datur de bonis communibus, uidetur michi: si non ualeant omnino de communibus sustentari, quod acciperent cum dolore cordis, cum licencia prelatarum que offeruntur uoluntarie ab amicis, et ponerent ea ante
pedes prepositorum, et facto et mente sincera sine ficcione cordis
liberam eis in predictis permitterent facere uoluntatem. Si tunc eis
illorum amministracio concederetur et permitteretur, et concessis
non sicut propriis sed sicut communibus eciam ad aliorum indi-
genciam, si alii magis indigerent, uterentur, semper tamen mallent
omnia ad commune reponi et de communibus quam de propriis
uiuere, et ut regule exquirunt fierent communia, laborare.

Tali moniali spero salutem, que raro inuenitur. Si alie sint se-
cure, ego non sum securus, sed multum eis timeo. Nec estimari
potest numerus uiciorum et singularitatum ex huiusmodi singula-
ritatibus oriencium.

129/132 cfr Thom., II-II, Q. 186 a. 2 co. (T. 10, p. 488, a. 2, c. 2, 9-19)   132/
134 cfr Thom., II-II, Q. 186 a. 2 co. (T. 10, p. 488, a. 2, c. 2, 19-21)

---

129 enim] *om. Kk*   teneantur] *marg. corr. L²*, *cett.*, tenentur
L¹ H1 Kk O2 P   132 fini] *add. K M O B O2 P Kk*, *om. L H2 H1*   134 radix] et
causa *add. M*   impedimentum – bona] indultum seu dispensacionem ad
propria *M*   135 praestare] dare *Kk*   136/148 si – inuenitur] *hanc partem
textus praebent Kk W*, 136/151 *om. M*   136 quare *K*   monialibus] monachis et *praem. Kk*   137 uestis *O*   bonis] *om. Kk W*   138 de communibus bonis omnino *W*   139 quod] si *add. W*   cordis] et *add. W*   139/
140 prelatarum] suarum *add. W*   140 que] ea *praem. Kk W*   ponerentur
O B   ea] *om. O B*   141 cordis ficcione *tr. K O B*   146 communi *Kk*
148 Tali – inuenitur] Talibus reuerendus doctor prescriptus sperat salutem, qui raro inueniuntur, ut fatetur. Hec ille *scripsit Conradus in Kk*   148/
151 Si – oriencium] *om. M Kk W*   150/151 singularitatibus] singularibus bonis *L H2 H1*

EPISTOLA (46) DE MONACHORVM INGRESSV ET EORVM RESIGNACIONE IN MONASTERIIS

CONSPECTVS SIGLORVM

H2 DEN HAAG, Koninklijke Bibliotheek, 78 J 55, s. XVa
Kk KÖLN, Historisches Archiv der Stadt Köln, GB 8° 152, a. 1438
L   LIÈGE, Bibliothèque de l'Université, 229 (c), a. 1451
W   WOLFENBÜTTEL, Herzog August Bibliothek, 203 Extravagantes, s. XVc

⟨EPISTOLA⟩
DE MONACHORVM INGRESSV
ET EORVM RESIGNACIONE IN MONASTERIIS

Predilecti mei in Christo, qui habent spiritualia dona de licencia abbatis, siue parati fuerint resignare cum abbas iusserit siue non, de iure communi non sunt excommunicati nec suspensi, et illi retinent usum clauium et realiter absoluunt.

1/21 Ger. hic THOM., II-II, Q. 186 a. 9 co. (T. 10, p. 500, a. 9, c. 1, 33 – c. 2, 20) sequitur, uerisimiliter sec. IOH. FRIB., *Summa Conf.*, L. 3 t. 33 q. 25 (f. 216r, c. 1-2) allegatum, qui praecipit quod "horum transgressio [i.e. quae pertinent ad actus uirtutum], quantum ad ea quae cadunt communiter sub praecepto, obligat ad mortale", quod ille facit [infra, 20-21] "qui non est paratus sua resignare"; ille enim transgreditur "quaedam ad quas obligatur religiosus ex uoto professionis [quod] respicit principaliter tria praedicta, scilicet paupertatem, continentiam et obedientiam. ... Et ideo transgressio horum trium obligat ad mortale. Aliorum autem transgressio non obligat ad mortale", quod pertinet ad illos "qui sic habent bona quod parati sunt ea resignare ad uoluntatem abbatis" [infra, 8-19], qui non transgrediuntur "uotum ... professionis". Illi enim uerisimiliter iussu abbatis bona habent, sicut exhibit *Decret.*, X 3.35.2 (c. II, 596, 59-61), ubi legitur: "Qui uero peculium habuerit, nisi ab abbate fuerit ei pro iniuncta administratione permissum, a communione remoueatur altaris". Iohannes hic porro sec. magistrum suum Vlricum elucidat (f. 216r, c. 2, 45-49): "Sic habere proprium est mortale peccatum. Recipere autem paruum quid sine licentia non cum animo occultandi potest: non contra preceptum est, et est ueniale peccatum". Postremo illi "qui habent spiritualia dona de licencia abbatis", neque uotum paupertatis neque uotum obedientiae transgrediuntur, quippe cum hic de donis non materialibus ab abbate permissis agatur. Cfr etiam HENR. BOIC, *Dist.*, sup. X 3.35.6 (p. 527, c. 2, 29-47 sub num. 18)   1/4 super monachos in saecularibus ecclesiis constitutos cfr GRAT., *Decr.*, C.16 q.1 p.c.19 (c. I, 765, 44 – 766, 5); c. 21-35 (c. I, 766-770); D.58 c.1-2 (c. I, 224); *Decret.*, X 3.35.5 (c. II, 598-599) et alias auctoritates a IOH. FRIB., *Summa Conf.*, L. 3 t. 28 q. 2 (f. 195r, c. 1 – 195v, c. 1) allegatas   4/6 cfr BENED., *Reg.*, c. 33 (p. 562, 1-14)

Tit. De monachorum ingressu et eorum resignacione in monasteriis *ante textum rubric. L*, nota, de proprietariis *marg. exponit L³*, Idem in quadam epistola *tit. in W*, prosequitur magister Gerardus Magnus de ista materia *ante* 8 *ut tit. ins. Conradus in Kk, tit. om. H2*   1/7 Predilecti – absoluendi] *non hab. fragmentum in Kk*   1 bona *W*   2 resignare] *corr. L³*, regnare *L¹*   2/3 siue non] *post* resignare *pos. W*

5 Si qui fuerint per constitucionem uestram et sic per denunciacionem proprietarii excommunicati, illi non haberent super corpus misticum uel in corpore mistico usum absoluendi.

Illi autem qui sic habent bona quod parati sunt ea resignare ad uoluntatem abbatis, licet periculose steterint, eos tamen nec con-
10 dempno nec assecuro, magnum uero eis est periculum. Tamen non dico quod sint *filii mortis* propter mortale, nec tamen dico quod sint filii uite. Illos dico habere usum clauium, et quos absoluunt absoluti sunt nisi aliud canonicum obstiterit. Tamen in confessione facienda, in quantum bono modo caritate mutua ser-
15 uata et pro parte, mallem alteri confiteri, sed in dubio nullus est uitandus. Propter dubiam ueritatem non est certa caritas frangenda nec ordo ca|ritatis relinquendus in tali dubio, quando suspiciones et rixe et dissensiones possint oriri. Hoc dico de parato sua resignare ad iussum abbatis.
20 De illo qui non est paratus sua resignare, dico quod est in mortali peccato et *filius perdicionis* pro tunc. Et ille nullo modo est trahendus aut inducendus ut confessionem alicuius audiat aut

---

11 cfr I Reg. 26, 16   21 II Thess. 2, 3 ; cfr Ioh. 17, 12

5/7 sc. cum in mortali peccato uiuant nisi proprietatem resignent, sec. auctoritates infra, 20-25, allatas   12/16 cfr fontes supra, 1-4, allegatos   13/15 cfr GRAT., *Decr.*, De pen., D.6 a.c.3 ; c.3 (c. I, 1244, 29-38)   16/18 cfr GRAT., *Decr.*, De pen., D.6 a.c.3 (c. I, 1244, 25-28), etiam C.16 q.1 p.c.19 (c. I, 765, 43-44)   16/21 cfr GER. MAG., *Stat.*, 122-126 ; 512-523 ; *Tract. paup.*, 986-990 ; *Ep.* 41, 83-88 ; 106-119, praesertim 112-114   20/21 cfr fontes supra, 1-21, allegatos

---

6 habent *W*   8 Illi] Religiosi sic primum uocabulum scr. Conradus in *Kk*   bona] propria *Kk*   10 periculum eis est *tr. W*   est] om. *L¹*, post periculum inser. *L²*   11 non] nec *Kk*   tamen] om. *Kk*   dico similiter *W*   12 Et tales usum habere dico clauium *W*   13 obsteterit *H2*   Tamen] Sunt *praem. L²*   14 modo] poteritis add. *W*   14/15 caritatem mutuo seruate *W*, seruata caritate mutua *tr. Kk*   14 fugiendi *L¹*, *uel fortasse ex* fugienda *corr. in ras. L²*   15 pro parte] sic *L¹ H2*, propterea *corr. L²*, pace *Kk*, sed pro parte saniori *W*, potest *fortasse legendum est, cfr Ep. 19, 54* in quantum potest et debet, *Focar.* 20 (2809/2810) in quantum licite potest quis mallem] hoc fieri possit *marg. suppl. L³*   16 Propter] Et *praem. W*   16/17 fugienda *Kk*   17 relinquendus] est add. *W*   in tali dubio] in illis. Dubito *W*   quando] ubi uel *praem. L³*   18 discensiones sic *L H2*   20 illo] uero add. *W*   20/21 peccato mortali *tr. Kk*   21 Et] sic add. *Kk*   nullo modo] a nullo *L*, nullo *H2*   22 inducendus] est *hic pos. W*

ut aliquid sui officii in persona ecclesie exerceat, quia talis in quolibet actu, secundum Thomam in *Quarto Sentencia|rum* et Albertum, mortaliter peccat, eciam si non esset excommunicatus. De excommunicacione talis uiri alias scripsi.

De mulieribus in grangiis. Si quis possit salua obediencia uitare eas, tenetur. Et si omnino esset propinquum periculum, esset recurrendum ad monasterium, eciam si displiceret abbati. Pocius esset *Deo quam hominibus* parendum, nec in foueam peccati mortalis deberet se quis precipitare propter cuiuscumque imperium, sed pocius omnia mala pati antequam hoc faceret. Sicut enim non deberet appropinquare mortali peccato propter alicuius iussum, sic nec deberet iussum superioris sine timore mali cadenti in constantem uirum declinare. Valete dilectissimi, memores mei in oracionibus uestris.

Cum timore dico quod iuuenes maneant usque uideant ad quantum abbas, prior et bursarius uelint et possint monasterium reformare. Forte Deus dabit ut *induantur* uberi *uirtute ex alto*

29/30 cfr Act. 5, 29   39 Luc. 24, 49

23/26 cfr GER. MAG., *Focar.* 23 (3190-3251), etiam 18 (2519-2531); *Artic.* 10 (77-84), etiam *Artic.* 2 (25-29); *Obseru.* (10-22)   cfr IOH. FRIB., *Summa Conf.*, L. 3 t. 22 q. 25 (f. 163v, c. 2, 19-35), qui allegat THOM., *Sent.*, L. 4 d. 24 q. 1 a. 3 qc. 5 CO. (p. 894, c. 1, 63-66); ibid., qc. 5 ad 4 (p. 894, c. 2, 16-19) et ALB. MAG., *Sent.*, L. 4 d. 24 art. 11 (Vol. 30, p. 45, c. 2 in fine); in *Obseru.* fere iidem loci certissime, in *Focar.* uerisimiliter allegantur sec. IOH. FRIB.   26 cfr GER. MAG., *Focar.* 18 (2539-2549)   30/31 cfr locos supra, 1-21; 23-26, allegatos   32 cfr GER. MAG., *Focar.* 19 (2663-2665; 2632), etiam 21 (2874-2875)   34/35 cfr formula iuridica "Vani timores sunt aestimandi, qui non cadunt in constantem uirum", primo in locutione comparabili e Gaio allegatum in IVST., *Dig.* 4, 2, 6 (p. 80, c. 1 [113, 31-32]), a Ger. uerisimiliter aliunde allegatum, e.g. uerbatim sec. *Decret.*, X 1.40 (de his quae ui metusue causa fiunt).4 (c. II, 220, 7-8 (rubr.); 19-21 (text.)) uel sec. THOM., II-II, Q. 125 (De timore) a. 4 arg. 2 (T. 10, p. 46, c. 1, art. 4, 8-9); cfr etiam duos locos locutionem eandem continentes, sed uere minus probabiles (cum de matrimoniis agant), a uiro docto Mulder propositos, sc. X 4.1.15 (c. II, 666, 54-56 (rubr.); 667, 11-14 (text.)); X 4.1.28 (c. II, 671, 42-43 (rubr.); 56-58 (text.), cfr postremo etiam THOM., II-II, Q. 98 (De periurio) a. 3 ad 1 (T. 9, p. 345, c. 2, 2-5)

---

23 personam *L H2*   26/41 De – sencientis] *om. Kk*   26 De – scripsi] *om. W*   uiri] *om. H2*   27 De mulieribus in grangiis] De uilibus personis, scilicet personis in grangiis *W*   28 propinquum esset *tr. W*   28/29 recurrendum esset *tr. W*   30 hominibus] *sic L*, homini *postea in ras. L*   35 declinare] et cetera *W*   35/105 Valete – omnibus] *om. W*

40 saluo tamen proprio iudicio cuiuscumque pericula | singularius uidentis et sencientis.

Proprietas monachorum proprietariorum, dummodo cum sciencia abbatis sua habeant, non nocet ueris monachis sine proprietate pauperibus quoad conuersacionem eorum ad extra. Nam 45 quoad homines non debent haberi pro excommunicatis, sed quoad Deum sunt ueri proprietarii, maxime tamen illi qui non sunt beniuoli ad resignandum scita uoluntate abbatis. Nullus debet eos petere uel trahere ad officiandum in aliquo officio ecclesiastico sacro uel eis confiteri, quia perdurant in continuo mortali 50 et scitur quod perdurant. Et talis officians uel celebrans in aliquo officio ecclesiastico sicut minister ecclesie mortaliter peccat. Ideo nullus | debet eum trahere ad mortale peccatum, maxime quia non potest presumi contritus quamdiu proprietatem tenet, imparatus resignare si abbas peteret, uel si uoluntarie non resignaret 55 ad peticionem uel ad solam uoluntatem abbatis nisi cogeretur, quia nullus coactus uere conteritur uel benefacit.

Propter grangias non uidetur recedendum, nisi periculum mortalis peccati immineat. Non dico: "si peccatum immineat", sed: "si periculum proximum mortali peccato immineat", et si tunc 60 possunt recurrere ad monasterium non exituri, *cessat quassacio*.

De monialibus ⟨est⟩ maximum periculum quia capto ho|mine a moniali non est potens se manifestare uel nodos disrumpere recedendo. Nullus enim potest ex se et per se resurgere a peccato, maxime carnis. Fortis armati hominem capientis potenciam euadere 65 non est uinculati hominis. Sunt duo alia pericula apud moniales, scilicet symonia ingressuum – et quis absoluet? – et proprietas earum – et quis, si absoluerit, absoluet sine claue sciencie et potencie mendaciter absoluentem? Ibi non uideo remedium,

---

60 Ps. 105 (106), 30 paene ad litt.

43/44 cfr *Decret.*, X 3.35.2 (c. II, 596, 59-61) supra in app. font. sup. 1-21 uerbatim citatam   44/56 eandem materiam Ger. supra, 20-25, tractauit   57/60 eandem materiam Ger. supra, 28-32, tractauit

---

42/43 sciencia] sci- *L¹*, scitu sui *suppl., partim in marg., L²*   43 sua] *om. Kk*   nocent *H2*   44 qui ad conuersionem *L H2*   eorum] excommunicacionem quoad extra *add. L H2*   49 mortali] peccato *add. Kk*   51 ministri *L H2*   57/105 Propter – omnibus] *om. Kk*   59 mortalis peccati *H2*   61 est] *sic legendum, in codd.*

nisi uel non exire ad moniales, eciam si abbas iusserit, uel si quis
70 iuerit, ut ad eas dumtaxat uadat quas sine proprietate uel symonia mundas estimauerit, quas omnes non inueniet, uel tercio ut
uadat et nullam absoluat non contritam uel auersam a predictis
malis.

Et sic reuertatur ad monasterium ut inutiles se possunt bene
75 constringere et iuramento se inuicem promittere ad omne id
seruandum quod regule beati Benedicti per se est annexum, quilibet in se, et quilibet alius audiente alio. Et ideo possunt et iurare
et promittere sub iuramento se numquam propria habituros. Et
hoc iam ex regula promiserunt et uouerunt uoto solempni impli-
80 cite, et uotum magis constringit et obligat quam iuramentum.
Vnde possunt se de nouo constringere ad hoc et iurare et promit-
tere, hoc est primum uotum firmare et ro|borare, et hoc est me- 241vb
ritorium.

Sequitur meo uidere quod possunt bene iurare et promittere se
85 numquam uelle consentire in redempcionem monachi alicuius
nisi proprietatem abiuret in professione facienda: non in recep-
cione, quia possit exire post recepcionem. Et maxime bonum
esset ⟨ut⟩ huic ultime compromissioni et iuramento abbas consen-
tiret, alias non possunt in manifesto iuramentum a recepto exigere
90 uel promissionem accipere in recepcione. | 187

De iuramento in promissione facienda. Quia iurare non est de
regula nec de essencia professionis, sed uouere, et ideo caucius
esset si abbas non uellet compromittere quod iurarent neminem
se accepturos, nisi qui se promitteret expresse in professione sua,
95 si maneret, renunciaturum omni proprietati et eciam tali proprietati palleate, aut non expresse uoueret paupertatem ueram aut
communibus omnino sustentari, ut uotum illud esset quedam ma-
nifestacio, declaracio et renouacio regule et caucio contra pericula
proprietatum palleatarum, et sic melius staret.

100 Vere, uere uellem quod bursarius manus aperiret et impleretur
omne animal benediccione, et ut pauperibus melius esset quam

78/79 cfr BENED., *Reg.*, c. 33, 1-6 (p. 562, 1-14)

70 iuerit] ad aliquas *marg. add. L²*   ad] *corr.* H2², aliquid H2¹   75 se] *sic* L¹H2, sibi *corr. in ras.* L²   84 quod] *om.* L¹H2, *suppl.* L²   88 ut] *sic legendum, et* L H2   92 professionis] *om.* L   96 non] *contra codd. om.* Mulder   101 animal] *om.* L¹, *suppl.* L³   hec magister Gerardus Magnus *expl. post* 35 declinare *in* W

proprietariis: omnes tunc recurrerent. Vere, rei sunt proprietatis
eciam illi qui non habent, qui ea faciunt quo magis timeant alii
renunciare propriis uel propria | magis firmiter teneant, si possunt   242ra
105 liberalius dispensare de omnibus.

SERMO IN FESTO PALMARVM DE PAVPERTATE

CONSPECTVS SIGLORVM

codex principalis

A   BRUSSEL, Koninklijke Bibliotheek van België, 1216-34 (1129), s. XVb

Familia α

L   LIÈGE, Bibliothèque du Grand Séminaire, 6 G 28, a. 1466
Z   WOLFENBÜTTEL, Herzog August Bibliothek, 314 Gud. Lat. 4°, s. XVa

Familia ε

Ek   BERLIN, Staatsbibliothek zu Berlin – Preußischer Kulturbesitz, lat. fol. 690, a. 1397-1402
El   BERLIN, Staatsbibliothek zu Berlin – Preußischer Kulturbesitz, lat. fol. 704, a. 1454-1460

Hos codices in plagulis phototypice expressis contulimus.

SERMO IN FESTO PALMARVM DE PAVPERTATE

Videant pauperes et letentur, Psalmo .LXVIII. Carissimi, hodiernus Domini aduentus seu introitus in Iherusalem et ad Syon, montem sanctum eius, quem hodierna die tam festiua solempnitate celebramus, quamuis allegoricis mysteriorum et typicis moralitatum refertus sit figuris, uerumptamen ea que in hoc Christi introitu patenter ad oculum gesta seu ostensa sunt, nos et omnium uoluntarie pauperum uisus aspectu delectant ac palatum paupertatis dulci congratulationis sapore reficiunt. Vnde ipsos pauperes hortamur ut pauperem regem Christum hodie aduentantem totis spiritualium oculorum obtutibus *uideant et letentur*.

In quo aduentu paupertas Christi maxima simul et maiestas regia quasi quedam, que quibusdam uidentur repugnantia, iuxta se tamen posita uere coniunctissima et amicissima simul nobis resplendent et irradiant. In tota namque uita Christi sicut humilitas, sicut et caritas, sic et ipsa claruit paupertas. Sed nescio si umquam ante Christi passionem in aliquo uno facto uel itinere Christi sicut in hoc aduentu tot paupertatis exterioris tam lucide patue-

---

1 Ps. 68 (69), 33   2/3 cfr Matth. 21, 1-9; Marc. 11, 1-10; Luc. 19, 29-44; Ioh. 12, 12-16   10 Ps. 68 (69), 33

Tit. Incipit sermo in festo palmarum de paupertate editus a domino Gerardo Groot in Dauantria uenerabili dyacono *tit. in A,* Incipit opusculum magistri Gherardi dicti Groet de paupertate *tit. in Z,* Sermo de paupertate magistri Gerardi Groet de festo palmarum *tit. in L,* Magister Gerardus (Johannes (*sic T*)) Groet de recommendacione uoluntarie paupertatis *tit. in K T,* Magister Gerhardus Groet Dauentriensis utriusque iuris doctor consultissimus, qui sepultus est Dauentrie aput eos uenerabiles patres quos fratres recte appellamus *super tit. ins. alia manus in K,* Sermo magistri Gerhardi Groet de paupertate *tit. in Ek,* Sermo eiusdem magistri Gherardi (de *postea del. ipse G*) Groet in die palmarum de Domini nostri Ihesu Christi humillima azinacione et eius altissima paupertate et ipsius paupertatis ammirabili recommendacione, et religiosorum proprietate *tit. in G, tit. om. El, sed cfr infra explicit, ubi hoc opus Gerardo attribuitur*   1 Karissimi *Z Ek*   2 siue *Z*   intruitus *sic Ek*   Ierusalem *El*   3 die hodierna *tr. El*   sollempnitate *Z L El*   4 allegoriter *El*   mysteriorum] et cetera *add. Ek*   5 refectus *A*   ea] *om. L*   8 gratulationis *Ek*   9 totis] hodie *iterum praem. Ek El*   11 simul et maiestas] *in ras. scr. L²*   16 passionem Christi¹ *tr. L*   in – Christi²] *om. A*

runt uestigia. Similiter e regione nescio si umquam a turba in tam solempni habitus reuerentia tantaue sibi fuerit attributa dignitas uel magnificentia tantaque altitudo et potentia, ut possit, ut uidetur, in dubium reuocari an in hoc aduentu maiestas fuerit depau|perata uehementius an paupertas excellentius exaltata. Quid enim sibi uult harum rerum quasi contrariarum hodierna in summo gradu iuxtapositio, nisi ut nobis summa ueritas suo facto et exemplo ostenderet quam multiplex nobilitas, quam excellens dignitas, quam pulchra rerum uere opulentarum uarietas uoluntarie inesset paupertati. Habeant hic oculos qui non habent loculos, ut *uideant et letentur*. |

Ecce, aduenit dominator Dominus suam sanctam et preelectam uisitare metropolim ciuitatem, et se singulariter et notanter magnificum et gloriosum ostendere in regia maiestate, triumphalibus uocibus ac imperialibus plausibus a turba uenerari atque ipse semper a Deo Patre benedictus iter benedictum in nomine Domini peragere, quo se benedictum et benedicte uenientem in nomine Altissimi toti turbe manifestando aperuit, quo et qui uere solus Rex est uoluit uideri et dici Rex in terris. Nam sequentium et precedentium turbe populorum eum *Regem, Luce* .XIX., *Regem Israel, Iohannis* .XII., *filium* Regis, *Mathei* .XXI., et iterum secundum *Lucam, benedictum*, quia *uenit* regnum patris nostri *Dauid*, proclamabant.

Quin ymmo et etiam clamari et precari uoluit Saluator in celis quia *osanna in excelsis*, id est obsecro salua nos in excelsis. Vestimentis etiam, quibus discipuli et turbe uel *uiam strauerunt* asino

---

18/20 cfr Matth. 21, 6-10 ; Marc. 11, 4-10 ; Luc. 19, 32-38   28 Ps. 68 (69), 33   37 cfr Luc. 19, 38   37/38 cfr Ioh. 12, 13   38 cfr Matth. 21, 9   38/39 cfr Luc. 19, 38 ; Matth. 21, 9   42 Marc. 11, 10 ; cfr Matth. 21, 9 ; Luc. 19, 38 ; Ioh. 12, 13   42/47 Matth. 21, 7-8 ; Marc. 11, 7-8 partim paene ad litt., cfr Luc. 19, 35-36

20/22 ad haec uerba Ger. infra, 1174-1176, in conclusione alludit   30 Hierusalem 'metropolis ciuitas' nuncupatur in e.g. HIER., *Comm. in Proph. Min.*, *in Abdiam* 20 (p. 372, 697) ; *Comm. in Ezech.* 4, 16, 6-7 (p. 167, 1022-1023)

---

18 uestigia] insignia siue *praem. A*   19 tanta sibi ne *sic El*   fuerit sibi *tr. Ek*   22 excellentius] *corr.* Z^2, uehementius Z^1 23 quasi] *om. A*   24 ueritas summa *tr. Z*   26/27 inesset uoluntarie *tr. A*   27 inessent *L*   29 Ecce] De regali aduentu *ut subtit. marg. adnot. L*   31 in] et *El*   35 aparuit *Z Ek*   39 quoniam *Z*   43 uiam] *om. A*

uel dorsum eius uestierunt, ac foliorum, frondium et ramorum palmarumque proiectione obedientiam et subiectionem omnium sub dominii sui pedibus, et in cunctis inuincibilem uictorem, quia palma olim signum uictorie erat, ostenderunt cantantes in uia Domini, quoniam uere magna est gloria Domini, quam *uideant pauperes et letentur.*

Nam hoc modo uehementer exaltatus regnique indutus decorem precinxit se | undique paupertate. Ecce, qualem habuit in hac gloria apparatum, qualem comitiuam. Comitiuam habuit rex uelut duces suos, comites et barones et satellites simplicissimos, abiectissimos et pauperrimos, apostolos dico et discipulos. Qualis uero reliquorum turba fuerit, beatus Anselmus in quodam sermone hodierne festiuitatis aperit: "Sola", inquit, "Christum pauperum turba prosequitur et innocentium comitatur, quia innocentia innocentiam, humilitas humilitatem, paupertas paupertatem libens complectitur". Innocentes ipsum fuisse comitatum indubitabile est, nam *ex ore infantium et lactentium* hodie laus perfecta est, *Mathei* .XXI. Quomodoue estimabile sit, nisi uoluntarie pauperes uel | paupertatis dilectores Christum in tanta paupertate constitutum tanta gloria extulisse? Ecce, eius semper memorabilis comitiua pauperrima, cum et infantes et lactentes, quia terrena bona in eorum potestate esse non sinuntur, uere pauperum numero possunt asscribi.

Apparatus autem eius pauper fuit undiquaque, a nudi capitis uertice ad plantam pedis cum tibiis nudis, nudam gerens et plantam. Nichil nisi stigmata ostendit paupertatis, nudus superius, nudus inferius, non auro uel purpura fulgens, sed uili, grosso et rudi panno cinctus in corpore. Non curru seu alia uectura uehitur,

---

48/49 Ps. 68 (69), 33   60/61 Matth. 21, 16 paene ad litt.   69/77 cfr Matth. 21, 2; Luc. 19, 30; Ioh. 12, 14-15

46/47 cfr e.g. Avg., *In Ioh. tract.* 51, 2 (p. 440, 7-8)   54/59 Ivo Carn., *Serm. 16 in ramis palmarum* (c. 587A-B) paene ad litt.

---

45 et] *om.* A   47 uictorie signum *tr.* Z   47/48 Domini¹ – gloria] *om.* L   51 se] *om.* El¹, *suppl.* El²   52 comitiuam²] *om.* El   53 et¹] *om.* A L   55 Ancelmus A L   56 pauperem Z Ek   57 et] *om.* A L   60 lactancium El   61 .XXI.] .XII. L   67 Apparatus] De apparatu Christi *ut subtitulum interposuit* K L   undequaque *sic* A   68 nudam cum tibiis nudis *tr.* Z L   nuda Ek   70 uel] non A   71 cincto K   seu] sed Z Ek, uel El

non altum ascendit dextrarium, sed nec equitat, sed basse asinat maiestas paupercula.

Humilis rex iumentum bassum, uile, grossum, rude et deforme, sed mansuetum et pacis conscendit amicum. O altitudo diuiciarum, cur in tanta tua gloria tam omnino uilissimum iumentum elegisti? Numquid tui fuerunt *et sunt omnes fere siluarum, iumenta in montibus et boues*? | Cur et illum asinum sine proprietate, quasi non tuum sed quasi alienum et communem, tuis regiis applicuisti usibus? Nam secundum sanctos doctores pullus et asella communes erant, multos habebant dominos. Nutriebantur ad communia pauperum opera, qui iumenta non habebant. Ideo quasi parata ad hoc stabant *ante ianuam in biuio* secundum euangelium, *Marci* .XI.

Asinaturus etiam Dominus in hoc impreciato iumentorum genere elegit uel sexu fragile et ad insedendum fedum, quia asinam femellam, uel etate imbecille, quia *pullum asine* seu asellum, ac uel sessioni et asinationi insuetum, quia *pullum, super quem nullus hominum sedit*, uel uilioribus et rusticioribus usibus coaptatum, quia asina subiugalis, id est iugi laboribus deputata. Hec aduertant pauperes, quibus in usu sunt communia, quibus uilia, quibus sordida, quibus inepta quelibet et fragilia. Et sic asinantem pauperem regem *uideant et letentur*. |

Talis ergo est regis asinus. Sed ubi sella regia, que deest cum phaleris? Cuius loco subsunt sibi quasi pauperi rustico illa non

---

77/78 Ps. 49 (50), 10   80/81 cfr etiam Luc. 19, 33   83/84 Marc. 11, 4
87 Luc. 19, 30   88/89 Marc. 11, 2; cfr Luc. 19, 30   93 Ps. 68 (69), 33
95/96 cfr Marc. 11, 7; Matth. 21, 7; Luc. 19, 36

80/82 cfr HIER., *In Matth.* 3 (p. 182, 1182-1191), quem locum uariatur a BEDA, *In Luc.* 19, 33 (p. 343, 1904-1907); *In Marc.* 11, 5 (p. 572, 1185-1191), et reiteratur a HRAB. MAVR., *Exp. in Matth.* 6 (p. 542, 65-70); auctoritates ambo se referunt ad *Luc.* 19, 33 "dixerunt domini eius ad illos"

74 Humilis] De iumento *ut subtitulum interposuit* L   difforme *A Ek*
75/76 diuiciarum] *om.* L, o iterum *praem. El*   77 Numquid] non *add.*
Ek El   tue *El*   78 montibus] oues *add.* Z   et] igitur *A*   azinum *El*
79 quasi²] *om.* A   81 azella *A El*   82 opera pauperum *tr.* A
83 Ideo – stabant] *om.* L   84 .XI.] capitulo *add.* Z   85 Asinaturus] De asino Christi *ut subtitulum interposuit* L   Dominus etiam *tr. Ek El*   86 insidendum *Ek*   azinam *El*   87 asine] *om.* L¹, *suppl.* L²   88 et] uel *L El*   asinacione *El*   90 Hoc *Ek*   91 in] *om.* L   92 quelibet] quibus *A L* et] *om. A L*

sua, sed communia discipulorum concessa uestimenta uilia, forte
laciniosa, forte repeciata, forte reconsuta. Non autem hec uel auro
nitent uel resplendent ebore. Hec sella non sella, sicut et sessor
omni caret ornatu et commodo omnique ad asinandum apto et
solito, si non omnino necessarium fuerit. Non habet rex quibus
uacillantes pedes uel sine ocreis et caligis nudas stringat tibias
uel corpus subleuet uel asinum. Non habet sella quibus femora
coaptet, latera. Desunt quibus tardum iumentum stimulet, calca-
ria. Absunt quibus pertinax animal et stultum dirigat, frenum | et   48va
capistra. *Videant pauperes* quid hic ornatum uoluptuosum sit uel
commodum. Hic summus ornatus inornatus est, hic magna uoluptas et commoditas est posse lete uti inuoluptuosis et incom-
modis.

    Sic progreditur hodie gloriosus rex et humilis, stature procere,
dimissis oculis, facie plana, pendulis tybiis et fere terram contin-
gentibus, necessario sibi asino insedens, uix necessariis usus, et
illis uilibus et illis communibus et illis paucissimis, ad que acci-
pienda seu acquirenda minime antea fuit sollicitus. Sed ipso in-
stanti necessitatis et indigentie hora pro asina et pullo mittit discipulos ad suam necessitatem, *quia Domino necessarius est*,
Marci .XI., uel *necessarium habet, Luce* .XIX. Eorum custodibus al-
legari iubet, fidens in Domino quod eos faciat discipulos placabi-
les, et confestim dimittant eos. Cumque regi hos adduxissent, non
quesiuit communiter itinerantibus apta, consueta et requisita, sed
contentus omnino presentibus et eis que ad manum erant uesti-
mentis non quesiuit uel misit pro aliis. In sua igitur necessitate
omnem anticipatam reiecit curam diuine prouidentie, et secun-

---

    109/115 cfr etiam infra, 445-446   111 cfr Marc. 11, 3 ; Luc. 19, 34   113/
115 cfr Matth. 21, 2 ; etiam Marc. 11, 2-3 ; Luc. 19, 30   115/116 Marc. 11, 3
116 Luc. 19, 34   116/118 cfr Matth. 21, 7 ; Marc. 11, 4-7 ; Luc. 19, 33-35
120/121 cfr Matth. 21, 7 ; Marc. 11, 7

    96/97 cfr infra, 797

---

    98 nitent] lucent *Z Ek El*   101 pedes] *om. L¹, suppl. L²*   stringit *A*
103 latera] *eras. Z*   104 quibus] *om. El*   105 capistrum *L*   110 oculis dimissis *tr. Z L*   plena *L*   113 seu acquirenda] *om. El*   aurea *El*
ipsa *A Z L*   114 hora] *om. El*   115 ad] et *A Ek El*   116 Luce] *om. L*
.XIX.] .III. *El*   117 discipulis *L*   118 et] ut *El*   119 communiter] consequenter *A*

dum hanc rectoris uoluntati in rerum usu se submisit, ac usu peracto amplius nichil in eis sibi reseruauit. |

125 Hunc *pauperes* religiosi modum in rebus *uideant* acquirendi, *uideant* et utendi, *uideant* et dimittendi, et *letabuntur* si nulla omnino habeant quibus preoccupati sunt propria, sed tantum necessaria a prepositis, diuine uoluntati et prepositorum discretioni plene et libenter petitiones eorum humiles confidenter committentes, postulent. Si que parare uel difficile uel longe uel non ad manum est, non requirant, sed | contenti presentibus, nichil per curam uel prouidentiam reseruantes, cum necessitati satisfactum fuerit, ea reiciant uel remittant. Cuius rei hic in Christo uideant mirabilem et dulcem ut in speculo ymaginem. Nam *beati qui intelligunt super* hunc *egenum et pauperem*, ut uideant, quia *in die malo* letentur, quia *liberabit eos Dominus*.

Hec ergo est illa stricte et immodice, sed exaltate dies paupertatis, ad quam cum suis circumstantiis tam signanter et uidendam et exaltandam, *Zacharie* .IX., idem prophetans hortatus est, dicens: *exulta satis, filia Syon, ecce, rex tuus ueniet iustus et saluator, ipse pauper et ascendens super asinam et pullum asine*. Non recolo quemquam Christi post infantie annos et ante passionem actum singularius et expressius annunciatum in prophetis, quo sancte religiosorum pauperum, qui infima despexerunt, congregationi, quia *filie Syon*, de pauperis regis progredientis regno, iustitia, saluatione et paupertate, sufficienter letandum, quia *exulta satis*, et uidendum, quia *ecce*, Spiritus Sanctus pronunciat.

Hec est et illa dies quam ore proprio Dominus, cum proxime et mortem suam in Iherusalem instantem, et super eam omnem

---

125/126 cfr Ps. 68 (69), 33   **134/136** Ps. 40 (41), 2 paene ad litt.   **139/141** Zach. 9, 9   **144/147** cfr Ps. 68 (69), 33   **148/150** cfr Matth. 27, 45-56, Luc. 23, 26-49

126/130 cfr BENED., *Reg*., c. 33, 1-6 (p. 562)

---

123 rectorum *Ek*   ac] at *A*   **125** Hunc] Ad religiosos admonitio *ut subtitulum interposuit L*   **126** si] *om. Ek*   **128** discretorum *A*   **129** humiles] et *add. El*   **129/130** committente *Ek*   **130** postulant *Z*   **131** requirant] querant nec *praem. Z Ek El*   nichil] uel *El*   **133** ea] eas *Z L El*, eos *Ek*   **137** Hec] Ad diem presentem *ut subtitulum interposuit L*   ergo] *om. A¹*, est ergo *suppl. et tr. A²*   **139** ibidem *A*, isdem *Z*   **140** uenit *Z*   **142** quemque *A Z Ek*   **144** qui] quo *Z El*   **145** quia] qui *El*   **146** iustitiam *Ek*

SERMO IN FESTO PALMARVM DE PAVPERTATE 431

150 sanguinem iustum uenturum eamque desertam futuram †***†, Iudeis tamquam consideratione magnam et uisu dignam premuniendo predixit. *Dico*, inquit, *uobis, ammodo non uidebitis me, donec dicatis: benedictus qui uenit in nomine Domini, Luce* .XIII. et *Mathei* .XXIII. |
155 Hanc etiam paupertatis diem, cum pauper rex appropinquasset hodie ciuitati, diem Iherusalem et diem uisitationis eius diemque pacis cognitione optabilem nominans nunciauit. *Si cognouisses*, | ait, *et tu*, quod *in hac die tua, que ad pacem tibi*, sed modo *abscondita sunt ab oculis tuis*, quasi diceret: "si cognosceres sicut
160 illi, qui me precedunt et comitantur pauperes, quod *hec dies tua* sit dies tua singularis, cognitione dignissima, et tue uisitationis promisse et uocationis ad regiam paupertatem, et que per ymaginem paupertatis hodie *tibi ad pacem*, id est ordinis tranquillitatem, preparantur, aut mecum cum pauperibus inops in pace
165 quiesceres et gloria, aut mecum ignorantiam tuam et delicta uehementer deplorares. Sed hec regie paupertatis bona *abscondita sunt ab oculis tuis*", et omnium uel auarorum, qui *spinis diuiciarum* secundum parabolam Christi *suffocati* sunt, uel potentium seu *principum* mundi, quorum *nemo* secundum apostolum Dei
170 *cognouit sapientiam*, uel prudentium secundum carnem uel astutorum secundum seculum, quorum alii inimici sunt Dei, alii legi *Dei* secundum apostolum *subiecti non sunt*. Omnibus hiis uelamen super oculos positum est, ne maiestatis in paupertate et pau-

437

49ra

152/154 Matth. 23, 39; cfr Luc. 13, 35 paene ad litt.   156/157 cfr Matth. 20, 18; Marc. 10, 33; Luc. 18, 31   157/159 Luc. 19, 42 paene ad litt.   167/168 cfr Matth. 13, 22   169/170 cfr I Cor. 2, 7-8   170/172 cfr Rom. 9, 32 – 10, 3

163/164 cfr THOM., II-II, Q. 29 a. 1 co., ad 1 (T. 8, p. 236, a. 1, c. 2, 7-26), ubi allegat AVG., *Ciu. Dei* 19, 13 (p. 679, 10-11) "pax est omnium rerum tranquillitas ordinis", *sed* "omnium rerum" *om. Thom. Ger.*, infra, 976-978, nominatim allegatum

---

150 *uerbum hic supplendum uidetur, e.g.* presciret, *ut Moll obseruat*   151 usu *A*   151/152 premuniendo] in *praem. Ek*   152 predixit – me] *om. El*   me] *om. Ek*   157 cognatione *Ek*   159 cognouisses *A*   160/161 sit tua *tr. El*   164 inops] et *praem. A L*   169/170 cognouit Dei *tr. Z*   170 uel¹] nec *A Z Ek*, seu *El*   prudenciam *Ek*   170/171 astitutorum *Ek*   172 non sunt subiecti *tr. sec. Rom. 10, 3 A*

pertatis in maiestate diem hodiernum tam solempnisabilem, tam
semper memorabilem recognoscant, *quem uideant pauperes, et
letentur.*

  Hec ergo dies apte et merito dies et festum paupertatis seu so-
lempnitas exaltationis paupertatis est et dici potest. Hec est dies
illa que a fideli populo ab exitu de Egypto et deinceps annua
obseruatione et, ut estimo, repetita, secundum quosdam semper prefiguratione prophetata presignatur. Nam legis imperio,
Exodi .XII., in huius diei prescisam et solempnem figuram et
typum agnus ille paschalis, quem populus Israel secundum | do-
mos et familias die quarta decima ad uesperam, id est incipiente
a uespera quarte decime diei, per esum immolare consueuit, *decima die mensis* eiusdem et non alia die reseruandus solebat sig-
nanter introduci, typicans et presignans quod | uerus ille *agnus
Dei* et Deus – die mensis quinta decima a precedentis diei quarte
decime uespere, a quo Iudei diem inchoant, initiante, scilicet feria sexta, cuncta restauraturus et consummaturus per passionem
immolandus – decima erat die mensis eiusdem, scilicet dominica
precedente, locum sue passionis tam semper memorabili introitu
triumphali, tam et stricta paupertate circumdatus, ingressurus.

  Hec namque Christi, agni pauperis, tam solempnis introductio
mortis et passionis eius proxima fuit dispositio et grandis occasio.
Nam tunc *pharisei dixerunt ad semetipsos*: *"Videte quia nichil
proficimus? Ecce, totus mundus post eum abiit", Iohannis* .XII. Sic
lucem et diem et amorem paupertatis necesse est in nobis prius
sollempniter illucescere, antequam hoc propter quod Christus pas-
sus est, relinquens scilicet nobis exemplum ut sequamur uestigia
eius, perficere atque passioni, cruci, et morti eius conformari et

---

  175/176 Ps. 68 (69), 33   178/181 memoriam huius diei obseruandam esse
praescribitur in Ex. 12, 14; 12, 17; 12, 25   181/187 cfr Ex. 12, 3-4   184/
187 cfr Ex. 12, 6; 8   187/188 e.g. Ioh. 1, 29; 36   196/197 Ioh. 12, 19

---

  174 hodiernum] *sic hic codd. omnes, et ob pron. rel.* 175 quem *preferen-
dum, contra alios locos propinquos hoc substantiuum in genere feminino
tradentes, et contra lectiones* hodiernam *et* quam *a uiro doct. Moll falso im-
primatas*   175 uident Z   178 potest dici *tr. El*   180 secundum quos-
dam] *om. A Z*   181 Nam] noui L   182 Dei Ek   precisam A
186 eius A   187 introduci] *ex* introducere *in ras. corr. Ek*   188 diei]
die *sic L Ek*   191 erat decima *tr. Z*   193 secreta Ek   195 eius] *om. Z*
proxima] proxime *fortasse potius legendum*   198/199 solempniter prius
tr. A   199 priusquam El   201 et²] atque El

SERMO IN FESTO PALMARVM DE PAVPERTATE 433

configurari secumque spiritualiter resurgere et ascendere ualeamus. Hanc uiam ascendant pauperes, uideant ad quam magna ducit, et quod tam grandi se conformat paupertas uoluntaria, gau-
205 deant! Quomodo potest se contempnere uel pati iniurias uel molestias, qui tam longe a corpore relegata et tam modicum ad hominem pertinentia bona prius spernere non ualuit? In cunctis uiam uite docet passionibus preuia paupertas, ductrix et magistra, quam optimam ducem *uideant* | *pauperes et letentur*.
210 O, efficacis paupertatis dies, que est dies spiritualis Iherusalem, interne uisionis et pacis, o, dies ingressus ad sapiendam tranquillitatem ordinis, o, dies progressus ad montem Syon et contemplationis promontorium, o, dies aggressus Domini in templum suum uiuum, numquid et tu dic, si sis illa paupertatis dies, in qua anima
215 sancta, quam diuicie *speluncam latronum* fecerunt, in *orationis domum*, sicut *scriptum est*, uocata et electa est? O, paupertatis dies, Dominus pauper, peracto in te glorioso itinere, tandem sicut paupertatis maiestatem, sic diuiciarum uilitatem et contemptum uoluit ostendere.
220 *Ingressus* enim *in templum ementes et uendentes*, id est res nummismate mensurantes seu transmutantes, non eduxit, sed *eiecit*. *Mensas nummulariorum et cathedras uendentium* non expor|tauit nec extulit, sed *euertit*. Ymmo, ut habetur *Marci* .XI., *non sinebat ut quis transferret uas per templum*, ut omnis rei tempo-
225 ralis fieret in templo mentis immotum et internum silentium et nodi et funiculorum diuiciarum non fieret solutio, sed plena ruptio et abscisio, mutabilium affectuum euersio, uariarum formarum

49va

439

---

209 Ps. 68 (69), 33   215/216 Matth. 21, 13 ; Marc. 11, 17 ; Luc. 19, 46 paene ad litt.   220 Luc. 19, 45   220/224 Marc. 11, 15 paene ad litt., cfr Matth. 21, 12 ; Luc. 19, 45

211/212 cfr Thom., II-II, Q. 29 a. 1 co., ad 1 (T. 8, p. 236, a. 1, c. 2, 7-26), ubi allegat Avg., *Ciu. Dei* 19, 13 (p. 679, 10-11) "pax est omnium rerum tranquillitas ordinis", *sed* "omnium rerum" *om. Thom. Ger.*, infra, 976-978, nominatim allegatum

---

202 specialiter *A*   203 Hac uia *Ek*   206 a corpore] composicione *Ek* religata *Ek El*, relegatus *Z*   210 dies²] *om. Z*   213 promotorium *Z L Ek El*   214 et] non *Z*   scis *Z*   dies] es *praem. Z*   218 utilitatem *Ek*   220 id est] et *A*   227 formarum uariarum *tr. A*

totalis eiectio. Quapropter – et nonne aptissime? – in hac die paupertatis, secundum sanctorum patrum pauperum iusta et congrua instituta, in monasteriis religiosorum, qui omnes paupertati sine proprietate ex solempni uoto sunt asstricti, quicunque inter eos cum quarumcunque rerum proprietate fuerint inuenti, a templo Dei, id est ecclesia sancta et fidelium participatione, excommunicationis sententia seu mucrone anime expelluntur, ceterosque ad eam quam promiserant paupertatem sermone paupertatis in hac die adhortantur, ut et paupertatis gloriam, sic et diuiciarum reiectarum carentiam una hec | dies presens solempnizet, quam tam multis et crebris paupertatis uexillis depictam *uideant pauperes*, atque tam magnis gaudiorum tripudiis adornatam *letentur*, ut simul eam *uideant pauperes et letentur*, que erant uerba nostri proposita thematis.

In quibus uerbis totiens et repetitis et introductis luce clarius duo explicantur. Primo, pauperis uite Christi ueritas actibus imitanda, quia *uideant*, cum nichil practico intellectus oculo recte uidetur quod uerum uite non sit et imitabile. Secundo, paupercule glorie dignitas laudibus extollenda, quia *letentur*, cum nichil

49vb

238/240 Ps. 68 (69), 33

228/234 cfr GER. MAG., *Simonia beg.*, 307-309 ; 987-993 ; *Ep.* 41, 44-47 ; *Ep.* 45, 12-26 ; 122-127   cfr e.g. THOM., II-II, Q. 186 a. 3 (paupertas requiritur ad perfectionem religionis) ; 6 (paupertas, continentia et obedientia cadunt sub uoto) (T. 10, p. 490 ; 496, quorum summarium praestat ibid., THOM., II-II, Q. 186 a. 7 CO. (T. 10, p. 497, c. 2, a. 7, 4-37)   231/234 cfr infra, 334-343 et GER. MAG., *Ep.* 41, 33-35 ; *Ep.* 42, 12-13 ; *Ep.* 45, 97-103   cfr praesertim *Decret.*, X 3.35.2 (c. II, 596, 59-61), ubi legitur : "Qui uero peculium habuerit, ... a communione remoueatur altaris", etiam GRAT., *Decr.*, C.12 q.1 c.5 (c. I, 678, 1-3) ; C.12 q.1 c.9 § 1 (c. I, 679, 28-37) ; C.12 q.1 c.10 § 3-4 (c. I, 680, 12-28) ; *Decret.*, X 3.35.6 § 2 (c. II, 599, 31-42) ; in locos a BERN. PARM., *ibid.* (c. 1291 (L. 3, p. 150), gl. f, l. 70-72) collectos (sc. GRAT., *Decr.*, C.12 q.1 c.11 ; C.18. q.1 c.1 ; C.27 q.1 c.32) excommunicatio transgredientibus non minatur   245/248 cfr infra, 569-571

---

229 pauperum] *om.* Z   iusta] multa A   230 monasteriis] quibusdam *add.* Ek El   232 quecunque El   inuenti] *om.* A Z   234 mucrone] *sic codd.*, microne *false* Moll   234/235 ceterique A   237 solempnizat presens una dies hec El   238 uexillis] et *praem.* Ek El   241 thematis] et cetera *add.* Ek   242 In] Diuisio *ut subtitulum interposuit* L   quibus] hiis El et¹] *om.* El   243 Christi uite *tr.* L, *falso, cfr infra*, 249/250   245 uerum] *sic* Ek, uere *corr.* Ek²   et] *om.* A Z   246 excolenda Z

SERMO IN FESTO PALMARVM DE PAVPERTATE

est de quo secundum affectum uere letandum sit quod bonum non sit et laudabile

Dico primo quod in uerbis propositis explicatur pauperis uite Christi ueritas actibus immitanda. Imitanda omnibus ueritatem cognoscentibus, precipue tamen christianis, quorum caput Christus pauper paupertatis forma est et fons paupertate abundans, in singula sua paupera membra paupertatis aquas influens, | maxime tamen religiosis, ad quos est sermo, quibus Christi consilia de paupertate et de diuiciis et aliis relinquendis per propria uota facta sunt precepta. Alios nam ad hanc eo quod expedit ad uitam, quod nociua resecat in uia, quod iter ad Deum accelerat, commonent et hortantur, sed religiosos ligant et obligant.

Quin ymmo, ipsis religiosis omnino ad salutem necessaria illa est paupertas, que rerum proprietatem excludit, sed bonorum cunctorum communitatem includit, cuius Christus erat speculum, imitatores apostoli et discipuli. Nam primitiue ecclesie multitudinis credentium nullus *suum aliquid esse dicebat, sed erant illis omnia communia. Diuidebant autem singulis, prout cuique opus erat,* | *Actuum* .IIII. Post quos religiosorum statuum institutores et regularis uite formatores, Basilius, Augustinus, Benedictus et alii, in eorum regulis inuiolabiliter obseruare hanc preceperunt sine proprietate rerum communitatem et paupertatem. Et suos successores et sequipedes quoscumque regularis uite obseruatores, cuiuscumque existunt religionis, sicut ad castitatem, sic ad obedientiam et paupertatem, ad tria hec omni religioni communia, uoluerunt

---

254/255 cfr Matth. 19, 21; Marc. 10, 21, locos infra, 611-612, uerbatim allegatos, etiam Luc. 18, 22, et generaliter Matth. 19, 23-30; Marc. 10, 23-31; Luc. 18, 24-30   262/265 Act. 4, 32; 4, 35, in *Ep.* 45, 48-52, allegatum sec. CASS., *Coll.* 18, 5 (p. 509, 19 – 510, 5; 510, 23 – 511, 8); cfr etiam Act. 2, 44-45

259/265 cfr GER. MAG., *Ep.* 45, 16-20; 43-52   cfr CASS., *Coll.* 18, 5 (p. 509, 19 – 510, 5; 510, 23 – 511, 8)   265/272 cfr GER. MAG., *Ep.* 45, 120-125   cfr BAS., *Reg.*, c. 5 (p. 35, 2 – 36, 12); BENED., *Reg.*, c. 33 (p. 562); AVG., *Reg.*, c. 1 (p. 418, 5-14)

---

247 sit¹] *om. A*   247/248 quod – non] *om. A*   249/250 Christi uite *tr. Ek El*   252 forma] *om. Ek*   paupertate] paupertatis *L*   253 aquas paupertatis *tr. El*   256 nam] namque *L Ek El*   259/260 est illa *tr. El*   261 spectaculum *A*   263 aliquid suum dicebat esse *tr. Ek El*   264 unicuique *Z*, cuiquam *L*   267 hanc preceperunt obseruare *tr. Z*   269 sequipede *A*   271 hec tria *tr. Ek*

solempni fore uoto constrictos. Quorum status et regule, a sancta Dei ecclesia confirmati, tamquam Christi et apostolorum uite conformes ymagines ⟨sunt⟩. Omnem proprietatem ab hiis statibus uniuersaliter, tamquam uite Christi et apostolorum dissonam et incongruam, eadem mater ecclesia semper quam uehementer abhorruit et, quantum potuit, districtius eiecit.

Ad cuius districtionis rigorisue habendum exemplum nutu Sancti Spiritus primus princeps apostolorum in primos inter discipulos proprietarios, Ananyam et Saphyram, primam et tam duram excommunicationem exercuit, que et mortem temporalem induxit et subitam, ut timor magnus in omnes qui audirent, precipue in futuros, fieret proprietarios.

Idcirco Extra, *De statu monachorum*, in decretali *Cum ad monas|terium*, sic precipit ecclesia: "Prohibemus districte in uirtute obedientie sub obtestatione diuini iudicii ne quis monachorum proprium aliquid possideat, sed si quid habet proprii, totum in continenti resignet. Quodsi proprietas apud quemquam inuenta fuerit in morte, ipsa cum eo in signum perditionis extra monasterium in sterquilinio subterretur, secundum quod beatus Gregorius narrat in *Dyalogo* se fecisse. Vnde si quid fuerit | alicui specialiter destinatum, non presumat illud accipere, sed abbati, priori uel cellerario destinetur". Hec decretalis uerba sunt.

Ad quam intelligendam ueniat in medium preallegatum factum Gregorii, in cuius monasterio, ut narrat quarto *Dyalogorum* libro, erat quidam monachus, medicina imbutus, Iustus nomine, habens tres florenos, quos se habere fratri suo germano, nomine Copi-

---

278/283 cfr Act. 5, 1-11

274/277 cfr *Decret.*, X 3.35.6 § 2 (c. II, 599, 27-42)   284/309 cfr GER. MAG., *Ep.* 41, 35-39   284/293 *Decret.*, X 3.35.6 § 2 (c. II, 599, 27-42), ubi Innoc. .III. sepulturam extra monasterium in sterquilinio praescribit, auctoritatem Gregorii .I. (GREG. MAG., *Dial.*, 4, 57, II, p. 190, 81-86) nominatim allegans   294/299 Gerardus hic summatim exponit GREG. MAG., *Dial.*, 4, 57, 8-10 (p. 188, 49-65)

---

274 sunt] *inserendum censuit Moll, om. codd.*   275 et²] *om. Ek*   278 rehabendum *L*   279 Spiritus Sancti *tr. Z*   280 Ananiam et Saphiram (Zaphiram *El*) *Z L Ek El*   283 fieret proprietarios] *om. L*   288 commune *El*   291 aliquid *L*   alicui specialiter fuerit *tr. Z*   specialiter] *om. El*   293 cellerario] *Z L, sic sec. X legendum,* cellario *A Ek El*   297/298 Copioso nomine *tr. Z*

oso, in fine uite constitutus reuelauit. Qui Copiosus deinde beato hec Gregorio retulit. Quapropter Gregorius precepit ut nec aliquis
300 de fratribus in morte se illi adiungeret, nec infirmum uisitaret aut quicquam consolationis ei uel operis impenderet, ut se propter tres aureos a cunctis fratribus horrendum et abhominatum cognosceret, quod et precise obseruatum est. Et dum ad mortem deueniret, facta est fossa in sterquilinio, in qua corpus eius cum
305 horrore proicitur. Desuper tres aurei iactantur cunctis fratribus astantibus ad tam lugubre spectaculum et clamantibus singulis: *"pecunia tua tecum sit in perditionem".* Ecce contra proprietarios executio, quam deinde sancta ecclesia propter proprietatis inexcusabile et enorme uicium tamquam legem de cetero statuit.
310 Vix tam grande uicium heresi excepta inueni, quod tam lamentabili etiam post mortem rigore punitur ad prescisius et artius religiosas mentes a lapsu ad proprietatem, ad quam tam inclinata est cupido, sub regula constringendas paupertatis. Nam duo hec, et habendi pronitas et uicii enormitas, strictam et acrem pe|nam
315 exigunt. Non est quid, cuius proprietas monacho conceditur. Nam ut in *Vitis patrum* dicitur: "monachus obulum quem habet non ualet".

Nam | monachatui adheret inseparabiliter paupertas, sicut et castitas indissolubili pene uinculo colligata est. Nec pretextu li-

307 Act. 8, 20

299/307 GREG. MAG., *Dial.*, 4, 57, 11 (p. 190, 74-86), partim paene ad litt. 307/309 sc. Innoc. .III. in *Decret.*, X 3.35.6 § 2 (c. II, 599, 27-42), supra, 287-290, allegatum   315 cfr BENED., *Reg.*, c. 33, 3-4 (p. 562, 4-7)   315/317 cfr GER. MAG., *Ep.* 41, 48-49   in *Vitis patrum* hoc prouerbium inuenire nequiui; prouerbium ab HELIN., *Serm.* 13 (*PL*, 212, 589C) originem ducit, cfr SINGER, *Thesaurus prouerbiorum*, Bd. 8, p. 227, sect. 1, 2 (der Mönch darf nicht nach Weltlichem streben), n. 25; hoc prouerbium neque in WALTHER, *Prouerbia*, T. 2 (p. 914-915, n. 15025-15029) uel T. 8 (p. 447, n. 38311-38326; cfr etiam numeros in indice, T. 6, p. 134, s.u. 'obolus' citatos), nec in WERNER, *Sprichwörter*, inuenire potui   318/325 eundem locum GER. MAG., *Ep.* 45, 89-94, uerbatim allegat, cfr insuper *Ep.* 41, 31-33

298 deinde] *om. Z*   298/299 hec beato *tr. El*, hoc beato *Z*   299 Gregorius] beatus *praem. Z*   300 illi] *om. A*   301 ei consolationis *tr. Z* uel] aut *Z*   opis *A*   302 abhominatum] *sic codd.*, abhominandum *El*, abhobinatum *false Moll*   305 aureos iactant *A*   306 singulis] *om. A* 308 sancta] mater *add. Z*   311/312 religiosas mentes prescisius et artius *tr. L*   312 inclina *A*   314 artam *Z*   316 ut] *om. A*   Vitas *Ek El* 319 indissolubilis *El*   prorsus *Z*

centie abbatis, abbatisse uel prioris excusari potest quo magis quis proprietatem habeat. Vnde sancta in predicta decretali premunit ecclesia, dicens: "Nec estimet abbas quod super proprietate possit dispensare, quia abdicatio proprietatis, sicut et custodia castitatis adeo est annexa regule monachali ut nec contra eam summus pontifex licentiam possit indulgere". Concordant et doctores quod summus pontifex non possit magis in proprietate quam in contrahendo matrimonio cum monacho dispensare, cum uix inueniatur sicut paupertatis, cui quis obligatur ex uoto, similiter et continentie obseruatio quicquam obligatis tam bonum uel utile.

Cum et in minoribus rebus et pene sine periculo dispensatio que ad maius bonum non dirigit, accipientibus et dantibus laqueus, periculum et peccatum est, quantum minus ergo in rebus ad quas nulla se pene humana extendit potentia, excusat licentia. Res namque que de scitu et licentia superiorum monacho de facto conceduntur, dicuntur monachi peculium, quas ne monachi habeant secundum Lateranense concilium sub penis predictis strictius prohibet, ut habetur in c. *Monachi*, Extra, *De statu monachorum*. Ait namque hoc uenerabile concilium: "Monachi non permittantur habere peculium. Qui uero peculium habuerint, nisi

---

321/325 *Decret.*, X 3.35.6 § 2 (c. II, 600, 15-19)   **325/329** cfr HENR. BOIC, *Dist.*, sup. X 3.35.6, in comm. sup. gl. 'et ita habes' (= BERN. PARM., *Glos. ord. in Decret.*, super X 3.35.6, comm. sup. 'abdicatio' (c. II, 600, 16), ed. 1582, c. 1297 (p. 154), gl. d) (p. 526, c. 1, 65 – c. 2, 47 sub num. 7-9), ubi allegat nouem doctores omnes unanimiter confirmantes papam cum monachis proprietariis et incastis dispensare non posse, sc. BERN. PARM., *loc. alleg.*, qui insuper testimonium Vincentii et Iohannis inuocat; HOST., *Summ.*, L. 3, t. 37, § 6 (ed. 1574, c. 1109-1110); Iohannem et Huguccionem sicut allegatos in BRIX., *Glos. ord. in* GRAT., *Decr.*, super C.25 q.1 c.6, comm. sup. 'apostoli' (c. I, 1008, 34) (c. 1899 (p. 1013), gl. a); INNOC., *Comm. Decret.*, super X 3.35.6 sub 2 (ed. Frankf., 1570, f. 432v, c. 2 – 433r, c. 1) (sed sec. Innoc. et Host., sicut et sec. Henr., papa potest dispensare "ex magna causa et deo placente" in uoto castitatis, non autem in uoto paupertatis); THOM., II-II, Q. 88 a. 11 co. (T. 9, p. 264-265, praesertim conclusio corporis, p. 265, c. 1, 1-23)   **334/343** cfr supra, 231-234, et GER. MAG., *Ep.* 41, 33-35; *Ep.* 42, 12-13; *Ep.* 45, 97-103   *Decret.*, X 3.35.2 (c. II, 596, 50-51; 596, 59 – 597, 4) paene ad litt.

---

320 uel] *om. Z*   **321** habet *A*   premuniuit *Z*   **322** ecclesia] *post* sancta *pos. Z*   **324** annexa est *tr. Z*   **325** et] *om. A*   **327** matrimonium *Ek*   dispensare cum monacho *tr. A*   **328** cuius *Ek El*   quis] quid *L*   **329** obligatis] obligat *A*, de *praem. Z*   **330** et¹] *om. L*   **333** se nulla *tr. L*   **334** scitu] *ex* statu *in ras. corr. A¹*   **335** concediatur *L*   **336** consilium *L Ek El*   **336/337** strictius] *om. L¹*, *marg. suppl. L¹ uel ²*   **338, 343** consilium *L Ek*

340 ab abbate fuerit sibi pro iniuncta amministratione commissum, a communione remoueantur altaris, et qui in extremis cum peculio inuentus fuerit, nec oblatio fiat pro eo, nec inter fratres accipiat sepulturam". Et addit hoc | concilium, se ipsum ut in hoc religiosos uniuersaliter interpretans includat: "hoc", quod predictum est, 345 "de omnibus religiosis precipimus obseruari".

Vnde sciendum quod qui res habent in peculio, non habent principale neque plenum neque integrum rerum proprietatis dominium. Non enim sibi, sed suis superioribus, ut seruus domino, filius patri, monachus abbati uel monasterio querunt, sed ex li- 350 centia eorum sub quibus sunt, | disponendi pro tempore et contractandi habent potestatem, que potestas quedam est, sed limitata et subiecta, sed non plena rei possessio, que tamen monachis nullo modo "nisi pro iniuncta amministratione" permittitur, ut secundum glosam Innocentii, qui est lucerna iuris, "uestiarius uel 355 elemosinarius fuerit" uel aliquod tale communi utilitati deseruiens habuerit officium. Tunc ex licentia superioris potest tale habere peculium, quod debet amministrare communiter fratribus, ut *fidelis et prudens dispensator, quem constituit dominus* abbas *super familiam suam* monachorum, *non querens que sua sunt*, sed 360 secundum indigentiam personarum et secundum debitum amministrationis sibi commisse disponere, prouidere, tractare et distribuere, et secundum apostolicam doctrinam et regulam *prout cuique opus est*, id est necessarium, *diuidere*.

357/359 Luc. 12, 42   359 Phil. 2, 4; 2, 21 a Ger. conflantur   362/363 cfr Act. 2, 45; etiam Act. 4, 35

---

353 Decret., X 3.35.2 (c. II, 596, 60)   354 lucerna iuris] sic Ger. Innoc. nominat in Focar. 1, 366   354/356 INNOC., Comm. Decret., super X 3.35.2, comm. sup. 'Administratione' (c. II, 596, 60) (ed. Frankf., 1570, f. 432r, c. 2, 16-18) paene ad litt.   357/359 cfr GER. MAG., Ep. 41, 71-72, ubi Ger. in contextu dissimili eosdem locos biblicos coniunctim citat   359/363 cfr supra, 259-267

---

340 sibi fuerit tr. Ek   342 recipiat L   343 se] id Z   344 dictum L 345 precipimus religiosis tr. contra decret. L Ek El   346 sciendum] est add. Z   350 dispensendi sic Ek   351 potestas] sic codd., proprietas contra codd. Moll   352 sed] et Z   354 uestiarius] si praem. A, suppl. Ek², contra intentionem Innocentii, qui in loco ut coniunctionis (a Ger. adhibitae) quia scripsit   356 habere tale tr. A   357 communiter amministrare tr. A   358 dominus] om. Z Ek El   359 suam] om. A   monachorum] suorum add. A   362/363 cuiquam L

Sed prolongantes iniquitatem eorum sub pretextu amministrationis ueri proprietarii et possessores efficiuntur. Ymmo, quod horribilius est, bona immobilia eorum specialiter faciunt usibus annuatim applicari, alii excusantes quia in cista abbatis uel prioris certi, tamen humano modo et consueto, eis reseruari, alii ad eorum amministrationem tamquam peculium commissum dicunt amministrandam rem – sed non amministrationem habentes, nisi amministratio dicatur ea que est ad | proprios tantum usus reseruatio et applicatio et contractio. Que uere proprietatis uidetur esse possessio, quam excusationem in peccatis sub nomine amministrationis, a quo nomen ipsum longissimum est, excusare nituntur. Hic est *lapis offensionis et scandali petra, meridianum demonium* ualde gyrouagum et terribile.

Et ut sciatur quid per nomen proprietatis uel proprietarii importetur, sciendum est quod res quas dicimur possidere uel in quibus habemus proprietatem seu dominium, que fere unum sunt, non subiciuntur nobis secundum se in earum natura | nec secundum motus earum naturales, sed solum secundum applicandi et disponendi quendam modum, in quantum homo per uoluntatem et rationem potest res que propter ipsum sicut ad finem create sunt, in suos uel aliorum hominum usus ordinare uel applicare. Talis applicationis uel ordinationis potestas, ratione uel consuetudine uel lege confirmata, iustum dominium uel proprietas hominis in rebus dicitur.

---

375 I Petr. 2, 8 (sec. Is. 8, 14), ubi sequitur: *his, qui offendunt verbo nec credunt in quod et positi sunt*   Ps. 90 (91), 6   377/387 cfr Gen. 1, 26-30

377/407 cfr GER. MAG., *Ep.* 41, 95-102   377/387 cfr THOM., II-II, Q. 66 a. 1 co. (T. 9, p. 84, c. 1-2)

---

365 uere *A Z*   proprietarii ueri *tr. Ek El*   efficiunt *Ek*   366 usibus faciunt *tr. Z*   367 excusantes] se *add. Z*   prioris] aut bursarii *add. Z*   370 nisi] si *A*   372 et¹] *om. A*   uidetur] dicitur *El*   373 excusatione *A*   374 nomine *Z*   est] *om. Z*   375 petra scandali *tr. L*   petra] *om. Ek El*   demonem *L*   377 Et] Quid est dominium uel proprietas *ut subtitulum interposuit L*   uel proprietarii] *om. L*   380 earum¹] eorum *A Z Ek El*   383 et] *corr. Z²*, uel *Z¹*   386 confirmata] *ex* firmata *corr. El²*

SERMO IN FESTO PALMARVM DE PAVPERTATE 441

Secundum autem dictamen recte rationis, prout habetur ex dictis Phylosophi, .II. *Politice*, et prout doctores sacre pagine et
390 Thomas in *Secunda secunde*, q. .LXVI., art. .II., determinant (nam una in communitate rerum et philosophorum et theologorum sententia est), duplex huiusmodi est in rebus potestas seu proprietas. Vna est potestas acquirendi res, procurandi, ordinandi, disponendi, transmutandi et alienandi, secundum quod licitum est
395 personis que se in contrarium uoto non strinxerunt. Hoc modo habere proprietates ratio quippe recta dictat, quia bonum et conueniens est quod rerum dominia et proprietates sint distincta propter tres causas, secundum Thomam et philosophum. Primo, ne regimen et cura rerum negligatur, cum sepe negligantur que
400 communi et plurimorum, | maxime omnium prudentie subdun- 51rb
tur, sed quilibet sibi sollicitus est et suis. Secundo, propter inordinationem et confusionem in rebus tractandis uitandam, que fieret si quidlibet esset in potestate cuiuslibet. Et rursum tertio, si omnia essent communia, maxima fieret inter homines discordia. Ideo
405 conuenit rerum procurationi ordinate et pacifico uite humane statui ut huiusmodi proprietates, id est potestates procurandi et disponendi, sint distincte.

Sed hee tres cause in monasteriis omnino cessant, etiam si uoto se ad paupertatem et communitatem non restrinxissent. Quare in
410 eis standum est naturali iuri, quod dominia et proprietates in rebus non distinguit. Nam huiusmodi proprietas est apud monaste-

---

388/407 cfr Thom., II-II, Q. 66 a. 2 co. (T. 9, p. 85, c. 1-2)   389 Ger. hic errat, alludit quidem ad Arist., *Pol. Lat.* 1, 3 § 6, quem locum in uersione latina a Guil. de Moerbeka facta (p. 31, 9-10 = 1256b7-8 Bekker) allegat Thom., II-II, Q. 66 a. 1 co. (T. 9, p. 84, art. 1, c. 2, 5-7), supra (377-387) citatum doctores] sc. Basilium et Ambrosium, ambo a Thom., *ibid.*, ad 2 ; ad 3, allegatos
394/395 i.e. laici, nam religiosi hic excluduntur, sicut infra, 408-416, patet

---

388 Secundum] Quod duplex in rebus est proprietas *ut subtitulum interposuit* L   dictum *El*   ex] in *El*   389 .II.] *sic codd.*, .I. *legendum est*   Pollicite *Ek*   prout] ut *Z*   392 in rebus est *tr. El*   393 potestas] *om. Z*   potestas] seu proprietas que est potestas *add. Ek*   395 in] *om. Ek¹, suppl. Ek²*   strinxerunt] *sic Ek¹*, astrinxerunt *corr. Ek²*   396 recta] *om. Ek*   397 est] *om. El*   399 rerum cura *tr. Z*   400 prouidencie *El*   402 fiet *A*   403 quodlibet *L*   404 inter homines fieret *tr. L*   407 distincti *A*   408 cessent *El*   cessant] ex regulari institucione *add. Z*   uoce *L*   409 non] se *iterum praem. El*   410 iuri naturali *tr. A*   potestates *Z Ek El*   410/411 non distinguit in rebus *tr. A*   411 proprietates *Ek*

rium et apud prepositos non nomine proprio, sed nomine communitatis, ut communia bona, que certorum cura et prouidentia ordinato | regimine tranquille gubernata, *prout cuiquam opus est* per regentes, cui se alii subiectos uouerunt, iuste distribuantur et dispensentur.

Aduertant religiosi quod proprietates rerum et potestates et propter alias causas distincte non sunt. Videant, si in rebus peculiaribus uel aliis habeant huiusmodi potestates, scilicet res uel procurandi uel regendi uel dispensandi et disponendi, emendi et uendendi, contrahendi uel alias transmutandi uel applicandi, et quantas et quot tales habent potestates, tantas et tot habent in rebus proprietates. Nam nichil aliud est proprietas, que districte religiosis prohibetur, nisi huiusmodi in rebus procurandi et ordinandi potestas libera.

Sed est alia proprietas, que est potestas utendi et ad usum immediate quasi applicandi, secundum quam iuxta diuinam et naturalem equitatem non est fas cuiquam | hominum habere propria. Nam usus rerum debet esse communis et non proprius, etiam secundum philosophos, ut non reputet quis ea que habet ad usum sibi dumtaxat fore concessa. Nec ea solus potest suis usibus applicanda reseruare, sed etiam ad aliorum usus et ad materiam uirtutum res possideat.

Et secundum quod ratio dictauerit, omnes debent se secundum primum modum proprietatis sicut rerum procuratores, rectores, dispensatores et dispositores rationabiles gerere, non autem sicut

---

414 cfr Act. 2, 45; etiam Act. 4, 35

423/425 Ger. hic reiterat opinionem supra (388-407) allegatam sec. THOM., II-II, Q. 66 a. 2 co. (T. 9, p. 85, c. 1, praesertim art. 2, l. 36-38)   426/440 cfr THOM., II-II, Q. 66 a. 2 co. (T. 9, p. 85, c. 2, praesertim art. 2, l. 12-18)   434/436 cfr locum ex Thoma supra, 388-398; 418-421, allegatum

---

414 ordinate *El*   415 nouerunt *A L*   416 dispensantur *Z*   417 et rerum *tr. Ek El*   418 distincta *El*   in] *om. A*   419 aliis] in *praem. Ek* habeant] pro se et non respectu communis boni per modum amministracionis *add. Z El, post* potestates *add. Ek*   420 disponendi et dispensandi *tr. Ek El*   et¹] uel *Z*   423 distincte *L*   423/424 prohibetur religiosis *tr. El*   424 et] uel *El*   425 libera] *om. A*   libera potestas *tr. El*   426 Sed] Secunda proprietas que nulli christiano licet *ut subtitulum interposuit Ek*   428 homini *Ek*   432 applicandi *A Z Ek*   436 dispensatores *pro* dispositores *iterum El*

usurpatores et congregatores in usus proprios tantum, sed res aliis ut in communem usum deputatas facile largiri, leuiter impertiri. Hoc est quod precipit apostolus, *.I. ad Timotheum* .VI., *facile tribuere et communicare.*

Naturalis igitur suadet ratio et diuina caritatis equitas ut in hoc quis sibi necessaria uite primo amministrare ualeat. De eo uero quod superest necessitati, secundum naturalem equitatem quilibet bonus uir, gentilis uel laycus, indigentibus tenetur impertiri, quanto magis christianus, quorum legifer et Dominus pauper et uerbo et exemplo docuit tantum necessitati satisfieri. Vnde secundum preceptum Domini christianus quantumcunque superest in elemosinam largiri tenetur, cum et infusa largitas seu liberalitas, ymmo | et proximi caritas de necessariis sibi cum pauperrima uidua subtrahit.

O, uos ergo, dilectissimi, proprietates abicite. Propria secundum modum primum nec naturalis ratio nec institutio regularis uos habere permittit, propria secundum modum alterum nec quisquam debet christianus uel uir bonus habere. Vtinam ab illa essetis liberi. Moneat uos ad propria relinquenda naturalis ratio, moneat euangelica inhibitio, mo|neat Christi et apostolorum conformatio, moneat proprietariorum per eos tam stricte punitorum dampnatio, moneat uos regularis institutio et uoti, moneat indis-

---

439/440 I Tim. 6, 18, allegatum sec. THOM., II-II, q. 66 a. 2 co., ut patet ex uoce 'et' inserto in THOM., sed non in apost.   445/446 cfr supra, 109-115, et locos ibi allegatos, sc. Matth. 21, 2 ; etiam Marc. 11, 2-3 ; Luc. 19, 30   446/450 cfr Matth. 19, 21 ; Marc. 10, 21   448/450 cfr Marc. 12, 41-44 ; Luc. 21, 1-4   456 cfr Matth. 19, 21 ; Marc. 10, 21   456/457 cfr Act. 5, 1-11 supra extensius allegatum

---

451/453 primum modum Ger. supra, 393-407, tractat   453/454 secundum modum Ger. supra, 426-433, tractat   455/468 cfr DON., *Mai.* 3, 5 (p. 664, 14 – 665, 2)   455 cfr supra, 434-450   456/457 cfr supra, 446-450   457/458 cfr supra, 278-283   458/459 cfr supra, 265-272

---

438 largire *El*   impertire *El*   441 igitur] ergo *A*   442 ualeat] *Z Moll*, ualet *A L Ek El*   uero] om. *L*   444 gentilis] siue praem. *A*   uel] siue *A* Iudaicus *L*   impertire *El*   446 docuit et exemplo *tr. Z*   448 cum et] tamen ut *Ek¹*, sic eciam *marg. suppl. et corr. Ek²*   fusa *Ek*   451 O] Exhortacio ad religiosos *ut subtitulum interposuit L*   453 nos *A*   alterum modum *tr. L*   455 relinquenda propria *tr. Z*   455/468 moueat *quater decies Z Ek*   458 uos] om. *A*   et uoti] Et non *sic El*

pensabilis solempnizatio, moneat sancte ecclesie tantum pro-
460 prietates abhorrentis dira comminatio, moneat tam crudelis gla-
dii, quia excommunicationis, hodierna percussio, moneat debite
sepulture in sterquilinio abhominatio, moneat uos tam frequens,
tam magna et infinita pene sanctorum patrum exhortatio, moneat
antiquorum et predecessorum uestrorum, in quorum loca succes-
465 sistis, paupertatis ad unguem obseruatio, moneat tota uita Christi
paupercula et inops eius hodierna asinatio, moneat uos paupertatis uexillum, dies hec atque nostra paupertatis solempnis festi-
uatio, et moneat uos ista eius imperialis exaltatio.

Nolite uos, religiosi, ubi non est timor, trepidare, sed fidenter
470 Christi, apostolorum et antecedentium paupertatis formam assu-
mite. Legimus de apostolis quod in necessariis multociens defi-
ciebant. Nam scriptum est quod *in fame, siti, frigore et nuditate*
Domino seruiebant, quia erant paucissimi christiani, omnes pauperes, in cuncto hominum genere abiectissimi et despecti. Nunc
475 uix et raro christianus a necessariis potest deficere inter christianos, precipue non uir bonus et uoluntarie pauper, maxime ut uoluntarie pauperem decet uirtuosus. Non tantum senuit christiana
religio, non tantum adhuc mala creuerunt ut non habeant homines uiscera pietatis, ut non cogat pauper sanctitas et humilis se
480 diligi, ymmo ammirari. Quis tam crudelis qui non cum tali uni-
cam panis crustulam partiatur? | Quanto minus religiosus potest   52ra
deficere de communi ui|uens, cui licet uel non uoluptuosa nec in   447
abundantia, tamen necessaria ministrantur.

O, quam modicis contentatur natura. O, si religiose uiueret,
485 etiam si nichil de communi haberet, quanta sibi cottidiana etiam

---

472 II Cor. 11, 27

459/460 cfr supra, 272-277 ; 284-307   460/461 cfr supra, 337-341, praesertim locum ex *Decret.*, X 3.35.2 (c. II, 596, 59-61)   461/463 cfr supra, 294-
307   465/468 cfr supra, 74-113   468 cfr supra, 29-49 ; 177-178

---

460 abhorrentes *L*   461 debite] uos *praem., sed postea exp. L*
464 loca] *om. El*, digne aliis *add. Ek*   464/465 succeditis *L*   465 ad
unguem] ad eorum exemplum *Ek*   466 eius] *om. El*   hodie *A*   moueat *A*   469 uos] ergo *L*, ergo *praem. Ek El*   470 Christi] et *add. Z*
471 quod] qui *Ek*   476 non] tamen *L*   maxime] non *add. A*
479 cogat] eum *praem. Ek*   481 crustulam panis *tr. Z*   482 non] si
praem. Ek²   482/483 nec – abundantia] *om. El*   483 necessaria tamen
tr. L

SERMO IN FESTO PALMARVM DE PAVPERTATE 445

ultra quam uellet a scientibus ei preberentur. Sed deficit in Domino confidentia, deficit et uita religiosa. Vnde ad congregandum bona temporalia nobis cupido imperat. Sed habeant christiani, qui uoluerint, necessaria tantum. Habundantia autem large accepta in
490 multa que excludit necessitas se diuidit. Paupertas contenta necessariis horret et contempnit multitudine et numero copiosa ut onera importabilia, spernit cara et preciosa ut natura uilia. Non cognoscit exquisita et curiosa, quia difficilia, despicit exteriori ornatu pulchra et speciosa, quia intus decore uacua. Reicit secun-
495 dum carnem sapida et uoluptuosa, quia finaliter sunt tristia et toxica. Repellit quieta corpori et commodosa sicut non rationi sed bestialitati obsequentia. Omnia hec rationem habentia quandam habundantie necessitati sunt contraria. Quorum omnium ymaginem *uideant pauperes* in hodierna Christi asinatione. Quid in hac
500 Christus habuit uel magnum uel multum, quid preciosum, quid curiosum, quid exquisitum, quid difficile parabile, quid ornatum uel pulchrum, quid uoluptuosum uel commodosum? Omnino non solum exclusa, sed longe omnis habundancie genera relegata sunt.
505 Nam, ut dicit beatus Bernhardus in libro *De diligendo Deum*: "superfluitas obuiante mandato Domini, cum dicitur: *diliges proximum tuum sicut te ipsum*, cohibetur. | Iustissime quidem, ut 52rb *consors nature* consors sit et gratie, presertim illius que nature insita est. Quod si quis grauatur non dico necessitatibus, sed uolup-
510 tatibus fraternis", commoditatibus et curiositatibus, copiose pulchris et preciosis rebus "subuenire, sibi illa, que aliis impertiri non

---

499 Ps. 68 (69), 33   506/507 Matth. 22, 39 ; Luc. 10, 27 ; Gal. 5, 14 ; Iac. 2, 8 uerbatim ; Marc. 12, 31 paene ad litt., allegatum sec. Bern.   508 II Petr. 1, 4, allegatum sec. Bern.

499/502 Ger. hic summatim paupertati contraria, supra, 490-497, fusius elaborata, reiterat   505/514 BERN., *Dil. Deo* 8, 23 (p. 138, 19 – 139, 2), partim uerbatim, partim minus accurate

---

489 uoluerunt *El*   491 multitudinem *Z*   et²] *om. Ek*   493 quia] et *A*
494 decora *El*   Reiecit *Ek*   497 hec] uel *add. Z*   501 parabile] quid *praem. Z*   502 uel¹] quid *El*   uel¹·²] quid *bis Z*   505 Nam] De communicando fratri temporalia *ut subtitulum interposuit L*   Bernhardus *Ek El*   506 Domini mandato *tr. Z*   diligis *Z Ek*   507 tuum] *om. Ek*
509 generatur *Ek*   dico] *sec. Bern. hab. A, om. cett.*   510 fratris *L*
511 rebus] *om. A*   impertire *El*

uult, non acquirat, si non uult esse dominici transgressor precepti. Quanta enim uel qualia sibi ipsi indulgeat, tantumdem Deo et proximo meminerit exhibendum." |

Ecce dominicum frenum omnis habundantie, ecce limitem diuiciarum et possessionum et usus earum, quo ex precepto caritatis (sine qua non est uita nec ordinata disciplina) *proximum sicut te ipsum* teneris *diligere*, ne post concupiscentias, auaritiam, gulam, iniustitiam, curiositatem et superbiam tuam abeas, ne bonis tuis hos hostes tuos, qui omnes in habundantia sicut pisces in aqua uiuunt, nutrias. Et si secundum apostoli doctrinam, *.I. ad Timotheum* .VI., *habentes alimenta et quibus tegamur, hiis contenti sumus*, si paulisper nos habundantiarum diuersis generibus et carnalibus desideriis, que militant aduersus animam, suspendere nos ipsos non grauamur, illud quod hostibus subtrahimus, fratri nostro, nature consorti, promptius impertimur. Tunc amor noster temperatus, iustus et de carnali socialis et communis efficitur et meritorius. "Porro et hoc" secundum Bernardum, ubi supra, "iusticie est, cum quo tibi natura communis est, munus nature non habere diuisum".

Si autem de tibi necessariis proximo communicas, habeas fiduciam in eo *qui dat omnibus affluenter et non improperat*, et *aperit manum suam et implet omne animal benedictione*. | *Noli timere, pusillus grex*, quod in necessariis, si salutifera tibi fuerint, desit qui omnia tam *fortiter disponit* quam *suauiter*. Et iterum, ut in canonica *.I. Iohannis* .III., *qui habuerit substantiam huius*

517/518 Matth. 22, 39 ; Luc. 10, 27 ; Gal. 5, 14 ; Iac. 2, 8 uerbatim ; Marc. 12, 31 paene ad litt.   521/523 I Tim. 6, 8   532 Iac. 1, 5   532/533 Ps. 144 (145), 16   533/534 Luc. 12, 32   535 Sap. 8, 1   535/538 I Ioh. 3, 17

515/528 cfr BERN., *Dil. Deo* 8, 23 (p. 139, 2-12), partim paene ad litt.   528/530 BERN., *Dil. Deo* 8, 24 (p. 139, 23-25)   531/533 cfr BERN., *Dil. Deo* 8, 24 (p. 139, 13-16)

---

512 precepti transgressor *tr. A*   517 proximum] tuum *add. sec. Bibliam Z*   519 eas *Ek*, adeas *Z El*   nec *Z*   521 apostolicam *L*   522 tegimur *L*   523 simus *sec. Tim. Z*   nos] *om. A*   habundantiarum] ab *praem. L*   525 nosmetipsos *El*   526 prompcius] *corr. Ek²*, promcius *Ek¹*   527 et communis] *om. L*   528 hec *El*   secundum] beatum *add. Z L El* Bernhardum *Ek El*   530 habere] *L sec. Bern.*, habete *cett.*   532 et²] sed *Ek*   533 suam] *om. Z El*   534 salutaria *L*   tibi salutifera *tr. Z*   535 ut] *om. Ek El*   536 .I. Iohannis] Iohannis.II. *A*

mundi, et uiderit fratrem suum necesse habere, et clauserit uiscera sua ab eo, quomodo caritas Dei est in eo? Sed cottidie in oculis nostris tot occurrunt egeni nutriendi, tot nudi uestiendi, tot capti liberandi, tot infirmi uariis necessariis indigentes uisitandi, etiam multi alii diuersis nostre mundane substantie remediis subleuandi, quomodo multa uel magna uel preciosa uel alia predicta habundantie genera ualent apud misericordie uiscera remanere uel apud corda caritate referta? Non enim caritas caritas est, si ordinata non est, quia ordo caritatis in precepto est.

Qui ergo suam habundantiam, uolup|tatem uel ornatum et similia spirituali lucro, quod in omni elemosina et subleuatione pauperum est, preponit, ordinem caritatis, quo spiritualia corporalibus debet preponere, peruertit, magis quod sue cupiditati quam quod Dei beneplacito deseruit, inquirit et eligit.

Sed tu, religiose, tu amator quisquis sis paupertatis, da liberaliter, da magnifice, da habunde, ymmo et effunde. Estimo quod hoc patres non propter bonum et meritum tantum quod dando quis acquirit hortati sunt, ut currentem in equo et preteruolantem sine munere pauperem non permitteremus preterire, sed multum etiam et maxime, ut cicius et rectiori uia ad paupertatis perueniremus optabile bonum, et ut amplius inter proprium bonum et caritatem, inter spirituale et corporale nulla oriretur repugnantia. Saltem | tantum da et effunde ut solum supersint necessaria et pauca et parua, quia sine pondere et cura leuia sunt, uilia et abiecta, quia secura sunt, simplicia et leuiter parabilia, quia ad manum delectabilia sunt, inculta, quia naturalia sunt, sine uoluptate nutrientia, quia non coinquinant, sine commoditate laboriosa, quia carnem reprimunt et mentem fortificant. Ad hec te ducit dux optima paupertas, que ista nec uult nec potest. Nam in ea secundum formam hodie in hac eius exaltatione per Christum datam

---

537 necessitatem *sec. .1. Ioh. Ek*   538 karitas *Ek*   est] manet *sec. Ioh.* Z   illo Z   543 genera] *om.* L   544 caritate] scilicet *add.* Z   547 spirituali lucro] spiritualiter L   549 debent *L Ek*   magisque L   551 Sed] *om. El*   552 hec *El*   554 currentem – preteruolantem] *spatio uacuo relicto om. El*   556 etiam] *om. Ek*   rectori *sic* Z   paupertatem L   557 bonum¹ – proprium] *om. Ek*   558 orietur A   560 sunt leuia et cura *tr. El*   cura] *om.* L   564 te] *om.* L   dux] *om. Ek*   565 nec uult nec potest ista *tr.* A   nec¹] non L   566 eius hac *tr.* Z   data *El*

est uite ueritas imitanda, ut *uideant pauperes*, quod erat primum diuisionis nostre.

Dixi secundo quod in uerbis propositis tangitur paupertatis dignitas laudibus extollenda, quia *letentur*, cum nichil sit de quo secundum affectum letandum est quod bonum non sit et laudabile. In laude enim paupertatis uix humanum sufficit eloquium, cum tam admirabilis uirtutis sit ut habeat promissionem presentis uite et future. Nam quantum ad uitam prosit et ueram et futuram, ex uerbis Christi propheticis innumerabiliter colligi potest.

Sed hoc unum sufficit, quod *beati sunt pauperes, quoniam ipsorum est regnum celorum, Luce* .VI. Sufficit, *quia | saturabuntur qui hic esuriunt*. Saciabuntur, cum apparuerit eius quem imitantur gloria regni, quod eis singulariter promittitur. Tunc *edent pauperes et saturabuntur, et laudabunt Dominum in seculum seculi*, quia *iudicabit* Dominus *pauperes populi, et saluos faciet filios pauperum*. Dominus enim pauper in retributione cunctorum in finali iudicio assumet sibi personas pauperum ut propriam. Iudicabit per pauperes, cum pauperibus et pro pauperibus. | Tunc et pauperes erunt iudices diuitum, erunt et Christi assessores, erunt et sunt intercessores et aliorum in eterna tabernacula receptores.

Diuicie uero quam miro modo nos a regno abducant, Veritas docet, *Mathei* .XIX.: *Amen dico uobis*, inquit, *diues difficile intrat*

---

567 Ps. 68 (69), 33   570 cfr Ps. 68 (69), 33   576/577 Matth. 5, 3 et Luc. 6, 20 paene ad litt.   577/578 Luc. 6, 21 paene ad litt.   579/580 Ps. 21 (22), 27   581/582 Ps. 71 (72), 4   585/586 cfr Luc. 16, 9   588/589 Matth. 19, 23

569/571 cfr supra, 245-248   576/586 cfr etiam infra, 1079-1086, et conclusionem secundae partis, infra, 1171-1173, ubi Ger. hoc thema resumit   cfr GER. MAG., *Ep.* 41, 68-69

---

567 pauperes] et cetera *add. Ek²*   primum] *om. Ek^r*, primum membrum *marg. suppl. Ek²*   569 Dixi] secundum membrum *ut subtitulum interposuit L*   570 excolenda *Z*   leutentur *sic El*   572 enim] *om. Ek El*   573 uite presentis *tr. A*   574 prosit] non tantum presentem, quia pater uester scit quia opus hiis habetis. et illud modice fidei multis passeribus meliores estis, ne ergo solliciti sitis, et cetera. M⟨agister⟩ G⟨erardus⟩. Sed et quantum ad uitam *marg. add. Ek²*   575 propheticis] et prophetis *Ek*, et prophetarum *L El*   576 sunt] *om. A*, sint *L*   578 qui] quia *L*   Saturabuntur *Z*   585 erunt²] *om. A*   accessores *A*   erunt³] erint *add. L*   587 quam miro] quantam *Ek*   regno] Dei *add. Z*   abducunt *L Z Ek*

in regnum celorum, et *Marci* .x.: *Quam difficile qui pecuniam habent, in regnum Dei intrabunt. Quam difficile est confidentes in pecuniis in regnum Dei introire. Iterum dico uobis: facilius est camelum per foramen acus transire quam diuitem intrare in regnum Dei.* Ve diuitibus, per Christum dicitur, *quia habent consolationem* eorum, quasi non essent inuenturi consolationem et uitam in futuro. Sed renunciantes hiis diuitiis et temporalibus secundum promissum Domini *centuplum* sine comparatione meliora, maiora et plura in hac uita *accipient, et uitam eternam possidebunt.*

Vnde restat ostendere quam admirabilis sit proficui paupertas in hac uita, et primo quantum ad latriam et ad Dei emulationem seu ad sibi seruiendum in hac uita proficiat, quantumque ad gratiam, dona et uirtutes obtinendas, ymmo ad ipsummet Deum in hac uita modo possibili comprehendendum et contemplandum oppido iuuat, quibus diuiciarum seruitus adeo est aduersa ut non possit quis, ut ait Veritas, *Mathei* .vi., simul *Deo et mammone*, id est diuiciis, *seruire*, quia *non potest* simul *seruire duobus dominis: aut enim unum*, scilicet Deum, *odiet et alterum*, scilicet diui|cias, *diliget, aut uni*, scilicet Deo, *adherebit et alterum*, scilicet diuicias, *contempnet.*

Paupertas uero est perfectionis uia, quia obseruanti mandata, dicente | Domino, *Marci* .x., *unum deest*; *si uis perfectus esse, uende omnia que habes et da pauperibus, Matthei* .iii. Paupertas est consiliorum Altissimi imitatrix, consequenter quoque omnis

---

589/591 Marc. 10, 23-24   589/590 etiam Luc. 18, 24, ubi uerbum 'intrabunt' melius loco Gerardi consonat quam uerbum 'introibunt', quod in Marc. 10, 23 adhibitur   591/593 Marc. 10, 25; etiam Matth. 19, 24; Luc. 18, 25   593/594 Luc. 6, 24   596/598 Matth. 19, 29 paene ad litt., cfr Marc. 10, 30; etiam Luc. 18, 30   605/609 Luc. 16, 13; etiam Matth. 6, 24 paene ad litt.   611 unum deest] Marc. 10, 21   611/612 Matth. 19, 21; etiam Marc. 10, 21 paene ad litt.

---

593 habent] hoc *falso add.* Z   593/594 consolationem] hic *add. Ek²*   594 eorum] suam *L*   596 centuplum] et *add. El*   596/597 meliora] et *add. Z Ek El*   597 et¹] *om. Ek El*   599 Vnde] Commendatio paupertatis *ut subtitulum interposuit L*   600 ad²] *om. El*   601 sibi] *om. A*   603 et] *om. A*   604 uiuat *A*   605 Mathei] *Ek*, Luce *cett.*   606 non] nemo *sec. Luc. A*   607 odit *El*   607/608 diliget (diligit *El*) scilicet diuicias *tr. Ek El*   608 scilicet¹] *om. L*, id est *Z*   Deo scilicet *tr. A*   609 contempnit *El*   610 uia perfectionis *tr. L*   612 .iii.] *A L*, .xx. *Z Ek El*, .xix. *legendum*,   613 communiter *Z*   quoque] *om. El*

religionis inicium et indiuiduus comes. Nam dixit Dominus: nisi quis *renunciauerit omnibus que possidet, non potest meus esse discipulus.*

Est etiam in paupertate accessus ad Deum securior, quia secundum apostolum non solum diuites in rebus, sed *uolentes fieri diuites* per auariciam *incidunt in laqueos diaboli.* Voluntarie pauper mundum uicit, et secundum Virgilium "strepitum Acherontis auari", arma carnis et subsidia abstulit. Contra dyabolum ut pugil stat, semper paratus ad pugnam, quia *in agone contendens* secundum apostolicam preparationem *ab omnibus se abstinet,* tanto inuincibilior quanto minus inuenit hostis quo eum teneat uel prosternat.

Vnde et uoluntaria paupertas est amica solitudinis. Pauperem diuites fugiunt, et pauperes non iuuantur exterius a paupere. Non habet pauper cur quis uel eum comitetur uel sequatur. In temporalibus accipere potest, non reddere. Societas deficit quando non est conuiuere, id est de eodem gaudere et tristari. Non permanens est contrariorum, sed uiolenta, non diu durans coniunctio. Quid est de quo communes gaudent, quod pauper non despicit? Ymmo, et crebros risus et iocunda secundum seculum uoluntarie pauper habet ut tristia.

Est igitur pauper in se et ad Deum tanto constrictior quanto ab hominibus corpore et mente separatior, quantoque in rebus collectior. Ideoque corde et mente purior, quia a concupiscentiis et inquinamentis elongatior. | *Nam ubi thesaurus tuus, ibi et cor tuum.* | Consequenter et in oratione et desideriis sanctis mundior, quia diuina lumina et angelicas impressiones ydola substantie

---

615/616 Luc. 14, 33   618/619 I Tim. 6, 9 paene ad litt.   622/623 I Cor. 9, 25 paene ad litt.   629/638 cfr Matth. 5, 11 ; Luc. 6, 22   638/639 Matth. 6, 21 paene ad litt.

620/621 Virg., *Geo.* 2, 492

---

615 esse meus *tr. contra* Bibl. *A L*   618/619 diuites] scilicet *add. Ek*   619 per auariciam] *om. A Z*   laqueum *sec. Bibl. L*   620 uicit mundum *tr. Ek El*   621 subsidia] eius *add. Z Ek El*   623 abstinuit *Ek*   624 uel] et *El*   626 amica est *tr. A*   629 non potest *tr. El*   632 gaudet *El*   634 ut] et *A*   635 ad] *om. Ek*   636 separabilior   in] *om. Ek*   638 et] *om. A L Ek*   639 communiter *Z*   desideriis] in *praem. A* sanctis desideriis *tr. El*

mundi transformant, ad quas et ad Deum intuendas nuda in rebus mens est et paratior et permanentior et fructuosior. Nam *uerbum* Dei auditum intus uel extra *sollicitudo huius seculi et fallacia diuiciarum suffocant, ut sine fructu efficiatur.*

645 Pauper uoluntarie et frugalis stat securus a uiciis et aptus in Domino manente uerbo stabiliri. Paupertas neminem per potentiam extulit, neminem superbia inflauit, non ualet alios supprimere. Paupertas, omnis pene glorie mundi inops, ornatum exteriorem, curiosa et uoluptatem nec uult nec potest.

650 Paupertas est tribulationis et humiliationis officina, de qua propheta in persona Christi et pauperum dixit: *infirmata est in paupertate* fortitudo seu *uirtus mea, et ossa mea conturbata sunt, Psalmorum* .xxx., qui loquitur de undique in temporalibus paupere, qui renunciauit non solum rebus, sed etiam humanis adiu-
655 toriis, cui dicitur, *Marci* .x., per Veritatem: *Nemo qui reliquerit domum aut fratres aut sorores aut patrem aut matrem aut filios aut filias aut agros propter me et propter euangelium, qui non accipiat centies in hoc tempore domos aut fratres aut sorores aut matrem aut filios aut agros cum persecutionibus, et uitam eternam*
660 *in futuro.* Et secundum supra dictum *Psalmum* talis est qui plus quam inimicus *factus est et obprobrium uicinis suis et timor notis suis,* quem *qui uident, foras* in plateis *fugiunt,* qui ab omnibus *obliuioni a corde datus est,* sicut *mortuus,* qui *factus | est* inter homines *tamquam uas perditum* et *uituperatio multorum com-*
665 *morantium in circuitu,* cuius et *animam,* id est uitam, *accipere consiliati sunt.*

Sed, Domine, quos dabis sibi *matres aut patres in hoc tempore?* Hoc, quod idem canit *Psalmus,* dabit *benedictus Dominus,*

53vb

642/644 Matth. 13, 22 paene ad litt.   645/646 cfr Eccli. 31, 11; etiam I Cor. 15, 58   651/653 Ps. 30 (31), 11   655/660 Marc. 10, 29-30   660/666 Ps. 30 (31), 12-14 paene ad litt.   667 cfr Marc. 10, 30, supra, 655-660, uerbatim allegatum   668/675 cfr Ps. 30 (31), 20-22

---

642 mens] pauperis *add. Z*   est] *om. Z¹, suppl. Z²*   643 seculi huius *tr. Z Ek*   645 securius *A*   647 per superbiam *El*   648 pene omnis *tr. A* ortum *sic Ek*   649 et] *om. A*   652 paupertatem *Ek*   uirtus] metus *A*   653 nudique *El*   654 qui renunciauit] *om. A*   solum] *om. Z*   655 cui] cum *A*   656/657 aut filias] *om. Z*   657/658 accipiet *Z Ek El*   659 filios] aut filias *sec. Bibl. suppl. L*   661 suis¹] *om. Ek El*   662 in plateis foras *tr. Z*   663 obliuione *El*   datus est a corde *tr. El*   665 id est] et *L*   668 Hoc] *om. L*

cen|ties tantum sibi in temporali adiutorio ualens sicut carnales
parentes uel propinqui; dabit, quia *mirificabit* in eo *misericordiam suam*, et ponet eum tamquam *ciuitatem munitam*. Et illam quam magnam multitudinem dulcedinis sue Dominus, *quam abscondit timentibus se*, ipsis *qui* in eo tantum *sperant, in conspectu filiorum hominum* perficit, et *abscondit eos in abscondito dulcis faciei* sue et *in* dilecto *tabernaculo* suo.

Predictum est quod paupertas operatur humiliationem et tribulationem. Tribulatio autem efficit *pacienciam, paciencia autem probationem, probatio spem. Spes autem non confundit, quia caritas diffusa est in cordibus nostris per Spiritum Sanctum, qui datus est nobis.* Hoc ordine et recto itinere paupertas ducit ad spem et caritatem, *Ad Romanos* .v., quibus nichil utilius est hominibus sub sole.

Paupertas etiam caritatem precedens ei uiam preparat, impedimenta et nociua sibi resecat, ipsa eam ad cellam ut dux cordis introducit, nutrit et roborat, que aucta et nutrita uersa uice cogit augeri paupertatem, quia est quidam diuini gustus effectus frugalitas, qui tanto facilius transitoria spernit quanto magis eternorum fragrat amore, tanto promptius effundit in proximum quanto constantius per spem confidit in Deum.

Mirabiliter paupertas et sperare in Domino docet et confidere. Experta est | paupertas quod melius est sperare uel confidere in Domino quam in homine uel humano adiutorio, *quia uana salus hominis*, et *maledictus homo qui ponit carnem, brachium suum* dico, in se uel in alio homine, et longe minus in adherentibus homini. Cogitur, sicut nauta fracto malo et gubernaculo, diuino iuua-

---

669/670 cfr Marc. 10, 30   677/681 Rom. 5, 3-5   690/692 cfr Ier. 17, 5-7
692/693 Ps. 59 (60), 13   693 Ier. 17, 5   695/696 cfr Ier. 9, 23

676/677 cfr supra, 650-651   683/685 cfr THOM., II-II, Q. 186 a. 3 co. (T. 10, p. 491, c. 1, praesertim 4-21), infra, 831-836, etiam allegatum, sicut ex indice fontium patet

---

669 adiutorio temporali *tr. Z*   670 mirificauit *sec. Bibl. L*   673 ipsi *L*, eis *Ek El*   674 eos] *om. A*   675 et] *om. Ek El*   679 diuisa *Z*   681 hominibus] *om. A*   686 augere *Z*   688 fragrauit *L*, fraglat *Z*   689 Deo *Ek El*   690 et¹] *om. Z*   et²] *om. Ek¹, suppl. Ek²*   691 est²] *om. A*   692 uana] noua *Ek*   694 dico] *Ek¹*, considero *corr. Ek²*   695 cogita *L*   695/696 iuuari *El*

SERMO IN FESTO PALMARVM DE PAVPERTATE 453

mini pauper inherere, cum non sit quod exterius spem promittat. Sed beatus uir pauper non gloriatur in multitudine diuiciarum nec in uanitate sua, sed est nomen Domini sui in suis necessitatibus adiutor eius, spes eius, *qui fecit celum*, id est animam, *terram*, id est | corpus, *mare*, id est uentrem, *et omnia que in eis sunt*, id est ad uentrem, corpus et animam pertinent. Iactat curam suam in Domino, ut ipse eum enutriat. Cumque necessariis, que panis nomine signantur, indiget, per cotidianam solum in Deo confidentiam spei inditur robur et continua renouatio. Et eo sapidius et largius quo in sensu suo frequentius cogitat circumspectionem Dei circa ipsum, quantum sui *Dominus sit sollicitus*, cum *mendicus* sit secundum *Psalmum* et *pauper*. *Cybabit illum* Dominus *pane uite et intellectus, et aqua sapientie salutaris potabit illum*, *Ecclesiastici* .XIIII.

Talis dicat cum Dauid: *Oculi mei semper ad Dominum, quoniam ipse euellet de laqueo*, scilicet diuiciarum, *pedes meos. Respice in me et miserere mei*, Deus, *quia unicus et pauper sum ego. Tribulationes cordis mei multiplicate sunt, de necessitatibus meis erue me. Vnicus* est cuius *oculus semper ad Dominum*, quia solitarius sine adiutoribus *pauper* est sine rebus, que ut causas dat quare ipse *oculis ad Dominum semper* aspiciat, et cur merito in ipsum | Dominus debeat *respicere* et *tribulationum* suarum multiplicium *misereri*, sibique ipse et non alius prouidere in *necessitatibus* et necessariis.

Et si necessaria sibi deficiant, accipit ea a quocunque ministrentur sicut a manu Domini. Si non assunt, longanimiter expectat.

699/700 Ex. 20, 11   706/707 cfr Ps. 39 (40), 18   707/709 Eccli. 15, 3
710/719 Ps. 24 (25), 15-17

---

697 pauper] solet *add. Ek²*   diuiciarum] suarum *add. Z*   698 sui] *om. A Z*   699/700 id est] *ter om. A Z Ek*   corpus terram *tr. A Z Ek*   700 id est³] et *Z Ek El*   701 ad] *om. L*   702 pane *El*   703 Domino *Z*   704 spei] *om. A*   inditur *A Ek*, induitur *Z*, inducitur *El*   eo] Deo sic *El*   705 circumspectione *El*   706 sit] *om. Z*   707 Dominus] *om. L*   708 et¹] *om. A*   salutaris] *om. A*   709 .XIIII.] .XV. *contra codd. legendum*   711 ipse] *om. A L*   meos] *om. L*   712 quoniam *Z*   713 sunt] et *add. El*   714 oculi *Z L El*   716 cui *Z Ek El*   717 debeat] igitur *add. Ek El*   aspicere *El*   718 multiplicium] petat *add. L Ek El*   prouidere] prouideat (preuideat *L*, prouidet ei *Ek*) Deus *L Ek El*   719 necessariis] deprecetur *add. L El*   720 Et] *om. Ek El*   sibi] non *add. A L*   accipit] *Z¹*, accipiat *corr. Z²*   ea] *om. L*   720/721 ministrentur] sibi *praem. A*   ministretur *L*   721 assint *A L*

Si diutius tardant et fame uel siti cruciant, scit *quoniam non in finem obliuio erit pauperis,* quia *patientia pauperis non peribit in finem.* Et qui in superfluis aliquando non deest, in necessariis non deficiet. Scit quia qui non est in natura, diuinitus abundat in gratia et gratuitis.

Non immerito in manibus Domini sortes sue sunt, quia *non uidit iustum derelictum, nec | semen eius querens panem.* Cuius *oculi in pauperem respiciunt, exsurget propter miseriam inopum et gemitum pauperum.* Cui *derelictus est pauper, desiderium pauperum exaudiet et preparationem cordis eorum audit auris eius,* quia *Dominus factus est refugium pauperis, adiutor in opportunitatibus, in tribulatione.* Diuites autem *egent et esuriunt,* quia eos *dimisit inanes. Repleti prius pro panibus se collocant, et famelici saturati sunt,* nimirum quia solus Dominus pauperem facit et ditat, humiliat et sublimat, *suscitans de puluere egenum et de stercore erigens pauperem, ut sedeat cum principibus et solium glorie teneat.*

Quippe sicut ad theologicas, sic et ad morales proficit non modicum uirtutes paupertas. Nam sicut humiliationis, ita et humilitatis causa est. Nam sepe in *Scriptura,* ut et in cantico Anne predicto, humilitas et paupertas sicut causa et effectus connectuntur. Sicut aurora solem, | sic humiliatio precedit patienciam, humilitatem, deinceps et mititatem. Eo mitior est quis quo suo uidetur bassior, eo bassior quo ex se impotentior, eo in omni terribili uel defectu durior et constantior quo malis consuetior.

722/724 Ps. 9, 19   727/728 Ps. 36 (37), 25 paene ad litt.   729 Ps. 10, 9   729/730 Ps. 11 (12), 6 paene ad litt.   730 Ps. 10, 14 paene ad litt.   730/731 Ps. 10, 17 paene ad litt.   732/733 Ps. 9, 10   733 Ps. 33 (34), 11   734 Luc. 1, 53   734/735 I Reg. 2, 5   736/738 I Reg. 2, 8 paene ad litt.   741/742 sc. I Reg. 2, 1-10

724/725 BERN., *Dil. Deo* 8, 24 (p. 139, 16-17) paene ad litt.

---

722 quia] quoniam *Ek,* et *praem. Z*   725 deficiet] Deus *add. A*   qui] *om. L*   diminutus *L*   730/731 pauperis *L*   731 audiuit *sec. Ps. A*   732 est] *om. Ek*   733 eguerunt et esurierunt *sec. Ps. A,* eguerunt et esuriunt *paene ad litt. sec. Ps. Ek,* egent et esurient *Z El*   734 prius] post *add. L* se pro panibus *tr. sec. Bibl. A*   736 ditat] et *add. A*   subleuat *L*   739 Quippe] Ad morales uirtutes proficit *ut subtitulum interposuit L*   theologicas] catholicas *Ek*   740 paupertas] ipsa *praem. EkZ,* et *praem. El*   741 et] *om. L Ek El*   744 suo] *om. L*   745 eo²] quod *add. El* terribili] tribulatione *Ek*

SERMO IN FESTO PALMARVM DE PAVPERTATE   455

Sic paupertas edificat *turrim fortitudinis a facie inimici*, que turris sicut alta in profectu et utilis in refugio, sic in Christo et humilitate firmiter fundata est, sic ab inimicis tuta, sic donis munita et gratia, sic et inaccessibilis, cum non habet per quod ad eam ingressus pateat.

Sic et paupertas sedem preparat prudentie, rationem excolit, carnem comprimit, bestialitatem restringit, appetitus carnalis minuit fomitem, oculos intellectui aperit, profunda reuelat, alta considerat, infectionem desideriorum rectificat et saporem diui|norum ministrat.

Est etiam imperatrix temperantie et effectus iusticie. Quomodo non iustus qui nichil sibi sed aliis omnia tribuit? Hec est iusticia, que suum non dicit quicquam, nec suum solum cuilibet tribuit, sed que *dispergit et dat pauperibus, et* que *manet in seculum seculi*. Quomodo et non erit liberalis cuius iusticia est effundere? Quomodo non magnificus qui omne temporale, quamuis altum uideatur, sicut nichil estimat?

Hec omnia opera una et eadem paupertas in singulis uirtutibus operatur, ut omnes simul, quia colligate sunt, uel in actiua diuise habeantur uel in contemplatione tamquam in quodam uno pleno congregentur, cuius immodica paupertas est ministra. Ministrat enim has anime diuicias radix paupertas, quas nullus hostium uel potentum conferre poterit uel auferre, | nec et ipsa quidem mors, que cetera tollit, potest has ab anima disiungere.

Sed ad hanc uitam in hoc tempore ⟨habentibus⟩ respectum dumtaxat et non ad eterna, sicut quidam non habebant gentilium, paupertas amministrat centuplum, id est oppido meliora, plura et maiora quam diuicie. Hoc nobis ualet naturalis ratio tam persua-

---

747 Ps. 60 (61), 4   759 cfr Act. 4, 32   760/761 Ps. 111 (112), 3 paene ad litt.

752/756 cfr infra, 981-982

---

747 efficit *Ek El*   748 in] est *L*, est in *Ek El*   sic] et *add*. *Ek*   Christo et] Christi *Ek El*   750 et¹] *om*. *Ek*   752 extollit *Ek*   753/754 fomitem minuit *tr. Z*   754 intellectui] *om. L*   profundat *L*   755 et] ac *L*   759 quamquam *L*   765 quia] quasi *L Ek*   sunt] *om. L Ek El*   diuerse *L El*   768 radix] ut *praem. A*   paupertatis *Ek*   771 Sed] In hoc mundo meliora prestat diuiciis *ut subtitulum interposuit L*   habentibus] *scripsi*, habentes *codd*.   773 oppido] operatur *Ek*   774 ualet nobis *tr. L*   774/775 persuadere tam *tr. Z*

dere lucide quam sapide. Naturalis nobis, sicut et omnibus animantibus, uniuersalis est paupertas, nature imitatrix. Nudos nos natura genuit, nudi egressi a matre nostra terra, nudi in naturam et matrem reuertimur. *Nichil intulimus in hunc mundum, haut dubium quia nec auferre quid possumus.* Sicut nos pauperes natura produxit, sic et nudos recipiet. Et nudos parentes in primeua rerum origine constituit Altissimus. Cayn uero ex agricultura primus sibi diuicias aggregauit, secundum Iosephum. Ortus autem in lucem non est quis progenitoribus tam diuitibus ut lacte et pannis inuolutus contentus non sit.

In omni uero etate naturales nobis terminos natura imposuit, ut contentaremur *habentes alimenta et quibus tegeremur.* Nature desiderium est "non esurire, non sitire, non algere", ut ait Seneca. Natura querit cibum ut famem depellat, non qui palatum delectet, non qui desiderium irritet uel uentrem ingurgitet. Potum querit ut sitim extinguat, non qui immergat uel ad sitiendum amplius prouocet, uestem ut frigus arceat. Quid ad hunc finem iuuat naturam, si auro intexta quoue colore intincta sit? Quid obest, si non tenui filo mollis lane britannice contexta, grossa et rudis sit? In quo agnine, quia pelles primos homines in paradyso uestiebant, minus nos tegunt uel defendunt a frigore quam uariarum pellium

---

777/778 cfr Iob 1, 21   778/779 I Tim. 6, 7   780/781 cfr Gen. 2, 25; 3, 7   786 I Tim. 6, 8 paene ad litt.   794 cfr Gen. 3, 21

776/806 elenchum locorum cum locis ex Senecae epistulis parallelorum ex commentariolo a Patre G. Meersseman O.P., *Seneca*, p. 122-128, scripto sumpsi   779/780 cfr SEN., *Ep.* 22, 14 (p. 72, 9-10); 22, 15 (p. 72, 15-16)   781/782 cfr FLAV. IOS., *Ant.* I, 2, 1, 53-54 (p. 130, 9-13 ed. Blatt; p. 19-20 tr. Feldman), quem locum Ger. allegat cum Iosephus Cain describat ut "ad lucra solummodo semper intentus", in loco biblico (Gen., 4, 2) autem Cain ut "agricola" tantummodo describatur   782/784 cfr SEN., *Ep.* 20, 13 (p. 65, 5-6)   785/787 SEN., *Ep.* 4, 10 (p. 9, 7-8), partim paene ad litt., cfr fortasse etiam *Ep.* 119, 7 (p. 579, 4-5)   788/791 cfr SEN., *Ep.* 8, 5 (p. 18, 8-11)

---

775 Nobis naturalis *tr. El*   777 nudi²] nude *El*   778 reuertemur *Ek El*   haud *A*   haut] id est non *add. El*   779 afferre *L*   paupertas *Ek*   780 nudos] nostros *add. Ek El*   781 rerum] creacionis *Ek*   781/782 primus ex agricultura *tr. El*   prius *L*   783 progenitoribus] de praem. *Z*   788 Natura] Nam *A*   788/789 delectat *LZ*   789 irritat *AL*   790 qui] quod *AZ*   791 arceatur *Ek*   792 tincta *Ek*   sit] Sic *AZL*   794 agmine *Ek*   795 minus] non praem. *Z*   nos] om. *Z*   uel] et *El*

SERMO IN FESTO PALMARVM DE PAVPERTATE 457

extranearum uaria excogitata cum syndone serico mollis uarietas? In quo minus repeciata seu reconsuta nature finem attingunt? Natura uult ut domos contra ymbres, cauma et infesta muniant. In hoc fere non opitulatur, si alte leuetur, si apte contignetur, si pic‑
800 turis uel ymaginibus uarietur, si metallo aut lapide contegatur, aut canna uel stramine. Quicquid autem legem nature eiusque terminos superest uel transgreditur, humana finxit imbecillitas.

Ad diuicias natura non impellit, quod facile conuincitur. Nam instantibus desideriis desinentibus, cum fami, siti, frigori presen‑
805 tibus dumtaxat satisfactum est, amplius nature motus habitibus presentibus cessant. Non famescimus nec sitimus de futuro, sed presenti tantum defectu. Quicquid ergo in futurum reseruatur uel prouidetur, ultra nature legem est. Similiter natura ad aurum, pecunias et artificiales diuicias non mouetur, quibus nec saciari nec
810 uestiri potest. Vnde nec acquisitiue industrie nec media quibus ad hec peruenimus, sunt nature amminicula.

Sed natura solum quod ad predictos fines necessarium est, quod et minimum est, expetit. Nam modicis ualde natura non solum fouet se, sed et contenta est. Quomodo non modicis, quo‑
815 niam omnino presentibus contenta est et illis paucis. Ad manum et facile parabile est, quo oblato nature motus desinunt. Quin ymmo, et iam paratum | est omnibus naturaliter uiuentibus, precipue iustis et bonis, ab origine mundi, et religiosis per huma|nam prouidentiam de pluribus quam lex nature exigit, prouisum est.
820 Vltra quam quicquid est, a malo est.

55rb
458

---

797 cfr supra, 96-97   797/798 cfr SEN., *Ep.* 8, 5 (p. 18, 10-11)   798/801 cfr fortasse SEN., *Ep.* 16, 8 (p. 50, 3-8)   801/802 cfr SEN., *Ep.* 4, 10 (p. 9, 7-8), supra, 785-786 paene ad litt. citatum   803/806 cfr SEN., *Ep.* 17, 4 (p. 51, 18-19)   812/831 elenchum locorum locis ex Senecae epistulis haustis parallelorum ex commentariolo a Patre G. Meersseman O.P., *Seneca*, p. 122-124, scripto sumpsi   812/813 cfr SEN., *Ep.* 17, 9 (p. 52, 25 – 53, 1)   815/816 cfr SEN., *Ep.* 4, 10 (p. 9, 12-13), supra, 785-786 paene ad litt. citatum

---

796 serico *om.* A   797 attingant *A Z*   798 domos ut *tr.* A   et] *om.* A   muniat *Ek El*   799 uere *Ek*, uero *El*   non] nichil *A*   leuatur *L*, leuentur *Ek*   configurentur *Ek*   800 uarientur *Ek*   contegantur *Ek*   801 stimulo *Ek*   804 fame *L*   fami] et *add.* Z   805 habitibus] *sic codd.*, habitis *coni.* Meersseman   806 nec] non *L*   807 defectui *L*   808 aurum] et argentum *add.* Z   813 expedit *El*   Nam] Anima *Ek*   814/815 quoniam] quomodo *Ek El*   816 ablato *Z Ek El*   820 quam] quamquam *El*   est¹] amplius *add.* L   820/821 a – Nam] *om. Ek El*

Nam hoc aut malefida carnis exquirit uoluptas seu concupiscentia, aut inquirit oculorum superbia aut inanis gloria, uel hoc ambicio extollit potentia; hoc trepide mentis sollicitus timor congregat, hoc superuacuus labor preparat, hoc ornat curiositas, hoc
825 auaricia multiplicat, hoc humanum fastidium eructans de hoc in illud uariat.

Hec omnia nos in tam multa precipitantia mala et tam longe a uia nature abducentia desiderium humanum ex falsa opinione et errore procedunt. Et sicut nec falsorum nec errorum quis est finis,
830 sic nec horum extraordinariorum et infectorum desideriorum ullus est terminus. Sicut pluribus datis erroribus et inconuenientibus plures contingunt et errores et inconuenientia, sic extraordinariis desideriis quantum plus conceditur seu offertur, tanto amplius nos irritant et nos stimulant. Sed non cessant ex concu-
835 pitis adeptis, sed rursum molestius inquietant et ueluti plus et plura indigentia et ut magis uacua ardentius conturbant.

Ex quo patet quod diuicie temporales indigentiam faciunt, paupertas uero sufficientiam tamquam amica et nature socia. Non deficit in necessariis, sicut nec comes eius optimus natura. Numquid
840 optimum in uia habens comitem et amicum fidelem, habundantem in cunctis necessariis, | potest deficere, qualis natura est? Numquid plenus comes plene ministrat comiti suo indiuiduo legi sue obtemperanti? Circumspice legem nature, quantum suis prouidet tam habundanter quam sagaciter. Attende quomodo
845 pullo in ouo et puero in utero alimenta preparat, quomodo exeunti fetui, mittens sanguinem ad mamillas, ut in congruum nutrimentum exeat, coquit in albedinem. Quis defert animalibus de loco se non mouentibus, ut conchilibus, alimentum? Quis pullis coruorum, antequam a parentibus cognoscantur nigri, alimenta

---

827/831 cfr SEN., *Ep.* 16, 9 (p. 50, 8-11)   831/836 cfr THOM., II-II, Q. 186 a. 3 co. (T. 10, p. 491, c. 1, praesertim 4-21), alibi etiam allegatum, ubi citat AVG., *Ep.* 31, 5 (p. 5, 18 – 6, 3) in uersione truncata   837/838 cfr infra, 855-861

---

821 autem *El*   seu] aut *L*   823 ambiciosa *L Z*   mentis] *om. L*
825 in] *om. A*   830 extra ordinatorum *A*   831 sicut] ac *Ek*, et *El*
833 quanto *A*   834 nos amplius *tr. A*   835 pluri *A*   837 faciunt] *om. L*   838 uero] *om. L*   839 optima *L*   840 habens comitem in uia *tr. A*   841 qualis] sicut *A*   842 comes plenus *tr. Ek El*   plene] plena *Z*
848 conchilibus] *sic codd.*, conchulibus *legendum*   849 alimenta] *om. A*

55va

SERMO IN FESTO PALMARVM DE PAVPERTATE 459

850 amministrat? Quis natare aliaque exercitia fetus auium docuit ad
alimenta in debitis locis | acquirenda, nisi illa in nullo deficiens
natura? Deus cuncta ordinate, sufficienter et ditissime disponens,
superhabundantissime et copiosissime effluens et ministrans,
cuius operationem paupertas imitatur et ipsa diues et plena.
855 Inde est frequens illa Epycuri et stoicorum uox crebro repe-
tenda, que, ut fert Seneca, non satis repeti uel dici potest: "diuicie
mundane sunt secundum nature legem composita paupertas."
Nam quid aliud sunt diuicie nisi contra legem nature, ut supra
dictum est, quodam errore opinata indigentia uel paupertas? Sed
860 uere, iuxta alteram uerbi legem Metodori et aliorum epycurorum,
diues est qui minime diuiciis eget. Diues ergo omnis uoluntarie
pauper, diues et sufficiens et plenus. Sufficit enim pauperibus paupertas, si diuicie computentur, id est si uoluntarie assumatur, et
estimentur diuicie esse in paupertate, ut confidat quod ea que
865 habet quecunque minima suffi|cienter magna sint. Cuius simile
ponunt hiis uerbis Epycurus et Seneca: "cui sua non uidentur am-
plissima, licet tocius mundi dominus sit, miser est", et iterum:
"uere miser est qui se ditissimum non iudicat." Tantum uero pauper est quantum aliquid sibi pro quo stat deficit.
870 Sed uoluntarie pauper quomodo non plenus est et diues,
qui quantum uult, tantum habet, qui minimum et presens uult?

459

55vb

855/869 cfr infra, 1143-1147   855/904 elenchum locorum locis ex Senecae epistulis haustis parallelorum ex commentariolo a Patre G. Meersseman O.P., *Seneca*, p. 124-125, scripto sumpsi   855/857 SEN., *Ep.* 27, 9 (p. 91,
14-15), ubi et Epicuri nomen refert, partim paene ad litt., cfr infra, 1025-1027;
idem prouerbium in *Ep.* 4, 10 (p. 9, 6-7) a SEN. citatur, sed sine nomine Epicuri; eadem epistula supra, 785-787; 801-802; 815-816, a Ger. allegatur   858/
859 cfr supra, 837-838   859/865 cfr GER. MAG., *Ep.* 41, 160   859/861 cfr
SEN., *Ep.* 14, 17 (p. 44, 3-6)   865/869 SEN., *Ep.* 9, 20 (p. 25, 22 – 26, 5) paene
ad litt., ubi Epicurus sec. Sen. non nomine adi. 'ditissimum', sed 'beatissi-
mum' utitur   870/873 cfr SEN., *Ep.* 2, 6 (p. 4, 9-10) "non qui parum habet,
sed qui plus cupit, pauper est"

---

850 omnium *Z*   docet *El*   ad] et *praem. Ek*   851 acquirendum *Ek El*
853 et¹] *om. A*   854 opus] operationem *A*   855 Inde] Quod pauper
uere est diues *ut subtitulum interposuit L*   stoycorum *Z L El*   858 nisi]
quam *Z*   859 quedam *A Z*   oposita *Ek*   860 Methodori *Z L*, Metro-
dori *El*   epicutorum *Ek*, epicurorum *Z El*   861 minimis *A Z*   indiget *L*
862 pauper] est *add. A Z*   863 computentur] paupertas *add. Ek*   as-
sumantur *El*   assumatur] paupertas *add. L*   864 que] qui *L*   866 ponuntur *Ek*   Epyturus *Ek*, Epicurus *Z El*, Epicuries *L*   867 est] *om. El*
868 uere *A*   est] *om. El*   869 aliquid] *om. L*   870 est plenus *tr. El*
et] sed *El*   871 qui²] *om. Ek*

Quomodo non plenus qui amplius non uult impleri uel ditari? Quomodo non sufficiens qui plenus et nullo uel minimo indiget? At uero ex alio pauperes diuites sunt, quia pauperes omnibus rebus dominantur, omnia subiciunt prout uolunt, secundum apostolum *nichil habentes et omnia possidentes*. Est et magna possessio et ⟨leta⟩ paupertas, que auferri non potest, contra indigentias diui|ciarum et insidias sicut quedam plenitudo, tuta possessio.

Temporales diuicias nos non, sed ipse nos habent, nobis dominantur et impellunt suis nos imperiis ad multa et extraordinarias molestias. Si tu eas te habere dixeris, non contendam de nomine, sed scias quod eo tunc modo quo febres habes, qui magis tibi quam tu eis dominantur et tyrannide. Ymmo, si ingentes sunt diuicie, sicut enormia gubernacula te mergunt et supprimunt in profundum, ut amplius proprie potestatis et respirationis uox non possit audiri. Et si quid dispositionis habet in hoc diues, potius diuiciarum procurator est quam dominus, sollicitus plus quomodo amplificet, quomodo congreget, quam quomodo usui naturali applicet uel quam quomodo sibi eas subiciat.

Item ex alio, quomodo diues est qui nulla bona habet. Nam exteriora | bona secundum Tullium, achademicos et stoicos omnino bona non sunt humana, uel minima ualde secundum peripatheticos, cum sine ueris bonis nullus est diues. Nam si bonum sit, tamen nostrum non est quicquid iure auferri potest. Non dedit nobis natura hec bona ut debitrix, alioquin quomodo fortuna, cui natura imperat, iuste possit repetere? Extra nos sunt hec bona, nostra sunt magis ex iuris positione et lege hominum quam in ue-

---

875/876 II Cor. 6, 10

876/877 cfr SEN., *Ep.* 2, 6 (p. 4, 8)   879/883 cfr SEN., *Ep.* 119, 12 (p. 580, 8-13)

---

874 sint *Ek*   quia] qui *El*   877 leta] *sic sec. Sen. emend. Meersseman*, lata *codd.*   879 Temporales] Quod diuicie magis obsunt *ut subtitulum interposuit L*   880 implent *El*   nos suis *tr. Z El*   impiis *Ek*   881 te] *om. Z*   886 habet] *om. El*   888 amplicet *El*   889 quam] *om. Z*   eas] *om. A L*   890 Nam] non *Ek*   891 tulium *El*   athe^tos et stoycos *Ek L*, athe^cos et stoycos *El*   stoycos *Z*   omnino] omnia *Ek*   892 bona] *om. L*   humana] *hab., sed postea exp. Z*   ualde] et *add. A*   892/893 peripathetitos *Ek*, parypoteticos *Z*, perypotheticos *El*   893 cum] *om. A*   893/894 tamen] *om. A*   896 posset *Z*

ritate, attributione nostra potius dicuntur quam sunt. Sed uoluntarie pauper scit sua non esse, sed dici, si quid habet. Quicquid boni extra nos est, uere nostrum non est.

Vnde Stilbon philosophus, cum "capta patria, liberis et uxore amissis et solus de incendio publico exiret, interroganti Demetrio si perdidisset omnia, respondens: 'bona omnia mea', inquit, 'mecum sunt' ". Nam nichil suum putare potuit quod eripi possit. Et sicut uere diues est pauper, cuius omnia bona inseparabilia sunt, sic fortunatus et felix, cui nichil de suis auferri potest, cui omnia que in motu fortune uult, succedunt prospere. Quomodo non felix? Ymmo, quicquid optat, habet. Nam hanc opinio uulgaris in excellenter diuite probationem solet inducere.

Hinc sequitur quod paupertas a curis soluta est nec sollicita. Pro quo sollicitus esse poterit, qui nichil uult, nichil cupit, cui sua satis sunt, qui diues, qui plenus est, qui solum presentem curat et non crastinam famem uel defectum depellere, forte numquam, si antea moriatur uel aliunde melius proueniat, futuram? Secundum iussum Christi, qui nos ad Patris remittit opera, *ne sit quis sollicitus quid manducet aut quo uestiatur. Considerat uolatilia celi, que neque serunt neque metunt neque congregant in horrea, et Pater celestis pascit ea. Considerat et lilia agri quomodo crescunt: neque laborant neque nent.* Tamen unum ex hiis est a Domino ita uestitum quod *Salomon in omni gloria sua ita non fuit coopertus.* Si hiis omnibus naturali rerum prouidentia Deus sollicitus est,

---

915/921 Matth. 6, 25-26; 6, 28-29 paene ad litt.

898/904 SEN., *Ep.* 9, 18 (p. 25, 5-9) paene ad litt.   904 SEN., *Ep.* 9, 19 (p. 25, 13) paene ad litt.

---

899 scit] sic *El*   901 Stilbon] *sec. Sen. legendum est, sic Z (etiam K) Ek*, Stibbon *A*, Scibbon *L*, Salbon *El*   libris *El*   902 sonus *sic Ek*   exiret] et *add. El*   903 mea omnia *tr. El*   904 nichil] non *Ek*   906 sic] sicud *El* cui²] ymmo *EkEl*, ymmo cui *Z, sed* ymmo *postea exp. Z*   907 uult] sunt *A*   908 Ymmo] qui *Z*   910 Hinc] soluta est curis *ut subtitulum interposuit L*   Hinc] Eciam *EkEl*   911 nichil²] uel *EkEl*   911/912 satis sua *tr. B*   912 curat] famem *add. Z*   914 antea] ante *EkEl*   915 qui] quis *Z* ad] a *El*   remittit ad Patris *tr. Z*   sic quis sit *sic Z*   916 considerans *A*   918 quomodo] que *El*   919 neque¹] non *sec. Matth. Z*   est] *om. L¹, marg. suppl. L¹ ᵘᵉˡ ²*, in *Ek*   919/920 a Domino uestitum *tr. El* 920 ita] *om. EkEl*   Solomon *A Ek*   921 Si] Pro *A,* Quod *praem., sed postea eras. Z*   Deus] *om. EkEl*

quanto magis pro nobis, ad quos tam hec quam illa sicut ad finem et in subsidium, ne sollicitemur, ordinata sunt.

Diuiti autem sollicitudo non deficit, angusta sibi uidentur cuncta que possidet, in longinquum fertur. Omnium etiam futurorum expectationi sicut inest sollicitudo, sic et afflictio, quia spes que differtur uel que frustratur, affligit animam. Sic et timor et anxietas ne dilatum non obtingat et ne contingens uel auferatur uel minoretur. Diues totus in futurum pendulus est, tanto sollicitior quanto prudentia sua ad ulteriora et ad plura adipiscenda astutior. Tanto prouidet longinquius quanto uidet acutius, tanto anxior et se affligens sibi molestior quanto in fortuitorum inconstantia perspicacior seu quanto euentuum uarietate experientior.

Adest de preteritis bonis dolor cum tristicia, que negante fortuna non obtinuit uel auferente perdidit uel non hortante neglexit. Se suosque cum non obtinet quod uult, frequenter accusat, et contra Deum, naturam et fortunam undique querulus murmurat. Quid mirum, cum tante uirtutes, uti rationis maioris prouidentia, intellectus perspicacitas, experiencie soliditas, memorie tena|citas, in malum sibi uertuntur et de afflictione, molestia et dolore sibi opponunt, sicut de cura, anxietate et timore addunt? Tormentum in cunctis hiis memoria renouat, prouidentia anticipat, intellectus augmentat, experientia multiplicat, et singula tanto crebrius quanto | in rebus magis est pluralis, ac quanto se plures res obtinendi offerant, occasiones et oportunitates. Et tormentum hoc illa que proueniunt ut optat, non dirimunt. Nam desiderium desiderium stimulat et spes spem prouocat, multo magis eum quam pauperem torquent et prius quam pauperem, et que nullo modo pauperem molestant.

Ymmo, ut frequentius, ubi non est timor, anxiatur et torquetur, de presencium dolore incontentus, appensus cura ad maliciam

---

950/953 cfr Matth. 6, 34

---

922 hoc *Ek*   924 Diuiti] Tormenta diuitium *ut subtitulum interposuit L*
927 que²] *om. Ek El*   928 aufferatur *Ek*   929 minoratur *Ek Z*
930 ad²] *om. Ek El*   adipiscenda plura *tr. Ek El*   931 longinquus *El*
uidit *L*   932/933 inconstantior *Ek*, inconstantior et *L El*   933 seu] seculi *El*   934 Adest] Atque *El*   935 aufferente *Ek*, auferenti *Z*
938 maior *L*   941 apponunt *L*, ponunt *El*   944 ac] 7 *Ek*, et *El*   se] *om. L*   946 diminuunt *A Z*   desiderium²] *om. El*   947 multa *El*
949 pauperi (pauperem *L*) molesta sunt *A Z L*

crastini, cui, secundum Christum, cum uenit, malicia sua et anxietas sufficit, si non antequam sit dolore nos preoccupat. Nam sicut cupitarum et possessarum, sicut attingendi, augendi et retinendi tam debiles, tam falsas, tam non contingentes quam impossibiles occasiones et causas cupido confingit errore, sic desideratarum et habitarum non accipiendi, diminuendi uel perdendi tam superfluos timores quam sine ratione timidas suspiciones fabricat. Cum animus in incertis estuat, eo pronius se inclinat qua coniectura fauentis cupidinis uel sperando uel timendo declinat. Humani metus plurimum sunt fantastici et pene limphatici, maxime diuitum, quia suspicionibus referti sunt. Nam plures humanos metus incutit menti uel fama illudens uel nostra fictio uel opinio.

Stat ergo paupertas, liberata ab hiis diuiciarum tormentis, intrepida, | tam tuta et secura. Nam quem timebit pauperculus? Non nichil cupientem concinnit, qui sibi rebus et corde amico applaudit ut simili; non sua cupidine uel rebus famescentem, cum nichil habeat, quod cum magno emolimento eripi ualet. Nullus paupertati inuidet. Tuta est a cunctis que delectant que uulgo placent, que qui spernit paupertatem amat. Nam uel amari uel misereri paupertas se cogit, atque ambo hec addunt tutamini.

Etiam non est de quo pauper metuat, cum tam ad parua et leuia redactus sit, a quibus cadere non potest. Non est ubi timeat, cum

---

964/975 elenchum locorum locis ex Senecae epistulis haustis parallelorum ex commentariolo a Patre G. Meersseman O.P., *Seneca*, p. 125-126, scripto sumpsi   964/965 cfr SEN., *Ep.* 17, 3 (p. 51, 10), fortasse etiam sicut Patri Meersseman uidetur *Ep.* 20, 12 (p. 64, 22-23)   967/968 SEN., *Ep.* 14, 9 (p. 41, 17-18) paene ad litt., quam epistulam Ger. etiam supra, 859-861, et infra, 987-988, allegat   972/973 SEN., *Ep.* 20, 8 (p. 63, 21-22) paene ad litt.   973/975 Ger. hic prouerbium ubique in medio quod dicitur aeuo diuulgatum in paraphrasi allegat, quod primo inuenitur in Ivv., *Sat.* 10, 22 "Cantabit uacuus coram latrone uiator"; exempla et uersiones deriuatiuae enumerantur in SINGER, *Thesaurus prouerbiorum*, Vol. I s.u. 'Arm (adj.)', 3.5.2 'Spez.: Der arme braucht keine Räuber', n. 433-451; uersio a Ger. praesentata praesertim cum n. 439; 443 consimilis est

---

952 cui] tui *El*   953 sic *El*   preoccupet *ZLEl*   954 et[1]] uel *AZL* sicut] *fortasse delendum*, sic *certe false hab. EkEl*   955 tam[3]] nam *A* 957 diminuendi] *om. EkEl*   958 suspicaciones *El*   Cum] tamen *A* 959 quo *AL*   960/961 motus *Ek*   962 referti] .i. repleti *add. El* 964 Stat] Libertas pauperum *ut subtitulum interposuit L*   965 tenebit *El*, ~~tenebit~~ timebit *corr. se ipsum Ek[1]*   966 concurrit *Ek*   969 que] quos *A Ek*   que delectant] *om. El*   972 non] nichil *EkEl*   ad tam *tr. ZEl*

464   SERMO IN FESTO PALMARVM DE PAVPERTATE

pauper in ter|ribili etiam cunctis uia, que latronibus obsessa est, 463
975 cantet uiator intrepidus.
   Est quasi pacis fundamentum assumpta uoluntate paupertas.
Nam, ut diffinit Augustinus, .XIX. *De ciuitate Dei*, "pax est tranquillitas ordinis", qui ordo ex concordia appetituum et appetibilium sine impedimento assecutione est. In paupertate uoluntaria est
980 uoluntatis, qui est appetitus intellectiuus et naturalium et uegetabilium, maxime contra rationem militantium appetituum, ut supra declaratum est, concors et amica consonantia, que uniri, quia extrema sunt, nisi per medios sensus concordes apte non possunt. In paupertate etiam appetibilium, que uel non uult uel minima uel
985 facilime parabilia, prosecutio minimum impeditur.
   Est ergo undique pacifica et cunctis fere concors. Nam lites et discordie non nisi a pronominibus 'meum' et 'tuum' oriuntur. Inter competitores rixa est, paupertas uero 'meum' non dicit, 'tuum' non uult, sibi contenta est, non laboriosa, | non occupata, sed 57ra
990 quieta.
   Omneque fortuitum bonum, quia natura sua tremulum est, suum, sicut ramus motus uel quassatus auem insedentem inquietat, possessorem et agitat. Sicut fluctus mari non deficiunt, ita nec habere cupienti et possidenti multa ire, tristicie, dissentiones
995 et occupationes desunt. Magno labore et operose parantur diuicie, obtente uariis premunt ponderibus. Nouis occupationibus ueteres renouantur, numquam deficiunt. Quibus, ut taceam de christianis uel philosophis, sed tyranni plurimi pressi occupationum premia et causas, gloriam uidelicet uel potentiam uel deposuerunt

---

   976/978 cfr GER. MAG., *Ep.* 41, 89-91   cfr THOM., II-II, Q. 29 a. 1 co., ad 1 (T. 8, p. 236, a. 1, c. 2, 7-26), ubi allegat AVG., *Ciu. Dei* 19, 13 (p. 679, 10-11) "pax est omnium rerum tranquillitas ordinis", *sed* "omnium rerum" *om. Thom. Ger.*   980/981 cfr e.g. THOM., II-II, Q. 24 a. 1 co. (T. 8, p. 174, c. 1-2)   981/982 cfr supra, 752-756   986/990 cfr GER. MAG., *Stat.*, 122-126 ; 512-523 ; *Ep.* 41, 83-88 ; 106-119, praesertim 112-114 ; *Ep.* 46, 16-21   cfr PS. SEN., *Mor.* 5 (p. 466 ed. Haase = *PL*, 72, 31A)   987/988 inter – est] SEN., *Ep.* 14, 9 (p. 41, 16-17) paene ad litt., quam epistulam Ger. etiam supra, 859-861 ; 967-968, allegat

---

   974 cunctis] a *ante suppl.* L²   est] *om. El*   975 cantat *A L Z*   uiator] *ex* uiatibus *corr.* Ek¹ ᵘᵉˡ ²   976 Est] Et *A*   977 Non *Ek*   978 appetibilis *Ek*   979 assecutus *Z*   980/981 uegitalium *Ek*   982 consors *El*   984 etiam] est *Ek*   985 persecucio *Ek*   minime *El*   987 meum] *scilicet praem. Ek*   et] *om. A*   991/992 suum est *tr. El*   995 occupationes] non *falso add.* L   desunt] *om. El*   996 premium *sic Ek*   998 occupationem *Ek*   999 uidelicet] *om.* L   uel¹] et *Z*   uel²] *om.* L

uel deponere habuerunt in desiderio, de quibus referte sunt hystorie. Domitor ille orbis Hercules imperium orbis grauatus baculo contentus pro comite et una pelle pro ueste deposuit, ut scribit Apologius in libro *De magia*. Quod ille qui uniuersum iussit orbem describi, bis in desiderio propositi habuit, ut scribit Suetonius in libro *De .XII. Cesaribus*.

Quam multi diuitum uel desidia uel tedio uel labore confecti uellent occupationes fugere, sed | premia et fines et causas et effectus occupationum ardenter cupiunt, rem uidelicet familiarem uberem, domum plenam, turbam seruorum, res preciosas, raras, ornatas, commodas et uoluptuosas, que non sine occupationibus uel parabiles uel conseruabiles sunt. Circa pauperem familia non constrepit. Nudum suum in uia latus est, cubiculum quietum est, et domus sua uacua est. Non est quo oneretur exportando, si irruat hostis uel incendium. Expeditus est, leuis est, natat | sine sarcina, sine impedimento ambulat. Quorsum se, sic sua ubilibet facile transfert. Liber est, non obligatus rebus, non alligatus loco. Ex qua libertate et facilitate transferendi paupertas pluribus Deo datis causa uagandi et occasio fuit et cadendi. Non seruit pauper quemadmodum diues cupidini, non uiolentatur occupationibus, non impellitur curis et anxietatibus, non affligitur, non molestatur, sibi nec alteri discors est, nichil sibi dampnosum est. Et pene cuncta que uult sibi, quia minima sibi uult, potest et optinet, tamquam ille cui pene ad uotum omnia contingunt.

1001/1003 cfr APVL., *Mag.* 22, 9-10 (p. 26, 19-25 ed. Ihm, p. 52, 13-18 ed. Hunink)   1003/1004 cfr SVET., *Caes., Aug.* 21, 1-3 (p. 57, 12 – 58, 7)   1003/1005 cfr SVET., *Caes., Aug.* 28. 1 (p. 62, 11-19)   1006/1071 elenchum locorum locis ex Senecae epistulis haustis parallelorum ex commentariolo a Patre G. Meersseman O.P., *Seneca*, p. 126-128, scripto sumpsi   1006/1013 cfr SEN., *Ep.* 22, 9 (p. 71, 5-11); Ger. in l. 1012-1013 SEN., *loc. cit.* (p. 71, 8-9) paene ad litt. allegat   1008/1009 cfr APVL., *Mag.* 22, 1-5 (p. 25, 17 – 26, 4 ed. Ihm, p. 51, 26-37 ed. Hunink), infra, 1140-1150, nominatim allegatum   1013/1016 cfr SEN., *Ep.* 22, 12 (p. 71, 23-26); Ger. in l. 1014-1015 SEN., *loc. cit.* (p. 71, 26) paene ad litt. allegat   1016/1018 cfr SEN., *Ep.* 22, 11 (p. 71, 17-21)

1001 domitor] *ex* dominator *corr. c. punct. del.* Z, dominice et *Ek*   orbis] *om.* El   Ercules *Ek*   imperio A   1003 Appoleglus L, Apulogius *Ek El*   Magna *Ek*   Quod] Et Z, dicens *praem. Ek*   iussit uniuersum *tr.* El   1004 bis] *om. Ek El*   1004/1005 Suetanius Z   1008 scilicet *El*   1009 ratas Z *El*   1010 que] *om.* L *El*   1012 constrepat A L Z   nidum sic *Ek*   1014 uel] aut A   uacat *El*   1015 sic] fert Z *Ek El*   1015/1016 facile] *om. Ek El*   1017 de eo *Ek*   1018 et¹] *om.* Z *Ek El*   1021 nichil] uel L

Et non solum leta res est paupertas ei qui cum ea bene conuenit, et delectabilis, sed plena gaudio et uoluptate. In huius testimonium inimicus tristicie et "magister uoluptatis" accedat, "Epycurus", qui cum omne quod uoluptatem afferre poterat, adprime exquireret, paupertatem in hoc miro modo diuiciis, ut predictum est, pretulit. Nam referente Seneca in mansiolis seu "ortulis" epycurorum "inscriptum" fuerat: " 'Hospes, hic bene manebis, hic summum bonum est uoluptas'. Paratus erit huius domicilii custos hospitalis, humanus, et te polenta excipiet et aquam quoque large ministrabit, et dicet: 'bene acceptus es'." Curauit Epycurus desideriis naturalibus, que consolationis receptiua sunt, tantum satisfieri solamine naturali et gratuito, que recipiendo optata quiescunt nec amplius molestant, naturali debito soluto.

Desideria autem diuiciarum aut uoluptatum extraordinaria sunt, quia | nequaquam finem, sicut nec error a quo procedunt, habent. | Diuersis, ut supra dictum est, tormentis, uoluptati uere contrariis, affligunt, maxime quando in consuetudinem ducte sunt. Tunc molestiores sunt, tunc non solum nos trahunt, sed cogunt in tantum ut sine eis non uidetur nobis uita nec quies. Vnde "uoluptatis magister" dicit quod "licet uoluptates", cum eis nichil debemus, "differre, castigare et comprimere", nam hoc est ad uere uoluptatis naturam se redigere. Habent etenim huiusmodi uoluptates illecebrose et superflue, ueluti commessationes, quandam delectationem. Habent, fateor, sed bestialem, breuem et fugacem, perfunctoriam. Cibus in gutturis transitu uix per trium digitorum spacium nos delectat. Talis delectatio continue reficienda est, quia

---

1024 cfr Sen., *Ep.* 2, 6 (p. 4, 8)   1024/1025 Sen., *Ep.* 4, 11 (p. 9, 16) paene ad litt.   1025/1027 Sen., *Ep.* 18, 9 (p. 56, 8-9), infra, 1043, etiam allegatum   1027/1029 cfr Sen., *Ep.* 27, 9 (p. 91, 14-15), etiam *Ep.* 4, 10 (p. 9, 6-7), locum supra, 855-857, nominatim Senecae attributum   1029/1033 Sen., *Ep.* 21, 10 (p. 68, 2-6)   1033/1039 cfr Sen., *Ep.* 21, 10-11 (p. 68, 9-15)   1039/1042 cfr supra, 924-963   1042/1045 cfr Sen., *Ep.* 21, 10 (p. 68, 12-13)   1043 Sen., *Ep.* 18, 9 (p. 56, 8-9), supra, 1025-1027, etiam allegatum

---

1026 accedit *L Ek*   1026/1027 Epiturus *Ek*   1027 auferre *Z Ek*   1029 in] *om. A Z*   mansiolis *Z*   1029/1030 Epiturorum *Ek*   1031 custos] *om. L*   1033 mistrabit *El*   Epyturus *Ek*   1037 autem] aut *Ek*   aut] ac *Z*   1038 finem nequaquam *tr. Z*   1042 ut] *om. Ek*, quod *Z*   1043 cum] tamen *L*   1044 castigare] sed *praem. L*   imprimere *A* (opprimere *Sen.*)   1045 Habent] *om. Ek El*   enim *L*   1048 perfunctoriam] sed *praem. A*   1049 continue] nature *Z*

debilis, et renouanda, quia preteriit. Longe maius hominem etiam in talibus occupat molestia quam uoluptas. Leue et in superficie in hoc et similibus gaudium est, sicut efficiens motus leuis est et mobilis.

Gaudium uerum solido innititur. Quomodo solidum est aliquid fortuitum, cum tam sit instabile? Quo altius surgit, oportunius cadit. Nichil casurum solide delectat, sicut nec motu instabile. Vnde patet in risu non esse uerum gaudium, quia res risum excitat non secundum quod bona, sed secundum quod bene mobiliter mota, secundum Aristotelem in *Probleumatibus*. Ridet quis si uentum emiserit, si quis ceciderit, non si diu optatum et magnum bonum attigerit. Tunc facies plana, tunc uultus submissus, quia uerum gaudium seuera res est. Habet securitatem gaudium pauperis, sine qua nichil est iocundum et sine anxietate et timore tutum, sine molestia et afflictione continuum, sine uanitate solidum, | sine motu stabile et quietum, sine turbatione in ea que omnem sensum superat, pace tranquillum, sine dolore purum et sincerum.

Stat pauper letus, animo alacer, erectus, fidens et iocundus. Nonne iocundum est nichil poscere, plenum, sufficientem et | diuitem esse, et nature numquam tristis, sed plene esse imitatorem et comitem? Et hoc iocundum est: minus iocundum, ut aquam et polentam, posse iocunde sumere. Vnde Ieronymus, *Contra Iouinianum*: "grandis", inquit, "exultatio anime est, cum paruo contentus fueris, mundum habere sub pedibus et omnem eius potentiam, epulas, libidines, propter que diuicie parantur, uilibus mutare cibis et grossiori tunica compensare".

1055 cfr SEN., *Ep.* 23, 5 (p. 74, 18-20)   1055/1056 cfr SEN., *Ep.* 23, 3 (p. 74, 4)   1056/1058 cfr Ps. ARIST., *Probl.*, part. 28, probl. 8 (p. electr. 555, c. 2 inferior, s.u. 'ultimum problema'); locus a Ger. directe allegatus est, quia in fontibus secundariis sicut Thom. Aq. locum nusquam inuenire potui   1061/1062 SEN., *Ep.* 23, 4 (p. 74, 6)   1067/1071 cfr SEN., *Ep.* 18, 10 (p. 56, 17-22)   1070/1071 Ger. hic ad SEN., *Ep.* 21, 10 (p. 68, 2-6), locum supra, 1029-1033, e Seneca sumptum alludit   1071/1075 HIER., *Adu. Iou.* 2, 11 (c. 301A-B)

1050 magis *Ek El*   hominem] *om. Z*   hominem etiam] scilicet *A*   1052 similibus] in *praem. Z*   1055 opotunius *Ek*   1056 solido *Z*   sicut] sic *A*   stabile *L*   1057 est *El*   res] nos *El*   1058 bona] bonum est *Ek*, bona est *El*   1059 Problemuatibus *El*   1060 non] nam *A*   1062 sonora *Ek*   1063 timore] sine *praem. LZ*   1064 uarietate *Ek*   1068 poscere] possidere *L*, nichil possidere *add. Ek*   1070 Et] *del.* $Z^{2?}$ iocundum²] *om.* Z^{1}, et iocunda uidetur *marg. suppl.* Z^{1}, iocunda *A*   ut] *om. Z*   1070/1071 aqua et polenta *Ek*

Voluptates et abundantie, si modum qui in eis sicut raro sic et difficile tenetur, excesserint, multum habent penitudinis et minimum plenitudinis. Inde est quod mordent cauda, et finali concludunt tristicia. Sed gaudium paupertatis est undique, sed in fine
1080 abundantius. Sed priuilegio speciali in christiano paupere alacris gaudiorum soliditas est et securitas, et longe maior et uerior leticia de regno celorum, de eternis gaudiis, de singulis bonis et uirtutibus, quibus sue delectationes connexe sunt, cum sine spirituali delectatione nec habitus est nec uirtus. De quorum gaudiorum
1085 immensitate, sicut de gaudentium eternitate, et in exemplum nos precedentium numero lingua sileat.

Sed ad corporis accedamus bona, sanitatem et uite longeuitatem, que ceteris corporalibus bonis et exterioribus | prestantiores sunt, ad que oppido magis paupertas rerum quam opulentia
1090 proficit. Nam longe plures morbi ex repletione quam inanitione fiunt. Multi morbi sunt qui secundum genus eorum uel numquam uel multo rarius cadunt in pauperem quam in diuitem. Vnde et hoc quam uerum prouerbium: "abstinentia", que pauperibus cotidiana est, "summa medicina est". Et cum gula tot occidat, ut fer-
1095 tur, plures quam gladius, quot hominum senium, quot morbos quorum occasio ignoratur, estimanda est inducere eadem gula, diuiciarum filia?

Eciam diuitum cura canos anticipat; similiter timores, anxietates, afflictiones, molestie, ire, tristicie, occupationes crebre,

58ra

1080/1086 cfr Matth. 5, 3 et Luc. 6, 20, supra, 576/577, uerbatim allegatos

---

1079/1086 securitas pauperis Christiani ex locis biblicis supra in initio secundae partis, 576-586, allegatis euidenter probatur   cfr GER. MAG., *Ep.* 41, 68-69   1092/1094 cfr SINGER, *Thesaurus prouerbiorum*, Bd. 2, p. 482, s.u. 'Enthaltsamkeit', n. 3-4, ubi uersio germanica "Enthabunge ist der best list, Der an der arzet buochen ist" (Cato germanicus) inuenitur; uersio latina huius prouerbii transmissa non est

---

1077 excesserint] si *praem. A Z*   excesserunt *Ek El*   penitudinis] plenitudinis *A*, punitudinis *El*   et] *om. Ek*   1080 specialiter *Z*   alacris] *om. Ek El*, alacer *Z*   1084 est] *om. Ek El*   uirtus] sit *add. Ek El*   1085 et] *om. A Z Ek*   1086 numero] *om. El*   1087 Sed] proficit ad corporis bona ut subtitulum interposuit *L*   1093 uerum] *om. A*, quidem *sine necessitate emend. Moll*   1094 est²] *om. L*   1095 plures] et *praem. Z*   1096 estimata *Z*   1098 Eciam] Et *El*   1099 occupationes] molestaciones *El*   crebres *L*

1100 labores superflui et alia numero plurima, que diuitibus sunt indiuidui | comites sed importuni, tam corporis quam sensuum inducunt discrasiam, quam uite addunt celerius terminum. Diuitibus etiam uita tota inordinatior est. Dietam pluries et tempore et quantitate et qualitate alterant, que non modica breuitatis uite hominis
1105 causa sunt.

Mors uiolenta a pauperibus longior est. Nam maris temptare pericula uel diuiciarum potentia uel amor habendi docuit. Cur temptaret maria nichil cupiens? Vnde rixe, unde discordie, nisi a diuiciis et potentia? A gladio uoluntarie pauper rege potentissimo,
1110 etiam defenso milibus, tutior est. Sed ea que diuicias consequuntur uicia, ut auaricia, luxuria, inanis gloria, mundana potentia, mutua inuidia, ira, superbia | et sensuum ebetudo seu stoliditas, quantos de uita educunt, quot impotentes corpore efficiunt, quot memoria et sensuum uiuacitate uel priuant uel debilitant. Hoc
1115 enucleare esset *pluuiarum guttas et arenas maris numerare*.

Voluntarie ergo pauper stat sanus, stat longeuus, stat memoria et sensibus integer, singula moderans et iuste ponderans, "paruo potens", consilio diues et benesuadus in singulis. Quis ergo paupertatem digne laudare possit, que tanta suo possessori tribuit
1120 bona, que etiam toti mundo sua distribuit? Vnde Apulogius in libro *De magia*: "paupertas apud pristina secula omnium ciuitatum fuit conditrix, omnium artium repertrix, omnium peccatorum inops, omnis glorie munifica, cunctis laudibus ⟨apud⟩ omnes nationes perfuncta. Paupertas populo Romano impe-

---

1115 Eccli. 1, 2 paene ad litt.

1117/1118 APVL., *Mag.* 18, 2 (p. 21, 17 ed. Ihm, p. 49, 9 ed. Hunink)   1120/1126 APVL., *Mag.* 18, 6 ; 8 (p. 22, 6-10 ; 13-15 ed. Ihm, p. 49, 18-21 ; 24-26 ed. Hunink) paene ad litt.

1100 qui *Z*   1100/1101 indiuidua *L*   1102 discursum *A*   quam] quamquam *Ek*   uite] ad *praem. El*   celerius addunt *tr. A*   1106 Mors] est omnino *add. A*, est *add. Z*   est] *om. A L*   1108 rixa *El*   discordia *A*   1109 regi *L*   potentissime *Z Ek El*   1110 milibus] a *praem. Ek El*   militibus *El*   ea] *om. A*   1115 pluuiarum] *Ek, sic sec. Bibl. legendum*, pluuias *A Z L*, pluuiorum *El*   enumerare *Ek*   1118 concilio *A*   diues] *om. El* et] *om. A*   bene suadens *L Ek*   1119 poterit *Ek El*   1120 Appolegius *L*   1122 reperatrix *El*   1123 apud] *sec. Apul. legendum, om. A*, apta *Z Ek El*   1124 perfuncta] *sec. Apul. Z L*, perfundens *A Ek El*   Paupertas] De Romanis pauperibus *ut subtitulum interposuit L*

1125 rium fundauit, pro cuius memoria fictili catino diis sacrificare consueuit."

Et secundum beatum Augustinum, .II. *De ciuitate Dei*, Deus uolens paupertatis amorem et uirtutum moralium exercitia premiari, eis temporale concessit imperium. Inter Romanos fuerunt 1130 multi consules illustres, multi censores et triumphatores uel pauperes uel paruis contenti, uel in argumentum modestie ymagine et colore paupertatis usi. Inter quos erant rectores summi et subiectores nationum, ad tale | culmen ab aratro uel semina iactantes assumpti, reuertentes ad id ipsum deuictis hostibus et adeptis 1135 uictoriis. Fuerunt duces inter eos maximi qui uel agros suos propriis non poterant colere sumptibus. Erant qui nec filias de suis locare ualebant matrimonio. Erant et de maximis uictoribus, quibus, quod | pauperius est, exequiarum expensa et rogus post mortem defuit. De hiis referunt cum nomine Augustinus et Plinius, 1140 similiter Apulogius et quarto suo libro Valerius Maximus.

1127/1139 cfr AVG., *Ciu. Dei* 5, 18 (p. 153, 97-119)   1133/1135 sc. Q. Cincinnatum, ab aratro ad officium dictatoris uocatum, ab AVG., *ibid.*, l. 102-107, in exempum prolatum; cfr praesertim LIV., *A.u.c.* 3, 26, 6 – 3, 29, 7 (p. 166-169)
1133/1135 sc. Atilium quendam sec. Val. in tempore Scipionis cuiusdam uiuentem, qui dum "semen spargeret" ad imperium arcessitus est, sicut VAL. MAX., *Mem.* 4, 4, 5 (p. 189, 15-25) narrat; quem Atilium Val. Max. cogitet, exquiri non iam potest; uocabula "semen spargentem" a Val. Max. tantum scribuntur, qui ideo sine dubio Gerardi fons hic est   1135/1136 sc. Atilium Regulum, cs. 256 a.C.n., cuius penuria a VAL. MAX., *Mem.* 4, 4, 6 (p. 190, 1-16) describitur; ab AVG., *ibid.*, l. 112-117, sine nomine exemplum datur   1136/1137 cfr APVL., *Mag.* 18, 9 (p. 22, 15-17 ed. Ihm, p. 49, 27-30 ed. Hunink)
1137/1139 sc. P. Valerium Publicolam et Agrippam Menenium, quorum modestia sicut et simplicitas describitur a VAL. MAX., *Mem.* 4, 4, 1-2 (p. 188, 5-28); quia uocabulum "rogus" a Val. Max. tantum scribitur, Ger. hoc fonte sine dubio usus est; ille Publicola, quater consul, a. 503 a.C.n. mortuus, ab AVG., *ibid.*, l. 100-102, in exempum profertur, sed ab eo falso L. Valerius appellatur; de eorum morte in extrema penuria cfr etiam praesertim LIV., *A.u.c.* 2, 16, 7 (p. 87); 2, 32, 8 – 33, 11 (p. 105-107)   1139 locum ex Augustino sumptum supra, 1127-1139, indicaui, eos e Plinio sumptos recuperare non potui
1140 locum ex Apuleio sumptum supra, 1117-1126; 1136-1137, indicaui, cfr VAL. MAX., *Mem.* 4, 3, 4-10 (p. 179 – 183, 14); 4, 4, 1-9 (p. 188, 5 – 191, 23)

1129 concessit temporale *tr. L*   1131 in argumentum] *om. Z*   argumentum] omni *L El*, animum *Ek*   1133 ad] *om. Ek*, in *Z El*   1135 uictoribus *L*   1136 filias] suas *add. Z*   1139 Plurius *A*   1140 Apulegius *L*

SERMO IN FESTO PALMARVM DE PAVPERTATE 471

Similiter apud Grecorum magnos magna et paupertas fuit, maxime apud philosophos fuit paupertas inopinanda. Strennua fuit in Focione, quo inter eos nullus benignior; fuit in Aristide, quo inter eos iustior nullus, fuit in Homero, quo nullus Grecorum
1145 disertior, fuit in Socrate, quo nullus secundum Tullium inter eos sapientior, qui deorum oraculis sapiens consecratus est, qui, ut fertur, aurum in mare proiecit, qui cum nobilis esset genere, grangias ornatas et uberem rem familiarem hereditarias rei publice Athenarum tribuens ipse baculo et pera contentus Cretam illus-
1150 trauit, quos flexis homericis uersibus laudibus extulit.

De philosophorum paupertate pene silendum puto, quia oppido philosophie paupertas fuit uernacula. Dicte sunt epycurorum sententie, de quibus quibusdam, suo errore deceptis, uidetur quod sint diuiciarum amicissimi, sed uere paupertati coniunctis-
1155 simi. De ceteris ergo philosophis quid fuerit, quilibet estimet. Accedat tamen et ille, a quo nomen philosophie impositum est, humilis Pytagoras, cuius pater prediues acquisitor non poterat

---

1141/1146 cfr APVL., *Mag.* 18, 7 (p. 22, 10-13 ed. Ihm, p. 49, 21-23 ed. Hunink), locum hic a Ger. in paraphrasi paene una ulla omissione allegatum; quia Ger. Phocionem tam benignum quam strenuum dicit, in codice ab eo uso nomen Epaminondae defuisse uidetur   1145/1146 cfr GER. MAG., *Conclusa* (Vol. 7, p. 91, 28-30 ed. Pohl)   cfr CIC., *Cato maior* 78 (p. 39, 13-17); haec sententia in pluribus fontibus inuenitur (e.g. VAL. MAX., *Mem.* 3, 4, 1 (p. 137, 15-17); PLIN., *Nat. hist.* 24, 36, 5 (Vol. 5, p. 172, 6-8), sed cum nomen Ciceronis nusquam in fontibus sententiae adiiciatur, Ger. ex ipso Ciceronis tractatu citat   1146/1150 cfr APVL., *Mag.* 22, 1-5 (p. 25, 17 – 26, 4 ed. Ihm, p. 51, 26-37 ed. Hunink), ubi editores contra testimonium codicum bis "Socrates" in "Crates" emendauerunt; quamuis emendatio iusta est, Ger. in fonte suo "Socrates" legit, et ideo textus suus – pace Moll – potius emendandus non est   1151/1155 cfr supra, 855-869   1156/1158 Ger. VAL. MAX., *Mem.* 8, 7, ext. 2 (p. 387, 9 – 388, 11) false interpretatus esse uidetur, alium locum inuenire nequiui; cfr de inuentione nominis philosophiae etiam AVG., *Ciu. Dei* 8, 2 (p. 217, 5-12), fortasse etiam LACT., *Diu. inst.* 3, 2, 6 (p. 180, 7-19)

1141 Similiter] De Grecis pauperibus *ut subtitulum interposuit L*   et] *om. El,* eciam *L*   1142 inopinando *L,* uel opinando *marg. emend. L²*   1143 fuit¹] affuit *L*   Focone *A,* Foncione *L,* Fricone *Z*   benignior] fuit *praem. Ek El*   1144 nullus iustior *tr. L*   Omero *Ek El*   1145 discretior *Z Ek El*   Tulium *El*   1146 sapientior] fuit *praem. El*   1148 et] *om. El*
1149 Troyam *A Z,* Creyam *L*   1151 De] De philosophorum paupertate *ut subtitulum interposuit L*   1152 Dicte] Decem *Z*   1153 deceptus *L*
1157 Pyctagoras *Ek,* Pictagoras *El*

tanta conquirere quanta filius contempnere. Ab eius dogmatibus inter Hebraicorum | philosophorum sectas et phariseis et saduceis meliores esseni instituti sunt, qui quanta rerum paupertate et communitate, quanta philosophia, quanto moderamine floruerunt, qui scire uoluerit in *Antiquitatibus* | legat Iosephum. Nam hii esseni apostolice uite in multis fuerunt similes.

A quibus omnibus tam ducibus quam philosophis gentilibus nobis christianis diuitibus incutitur uerecundia et stupor. Mirum est quod tam magnam rem, tam altam dignitate, tam profundam uirtute, tam latam exemplo hominum, tam longam uetustate temporum non uidemus. Mirum est quod tam efficacem rem et uiuacem non percipimus, quod tam dulcia paupertatis fluenta et ampla non sapimus, quod qui in lato et libero campo paupertatis flores et fructus nascuntur, non carpimus; super omnia, quod ad hoc singulare paupertatis promissum et terminum, celorum regnum, per eam ingredi non nitimur.

Cuius ingressus speculum et forma per hodiernam et maiestatis Christi depauperationem et paupertatis exaltationem non diuitibus sed pauperibus preponitur, ut qui eum hodie oculis intellectus *uident pauperes, et letantur* in terris, supernam Iherusalem

---

1172/1173 cfr Matth. 5, 3 et Luc. 6, 20, supra, 576/577, uerbatim allegatos 1177 Ps. 68 (69), 33

1158/1163 cfr praesertim FLAV. IOS., *Ant.* 18 [II], 18-22; sed etiam 15 [10.4], 371 (locum unum et solum ubi Ios. nomen Pyth. nuncupat (cfr tr. et comm., Vol. 7B, p. 275-277, praesertim adnot. 2602; 2607 (super Pyth.)); textus latinus in medio aeuo ubicumque diffusus et a Ger. consultus hodie in ed. a Frobenio praelo data praesto est (ed. 1524, l. 18, c. 2 (p. 514, 8 – 515, 4); ed. 1524, l. 15, c. 13 in fine (p. 451, 15-19)); summatim super Essenos, Phariseos et Saduceos etiam legitur in l. 13, c. 8 (p. 572, 18-27); cfr etiam textum graecum in ed. Loeb (l. 18 [II], 18-22 super Essenos (p. 14-20), super Phariseos et Saduceos ibid., 18, [10], 12-17 (p. 10-14); 15 [10.4], 371 (p. 434)) 1171/1173 in conclusione Ger. se ad initium secundae partis refert, cfr supra, 576-586 cfr GER. MAG., *Ep.* 41, 68-69 1174/1176 his uerbis Ger. supra, 20-22, in exordio etiam usus est

---

1159 phariseos *A L* et²] etiam *L* 1160/1161 coniunctate *Ek* 1164 A] Conclusio *ut subtitulum interposuit L* 1165 diuitibus] *om. El* 1166 alta *El* 1168 est] *om. El* 1169/1170 et ampla] *om. Ek El* 1170 paupertatis campo *tr. Ek El* 1172 terminum] eternum *Ek* 1172/1173 regnum celorum *tr. Z El* 1176 ut] et *El* ut qui] Vide *L*

cum eo ingredientes, uisione facie ad faciem uideant et fruitione eius sempiterna letentur in celis, qui cum Deo patre et Spiritu
1180 Sancto uiuit et regnat per omnia secula seculorum. Amen.

1178 uisionem *Z* faciei *A* uideatur *El* 1180 et] *om. El* regnat] Deus *add. Ek El* secula] *om. Ek* Explicit sermo magistri gerardi groet in die palmarum de paupertate predicatus. Deo gratias *expl. in L*, Explicit sermo pulcher seu compendium notabile super recommendacione uolunta-rie (*corr. ex* uoluntatis) paupertatis, per magistrum Gherardum (magistri Johannis *T*) dictum (*om. T*) Groet literatum [in omni facultate, *postea eras. K*] et multum deuotum editus seu compilatum (literatum − compilatum] et cetera *T*) *expl. in KT*, Explicit sermo de paupertate magistri Gerardi dicti Magni *expl. in Ek*, Explicit sermo uenerabilis uiri magistri Gherardi dicti Groet dyaconi de paupertate in festo palmarum ad religiosos quosdam *expl. in El*, *expl. om. A Z*

INDICES

Index Locorvm S. Scriptvrae

Index Fontivm

INDEX LOCORVM SACRAE SCRIPTVRAE*

		Op.	*lin.*	*pag.*
Genesis				
1, 26-30	cfr	*Tract. paup.*	377-387	440
2, 25	cfr	*Tract. paup.*	780-781	456
3, 7	cfr	*Tract. paup.*	780-781	456
3, 21	cfr	*Tract. paup.*	794	456
18, 10-15	cfr	*Ep.* 41	9	385
21, 8-13	cfr	*Ep.* 41	23-24	386
22, 17		*Ep.* 41	213-214	394
25, 27-34	cfr	*Ep.* 41	21-22	386
27, 1-40	cfr	*Ep.* 41	21-22	386
Exodus				
12, 3-4	cfr	*Tract. paup.*	181-187	432
12, 6; 8	cfr	*Tract. paup.*	184-187	432
12, 14; 17; 25	cfr	*Tract. paup.*	178-181	432
16, 2-3	cfr	*Ep.* 41	126-129	390
	cfr	*Ep.* 41	135-136	391
17, 3	cfr	*Ep.* 41	126-129	390
20, 11		*Tract. paup.*	699-700	453
29, 41	cfr	*Ep.* 19	43	300
Leuiticus				
2, 9	cfr	*Ep.* 19	43	300
4, 31	cfr	*Ep.* 19	43	300
17, 6	cfr	*Ep.* 19	43	300
Numeri				
15, 3	cfr	*Ep.* 19	43	300
15, 7	cfr	*Ep.* 19	43	300
I Regum				
1, 24-28	cfr	*Ep.* 41	162-164	392
2, 1-10	cfr	*Tract. paup.*	741-742	454
2, 5		*Tract. paup.*	734-735	454
2, 8		*Tract. paup.*	736-738	454
16, 7	cfr	*Cura past.*	130	287
26, 16	cfr	*Ep.* 46	11	418
IV Regum				
5, 20-27	cfr	*Simonia beg.*	855-859	356

---

* The asterisk indicates a source that is indirectly quoted.

			Op.	lin.	pag.
Iob					
1, 21		cfr	Tract. paup.	777-778	456
5, 14		cfr	Ep. 41	136-137	391
Psalmi					
9, 10			Tract. paup.	732-733	454
9, 19			Tract. paup.	722-724	454
10, 9			Tract. paup.	729	454
10, 14			Tract. paup.	730	454
10, 17			Tract. paup.	730-731	454
11 (12), 6			Tract. paup.	729-730	454
21 (22), 27			Tract. paup.	579-580	448
24 (25), 15-17			Tract. paup.	710-719	453
25 (26), 5			Ep. 44	11-12	399
30 (31), 11			Tract. paup.	651-653	451
30 (31), 12-14			Tract. paup.	660-666	451
30 (31), 20-22		cfr	Tract. paup.	668-675	451-452
33 (34), 11			Tract. paup.	733	454
36 (37), 25			Tract. paup.	727-728	454
39 (40), 18		cfr	Tract. paup.	706-707	453
40 (41), 1			Simonia beg.	753-755	353
40 (41), 2			Tract. paup.	134-136	430
44 (45), 14-15		cfr	Ep. 41	216-219	394
49 (50), 10		cfr	Tract. paup.	77-78	428
59 (60), 13			Tract. paup.	692-693	452
60 (61), 4			Tract. paup.	747	455
68 (69), 33			Tract. paup.	1	425
			Tract. paup.	10	425
			Tract. paup.	28	426
			Tract. paup.	48-49	427
			Tract. paup.	93	428
		cfr	Tract. paup.	125-126	430
		cfr	Tract. paup.	144-147	430
			Tract. paup.	175-176	432
			Tract. paup.	209	433
			Tract. paup.	238-240	434
			Tract. paup.	499	445
			Tract. paup.	567	448
		cfr	Tract. paup.	570	448
			Tract. paup.	1177	472
71 (72), 4			Tract. paup.	581-582	448
74 (75), 9		cfr	Ep. 42	6-7	402
76 (77), 11			Ep. 41	243-244	395
80 (81), 13			Ep. 41	138-140	391
82 (83), 6		cfr	Simonia beg.	681-683	351
90 (91), 6			Tract. paup.	375	440
			Ep. 41	55-56	387
93 (94), 15			Ep. 42	26	403
105 (106), 30			Ep. 46	60	420
*109 (110), 4			Cura past.	140-141	288
111 (112), 3			Tract. paup.	760-761	455
132 (133), 1			Simonia beg.	1016-1017	362

		Op.	*lin.*	*pag.*
136 (137), 2	cfr	*Ep.* 44	56	401
140 (141), 4		*Ep.* 41	54-55	387
140 (141), 5		*Ep.* 41	57	387
144 (145), 16		*Tract. paup.*	532-533	446

Prouerbia
| 8, 14-16 | | *Simonia beg.* | 607-612 | 348 |

Ecclesiastes
| 1, 15 | | *Cura past.* | 300-301 | 296 |
| 5, 3-4 | | *Ep.* 45 | 22-26 | 408 |

Canticum Canticorum
1, 1-2	cfr	*Ep.* 41	73	388
4, 1; 3	cfr	*Ep.* 41	116-117	390
		Ep. 41	215	394

Sapientia
| 7, 11 | cfr | *Ep.* 41 | 209 | 393 |
| 8, 1 | | *Tract. paup.* | 535 | 446 |

Ecclesiasticus
1, 2		*Tract. paup.*	1115	469
15, 3		*Tract. paup.*	707-709	453
30, 24		*Cura past.*	95-96	285
31, 11	cfr	*Tract. paup.*	645-646	451

Isaias
*6, 8		*Cura past.*	37-38	283
6, 9-10	cfr	*Ep.* 41	137-138	391
8, 14		*Tract. paup.*	375	440
10, 1-2		*Simonia beg.*	744-748	353
29, 13		*Simonia beg.*	739-740	352-353
40, 9		*Cura past.*	256-257	294
64, 4		*Ep.* 41	220-222	394

Ieremias
1, 10	cfr	*Ep.* 41	231	394
9, 23	cfr	*Tract. paup.*	695-696	452-453
15, 19		*Simonia beg.*	1000-1002	361
17, 5		*Tract. paup.*	693	452
17, 5-7	cfr	*Tract. paup.*	690-692	452

Ezechiel
34, 2-4		*Ep.* 41	232-239	394-395
34, 4	cfr	*Ep.* 17	76-78	278
34, 8	cfr	*Ep.* 17	27-29	276
		Ep. 17	73-74	278
34, 10-11	cfr	*Ep.* 41	239-241	395

Daniel
| 3, 26 | cfr | *Ep.* 44 | 71-72 | 401 |

		Op.	lin.	pag.
3, 52	cfr	Ep. 44	71-72	401

Zacharias
9, 9		Tract. paup.	139-141	430

Malachias
*2, 7		Cura past.	218-220	292

Matthaeus
5, 3		Tract. paup.	576-577	448
	cfr	Tract. paup.	1080-1086	468
	cfr	Tract. paup.	1172-1173	472
5, 3; 6	cfr	Simonia beg.	281-282	337
5, 11	cfr	Tract. paup.	629-638	450
6, 21		Tract. paup.	638-639	450
6, 23		Cura past.	157-159	288-289
6, 24		Tract. paup.	605-609	449
6, 25-29		Tract. paup.	915-921	461
6, 34	cfr	Tract. paup.	950-953	462
7, 15	cfr	Ep. 41	142-143	391
7, 16; 20		Ep. 41	144-145	391
7, 22	cfr	Simonia beg.	800-804	355
11, 29		Simonia beg.	814-815	355
		Simonia beg.	817-821	355
13, 22	cfr	Tract. paup.	167-168	431
		Tract. paup.	642-644	451
13, 29-30	cfr	Locat.	598-599	266
	cfr	Locat.	612	267
15, 1-20	cfr	Simonia beg.	311-314	338
*15, 1		Simonia beg.	735-736	352
15, 1-3	cfr	Simonia beg.	705-711	351-352
*15, 13		Simonia beg.	731-734	352
*15, 14		Cura past.	206-208	291
		Ep. 17	36	276
		Simonia beg.	734-735	352
18, 6		Locat.	585-589	266
18, 7		Ep. 41	58-60	387-388
18, 20		Simonia beg.	1031-1033	362
19, 21		Simonia beg.	305-306	338
	cfr	Tract. paup.	254-255	435
	cfr	Tract. paup.	446-450	443
	cfr	Tract. paup.	456	443
		Tract. paup.	611-612	449
19, 23		Tract. paup.	588-589	448-449
19, 23-30	cfr	Tract. paup.	254-255	435
19, 24		Tract. paup.	591-593	449
19, 29		Tract. paup.	596-598	449
20, 1-16	cfr	Simonia beg.	649-650	350
20, 18	cfr	Tract. paup.	156-157	431
21, 1-9	cfr	Tract. paup.	2-3	425
21, 2	cfr	Tract. paup.	69-77	427-428
	cfr	Tract. paup.	113-115	429

		Op.	lin.	pag.
	cfr	Tract. paup.	445-446	443
21, 6-10	cfr	Tract. paup.	18-20	426
21, 7	cfr	Tract. paup.	95-96	428-429
	cfr	Tract. paup.	116-121	429
21, 7-8		Tract. paup.	42-47	426
21, 9	cfr	Tract. paup.	38-39	426
	cfr	Tract. paup.	42	426
21, 12	cfr	Tract. paup.	220-224	433
21, 13		Tract. paup.	215-216	433
21, 16		Tract. paup.	60-61	427
*21, 28-31	cfr	Simonia beg.	1083-1087	364
*22, 39		Tract. paup.	506-507	445
		Tract. paup.	517-518	446
23, 23		Simonia beg.	756-760	353
23, 25-26	cfr	Locat.	513-515	263
	cfr	Locat.	526	263
	cfr	Locat.	736-737	272
23, 26	cfr	Cura past.	131-132	287
23, 39		Tract. paup.	152-154	431
25, 1-12	cfr	Cura past.	278-279	295
25, 31-46	cfr	Simonia beg.	318-320	339
27, 45-56	cfr	Tract. paup.	148-150	430-431
28, 18		Locat.	209	250

Marcus

4, 12	cfr	Ep. 41	137-138	391
7, 1-23	cfr	Simonia beg.	311-314	338
7, 5-9	cfr	Simonia beg.	705-711	351-352
		Simonia beg.	737-743	352-353
10, 21		Simonia beg.	305-306	338
	cfr	Tract. paup.	254-255	435
	cfr	Tract. paup.	446-450	443
	cfr	Tract. paup.	456	443
		Tract. paup.	611-612	449
10, 23-24		Tract. paup.	589-591	449
10, 23-31	cfr	Tract. paup.	254-255	435
10, 25		Tract. paup.	591-593	449
10, 29-30		Tract. paup.	655-660	451
10, 30	cfr	Tract. paup.	596-598	449
	cfr	Tract. paup.	667	451
	cfr	Tract. paup.	669-670	452
10, 33	cfr	Tract. paup.	156-157	431
11, 1-10	cfr	Tract. paup.	2-3	425
11, 2		Tract. paup.	88-89	428
11, 2-3	cfr	Tract. paup.	113-115	429
	cfr	Tract. paup.	445-446	443
11, 3	cfr	Tract. paup.	111	429
		Tract. paup.	115-116	429
11, 4		Tract. paup.	83-84	428
11, 4-7	cfr	Tract. paup.	116-118	429
11, 4-10	cfr	Tract. paup.	18-20	426
11, 7	cfr	Tract. paup.	95-96	428-429

		Op.	lin.	pag.
	cfr	Tract. paup.	120-121	429
11, 7-8		Tract. paup.	42-47	426-427
11, 10		Tract. paup.	42	426
11, 15		Tract. paup.	220-224	433
11, 17		Tract. paup.	215-216	433
*12, 31		Tract. paup.	506-507	445
		Tract. paup.	517-518	446
12, 41-44	cfr	Tract. paup.	448-450	443

Lucas

1, 53		Tract. paup.	734	454
6, 20-21	cfr	Simonia beg.	281-282	337
		Tract. paup.	577-578	448
	cfr	Tract. paup.	1080-1086	468
	cfr	Tract. paup.	1172-1173	472
6, 22	cfr	Tract. paup.	629-638	450
6, 24		Tract. paup.	593-594	449
9, 62		Sim. beg.	95-97	332
10, 25-37	cfr	Ep. 41	73-82	388
*10, 27		Tract. paup.	506-507	445
		Tract. paup.	517-518	446
10, 34	cfr	Ep. 41	73	388
12, 32		Tract. paup.	533-534	446
12, 42	cfr	Ep. 19	131-132	304
		Tract. paup.	357-359	439
		Ep. 41	71-72	388
12, 42-44		Simonia beg.	345-351	339-340
12, 45-47	cfr	Simonia beg.	352	340
12, 48		Simonia beg.	352-355	340
13, 35		Tract. paup.	152-154	431
*14, 28-30		Ep. 45	27-32	408
	cfr	Ep. 45	76-78	410
14, 33		Tract. paup.	615-616	450
		Ep. 45	32-35	408
	cfr	Ep. 45	40-41	409
		Ep. 45	78-79	410
	cfr	Ep. 45	124-125	412
16, 9	cfr	Tract. paup.	585-586	448
16, 10		Simonia beg.	158-159	334
16, 11-12		Simonia beg.	358-362	340
16, 13		Tract. paup.	605-609	449
18, 22		Simonia beg.	305-306	338
	cfr	Tract. paup.	254-255	435
18, 24		Tract. paup.	589-590	449
18, 24-30	cfr	Tract. paup.	254-255	435
18, 25		Tract. paup.	591-593	449
18, 30	cfr	Tract. paup.	596-598	449
18, 31	cfr	Tract. paup.	156-157	431
19, 29-44	cfr	Tract. paup.	2-3	425
19, 30	cfr	Tract. paup.	69-77	427-428
		Tract. paup.	87	428
	cfr	Tract. paup.	88-89	428

INDEX LOCORVM SACRAE SCRIPTVRAE 483

		Op.	lin.	pag.
	cfr	Tract. paup.	113-115	429
	cfr	Tract. paup.	445-446	443
19, 32-38	cfr	Tract. paup.	18-20	426
19, 33	cfr	Tract. paup.	80-81	428
19, 33-35	cfr	Tract. paup.	116-118	429
19, 34	cfr	Tract. paup.	111	429
		Tract. paup.	116	429
19, 35-36	cfr	Tract. paup.	42-47	426-427
19, 36	cfr	Tract. paup.	95-96	428-429
19, 38	cfr	Tract. paup.	37	426
	cfr	Tract. paup.	38-39	426
	cfr	Tract. paup.	42	426
19, 42		Tract. paup.	157-159	431
19, 45		Tract. paup.	220-224	433
19, 46		Tract. paup.	215-216	433
21, 1-4	cfr	Tract. paup.	448-450	443
23, 26-49	cfr	Tract. paup.	148-150	430-431
24, 49		Ep. 46	39	419

Iohannes
1, 29; 36	cfr	Tract. paup.	187-188	432
3, 6		Simonia beg.	849-851	356
3, 9-20	cfr	Simonia beg.	683-684	351
3, 31		Ep. 44	48-49	400
6, 7		Locat.	259-260	252
8, 34	cfr	Simonia beg.	683-684	351
8, 44	cfr	Cura past.	141-142	288
10, 1	cfr	Ep. 17	25	276
10, 10		Locat.	242-243	251
10, 11-14	cfr	Locat.	372-374	257
*10, 12-13	cfr	Locat.	242-243	251
*		Cura past.	302-304	296
12, 12-16	cfr	Tract. paup.	2-3	425
12, 13	cfr	Tract. paup.	37-38	426
	cfr	Tract. paup.	42	426
12, 14-15	cfr	Tract. paup.	69-77	427-428
12, 19		Tract. paup.	196-197	432
15, 12		Simonia beg.	838	356
15, 19		Simonia beg.	662-664	350
17, 12	cfr	Ep. 46	21	418
21, 15-17	cfr	Cura past.	259-261	294

Actus Apostolorum
1, 1		Cura past.	246-247	293
2, 44-45	cfr	Stat.	122-126	312
	cfr	Stat.	512-523	322
		Simonia beg.	291-292	338
	cfr	Tract. paup.	262-265	435
	cfr	Tract. paup.	362-363	439
	cfr	Tract. paup.	414	442
	cfr	Ep. 41	162-164	392
	cfr	Ep. 45	17-18	408

	Op.		lin.	pag.
	cfr	*Ep.* 45	124-125	412
4, 32	cfr	*Tract. paup.*	759	455
	cfr	*Ep.* 41	162-164	392
	cfr	*Ep.* 41	224-225	394
*		*Ep.* 45	48-51	409
	cfr	*Ep.* 45	124-125	412
4, 32; 35	cfr	*Stat.*	122-126	312
	cfr	*Stat.*	512-523	322
		Tract. paup.	262-265	435
	cfr	*Ep.* 45	17-18	408
*4, 34		*Ep.* 45	51-52	409
4, 35	cfr	*Tract. paup.*	362-363	439
	cfr	*Tract. paup.*	414	442
5, 1-11	cfr	*Tract. paup.*	278-283	436
	cfr	*Tract. paup.*	456-457	443
5, 29	cfr	*Ep.* 46	29-30	419
8, 19		*Locat.*	63-65	244
8, 20	cfr	*Locat.*	65-68	244
*		*Locat.*	69-70	244
		Tract. paup.	307	437
8, 21; 23		*Locat.*	96-99	245
8, 23		*Locat.*	103	245

Ad Romanos

2, 11		*Simonia beg.*	430-432	342
5, 3-5		*Tract. paup.*	677-681	452
8, 1	cfr	*Ep.* 41	21-22	386
8, 4	cfr	*Ep.* 41	21-22	386
9, 5	cfr	*Ep.* 44	71-72	401
9, 32 – 10, 3	cfr	*Tract. paup.*	170-172	431

I ad Corinthios

1, 26-29		*Simonia beg.*	271-280	337
2, 7-8	cfr	*Tract. paup.*	169-170	431
2, 9		*Ep.* 41	220-222	394
4, 1-2		*Simonia beg.*	341-345	339
9, 13-14	cfr	*Ep.* 41	162-164	392
9, 25		*Tract. paup.*	622-623	450
11, 21		*Ep.* 41	126	390
13, 8		*Ep.* 41	216	394
13, 13	cfr	*Simonia beg.*	796-797	354
		Simonia beg.	809-810	355
		Simonia beg.	831	356
15, 58	cfr	*Tract. paup.*	645-646	451

II ad Corinthios

6, 10	*Tract. paup.*	875-876	460
6, 17	*Ep.* 27	14-15	379
11, 14	*Ep.* 41	56-58	387
11, 27	*Tract. paup.*	472	444
12, 17	*Ep.* 41	56	387

INDEX LOCORVM SACRAE SCRIPTVRAE 485

		Op.	*lin.*	*pag.*
Ad Galatas				
3, 16	cfr	*Ep.* 41	17-18	385
4, 22-31	cfr	*Ep.* 41	23-24	386
*4, 23		*Simonia beg.*	641	349
*		*Simonia beg.*	643	349
	cfr	*Ep.* 41	21-22	386
4, 28		*Ep.* 41	16-17	385
4, 29	cfr	*Ep.* 41	21-22	386
*5, 14		*Tract. paup.*	506-507	445
		Tract. paup.	517-518	446
Ad Ephesios				
4, 22	cfr	*Ep.* 44	5	399
	cfr	*Ep.* 42	18	402
4, 23		*Ep.* 42	21	403
5, 2	cfr	*Ep.* 19	43	300
	cfr	*Ep.* 42	6-7	402
*6, 9		*Simonia beg.*	430-432	342
6, 12		*Ep.* 41	14-15	385
Ad Philippenses				
2, 4		*Tract. paup.*	359	439
		Ep. 41	72	388
2, 21	cfr	*Cura past.*	191	290
		Tract. paup.	359	439
		Ep. 41	72	388
*		*Ep.* 41	98	389
3, 10	cfr	*Ep.* 17	85-86	278
Ad Colossenses				
2, 8	cfr	*Locat.*	737-738	272
3, 5		*Ep.* 41	28	386
3, 9	cfr	*Ep.* 44	5	399
	cfr	*Ep.* 42	18	402
II ad Thessalonicenses				
2, 3		*Ep.* 46	21	418
3, 6-12	cfr	*Stat.*	348-352	318
I ad Timotheum				
6, 7		*Tract. paup.*	778-779	456
*6, 8	cfr	*Ep.* 19	58-59	301
	cfr	*Stat.*	64-80	310-311
		Tract. paup.	521-523	446
		Tract. paup.	786	456
6, 9	cfr	*Cura past.*	73-74	285
		Tract. paup.	618-619	450
*6, 18	cfr	*Tract. paup.*	439-440	443
Ad Hebraeos				
1, 3	cfr	*Cura past.*	162	289
5, 4		*Cura past.*	136-138	287-288

		Op.	lin.	pag.
*5, 5		Cura past.	139-140	288
*7, 17		Cura past.	140-141	288

Epistula Iacobi

		Op.	lin.	pag.
1, 5		Tract. paup.	532	446
1, 17		Ep. 19	88	302
	cfr	Simonia beg.	616-619	349
2, 1-6		Simonia beg.	434-447	342-343
2, 4		Simonia beg.	456-457	343
*2, 8		Tract. paup.	506-507	445
		Tract. paup.	517-518	446

I Petri

		Op.	lin.	pag.
2, 8		Tract. paup.	375	440

II Petri

		Op.	lin.	pag.
*1, 4		Tract. paup.	508	445

I Iohannis

		Op.	lin.	pag.
3, 17		Tract. paup.	535-538	446-447

Apocalysis

		Op.	lin.	pag.
1, 8	cfr	Ep. 19	1-2	299
21, 6	cfr	Ep. 19	1-2	299
22, 13	cfr	Ep. 19	1-2	299

INDEX FONTIVM*

	Op.	lin.	pag.
ALBERTVS MAGNVS			
Sent.			
*L. 4 d. 24 art. 11 (Vol. 30, p. 45, c. 2 in fine)	cfr *Ep. 46*	23-26	419
AMBROSIVS MEDIOLANENSIS			
De officiis			
*1, 30, 147 (p. 53, 31-32)	*Locat.*	193-196	249-250
*	*Locat.*	374-376	257
APVLEIVS			
Pro se de magia (Apologia)			
18, 2 (p. 21, 17 ed. Ihm, p. 49, 9 ed. Hunink)	*Tract. paup.*	1117-1118	469
18, 6; 8 (p. 22, 6-10; 13-15 ed. Ihm, p. 49, 18-21; 24-26 ed. Hunink)	*Tract. paup.*	1120-1126	469
18, 7 (p. 22, 10-13 ed. Ihm, p. 49, 21-23 ed. Hunink)	cfr *Tract. paup.*	1141-1146	471
18, 9 (p. 22, 15-17 ed. Ihm, p. 49, 27-30 ed. Hunink)	cfr *Tract. paup.*	1136-1137	470
22, 1-5 (p. 25, 17 - 26, 4 ed. Ihm, p. 51, 26-37 ed. Hunink)	cfr *Tract. paup.*	1008-1009	465
	cfr *Tract. paup.*	1146-1150	471
22, 9-10 (p. 26, 19-25 ed. Ihm, p. 52, 13-18 ed. Hunink)	cfr *Tract. paup.*	1001-1003	465
ARCHIDIACONVS (GVIDO DE BAYSIO)			
Rosarium, seu in Decretorum uolumen Commentaria			
super C.16 q.7 c. 11 comm. sup. 'prebendas ecclesiae' (c. I, 804, 6-7) (f. 271r¹, c. 2, 10-31)	cfr *Locat.*	137-142	247
In Sextum Decretalium Commentaria			
super *Decret.*, VI 1.6.14 comm. sup. 'alii' (c. II, 954, 6) (f. 25v, c. 1, 9-11)	cfr *Ep. 17*	57-62	277

---

* The asterisk indicates a source that is indirectly quoted.

	Op.	lin.	pag.

ARISTOTELES LATINVS

Ethica Nicomachea. Translatio Roberti Grosseteste Lincolniensis siue 'Liber ethicorum', Recensio recognita, a Guill. Morbeka reuisa

*(fasc. 4, p. 141, 18-19 (ARIST., Ethic., A, 1, 4, 1094a13-15 Bekker))		Cura past.	117-119	287

Politicorum libri octo, in uersione latina a Guil. de Moerbeka facta

*1, 3, 4 (p. 31, 9-10 lat. (= p. 31, 7-8 gr.)) (ARIST., Pol., A, 8 (1256b7-8 Bekker))	cfr	Ep. 41	95-102	389
*	cfr	Tract. paup.	389	441
*3, 5, 6 (p. 171, 4-6) (ARIST., Pol., Γ, 5, 3 (1278a18-21 Bekker))	cfr	Cura past.	244-246	293

Analytica posteriora, Recensio Guillelmi de Moerbeka

*1, 2 (p. 287, 29-30, cfr p. 9, 13-14 (ARIST., Post. 1, 2, 72a29-30 Bekker))		Locat.	353-357	256
*		Cura past.	116-117	286-287
*	cfr	Ep. 19	15-18	299-300

ARISTOTELES (Ps.)

Problemata

part. 28, probl. 8 (p. electr. 555, c. 2 inferior, s.u. 'ultimum problema')	cfr	Tract. paup.	1056-1058	467

AVGVSTINVS HIPPONENSIS

De ciuitate Dei

5, 18 (p. 153, 97-119)	cfr	Tract. paup.	1127-1139	470
8, 2 (p. 217, 5-12)	cfr	Tract. paup.	1156-1158	471
*10, 1 (p. 273, 67-75)	cfr	Sim. beg.	929-935	359
*10, 3 (p. 275, 27-28)	cfr	Sim. beg.	1144-1145	366
*19, 13 (p. 679, 10-11)	cfr	Ep. 41	89-91	389
*	cfr	Tract. paup.	163-164	431
*	cfr	Tract. paup.	211-212	433
*	cfr	Tract. paup.	976-978	464
*19, 19 (p. 687, 31-33)		Locat.	290-292	253-254
*		Cura past.	54-56	284

Contra Faustum

*22, c. 27 (p. 621, 12-13)	cfr	Sim. beg.	672-675	350

Epistulae

*31, 5 (p. 5, 18 - 6, 3)	cfr	Tract. paup.	831-836	458
*167 (p. 605, 13-17)	cfr	Sim. beg.	448-451	343

Expositio epistulae ad Galatas

15 (= in Gal. 2, 11-16) (p. 70, 24 - 71, 8)		Sim. beg.	813-828	355
40 (= in Gal. 4, 21-24) (p. 109, 2-9)	cfr	Sim. beg.	641-644	349

In Iohannis euangelium tractatus

51, 2 (p. 440, 7-8)	cfr	Tract. paup.	46-47	427

INDEX FONTIVM 489

	Op.	lin.	pag.
De libero arbitrio *1, 5, 13 (p. 219, 73-77)	cfr *Locat.*	251-254	252
Regula tertia uel Preceptum 1 (p. 418, 5-14)	cfr *Ep. 45*	120-122	412
	cfr *Tract. paup.*	265-272	435
5, 2 (p. 428-430, 153-157)	cfr *Stat.*	122-126	312
	cfr *Stat.*	512-523	322
	Ep. 41	97-99	389
Sermones de uetere testamento 47, 8 (p. 579, 221-222)	cfr *Ep. 42*	27-28	403
De trinitate libri XV *2, 17 (28) (p. 119, 37-41)	cfr *Sim. beg.*	1002-1007	361
De uera religione *55, 113 (p. 259, 122)	cfr *Sim. beg.*	929-935	359
	cfr *Sim. beg.*	1145	366

AVGVSTINVS HIPPONENSIS (PS.)

Sermo 393
PL, 39, c. 1715, 18 — *Ep. 19* — 77-78 — 302

BARTHOLOMAEVS BRIXIENSIS

Glossa ordinaria in Decretum Gratiani
super C.1 q.3 c.8   cfr *Locat.*   13   241
expositio casus (c. 758 (p. 447),
    ante gl. o)
comm. sup. 'Quisquis' (c. I, 414,
    12) (c. 759 (p. 448), gl. d)
super C.25 q.1 c.6   cfr *Tract. paup.*   325-329   438
comm. sup. 'apostoli' (c. I, 1008,
    34) (c. 1899 (p. 1013), gl. a)

BASILIVS

Regula a Rufino latine uersa
5 (p. 35, 2 - 36, 12)   cfr *Tract. paup.*   265-272   435

BEDA VENERABILIS

In Lucae Euangelium expositio
comm. in Luc. 19, 33 (p. 343, 1904-   cfr *Tract. paup.*   80-82   428
    1907)

In Marci Euangelium expositio
comm. in Marc. 2, 7 (p. 520, 1246-   cfr *Sim. beg.*   711-717   352
    1250)
comm. in Marc. 11, 5 (p. 572, 1185-   cfr *Tract. paup.*   80-82   428
    1191)

BENEDICTVS DE NVRSIA

Regula
c. 33, 1-6 (p. 562, 1-14)   cfr *Ep. 45*   120-122   412

		Op.	lin.	pag.
	cfr	Ep. 46	4-6	418
	cfr	Ep. 46	78-79	421
	cfr	Tract. paup.	126-130	430
	cfr	Tract. paup.	265-272	435
c. 33, 3-4 (p. 562, 4-7)	cfr	Tract. paup.	315	437

BERNARDVS CLARAEVALLENSIS

Liber de diligendo Deo
8, 23 (p. 138, 19 - 139, 2)		Tract. paup.	505-514	445-446
8, 23 (p. 139, 2-12)	cfr	Tract. paup.	515-528	446
8, 24 (p. 139, 13-16)	cfr	Tract. paup.	531-533	446
8, 24 (p. 139, 16-17)		Tract. paup.	724-725	454
8, 24 (p. 139, 23-25)		Tract. paup.	528-530	446

Epistola 7 ad Adam monachum
7, 4 (p. 34, 6-9)	cfr	Ep. 45	109-113	412
7, 4 (p. 34, 16-17)		Ep. 45	113-116	412

Epistola 11 ad Cartusienses et Guigoni priori
11, 3 (p. 55, 10-11)		Ep. 45	116-119	412

De praecepto et dispensatione
3, 6 (p. 257, 25 - 258, 2)	cfr	Ep. 45	109-113	412

Sermones super Cantica Canticorum
18, 1, 2-3 (Vol. 1, p. 104, 8-28)	cfr	Cura past.	266-270	294

BERNARDVS PARMENSIS

Glossa ordinaria in Decretales Gregorii IX
super X 1.14.2	cfr	Ep. 17	4-7	275
comm. sup. 'aetatem' (c. II, 126, 23) (c. 265 (p. 133), gl. b)				
super X 1.14.3	cfr	Ep. 17	4-7	275
comm. sup. 'aetatem' (c. II, 126, 42) (c. 266 (p. 133), gl. d)				
super X 1.14.5	cfr	Locat.	128-132	246
comm. sup. 'breue tempus' (c. II, 457, 7) (c. 267 (p. 134), gl. b, l. 12-20 in gl.)				
super X 1.23.4	cfr	Locat.	137-142	247
comm. sup. 'consuetudinis' (c. II, 150, 57) (c. 313 (p. 157), gl. c)				
super X 3.35.2	cfr	Ep. 41	35-39	386-387
comm. sup. 'sepulturam' (c. II, 597, 2) (c. 1292 (p. 151), gl. g, l. 4-5)				
super X 3.35.6	cfr	Tract. paup.	325-329	438
comm. sup. 'abdicatio' (c. II, 600, 16) (c. 1297 (p. 154), gl. d)				
super X 5.3.34	cfr	Sim. beg.	503-511	345
comm. sup. 'pure consentiant' (c. II, 763, 35) (c. 1637 (p. 33), gl. d)				

INDEX FONTIVM

		Op.	lin.	pag.
*super X 5.3.40 comm. sup. 'paupertatis' (c. II, 765, 48-49) (c. 1641-1642 (p. 35), gl. c)	cfr	Sim. beg.	534-535	346
*	cfr	Leeringhe	183-185	375
super X 5.4.3 comm. sup. 'regimen statuantur'; 'sacerdotium' (c. II, 768, 24; 25) (c. 1648 (p. 38), gl. g; i)	cfr	Locat.	12-13	241
super X 5.4.4 comm. sup. 'praefatam ecclesiam' (c. II, 767, 40) (c. 1649 (p. 39), gl. c)	cfr	Locat.	605-607	267
super X 5.39.44 expositio casus (c. 1916 (p. 172) 65-68) comm. sup. 'humiliter sustinere' (c. II, 908, 13) (c. 1916 (p. 172), gl. h, 69-71)	cfr	Locat.	276-279	253

BONIFACIVS PAPA VIII

Liber sextus decretalium

VI 1.6.14 (c. II, 953, 42 - 954, 22)	cfr	Ep. 17	4-7	275
	cfr	Ep. 17	23-24	276
	cfr	Cura past.	8-10	281
VI 1.6.14 (c. II, 954, 1-2)	cfr	Ep. 17	67-68	277
VI 1.6.14 (c. II, 954, 13-20)	cfr	Locat.	128-132	246
VI 1.6.22 (c. II, 961, 8-15)	cfr	Locat.	128-132	246
VI 1.6.35 § 4 (c. II, 965, 45-53)	cfr	Locat.	689-693	270
	cfr	Ep. 17	49-65	277
	cfr	Ep. 19	47-52	301
VI 2.14.1 (c. II, 1007, 39-43)	cfr	Cura past.	294-295	295-296
VI 3.17.1 § 0 (C. II, 1054, 74 - 1055, 13)	cfr	Stat.	10-12	309
VI 5.11.1 (c. II, 1094, 12-15)	cfr	Cura past.	294-295	295-296

IOHANNES CASSIANVS

Collationes XXIIII

18, 5 (p. 509, 19 - 510, 5; 510, 23 - 511, 8)	cfr	Ep. 45	16-20	408
		Ep. 45	43-68	409-410
	cfr	Tract. paup.	259-265	435

MARCVS TVLLIVS CICERO

Cato maior de senectute

78 (p. 39, 13-17)	cfr	Tract. paup.	1145-1146	471

CLEMENS PAPA V

Constitutiones

1.6.3 (c. II, 1140, 21-26)	cfr	Ep. 17	4-7	275

	Op.	lin.	pag.
	cfr Ep. 17	23-24	276
	cfr Cura past.	8-10	281
3.11.1 (c. II, 1169, 30-52)	cfr Stat.	12-17	309
	cfr Stat.	228-261	315-316
	cfr Sim. beg.	64-68	331

Codex Iustiniani

*?Dig. 1.3.29-30 (p. 34, c. 2 [13, 22-28])	Ep. 17	57-62	277

Decretales, uide CLEMENS PAPA V, GREGORIVS PAPA IX uel BONIFACIVS PAPA VIII

Decretum magistri Gratiani, uide GRATIANVS, *Decretum*

DIONYSIVS AREOPAGITA

    De caelesti hierarchia sec. transl. Iohannis Scoti Eriugenae

*3, 1 (p. 785, c. 4 (l. 3))	Locat.	41-42	243
*3, 1 (p. 785, c. 5-6 (l. 3))	Cura past.	204-206	291

    De diuinis nominibus sec. transl. Iohannis Saraceni

*8 (p. 437, c. 2 - p. 438, c. 1 (l. 4))	cfr Sim. beg.	219-232	336

    De ecclesiastica hierarchia sec. transl. Iohannis Saraceni

1 (p. 1074, c. 7 (l. 4) - p. 1077, c. 7 (l. 4))	cfr Cura past.	247-250	293
1 (p. 1080, c. 3 (l. 4) - p. 1081, c. 4 (l. 4))	cfr Cura past.	242-244	293
1 (p. 1087, c.13 (l. 4) - p. 1088, c. 10 (l. 4))	cfr Cura past.	250-251	293
5 (p. 1361, c. 7 (l. 3 uel 4) - p. 1362, c. 1 (l. 3 uel 4))	Cura past.	138-141	288

    Ibid., sec. transl. Iohannis Scoti Eriugenae

*5 (p. 1345, c. 4 - p. 1346, c. 2 (l. 3))	cfr Locat.	152-154	248
*5 (p. 1369, c. 1 (l.3))	cfr Locat.	152-154	248

    Epistula 8, ad Demophilum monachum

(p. 1533, c. 3 (l. 4) - p. 1535, c. 3 (l. 4))	Cura past.	223-234	292

AELIVS DONATVS

    Ars maior

3, 5 (p. 664, 14 - 665, 2)	cfr Tract. paup.	455-468	443

Extrauagantes decretales, quae a diuersis Romanis pontificibus post .VI. emanauerunt

3.9.1 (c. II, 1279, 33 - 1280, 17)	cfr Stat.	12-17	309
	cfr Sim. beg.	68-69	331
3.9.1 (c. II, 1279, 46-61)	cfr Sim. beg.	71-73	331
5.1.1 (c. II, 1287, 40-52)	cfr Sim. beg.	518-521	345
	cfr Leeringhe	159-165	374
5.1.1 (c. II, 1287, 58 - 1288, 47)	cfr Sim. beg.	522-526	345
	cfr Leeringhe	166-172	374
5.1.1 (c. II, 1288, 2-20)	cfr Ep. 41	189-193	393
	cfr Ep. 44	33-42	400
	cfr Ep. 44	55-60	401

INDEX FONTIVM

	Op.	lin.	pag.

FLAVIVS IOSEPHVS

Antiquitates

I, 2, 1, 53-54 (p. 130, 9-13 ed. Blatt; p. 19-20 tr. Feldman)	cfr *Tract. paup.*	781-782	456
8 [11], 18-22 (ed. 1524, l. 18, c. 2 (p. 514, 8 - 515, 4))	cfr *Tract. paup.*	1158-1163	472
13, c. 8 (ed. 1524, l. 13, c. 8 (p. 572, 18-27))	cfr *Tract. paup.*	1158-1163	472
15 [10.4], 371 (ed. 1524, l. 15, c. 13 in fine (p. 451, 15-19))	cfr *Tract. paup.*	1158-1163	472

GAVFRIDVS (PS. BERNARDVS CLARAEVALLENSIS)

Declamationes de colloquio Simonis cum Iesu

2, 2 (*PL*, 184, c. 438C)	cfr *Cura past.*	192-201	290-291
11, 12 (*PL*, 184, c. 444C-D)	cfr *Cura past.*	259-264	294
15, 18 (*PL*, 184, c. 447C-448B)	cfr *Cura past.*	297-306	296
16, 19 (*PL*, 184, c. 448B-D)	cfr *Cura past.*	309-311	296
21, 24 (*PL*, 184, c. 451C)	cfr *Cura past.*	220-223	292

GERARDVS MAGNVS

Articuli uiginti quattuor de focaristis (Artic.)

2 (p. 520-521, 25-29)	cfr *Ep. 46*	23-26	419
10 (p. 524, 77-84)	cfr *Ep. 46*	23-26	419
18 (p. 531, 156-162)	cfr *Cura past.*	294-295	295-296

Conclusa et proposita, non uota

p. 91, 28-30	cfr *Tract. paup.*	1145-1146	471
p. 98, 5-8	cfr *Cura past.*	273-277	294-295

Consilium de cura pastorali (Cura past.)

8-10	cfr *Ep. 17*	4-7	275
42-46	cfr *Locat.*	305-312	254
52-59	cfr *Locat.*	289-304	253-254
	cfr *Locat.*	570-571	265
84-88	cfr *Locat.*	413-416	259
85-98	cfr *Locat.*	408-410	258-259
92-98	cfr *Locat.*	50-53	243
97-102	cfr *Locat.*	334-338	255
	cfr *Locat.*	507-515	262-263
	cfr *Ep. 17*	68-73	278
113-122	cfr *Ep. 19*	15-18	299
114-117	cfr *Locat.*	353-357	256
123-130	cfr *Locat.*	383-388	258
	cfr *Locat.*	481-494	261-262
131-132	cfr *Locat.*	513-515	263
161-168	cfr *Locat.*	54-61	243
164-168	cfr *Locat.*	186-193	249
	cfr *Locat.*	368-370	257
178-188	cfr *Locat.*	406-419	258-259
203-251	cfr *Locat.*	410-413	259
204-206	cfr *Locat.*	41-42	243

	Op.	lin.	pag.
206-209	cfr *Ep. 17*	34-36	276
265	cfr *Locat.*	370-374	257
	cfr *Ep. 17*	26-29	276
284-290	cfr *Sim. beg.*	407-416	341-342

Epistola 15

| 15, 13-14 | cfr *Ep. 27* | 15 | 379 |

Epistola 17

4-7	cfr *Cura past.*	8-10	281
26-29	cfr *Locat.*	370-374	257
	cfr *Cura past.*	265	294
34-36	cfr *Cura past.*	206-209	291
49-65	cfr *Locat.*	689-696	270
	cfr *Ep. 19*	47-52	301
68-73	cfr *Locat.*	334-338	255
	cfr *Locat.*	507-515	262-263
	cfr *Cura past.*	97-102	286

Epistola 19

15-18	cfr *Locat.*	353-357	256
	cfr *Cura past.*	113-122	286-287
24-34	cfr *Locat.*	364-365	257
24-25	cfr *Locat.*	173-177	249
32-34	cfr *Locat.*	173-177	249
47-52	cfr *Locat.*	689-696	270
	cfr *Ep. 17*	49-65	277
56-59	cfr *Stat.*	64-80	310
81-103	cfr *Locat.*	337-342	255
104-106	cfr *Stat.*	64-80	310

Epistola 23

| p. 101, 15 ed. Mulder | cfr *Ep. 27* | 30-31 | 380 |

Epistola 27

| 17-18 | cfr *Ep. 41* | 230-231 | 394 |

Epistola 41

31-33	cfr *Ep. 45*	89-94	411
	cfr *Tract. paup.*	318-325	437-438
33-35	cfr *Ep. 42*	12-13	402
	cfr *Ep. 45*	97-104	411
	cfr *Tract. paup.*	231-234	434
	cfr *Tract. paup.*	334-343	438-439
35-39	cfr *Tract. paup.*	284-309	436-437
44-47	cfr *Sim. beg.*	307-309	338
	cfr *Sim. beg.*	987-993	361
	cfr *Ep. 45*	12-15	407
	cfr *Ep. 45*	122-127	412
	cfr *Tract. paup.*	228-234	434
48-49	cfr *Tract. paup.*	315-317	437
68-69	cfr *Tract. paup.*	576-586	448
	cfr *Tract. paup.*	1079-1086	468
	cfr *Tract. paup.*	1171-1173	472
71-72	cfr *Tract. paup.*	357-359	439
83-88	cfr *Stat.*	122-126	312

INDEX FONTIVM

		Op.	lin.	pag.
	cfr	Stat.	512-523	322
	cfr	Ep. 46	16-21	418
	cfr	Tract. paup.	986-990	464
89-91	cfr	Tract. paup.	976-978	464
95-102	cfr	Tract. paup.	377-407	440
106-119	cfr	Stat.	122-126	312
	cfr	Stat.	512-523	322
	cfr	Ep. 46	16-21	418
	cfr	Tract. paup.	986-990	464
160	cfr	Tract. paup.	859-865	459
194-206	cfr	Sim. beg.	191-490	335-344
230-231	cfr	Ep. 27	17-18	379
Epistola 42				
12-13	cfr	Ep. 41	33-35	386
	cfr	Ep. 44	55	401
	cfr	Ep. 45	97-104	411
	cfr	Tract. paup.	231-234	434
	cfr	Tract. paup.	334-343	438
Epistola 45				
12-15	cfr	Sim. beg.	307-309	338
	cfr	Sim. beg.	987-993	361
	cfr	Ep. 41	44-47	387
12-26	cfr	Tract. paup.	228-234	434
16-20	cfr	Tract. paup.	259-265	435
43-52	cfr	Tract. paup.	259-265	435
89-94	cfr	Ep. 41	31-33	386
	cfr	Tract. paup.	318-325	437-438
97-103	cfr	Ep. 41	33-35	386
	cfr	Ep. 42	12-13	402
	cfr	Tract. paup.	231-234	434
	cfr	Tract. paup.	334-343	438-439
120-125	cfr	Tract. paup.	265-272	435
122-127	cfr	Sim. beg.	307-309	338
	cfr	Sim. beg.	987-993	361
	cfr	Ep. 41	44-47	387
	cfr	Tract. paup.	228-234	434
Epistola 46				
16-21	cfr	Stat.	122-126	312
	cfr	Stat.	512-523	322
	cfr	Ep. 41	83-88	388-389
	cfr	Ep. 41	106-119	390
	cfr	Tract. paup.	986-990	464
Sermo ad clerum Traiectensem de focaristis (Focar.)				
o (p. 299, 11-12)	cfr	Ep. 27	15	379
o (p. 303, 85-92)	cfr	Sim. beg.	604-612	348
	cfr	Sim. beg.	761-770	353-354
o (p. 304, 130-131)	cfr	Locat.	231-232	251
o (p. 304, 135-136)	cfr	Locat.	220-221	250
o (p. 305, 148-150)	cfr	Cura past.	218-220	292
o (p. 305, 152)	cfr	Cura past.	241	293

		Op.	lin.	pag.
0 (p. 307, 195-196)	cfr	Locat.	230-231	251
1 (p. 315, 366)	cfr	Ep. 19	74-75	302
	cfr	Tract. paup.	354	439
4 (p. 330, 646-902)	cfr	Cura past.	294-295	295-296
4 (p. 334, 708-720)	cfr	Cura past.	291-295	295-296
18 (p. 418-419, 2519-2527)	cfr	Cura past.	182-184	290
18 (p. 419, 2519-2531)	cfr	Ep. 46	23-26	419
18 (p. 420, 2539-2549)	cfr	Ep. 46	26	419
18 (p. 421, 2563-2567)	cfr	Cura past.	218-223	292
19 (p. 425, 2663-2665; p. 424, 2632)	cfr	Ep. 46	32	419
21 (p. 433, 2858)	cfr	Locat.	242-243	251
21 (p. 434, 2874-2875)	cfr	Ep. 46	32	419
23 (p. 449-451, 3190-3251)	cfr	Ep. 46	23-26	419

Tractatus de simoniaca receptione sororum in conuentibus Tertii Ordinis (Leeringhe)

51-96	cfr	Stat.	81-82	311
51-73		Sim. beg.	1-16	329
74-89		Sim. beg.	17-32	329-330
89-112		Sim. beg.	33-48	330
113-127		Sim. beg.	49-57	331
128-132	cfr	Sim. beg.	99-113	332-333
131-132	cfr	Locat.	608-613	267
	cfr	Locat.	654-660	269
	cfr	Locat.	699-705	270
132-156		Sim. beg.	110-129	332-333
157-183		Sim. beg.	517-533	345-346
183-190		Sim. beg.	534-540	346
192-215		Sim. beg.	548-568	346-347

Consilium de locatione cure pastoralis (Locat.)

13	cfr	Sim. beg.	6-11	329
	cfr	Leeringhe	58-64	371
41-42	cfr	Cura past.	204-206	291
50-53	cfr	Cura past.	92-98	285-286
54-61	cfr	Cura past.	161-168	289
62-63	cfr	Sim. beg.	860	357
66-70	cfr	Sim. beg.	860-863	357
69-73	cfr	Sim. beg.	863-865	357
173-177	cfr	Ep. 19	24-25	300
	cfr	Ep. 19	32-34	300
186-193	cfr	Cura past.	164-168	289
290-304	cfr	Cura past.	52-59	284
305-312	cfr	Cura past.	42-46	283
334-338	cfr	Ep. 17	68-73	278
	cfr	Cura past.	97-102	286
337-342	cfr	Ep. 19	81-103	302-303
353-357	cfr	Cura past.	113-122	286-287
	cfr	Ep. 19	15-18	299
357	cfr	Cura past.	116-117	286-287
364-365	cfr	Ep. 19	24-25	300
	cfr	Ep. 19	32-34	300
370-374	cfr	Ep. 17	26-29	276

INDEX FONTIVM

		Op.	lin.	pag.
370-372	cfr	Cura past.	265	294
382-405	cfr	Sim. beg.	888-898	358
383-388	cfr	Cura past.	123-130	287
406-419	cfr	Cura past.	85-91	285-286
	cfr	Cura past.	178-188	289-290
406-410	cfr	Cura past.	92-98	285
410-413	cfr	Cura past.	203-251	291-293
481-494	cfr	Cura past.	123-130	287
507-510	cfr	Cura past.	97-102	286
	cfr	*Ep. 17*	68-73	278
513-515		Cura past.	131-132	287
531-543	cfr	Sim. beg.	377-393	340-341
570-571	cfr	Cura past.	52-59	284
608-613	cfr	Sim. beg.	108-109	332
	cfr	Sim. beg.	160-166	334
	cfr	*Leeringhe*	131-132	373
654-660	cfr	Sim. beg.	108-109	332
	cfr	Sim. beg.	160-166	334
	cfr	*Leeringhe*	131-132	373
689-696	cfr	*Ep. 17*	49-65	277
	cfr	*Ep. 19*	47-52	301
699-705	cfr	Sim. beg.	108-109	332
	cfr	Sim. beg.	160-166	334
	cfr	*Leeringhe*	131-132	373

Een merckelijc onderwijs

7-177 (p. 131-135)	cfr	*Leeringhe*	1-7	369
	cfr	*Leeringhe*	11-12	369

Obseruationes quattuor de presbyteris fornicariis notoriis

p. 571-572, 10-22	cfr	*Ep. 46*	23-26	419

Sermo in festo palmarum de paupertate (Tract. paup.)

163-164	cfr	*Ep. 41*	89-91	389
211-212	cfr	*Ep. 41*	89-91	389
228-234	cfr	Sim. beg.	307-309	338
	cfr	Sim. beg.	987-993	361
	cfr	*Ep. 41*	44-47	387
	cfr	*Ep. 45*	12-15	407
	cfr	*Ep. 45*	122-127	412
231-234	cfr	*Ep. 41*	33-35	386
	cfr	*Ep. 42*	12-13	402
	cfr	*Ep. 45*	97-104	411
259-265	cfr	*Ep. 45*	16-20	408
	cfr	*Ep. 45*	43-52	409
265-272	cfr	*Ep. 45*	120-122	412
284-309	cfr	*Ep. 41*	35-39	386-387
315-317	cfr	*Ep. 41*	48-49	387
318-325	cfr	*Ep. 41*	31-33	386
	cfr	*Ep. 45*	89-94	411
334-343	cfr	*Ep. 41*	33-35	386
	cfr	*Ep. 42*	12-13	402
	cfr	*Ep. 45*	97-104	411
357-359	cfr	*Ep. 41*	71-72	388

		Op.	lin.	pag.
377-407	cfr	*Ep. 41*	95-102	389
576-586	cfr	*Ep. 41*	68-69	388
786-797	cfr	*Ep. 27*	18-20	380
859-865	cfr	*Ep. 41*	160	392
976-978	cfr	*Ep. 41*	89-91	389
986-990	cfr	*Stat.*	122-126	312
	cfr	*Stat.*	512-523	322
	cfr	*Ep. 41*	83-88	388-389
	cfr	*Ep. 41*	106-119	390
	cfr	*Ep. 46*	16-21	418
1079-1086	cfr	*Ep. 41*	68-69	388
1171-1173	cfr	*Ep. 41*	68-69	388

De simonia ad beguttas (Simonia beg.)

1-39	cfr	*Stat.*	81-82	311
1-16		*Leeringhe*	51-73	370-371
6-11	cfr	*Locat.*	13	241
17-32		*Leeringhe*	74-89	371-372
33-48		*Leeringhe*	89-112	372
49-57		*Leeringhe*	113-127	373
64-73	cfr	*Stat.*	228-261	315-316
64-68	cfr	*Stat.*	12-17	309
99-113		*Leeringhe*	128-132	373
108-109	cfr	*Locat.*	608-613	267
	cfr	*Locat.*	654-660	269
	cfr	*Locat.*	699-705	270
110-129		*Leeringhe*	132-156	373-374
160-166	cfr	*Locat.*	608-613	267
	cfr	*Locat.*	654-660	269
	cfr	*Locat.*	699-705	270
	cfr	*Leeringhe*	131-132	373
191-490	cfr	*Ep. 41*	194-206	393
307-309	cfr	*Ep. 41*	44-47	387
	cfr	*Ep. 45*	12-15	407
	cfr	*Ep. 45*	122-127	412
	cfr	*Tract. paup.*	228-234	434
377-393	cfr	*Locat.*	531-543	263-264
407-418	cfr	*Cura past.*	284-290	295
419-490	cfr	*Stat.*	82-88	311
517-526		*Leeringhe*	158-172	374
527-533		*Leeringhe*	173-183	375
534-540	cfr	*Leeringhe*	183-190	375
548-568		*Leeringhe*	192-215	375-376
860-865		*Locat.*	66-72	244
860		*Locat.*	62-63	244
888-898	cfr	*Locat.*	382-405	258
987-993	cfr	*Ep. 41*	44-47	387
	cfr	*Ep. 45*	12-15	407
	cfr	*Ep. 45*	122-127	412
	cfr	*Tract. paup.*	228-234	434

Statuta domus a magistro Gerardo feminis deuotis destinatatae (Stat.)

12-17	cfr	*Sim. beg.*	64-68	331

INDEX FONTIVM

		Op.	lin.	pag.
64-80	cfr	*Ep. 19*	56-59	301
	cfr	*Ep. 19*	104-106	303
81-83	cfr	*Sim. beg.*	1-39	329
	cfr	*Leeringhe*	51-96	370-371
122-126	cfr	*Ep. 41*	83-88	388-389
	cfr	*Ep. 41*	97-99	389
	cfr	*Ep. 41*	106-119	390
	cfr	*Ep. 46*	16-21	418
	cfr	*Tract. paup.*	986-990	464
228-255	cfr	*Sim. beg.*	64-68	331
512-523	cfr	*Ep. 41*	83-88	388-389
	cfr	*Ep. 41*	97-99	389
	cfr	*Ep. 41*	106-119	390
	cfr	*Ep. 46*	16-21	418
	cfr	*Tract. paup.*	986-990	464

Contra turrim Traiectensem

57-62	cfr	*Sim. beg.*	604-612	348
	cfr	*Sim. beg.*	761-770	353-354
388-391	cfr	*Sim. beg.*	761-770	353-354

Glossa ordinaria in ius canonicum, uide Bernardvs Parmensis; Bartholomaevs Brixiensis; Gratianvs

Gratianvs

Decretum

D.38 c.5 (c. I, 142, 2-3)	cfr	*Cura past.*	206-208	291
D.47 c.3 (c. I, 170, 8-36)	cfr	*Cura past.*	273-277	294-295
D.49 a.c.1 (c. I, 175, 5-15)	cfr	*Cura past.*	273-277	294-295
D.60 c.1-3 (c. I, 226, 30-44)	cfr	*Locat.*	137-138	247
D.77 c.1-7; D.78 c.1-5 (c. I, 272, 1 - 276, 19)	cfr	*Ep. 17*	4-7	275
	cfr	*Cura past.*	8-10	281
C.1 q.1 c.6 (c. I, 359, 5-9)	cfr	*Locat.*	118-119	246
C.1 q.1 c.7 (c. I, 359, 13-33)	cfr	*Locat.*	121-123	246
C.1 q.1 c.8 (c. I, 359, 37 - 360, 14)	cfr	*Locat.*	107-123	245-246
C.1 q.1 c.11 (c. I, 361, 1-3)	cfr	*Sim. beg.*	855-859	356
C.1 q.1 c.30-33 (c. I, 371, 28 - 372, 12)	cfr	*Locat.*	54-61	243
C.1 q.1 c.84 § 4 (c. I, 388, 15-29)	cfr	*Locat.*	54-61	243
C.1 q.2 a.c. 1 (c. I, 407, 19-28)	cfr	*Ep. 41*	161-162	392
C.1 q.2 c.2 (c. I, 408, 12-38)	cfr	*Sim. beg.*	503-511	345
C.1 q.2 c.8-9 (c. I, 411, 13-19; 39-51)	cfr	*Ep. 41*	161-162	392
C.1 q.3 c.7 (c. I, 413, 16-18)		*Locat.*	454-457	260
C.1 q.3 c.8 (c. I, 413-415)	cfr	*Sim. beg.*	6-11	329
	cfr	*Leeringhe*	58-64	371
C.1 q.3 c.8 § 1 (c. I, 413, 35 - 414, 11)	cfr	*Sim. beg.*	860-865	357
C.1 q.3 c.8 § 1 (c. I, 414, 6-8)		*Locat.*	66-73	244
C.1 q.3 c.8 § 1 (c. I, 414, 12-34)	cfr	*Locat.*	13	241
*C.1 q.3 c.8 § 1 (c. I, 414, 12-19)	cfr	*Locat.*	298	254
C.1 q.3 c.8 § 1 (c. I, 414, 30-33)		*Locat.*	454-457	260
C.1 q.3 c.15 (c. I, 418, 11-22)	cfr	*Locat.*	442-443	260
C.3 q.7 p.c.2 § 3 (c. I, 526, 41)	cfr	*Cura past.*	241-242	293

	Op.	lin.	pag.
*C.8 q.1 c.9 (c. I, 592, 22-23; 28-29)	cfr *Locat.*	292-300	254
C.8 q.1 c.11 (c. I, 594, 9-12)	cfr *Locat.*	290-292	253-254
C.12 q.1 c.5 (c. I, 678, 1-3)	cfr *Ep. 41*	33-35	386
	cfr *Ep. 42*	12-13	402
	cfr *Tract. paup.*	231-234	434
	cfr *Tract. paup.*	334-343	438-439
C.12 q.1 c.9 § 1 (c. I, 679, 28-37)	cfr *Ep. 41*	33-35	386
	cfr *Ep. 42*	12-13	402
	cfr *Tract. paup.*	231-234	434
	cfr *Tract. paup.*	334-343	438-439
C.12 q.1 c.10 § 3-4 (c. I, 680, 12-28)	cfr *Ep. 41*	33-35	386
	cfr *Ep. 42*	12-13	402
	cfr *Tract. paup.*	231-234	434
	cfr *Tract. paup.*	334-343	438-439
C.16 q.1 p.c.19 (c. I, 765, 43-44)	cfr *Ep. 46*	16-18	418
C.16 q.1 p.c.19 (c. I, 765, 44 - 766, 5)	cfr *Ep. 46*	1-4	417
C.16 q.1 c. 21-35 (c. I, 766-770)	cfr *Ep. 46*	1-4	417
C.19 q.1 c.1; q.2 c.1-2 (c. I, 839, 17 - 840, 18)	cfr *Locat.*	328-330	255
De pen., D.6 a.c.3 (c. I, 1244, 25-28)	cfr *Ep. 46*	16-18	418
De pen., D.6 a.c.3; c.3 (c. I, 1244, 29-38)	cfr *Ep. 46*	13-15	418
C.2 q.33 c.3 (De pen., D.7 c.4) (c. I, 1245, 33-34)	cfr *Ep. 19*	77-78	302

GREGORIVS MAGNVS

Dialogorum libri 4

1, 4, 8 (T. 2, p. 44, 84-99)	cfr *Cura past.*	48-50	283
4, 57, 8-10 (p. 188, 49-65)	cfr *Tract. paup.*	294-299	436-437
*4, 57, 11 (p. 190, 74-86)	cfr *Ep. 41*	35-39	386-387
	cfr *Tract. paup.*	299-307	437

Homiliae in Euangelia

*12, 1 (p. 82, 36-37)	cfr *Cura past.*	241-242	293
19, 2 (p. 145, 57-65)	cfr *Ep. 17*	73-75	278
19, 2 (p. 145, 57-60)	*Sim. beg.*	649-655	350
27, 1 (p. 229, 6-9)	*Sim. beg.*	837-841	356
*28, 2 (p. 241, 31-33)	cfr *Sim. beg.*	448-451	343

Homiliae in Hiezechihelem prophetam

*Ez., 2, 8 (p. 348, 465-468)	*Sim. beg.*	975-978	360

Moralia in Iob

*19, 27 (p. 995-996, 46-74)	cfr *Cura past.*	273-277	294-295
24, 25, 53 (p. 1227, 32-38)	cfr *Cura past.*	273-277	294-295

Regula pastoralis

Prol. (p. 126, 27-30)	*Cura past.*	211-214	291
1, 1 (p. 128, 4-5)	*Cura past.*	209-210	291
1, 1 (p. 128, 6-9)	*Cura past.*	214-217	291
1, 7 (p. 150, 9-11, cfr *PL*, 77, 20B)	cfr *Cura past.*	37-38	283
1, 7 (p. 152, 25-31, cfr *PL*, 77, 20C)	*Cura past.*	59-64	284
*1, 9 (p. 160, 38-39, cfr *PL*, 77, 22C)	*Locat.*	289-290	253
*	cfr *Locat.*	570-571	265

INDEX FONTIVM

		Op.	lin.	pag.
*		*Cura past.*	52-54	284
*1, 10-11 (p. 164, 33-39; 1-5)	cfr	*Cura past.*	273-277	294-295
2, 7 (p. 222, 56-70)	cfr	*Cura past.*	273-277	294-295

GREGORIVS PAPA IX
Decretales

X 1.6.7 § 2 (c. II, 52, 9-19)	cfr	*Locat.*	137-138	247
	cfr	*Ep. 17*	4-7	275
	cfr	*Cura past.*	8-10	281
X 1.6.7 § 2 (c. II, 52, 14)	cfr	*Ep. 17*	67-68	277
X 1.14.1 (c. II, 125, 45-46)	cfr	*Locat.*	137-138	247
X 1.23.1 (c. II, 149, 60 - 150, 6)	cfr	*Locat.*	143-145	247
X 1.23.4 (c. II, 150, 53-61)	cfr	*Locat.*	137-142	247
X 1.23.7 § 1-5 (c. II, 151, 35-59)	cfr	*Locat.*	164-165	248
X 1.23.7 § 2-3 (c. II, 151, 41-48)	cfr	*Locat.*	143-145	247
X 1.40.4 (c. II, 220, 7-8 (rubr.); 19-21 (text.))	cfr	*Ep. 46*	34-35	419
X 3.5.4 (c. II, 465, 26-31)	cfr	*Ep. 19*	52-54	301
X 3.35.2 (596, 50-51; 596, 59 - 597, 4)	cfr	*Tract. paup.*	334-343	438-439
X 3.35.2 (c. II, 596, 59-61)	cfr	*Ep. 41*	33-35	386
	cfr	*Ep. 42*	12-13	402
	cfr	*Ep. 45*	95-96	411
		Ep. 45	97-104	411
	cfr	*Ep. 46*	1-21	417-418
	cfr	*Ep. 46*	43-44	420
	cfr	*Tract. paup.*	231-234	434
X 3.35.2 (c. II, 596, 60)		*Tract. paup.*	353	439
X 3.35.2 (c. II, 597, 1-2)	cfr	*Ep. 41*	35-39	386-387
X 3.35.4 (c. II, 598, 18-32)	cfr	*Ep. 41*	35-39	386-387
X 3.35.5 (c. II, 598-599)	cfr	*Ep. 46*	1-4	417
X 3.35.6 § 2 (c. II, 599, 27-42)	cfr	*Tract. paup.*	274-277	436
	cfr	*Tract. paup.*	284-293	436
X 3.35.6 § 2 (c. II, 599, 31-42)	cfr	*Ep. 41*	33-35	386
	cfr	*Ep. 42*	12-13	402
	cfr	*Tract. paup.*	231-234	434
	cfr	*Tract. paup.*	334-343	438-439
X 3.35.6 § 2 (c. II, 599, 35-38)	cfr	*Ep. 41*	35-39	386-387
X 3.35.6 § 2 (c. II, 599, 40-42)	cfr	*Ep. 45*	104-106	411
X 3.35.6 § 2 (c. II, 600, 15-19)	cfr	*Ep. 41*	31-33	386
		Ep. 45	89-94	411
		Tract. paup.	321-325	438
X 3.35.6 § 2 (c. II, 600, 16-18)	cfr	*Ep. 45*	104-106	411
X 5.3.8 (c. II, 750, 45 - 751, 11)	cfr	*Sim. beg.*	3-6	329
	cfr	*Leeringhe*	53-58	370-371
X 5.3.15 (c. II, 753, 32-55)	cfr	*Locat.*	14-19	242
X 5.3.30 (c. II, 759, 39-57, praesertim l. 54-57)	cfr	*Sim. beg.*	49-57	331
	cfr	*Leeringhe*	113-127	373
X 5.3.34 (c. II, 763, 21-45)	cfr	*Sim. beg.*	503-511	345
X 5.3.38 (c. II, 765, 15-20)	cfr	*Sim. beg.*	49-57	331
	cfr	*Leeringhe*	113-127	373
X 5.3.40 (c. II, 765, 47-66)	cfr	*Sim. beg.*	49-57	331

	Op.	lin.	pag.
*	cfr *Sim. beg.*	534-535	346
	cfr *Leeringhe*	113-127	373
*	cfr *Leeringhe*	183-185	375
X 5.3.46 (c. II, 767, 41-50)	cfr *Sim. beg.*	121-125	333
	cfr *Leeringhe*	148-153	374
X 5.3.46 (c. II, 767, 44-50)	cfr *Locat.*	388-392	258
	Locat.	599-602	266
	Locat.	625-627	267-268
	cfr *Locat.*	678-679	269
	cfr *Locat.*	711-714	271
X 5.4.1 (c. II, 767, 52-53)	*Locat.*	10-11	241
X 5.4.3 (c. II, 768, 22-23; 25-26)	cfr *Locat.*	12	241
	Locat.	648-650	268
X 5.4.4 (c. II, 768, 31-43)	cfr *Locat.*	4-7	241
X 5.4.4 (c. II, 768, 44-50)	cfr *Locat.*	605-607	267
X 5.39.44 (c. II, 908, 12-14)	cfr *Locat.*	276-279	253

GVILLELMVS ALTISSIODORENSIS

Summa aurea

3, 49, 1 (T. 3.2, p. 940, 35-42)		*Sim. beg.*	783-795	354
3, 49, 2, 3 (T. 3.2, p. 954, 57-59)	cfr	*Sim. beg.*	913-915	358
3, 49, 2, 4 (T. 3.2, p. 960, 179-180)		*Sim. beg.*	1030-1031	362

GVILLELMVS RHEDONENSIS

Apparatus ad Summam Raymundi

*L. 1 t. 1 § 22, comm. sup. 'offerat se' (ed. 1603, p. 23, gl. x)	cfr *Sim. beg.*	527-533	346
*	cfr *Leeringhe*	173-183	375
*L. 1 t. 1 § 26, comm. sup. 'mancipatus' (ed. 1603, p. 27, c. 2, 42-59)	cfr *Sim. beg.*	17-32	329-330
*	cfr *Leeringhe*	74-89	371-372

HELINANDVS FRIGIDI MONTIS

Sermones

13 (*PL*, 212, 589C)	cfr *Tract. paup.*	315-317	437

HENRICVS BOHIC

Distinctiones in quinque libros Decretalium

sup. X 3.5.4 (c. II, 465, 26-31) (p. 386, c. 1, 15-25; 47-54 sub num. 1; 4)	cfr *Ep. 19*	72-73	302
sup. X 3.35.6 (p. 527, c. 2, 29-47 sub num. 18)	cfr *Ep. 46*	1-21	417-418
sup. X 3.35.6, in comm. sup. gl. 'et ita habes' (= BERN. PARM., *Glos. ord. in Decret.*, super X 3.35.6, comm. sup. 'abdicatio' (c. II, 600, 16), ed. 1582, c. 1297 (p. 154), gl. d) (p. 526, c. 1, 65 - c. 2, 47 sub num. 7-9)	cfr *Tract. paup.*	325-329	438

INDEX FONTIVM

	Op.	lin.	pag.

HENRICVS DE GANDAVO

Quodlibet 2
q. 18 (p. 136, 7-8)	cfr	*Locat.*	290-292	253-254
	cfr	*Cura past.*	54-56	284
q. 18 (p. 139, 66-68)	cfr	*Locat.*	292-294	254
q. 18 (p. 139, 83-85)		*Locat.*	289-290	253
	cfr	*Locat.*	570-571	265
	cfr	*Cura past.*	52-54	284
q. 18 (p. 139, 88 - 141, (1)26)	cfr	*Locat.*	305-312	254
	cfr	*Cura past.*	42-46	283
q. 18 (p. 140, 8 - 10)	cfr	*Cura past.*	37-38	283

HIERONYMVS PRESBYTER

Aduersus Iouinianum
2, 11 (c. 301A-B)		*Tract. paup.*	1071-1075	467

Commentariorum in Hiezechielem libri 14
4, 16, 6-7 (p. 167, 1022-1023)	cfr	*Tract. paup.*	30	426

Commentarii in prophetas minores
In Abdiam 20 (p. 372, 697)	cfr	*Tract. paup.*	30	426

Commentariorum in Mattheum libri 4
1 (in Matth. 6, 11, p. 37, 783-786)	cfr	*Ep. 19*	58-59	301
2 (in Matth. 15, 3, p. 127, 1407-1411)	cfr	*Sim. beg.*	711-717	352
3 (in Matth. 21, 2, p. 182, 1182-1191)	cfr	*Tract. paup.*	80-82	428

HOSTIENSIS (HENRICVS DE SEGVSIO CARDINALIS HOSTIENSIS)

Summa (aurea) super titulis decretalium
L. 3, t. 37, § 6 (ed. 1574, c. 1109-1110)	cfr	*Tract. paup.*	325-329	438
L. 5 t. 1 § 1 (ed. 1537, f. 231v, c. 2, 61-68)		*Sim. beg.*	473-477	344
L. 5 t. 8 § 3 (ed. 1537, f. 232r, c. 2, 51-61)	cfr	*Sim. beg.*	503-511	345

HRABANVS MAVRVS

Expositio in Matthaeum
6 (p. 542, 65-70)	cfr	*Tract. paup.*	80-82	428

INNOCENTIVS PAPA IV

In quinque libros Decretalium commentaria
*super X 3.5.4 comm. sup. gl. 'consideratis facultatibus' (ed. Frankf., 1570, f. 355r, c. 2)	cfr	*Ep. 19*	73-75	302
super X 3.35.2 comm. sup. 'peculium' (c. II, 596, 50-51) (ed. 1570, p. 516, c. 2, 64-65)	cfr	*Ep. 45*	107-108	411
super X 3.35.2		*Tract. paup.*	354-356	439

		Op.	*lin.*	*pag.*
comm. sup. 'Administratione' (ed. 1570, p. 516, c. 2, 68-69; ed. Frankf., 1570, f. 432r, c. 2, 16-18)	cfr	*Ep. 45*	107-108	411
super X 3.35.6 § 2	cfr	*Ep. 45*	107-108	411
comm. sup. 'Summus' (ed. 1570, p. 517, c. 2, 17-22)				
super X 3.35.6 sub 2 (ed. Frankf., 1570, f. 432v, c. 2 - 433r, c. 1)	cfr	*Tract. paup.*	325-329	438
*super X 5.3.34	cfr	*Sim. beg.*	534-535	346
comm. sup. 'consentiant' (ed. 1570, p. 599, c. 1, 21-27)				
*	cfr	*Leeringhe*	183-185	375
super X 5.4.3	cfr	*Locat.*	12-13	241
comm. sup. 'regimen' (ed. 1570, p. 602, c. 1, sub num. 3, 22-27)				
(ed. 1570, p. 602, c. 1, sub num. 3, 27-36)		*Locat.*	630-637	268

Apparatus in vium

super VI 5.11.1	cfr	*Cura past.*	291-295	295-296
comm. sup. 'irregularitatem' (c. II, 1094, 13) (f. 213v, c. 1 in fine, sub num. 4)				

IOHANNES ANDREAE

Glossa ordinaria in Clementinas

super *Clem.* 1.6.3	cfr	*Ep. 17*	4-7	275
comm. sup. 'Generalem' (c. II, 1140, 21) (c. 65 (p. 474), gl. e)				
	cfr	*Cura past.*	8-10	281
super *Clem.* 3.11.1	cfr	*Sim. beg.*	43-47	330
comm. in expositione casus (c. II, 1169, 30) (c. 216 (p. 549)), 14-36)				
	cfr	*Sim. beg.*	1095-1098	364
	cfr	*Leeringhe*	38-43	370
	cfr	*Leeringhe*	105-110	372
comm. sup. 'obedientiam' (c. II, 1169, 31) (c. 216-217 (p. 549-550), gl. u)	cfr	*Sim. beg.*	43-47	330
	cfr	*Sim. beg.*	1095-1098	364
	cfr	*Leeringhe*	38-43	370
	cfr	*Leeringhe*	105-110	372

IOHANNES CHRYSOSTOMVS (Ps.)

Opus imperfectum

Hom. 51, 1 (in Matth. 15, 1-20) (*PG*, 58, c. 510, 1-10)		*Sim. beg.*	718-730	352
Hom. 51, 3 (in Matth. 15, 1-20) (*PG*, 58, c. 514, 35-36; 43-47)	cfr	*Sim. beg.*	732-734	352

INDEX FONTIVM

	Op.	lin.	pag.
Hom. 51, 4 (in Matth. 15, 1-20) (*PG*, 58, c. 514, 48-56)	cfr *Sim. beg.*	734-736	352

IOHANNES FRIBVRGENSIS

Summa Confessorum

L. 1 t. 1 q. 7 (f. 5r, c. 1, 18-22)	cfr *Cura past.*	14-17	282
L. 1 t. 1 q. 10, c. 1 (f. 5r, c. 2, (49-) 54 - 5v, c. 1, 3)	cfr *Sim. beg.*	877-878	357
L. 1 t. 1 q. 14 (f. 6r, c. 1, 17-46)	cfr *Cura past.*	12-30	282
L. 1 t. 1 q. 14 (f. 6r, c. 1, 46 - c. 2, 7)	cfr *Cura past.*	33-40	283
L. 1 t. 1 q. 32 (f. 9v, c. 1, 18-27)	cfr *Sim. beg.*	503-511	345
L. 1 t. 1 q. 48 (f. 11r, c. 2, 46 - 11v, c. 1, 7)	cfr *Sim. beg.*	503-511	345
L. 1 t. 1 q. 49 (f. 11v, c. 1, 8 - c. 2, 15)	cfr *Sim. beg.*	527-533	346
	cfr *Leeringhe*	173-183	375
L. 1 t. 1 q. 49 (f. 11v, c. 1, 38-60)	cfr *Sim. beg.*	534-535	346
	cfr *Leeringhe*	183-185	375
L. 1 t. 1 q. 75 (f. 13v, c. 1, 47 - c. 2, 1)	cfr *Sim. beg.*	17-32	329-330
	cfr *Leeringhe*	74-89	371-372
L. 3 t. 22 q. 12 (f. 162r, c. 2 in fine, 54-58)	cfr *Ep. 17*	4-7	275
	cfr *Cura past.*	8-10	281
L. 3 t. 22 q. 25 (f. 163v, c. 2, 19-35)	*Cura past.*	182-184	290
	cfr *Ep. 46*	23-26	419
L. 3 t. 27 q. 10 (f. 194r, c. 1-2)	cfr *Locat.*	180-181	249
L. 3 t. 28 q. 2 (f. 195r, c. 1 - 195v, c. 1)	cfr *Ep. 46*	1-4	417
L. 3 t. 33 q. 25 (f. 216r, c. 1-2)	cfr *Ep. 46*	1-21	417-418

ISIDORVS HISPALENSIS

Etymologiarum siue Originum Libri XX

*10, 234	cfr *Sim. beg.*	1140-1143	365

D. IVNIVS IVVENALIS

Saturae

*10, 22	cfr *Tract. paup.*	973-975	463

IVO CARNOTENSIS

De ecclesiasticis sacramentis et officiis ac praecipuis per annum festis sermones

Serm. 16 in ramis palmarum (*PL*, 162, c. 587A-B)	*Tract. paup.*	54-59	427

IVSTINIANVS, uide *Codex Iustiniani*

L. CAELIVS FIRMIANVS LACTANTIVS

Diuinae institutiones

3, 2, 6 (p. 180, 7-19)	*Tract. paup.*	1156-1158	471-472
6, 6, 24-28 (p. 504, 2 - 505, 7)	cfr *Locat.*	537-543	264

	Op.	lin.	pag.

Liber sextus decretalium, uide BONIFACIVS PAPA VIII

PETRVS LOMBARDVS

Sententiae in IV libris distinctae

L. 2 d. 1 c. 4 qc. 4 (T. 1.2, p. 332, 26-28)	cfr *Cura past.*	106-108	286

PLINIVS MAIOR (CAIVS PLINIVS SECVNDVS)

Naturalis historia

*24, 36, 5 (Vol. 5, p. 172, 6-8)	cfr *Tract. paup.*	1145-1146	471

Prouerbia (S. SINGER, *Thesaurus prouerbiorum*)

Bd. 1, p. 200-201, s.u. 'Arm (adj.)', 3.5.2 'Spez.: Der arme braucht keine Räuber', n. 433-451	cfr *Tract. paup.*	973-975	463-464
Bd. 2, p. 482, s.u. 'Enthaltsamkeit', n. 3-4	cfr *Tract. paup.*	1092-1094	468
Bd. 6, p. 188, s.u. 'Hören', n. 67	cfr *Ep. 27*	31-32	380
Bd. 8, p. 227, sect. 1, 2, s.u. 'der Mönch darf nicht nach Weltlichem streben', n. 25	cfr *Ep. 41*	48-49	387
	cfr *Tract. paup.*	315-317	437

PS. ARISTOTELES, PS. AVGVSTINVS HIPPONENSIS, PS. SENECA, uide locos post ARISTOTELES, AVGVSTINVS HIPPONENSIS, SENECA

RAIMVNDVS DE PENNAFORTE

Summa de paenitentia

*L. 1 t. 1 § 7 (c. 284-285 ed. Ochoa)	cfr *Cura past.*	12-30	282
*L. 1 t. 1 § 22 (c. 299-300 ed. Ochoa; ed. 1603, p. 23, c. 2, 22 - p. 24, c. 1, 22)	cfr *Sim. beg.*	527-533	346
*	cfr *Leeringhe*	173-183	375

Regula ordinis tertii

c. 1-20 (p. 90-95)	cfr *Leeringhe*	35-38	370
c. 8; 13 (p. 92; 93)	cfr *Leeringhe*	38-43	370

RVPERTVS TVITIENSIS

Commentarium in Apocalypsim Iohannis apostoli

2, 2 (*PL*, 169, c. 879, 19)	Locat.	86	245

L. ANNAEVS SENECA

Epistulae morales ad Lucilium

2, 6 (p. 4, 8)	cfr *Tract. paup.*	876-877	460
	cfr *Tract. paup.*	1024	466
2, 6 (p. 4, 9-10)	cfr *Tract. paup.*	870-873	459-460
4, 10 (p. 9, 6-7)	cfr *Tract. paup.*	855-857	459

INDEX FONTIVM

		Op.	lin.	pag.
	cfr	Tract. paup.	1027-1029	466
4, 10 (p. 9, 7-8)	cfr	Ep. 27	18-20	380
		Tract. paup.	785-787	456
	cfr	Tract. paup.	801-802	457
4, 10 (p. 9, 12-13)	cfr	Tract. paup.	815-816	457
4, 11 (p. 9, 16)		Tract. paup.	1024-1025	466
8, 5 (p. 18, 8-11)	cfr	Tract. paup.	788-791	456
8, 5 (p. 18, 10-11)	cfr	Tract. paup.	797-798	457
9, 18 (p. 25, 5-9)		Tract. paup.	898-904	461
9, 19 (p. 25, 13)		Tract. paup.	904	461
9, 20 (p. 25, 22 - 26, 5)		Tract. paup.	865-869	459
14, 9 (p. 41, 16-17)		Tract. paup.	987-988	464
14, 9 (p. 41, 17-18)	cfr	Tract. paup.	967-968	463
14, 17 (p. 44, 3-6)	cfr	Ep. 41	160	392
	cfr	Tract. paup.	859-861	459
16, 8 (p. 50, 3-8)	cfr	Tract. paup.	798-801	457
16, 9 (p. 50, 8-11)	cfr	Tract. paup.	827-831	458
17, 3 (p. 51, 10)	cfr	Tract. paup.	964-965	463
17, 4 (p. 51, 18-19)	cfr	Tract. paup.	803-806	457
17, 9 (p. 52, 25 - 53, 1)	cfr	Tract. paup.	812-813	457
18, 9 (p. 56, 8-9)	cfr	Tract. paup.	1025-1027	466
		Tract. paup.	1043	466
18, 10 (p. 56, 17-22)	cfr	Tract. paup.	1067-1071	467
20, 8 (p. 63, 21-22)	cfr	Tract. paup.	972-973	463
20, 12 (p. 64, 22-23)	cfr	Tract. paup.	964-965	463
20, 13 (p. 65, 5-6)	cfr	Tract. paup.	782-785	456
21, 10-11 (p. 68, 9-15)	cfr	Tract. paup.	1033-1039	466
21, 10 (p. 68, 2-6)		Tract. paup.	1029-1033	466
	cfr	Tract. paup.	1070-1071	467
21, 10 (p. 68, 12-13)	cfr	Tract. paup.	1042-1045	466
22, 9 (p. 71, 5-11)	cfr	Tract. paup.	1006-1013	465
22, 11 (p. 71, 17-21)	cfr	Tract. paup.	1016-1018	465
22, 12 (p. 71, 23-26)		Tract. paup.	1013-1016	465
22, 14 (p. 72, 9-10)	cfr	Tract. paup.	779-780	456
22, 15 (p. 72, 15-16)	cfr	Tract. paup.	779-780	456
23, 3 (p. 74, 4)	cfr	Tract. paup.	1055-1056	467
23, 4 (p. 74, 6)		Tract. paup.	1061-1062	467
23, 5 (p. 74, 18-20)	cfr	Tract. paup.	1055	467
27, 9 (p. 91, 14-15)		Tract. paup.	855-857	459
	cfr	Tract. paup.	1027-1029	466
119, 7 (p. 579, 4-5)	cfr	Tract. paup.	785-787	456
119, 12 (p. 580, 8-13)	cfr	Tract. paup.	879-883	460

SENECA (Ps.) (Ps. MARTINVS BRACCARENSIS)

Libellus de moribus

5 (p. 466 ed. Haase = PL, 72, 31A)	cfr	Ep. 41	112-114	390
	cfr	Ep. 46	16-21	418
	cfr	Tract. paup.	986-990	464

Statuta synodalia Leodiensia

| tit. 16, c. 4 (p. 158, 7-17 ed. Avril) | cfr | Locat. | 137-142 | 247 |

		Op.	*lin.*	*pag.*
	cfr	*Ep. 17*	4-7	275
	cfr	*Cura past.*	8-10	281

C. SVETONIVS TRANQVILLVS

De uita Caesarum libri 8

Aug. 21.1-3 (p. 57, 12 - 58, 7)	cfr	*Tract. paup.*	1003-1004	465
Aug. 28.1 (p. 62, 11-19)	cfr	*Tract. paup.*	1003-1005	465

HENRICVS SVSO

Horologium sapientiae

1, 5 (p. 408, 21-26)	cfr	*Sim. beg.*	1107-1112	365

THOMAS AQVINAS

De perfectione spiritualis vitae

c. 27 co (T. 41, p. B 106, 289-301)	cfr	*Locat.*	50-53	243
	cfr	*Cura past.*	92-98	285-286

Scriptum super primo - quarto libro Sententiarum magistri Petri Lombardi

L. 2 d. 1 q. 2 pr. (p. 44, 22-23)	cfr	*Cura past.*	106-108	286
L. 2 d. 40 q. 1 a. 2 arg. 2-3 (T. 2, p. 1013)	cfr	*Locat.*	193-196	249-250
	cfr	*Locat.*	374-376	257
L. 4 d. 18 q. 1 a. 3 qc. 1 co.	cfr	*Ep. 19*	54-56	301
L. 4 d. 24 q. 1 a. 1 qc. 1 arg. 1; qc. 1 co.; qc. 2 co.; ad 1 (T. 7,2, p. 887, c. 2; p. 888, c. 2)	cfr	*Locat.*	54-61	243
L. 4 d. 24 q. 1 a. 1 qc. 3 s.c. (T. 7,2, p. 888, c. 1, 3-7)	cfr	*Locat.*	353-357	256
	cfr	*Cura past.*	116-117	286-287
	cfr	*Ep. 19*	15-18	299-300
L. 4 d. 24 q. 1 a. 2 qc. 2 arg. 2 (p. 890, c. 1); qc. 3 ad 2 (p. 891, c. 2)	cfr	*Locat.*	173-177	249
	cfr	*Locat.*	364-365	257
	cfr	*Ep. 19*	24-25	300
	cfr	*Ep. 19*	32-34	300
L. 4 d. 24 q. 1 a. 3 qc. 1-2 (T. 7,2, p. 892-893)	cfr	*Cura past.*	79-82	285
L. 4 d. 24 q. 1 a. 3 qc. 1 arg. 1 (T. 7,2, p. 892, c. 1)	cfr	*Cura past.*	163-164	289
L. 4 d. 24 q. 1 a. 3 qc. 1 arg. 1; co.; ad 1 (T. 7,2, p. 892, c. 1; p. 893, c. 1)	cfr	*Locat.*	54-61	243
L. 4 d. 24 q. 1 a. 3 qc. 4 s.c. 2 (T. 7,2, p. 893, c. 1, 3-5)	cfr	*Cura past.*	241-242	293
L. 4 d. 24 q. 1 a. 3 qc. 5 s.c. 1 (T. 7,2, p. 893, c. 1)	cfr	*Cura past.*	223-234	292
*L. 4 d. 24 q. 1 a. 3 qc. 5 co. (T. 7,2, p. 894, c. 1, 63-66)		*Cura past.*	182-184	290
	cfr	*Ep. 46*	23-26	419

	Op.	lin.	pag.
*L. 4 d. 24 q. 1 a. 3 qc. 5 ad 4 (T. 7,2, p. 894, c. 2, 16-19)	cfr *Cura past.*	182-184	290
	cfr *Ep. 46*	23-26	419
L. 4 d. 24 q. 2 a. 2 co.; ad 1; ad 4-5; ad 8; ibid., a. 3 co.; ad 2 (p. 897, c. 2 - 899, c. 1)	cfr *Locat.*	173-177	249
	cfr *Locat.*	364-365	257
	cfr *Ep. 19*	24-25	300
	cfr *Ep. 19*	32-34	300
L. 4 d. 25 q. 3 a. 1 qc. 1 ad 1 (T. 7,2, p. 910, c. 2, 57 - p. 911, c. 1, 9)	cfr *Cura past.*	129-132	287
*L. 4 d. 25 q. 3 a.3 ad 4 (T. 7,2, p. 915, c. 1)	cfr *Cura past.*	12-30	282
L. 4 d. 49 q. 3 a. 4 qc. 3 arg. 1 (T. 7,2, p. 1221, c. 1, 6-8)	cfr *Cura past.*	117-119	287
L. 4 d. 49 q. 3 a. 4 qc. 3 co. (T. 7,2, p. 1222, c. 1, 47-58)	cfr *Cura past.*	117-119	287
Pars prima summae theologiae			
q. 21 a. 1 co. (T. 4, p. 258, c. 1, 24-31)	cfr *Sim. beg.*	219-232	336
	cfr *Sim. beg.*	634-637	349
q. 21 a. 1 co. (T. 4, p. 258, c. 2, 1-4)	cfr *Sim. beg.*	219-232	336
q. 21 a. 1 ad 3 (T. 4, p. 259, c. 1, 14 - c. 2, 7)	cfr *Sim. beg.*	224-238	336
q. 108 a. 1 arg. 2 (T. 5, p. 494, c. 1, l. 28-29)	cfr *Locat.*	41-42	243
	Cura past.	204-206	291
Prima secundae summae theologiae			
q. 19 a. 4 s.c. (T. 6, p. 144, c. 1, art. 4, 19-22)	cfr *Sim. beg.*	672-675	350
q. 62 a. 1 co. (T. 6, p. 401, a. 1, c. 1, 29 - 2, 17)	cfr *Sim. beg.*	841-847	356
	cfr *Sim. beg.*	905-907	358
q. 93 a. 3 sed c, co. (T. 7, p. 164, c. 1-2)	cfr *Sim. beg.*	604-612	348
q. 93 a. 3 co. (T. 7, p. 164, c. 1, 16 - c. 2, 5)	cfr *Sim. beg.*	233-238	336
q. 93 a. 3 co., ad 1, ad 2 (T. 7, p. 164, c. 2)	cfr *Sim. beg.*	619-625	349
q. 93 a. 3 co., ad 2 (T. 7, p. 164, c. 1-2)	cfr *Sim. beg.*	761-770	353-354
q. 95 a. 2 co (T. 7, p. 175, c. 2)	cfr *Sim. beg.*	764-767	353
q. 96 a. 2 co (T. 7, p. 181, c. 2, 3-12)	cfr *Locat.*	249-253	252
q. 96 a. 2 ad 3 (T. 7, p. 181, c. 2)	cfr *Locat.*	253-254	252
q. 105 a. 1 co. (T. 7, p. 262, c. 2, co., l. 9-16)	cfr *Cura past.*	244-246	293
Secunda secundae summae theologiae			
q. 23 a. 6 co. (T. 8, p. 170, c. 1, 32 - 2, 3)	cfr *Sim. beg.*	830-837	356
q. 24 a. 1 co. (T. 8, p. 174, c. 1- 2)	cfr *Tract. paup.*	980-981	464

		Op.	*lin.*	*pag.*
q. 29 a. 1 co., ad 1 (T. 8, p. 236, a. 1, c. 2, 7-26)	cfr	*Ep. 41*	89-91	389
	cfr	*Tract. paup.*	163-164	431
	cfr	*Tract. paup.*	211-212	433
	cfr	*Tract. paup.*	976-978	464
q. 43 a. 1 ad 4 (T. 8, p. 323, c. 1-2)	cfr	*Locat.*	574-578	265
q. 63 a. 1-2 co. (T. 9, p. 62-63)	cfr	*Sim. beg.*	419-451	342-343
q. 63 a. 1 co. (T. 9, p. 62, art. 1, c. 1, 26 - c. 2, 28)	cfr	*Sim. beg.*	219-232	336
	cfr	*Sim. beg.*	693-695	351
q. 63 a. 1 co. (T. 9, p. 62, art. 1, c. 2, 2-9)		*Sim. beg.*	422-429	342
q. 63 a. 1 co. (T. 9, p. 62, art. 1, c. 2, 10-15)	cfr	*Sim. beg.*	419-422	342
q. 63 a. 1 co. (T. 9, p. 62, art. 1, c. 2, 24-28)		*Sim. beg.*	429-432	342
q. 63 a. 2 sed c. (T. 9, p. 63, art. 2, c. 1, 34 - c. 2, 2)	cfr	*Sim. beg.*	448-451	343
q. 63 a. 2 co. (T. 9, p. 63, c. 2, 3-30)	cfr	*Sim. beg.*	219-232	336
	cfr	*Sim. beg.*	634-637	349
q. 63 a. 3 arg. 3. (T. 9, p. 65, art. 3, c. 1, 8-11)	cfr	*Sim. beg.*	448-451	343
q. 66 a. 1 co. (T. 9, p. 84, c. 1-2)	cfr	*Tract. paup.*	377-387	440
q. 66 a. 1 co. (T. 9, p. 84, art. 1, c. 2, 5-7)	cfr	*Ep. 41*	95-102	389
	cfr	*Tract. paup.*	389	441
q. 66 a. 2 co. (T. 9, p. 85, c. 1-2)	cfr	*Ep. 41*	95-102	389
	cfr	*Tract. paup.*	388-407	441
	cfr	*Tract. paup.*	434-436	442
q. 66 a. 2 co. (T. 9, p. 85, c. 1, art. 2, 36-38)	cfr	*Tract. paup.*	423-425	442
q. 66 a. 2 co. (T. 9, p. 85, c. 2, art. 2, 12-18)	cfr	*Tract. paup.*	426-440	442-443
q. 81 a. 1 arg. 2 (T. 9, p. 177, c. 1, a. 1, 13-22)	cfr	*Sim. beg.*	929-935	359
q. 81 a. 1 co. (T. 9, p. 177, c. 2, a. 1, 16-29)	cfr	*Sim. beg.*	1136-1145	366
q. 81 a. 1 co. (T. 9, p. 177, c. 2, a. 1, 23-29)	cfr	*Sim. beg.*	929-935	359
q. 81 a. 1 ad 2 (T. 9, p. 178, c. 1, a. 1, 27-33)	cfr	*Sim. beg.*	929-935	359
q. 81 a. 2 co. (T. 9, p. 179, c. 2, 6-8)	cfr	*Sim. beg.*	917-922	358-359
q. 81 a. 4 co., ad 1-3 (T. 9, p. 181, c. 1, 2 - c. 2, 15)	cfr	*Sim. beg.*	917-922	358-359
q. 81 a. 5 co. (T. 9, p. 182, c. 1, 8-14)	cfr	*Sim. beg.*	944-946	359
q. 81 a. 5 ad 1 (T. 9, p. 182, c. 1, 21 - 2, 4)	cfr	*Sim. beg.*	809-811	355
	cfr	*Sim. beg.*	923-924	359
q. 81 a. 6 co. (T. 9, p. 183, c. 2, 4-13)		*Sim. beg.*	923-928	359
q. 81 a. 7 (T. 9, p. 184, c. 1, 1 - c. 2, 36)	cfr	*Sim. beg.*	936-939	359

INDEX FONTIVM

		Op.	lin.	pag.
q. 88 a. 11 co. (T. 9, p. 265, c. 1, 1-23)	cfr	Tract. paup.	325-329	438
q. 100 a. 1 ad 4 (T. 9, p. 353, c. 2, 13-17)	cfr	Sim. beg.	855-859	356
*q. 100 a. 3 ad 4 (T. 9, p. 359, c. 2, 30-46)	cfr	Sim. beg.	527-533	346
*	cfr	Leeringhe	173-183	375
q. 100 a. 5 s.c. (T. 9, p. 362, a. 5, c. 1, 28-32)	cfr	Locat.	298	254
*q. 100 a. 5 co.; ad 3 (T. 9, p. 362, a. 5, c. 1, 33 - c. 2, 8; 32-40)	cfr	Cura past.	12-30	282
q. 100 a. 5 co. (T. 9, p. 362, c. 2, 13-20)	cfr	Locat.	295-300	254
q. 100 a. 5 ad 3 (T. 9, p. 362, c. 2, 53 - 363, c. 1, 2)	cfr	Locat.	305-312	254
	cfr	Cura past.	42-46	283
q. 100 a. 5 ad 3 (T. 9, p. 363, c. 1, 4-7)		Locat.	300-304	254
	cfr	Cura past.	56-59	284
q. 100 a. 6 ad 5 (T. 9, p. 365, c. 1, 19-26)	cfr	Sim. beg.	49-57	331
	cfr	Leeringhe	113-127	373
q. 125 a. 4 arg. 2 (T. 10, p. 46, c. 1, art. 4, 8-9)	cfr	Ep. 46	34-35	419
q. 184 a. 4 co. (T. 10, p. 455, c. 2, a. 4, 15-32)	cfr	Sim. beg.	1073-1092	364
q. 184 a. 5 co. (T. 10, p. 456, a. 5, c. 2, 9-24)	cfr	Ep. 45	122-127	412
q. 184 a. 5 co. (T. 10, p. 457, c. 1, 3-11)	cfr	Locat.	152-154	248
q. 184 a. 6 s.c. (T. 10, p. 458, c. 1, 18-22)	cfr	Locat.	152-154	248
q. 184 a. 6 co. (T. 10, p. 458, c. 1-2)	cfr	Locat.	145-152	247-248
q. 184 a. 6 ad 2; ad 3 (T. 10, p. 458, c. 2 - 459, c. 2)	cfr	Locat.	140-145	247
q. 185 a. 1 s.c. (T. 10, p. 466, c. 1 - 467, c. 2)	cfr	Locat.	290-292	253-254
q. 186 a. 1 co. (T. 10, p. 486, c. 2, a. 1, 17-22)		Sim. beg.	957-965	360
q. 186 a. 1 co. (T. 10, p. 486, c. 2, a. 1, 22 - p. 487, c. 1, 1)		Sim. beg.	970-980	360
q. 186 a. 1 co. (T. 10, p. 487, c. 1, 1-5)	cfr	Sim. beg.	983-985	361
q. 186 a. 2 co. (T. 10, p. 488, a. 2, c. 1, 31 - c. 2, 24)	cfr	Ep. 27	52-57	381
q. 186 a. 2 co. (T. 10, p. 488, a. 2, c. 2, 3-24)	cfr	Ep. 45	122-127	412
q. 186 a. 2 co. (T. 10, p. 488, a. 2, c. 2, 9-21)	cfr	Ep. 45	129-134	413
q. 186 a. 3 co. (T. 10, p. 491, c. 1, 4-21)	cfr	Ep. 41	44-47	387
	cfr	Tract. paup.	683-685	452
	cfr	Tract. paup.	831-836	458

		Op.	lin.	pag.
q. 186 a. 7 co. (T. 10, p. 497, c. 2, a. 7, 4-37)	cfr	Sim. beg.	307-309	338
	cfr	Sim. beg.	987-993	361
	cfr	Sim. beg.	1048-1051	363
	cfr	Sim. beg.	1071-1072	363
	cfr	Ep. 45	12-15	407
	cfr	Ep. 45	122-127	412
	cfr	Tract. paup.	228-234	434
q. 186 a. 9 co. (T. 10, p. 500, a. 9, c. 1, 33 - c. 2, 20)	cfr	Ep. 46	1-21	417-418
q. 186 a. 9 co. (T. 10, p. 500, a. 9, c. 2, 6-20)	cfr	Ep. 27	52-57	381
q. 188 a. 6 co.; ad 3 (T. 10, p. 529, c. 2)	cfr	Sim. beg.	43-48	330
	cfr	Leeringhe	105-111	372
q. 189 a. 10 arg. 3; ad 3 (T. 10, p. 552, c. 1, a. 10, 20-36; p. 553, c. 2, 3-17)	cfr	Ep. 45	35-37	408-409

Summae theologiae tertia pars

q. 63 a. 4 co. (T. 12, p. 36, c. 1 - c. 2)	cfr	Cura past.	162-163	289
q. 64 a. 1 co. 2 (T. 12, p. 41, c. 2, co. 14-20)	cfr	Cura past.	162-163	289
q. 64 a. 5 co. (T. 12, p. 46, c. 1 - c. 2)	cfr	Locat.	54-61	243
	cfr	Cura past.	163-164	289
q. 64 a. 6 s.c. (T. 12, p. 47, c. 1 - c. 2)	cfr	Cura past.	223-234	292

THOMAS A KEMPIS

Chronica Montis S. Agnetis

1 (p. 337, 23-30)	cfr	Ep. 42	15-16	402

Dialogus nouiciorum

4, 1 (p. 216, 20-25)	cfr	Ep. 19	58-59	301

VALERIVS MAXIMVS

Facta et dicta memorabilia

3, 4, 1 (p. 137, 15-17)	cfr	Tract. paup.	1145-1146	471
4, 3, 4-10 (p. 179 - 183, 14)	cfr	Tract. paup.	1129-1140	470
4, 4, 1-9 (p. 188, 5 - 191, 23)	cfr	Tract. paup.	1129-1140	470
8, 7, ext. 2 (p. 387, 9 - 388, 11)	cfr	Tract. paup.	1156-1158	471

P. VIRGILIVS MARO

Georgicon liber

2, 492		Tract. paup.	620-621	450

CONSPECTVS MATERIAE

PREFACE	5-6
BIBLIOGRAPHY	7-21
PRIMARY SOURCES	7-16
SECONDARY SOURCES	16-22
INTRODUCTION	23-236
I. GEERT GROTE AND THE PROBLEM OF SIMONY AND PROPRIETARISM	23-61
1. Introduction	23-30
1.1. A summary of the more conspicuous new insights presented in this volume	25-26
1.2. Some further observations on the *Letters* and the 'letter collections'	26-30
2. Views on simony in the second half of the Middle Ages	30-38
3. Has Grote committed simony himself according to his own standards before his conversion?	38-49
4. Some notes on Grote's use of sources	49-53
5. Editorial principles	53-61
5.1. Orthography and related matters in Latin texts	56-58
5.2. Editorial policy with regard to texts in Middle Dutch	58-61
II. A *CONSILIVM* ON THE LEGITIMACY OF LETTING AN ECCLESIASTICAL POSITION INVOLVING PASTORAL CARE	62-80
1. Summary of contents	62-68
2. Editorial history, supplement	68
3. The manuscripts	69-72
3.1. Manuscripts used for the edition	69-71
3.2. Other manuscript witnesses	71-72
4. Procedure in establishing a stemma	73-80
4.1. Choosing a basic manuscript	73-77
4.2.1. Conglomerate ζξ	77-79
4.2.2. Group υ (MSS *Kb V – C – AL*)	79-80

III. A LETTER ON SIMONIACAL ACQUISITION OF A PASTORAL
POSITION (*EP*. 17) 81-90
1. Summary of contents, and context of *Ep*. 17 81-83
2. The manuscripts 83-90

IV. A *CONSILIVM* ON PASTORAL CARE (*EP*. 73) 91-105
1. Summary of contents 91-93
2. Editorial history, supplement 94
3. The manuscripts 94-98
   3.1. Manuscripts used for the edition 94-95
   3.2. Other manuscript witnesses 96-98
4. Procedure in establishing a stemma 98-105
   4.1. Choosing a basic manuscript 98-101
   4.2. Grouping the various manuscripts 101-105
      4.2.1. Group δ 101-102
      4.2.2. Group κ 102-104
      4.2.3. Group ξ 104-105

V. A LETTER (*EP*. 19) ABOUT PRIEST JOHN AND HENRY FROM
SCHOONHOVEN, EPISCOPAL COMMISSIONER, ON SIMONY . 106-113
1. Summary of contents 106-107
2. Attempt at identification, and editorial history ... 108-113
3. The manuscripts 113

VI. THE *STATUTES* OF THE MEESTER GEERTSHUIS 114-120
1. Introduction, with an analysis of the *Statutes* 114-117
2. Summary of contents 117-118
3. Editorial history 118-119
4. The manuscripts 119-120
5. Transcription and editorial policy 120

VII. A TREATISE ON SIMONY FOR A COMMUNITY OF BEGUINES
(*DE SIMONIA AD BEGVTTAS*) 121-135
1. Character of the treatise and summary of
   contents 121-131
2. Editorial history, supplement 131-132
3. The manuscript 133-134
4. Transcription and editorial policy 135

VIII. A TREATISE ABOUT AND DESCRIPTION OF THE SIN OF
SIMONY 136-164
1. Summary of contents 136-138
   2.1. The scribe of *Leeringhe ende onderscheit
        van der sonden der symonien* 138-140

CONSPECTVS MATERIAE

2.2. *Een merckelijc onderwijs* and *Leeringhe*	140-141
3.1. Scribe, translator, revisor	142-145
3.2. From IJssellandish to Brabantine	146-150
3.3.1. The changes introduced by Peter Jansz	150-155
3.3.2. Spelling and use of words	155-157
3.3.3. Additions	157-161
3.3.4. Transpositions	161-162
3.4. Conclusion and summary	162-163
4. The manuscript	163-164

IX. A LETTER TO A CORRESPONDENT WHO HAS DONE PROFESSION (*EP.* 27) 165-181
1. Summary of contents, and context of *Ep.* 27 165
2. Editorial history, supplement, and the recipient of *Ep.* 27 165-168
3. The manuscripts 168-179
    3.1. Manuscripts used for the edition 168-172
    3.2. Other manuscript witnesses 172-179
4. Relations among the manuscripts 179-181

X. A LETTER ABOUT PROPRIETARISM, WRITTEN TO THE ABBOT OF THE CISTERCIAN ABBEY IN KAMP-LINTFORT (*EP.* 41) .. 182-189
1. Summary of contents 182-184
2. Editorial history, supplement 184-185
3. The manuscripts 185-186
4. Relations among the manuscripts 186-189

XI. TWO LETTERS ON SIMONY AMONG THE CISTERCIAN SISTERS IN TER HUNNEPE NEAR DEVENTER 190-195
1. Summary of contents 190-191
2. Editorial history, supplement 191-192
3. The manuscripts 192-194
4. Relations among the manuscripts 194-195

XII. A LETTER TO THE ABBESS OF THE CISTERCIAN ABBEY TER HUNNEPE NEAR DEVENTER ON PROPRIETARISM (*EP.* 45) .. 196-204
1. Summary of contents 196-198
2. Editorial history, supplement 198-199
3. The manuscripts 199-201
4. Relations among the manuscripts 201-204

XIII. A LETTER TO A MONASTIC COMMUNITY (*EP.* 46) 205-210
1. Summary of contents 205-208

2. The manuscripts...............................	208
3. Relations among the manuscripts	208-210
XIV. A SERMON ON THE OCCASION OF PALM SUNDAY ABOUT VOLUNTARY POVERTY..............................	211-236
1. Possible occasion and date of the text, composition, sources and summary of contents	211-222
1.1. Possible occasion and date of the text	211-214
1.2. Composition of the text.....................	214-215
1.3. Sources used in the text	215-217
1.4. Summary of contents.......................	217-222
2. Editorial history, supplement...................	223-224
3. The manuscripts...............................	224-229
4. Relations among the manuscripts	229-236

SCRIPTA CONTRA SIMONIAM ET PROPRIETARIOS

Consilium de locatione cure pastoralis	237-272
Epistola (17) ad Wilhelmum Vroede de cura pastorali recusanda a minoribus aetate	273-278
Consilium de cura pastorali (Epistola 73)	279-296
Epistola super Iohannem presbyterum et dominum Henricum de Scoenhove de Gouda (de simonia euitanda in cura pastorali	297-305
Statuta domus a magistro Gerardo feminis deuotis destinatae	307-326
De simonia ad beguttas	327-366
Tractatus de simoniaca receptione sororum in conuentibus tertii ordinis, uulgari lingua 'leeringhe ende onderscheit van der sonden der symonien' nuncupatus ..	367-376
Epistola (27) de proprietate monachorum ad quendam professum	377-381
Epistola (41) ad abbatem in Camp de proprietatibus uitandis	383-395
Epistolae duae ad abbatem (44) et fratres (42) in Camp de sororibus cisterciensibus in Ter Hunnepe	397-403
Epistola (45) ad rectricem monialium de proprietariis	405-413

Epistola (46) de monachorum ingressu et eorum resignacione in monasteria 415-422
Sermo in festo Palmarum de paupertate 423-473

INDICES 475-512

Index locorum S. Scripturae 477-486
Index fontium 487-512

GERARDI MAGNI
OPERA OMNIA

cura et studio
Instituti Titus Brandsma
in Vniuersitate Radbodi Nouiomagensi
ad fidem codicum manu scriptorum
edita

Corpus Christianorum
Continuatio Mediaeualis

I   *Prolegomena ad Gerardi Magni opera omnia,*
    conscripsit Rudolf Th. M. VAN DIJK
    Contra turrim Traiectensem,
    ed. Rijcklof HOFMAN

    Turnholti, 2003
    (*CCCM* 192)

II 1. *Sermo ad clerum Traiectensem de focaristis,*
    ed. Rijcklof HOFMAN

    Turnholti, 2011
    (*CCCM* 235)

    2. *Scripta contra simoniam et proprietarios,*
    ed. Rijcklof HOFMAN et Marinus VAN DEN BERG

    Turnholti, 2016
    (*CCCM* 235A)

V   1. *Ioannis Rusbrochii Ornatus spiritualis desponsationis Gerardo Magno interprete,*
    ed. Rijcklof HOFMAN
    adhibita editione preliminaria a H. A. M. DOUWES inchoata

    Turnholti, 2000
    (*CCCM* 172)

CORPVS CHRISTIANORVM
CONTINVATIO MEDIAEVALIS

ONOMASTICON

Adalboldus Traiectensis 171
Adelmannus Leodiensis 171
Ademarus Cabannensis 129, 245, 245A
Adso Dervensis 45, 198
Aelredus Rievallensis 1, 2A, 2B, 2C, 2D
Agnellus Ravennas 199
Agobardus Lugdunensis 52
Alcuinus Eboracensis 249
Alexander Essebiensis 188, 188A
Alexander Neckam 221, 227
Ambrosius Autpertus 27, 27A, 27B
Andreas a S. Victore 53, 53A, 53B, 53E, 53F, 53G
Anonymus Bonnensis 171
Anonymus Einsiedlensis 171
Anonymus Erfurtensis 171
Anonymus in Matthaeum 159
Anselmus Laudunensis 267
Arnoldus Gheyloven Roterdamus 212
Arnoldus Leodiensis 160
Ars Laureshamensis 40A
Ascelinus Carnotensis 171

Balduinus de Forda 99
Bartholomaeus Exoniensis 157
Beatus Liebanensis 58
Benedictus Anianensis 168, 168A
Beringerius Turonensis 84, 84A, 171
Bernoldus Constantiensis 171
Bovo Corbeiensis 171
Burchardus abbas Bellevallis 62

Caesarius Heisterbacensis 171
Carmen Campidoctoris 71
Christanus Campililiensis 19A, 19B
Chronica Adefonsi imperatoris 71
Chronica Hispana 71, 71A, 73
Chronica Naierensis 71A
Chronica Latina Regum Castellae 73
Claudius Taurinensis 263
Collectaneum exemplorum et uisionum Clarevallense 208
Collectio canonum in V libris 6
Collectio exemplorum Cisterciensis 243
Commentaria in Ruth 81
Conradus Eberbacensis 138
Conradus de Mure 210

Constitutiones canonicorum regularium ordinis Arroasiensis 20
Consuetudines canonicorum regularium Springiersbacenses-Rodenses 48
Constitutiones quae uocantur Ordinis Praemonstratensis 216

Dionysius Cartusiensis 121, 121A
Donatus ortigraphus 40D

Eterius Oxomensis 59
Excerpta isagogarum et categoriarum 120
Excidii Aconis gestorum collectio 202
Explanationes fidei aevi Carolini 254
Expositiones Pauli epistularum ad Romanos, Galathas et Ephesios 151
Expositiones Psalmorum duae sicut in codice Rothomagensi 24 asseruantur 256

Florus Lugdunensis 193, 193A, 193B, 220B, 260
Folchinus de Borfonibus 201
Frechulfus Lexoviensis 169, 169A
Frowinus abbas Montis Angelorum 134

Galbertus notarius Brugensis 131
Galterus a S. Victore 30
Garnerius de Ruperforti 232
Gerardus Cameracensis 270
Gerardus Magnus 172, 192, 235, 235A
Gerardus Moresenus seu Csanadensis 49
Gerlacus Peters 155
Germanus Parisiensis episcopus 187
Gesta abbatum Trudonensium 257, 257A
Gillebertus 171A
Giraldus Floriacensis 171A
Gislebertus Trudonensis 257A
Glosa super Graecismum Eberhardi Bethuniensis 225
Glossa ordinaria in Canticum Canticorum 170.22

Glossae aeui Carolini in libros I-II Martiani Capellae De nuptiis Philologiae et Mercurii 237
Glossae biblicae 189A, 189B
Gozechinus 62
Grammatici Hibernici Carolini aevi 40, 40A, 40B, 40C, 40D
Magister Gregorius 171
Guibertus Gemblacensis 66, 66A
Guibertus Tornacensis 242
Guillelmus Alvernus 230, 230A, 230B, 230C
Guillelmus de Conchis 152, 158, 203
Guillelmus Durantus 140, 140A, 140B
Guillelmus de Luxi 219
Guillelmus Petrus de Calciata 73
Guillelmus a S. Theodorico 86, 87, 88, 89, 89A, 89B
Guitbertus abbas Novigenti 127, 127A, 171

Haymo Autissiodorensis 135C, 135E
Heiricus Autissiodorensis 116, 116A, 116B
Henricus a S. Victore 30
Herimannus abbas 236
Hermannus de Runa 64
Hermannus Werdinensis 204
Hermes Trismegistus 142, 143A, 144, 144C
Hieronymus de Moravia 250
Hieronymus de Praga 222
Hildebertus Cenomanensis 209
Hildegardis Bingensis 43, 43A, 90, 91, 91A, 91B, 92, 226, 226A
Historia Compostellana 70
Historia translationis S. Isidori 73
Historia Roderici vel Gesta Roderici Campidocti 71
Homiletica Vadstenensia 229
Homiliarium Veronense 186
Hugo Pictaviensis 42
Hugo de Miromari 234
Hugo de Sancto Victore 176, 176A, 177, 178, 269
Humbertus de Romanis 218
Hieronymus de Moravia 250

Iacobus de Vitriaco 171, 252, 255
Iohannes Beleth 41, 41A
Iohannes de Caulibus 153
Iohannes de Forda 17, 18
Iohannes Hus 205, 211, 222, 238, 239, 239A, 253, 261, 271
Iohannes Rusbrochius 101, 102, 103, 104, 105, 106, 107, 107A, 108, 109, 110, 172, 207

Iohannes Saresberiensis 98, 118
Iohannes Scottus (Eriugena) 31, 50, 161, 162, 163, 164, 165, 166
Iohannes Soreth 259
Iohannes Wirziburgensis 139

Lanfrancus 171
Liber de gratia Noui Testamenti 195 + suppl.
Liber ordinis S. Victoris Parisiensis 61
Liber prefigurationum Christi et Ecclesie 195 + suppl.
Liber Quare 60
Liber sacramentorum excarsus 47
Liber sacramentorum Romane ecclesiae ordine exscarpsus 47
Liudprandus Cremonensis 156
Logica antiquioris mediae aetatis 120
Lucas Tudensis 74, 74A

Magister Cunestabulus 272
Margareta Porete 69
Martianus Capella 237
Metamorphosis Golie 171A
Metrum de vita et miraculis et obitu S. Martini 171A
Monumenta Arroasiensia 175
Monumenta Vizeliacensia 42 + suppl.
Muretach 40

Nicolaus Maniacoria 262

Opera de computo s. XII 272
Oratio S. Brandani 47
Oswaldus de Corda 179
Otfridus Wizemburgensis 200

Pascasius Radbertus 16, 56, 56A, 56B, 56C, 85, 94, 96, 97
Paulinus Aquileiensis 95
Petrus Abaelardus 11, 12, 13, 14, 15, 190, 206
Petrus de Alliaco 258
Petrus Blesensis 128, 171, 194
Petrus Cantor 196, 196A, 196B
Petrus Cellensis 54
Petrus Comestor 191
Petrus Damiani 57
Petrus Iohannis Oliui 233, 275
Petrus Marsilii 273
Petrus Pictaviensis 51
Petrus Pictor 25
Petrus de S. Audemaro 25
Petrus Venerabilis 10, 58, 83
Polythecon 93
Prefatio de Almaria 71

Psalterium adbreviatum Vercellense 47
Psalterium Suthantoniense 240

Rabanus Maurus 44, 100, 174, 174A
Radulfus Ardens 241
Radulfus phisicus 171A
Radulphus Cadomensis 231
Raimundus Lullus 32, 33, 34, 35, 36, 37, 38, 39, 75, 76, 77, 78, 79, 80, 111, 112, 113, 114, 115, 180A, 180B, 180C, 181, 182, 183, 184, 185, 213, 214, 215, 246, 247, 248, 264, 265
Rainherus Paderbornensis 272
Ratherius Veronensis 46, 46A
Reference Bible – Das Bibelwerk 173
Reimbaldus Leodiensis 4
Remigius Autissiodorensis 136, 171
Reynardus Vulpes 171A
Robertus Grosseteste 130, 268
Rodericus Ximenius de Rada 72, 72A, 72B, 72C
Rodulfus Trudonensis 257, 257A
Rogerus Herefordensis 272
Rudolfus de Liebegg 55
Rupertus Tuitiensis 7, 9, 21, 22, 23, 24, 26, 28, 29

Saewulf 139
Salimbene de Adam 125, 125A
Scriptores Ordinis Grandimontensis 8

Sedulius Scottus 40B, 40C, 67 + suppl., 117
Sermones anonymi codd. S. Vict. Paris. exarati 30
Sermones in dormitionem Mariae 154
Sicardus Cremonensis 228
Sigo abbas 171
Smaragdus 68
Speculum virginum 5
Stephanus de Borbone 124, 124A, 124B

Testimonia orationis christianae antiquioris 47
Teterius Nivernensis 171
Thadeus 202
Theodericus 139
Thiofridus Epternacensis 133
Thomas de Chobham 82, 82A, 82B
Thomas Gallus 223, 223A
Thomas Migerius 77

Vincentius Belvacensis 137
Vitae S. Katharinae 119, 119A
Vita S. Arnulfi ep. Suessionensis 285
Vita S. Hildegardis 126

Walterus Tervanensis 217
Wilhelmus Iordani 207
Willelmus Meldunensis 244
Willelmus Tyrensis 63, 63A

October 2016